The International Economy

The

International Economy

THIRD EDITION

P. T. ELLSWORTH
University of Wisconsin

THE MACMILLAN COMPANY, NEW YORK
COLLIER-MACMILLAN LIMITED, LONDON

Earlier editions entitled *International Economics,* copyright 1938 by The Macmillan Company, and *The International Economy,* copyright 1950 and 1958 by The Macmillan Company.

83442

HF 1408
C

Library of Congress catalog card number: 64-16046

THE MACMILLAN COMPANY, NEW YORK
COLLIER-MACMILLAN CANADA, LTD., TORONTO, ONTARIO

Printed in the United States of America

PREFACE TO THE THIRD EDITION

Rapid change, which outdated the later chapters of the 1958 edition of this text, made a revision imperative. At first, I hoped to limit the revision to these chapters on current problems. But critical comments from others, together with self-imposed criticism, caused me to undertake extensive alterations. I have, however, retained the basic structure of the two earlier editions —one that combines history and theory.

The historical chapters, contained in Parts I, III, and V, are changed but little. They provide many illustrations of theoretical principles and serve as well, I hope, to stress the ever-present conflict between the forces of nationalism and the requirements of a world made increasingly interdependent by its industrial transformation since the eighteenth century. Nationalist forces, meeting little effective opposition, triumphed in the early twentieth century. In the 1930's they overwhelmed the growing, but ineffectual, efforts at international cooperation epitomized by the League of Nations. Increasingly, since the catastrophe of World War II, the needs of an interdependent world have been expressed in a series of conscious attempts to organize effective forms of international cooperation directed toward reconstruction, the liberalization of trade and payments, and the economic development of the poorer nations. The conflict between nationalist impulses and international requirements goes on, overshadowed by the deeper conflict between the rival communist and capitalist systems.

In Part II are gathered the chapters that present the theoretical bases upon which international specialization and trade rest, and that explain the advantages of such trade. As in the 1958 edition of this book, the development of international trade theory is presented, from its beginnings in the hands of Adam Smith and David Ricardo to its modern formulation in terms of factor endowments and production functions. The continuity of this development is made clearer by the inclusion of a new chapter on the modernization of the comparative cost doctrine through its formulation in terms of opportunity cost. The remaining chapters on international trade theory are either completely or partly rewritten, and a new chapter on dynamic aspects of international trade has been added that attempts to take into account some criticisms of the factor proportions theory.

Part IV comprises the chapters dealing with the balance of payments: the meaning and significance of the concept, the character of disturbances to international payments, and alternative means of adjustment. Chapter 14, on the national income and its relation to the balance of payments, is completely new, while Chapter 15, presenting the foreign trade multiplier, has been considerably revised and expanded. Chapters 19 and 20, which are concerned with the mechanism of adjustment under fixed and flexible exchange rates, have also been extensively revised.

Part VI considers the major international economic problems of current and continuing interest. Chapter 25 condenses and brings up to date the discussion of postwar reconstruction and its consequences for national balances of payments, while Chapter 28 (completely rewritten) stresses the international aspects of economic development.

Nowhere is the conflict between the forces of nationalism and the needs of an international economy clearer than in the search for a means of reconciling the national goals of full employment, price stability, and optimum growth with the maintenance of balance of payments equilibrium. This conflict is discussed at some length in Chapters 26 and 27, which deal with postwar monetary problems and with alternative paths to international monetary reform. A new form of potential conflict with the efficient economic organization of the free world may be emerging in the establishment of the European Common Market and other regional organizations. Chapters 29 and 30 deal with this and related topics.

For valuable critical comments preparatory to revision, I am indebted to Dr. David Carney of the United Nations Economic Commission on Africa.

My colleagues, Theodore Morgan and Hans Schmitt, have been generous in taking time to read and comment on many parts of the manuscript. For this help, I am grateful.

P. T. ELLSWORTH

Madison, Wisconsin

TABLE OF CONTENTS

The International Economy

I

WHAT INTERNATIONAL ECONOMICS IS ABOUT

Economics deals with man's daily activities in getting a living, in general with the problems of productivity, of depression and inflation, monopoly, and of inequality of incomes. The exact content of the subject, however, as with any broad field of knowledge, cannot be known until we have actually studied it.

This is equally true of the branch of economics that we call international economics. Its name indicates that it concerns itself with the economic relations between nations. But what precisely do these relations include? Is a separate study of international economics necessary?

This chapter gives a first-approximation answer to the above questions. It surveys some of the principal problems we shall encounter, and shows how we will attack them. Here we will sketch the outlines only. You will get a fuller grasp of what it is all about as you become better acquainted with the critical problems and opportunities of our international economy.

WHY SHOULD WE TRADE?

The Role of Trade

Nations cannot live alone any more effectively than can individuals. A single family, living in isolation and providing for all its needs, can obtain only a meager and primitive living. So compelling is this fact that even among primitive peoples there is some rudimentary specialization, together with an inevitable sharing or exchange of its fruits. With the progress of technology, from the discovery of fire and invention of the grinding stone and the wheel, down to the perfection of the latest electronic device, the scope of specialization has increased—and with it the abundance of goods and services to satisfy our wants. The specialized producer uses only part—maybe none—of his own output. He exchanges his surplus for the things he wants of the specialized out-

[1]

puts of others. In other words, specialization implies trade and cannot occur without it.

A large part of total trade, of course, is among the inhabitants of a single locality or region. In the Middle Ages, when perhaps nine-tenths of the world's population lived and worked on farms, when the techniques of production were relatively simple and incomes were correspondingly low, the volume of goods that travelled long distances—mainly luxuries of the rich— was only a minute part of total trade. Even today international trade, or trade that crosses national boundaries, represents only five to six per cent of the total exchange of goods. Yet that small percentage is crucial and amounts to many billions of dollars a year. Indeed, it is considered small only because of the immensity of the day-to-day transactions inside each country.

Trade or Perish

For many countries, as we shall see, international trade is a matter literally of life or death. Thus western Europe in the middle of the twentieth century consists of some 300 million people inhabiting a comparatively small land area with limited physical resources. This densely populated community cannot even feed itself. Most of its textile fibers—cotton, silk, jute, even wool— must be obtained from overseas. Without the rubber of Malaya and the petroleum of the Middle East and the Western Hemisphere, its cars and buses would be immobilized. Many of its luxuries, if they really can be called that —tea, coffee, cocoa, tobacco—would be unobtainable without far-reaching trade.

This point can be put in another way. Had Europe been unable to draw upon the resources of other continents for a constantly increasing flow of raw materials and foodstuffs, the industrial revolution—which transformed its industry and made western Europe by the end of the nineteenth century the workshop of the world—would either have been impossible or restricted within exceedingly narrow limits. Population might have increased some 50 per cent over the 100 million or so alive in 1800, instead of trebling. European people would be enjoying a standard of living half that available today, or less.

Trade or Be Poorer

At the other extreme from regions so dependent on international trade as Europe are nations of huge area such as the United States and the Soviet Union. Yet even to them, external trade is extremely important and in some respects essential. Were it not for foreign trade, the people of the United States, like Europeans, would have to do without many of their conventional comforts, such as coffee, tea, chocolate, bananas and other tropical fruits. Even sugar would be scarce and costly. Though formerly self-sufficient in iron ore, this country's deposits have been used up to such an extent that it is increasingly dependent on supplies from Canada, Venezuela, Brazil, and Chile. A Presidential Commission has estimated that by 1975, with consumption of iron ore up by more than 50 per cent, the United States will have to import nearly all its requirements of this most basic of industrial raw materials. We lack deposits of nickel and tin, and are entirely dependent on imports of these important materials. There are dozens of other materials for which we depend heavily upon foreign trade and will become increasingly dependent.

Most of the commodities cited so far have been of a kind unobtainable in the importing countries, or obtainable in insufficient amounts. Such items, however, comprise only a part, though an important part, of world trade. Much the greater portion of its volume consists of articles which could be produced at home, but which instead are imported. They are imported because foreign producers can supply them more cheaply than home producers. As will be explained more fully later, foreign producers can quote low prices because the kind and quality of the resources available to them are more suited to the production of these exported goods than are the resources of the importing country. Not only does specialization among individual producers within a country lead to more efficient and hence abundant output, but so also does geographical specialization between countries.

The basic reasons for the importance of international trade should now be clear. Goods can be obtained from abroad that cannot be produced at home. Finally, also, goods that *could* be produced at home can be obtained at lower cost from other countries. In short, international trade permits more people to live, to gratify more varied tastes, and to enjoy a higher standard of living than would be possible in its absence.

THE INTERNATIONAL MOVEMENT OF RESOURCES AND TECHNIQUES

Trade between nations is important, but it does not exhaust even the purely economic ways in which their economies react upon one another. Not only goods, but also some of the resources that make them, move across national frontiers. So too does that vast accumulation of the product of man's intellect, knowledge of how to produce things. These movements bring about great changes in the world's economy. Thus during the middle half of the nineteenth century, the United States obtained large amounts of capital from Britain. These savings of the British people were transferred to us in the form of money, or unearmarked purchasing power. American borrowers chose to spend it in England on steel rails, railway rolling stock, and machinery for their growing factories. This foreign capital considerably hastened the transformation of our predominantly agrarian economy. Later the flow of British capital turned toward Canada, Latin America, and the colonies; the French invested heavily in Russia and the Germans in central and eastern Europe.

Along with the capital went engineers, construction workers, and some skilled labor. They built railways and factories, put new plants in operation, and trained local personnel to replace them. Besides these temporary migrants possessing technical qualifications, some proportion of the huge numbers of immigrants who left the relatively crowded nations of Europe carried with them skills that helped the expansion of mechanized industry in the newer countries.

Most of the labor that left Europe in search of better opportunties in the open areas of the world, however, was unskilled, or skilled mainly in agricultural practices. These workers brought with them little capital and not much technical knowledge. Their contribution to the equalization of the productive power of nations, however, was immense. In the hundred years between 1830 and 1930, approximately 60 million people left Europe and Asia to take up residence abroad, mainly in North and South America and Australia. Lands that had been nearly empty became populated; their agricultural production expanded, providing ever more abundant supplies of wheat, corn, beef, and butter for the markets of Europe; cities and factories sprang up in hitherto deserted spots.

This was the era of the economic development of the "newer" regions of the world—the United States, Canada, Australia, New Zealand, Argentina, South Africa. Like the trade in goods that preceded and accompanied these movements of labor and capital, their flow benefited both the giver and the receiver. Emigration from Europe reduced somewhat the pressure of rising population on resources; as the migrants arrived overseas, their additional labor permitted more effective use of the abundant resources awaiting them. European capital sent abroad earned a higher return for its lenders, and at the same time enhanced the productivity of the labor and land with which it was combined.

These great intercontinental movements of capital and labor, and of the technical knowledge that makes them productive, were a unique feature of the nineteenth century. Since World War I, immigration has fallen to a mere trickle, and international investment has not approached the relative importance it had before 1914. Yet some countries, such as Egypt, have a surplus of population for which really productive employment cannot be found at home; others, such as Venezuela and Brazil, could benefit from additions to their labor force. More striking yet is the need for capital in the so-called "underdeveloped" areas—most of Asia, Africa, and Latin America—where a keen desire to share in the material progress of the more advanced nations has been awakened. Much effort and ingenuity are being devoted to discovering ways and means of enlarging and supplementing the sluggish flow of private capital, and of making available to the underdeveloped regions the technical knowledge of the West.

THE GROWTH OF RESTRICTIONS IN THE
TWENTIETH CENTURY

During most of the nineteenth century, the world gladly accepted the benefits of international trade and of the intercontinental flow of labor and capital. It interposed few restrictions on this traffic. Subject only to relatively moderate and quite stable tariffs, buyers could seek out the cheapest and most suitable supplies of raw materials or manufactured goods, place an order, and expect to receive their purchase promptly and with a minimum of formalities. Travelers could obtain as large quantities of any currency as their means would allow and could proceed to their destination without passports, impertinent inquiries, or required declarations of currency holdings and even of political views. Immigrants were welcomed, and investors could invest their funds or remove them at will.

After 1914, all this changed. Tariffs became generally higher and, in many countries, subject to sudden variation. For the better part of the next half century, direct quantitative restrictions became an important element of trade policy. Some nations prohibited altogether the import of particular commodities, while a great many established long lists of goods for which import licenses were necessary and reinforced these restrictions by controls over spending abroad. Immigration even today is restrained by rigid national quotas and by various processes of screening the applicants. Even those countries most in need of capital often seem to do their best, by a variety of onerous restraints and limitations, to scare off foreign investors.

Passports and visas have been the least of a traveler's worries. Most countries until recently severely limited the amount of foreign currency the traveler could acquire for his journey, and a number still do. Upon entering other countries, he must declare how much of its money he has and account for it when he leaves. Compare all this with the ease and freedom of trade and travel before 1914.

Fortunately, this era of restrictionism, during which it has sometimes appeared as though the world had lost its wits, has in recent years moderated appreciably. Many of the more onerous restrictions have been removed, and customs officials (especially in western Europe) no longer examine one's luggage with such suspicious zeal. Perhaps we are about to enter another period of liberality in international dealings. This is a question that will concern us deeply.

CHANGES IN THE STATUS OF NATIONS

British Dominance

During the nineteenth century, or more accurately, the hundred years (1814-1914) between the Napoleonic War and World War I, the role of outstanding leader among nations fell to Great Britain. After defeating Napoleon at Waterloo, Britain pursued the strategy of preserving a balance of power in Europe, shifting her weight from one side to another when it appeared that any single country might achieve a position of dominance. A century of uneasy peace resulted, broken—except for minor struggles—only by the Franco-Prussian War and the American Civil War.

If Britain was a movable counterweight in the politico-military sphere, in the economic sphere she could justly be called that century's stable but ever-expanding center. Her insular position, her role as the world's leading trader, her free institutions, and her rapidly growing population all combined to stimulate that revolution in the industrial arts which—at first slowly and imperceptibly, then with rapidly increasing tempo—made her by mid-century the outstanding industrial nation of the world.

Her economic predominance extended also to matters of trade and finance. British ships roamed everywhere, carrying British manufactures to the most distant markets and returning laden with wool, cotton, tobacco, sugar, and all the multitude of foods and materials required by a rapidly expanding industry and a multiplying population. London became a great central marketplace of the world, where anything known and desired could be bought or sold. Complementing this commercial preeminence was an equal financial preeminence, based on a currency fixed and stable in relation to gold and a financial market incomparable in its degree of specialization and efficiency.

Until after 1914 Britain retained her outstanding position as trader and banker to the world, though her rank as industrial producer had been successfully challenged. First the United States, then Germany, surpassed Britain in manufacturing output. American industrial superiority, though it came as early as 1890, brought no threat to Britain's international position, for the United States, isolated by distance, was too busy with her own internal growth and expansion to have much concern for foreign markets. Germany, a keen rival, was thrust back temporarily by the war of 1914-1918.

American Leadership

It is in the four decades since that war that the United States has become— as a result of the growth of its own wealth and power and of the destruction in Europe of two major wars—the successor to Britain's role of leadership. We play this part, however, in circumstances far different and far more dangerous than those that confronted England. Though the nations of the nineteenth century were divided by conflicting rivalries, they operated within a framework of substantial agreement as to the desirable character of social organization. Capitalism was dominant everywhere, and though challenged by socialist movements, it showed itself flexible and capable of accommodation to criticism.

Today there is no such agreement. Two rival philosophies divide the world.

One acclaims the superior merits of the totalitarian state, where the state is everything, the individual nothing, and aspires to impose its views universally by force or by subversion. The other believes in the right of the individual to choose his government by a free vote, and in the economic field, it believes in individual freedom tempered by controls and by varying degrees of democratically determined state action.

This cleavage would not be too disturbing were it not for the Communist aim of world domination. Given that aim, backed by the military and economic strength developed in the past thirty years by the Soviet Union, every decision on foreign affairs made by any government of the free world must inevitably be conditioned by its probable effect on the struggle against Communist expansion. This conclusion applies, of course, with particular force to the foreign policies of the United States.

The mid-twentieth century differs from the nineteenth not only in that ideological division has replaced agreement on the fundamentals of political and economic thought, but there is also the economic fragmentation to which we have already alluded. A highly integrated world economy, based on relatively free trade focused upon the great center at London, gave way after 1914 to restrictionism and separation. True, the situation has improved greatly from the chaos of the depressed 1930's. Western Europe achieved economic reconstruction in the early postwar years, then enjoyed more than a decade of rising productivity and rapid expansion, and now is moving toward a substantial degree of economic unity. Notable progress has been made toward lowering tariffs and removing trade restrictions; but the ideological split has separated the Communist and the non-Communist blocs, between which there is relatively little trade. The free world is no longer linked through freely operating market forces with a single dominant center. Instead, there are several centers, among which a precarious equilibrium is preserved by various cooperative devices. As these efforts at cooperation become established in international institutions and agreed procedures, we may again achieve a stable and workable international economic system. That is one of the topics into which we shall enquire.

INTERNATIONAL ECONOMIC PROBLEMS OF THE MID-TWENTIETH CENTURY

In the preceding pages we have tried to show how nations depend on international trade, what they gain from it, and how, in spite of these gains, they have in the past half-century partially turned their backs on it. We have also examined briefly the effects of international movements of capital and labor, and the great change in the relative economic status of nations that these movements, together with the spread of modern industrial technology, have helped to bring about.

This review makes clear the divisions and instability that characterize the relations of nations today, and it shows how this situation is the product of deep-seated changes during the past century and more. It also enables us to indicate the principal problems of today that arise out of the ways in which the economic activities and policies of different countries affect one another.

Economic Regionalism

During the years immediately following World War II, the most critical economic problem facing the free world was how to restore health and strength to the enfeebled economy of western Europe. Its productive power had been greatly reduced by nearly six years of war; trade was compressed into narrow, bilateral channels; inflation was serious in every country and extreme in some; and imports of badly needed supplies of all kinds far exceeded the region's ability to pay for them. Fortunately, a combination of American aid and European organization and energy brought quick and effective results. By 1950, western Europe's production exceeded prewar production by a modest margin, and her international payments and receipts were in balance. During the 1950's, the nations in this group enjoyed rapid expansion, with per capita incomes in several of the countries rising at a gratifying rate.

This prosperity furnished a favorable environment for the discussion and later for the realization of a concept that had attracted a wide following: a permanent strengthening of western Europe through some form of economic and political union. In 1957, six nations (France, Germany, Italy, Belgium, Netherlands, and Luxembourg) signed a treaty under which they were to form a customs union, with no tariffs on trade among members and with a single tariff against the outside world. The nations agreed to eliminate barriers to the movement of labor and capital within the Community and to cooperate closely in the determination of national monetary and fiscal policies. The European Economic Community became a reality in 1958, and since then has made rapid progress toward achieving its stipulated goals.

Spurred by this daring action, seven other European nations,[1] unwilling or unable to move so far or so fast, formed the European Free Trade Association. Its goal was limited to the elimination of tariffs among members on industrial products, and it did not provide for the establishment of a common tariff on trade with nonmembers.

The appeal of economic union has not been limited to Europe, but has spread to the Americas. In 1962, eight nations of South America, which had already united in a customs union, introduced the first stage of tariff reductions against one another's products; five of the Central American Republics simultaneously took a similar step.

The European union appears to be bringing tangible benefits to its mem-

[1] Austria, Denmark, Norway, Portugal, Sweden, Switzerland, and the United Kingdom.

bers in the form of stimulus to increased productivity of more lively competition, gains of increased specialization of industrial plants, and greater mobility of labor and capital. Perhaps the same will be true of the unions formed in Latin America.

But what of the effects of this formation of regional blocs upon the rest of the world? Even though the tariff of such a region is no higher than the average preunion national tariffs, the very formation of a customs union enables some of its producers, with duty-free access to all parts of the common market, to displace imports that remain subject to duty.

Whether the formation of regional trade blocs will affect the rest of the world adversely or favorably will depend partly upon the extent to which production within each region displaces external trade, and partly upon the future tariff policy of these regions. The answers to those questions are of great importance for the future of world trade and world stability.

International Monetary Problems

Until the completion of European reconstruction by the beginning of the 1950's, the chief international monetary problem had been the restoration of some sort of balance in the international payments of western European nations. Indeed, the belief was widespread that in the face of superior United States productive power, western Europe's payments difficulties were chronic and almost insoluble. Actual developments, however, belied this fear. The recovery of European capacity to export—together with the continuance of large United States foreign aid, military expenditures, and private foreign investment—turned western Europe's international deficit into a surplus, enabling those nations to add $10 billion to their reserves by 1956. Simultaneously, the United States ran a modest annual international payments deficit of a little over a billion dollars.

Beginning in 1958, the United States became the problem area. During each of the next three years, its international payments deficit fell only a little short of $4 billion, and despite many countermeasures, amounted to $2.5 billion in 1961 and $2.1 billion in 1962. From an impregnable total of $24.6 billion in 1950, its gold reserves fell to $16.1 billion by the end of 1962, while short-term foreign claims against the dollar rose from a mere $8.2 billion to nearly $22 billion.

Although the mounting short-term claims on the dollar resulted from the imbalance in U.S. international payments, they reflected confidence in and a desire to use the dollar as a "reserve currency"; that is, many countries preferred to hold a substantial portion of their reserves in the form of short-term dollar assets rather than in gold. An indefinite rise in those claims, however, could not be allowed, for it would destroy confidence in the reserve currency and lead to a conversion of claims into gold, exhaustion of U.S. gold reserves, and international monetary chaos.

How to eliminate the deficit in the international accounts of the United States and yet to provide for adequate growth of international reserves became one of the dominant problems of the early 1960's. Numerous international conferences and congressional inquiries considered this problem in detail, and a wide range of suggestions for reform of the international monetary system emerged.

Economic Development

Another broad set of issues is presented by the desire and determination of the underdeveloped countries of the world to raise their national prestige and the welfare of their people by modernizing and improving their stagnant economies. This concerns not only these countries themselves, but also advanced countries of the West as well. The task confronting the underdeveloped regions is formidable—so formidable that successful economic development probably depends upon substantial and continuing aid from the richer nations. The need for this aid by now has become generally accepted, but troublesome questions remain. Should such aid be unconditional, or should some test of performance by the recipient of aid be required by the donor? How far should the nation rendering aid participate in the planning and programming of the recipient's development effort? If it does participate in these activities, how far does it commit itself to the program's success? As the structure of the underdeveloped countries changes—in particular, as they become more industrialized—what adjustments will the industrial nations have to face, and what policy changes will be called for?

A particularly stubborn problem of the underdeveloped nations arises from the character of and movements in their trade. Exports of these nations consist principally of primary products. Although they have continued to expand in recent years, their rate of expansion has been less than that of exports of the developed nations. Imports of the underdeveloped countries, however, have grown more rapidly than their exports, especially imports of capital goods needed for their development. The resulting excess of foreign payments has been met in large part by foreign loans. But since these will some day have to be repaid, and in the meantime add a burden of interest charges, the underlying problem of exporting sufficient to pay for needed imports remains unsolved.

These are some of the broader and more pressing economic problems of international scope. There are others of more limited concern to citizens of the United States. Among these is the ever-present question of the tariff. Decade after decade the tariff question has stimulated more enthusiastic political battles than any other issue in American political history, and the issue is just as alive today as it ever was. Should tariffs be reduced, in our own long-range national interest, as a contribution to the increased viability of Europe and Japan? And if this were done, who would be injured, and how much? Another issue is the problem of reconciling our policy of maintaining an artificial level of agricultural prices, which requires restrictions on the entry of foreign farm products into our market, with our advocacy of a liberal international trade policy.

All of these problems would exist, and national decisions on relevant policies would be required, even if Communism had never been heard of. Yet the challenge Communism presents gives a special urgency to almost every international issue. Thus it may be that European Economic Union is not only desirable as a means to increased efficiency and prosperity, but also in view of rising productivity in Russia is perhaps even a necessity for western Europe's survival as part of the free world. Liberalization of trade policies is also given added force as a possible contribution to the economic strength of the non-Communist nations. Finally, is not economic aid to underdeveloped countries (justifiable on independent grounds) made doubly necessary if they are not to succumb to the attraction of Communist planning and regimentation?

FIRST THINGS FIRST

The issues surveyed in the foregoing paragraphs are among the most vital of our age. It would be perfectly possible to attack them directly and immediately, and to make this book a survey of contemporary international economic problems. Many such books have been written. Their purpose is to inform, and generally to mold opinion in favor of a particular viewpoint or course of action. The best ones are written by experts, and the position they defend may well be the most sensible of the alternatives open. But because the problems in this field are complex and difficult, they have to take much for granted—in particular, the principles on which their specific analyses and conclusions are based.

Essential Tools, Not Conclusions

The purpose of this book is to do something more than provide ready-made solutions to current international problems. It is to furnish you with the principles that underlie these vital issues, so that you can make up your own mind as to the relative merits of alternative ways of dealing with them. With proper study, you should acquire the tools essential to an informed judgment, rather than a ready-made conclusion, however well-grounded. We will not avoid the problems, but the foundations come first.

Principles of Trade

Among the "first things" are a few, but only a few, basic theoretical principles. The first of these shows the foundations on which the trade between nations rests. It explains what factors determine the commodities upon which a country can with greatest advantage specialize and thus export, and those which it should, in its own interest, import. An understanding of this theory is essential if we are properly to evaluate policies that alter the international flow of goods, such as protective tariffs or other import restrictions. It must also be given full consideration by a country engaged in economic development if that development is to lead to efficiency, not waste, in the use of scanty resources.

This part of our theoretical study is mainly static in character; that is, it deals with what is true under given conditions. This is not to say that it cannot deal with changes; our reasoning will show how changes in costs and demands will lead to changes in a country's exports and imports.

Balance of Payments Analysis

Changes in the quantity of exports a country sells, or in the value of its imports, will clearly have an immediate effect on its international payments and receipts—its balance of payments. So too will a decline in its earnings from foreign investments, or in the volume of its borrowing or lending. But the effects do not stop here; they have substantial repercussions on the country's internal economy—on the level of employment and business activity, on prices, and hence on its ability to compete in international markets.

A second important area of theory deals with these phenomena. Since their impact differs a good deal when the currency of the country in question is fixed in value in terms of other currencies, as under the gold standard, and when it is free to fluctuate, we shall have to study balance of payments problems under both fixed and variable exchange rates. Such study should enable us to understand why the gold standard was widely abandoned during three of the past four decades, why in its restored form it proved far from satisfactory, and what issues underlie the many proposals for international monetary reform.

Knowledge of Institutions Also Needed

A firm grasp of international trade and balance of payments theory will go far toward providing you with the tools you need for attacking independently the major economic issues that transcend national boundaries. Most of this essential analytical equipment, however, is abstract in character. Yet it must always be applied to a concrete situation—a situation that has its roots in the past and that can only be fully understood if one sees how it developed from its origins. Moreover, the general principles that emerge from theoretical analysis rest upon an unavoidable simplification of reality. When it comes time to apply them in the devising of a specific policy, allowance must be made for the differences between the simplified world of theory and the complex world of reality. Sometimes the differences will not be so great as to rule out a solution suggested by the most general principles. But sometimes the institutional environment will require substantial adjustments, and on other occasions it may render totally inapplicable a policy based on assumptions that do not fit the concrete case.

To illustrate, some people, especially those concerned with the dangers of inflation, would still welcome the restoration of a gold standard similar to that before 1914; for this monetary system provides not only stable rates of exchange, but also (when allowed to work as it is supposed to do) automatic control over a country's money supply. It does this by establishing a fixed relationship between gold reserves and the total amount of money. An expansion of money and credit, especially if accompanied by inflationary symptoms, will lead to a loss of reserves and contraction of the money supply—that is, to automatic deflation. Though this system worked relatively well in the nineteenth century, its applicability to vastly different twentieth-century conditions is at least dubious. To mention only one difference, many more people are affected today by any deflationary process, and for a number of reasons they have become far more sensitive to its impact. A type of policy that in an earlier day won public acceptance now encounters strenuous opposition. The reasoning underlying the gold standard (its theoretical foundation) is sound enough, but the environment it needs in order to work effectively no longer exists.

A second illustration shows how cultural and institutional differences affect a country's economic growth. In the early part of the nineteenth century, when most Latin American countries achieved their independence, their economic status was not radically different from that of the United States. Yet in the intervening century and a half, the United States has enjoyed a phenomenal increase in wealth and productivity, while until very recently the Latin American nations remained very much as they always had been—predominantly agrarian, static, and poor. This striking difference cannot be attributed mainly to a difference in resources, though that is certainly a factor. The explanation is to be found principally in the cultural characteristics of the two regions. The early settlers who came to North America were mainly from the lower middle classes—shopkeepers, artisans, small farmers. They brought with them a tradition of individual striving, a questioning of authority, and a desire for economic improvement. Except in the South, they established small farms suitable to operation with the labor of the family. The indigenous Indians, few and scattered, they exterminated or drove back into the interior.

The Spanish conquistadores, on the other hand, were either members of a feudal aristocracy or aspired to enter its ranks. This could be done by acquiring large estates, and these the crown granted liberally as a reward for the conquest of the New World. Along with the land went a labor force, supplied (in the principal areas of colonization) by a settled and numerous Indian population. Here were the ingredients of the hacienda system, under which rich owners of huge estates monopolized the best land, dominated the political scene, and caused economic life to stagnate.

The significance of these striking differences is this: whereas in the United States a policy of laissez faire, of governmental inaction, produced rapid economic development, a similar policy could not, in the Latin American environment, be expected to have the same result; for there was no aspiring and energetic middle class to supply the business leadership that was such an important element in our economic growth. This agency of change either had to be created, or a substitute for it had to be found. Its comparative absence today hampers the development of Latin America. Thus we see that to be properly equipped to deal with the issues in question, a coupling of historical with theoretical analysis is essential.

Our study begins with a glimpse back in time, to the ideas of the Mercantilists of the sixteenth and seventeenth centuries. This starting point is chosen because their ideas, though often wrong, have led a hardy life—many are still with us today—and because an understanding of Mercantilist views serves to set in bold relief the accomplishments of the classical economists, who were the first to achieve a reasonably satisfactory understanding of international trade.

PART I

From Restriction Toward Freedom
in Trade and Enterprise

2

REGULATED TRADE:
MERCANTILISM

Attitudes and policies of governments toward international trade have undergone sweeping changes within modern times. One of our major interests will be to understand present-day government trade policies and the arguments that support them. We should be able to throw light on this topic by contrasting what nations do today with what they have done in the past under circumstances in some respects similar and in some, different. Moreover, many views held in the past grew tenacious roots; they still live on and influence current decisions. It is important to show their origins and to see whether, if they suited conditions when they first arose, they still do so.

A Starting Point

We start with the era of Mercantilism. This period includes roughly the years 1500 to 1750, when western Europe emerged from the comparative stagnation of the Middle Ages, gradually discarded its feudal institutions, and acquired many of the characteristics of modern nationalism. We first review briefly the major characteristics of western European society at the beginning of the sixteenth century, together with the leading events that shaped its development during the next two and a half centuries.

SOCIAL AND ECONOMIC CHARACTERISTICS
OF THE MERCANTILIST PERIOD

In 1500: an Agrarian Society

In 1500, western Europe probably had a population between 55 and 60 million. Most of these people earned a meager living tilling the soil, either as serfs on the large estates of the nobility or as independent peasant farmers. Probably 80 to 90 per cent of them were so occupied. Of the remainder, most were employed as craftsmen, shopkeepers, or servants of the relatively small number of nobles, higher clergy, and well-to-do merchants who enjoyed ample incomes and who held the reins of political and economic power.

Household Manufacture

Society was thus preponderantly agrarian. Only four cities had attained a population of close to or slightly above 200 thousand: London, Paris, Naples, Milan. Six had a population of about 100 thousand: Antwerp, Amsterdam, Lisbon, Seville, Rome, Palermo. There were relatively many towns of a few thousand to 40 thousand or 50 thousand population, but even these were widely scattered. In these cities and towns, industry as we know it today did not exist. With few exceptions, manufacturing processes took place in the shop of the craftsman employing a few journeymen and apprentices, or in the home of the peasant. This was true of furniture, kitchen utensils, pottery, candles, hardware, and clothing. But in the manufacture of woolen textiles—which was the dominant industry of the thriving commercial cities of northern Italy and Flanders, and of England as well—the craft gild system had given way to the "domestic" or "putting-out" system. Here the trader or mechant-capitalist purchased raw wool; placed it in the homes of spinners and weavers to be worked up; collected the crude cloth and put it out with other workers for fulling, dyeing, and finishing; and marketed the completed product. In a few instances, an even more capitalistic method had been developed: the capitalist provided not only the raw materials but also the tools and a large building where he employed as many as several hundred workers on the various processes of textile manufacture. In some other industries, such as mining and the production of armor, the capitalist owner had achieved a position of dominance. Otherwise, the craft method of the Middle Ages continued relatively unchanged.

The Character of Trade

Because most people had an income sufficient only to provide the bare needs for food, clothing, and shelter, trade in the fifteenth century was confined mainly to the towns and their immediately surrounding countryside. Such trade as was carried on over greater distances could be divided into the movement of such staples as grains from the Baltic region and salt fish from the Baltic and North Seas to supplement the food requirements of city dwellers, and the flow of luxuries to supply the wants of the comparatively rich. The latter included the long established trade with the East in fine cotton and silk fabrics, spices, drugs, dyes, and perfumes, the movement northward of the wines and fruits of the Latin countries, and the exchange for these—and for other products such as armor, leather goods, Venetian glassware, and furs—of the famous woolens of northern Italy, Flanders, and England.

At about the turn of the fifteenth century, the earlier slow tempo of change became suddenly accelerated; in economic life, and especially in the scope and conduct of trade, it effected no less than a revolution. Though this relatively sudden speeding-up of man's way of life had many roots, three stand out as of primary importance. There was an intellectual awakening that advanced human understanding with a rapidity hitherto unknown; there occurred the great series of geographical discoveries that opened up an entire new world to exploitation and settlement; there was a sharp increase in population.

The Renaissance

The intellectual awakening that culminated in the sixteenth century represented a fundamental change in attitudes and ways of thinking. Starting in northern Italy in the fourteenth century, there occurred a rebirth of interest in the art, literature, and civilization of Greece and Rome that differed radically from the medieval interest in Aristotelian logic and metaphysics. What now captured attention was the poetic and aesthetic aspects of Greek and Roman writings, the classical ideal of the full, well-rounded life. The literature that embodied these elements appealed to the wealthy burghers and princes who were the chief patrons of the arts. This was scarcely surprising, for although they were still loyal to the Church, their absorption in the affairs of business and the court bred a more secular view, while their greater wealth enabled them fully to enjoy pleasures not available to their medieval forebears. Concern with the after-life gave way to a concern with the here-and-now.

This secular influence was increasingly reflected not only in the literature of the times, but also in the work of scholars in many fields. Exhibiting a lively curiosity about the actual world, they began to examine the facts of nature instead of spinning out the logical implications of established doctrine. A number of important technical discoveries—the clock, the microscope, the telescope, the barometer—by making observation and experiment more accurate and even possible, immensely aided the increasingly popular study of the physical world. By the end of the sixteenth century, the foundations of modern science had been securely laid.

Effects of the Geographical Discoveries

Just when the leading intellects of the late fifteenth and early sixteenth centuries began to examine the world instead of what others had said about it, adventurous men commenced the series of geographical explorations that led to the discovery of the New World and of a new route to the East.

The discovery of the Americas was soon followed by the Spanish conquest of Mexico and Peru. From their art treasures and mines flowed a swelling stream of gold and silver that bulwarked Spain's power for over a century. Settlements, and with them the chance to sell European goods, grew first in the Spanish colonies. About a century later, emigrants from England, Holland, and France pitted themselves against the wilderness and the Indians to the north and gradually built up tobacco plantations, fisheries, lumbering, and the fur trade.

Vasco da Gama's voyage to India around the Cape of Good Hope (1498) brought Portugal to a position of affluence and power and established Lisbon rather than Venice as the central mart for trade with India and the Spice Islands. Together with the discovery and settlement of the Americas, da Gama's achievement meant that commerce was no longer confined to the Mediterranean galleys of Venice, to the camel caravans of the Near East, and to the pack trains winding their way northward over the Alps. Now commerce could take to the high seas in vessels of increasing size, at a diminishing cost of operation.

New opportunities for trade appeared over the widening horizon and under the very noses of the merchants. This trade became increasingly profitable, for with the flow of the precious metals into Spain, whence they seeped out into the rest of western Europe, prices rose steadily if somewhat irregularly, while wages characteristically lagged behind. This is a situation made to order for business men. The mild but steady inflation continued until 1650 or later, reenforcing the tendency toward expansion caused by the opening up of new markets both at home and abroad. And with high profits, the accumulation of capital was greatly accelerated. Large individual fortunes became more common, and their owners became increasingly powerful in political and economic affairs.

The Growth of Population

The third factor which operated to speed up the economic life of Europe, a rapid increase in population, paralleled the beginnings of science and the voyages of discovery. In 1300, the population of western Europe appears to have been about 53 million. It could scarcely have increased much in the next hundred and fifty years, for the Black Death and other plagues took a huge toll of lives, while the Hundred Years' War (1337-1453) kept France in a turmoil. Since the population of this area amounted to some 70 million in 1600, it follows that most of the increase of 17 million (nearly a third) took place after 1450.[1]

More people meant a more rapid migration from the country to the towns, thus furnishing more hands for the rising industries. It meant more hands to man the ships, more recruits to fill the ranks of the armies, more colonists to settle overseas. It meant, in turn, a larger demand for fish, grain, and meat, for textiles, pottery, and muskets, for shoes, knives, and Bibles. It meant more profits for those who made and handled these goods, more capital from the profits that were saved, and an increased demand for the luxuries that the profits made possible.

[1] Shepard B. Clough and Charles W. Cole, *Economic History of Europe*, pp. 98-99. Copyright 1941 by D. C. Heath & Co., Boston.

Rise of the Commercial Class

One of the most significant developments of the period was the rise to positions of prominence and power of the new capitalist class. All the influences to which we have called attention worked in this direction: the new secular view, by creating a climate of opinion more favorable to commercial activity; the geographical discoveries and the growth of population, by providing expanding opportunities for men of enterprise; the fresh supplies of the precious metals, by making profits more abundant and secure, and capital accumulation easy. The capitalist organizer expanded his activities in all directions. He increased his trade in such staples as grain, fish, and timber. The need for nails, chains, and miscellaneous hardware such as locks, keys, hinges, and lanterns stimulated the rise of many small industries making these articles in Birmingham as early as 1538. Sugar, which in the Middle Ages appeared only on the tables of the very rich, by the middle of the seventeeth century became a common article of diet for all but the poor. Sugar, molasses, and rum were mainstays of the trade with the West Indies at that time. The closely associated traffic in Negro slaves, which began in 1510, rose to a volume of 15 thousand a year in the seventeenth century and 30 thousand, in the eighteenth.

In his role as trader, the capitalist also introduced totally new commodities to Europe: tea, coffee, cocoa, and indigo from the East; tobacco, tomatoes, corn, and potatoes from the Americas. As organizer of industry, he constantly invaded new fields. The putting-out system or the large but unmechanized "factory" became dominant, not only in woolen textiles, armor, and mining, but also in firearms, cutlery, hardware, shipbuilding, and many other industries. The merchant-capitalist became an ever more important figure, both as investor and entrepreneur and as lender to and counselor of ruling kings and princes.

The Rise of National States

Quite as important as the economic expansion of the sixteenth century and the concomitant rise to a position of prominence and influence of the merchant-capitalist was the outstanding political fact of the period—the appearance in western Europe of powerful national states. Until after the middle of the fifteenth century, the terms "England," "France," "Spain," and "Netherlands" had principally geographical and linguistic significance—they carried little political meaning. Although there had been kings of England and of France since at least the Norman Conquest, their power to command the loyalty of their subjects was constantly in dispute, ever challenged by the strong feudal nobility. Spain was divided into Castile, Aragon, and regions still dominated by the Moors, while the Low Countries were principalities of the dukes of Burgundy.

Yet during the late medieval period, even while authority remained dispersed among countless feudal nobles, the bases of their power were being gradually eroded. The slow but steady growth of trade brought with it and was supported by an increase in the supply of money. Towns grew and multipled, expanding the numbers and influence of the wealthy burgher class. The use of money spread, invading even the institutions of feudalism, where it led to the conversion of mutual rights and obligations between lord and vassal into contractual payments. With the spread of the money economy, royal monarchs no longer had to depend on feudal levies of armed knights for military support, but could hire mercenaries, using the proceeds of the taxes that replaced contributions in kind. And in the rising burgher class, they found men experienced in business and finance to administer their increasingly complex affairs and to provide, when needed, substantial loans. Finally, the introduction of gunpowder from China, together with the invention of muskets and cannon, destroyed the impregnability of the castle stronghold and relegated chain mail and plate armor to quiet corners of museums.

In spite of these developments favorable to centralized authority, it required the firm hand and strenuous efforts of Henry VII (1485-1509) to establish the royal power and to unify England. His work of national unification was strengthened and consolidated by his great successors, Henry VIII (1509-47) and Elizabeth (1558-1603). In France, it was not until the end of the Hundred Years' War in 1453, when the English claims to almost half of France were liquidated, that it became possible to weld the numerous duchies and counties into a national state subject to a single ruler. Then, building on the long struggle of his predecessors to subdue the feudal nobles, Louis XI (1461-83) used shrewdness and treachery to consolidate the kingdom. From his time on, the authority of the French king was never in serious doubt, and France became one of the major powers of Europe.

Spain's entry upon the international scene was sudden. Though the separate feudal kingdoms of Castile and Aragon spent several centuries in pushing back the Moors, national unity came all at once, with the marriage in 1469 of Ferdinand of Aragon and Isabella of Castile. In the same year that Columbus discovered America, his royal master's troops were engaged in the conquest of Granada, the last remaining stronghold of the Moors. Thereby all of the Iberian peninsula, with the exception of independent Portugal, came under the rule of a single Spanish king.

The Dutch Republic, the fourth of the great powers of Europe in the early modern period, did not emerge until more than a century later. By a succession of marriages, the Low Countries passed from the hands of the last of the dukes of Burgundy to those of Charles V, King of Spain. The intolerance and persecution that Charles's son Philip II visited upon the Dutch Protestants, culminating in the infamous cruelty and butcheries of his delegate, the Duke of Alva, provoked the Dutch into rebellion. For forty years, their bloody struggle against their Spanish oppressors continued, until in 1609 they won effective independence.

Less powerful and populous than the Big Four of the early modern period, yet important constituents of the emerging international community, were five other national states. Sweden achieved a position of power and influence in central Europe in the sixteenth and seventeeth centuries, while Norway and Denmark attained national unity by the beginning of the sixteenth century. The Swiss cantons shook off Hapsburg domination and became independent in 1499, though much time had to elapse before their confederation became strong and well organized. Portugal, as we have seen, had reached a vigorous nationhood by the time of the great geographical discoveries.

The rise of national states led not only to the subjugation of the feudal nobles and their transformation into courtiers of the king, but also to serious conflict with the Church. For the Church was a great landowner, and as such, it exerted temporal as well as spiritual authority, and was the recipient of large incomes. Moreover, as the sole unifying element in western Christendom, it had long exerted the strongest claim to men's loyalties. But the monarchs of the national states, faced with the need to raise large revenues and to enforce their authority over all their numerous subjects, asserted their right to tax the hitherto exempted clergy as well as Church lands. They insisted that temporal authority was theirs exclusively. The resulting struggle ended in victory for the crown. Together with the Reformation and the consequent transfer of religious affiliation in many of the northern countries to Protestantism, it brought an end to the universal authority of the Catholic Church.

THE BASES AND CHIEF ELEMENTS OF MERCANTILIST THOUGHT

We now have before us the chief elements that shaped the economic ideas of the sixteenth and seventeenth century. One of them was economic expansion, witnessed in ever-widening channels of trade bringing a growing volume of goods, both old and new, to the burgeoning ports of western Europe; in a flood of gold and silver from the New World boosting prices and profits and supporting rapid capital accumulation; and in a growing population supplying more customers to buy the goods, more workers to make them, more settlers to exploit the resources of the Americas. Another element was the rise of the merchant-capitalist class, which furnished the organizers of commercial, shipping, and manufacturing enterprises, and financial advisers and financial sources to royal courts. A third was the new national states, each eager to augment its power, to expand its possessions, and to increase its trade.

Had these features sufficed to describe the main outlines of western Europe in their period, it might well have been an era of peaceful accumulation of wealth, peaceful settlement of the new lands to the West, and rising standards of living. For there was plenty of room for all, ample resources, and un-bounded opportunity.

Accumulation and settlement there was, and improvement in living con-ditions. But there was no peace:

> War was almost a normal relationship among national states. From 1494 to 1559 there was fighting nearly every year in some part of Europe; the seven-teenth century enjoyed only seven calendar years of complete peace, and England was at war during eighty-four of the 165 years between 1650 and 1815.[2]

A Static View of the World

In part, no doubt, this prevalence of war can be attributed to the very human rivalry of ambitious monarchs, in part to religious zeal and intoler-ance. Yet in large measure, what was responsible was an essentially static view of the world and its resources. There was no conception, until relatively late, of the immense size of the American continents, of the room for expan-sion, of the increase in wealth that all could hope to share. Within each country, on the other hand, the desire for growth was strong. Merchants, manufacturers, and shippers all wanted to increase the scope of their activities. The kings and ministers of each of the new national states sought to build up its strength and to improve its position. But if the resources available for expansion were strictly limited, as they were thought to be, the desires of one nation were bound to collide with those of others. International conflict was inevitable.

One of the leading students of Mercantilism has described the situation this way:

> *Within* the state, mercantilism consequently pursued thorough-going dy-namic ends. But the important thing is that this was bound up with a static conception of the total economic resources in the world; for this it was that created that fundamental disharmony which sustained the endless commercial wars. Both elements together implied that the position of a particular country could change and was capable of progress, but that this could only happen through acquisitions from other countries. This was the tragedy of mercan-tilism. Both the Middle Ages with their universal static ideal and *laissez faire* with its universal dynamic ideal avoided this consequence. Without grasping this it is impossible to understand mercantilism either in theory or practice.[3]

The Doctrine of State Power

The common desire of the new states of western Europe to expand their wealth, their population, and their territory, combined with the conviction

---

[2] Herbert Heaton, *Economic History of Europe*, p. 228. Copyright 1936 by Harper & Brothers, New York.

[3] August Heckscher, *Mercantilism*, Vol. II, pp. 25-26. Copyright 1936 by George Allen & Unwin Ltd., London.

that the opportunity for such growth was severely circumscribed, set the overriding goal of national policy. To increase the power of the state by all possible means must be a nation's primary objective.

This goal, and the world view on which it rested, gave shape and content to Mercantilist ideas and practice. If national power was essential in a narrow and hostile world, how could it best be realized? Military strength is, of course, an important component of national power. Great stress therefore, was laid on the recruitment, training, and supplying of a sizeable army. A large navy was even more important, for the mines providing the vital flow of gold and silver lay overseas, and shipments of these precious metals had to be protected—as likewise the merchant vessels carrying the profitable cargoes of goods of all kinds. Colonies furnished an outlet for a growing population and could supply timber, ships' spars, and other naval stores, as well as an ever-widening variety of raw materials for processing by the skilled workers of the mother country. Colonies were therefore important in their own right, and they also required the protection of strong naval forces.

To feed and supply numerous and unproductive soldiers and sailors, one must be sure of a steady production of muskets, cannon, gunpowder, ships, clothing, and rations. A country therefore has to be economically strong. It must have available a wide range of manufactures and assured supplies of all the raw materials they need. National wealth, in other words, was seen to be the very foundation of national power.

The Necessity of Regulation

If all these things are necessary to ensure the strength of the nation, the question next arises: what is the best way of making certain that a nation has them?

Of one thing Mercantilist statesmen were sure: their provision could not be left to chance, or to the unguided efforts of the individual. His activities must be regulated by the state—they must be subordinated and made to conform to the goal of national power. There was another reason for this preference for regulation of economic activity: no one had much experience with any other policy. Throughout the Middle Ages, the methods used by craftsmen and the quality of their product had been closely controlled by the craft gilds. Choice of an occupation by an individual was free for comparatively few; most people were compelled by tradition to follow in the footsteps of their fathers. Trade, too, had always been subject to jealous and detailed regulation. Thus, regulation of economic activity not only appeared to the statesman of Mercantilist times to be logically necessary; it also had the strong appeal of familiarity.

We can express the gist of the Mercantilist philosophy by describing it as *giving first rank to the goal of national power and adopting regulation of economic life as the preferred means of ensuring the desired increase of wealth.*

Expressions of this viewpoint are abundant in pamphlets and books that poured from the presses of Europe throughout the sixteenth and seventeenth centuries. Interest in economic affairs was keen, especially in matters of current government policy. Contributions to a lively discussion came from prominent merchants, lawyers, financial advisers to governments, and state officials. It is this miscellany of writers who later became known as Mercantilists. In spite of differences on details, they shared a substantial area of agreed opinion, which included the views we have just summarized as the core of Mercantilist doctrine. This concensus is not surprising, for their assumptions were based on the world situation they confronted and which, as members of the same social class, they tended to see in a common light.

The Balance-of-Trade Theory

In addition to their agreement on the goal of national power, on an abundance of riches as its essential support, and on regulation of economic activity as the best means of attaining national wealth, Mercantilists also shared—what is of particular interest to us—a common theory of international trade. This may be summarily stated as follows: *that a nation could only gain through foreign trade if it had a favorable balance, or an excess in the value of exports over imports.* The gain arose from the fact that an excess of exports over imports had to be paid for with gold and silver, and for a nation to acquire those precious metals, or treasure, was the surest way of enriching itself. For a nation without gold and silver mines, it was the *only* way.

Clearly, the favorable balance-of-trade doctrine rested upon the conviction that the precious metals were of paramount importance. To the Mercantilists, wealth consisted above all else in gold and silver. Clement Armstrong, an English Mercantilist of the early sixteenth century, asserted that it is "better to have plenty of gold and silver in the realm than plenty of merchants and merchandizes," and Monchrétien, a Frenchman writing a century later, said: "We live not so much from trade in raw materials as from gold and silver."[4]

Why the Stress on the Precious Metals?

Today we think differently. We recognize that gold and silver are minor components of a nation's wealth, that what really counts is abundance of goods capable of satisfying human wants, and even more, of the productive resources that make a continued flow of such goods possible.

Likewise, we regard the gains from trade as resting not on the accumulation of gold and silver, but on the possibility of taking advantage of international specialization. A country benefits from trade because it can obtain its imported goods more cheaply through trade than by producing them itself; therefore, its real income is larger if it trades than if it tries to be self-sufficient.

What led the Mercantilists to take their extreme and untenable position?

[4] Cited in Heckscher, *op. cit.,* p. 187.

Probably the most important reason was simply the use of imprecise terms, a practice that is almost unavoidable when a science is in its infancy, but which still plagues economics today. "Wealth" means many things, including the precious metals. But when the Mercantilists lived, money consisted almost exclusively of gold and silver; bank notes and bank credit were yet but little used. And since wealth is measured in money and is constantly being exchanged for it, their confusion is understandable, especially since many Mercantilists were themselves traders.

In addition to confusion as to the meaning of wealth, there were other reasons for according the precious metals a position of paramount importance. They are very durable, and thus serve well as a means of storing up or hoarding wealth. The Mercantilists highly approved saving as a means to the accumulation of wealth, but since their concept of saving was closely akin to hoarding, gold and silver naturally appeared in a preferred light. Most obviously of all, money could buy arms, supplies, and the services of troops; as a war chest, it had a strong appeal to nations almost constantly engaged in or planning military campaigns.

Given the premise that gold and silver together comprise the most important form of wealth, the balance-of-trade doctrine follows logically and fits perfectly into the more general principles of Mercantilist thought. If the state must be powerful, if wealth is the necessary bulwark of such power, and if money is wealth *par excellence,* then ministers of state must bend every effort to ensure their country an abundant supply of the precious metals.

An Element of Truth in the Balance-of-Trade Doctrine

With respect to the short-run monetary effects of a favorable balance of trade, a widely held Mercantilist view was closer to the truth than that held by their successors, the classical economists. As we know today, when unemployment is high and the inducement to invest is weak, a lowering of interest rates may stimulate an increase in investment and in employment. And in the short run, at least, an increase in the supply of money can often effect a lowering of interest rates.

The Mercantilists generally were convinced that a close connection existed between the supply of money and the interest rate, though only the more perspicacious were at all clear as to the reason.[5] Abundance of money meant low interest rates, expanding investment, and employment; scarcity of money meant the opposite. Here, then, was another and more valid reason for desiring—especially in a time when metallic money was the principal kind in use—a favorable balance of trade.[6]

Note, however, that this reason is valid only at times of substantial unem-

[5] Heckscher, *op. cit.,* p. 200.
[6] For a fuller discussion of this and related points, see J. M. Keynes, *The General Theory of Employment, Interest and Money,* Ch. 23. Copyright 1936 by Macmillan & Co., London.

ployment. When most workers are occupied, any lowering of interest rates through an increase in the supply of money can have little effect on employment. The principal effect will then be on prices. We shall return to this point later.

Some reader may raise the question: if an increase in the supply of money will lower interest rates and stimulate employment, why not simply expand credit and paper money, instead of striving through complex devices to ensure an expansion of the supply of metallic money through a favorable balance of trade? This is just the question raised by some of the later Mercantilists, around 1700, and it caused them to abandon the favorable balance-of-trade doctrine. Surely that doctrine would have been set aside far earlier had there been a clearer perception of the role of money and of the relation of money to other forms of wealth.

Balance-of-Trade Corollaries

From the basic economic doctrine that the primary goal of economic policy should be the attainment of a favorable balance of trade, there followed a number of corollaries. The value of exports should be made as great as possible; this meant that not only should the greatest possible amount of goods be exported, but also that exports of high value were to be preferred to those of low value. For this reason, exports of raw materials were decried; every effort was made to bring about their production at home, and to export the finished product. Imports, of course, must be kept to the minimum; raw materials were to be preferred to manufactures, as being of less value. Imports of the latter, especially of luxury manufactures, were to be severely restricted, if not completely prohibited.

Perhaps the clearest and most concise expression of these ideas is to be found in the work of an Austrian Mercantilist, Von Hornick (1638-1712):

> . . . all commodities found in a country, which cannot be used in their natural state, should be worked up within the country; since the payment for manufacturing generally exceeds the value of the raw material by two, three, ten, twenty, and even a hundred fold. . . .
>
> The inhabitants of the country should make every effort to get along with their domestic products, to confine their luxury to these alone, and to do without foreign products as far as possible (except where great need leaves no alternative, or if not need, wide-spread, unavoidable abuse, of which Indian spices are an example). . . .
>
> Such foreign commodities should in this case be imported in unfinished form, and worked up within the country, thus earning the wages of *manufacture* there. . . .
>
> Opportunities should be sought night and day for selling the country's superfluous goods to these foreigners in manufactured form, so far as this is necessary, and for gold and silver; and to this end, *consumption,* so to speak, must be sought in the farthest ends of the earth, and developed in every possible way. . . .

Except for important considerations, no importation should be allowed under any circumstances of commodities of which there is a sufficient supply of suitable quality at home; and in this matter neither sympathy nor compassion should be shown foreigners, by their friends, kinsfolk, *allies,* or enemies. For all friendship ceases, when it involves my own weakness and ruin. And this holds good, even if the domestic commodities are of poorer quality, or even higher priced. For it would be better to pay for an article two dollars which remain in the country than only one which goes out, however strange this may seem to the ill-informed.[7]

Get the foreigner to pay you as much as possible, pay him as little as you can—this rule extended not only to all goods traffic, but also to other kinds of international payments. The "invisible items," such as freight earnings, insurance payments, travelers' expenses, diplomatic and military expenditures abroad, and so on, were recognized early, and most of the leading Mercantilists urged the necessity of including these in the calculation of a country's favorable balance. The balance they had in mind was therefore a balance of international payments of all kinds, not just a balance of trade items. Thus Mun stated:

The value of our exportations likewise may be much advanced when we perform it ourselves in our own Ships, for then we get not only the price of our wares as they are worth here, but also the Merchants gains, the charges of ensurance, and fraight to carry them beyond the seas.[8]

MERCANTILISM IN ACTION: CONCRETE POLICIES

From the doctrine of state power and the derived theory of the balance of trade followed most of the concrete policies of Mercantilism.

Regulation of Trade

To anyone who regards trade principally as a means of obtaining a continuous inflow of the precious metals, it cannot be left to itself to develop naturally, but must be constantly watched and regulated. The Mercantilists developed a formidable apparatus of trade regulations; scarcely any measure that would promote exports or diminish imports, no matter how petty or annoying, was overlooked.

BULLIONISM One of the earliest, and certainly the crudest, of Mercantilist restrictions consisted in the direct prohibition of exports of gold or silver bullion. The reasoning underlying bullionism, as it came to be called, was simple, obvious, and naive: if the precious metals do enter the country, keep them there.

[7] Phillip W. Von Hornick, "Austria Over All If She Only Will," reprinted in Arthur Eli Monroe, *Early Economic Thought,* pp. 223-25. Copyright 1927 by Harvard University Press, Cambridge, Mass.

[8] *Ibid.,* p. 174.

Bullionist restrictions go back to the Middle Ages, but were common in the sixteenth and seventeenth centuries. Spain, the recipient of most of the gold and silver from the Americas, applied these restrictions over the longest period and with the greatest severity; it imposed the death penalty for the export of bullion or coin, established rewards for informers, and prohibited the purchase of bullion by foreigners. Yet so great was the appetite for goods in her growing colonies, and even among her own citizens, and so feeble the ability of her backward economy to produce them, that in the face of the flood of gold and silver, prices of commodities soared. Importing became so profitable, corruption of officials so common, that large amounts of specie moved surreptitiously into the hands of foreigners. Spain finally licensed limited exports of gold and silver. In England and Holland, bullionist restrictions virtually came to an end by about the middle of the sixteenth century.

THE MONOPOLY OF TRADE   Prominent among Mercantilist measures were those designed to exclude all foreigners from certain areas of trade. Portugal made the monopoly of trade with the East the backbone of her policy throughout the sixteenth century, even going so far as to capture or destroy the ships of interlopers. The king, moreover, kept the trade in his own hands; private traders could carry on only petty dealings, being limited to what they could transport in their cabins on royal ships.

Spain, too, attempted to monopolize the trade with its colonies, though unlike Portugal, it did not try to keep all commerce in royal hands. Private traders bought goods in Spain and shipped them to the colonies to an agent, who sold them and shipped back specie or colonial produce. All goods had to be carried, however, in royal ships, and traders' activities were subject to the closest inspection and regulation. To make this control more effective, colonial trade was confined to one port in Spain, Seville, and to a limited number of American ports. For protection against pirates, privateers, or organized attack by other nations, after 1560 all west-bound vessels sailed twice annually in great fleets accompanied by warships. When they arrived in the Indies, their shipments were sold at great fairs, the return cargo was loaded aboard, and the fleet sailed back to Spain.

This system worked quite well in the sixteenth century, in spite of considerable smuggling, but broke down in the seventeenth, owing to Spain's increasing economic weakness. Its land eroded by the overgrazing of sheep, its most industrious citizens and most skilled artisans—the Jews and Moors—expelled from the country, its economy ridden by inflation and by heavy taxation to support foreign wars, Spanish industry simply could not produce the goods demanded in its colonial markets. Dutch, English, and French traders, with the connivance of local governors, took over a large share of the trade with Spain's colonies by illegal methods.

Dutch Mercantilism revolved around the monopoly of the East India Company (founded in 1602). Its officials established trading posts in Java,

Amboina, and other islands of the East Indies, drove out traders of other nationalities, and thereafter successfully bent every effort to keep them out. In addition to making the Indies its private preserve, the Company practiced every other device of monopoly. It limited the production of certain commodities, such as coffee, pepper, nutmeg, cloves, and indigo, to specific areas, destroying crops raised elsewhere; it used its strong bargaining power to hold to a minimum the prices it paid native growers. The artificially scarce but cheap goods were then sold at high prices in the European market. Small wonder that the Company established a dividend record unequalled in history.

DIRECT REGULATION OF TRADE   Through their trading monopolies, the various nations sought to improve the balance of trade by obtaining needed supplies within an imperial area and by buying cheap—and selling dear—things needed by the rest of the world. This same objective was also pursued by the many detailed regulations applied to exports and imports. All the countries of western Europe, with the sole exception of Holland, used these measures extensively, but they were probably more widespread and more highly developed in England than elsewhere.

Thus British exports that could not meet foreign competition unaided were supported at the very least with refunds ("drawbacks") of taxes, internal or external, previously paid on raw materials. If more help was necessary, a subsidy was not hard to get. A more indirect stimulus to exports was sought in obstacles to the export of raw materials. It was thought that by keeping them at home, they would be made abundant and cheap, to the advantage of the exporter of finished products. Export duties were levied on a long list of raw materials and semifabricated articles, but total prohibition of such exports was common. The English woolen textile industry, accounting in 1700 for half the country's exports, was thus favored; we find sheep, wool, woolen yarn and worsted, as well as fuller's earth (used in cleaning wool) all on the list of prohibited exports. Enforcement of the law was Draconian in its severity; for the first offense the transgressor was to have his left hand cut off; the second offense carried the death penalty.

Measures aimed at imports paralleled those affecting exports. Instead of receiving a subsidy, practically every good imported into England paid a heavy duty, in a very large number of cases so high as to be prohibitive. As we might expect, direct prohibition of imports applied to England's most important manufactures, both woolen and silk textiles being so favored. Imports of raw materials, on the other hand, were permitted duty-free entry; some (principally naval stores and indigo from the American colonies) were even given bounties.

Each particular regulation, taken by itself, worked to the advantage of some specific industry. Special interests, therefore, worked unremittingly to maintain and extend the system that protected and favored them, yet in so doing they also worked to further the general interest, as it was understood in the Mercantilist economic philosophy.

Here, with a reverse twist, is that coincidence of selfish and public interests that Adam Smith later attributed to the working of laissez faire. He denied it to Mercantilism simply because he refused to accept either its principal goal, the increase of the power of the state, or its basic assumption, the supreme importance of the precious metals.

The Navigation System

If the complex system of trade regulation followed logically from the Mercantilist balance-of-trade doctrine, so likewise did the laws adopted by various countries to foster a native shipping industry. For as it was early recognized, ocean freights could substantially add to or subtract from a country's balance of international payments. Reenforcing this contribution of a merchant fleet to a nation's economic strength was its equally important contribution to its physical strength: merchant vessels—and the fisheries, too— reared up a force of seamen to man the navy, while the ships themselves could be converted into privateers or auxiliary men-of-war, or provide an assured means of bringing in needed foreign supplies. Laws affecting navigation, therefore, bulked large in Mercantilist economic policy. Nowhere did this aspect of national power receive closer attention or fuller expression than in England, whose insular position from early times aroused keen interest in matters relating to the sea.

Although England took her first steps in the regulation of maritime traffic as early as the late fourteenth century, and imposed increasingly exclusive controls as her colonial system developed, two and a half centuries passed before they were strengthened and consolidated in the famous Navigation Acts of 1651 and 1660. The motive leading to the adoption of these laws was the severe inroads on the British-carrying trade made by the Dutch while England was preoccupied with the Civil War of 1642-46. Their purpose and effect was to reserve, with as few exceptions as possible, the carriage of freight to and from British and colonial ports to British (including colonial) vessels.

The Navigation Acts succeeded in excluding foreign ships from the British coastal trade, from trade between the colonies and Britain, and from carrying imports from Asia, Africa, or the Americas to Britain or her colonies. British ships, moreover, had to be British built and three-quarters British manned. It was felt unwise, however, to prevent foreigners from taking English exports to noncolonial destinations, for this could mean larger exports, a goal at least as important as a monopoly of the shipping trade. Yet if foreign ships were to be allowed to call at English ports, they must be allowed to bring goods in. Hence imports into the British Isles from the continent were permitted, though they had to pay double duties on arrival, and, to hold down the Dutch entrepot trade, they also had to come direct from the country of origin. Certain specific exceptions to the British monopoly of shipping also had to be granted for practical reasons. Thus, because they needed the spices produced in the Dutch East Indies, goods from the Spanish and Portuguese colonies, commodities coming to Holland overland from Italy, and naval stores, these could be brought to Britain from entrepot centers, even in the ships of their Dutch rivals.

Monopoly of the colonial trade was reenforced by the establishment of a list of "enumerated" commodities, comprising the most important colonial products, which the colonies could export only to other British possessions.[9] This regulation had particular relevance to the extremely profitable trade in sugar and molasses with the Spanish and French West Indies, which the sugar planters of the British West Indies wanted to reserve for themselves. These products went to the American colonies for conversion into rum, which in turn was shipped to Africa, there exchanged for slaves, who were transported to the West Indies. Since a single complete voyage yielded a profit as high as 1000 per cent, no wonder Yankee smuggling proved impossible to stop.

Although Spain and France also endeavored to enforce a monopoly of trade with their colonies, their policy was less rigorous than the British, and less successful.

The Dutch, on the other hand, showed a liberality unusual for this period. Except in the cherished East Indies trade, they relied not upon monopoly but upon competition. They developed the light, easily handled flyboat to replace the clumsy, armed tub in general use, standardized its design, bought construction materials in bulk, and built it by methods resembling the modern assembly line. Besides cheap construction, the need for a small crew and willingness to hire sailors of any nationality at the lowest possible wage—in contrast to the 'nationality requirements of their rivals—kept operating costs low and Dutch freight rates at levels half to two-thirds those of their competitors. No wonder that in the late seventeenth century perhaps half of Europe's shipping tonnage was Dutch, and that Holland was the shipbuilder to Europe.

The Old Colonial System

In the management of their colonies, the English felt that since they furnished the people and the capital needed for colonial development, they had a right to guide this development in such a way as to serve their major political objective, the increase of national power. According to Mercantilist doctrines, this meant using the colonies as a base of supplies needed by the mother country, as a source of raw materials that could be worked up into manufactures for export, and as a market for the products of English labor.

---

[9] At first including only sugar, tobacco, cotton, ginger, indigo, and dye-woods, this list was expanded by a score of commodities in the eighteenth century, and in 1766, all colonial exports to any port north of Cape Finisterre were forbidden.

The means to this end of making colonies serve as the economic complement of the home country were numerous, and we have considered some of
them already. Thus the navigation system, in addition to establishing a semi-
monopoly of the carrying trade for British subjects, also formed an integral
part of the colonial system. The principle of enumerated commodities, in
particular, guaranteed that England would have her pick of these major
products of the colonies and that her merchants would secure the profits to
be gained from the reexport of any surplus.

In addition to the close regulation of colonial trade contained in the navigation acts, controls were established over the development of colonial industry. Positive encouragement of colonial production of articles wanted in
England for consumption or reexport took the form of bounties or of preferential duties on their import into the British Isles. Negative measures of control aimed at the suppression of colonial manufactures in favor of producers
in the mother country; these included the prohibition of colonial exports of
woolen products and hats and of colonial processing of iron.

In spite of the burdens to which Britain's colonial subjects had to submit,
we must remember that the special privileges possessed by English merchants
and shippers were shared equally with colonials. The colonial system most
injured the interests of consumers: English consumers, like colonial consumers, were sacrificed to the requirements of Mercantilism. Yet as the
population and wealth of the colonies increased to the point where local manufacturing industries became significant, their suppression added one more element to the conflict of interests that led to the American Revolution.

The Internal Regulation of Industry

French Mercantilism stressed the guidance and control of domestic industry. Policy in this field followed two principal lines: the deliberate encouragement of manufactures, and the close regulation of almost every aspect of
production.

In the seventeenth century, stimulation of manufactures first took the form
of grants of tax exemptions, subsidies, and privileges and of the liberal investment of royal funds—as in the establishment of the raw silk and silk manufacturing industry and in many other luxury industries for which France is
still famous.

Under Colbert, Louis XIV's great minister, the policy of fostering industrial development was intensified and expanded. Many businesses were made
"royal manufactures" (the Gobelins' tapestry works is the best known), a
title that carried with it the assurance of sales to the crown as well as the
luster and prestige that went with royal patronage.

Colbert carried even further the second aspect of French industrial policy,
the state regulation of industry. Building on existing gild controls, he drew
up a comprehensive system of uniform regulations for each type of produc-

tion, imposed them by decree, and tried—with indifferent success—to enforce them through local inspectors appointed from Paris.

England as well as France tried centralized regulation of industry. In the reign of Elizabeth, a major piece of legislation, the Statute of Artificers (1563), brought together and codified into a national system the workable parts of earlier national laws and local regulations. Its more important purposes were the provision of adequate training for industrial workers, who had suffered from the decay of the gilds and the spread of industry to villages and country districts; the ensurance of an ample supply of agricultural labor; and the establishment of greater security of employment. It met these goals by requiring, in every branch of industry, an apprenticeship of seven years; by prescribing in general terms a uniform training in each craft for all England; by making compulsory the employment in agriculture of all workers not engaged in some specific industry; and by setting up as the minimum hiring period the term of one year. In addition it continued the regulation of wages, established in the mid-fourteenth century to cope with the great shortage of labor resulting from the Black Death.

Two other devices were also tried in England, though much less extensively than in France. Regulation of the quality of goods produced had been practiced in the woolen industry from its early days. To ensure the high quality of English exports, fabrics were subject to inspection by a royal official, the alnager; failure to meet standard specifications resulted in fines and confiscation of unsatisfactory goods. The first decades of the seventeenth century saw the extension of official supervision to the silk trade, to the smelting of iron, tin, and lead, and to the mining of coal.

Industrial policy was never as important in Holland or Spain as in either France or England. Holland, as we have seen, concentrated upon securing and maintaining a monopoly of the trade with the East Indies. At home, she followed a policy of relatively free trade and free conduct of industry. Spain likewise strove, though much less successfully, to rivet a monopoly control upon the trade of her American colonies; this implied the exclusion of foreign wares and merchants from Spanish markets. But Spanish industry simply could not deliver the goods, and her colonial markets were increasingly supplied by imports from other parts of Europe.

Labor Under Mercantilism

Trade, colonial, and navigation policies were, as we have stressed, shaped by the Mercantilist balance-of-trade theory. So too were the views and policies of Mercantilists toward labor, which in an age when capital equipment was limited mainly to comparatively simple tools, was clearly the chief factor of production, especially in manufacturing. Since exports of manufactures ranked high as a means of obtaining the precious metals, it is, therefore, only natural that Mercantilists stressed the need for a large and growing population to ensure an ample supply of labor, or that they advocated measures to stimulate its increase, such as rewards for marriage, bounties for children, and penalties on the unmarried. Indeed, they even went so far as to concede labor "a position of strategic importance."[10] Expressions such as the following were common:

> The people are the riches and strength of the country. (Nicholas Barbon)
> Is not that country richest which has the most labor? (Josiah Tucker)
> That the strength and riches of a society consists in the numbers of the people is an assertion which hath attained the force of a maxim in politics. (Henry Fielding)

If the quantity of labor was important, its skill and industriousness were equally so, for these qualities would enable it to produce more and better exports. Almost without exception, economic writers of the Mercantilist period emphasized the need for habits of industry and the acquisition of manufacturing skills.

But what of wages? It would appear that those who hold that "the people are the riches and strength of the country" should also want to see them well paid, comfortable, and satisfied with their lot. Most Mercantilists, however, held quite the contrary view. In order to have a favorable balance of trade, it was necessary to be able to undersell the foreign rival. Labor, being the largest element in cost, therefore must be cheap. Large numbers of workers were needed, not only to ensure a large volume of manufactures for export, but also to guarantee low wages, low cost, and strong competitive ability.

We know today that it does not necessarily follow that labor costs will be low only if wages are low. High wages are consistent with low labor costs if the productivity of labor is high. But among Mercantilists the opinion was widespread that high wages induced, not greater industry, but idleness and sloth. Thus, Arthur Young, a widely traveled and intelligent observer of the middle of the eighteenth century, merely expressed the common viewpoint of many other contemporary and earlier writers when he said:

> Every one but an idiot knows that the lower classes must be kept poor or they will never be industrious; I do not mean, that the poor of England are to be kept like the poor of *France,* but, the state of the country considered, they must (like all mankind) be in poverty or they will not work.[11]

A low opinion of the motives that stimulated the workman to effort thus combined with the balance-of-trade theory (and with the self-interest of the employing classes) to establish the necessity of low wages as a firmly held doctrine. At the same time, it was believed with equal conviction that labor was of vital importance in the national economy. There is no inconsistency

---

[10] Edgar S. Furniss, *The Position of the Laborer in a System of Nationalism,* p. 31, Copyright 1930 by Houghton, Mifflin Co., Boston. The quotations immediately following are from p. 22n.

[11] Arthur Young, *Eastern Tour* (1771), p. 361, cited in Furniss, *op. cit.,* p. 118.

in the two ideas, however. An abundance of labor, as a source of exports and thus of treasure, was a necessary condition of national wealth and power. But this labor must be industrious and productive; if poverty is essential to make the laborer work, then low wages are just as much a necessary condition as an ample supply of labor.

Although it was easy for the Mercantilist to accord labor a position of great importance while at the same time denying it a reward much above mere subsistence, how could he possibly reconcile "the riches of the nation" with a people many of whom were in rags, and most of whom were poorly clad, badly housed, and ill fed? The reconciliation was simple. To the typical Mercantilist, the welfare of the common man had nothing to do with national wealth. That nation was rich which had, not a prosperous and well-fed population, but abundance of "treasure." To a person obsessed with the importance of gold and silver, convinced of the necessity of having a favorable balance of trade to obtain the precious metals, and sure that the only way to make people work hard was to keep them poor, the poverty of the common man was a national asset. A rich nation and a poor people were not incompatible, but actually complementary. To such paradoxical lengths were they led by a short-sighted view of the nature of wealth.

SELECTED REFERENCES

Clough, Shepard B. and Charles W. Cole, *Economic History of Europe*. Boston: D. C. Heath & Co., 1941.

Ferguson, W. K., *The Renaissance*. New York: Henry Holt & Co., 1940. An excellent brief statement of the major changes western society underwent in this exciting period.

Furniss, Edgar S., *The Position of the Laborer in a System of Nationalism*. Boston: Houghton, Mifflin Co., 1930. This book, especially Chapter II, contains a full and eminently readable account of the laborer in Mercantilist thought.

Heaton, Herbert, *Economic History of Europe*. New York: Harper & Bros., 1936. Both this and the text by Clough and Cole contain good chapters on the background of the Mercantilist period.

Heckscher, August, *Mercantilism*, 2 vols. London: Geo. Allen & Unwin, Ltd., 1936. This is the most comprehensive study of Mercantilism available, both with respect to theory and practice.

Lipson, E., *A Planned Economy or Free Enterprise,* 2nd ed. London: Adam & Chas. Black, 1946. Chapter II is interesting for its argument that Mercantilism was a "planned economy."

Mosse, George L., *The Reformation*. New York: Henry Holt & Co., 1953. An excellent brief special study.

Viner, Jacob, *Studies in the Theory of International Trade*. New York: Harper & Bros., 1937. Chapters I and II provide the best discussion available of the Mercantilist theory of foreign trade as it was expressed in England.

3

THE TRANSITION TO
ECONOMIC LIBERALISM

Any period of history is transitional, in the sense that it is not static, but is undergoing changes that foreshadow what is to come, while at the same time it clings to and only gradually sheds habits and institutions of an earlier age. Thus in the period from 1500 to 1750, Mercantilist views were dominant, but were themselves permeated and also in conflict with medieval doctrines and practices. Simultaneously, the theory and practice of Mercantilism underwent change, as the social class that spawned it, the merchant capitalists, became more numerous, more powerful, and more confident. The parallel institution of princely rule was also drastically modified, especially in England, as the national state to whose needs it ministered became more firmly established and secure in its power. And both economic ideas and the principles and practices of government reflected the influence of the spread of the scientific spirit and the changes it wrought in men's outlook on the world.

Continuity of History

In sum, the Middle Ages did not end in 1500, nor did the age of laissez faire begin with Adam Smith. The one extended its hold far into modern times; the other began as a seedling long before it came to flower. The historian G. M. Trevelyan clearly expresses this continuity of history in the following passage:

It is indeed useless to look for any date, or even for any period, when the Middle Ages "ended" in England. All that one can say is that, in the Thirteenth Century, English thought and society were mediaeval, and in the Nineteenth Century they were not. Yet even now we retain the mediaeval institutions of the Monarchy, the Peerage, the Commons in Parliament assembled, the English Common Law, the Courts of Justice interpreting the rule of law, the hierarchy of the established Church, the parish system, the Universities, the Public Schools and Grammar Schools. And unless we become a Totalitarian State and forget all our Englishry, there will always be something mediaeval in our ways of thinking, especially in our idea that people and corporations

[38]

have rights and liberties which the State ought in some degree to respect, in spite of the legal omnicompetence of Parliament. Conservatism and Liberalism, in the broadest sense, are both mediaeval in origin, and so are trade unions. The men who established our civil liberties in the Seventeenth Century, appealed to mediaeval precedents against the "modernizing" monarchy of the Stuarts. The pattern of history is indeed a tangled web. No single diagram will explain its infinite complication.[1]

Just as no powerful social habits have suddenly lost their influence, so none has suddenly sprung into being. The individualistic age which was to follow Mercantilism was not the creation of the "classical" economists, but was germinating and slowly taking shape in an environment of state regulation and of restrictions aiming at the maximum favorable balance of trade.

The problem of this chapter is to trace the major strands out of which there grew a new philosophy of government and a new economic viewpoint that were to achieve dominance for a time, and then become modified, qualified, and eventually, perhaps, superseded by still other philosophies of government and economics more suited to the changed society they both shaped and mirrored.

THE INFLUENCE OF THE RISING CAPITALIST CLASS

The most important single contribution to the decline of the Mercantilist system of ideas and regulations and to the rise of economic individualism came from the growth in the numbers, wealth, and influence of the rising class of business men. Comparatively few and unimportant as a class in the late fifteenth century, by the eighteenth they were numerous, rich, and powerful. They then dominated the affairs of cities and towns, were heavily represented in Parliament, and carried great weight in councils of state.

Challenge and Response

Their rise was made possible by the rapid expansion to whose increasing opportunities they responded vigorously and successfully. We have seen how the great geographical discoveries opened up a new world of trade, both in the Americas and in the East. To the stimulus of an expanding trading area was added the further stimulus of rising prices, supported by the seepage of the precious metals out of Spain and by occasional large leaks engineered by the daring piracy of men such as Drake, Hawkins, and Frobisher. Trade offered rich rewards, capital accumulation proceeded in almost geometrical progression, and merchants, manufacturers, shippers, and bankers, English and Dutch above all, waxed prosperous and powerful.

As the older industrial organizations of the craft gilds proved incapable of meeting the demands of an expanding economy, its place was taken, in

[1] G. M. Trevelyan, *English Social History*, pp. 95-96. Copyright 1942 by Longmans, Green and Co., New York. Reprinted by permission of the publisher.

industry after industry, by individual enterprise. The domestic system, with the merchant capitalist in the central guiding role, became common and eventually predominant, not only in the woolen trade, but also in shipbuilding, iron production and manufacture, mining, and in occupation after occupation, until by the eighteenth century, this system, supplemented and sometimes overshadowed here and there by small factories, was typical, and gild organization was an occasional survival of the past.

The substitution of the individual businessman for the corporate gild led to a radical change in the ideals by which men measured their accomplishments. The new aim of getting rich quick replaced the older ideal of a "suitable" income. The medieval notion of the regulation of economic activity according to moral principles gave way to the pursuit of wealth for its own sake.

At first this led, as we have seen, to the near-worship of the precious metals and to the regulation of trade so as to create a favorable balance of trade and an inflow of gold and silver.

Freedom Favors Expansion

Yet at the very time that these Mercantilist tendencies were strongest, individuals here and there perceived that their desire for gain would best be served by freedom. A free market, it became slowly but increasingly apparent, offered greater scope for individual initiative, and where individual initiative was least hampered, output could be most rapidly increased, costs could be lowered by using new methods and new sources of supply, and gain could be maximized. The desire of particular business men for freedom to expand their activities led to pronouncements and appeals in favor of the relaxation of Mercantilist restrictions.

This dislike of regulation appeared early. Thus, in 1550, Sir John Masone, expressing himself with respect to a proclamation regulating the price of butter and cheese, said:

> I have seen so many experiences of such ordinances; and ever the end is dearth, and lack of the thing that we seek to make *good cheap*. Nature will have her course, . . . and never shall you drive her to consent that a *penny-worth* of new shall be sold for a *farthing*. . . . For who will keep a cow that may not sell the milk for so much as the merchant and he can agree upon?[2]

Another illustration, a half century later in date, is furnished by the comment of Sir Walter Raleigh on a bill making compulsory the sowing of a certain proportion of hemp:

> For my part, I do not like this constraining of men to use their grounds at our wills. Rather let every man use his ground to that which is most fit for, and therein use his own discretion.[3]

[2] Cited in H. M. Robertson, *Aspects of the Rise of Economic Individualism*, p. 70. Copyright 1933 by Cambridge University Press, New York.
[3] *Ibid.*

The slow accretion of such views as these went on steadily, building up, bit by bit, a widening sentiment in favor of freedom. At the same time, the belief that regulation and restriction of industry and of *internal* trade was necessary underwent gradual erosion.

Decline of State Control

The spreading dislike of regulation was strongly reenforced by experience, especially in England. For state control of industry, in particular the system of monopoly grants, had worked badly. Partly to domesticate industries that had grown up abroad or to develop new industries, partly to obtain revenue, the crown had adopted the system of granting monopolies to individuals or groups in return for a lump payment or a share of the profits. During the late sixteenth and early seventeenth centuries, such English industries as glass, salt, soap, alum mining, pin manufacturing, the production of wire, and the sale of coal came under this system. The result, quite generally, was high prices, poor quality, and inadequate supplies. "Nearly all the monopolists promised to supply a better quality more cheaply. In no single case was this promise fulfilled."[4] But not only were the monopolies grasping; they were also inefficient and corrupt, frequently being given, not to the most promising enterpriser, but to court favorites and their friends.

Public indignation mounted, became vocal, and expressed itself vigorously in meetings, pamphlets, and speeches in Parliament. Finally, with the establishment of that body's supremacy by the Revolution of 1688, the royal right of dispensation was abolished. Thereafter the individual was free to develop any industry to which he might be attracted.

But dislike of regulation did not stop at government-supported monopolies; it extended also to those survivals of the Middle Ages, wage and price regulations. The central agency that supervised and administered these ordinances was the Privy Council, a sort of super-cabinet. Their local enforcement was in the hands of the Justices of the Peace. With the abolition of the Privy Council at the time of the Cromwellian Revolution (1642-46), the whole system of regulation lost its head; its hands and feet continued to function as before for a time, but showed increasing feebleness and lack of coordination. The Justices of the Peace were overburdened with a multitude of duties; where opposition to the wages and price legislation was strong, they tended to permit it to become a dead letter. Its enforcement became more and more sporadic. By the eighteenth century, the system of regulation was in an advanced stage of decay.

Other aspects of state control also declined or disappeared in the latter part of the seventeenth or in the eighteenth century. Thus the regulation of the quality of various kinds of goods, which had been enforced by agents of the

---

[4] Herman Levy, *Economic Liberalism,* p. 30. Copyright 1913 by The Macmillan Company, London.

crown, was abandoned when Parliament became the dominant institution of government. Even the Elizabethan Statute of Artificers, which regulated the conditions of apprenticeship, became more limited in its application, trade after trade being exempted by Parliament from its scope.

Thus, by the end of the seventeenth century there had been a strong growth of sentiment in favor of economic freedom and a great increase in the actual area of freedom. These tendencies were the result of the rise of an important capitalist trading and industrial class, itself the response of the individualist side of human nature to the expanding opportunities that appeared after the great geographical discoveries.

RELIGION

All during the Middle Ages, the influence of religion had been on the side of society against the individual. It had supported with its authority the medieval system of status, in which each person had his place, with established rights and established responsibilities, and it also contributed greatly to the framework of social organization. The Church refused to countenance the taking of interest on loans, or usury, or the charging of more than the "just price." To do either was to be guilty of extortion and thus of the sin of avarice. Indeed, the Church and its ethical teachings permeated society and the daily lives of men.

As the opportunities for commercial activity increased and the commercial motive of gain became an ever more powerful force, the growing desire for individual freedom began to push against all obstacles that stood in its way. We have just seen how this force modified law and opinion in the sixteenth and seventeenth centuries. Religion was by no means excepted from its influence. Even in the Middle Ages, the doctrines of usury and of "just price" underwent a gradual softening which made them more agreeable to the investor and the trader. As the commercial and industrial classes became more numerous and more influential, their views, reflecting the changing facts of economic life, forced the Churches, both Catholic and Protestant, into a step-by-step retreat.

> . . . The Churches, one and all, have had to accommodate themselves to an extraneous development of a busy commercial spirit, . . . capitalism has created, or found already existent, its own spirit, and set the Churches the task of assimilating it.[5]

Religion generally fought a losing battle with the individualism of the shop or the market place. In the case of the Protestant churches, individualism actually invaded the sacred precincts, turning them to its own purposes. Al-

[5] H. M. Robertson, *Aspects of the Rise of Economic Individualism,* p. 165. Copyright 1933 by Cambridge University Press, New York.

though, as Tawney shows, conservatism and communal discipline were strong in the early days of Protestantism, by the seventeenth century they had succumbed to the demand for economic freedom.[6] The later Protestant church actively facilitated the spread of individualism. Thus the Puritan doctrine of work stressed the virtues of economic activity and regarded indolence as a sin. Puritanism ridiculed and abhorred sport, license, and loose living, and exhorted its members to frugality, close attention to business, and productive effort. Rather than being tolerated as necessary to life, business was exalted as a suitable calling for a Christian.

Protestantism strengthened the forces of individualism in another way, for an essential feature of Protestantism was its challenge to authority. By stressing individual freedom of conscience, it stimulated an individualist and anti-authoritarian attitude toward religion. It was no accident that the most numerous element in the prosperous English middle class was the Dissenters, nor that their opposition to the Church of England led them into opposition to its ally, the monarchy, and to the rebellion that ended in the supremacy of Parliament.

THE DECAY OF MERCANTILIST VIEWS

Our study of Mercantilism showed how a tendency to identify wealth with money led to undue stress on the importance of the precious metals, and how this fallacy, in turn, lay at the root of that unique Mercantilist doctrine, the need for a country without mines to have a favorable balance of trade.

Under the influence of a rising volume of criticism, Mercantilist writers gradually clarified their opinion as to the relative importance of money and other forms of wealth. Although the view that money was all-important continued to be expressed well into the eighteenth century, a broader understanding of the real nature of wealth became steadily more widespread.

The Quantity of Money and the Price-Specie-Flow Theory

Thus the need for an abundant supply of money as a stimulus to trade and investment remained the sole prop of the balance-of-trade doctrine. This concept, as we have noted, is only valid under conditions of unemployment. Its supporters, however, did not specify any such limitation; they seemed to think that continual additions to the money supply would constantly raise the volume of production and trade. This was because they had no clear understanding of the quantity theory of money. Although this theory had been stated in simple terms several times during the seventeenth century, it had not been thoroughly incorporated into current thought; hence its inconsistency with an unqualified balance-of-trade doctrine was not perceived.

[6] See R. H. Tawney, *Religion and the Rise of Capitalism,* especially Ch. IV. Copyright 1926 by Harcourt, Brace & Co., New York.

A series of writers provided the necessary corrective. John Locke, writing in the 1690's, gave a clear and emphatic statement of the quantity theory, but he failed to connect it with the balance of trade.[7] A contemporary of Locke's, Dudley North, contributed a statement to the effect that the supply of money adjusts itself automatically among nations according to the needs of trade.[8] But since he lacked a grasp of the quantity theory of money, the logical conclusion eluded him.

It was David Hume who, by bringing the quantity theory of money and the balance-of-trade doctrine into direct juxtaposition, effectively undermined the latter:

> Suppose four fifths of all the money in Great Britain to be annihilated in one night . . . what would be the consequence? Must not the price of all labour and commodities sink in proportion . . . ? What nation could then dispute with us in any foreign market, or pretend to navigate or to sell manufactures at the same price, which to us would afford sufficient profit? In how little time, therefore, must this bring back the money which we had lost and raise us to the level of all the neighboring nations? Where, after we arrived, we immediately lose the advantage of the cheapness of labour and commodities; and the farther flowing in of money is stopped by our fullness and repletion.[9]

Here we have the essentials of what is known as the classical price-specie-flow analysis. Prices in any one country are determined by the quantity of money; prices in different countries are interdependent—a low-price country can undersell a high-price country; such underselling will lead to a flow of specie to the low-price country, raising prices there and lowering them in the other country. Equilibrium is finally reached with some common relationship between national price levels.

A Reconciliation

Just as the balance-of-trade doctrine dominated international trade theory during the Mercantilist period, so the price-specie-flow analysis ruled supreme throughout the nineteenth and first third of the twentieth century. Both were extreme views. The balance-of-trade theory, in its more sophisticated "stimulus to employment" version, failed to recognize that as full employment is approached, increased supplies of money can add little to employment but much to the rise of prices. The price-specie-flow theory, on the other hand, assumed full employment as the normal equilibrium situation, departures from which would be corrected through the effect of the inflow or outflow of money upon prices and through them on the demand for commodities. It was not until after the publication in 1937 of Lord Keynes' *General Theory*

---

[7] John Locke, *Some Considerations, etc.*, in *Works*, Vol. 5, p. 43.

[8] See James W. Angell, *The Theory of International Prices*, pp. 16-18. Copyright 1926 by Harvard University Press, Cambridge.

[9] David Hume, *Essay of the Balance of Trade*, cited in Arthur Eli Monroe, *Early Economic Thought*, p. 325. Copyright 1927 by Harvard University Press, Cambridge.

of Employment, Interest and Money, and the subsequent extension of his doctrines into the field of foreign trade, that the previously rival views were reconciled. Today we recognize that the development of a favorable balance of trade (or, for that matter, an expansion of exports) can have a stimulating effect on employment—provided there are idle resources to begin with. If the initial position, however, is one of full employment, the effect of such a stimulus is upon prices and not upon employment.

INDIVIDUALISM IN POLITICAL THOUGHT

Modern philosophy starts with Descartes, and with good reason. To him, writing at the time (the 1630's and '40's) when scientific inquiry was replacing reliance on authority as the source of knowledge, the universe appeared ruled by laws discoverable by human reason. Since the use of reason was an individual matter, the independence and importance of the individual as a discoverer and interpreter of the world about him were vastly stimulated.

Locke and Limits on Government

This modern view of the world was accepted by and applied to the problems of politics by John Locke. In the state of nature, governed by its own laws, he assumed all men were equal. Because of this equality, men were endowed with certain natural rights, which Locke identified—as a citizen of seventeenth century England—with life, liberty, and the enjoyment of property. But since men, though equal in their rights, are unequal in intelligence, they will interpret natural law differently. The result is chaos and confusion. Government is necessary to ensure order and the peaceful pursuit by each man of his natural rights. Men instituted government by a social contract, endowing it with the power to make laws to secure life, liberty, and property, but no more. Government thus has a distinctly limited function—to permit individuals to live, not as they would in a state of nature, but according to the underlying laws of nature.

Revolution against a tyrannical government is implicit in such a concept, for a tyrannical government oversteps the limits of the social contract. But revolution, if necessary, should be the act of a majority. And to avoid tyranny, government should be democratic—it should reflect the will of the majority.

Thus Locke was the exponent of limited, democratic government, designed to serve the interest of individuals. His political liberalism, applied to the relations of Parliament and King in the English Revolution of 1688 and copied and elaborated by numerous followers, became the intellectual foundation of the British government, of the American Declaration of Independence, and as interpreted by Rousseau, of the French Revolution.

ADAM SMITH AND THE NEW ECONOMICS

Production for the Market

By the middle of the eighteenth century, the commercial and political revolutions of early modern times had completed their work. In England and Holland, and to a lesser extent in other countries, a simple agricultural society had been transformed into a complex economy with a thriving industry and commerce. Trade, no longer confined mainly to local markets, was conducted on a national and worldwide scale. Instead of wool and wheat, England now exported textiles, wares of iron and pewter, shoes, hats, leather goods, and coal. The domestic system of industry, supplemented here and there by small mills and factories, was now predominantly capitalistic. Labor received its raw materials, its orders, and often its tools from a capitalist employer; it received a money wage, fixed mainly by market forces, for its skill and effort. A developed system of banking, involving the widespread use of bills of exchange and the issue of bank notes, and headed by the Bank of England (established 1694) had come into being to serve the needs of industry and trade.

Above all, the guidance of economic activity was no longer subject to the control of gild, town authority, or church, or king. The questions of what to produce, by what methods, and at what price were now decided by the individual enterpriser serving an impersonal and ever-growing market.

Even in agriculture, production for the market had replaced the old communal system of the manor. Transfer of property had become increasingly free, and many small holdings had been bought up and consolidated by the more enterprising peasants. Serfdom had ceased with the reign of Elizabeth, and farming was now carried on by small freeholders and by tenants working the large- and medium-sized farms of the gentry. The numbers of the latter were steadily augmented by the purchase of farms by well-to-do businessmen desirous of acquiring the status of landowners. The enclosure movement, involving the union into a few large properties of the scattered small holdings of the manorial open-field system, had begun with the scarcity of labor after the Black Death (1348-49). As the English woolen industry became more important, the demand for its raw materials became steadily greater, sheep-raising became more profitable than arable farming, and enclosures increased rapidly under the Tudors. Yet the amount of land enclosed by the end of the seventeenth century was probably only a small proportion of the total.[10] The disappearance of the old open-field system awaited the tremendous burst of enclosures in the latter half of the eighteenth century.

The modern state, no longer new and untried, but secure and well-estab-

---

[10] On the enclosure movement, see W. H. R. Curtler, *A Short History of English Agriculture*, especially Ch. VII, IX, and XI. Published 1909 by Clarendon Press, Oxford.

lished, had less need to shape every policy with an eye to the increase of its power. It could tolerate greater freedom of the individual to pursue his own interests. Moreover, in Holland, the machinery of government had been taken over by the commercial classes, while in England they shared its control with landed proprietors. Mercantilist restrictions on internal trade and industry, together with those medieval survivals that Mercantilism supported, disappeared with the declining interest of government in their retention and the rising interest of traders and manufacturers in their abolition. With the progress of economic inquiry, even that pillar of the Mercantilist ideology, the favorable balance of foreign trade—a concept not unwelcome to the exporting classes—was rudely shaken.

Adam Smith and "the Invisible Hand"

Though the spirit of individualism was already dominant in the mid-eighteenth century and had received its political expression in the writings of Locke, it still awaited formulation as a rounded economic philosophy. This was the great task that Adam Smith was to perform. What Locke had done for government, he did for economics. Taking the prevalent view of the universe as ruled by natural law, and of individual enterprise as the most efficient means of getting goods produced, he constructed a thorough-going, individualist economic system. The central core of his ideas may be summarized in the following propositions:

Each man is best fitted to be the judge of his own actions.

Individual interests are not in conflict, but are subject to a natural harmony.

Therefore, the selfish actions of individuals lead to the welfare of all, and the continuous regulation of government is unnecessary. The best results can be obtained if the state follows a policy of let-alone, of laissez faire.

But let Adam Smith speak for himself:

> As every individual endeavors as much as he can both to employ his capital in the support of domestic industry, and so to direct that industry that its produce may be of the greatest value; every individual necessarily labours to render the annual revenue of the society as great as he can. He generally, indeed, neither intends to promote the public interest, nor knows how much he is promoting it. By preferring the support of domestic to that of foreign industry, he intends only his own gain, and he is in this, as in many other cases, led by an invisible hand to promote an end which was no part of his intention. Nor is it always the worse for the society that it was no part of it. By pursuing his own interest he frequently promotes that of the society more effectually than when he really intends to promote it.[11]

From this reasoning comes a major conclusion. The "Wealth of Nations" is best served, not by minute regulation—of which there were many survivals,

---

[11] Adam Smith, *The Wealth of Nations,* p. 400, Modern Library Edition.

especially in the field of foreign trade—but by the greatest possible freedom of enterprise. The businessman's yearning for economic freedom is now entirely justified. Full release of his energies is the right prescription for a prosperous society.

No wonder that Adam Smith's philosophy of laissez faire received wide acceptance, becoming the ruling economic doctrine of the nineteenth century. For it told the rising commercial and industrial classes, who were soon to achieve political dominance, to do what they wanted to do.

Protection Survives

Adam Smith did not confine his recommendation of freedom to internal economic affairs—he also vigorously advocated a policy of free trade.[12] But his prescription had little in the way of immediate, practical results. Beneficiaries of protection were loath to give it up, even though they did not need it, and even though they agreed with his basic philosophy. Moreover, the most significant restrictions on foreign trade, the very core and center of English protectionism, were the duties on grain, or, as they were generally known, the Corn Laws. The landowning classes, whose interests these served, were still the numerically dominant group in Parliament.

Not until the Reform Act of 1832, which gave wider representation to the urban middle class, was a frontal assault on the Corn Laws politically possible. And not until the interests of merchants and manufacturers in free trade were more clearly apparent than in 1776, when Adam Smith wrote, could a powerful body of opinion be marshaled behind a free-trade movement. The growth of this opinion had to await the impact of the Industrial Revolution.

THE INDUSTRIAL REVOLUTION: TECHNICAL ASPECTS

Although individualism was the dominating philosophy in politics, economics, and religion by the time Adam Smith wrote *The Wealth of Nations,* the full consequences of the unleashing of the individual's energies were not brought out until the Industrial Revolution had transformed England from an economy of household industry, based on skilled labor adept in the use of tools, to an economy of factories and mills, based on machines and steam power.

Inventions: A Chain Effect

On the technical side, the Industrial Revolution was a series of interrelated inventions, each meeting some immediate and pressing industrial need, but upsetting the balance of industry so that additional inventions became an

---

[12] For a brief discussion of his theory of international trade, see Chapter 4 of this book.

urgent necessity. Consider, for example, the sequence of development in the cotton textile industry. The production of cotton fabrics (actually fustians, a cloth half linen and half cotton) had first been established in England about 1600, on the same household basis as its older rival, the woolen industry. For a century, its growth was very gradual until, in the opening years of the eighteenth century, the importation of cotton prints, and even their wear, was prohibited. These colorful prints, a product of Indian hand looms, had become so popular that they aroused the strenuous opposition of the woolen and silk industries. English-made fustians, however, met no such obstacles; with the elimination of the competition of pure cotton fabrics, for which they were a fairly satisfactory substitute, their production expanded swiftly.

The first of the textile inventions was a simple improvement in the old loom designed to remedy a defect that hampered the expansion of production. Hitherto, the width of the fabric that could be made by a single workman had been limited by the length of his arms, for he had to throw the shuttle containing the cross thread, or woof, from one hand to the other. For wider fabrics, two or more men had to be employed. In 1733, John Kay, a weaver with mechanical talent, developed the flying shuttle, fitted with wheels and propelled mechanically with sufficient force so that a much wider stretch of warp threads could be traversed.

Because the flying shuttle permitted a considerable expansion in the output of the weaving branch of the textile industry, it upset its balance. The spinning process had always required five or six men to supply one weaver with thread. Now the spinners found it impossible to keep up with the demand. The need for improvement in this stage of the industry became acute. The Society for the Encouragement of Arts and Manufactures offered a prize for a suitable invention,[13] and many men worked intensely on the problem.

Finally, between 1769 and 1779, three inventions revolutionized spinning —Hargreaves' spinning jenny, Arkwright's water frame, and Crompton's mule. The jenny made possible the spinning by one operator of several threads, of fine quality, but too weak to replace linen in the warp. Arkwright's water frame furnished a coarser but stronger thread which could be spun by power-driven machinery and which permitted for the first time the manufacture in England of pure cotton goods.[14] The mule combined the principles of the jenny and the water frame and made a thread that was both fine and strong. It soon came to be fitted with three to four hundred spindles, so that a single machine did the work of that many individual spinners, each working with a single spinning wheel. Fortunately, at about the time that

[13] Paul Mantoux, *The Industrial Revolution in the Eighteenth Century,* p. 220. Copyright 1927 by Harcourt, Brace & Co., New York. This book contains one of the best accounts available of the role played by inventions in the Industrial Revolution. I am much indebted to it.

[14] It was Arkwright's defense of his industry before Parliament that resulted in freeing it from the prohibition against cotton manufactures.

these advances in spinning made it possible to work up much larger quantities of the raw material, an American, Eli Whitney, developed his cotton gin (1793). By permitting the easy extraction of the rough seeds from the boll, his invention enabled the processing of enough cotton to keep up with rapidly expanding demand.

The new spinning machines gave a great impetus to factory production, since they could be operated most economically by water (later steam) power, and thus had to be brought together in large numbers where the power was available. Arkwright, whose claims as an inventor are at least dubious, was above all else a man of great business ability. He suceeded in raising capital, training workmen, and building and setting into operation a large number of factories, employing from 150 to 600 hands. His fame thus has a legitimate basis mainly in the fact that he was the first of the new class of industrial capitalists who, seizing upon the inventions of others, were to transform Britain's cottage industry in the next hundred years. Even in the cotton textile industry, his example was soon followed by many others, while similar men-of-business made over the iron and steel trades.

By 1790, when the inventions in spinning were widely used, the different parts of the textile industry were again badly out of balance. Whereas thirty years earlier, thread had been scarce, now there were not enough weavers to work up all the thread streaming out of the spinning mills. A chance discussion set a country parson named Cartwright to proving that a power loom was not, as the company present had alleged, an impossibility. After several years of effort, he proved his point in 1785; but it took years more for his invention to make its way in industry, owing mainly to the violent opposition it met from handloom weavers. Not until about 1810 was the power loom widely used, but within a few years more, it was universal in the cotton industry.

In the manufacture of wool, the spinning inventions took hold rapidly, especially in Yorkshire, where wages rose from the competition of the neighboring Lancashire cotton districts and where abundant water power was to be found. The power loom, partly because of strenuous opposition to its introduction, partly because it was less adapted to weaving woolen fabrics, made much slower progress. In 1803, according to Mantoux, only one-sixteenth of the cloth production of the main Yorkshire woolen district was factory-made. Large numbers of handlooms continued to be operated until late in the nineteenth century.

As in the textile industries, a succession of inventions upset the balance of the iron industry, each leading to further development. Thus the opening years of the eighteenth century found the English iron industry quite incapable of meeting the demands of the Midland iron workers for pig iron; it was even on the point of disappearing. Ever since prehistoric man discovered how to extract the metal from its ore, its manufacture had been dependent on charcoal for smelting. By 1720, almost all wooded areas near enough to iron mines to permit economic production had been destroyed. In that year, but sixty blast furnaces, producing only some 17 thousand tons of pig iron annually, were in operation in England.[15] The country was becoming increasingly dependent on imports of pig iron from Sweden, Germany, Spain, and the American colonies. Coal was abundant and was widely used as a fuel in many countries, but it could not be combined with iron ore to smelt pig iron because its sulphur content made the product too brittle for use. A method of making coal into a serviceable smelting agent had to be devised and was actively sought throughout the seventeenth century. Finally, about 1709, an English iron-master named Abraham Darby succeeded in making a coke that could be used in the smelting process.

Apparently, in spite of its great utility, the manufacture of pig iron with coke did not become common until some seventy years had passed. By that time, the supply of pig iron outstripped the ability of refiners to make it into malleable iron, the type necessary in the many uses requiring a low carbon content. Research became actively stimulated, and in 1784, the process of "puddling," or heating and stirring molten pig iron mixed with iron oxide to burn out the carbon left by the coke, was invented by a contractor named Cort, together with a rolling mill that eliminated the tedious labor of hammering the refined metal.

Along with these basic discoveries, there were many auxiliary ones, such as the development of air pumps to deliver an adequate blast in the blast furnace, the invention of the steam hammer, and of metal-turning lathes. They made possible a rapid expansion in the output of iron and a lowering of its cost, as well as greater precision in machine manufacture. The use of machines made of iron grew rapidly; the iron industry itself furnished an increasing number of applications of the new technique, while the superior strength, accuracy, and durability of machinery made of this material led, after a beginning was made in 1785, to the rapid replacement of the early wooden spinning mules and water frames.

Advent of the Steam Engine

The invention which removed all limitations to the spread of machinery, and which, combined with the chemical discoveries of coking and puddling, laid the foundations of England's industrial greatness, was the steam engine. At about the beginning of the eighteenth century, two primitive steam engines had been developed in England, and these became quite widely used. Owing to mechanical defects, however, and to the lack of any means of transmitting power from the engine to a driving wheel, their use was limited mainly to pumping water.

The problems of designing an engine of sufficient power and accuracy and of translating the straight thrust of a piston into rotary motion were solved

[15] Mantoux, *op. cit.,* p. 278.

by James Watt. His person united scientific training, intelligence, and a rare intellectual curiosity. A maker of scientific instruments at the University of Glasgow, a student, and the friend of distinguished scientists, he devoted years of study and patient research to making the inefficient Newcomen engine an effective source of motive power. Success came in 1769 when he registered his first patent. A great gap, however, separates an invention from it effective application to industry. In Watt's case this gap was overcome by a fortunate partnership with Boulton, a Birmingham manufacturer of small metal wares. His financial aid brought the new engine past the test stage, his business connections established its first market, and his exceptionally well-equipped and well-managed shops furnished the accuracy of construction required for a satisfactory engine. After initial difficulties, the partnership throve, and the firm of Boulton and Watt became the producer of steam engines for all of Britain. By 1800, when their patents expired, steam power was really beginning to displace water power.

> With this new great event, the invention of the steam engine, the final and most decisive stage of the industrial revolution opened. By liberating it from its last shackles, steam enabled the immense and rapid development of large-scale industry to take place. For the use of steam was not, like that of water, dependent on geographical position and local resources. Wherever coal could be bought at a reasonable price a steam engine could be erected. England had plenty of coal, and by the end of the eighteenth century it was already applied to many different uses, while a network of waterways, made on purpose, enabled it to be carried everywhere very cheaply: the whole country became a privileged land, suitable above all others for the growth of industry. Factories were now no longer bound to the valleys, where they had grown up in solitude by the side of rapid-flowing streams. It became possible to bring them nearer the markets where their raw materials were bought and their finished products sold, and nearer the centres of population where their labour was recruited. They sprang up near one another, and thus, huddled together, gave rise to those huge black industrial cities which the steam engine surrounded with a perpetual cloud of smoke.[16]

THE INDUSTRIAL REVOLUTION: SOCIAL AND ECONOMIC ASPECTS

The mechanical inventions in the textile and iron industries, the chemical discoveries in the use of coal and the manufacture of iron, set in motion a technological revolution, a revolution that was to alter completely the physical bases of industry. From its dependence for thousands of years upon wood as a material and as a fuel, upon water, animals and men for power, upon human dexterity and skill for the scope of its processes, it now became liberated. Coal, iron, and machinery replaced these less reliable, less accurate resources and opened up a century of industrial growth and progress that made earlier periods of expansion look stagnant.

[16] Mantoux, *op. cit.,* pp. 344-45.

The Factory System

If the Industrial Revolution had had no other effects than these, it would have earned its title. But it was at least as revolutionary in the social and economic sphere as in the purely technical. The new industrial machinery and methods could be used effectively only in establishments where large numbers of machines could be assembled, both because of the close relationship of the various processes of manufacture and because of the large volume of power made available by a single steam engine. This meant, of course, the grouping together under a single roof of hundreds of workmen and the development of a system of factory discipline that tolerated little deviation from a standard norm, whether in the matter of hours, of shop practice, or of quality of performance. Paradoxically, the industrial changes that gave the freest rein to the individual, provided he belonged to the managing and directing class, imposed an iron conformity of behavior on the great mass of the workers.

The new working environment came gradually, since the factory system supplanted the old cottage industry only in the course of decades. But by 1830, the cotton textile industry had become thoroughly mechanized, the production of iron was a relatively large-scale operation, and even in iron manufacturing, the small shop of the skilled craftsman was fast disappearing. Not until after the middle of the century, as we have noted, were the handloom weavers of woolen fabrics finally vanquished.

What is important is not the time required for the spread of the factory system, but its inevitability. With minor exceptions, the progress of the steam engine, the machine, and the new factory discipline was remorseless. Within the span of a century, most men who earned their living by making things ceased to work in their own homes, at hours they themselves set, and often with their own tools, and instead, entered the factory gates at a set hour, took their places before expensive machines in which they had no share of the ownership, and worked for a period, in a manner, and at a speed determined by the iron constitution of an inhuman engine. Machines and steam power spawned a new class, the industrial proletariat, with a new way of life, and in so doing gave a tremendous impetus to the growth of cities.[17]

[17] If we put the figure for the population of a town at 2,000, in 1801 there were in England and Wales 283 towns containing approximately 31 per cent of the total population. By 1841 these towns contained 46 per cent of the people. This later figure may exaggerate the situation somewhat, but it is probably not excessive. [G. P. Jones and A. G. Pool, *A Hundred Years of Economic Development in Great Britain,* p. 19. Published 1940 by Gerald Duckworth and Co. Ltd., London.]

For the United States, comparable figures are available for the period 1820-1940. In 1820, 82 per cent of the country's labor force was engaged in agriculture, only 18 per cent in nonagricultural pursuits. In 1940, the figures were exactly reversed—18 per cent of the labor force was employed in agriculture, 82 per cent in nonagricultural pursuits. (These latter include, besides industry, also transportation, trade, government, the professions, etc., all of which have expanded with the expansion of industry.)

Industrial Leadership

Urbanization and the growth of an urban industrial proletariat were two of the social consequences of the Industrial Revolution. Still another was a tremendous increase in the importance of capital and the capitalist. We have seen that even the earlier cottage or domestic system of industry was dominated by the capitalist, who organized and directed the various processes of manufacture. He was, however, essentially still a merchant, and was generally so called, even though he might direct extensive manufacturing operations. With the replacement of tools by machines, and of hand or water power by the steam engine, thousands of pounds or dollars had to be invested in plant and equipment where hundreds or tens had formerly sufficed. The men who raised these vaster sums and who directed their use were a very different type from the earlier merchants.[18] Besides a knowledge of markets, they had to know a good deal about the technology of industry, they had to possess organizing ability, and, if they were to succeed, they had to have, or to understand how to raise, large amounts of capital. Men like Arkwright, the cotton manufacturer, and like the ironmasters Boulton and Wilkinson, were typical of the new "captains of industry" who became the innovators, the entrepreneurs of the new age of iron and coal.

What made the innovating activity of this class of industrial capitalists possible was an inheritance of the previous century—the "liberal" view of society that had arisen out of the constant pressure of business interests seeking to take advantage of expanding opportunities, and out of the stimulus to individual freedom of thought and action furnished by the rise of scientific thought and the parallel decline in the hold of religion and authority. Without the favorable climate of opinion known today as political and economic liberalism (formulated in the writings of Locke, Hume, Adam Smith, and Jeremy Bentham), the freedom necessary for introducing the radical changes in industry required by the mechanical inventions would have been lacking. Bound by old rules of handicraft manufacture, industry would have continued along lines laid down in the Middle Ages. Evasion of these rules had made possible the rise of the domestic system; their continued evasion, and the repeal of the restrictions introduced during the Mercantilist period, was essential to the rise of the new industry.

The Combination Act

So far had the philosophy of individualism gone by the end of the eighteenth century that intervention by the state was largely discredited, and

---

[18] At first, the capital came from accumulations already made in trade or industry, frequently pooled in partnerships containing from two to several partners. As the profits of the new enterprises mounted, large sums were ploughed back into the expansion of old, or the erection of new plants. It was not until after the middle of the nineteenth century that the corporate form of organization, with its limited liability and its power of attracting many small streams of savings, became at all common in England.

laissez faire was widely accepted as the foundation of economic relations. In the Combination Act of 1799, all combinations of workmen to improve their condition of labor were outlawed. Henceforth, it was assumed, individual pursuit of individual interest would ensure economic justice to all. Forbidden to unite their strength to offset the greater bargaining power of the employer, workers tried to obtain remedy for low wages, long hours, and wretched working conditions by appealing for enforcement of such old laws as the Elizabethan Statute of Artificers. But though many such laws remained on the books of Parliament or were technically in force in various towns and trades, the spirit that had created them was dead. Besides, fixed numbers of apprentices and regulation of methods of production were inconsistent with the needs of a rapidly changing industry and with the interests of its owners and directors. The old laws were suspended, then repealed.[19] The "simple system of natural liberty" had prevailed. The character of industry and the status of labor were to be determined in a free market by free competition. Government was to combat ignorance by providing instruction, to stimulate progress by encouraging science and invention, and to protect the unsuspecting against fraud. With government thus limited, all restraints on the spread of the factory system vanished.

SELECTED REFERENCES

Halévy, Elie, *The Growth of Philosophic Radicalism*. London: Faber & Gwyer, Ltd., 1928. Chapter III, Section I, has a good discussion of the views of Adam Smith, especially his principle of the natural identity of interests.

Mantoux, Paul, *The Industrial Revolution in the Eighteenth Century*. New York: Harcourt, Brace & Co., 1927. One of the outstanding studies of the Industrial Revolution.

Polanyi, Karl, *The Great Transformation*. New York: Farrar & Rhinehart, 1944. A provocative study of the development of the market economy in the eighteenth and nineteenth centuries, and of its subsequent decline.

Robertson, H. M., *Aspects of the Rise of Economic Individualism*. New York: Cambridge University Press, 1933. This book contains a full account, with many illustrations, of how individualism displaced the philosophy of state regulation.

Smith, Adam, *The Wealth of Nations*, Chapters I-III, on the division of labor, and its relation to the extent of the market, are well worth reading.

Tawney, R. H., *Religion and the Rise of Capitalism*. New York: Harcourt, Brace & Co., 1926. See especially Chapter IV, Sections II & III, for a discussion of religion, trade, and the economic virtues.

Trevelyan, G. W. *English Social History*. New York: Longmans, Green & Co., 1942. Chapters VI to XIII provide a vivid picture of the social background of this period.

[19] The Statute of Artificers was repealed in 1809, thus finally doing away with national regulation of apprenticeships and of wages.

PART II

The Bases of Specialization and Trade:
The Theory of International Trade

4

THE CLASSICAL DOCTRINE
OF COMPARATIVE COST

State regulation of internal industry and trade within England had, as we have seen, a limited scope and a relatively short life. After the Cromwellian Revolution, it expired. By the end of the eighteenth century, businessmen possessed almost unlimited freedom in the choice of their field of activity and the manner in which they carried it out; the philosophy of individualism permeated the intellectual classes and was beginning to influence both statesmen and leaders of industry.

From this time on, the controls of Mercantilism affected chiefly the country's external trade by means of tariffs, bounties, prohibitions, and the Colonial and Navigation systems. Although a beginning had been made, in the Eden Treaty of 1786 with France, toward the relaxation of restrictions on foreign trade, commercial and industrial opinion was divided on this topic; during the long interval, from 1793 to 1815, of wars with France, further progress in this direction was impossible.

Yet during these war years expansion and mechanization of England's newer industries, cotton, iron and steel, coal, and engineering, continued rapidly, and the new machine processes began to take hold in the old woolen textile industry. On the continent of Europe, the war retarded development in these lines. With the end of the military conflict, therefore, Britain's leading industries held an unchallengeable position. No one anywhere was in a position to offer them effective competition. On the other hand, the termination of the war brought with it a collapse of markets. Steel was no longer needed for muskets and cannon, the demand for soldier's uniforms and blankets vanished, and prostrate Europe was in no position to buy large quantities of English goods. Concern for markets, therefore, caused a strengthening of sentiment in favor of freer trade among merchants and manufacturers, a change in opinion which was to have important consequences, as we shall see.

[59]

ADAM SMITH

At the same time that economic developments were preparing the ground for an attack on Mercantilist foreign trade policies, the intellectual weapons necessary for this attack were being sharpened and improved. Adam Smith stressed the absurdities of Mercantilist restrictions and had laid the groundwork for the free trade argument when he showed that trade between nations enables each to increase its wealth—in the sense of real income—by taking advantage of the principle upon which all increase of wealth rests, the division of labor.

It is the maxim of every prudent master of a family, never to attempt to make at home what it will cost him more to make than to buy. The taylor does not attempt to make his own shoes, but buys them of the shoemaker. The shoemaker does not attempt to make his own clothes, but employs a taylor. The farmer attempts to make neither the one nor the other, but employs those different artificers. All of them find it for their interest to employ their whole industry in a way in which they have some advantage over their neighbours, and to purchase with a part of its produce, or what is the same thing, with the price of a part of it, whatever else they have occasion for.

What is prudence in the conduct of every private family, can scarce be folly in that of a great kingdom. If a foreign country can supply us with a commodity cheaper than we ourselves can make it, better buy it of them with some part of the produce of our own industry, employed in a way in which we have some advantage. . . .

The natural advantages which one country has over another in producing particular commodities are sometimes so great, that it is acknowledged by the world to be in vain to struggle with them. By means of glasses, hotbeds, and hotwalls, very good grapes can be raised in Scotland, and very good wine too can be made of them at about thirty times the expense for which at least equally good can be bought from foreign countries. Would it be a reasonable law to prohibit the importation of all foreign wines, merely to encourage the making of claret and burgundy in Scotland? But if there would be a manifest absurdity in turning towards any employment, thirty times more of the capital and industry of the country, then would be necessary to purchase from foreign countries an equal quantity of the commodities wanted, there must be an absurdity, though not altogether so glaring, yet exactly of the same kind, in turning towards any such employment a thirtieth, or even a three hundredth part more of either. Whether the advantages which one country has over another, be natural or acquired, is in this respect of no consequence. As long as the one country has those advantages, and the other wants them, it will always be more advantageous for the latter, rather to buy of the former than to make. It is an acquired advantage only, which one artificer has over his neighbour, who exercises another trade; and yet they both find it more advantageous to buy of one another, than to make what does not belong to their particular trades.[1]

[1] Adam Smith, *The Wealth of Nations,* Modern Library Edition, pp. 424-26.

Absolute Advantage Assumed

This statement, vigorous and clear though it was, lacked something in sharpness. Excellent as far as it went, it did not go far enough. It assumed without argument that international trade required a producer of exports to have an *absolute* advantage; that is, an exporting industry must be able to produce, with a given amount of capital and labor, a larger output than any rival.

But what if a country had *no* line of production in which it were clearly superior? Suppose a relatively backward country whose "capital and industry" in the broadest sense (compared with its more advanced neighbors) were inefficient, capable of producing less in all lines of activity—a not too hypothetical case. Would it be forced to insulate itself against more efficient outside competition or see all its industry and agriculture subjected to ruinous competition? Adam Smith's analysis was incapable of dealing with this kind of situation, and it was not until David Ricardo undertook a more precise formulation of the theory of international trade (*Principles of Political Economy,* 1817) that a *general* theory of the subject became available.

DAVID RICARDO

Labor Cost Determines Domestic Value

The logical point of departure for considering Ricardo's explanation of international trade is his theory of value. According to this, the value of any commodity depended upon its labor costs: "It is the comparative quantity of commodities which labour will produce that determines their present or past relative value."[2] In the domestic trade of a country, this rule held good. Thus suppose that in Yorkshire, a certain quantity of cloth (x yds.) could be produced at a cost of 60 days' labour, in London at a cost of 100 days, while in Yorkshire the labor cost of cheese (y lbs.) was 30 days, in London 90 days. Both commodities would be produced in Yorkshire, since the costs there are lowest, and they would exchange in the proportions of 1 unit of cloth for 2 units of cheese.

If these were the only commodities that could conceivably be produced in either region (or if the costs or producing all other commodities were lower in Yorkshire), labor and capital would desert London for the more productive Yorkshire area. In reality, however, other possibilities would doubtless exist in London for a more effective application of labor and capital than in Yorkshire. Suppose one of these to be the manufacture of hardware, at a cost of 20 days' labor as compared with 60 in Yorkshire. A table of costs would look like this:

[2] David Ricardo, *Principles of Political Economy,* Everyman's Edition, p. 9.

	Labor Costs of Producing		
	(x yd.) Cloth	(y lb.) Cheese	(z units) Hardware
Yorkshire	60	30	60
London	100	90	20

The hardware industry would then locate in London, the cloth and cheese industries in Yorkshire, and their products would exchange for one another in the proportions of 1 cloth for 2 cheese for 3 hardware.

In international trade, however, the labor-cost principle does not govern value in exchange, according to Ricardo.

> The same rule which regulates the relative value of commodities in one country does not regulate the relative value of the commodities exchanged between two or more countries. . . . The quantity of wine which (Portugal) shall give in exchange for the cloth of England is not determined by the respective quantities of labour devoted to the production of each, as it would be if both commodities were manufactured in England, or both in Portugal.[3]

What, then, does determine values in international exchange? Ricardo assumes the following figures for labor costs of producing wine and cloth in Portugal and England:

	Labor Costs of Producing	
	Wine (x bbl.)	Cloth (y yd.)
Portugal	80	90
England	120	100

Costs of producing both commodities are lower in Portugal. In spite of this, it will pay Portugal to specialize in the production of wine and to exchange it for cloth made in England. For by so doing, Portugal would procure for an outlay of 80 days of labor (in Ricardo it is man-years) what would cost her 90 days to produce at home. England would also gain from the exchange, for by concentrating on the production of cloth and exchangeing it for wine, she could get for a cost of 100 days labor what would, in the absence of trade, cost her 120 days.

International Immobility of the Factors

Why should there be such a remarkable difference in the principles regulating exchange within and between countries? The explanation is simple.

> The difference in this respect, between a single country and many, is easily accounted for, by considering the difficulty with which capital moves from one country to another, to seek a more profitable employment, and the activity with which it invariably passes from one province to another in the same country.

[3] *Ibid.*, pp. 81-82.

It would undoubtedly be advantageous to the capitalists of England, and to the consumers in both countries, that under such circumstances the wine and the cloth should both be made in Portugal, and therefore that the capital and labour of England employed in making cloth should be removed to Portugal for that purpose. . . .

Experience, however, shows that the fancied or real insecurity of capital, when not under the immediate control of its owner, together with the natural disinclination which every man has to quit the country of his birth and connections, and intrust himself, with all his habits fixed, to a strange government and new laws, check the emigration of capital. These feelings, which I should be sorry to see weakened, induce most men of property to be satisfied with a low rate of profits in their own country, rather than seek a more advantageous employment for their wealth in foreign nations.[4]

In more modern terms, it is the immobility of labor, capital, and enterprise which tends to keep them at home, and thus to prevent production from taking place where labor costs are absolutely lowest. The localization of production as between different countries follows the principle of *comparative costs:* each country will tend to specialise in the production of those commodities for which its (labor) costs are comparatively lowest.

At bottom this is simply an extension of the principle of the division of labor. In general terms, applicable to both nations and individuals, competence should specialize where competence counts most, and incompetence where incompetence counts least. As Ricardo expressed the matter in an illustration:

Two men can both make shoes and hats, and one is superior to the other in both employments, but in making hats he can only exceed his competitor by one-fifth or 20 per cent, and in making shoes he can excell him by one-third or 33 per cent;—will it not be for the interest of both that the superior man should employ himself exclusively in making shoes, and the inferior man in making hats?[5]

It is clear that the doctrine of comparative cost marks a real advance over Adam Smith's statement of the basis of international trade. It is more general; it explains situations not covered by Smith's formulation and includes the latter as a special case, one where a country's *comparative* cost advantage is also an absolute advantage.

Yet as it left the hands of Ricardo, though the principle gave a more convincing and adequate proof of the benefits of trade, it left the actual ratios of international exchange, or international prices, undetermined. Ricardo simply assumed that Portugal would exchange wine costing 80 units of labor (x bbl.) for English cloth costing 100 labor units (y yd.). That is, he focused exclusively upon the supply or cost side of international trade and paid no attention to the demand side. Perhaps he failed to go further and

[4] *Ibid.,* p. 83.
[5] *Ibid.,* p. 83.

establish the precise terms of profitable exchange because he was mainly interested in showing that only a comparative and not an absolute difference in labor costs is necessary for gainful international trade. Or it may have been because the way in which he set up his illustration tended to obscure the problem of the terms of trade. Whatever the reason, this further step awaited the attention of Ricardo's illustrious successor, John Stuart Mill.

JOHN STUART MILL

When, after restating Ricardo's doctrine of comparative cost in a clearer fashion, Mill proceeded to examine the question of international values, or the ratios at which commodities would exchange for one another, he used an illustration whose very form focused attention upon this problem. Instead of taking as *given* the output of each commodity in two countries, with the labor costs different, he assumed a given amount of labor in each country, but differing outputs.[6] Thus his formulation ran in terms of comparative advantage, or comparative effectiveness of labor, as contrasted with Ricardo's comparative labor cost.

Mill's formulation can be illustrated as follows:[7]

Input of Labor (man-years)	Country	Output of: Steel (tons)	Wheat (tons)
10	Belgium	20	20
10	France	10	15

For the same input of labor, Belgium and France produce quite different outputs of steel and wheat. Belgium has an absolute advantage in the production of both commodities (20 tons of steel against 10, and 20 tons of wheat against 15), but a clear comparative advantage in steel (2 to 1, as compared to 4 to 3 or 2 to 1.5). France's least comparative disadvantage is in wheat. It is *comparative advantage* that indicates the lines of profitable specialization if trade is permitted to develop.

6 " 'Suppose that 10 yards of broadcloth cost in England as much labour as 15 yards of linen, and in Germany as much as 20. . . .' This supposition then being made, it would be in the interest of England to import linen from Germany, and of Germany to import cloth from England." J. S. Mill, *Principles of Political Economy,* Ashley edition, Book III, Ch. XVIII, Sec. 8, pp. 584-85. Published 1921 by Longmans, Green & Co., London.

7 Ricardo would have expressed this illustration in some such form as the following:

	Cost of: Steel (1 ton)	Wheat (1 ton)
Belgium	½ man-year	½ man-year
France	1 man-year	⅔ man-year

Possible Terms of Trade

In the absence of trade, 10 tons of steel will exchange in France for 15 tons of wheat, since these quantities represent an equal labor cost. In Belgium, 10 tons of steel will command only 10 tons of wheat, each of these quantities being the product of 5 man-years of labor. Clearly, however, trade will benefit Belgium if for 10 units of steel anything more than 10 units of wheat can be obtained, while France will gain if it can get 10 tons of steel by exporting any less than 15 tons of wheat. That is, *the limits to the possible barter terms of trade* (the international exchange ratio) *are set by the domestic exchange ratios established by the relative efficiency of labor in each country.*

The range of possible barter terms can be shown as:

Steel	Wheat
10	10+
	15—

Within this range, any single ratio may rule. The question Mill sought to answer was: What factors determine *the actual terms* on which the commodities will trade?

Reciprocal Demand

Stated briefly, Mill's answer was: The actual ratio at which goods are traded will depend upon the strength and elasticity of each country's demand for the other country's product, or upon reciprocal demand. This ratio will be stable when the value of each country's exports just suffice to pay for its imports.

The operation of Mill's principle of reciprocal demand can be shown most clearly if we introduce money wages into our illustration.[8] Let us assume that wages in Belgium are 10,000 francs per man-year, and in France 6,000. We now obtain determinate money costs from which the barter terms can easily be computed.

Input of Labor	Wages Per Man-Year	Total Cost	Country	Steel Output	Steel Unit Cost	Wheat Output	Wheat Unit Cost
10	10,000 fr.	100,000 fr.	Belgium	20	5,000 fr.	20	5,000 fr.
10	6,000 fr.	60,000 fr.	France	10	6,000 fr.	15	4,000 fr.

[8] Mill's answer took a somewhat different form from the presentation given here, which is chosen for the purpose of clarity. He did not introduce money wages, but reasoned in terms of barter trade. Thus he would say that the ratio of 10 steel for 12.5 wheat would be stable provided each country's requirements are a common multiple of the terms of trade, say, when Belgium wants 1,000,000 × 12.5 units of wheat or 12,500,-000 wheat and when France at the same time wants 1,000,000 × 10 steel or 10,000,000 steel.

At these costs, 10 tons of steel will come to 50,000 francs in Belgium. For this sum, 12.5 tons of wheat can be obtained in France (at 4,000 francs a ton). If, at these barter terms of 10 steel for 12.5 wheat, total Belgian demand for wheat is, say, 12.5 million units or 50,000 million francs worth, and French demand for steel is 10 million tons, also 50,000 million francs worth, the value of each country's exports is just equal to the value of its imports, its trading account is in balance, and the barter terms of trade will be stable.[9]

Suppose, however, that at these prices and barter terms, France's demand amounted to 12 million tons of steel, with a total value of 60,000 million francs. France would have to send Belgium a net sum of 10,000 million francs in gold. This would cause wages and prices to rise in Belgium and to fall in France. Suppose Belgian wages were to go up to 10,500 francs. French wages to fall to 5,500 francs. Our illustration changes as follows:

Input of Labor	Wages Per Man-Year	Total Cost	Country	Steel		Wheat	
10	10,500 fr.	105,000 fr.	Belgium	20	5,250 fr.	20	5,250 fr.
10	5,500 fr.	55,000 fr.	France	10	5,500 fr.	15	3,667 fr.

At the now higher price of 5,250 francs for steel, French buyers will reduce their purchases somewhat, while Belgian purchases of wheat will expand at the lower price of 3,667 francs. If French demand now amounts to 11 million tons of steel, the total value of their imports will be 57,750 million francs. Should Belgian demand for wheat at a price of 3,667 francs a ton chance to be 15,750 million tons (approximately), the value of Belgian imports would also be just 57,750 million francs. Trade would be in balance, and so would the barter terms, which now stand at 10 steel = 14.32 wheat. If, however, Belgian demand at this new price were smaller or larger, the adjustment of wages and prices to international demands would have to continue until a stable position was reached.

In summary, (1) the possible range of barter terms is given by the respective domestic terms of trade as set by comparative efficiency in each country; (2) within this range, the actual terms depend on each country's demand for the other country's product; (3) finally, only those barter terms will be stable at which the goods demanded by one country are equal in value to the goods demanded by the other.

Limits to Wage Differences

It is convenient to go one step further. At the same time that the comparative efficiency of labor in each country establishes the limits to the

---

[9] In this simplified illustration, trade is, of course, assumed to be confined to these two countries and these two commodities. We are also abstracting from transport costs. A gold currency is postulated, with 1 Belgian franc = 1 French franc.

barter terms of trade, it also sets bounds on relative wages. Consider the illustration we have been using. The ratio of labor efficiency in producing steel is 2 to 1, in producing wheat only 2 to 1.5. Wages in Belgium could never be twice as high as in France, for this would fully counteract the Belgian comparative advantage in steel and make its export impossible. France would make her own steel, at the same cost as in Belgium, and would export wheat, for which Belgium would pay with gold. Nor could the ratio of Belgian to French wages ever fall as low as 2 to 1.5, for at that ratio Belgian money costs for wheat would be equal to costs in France. Belgium would produce both steel and wheat, and export the latter, receiving gold in payment.

In both instances, balanced trade is impossible. The price-specie-flow mechanism would operate to reduce wages and prices when they were high and to raise them when they were low, until prices were such that reciprocal demands just balanced.

ELABORATION AND REFINEMENT OF THE CLASSICAL DOCTRINE

From the time of Ricardo and Mill down to the present, the essentials of their theory of international trade have remained relatively intact. The theory has, however, been elaborated and refined in a number of ways. Of most importance have been the refinements introduced by Taussig to deal with the problems raised by noncompeting groups of labor and by the existence of capital charges.

Noncompeting Groups

In the basic theory, labor in each country is assumed to be homogeneous, and to differ between countries only in productivity. Yet it has long been recognized that any country's labor force consists of many different groups of labor (technical, skilled, semiskilled, and unskilled, to mention one common classification) among which mobility is far from perfect. These distinct categories of labor, with rather well-marked and enduring differences in wages, became known as "noncompeting" groups.

The mere existence of such groups would not affect the theory of international trade, provided that in each country the relative scale of wages were the same. But if, for example, wages of unskilled labor were especially low in one country, because this kind of labor was unusually abundant, that country could produce some commodity or commodities at a lower money cost than its competitors, even though it had no comparative advantage. The same would be true were skilled labor, or any other of the noncompeting groups, the one with abnormally low wages, or if wages of *all* groups were especially depressed in some particular industry. Abnormally low wages for a particular kind of labor, in other words, act as a substitute for *real* comparative advantage.

Taussig developed this point at some length, yet he thought noncompeting groups served to explain only special situations, such as existed in the German chemical industry and in the U.S. iron and steel industry before 1914. In the former, employers could obtain highly-skilled chemical workers at abnormally low rates of pay, while in the latter, an unusually large supply of unskilled immigrant labor reduced its wage level to an extraordinary degree. To a considerable extent, Taussig felt, the ability of both industries to export rested upon these facts. Barring a few such exceptional cases, however, the basic doctrine of comparative advantage required no modification. This was because—at least in the Western nations—the hierarchy of noncompeting groups and the relative differences in their wages were about the same.[10]

Capital Charges

Taussig treated capital charges in a similar manner. While admitting interest on capital as an element in money costs, he held that it would have no effect on the relative prices of commodities unless it bore with *unequal weight on different goods.*

For this to be true, (1) interest rates have to differ among countries, and (2) the relative use made of capital as compared with labor would have to vary from one industry to another. Thus a country enjoying low interest rates would have a price advantage equivalent to one caused by the basic principle of comparative costs only in industries in which capital was used in relatively large quantities. Since national differences in interest rates were judged to be "not considerable," and since Taussig implied that the relative use of capital did not vary greatly between industries, the range of influence of interest rates "is restricted to a special set of circumstances." As with noncompeting groups, its introduction "does not lead to a radical modification of our first conclusions."[11]

By permitting diversity of wages between different groups of labor and differences in interest rates to play a role only in exceptional circumstances, Taussig was able to retain the doctrine of comparative labor costs as the dominant principle explaining international price differences and thus the direction of specialization and trade.

Limitations of the Classical Theory

The principle of comparative cost has served well as a tool of analysis for more than a century, and with the necessary qualifications it can be applied to a wide range of problems. It suffers, however, from the serious defect of

[10] See F. W. Taussig, *International Trade,* Ch. 6. The trade between Western nations Taussig regarded as determined by the principle of comparative costs, whereas in the trade with the tropics and other overseas areas, differences in costs or advantage were absolute rather than comparative only.

[11] *Ibid.,* pp. 67-68.

resting on the labor theory of value and therewith of being expressed in terms of the single factor, labor. The labor theory of value, which is presumed to explain *domestic* prices or exchange ratios, has been long discarded. To limit inputs to labor alone flies in the face of such well-known facts as that there are many factors of production and that even labor is not a single homogeneous factor. To take these facts into account by treating them as exceptional fails to do them justice; moreover, this method has the disadvantage of being roundabout and cumbersome.[12]

Finally, we should note that the classical economists were more interested in showing the gains from international trade than in explaining its mechanism. Their theory served adequately to show the effects of trade upon welfare, but it had serious shortcomings as an explanatory device. Thus the classical model showed how, with relative differences in labor costs *given,* trade would benefit both trading partners. But it did nothing to explain why costs were lower or labor was more efficient in one country than in another. When this is attempted, one is inevitably driven to appeal to such factors as superior resources, the use of elaborate machinery, or the presence of more abundant and better managerial talent.[13] But this is to introduce the abundance of *other* factors of production to explain the greater productivity of *one* of them— labor.

Would it not be more fitting and overcome, at the same time, the objection to the stress on a single factor involved in the comparative cost theory if we founded our explanation of international trade on the striking differences with which different nations are endowed with *all* the productive agents?

SELECTED REFERENCES

Ellsworth, P. T., *International Economics*. New York: Macmillan, 1938. Chapter II reviews the contributions of the classical economists to the development of international trade theory. Chapter III is a synopsis of the modern classical position, with all its qualifications.

Haberler, G., *The Theory of International Trade*. London: Wm. Hodge & Co.,

---

[12] Another approach attempts to meet the problem posed by the existence of numerous factors by resort to the concept of "real costs." These are the subjective costs attached to different kinds of inputs of human origin—the effort or disutility of various kinds of labor and the abstinence involved in saving. Since these costs are incommensurable (the disutility of labor and the disutility of saving are different in kind and therefore cannot sensibly be added), either one must assume that the proportions in which capital and different kinds of labor are combined are the same in all industries, or that the valuations given them by the market (wages, interest) are proportional to the disutilities involved (so that the sum of their prices accurately reflects the sum of real costs). Since it is impossible to admit the realism of either of these alternatives, the real costs approach cannot be justified. Furthermore, it cannot take into account costs which are "real" but involve no disutility, such as the necessity of using land to produce tobacco instead of cotton.

[13] See, for example, the numerous illustrations of this sort given by Taussig in his *International Trade,* Chs. 15 and 16.

Ltd., 1936. Chapters IX-XI contains an excellent elaboration of the classical theory. A much briefer statement is to be found in the same author's *A Survey of International Trade Theory, Special Papers in International Economics,* No. 1. Princeton, N.J.: International Finance Section, Princeton University, 1961.

Marsh, Donald B., *World Trade and Investment.* New York: Harcourt, Brace & Co., 1951. Chapters 19 and 20 give a rigorous statement of the theory of international trade in terms of real cost. Difficult, but rewarding.

Mill, John Stuart, *The Principles of Political Economy.* Book III, Ch. XVIII, contains Mill's theory of reciprocal demand.

Ohlin, Bertil, *Interregional and International Trade.* Cambridge, Mass.: Harvard University Press, 1933. Appendix III is a vigorous criticism of the classical theory.

Ricardo, David, *The Principles of Political Economy and Taxation.* Chapter VII contains the famous statement of the doctrine of comparative cost.

Viner, Jacob, *Studies in the Theory of International Trade.* New York: Harper & Bros., 1937. See Chapter VIII, Sections I, VII, VIII, X, XI, and XII, for a defense of the real-cost approach to international trade.

5

THE MODERNIZATION
OF COMPARATIVE COST

Toward a More Comprehensive Theory

It is precisely in terms of relative factor endowment that modern theories of international trade have developed. We shall present two of these theories, both widely used. The first of these, known as the opportunity cost theory, originated with Professor Gottfried Haberler. It is derived directly from the older comparative cost theory, and we can best begin its exposition by re-stating that theory in terms of a concept that plays an important role in Haberler's exposition—that of the production possibilities or product substitution curve.

The illustration used in the last chapter shows, for both Belgium and France, the output of steel and wheat obtainable for a given input of labor— 10 man-years. Were we to vary the inputs, the outputs would of course also vary, and if we assumed constant returns to labor as the amount employed was varied, we would have the case of constant costs of production. We could draw up a table for each country showing a constant proportionality of output to input over any desired range. Such tables would take the following form:

| | OUTPUT | | | |
| | Belgium | | France | |
Input of Labor (millions of man-years)	Steel (million tons)	Wheat (million tons)	Steel (million tons)	Wheat (million tons)
20	——	——	20	30
10	20	20	10	15
8	16	16	8	12
6	12	12	6	9
4	8	8	4	6
2	4	4	2	3

Note first that we have put the illustration on a more truly national scale by expressing inputs in terms of millions of man-years of labor and output in millions of units. Constant returns to inputs of labor is implicit in the table: if we start with 2 million labor units, we obtain in Belgium 4 million tons of steel or 4 million tons of wheat and in France 2 million tons of steel and 3 million tons of wheat; if we increase the input of labor from 2 million to 4 million units, we double the output of each commodity in each country, and so on.

These facts can be expressed more conveniently and briefly in a diagram. In Figure 5.1, units of steel are measured on the vertical axis, units of wheat on the horizontal axis. Units of labor employed are not shown, but are assumed to be related to output as set forth in the table.[1] Thus on the diagram for Belgium, if all of 2 million workers are employed for a year in making steel, 4 million tons can be obtained, while if the same 2 million workers devote their labor to raising wheat, they can also produce 4 million tons. The outputs for France corresponding to an input of 2 million man-years of labor are 2 million steel and 3 million wheat. But suppose the labor force in question were not allocated entirely to steel or to wheat, but were divided

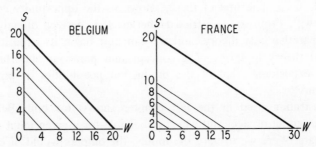

FIGURE 5.1   Production Possibilities Curves: Constant Costs

in some proportion between the two commodities. If half of the 2 million workers in the Belgian steel industry were shifted to growing wheat, the output of steel would shrink by half, to 2 million tons, and the output of wheat would be 2 million tons.[2] The labor could be allocated between the two commodities in any proportions desired. The particular allocation chosen in fact would correspond to the community's demands for these products.

The line or "curve" we have been considering, that corresponding to an

[1] Were we to use a three-dimensional diagram, labor could be measured on the axis vertical to the plane of the other two axes. Output of the two commodities would then be shown as rising along a plane with constant slope, starting at the origin.

[2] Thus, to anticipate the next stage in our argument, the cost of obtaining 2 million tons of wheat could be regarded as the 2 million tons of steel that had to be given up in order to get the wheat. This is another way of measuring cost alternative to the amount of labor required to produce a commodity.

input of 2 million man-years of labor, is known as a *production possibilities* or product substitution curve. There is a whole family of such curves, of which we have shown five for Belgium and six for France. Suppose we assume that the total labor supply in Belgium is 10 million and in France 20 million man-years. Then when Belgium's labor force is fully employed, it could produce either 20 million tons of steel or 20 million tons of wheat, or a combination represented by some point on the topmost line of its diagram. France could produce 20 million tons of steel, 30 million tons of wheat, or some combination of the two. These would be the maximum or optimum production possibilities curves for these countries. It is these optimum production possibilities curves that are normally used, since full employment is generally assumed. Then all the other curves or lines, for lower levels of employment and output, can be ignored.

Graphical Representation of Constant Cost

In Figure 5.2 we have reproduced the optimum production possibilities curves for Belgium and France. Let us suppose that demand for the two commodities in Belgium is such that, in isolation, the production point P on the production possibilities curve is realized, with 10 million units each of steel and wheat produced. In France, assume a relatively greater demand for wheat, with the corresponding production point P, where output of the two commodities is $6\frac{2}{3}$ million of steel and 20 million of wheat.

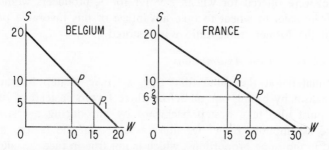

FIGURE 5.2   Production at Constant Costs

Since each production possibilities curve is a straight line, its slope is constant. Each curve therefore reflects a condition of constant costs. Thus if, in Belgium, the community's demand for wheat were to increase and its demand for steel to diminish, the production point would move downward along the curve, say to the point P_1, corresponding to the production of 5 million units of steel and 15 of wheat. If the opposite shift in demands occurred in France, the production point would move upward to a new position such as P_1, where output is 10 million of steel and 15 million of wheat. If we wished to continue our analysis along classical lines, in terms of labor cost, we could do so, and we could show that in each country, the unit labor cost of each commodity remains constant.[3]

Now is a good time to drop the labor-cost assumption. We can regard the cost of Belgium's increased wheat output as the amount of steel production that must be sacrificed to obtain it. The steel forgone is the *opportunity cost* of obtaining the additional wheat. And since the production possibilities curve is a straight line, the opportunity cost of either commodity is constant—in the case of Belgium, it is 1 unit of steel for each unit of wheat, or vice versa; in France, it is 1 unit of steel for 1.5 units of wheat.

We can now also get rid of one more of the narrow assumptions of the classical theory. Instead of assuming that steel and wheat are produced by labor alone, we can take as the input the total economic resources of each country—all its land, labor, and capital. Our model is now more realistic in that it takes into account the fact that all commodities require the employment not only of labor, but also of the other factors of production. It is also more general in that it expresses cost in terms of alternative production forgone rather than in terms of labor.

The production possibilities curve, under conditions of constant cost, can be given an additional meaning. For a country in isolation, before international trade is introduced, its slope reflects a constant exchange ratio between commodities, or constant relative prices. In Belgium, steel will exchange for wheat at a 1:1 ratio, in France at a ratio of 1:1.5. If in Belgium more steel were offered for wheat, say 1.1 for 1, producers would shift resources from steel to wheat to take advantage of this favorable price situation, until the former stable ratio was restored.

A Short Digression on Assumptions

Unfortunately, at the same time that we take a step forward toward greater realism by basing our model on three factors instead of on a single one, we must also take a step backward by introducing a restrictive and unrealistic assumption. Either we must assume that the factors are always combined in the same proportions, which is not true in fact, or, alternatively, we must assume that each factor of production is equally suited to the production of all commodities. One of these assumptions is necessary as long as we wish to adhere to the case of constant costs, whether costs be expressed in terms of alternative production forgone, or in terms of the resources required to produce a unit of a commodity.

We shall dispense with any such assumption shortly. Then it will be shown that when a given resource (for example, land) is better suited to the produc-

---

[3] Thus in Belgium, at production point *P,* the labor force is evenly divided between steel and wheat, with 5 million man-years devoted to the production of each commodity. Unit cost of each commodity is ½ man-year. If the output of wheat is increased by 5 million units and that of steel diminished by the same amount, 2½ million man-years of labor must be shifted from steel to wheat. The unit cost of the *additional* wheat is constant at ½ man-year. Similar reasoning applies in the case of France.

tion of some commodities (for example, foodstuffs) than others, increasing costs will rule. When one assumes homogeneity of factors with respect to all types of production, then to explain comparative advantage one is obliged—as in the classical case—to appeal to the presence of determinants other than those specified in the analysis, such as climate or national differences in ability.

International Trade Under Conditions of Constant Costs

We can now modify our diagrams to take account of international trade. In Figure 5.3 we reproduce the production possibilities curves for Belgium and France, with each country allocating resources to the production of the two commodities, as indicated by the production points P. Prices or exchange ratios in each country before trade are indicated by the slopes of these curves; they are 1 steel $= 1$ wheat (or $20\ S = 20\ W$) in Belgium, and 1 steel $= 1.5$ wheat (or $20\ S = 30\ W$) in France. Since Belgium has a comparative advantage in steel, when trade between the two countries is opened up, it will specialize completely in the production of that commodity; its production point will move from P to P_1. France, on the other hand, will specialize in wheat production, at P_1 in the diagram for France.[4]

If Belgium is to benefit from trade, it must get a better price (in terms of wheat) than 1 : 1, or 20 : 20. The best terms it could possibly get would be

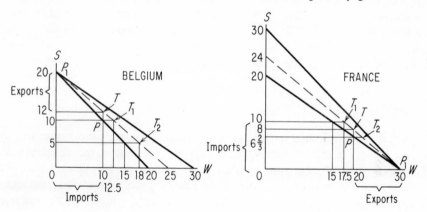

FIGURE 5.3 International Trade: Constant Costs

20 : 30, which are the terms (or "price") at which the two products exchange in France. This price line is shown on Belgium's diagram. Correspondingly, France must get better terms than $20\ S$ for $30\ W$ (the domestic exchange

[4] Complete specialization will occur only if the trading countries are of comparable size. If one were a large nation and the other small, the demand of the small nation would be insufficient to justify complete specialization by the large nation. Only the small country would confine its production to exports, and since trade would take place at the price ratio ruling in the larger country, the smaller one would enjoy all the gains from trade.

ratio); the maximum possible terms for France will be the exchange ratio that rules in Belgium, of 30 S = 30 W (or 1 : 1). The lines with slopes of 20 : 30 and 30 : 30 indicate the *limits* to the terms of international trade for each country. The actual international price, exchange ratio, or terms of trade can be anywhere between these limits.

As we know, the ruling exchange ratio will be determined by reciprocal demand. Let us assume that it settles at 20 S = 25 W (10:12.5, or 1:1.25), and that at this international price, Belgium will take 10 million tons of wheat. For imports of this amount, it will have to provide exports of 8 million tons of steel (8 : 10 : : 10 : 12.5). Belgium's trading position on the international price line will then be T. France will export 10 million tons of wheat in exchange for imports of 8 million tons of steel, a position also represented by the point T on France's diagram.

It may help to clarify this discussion if we express the conditions before and after the opening of trade in the form of tables. The point to note is that after trade is opened, Belgium obtains the same amount of wheat through

| | Belgium | | France | |
	Steel (million tons)	Wheat (million tons)	Steel (million tons)	Wheat (million tons)
Before Trade:				
Production	10	10	6⅔	20
Consumption	10	10	6⅔	20
After Trade:				
Production	20	——	——	30
Consumption	12	10	8	20
Exports	8	——	——	10
Imports	——	10	8	——

importation as she obtained before trade from domestic production, but at a cost of only 8 million tons of steel exports. This leaves the country with 12 million tons of steel (out of a total production of 20 million tons) for consumption—a gain of 2 million tons. France gains in the same manner: her consumption of wheat remains the same as before trade, but she obtains 1⅓ tons more of steel.

Consider another possible situation. Suppose that reciprocal demands are such that at the given international price of 20 : 25, Belgium imports 12.5 million tons of wheat while France imports in exchange 10 million tons of steel. This puts the trading points at T_1 in each diagram. Belgium now obtains the same amount of steel as before trade (10 million tons), but imports for consumption 12.5 million tons of wheat, a gain of 2.5 million of wheat. At any point on Belgium's trade line between T and T_1, the gain is clear: the country has more of both commodities. At the limiting points, T and T_1, she obtains more of one and the pretrade amount of the other.

But what about France? Her new trading point (T_1) lies outside the limits (in the case of France, $T - T_2$) at which she obtains more of one commodity and the same amount of the other, and within which she gets more of both commodities. At T_1, France imports 10 million tons of steel and exports 12.5 million tons of wheat, which leaves her with only 17.5 million tons of wheat for home consumption. French consumers thus have considerably more steel than before (10 million as against 6⅔ million tons), but 2½ million tons less of wheat. Is France better off as a result of trade? Surely she must be. French consumers must—at the new exchange ratio between wheat and steel—prefer to take a substantially larger quantity of steel, along with some reduction in their consumption of wheat. Otherwise, had they been less willing to reduce their consumption of wheat and to increase their consumption of steel, the amounts exchanged would have been brought within the limits where the gain is clear.[5]

Increasing Costs

Up to now, we have assumed that production takes place under conditions of constant cost. This means that the efficiency of the resources used remains the same whatever the relative output of the two commodities. But this must imply, as we have noted, either that these resources (land, labor, and capital) are combined in fixed proportions in all industries, or that factors can be substituted for one another with no loss of efficiency. (In technical terms, there is perfect substitutability of the factors.) But neither assumption is true for the real world.

Thus in the production of vegetables, land is a particularly important factor, though it must be supplemented, of course, with labor and with some capital in the form of garden equipment and fertilizers. As production is increased in a given region and as all the suitable land is brought under cultivation, output can be still further increased by more intensive application of capital and labor—that is, by substituting these factors for additional land. Output will not increase proportionately, however, but only at rapidly diminishing returns. Under these conditions, labor and capital are very inadequate substitutes for land.

Or consider manufacturing, in which capital in the form of plant and equipment is a critical factor. Especially in the short run, during which the types of equipment used cannot be changed, the attempt to increase output in the absence of additional capital by substituting labor in its stead will yield reduced returns. With the passage of time, equipment wears out and can be

---

[5] There is another way of showing the gain—a way that takes into account the possibility that different groups of consumers may be affected by the change in consumption. In our last illustration, consumers of steel enjoy an increase in their consumption because steel is cheaper at the new international price, while since wheat is dearer, consumers of wheat reduce their consumption. The government could, however, impose a tax on steel consumers and use the proceeds to subsidize the consumers of wheat. By this means, it could bring the welfare position of the consumers down to T, or even beyond.

replaced out of depreciation reserves with simpler and less complex machinery, with which greater amounts of labor could be combined efficiently. Thus over the longer run, the substitutability of labor for capital would be higher, though still far from perfect.

This imperfect substitutability of the factors for one another in different lines of production gives rise to the phenomenon of increasing costs. We represent this situation by Figure 5.4, which shows a production possibilities curve for some country with respect to food and manufactures. Let us start by

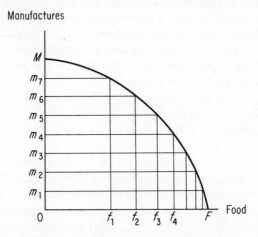

FIGURE 5.4   Increasing Opportunity Cost

assuming that all the country's resources are employed in the manufacturing industry. As we have suggested, this is a capital-using or capital-intensive type of productive activity. With only manufactures being produced, all the country's capital will be fully employed, and the demand for capital being great, the return on capital will be high. Therefore every effort will be made to economize in its use by substituting land and labor for it. Presumably all the country's labor force will be employed, too, and the methods of production adopted will use as much labor as possible in combination with the expensive capital. Relatively little land can be used in manufacturing, however, so that although factories and warehouses can be allowed to sprawl over as large areas as is desirable, most of the nation's land will stand idle. Land will be a free good.

Now let us reduce the output of manufactures somewhat, say to Om_7, and transfer the productive resources released to the production of food. Land, which is the vital factor in food production, will be readily available, and its transfer to (or rather, its initial employment in) this activity will be accompanied by the transfer of relatively small amounts of labor and capital. The production of foodstuffs will rise by a relatively large amount, Of_1. This is especially true since the land best suited to agriculture (the most fertile and the nearest to urban markets) will be employed first. If this process is repeated, with the output of manufactures successively reduced by equal decrements, the amounts of food obtained for each installment of released resources will progressively diminish, as shown by the diminishing distances f_1f_2, f_2f_3, and so forth, on the food axis.[6]

The reason for the diminishing returns in food to the resources transferred is to be found in the increasingly unsuitable factor "mix" as more and more resources are devoted to food production. If all the country's land is assumed to be employed either in manufacturing or in agriculture when Om_6 of manufactures and Of_2 of food are produced, from then on each reduction of manufactures' output will release relatively little land but relatively large amounts of capital. Capital, however, is a poor substitute for land in agricultural production. Therefore the resources released will be decreasingly effective in the production of foodstuffs.

Increasing costs are reflected in the concave shape of the production possibilities curve and are to be interpreted as increasing opportunity costs. As we progress from left to right along the curve, for each unit quantity of manufactures given up, a smaller and smaller quantity of food is obtained. This means that for each unit that food production is increased, a larger quantity of manufactures must be forgone. The cost of food in terms of alternative production steadily increases.

It is convenient at this point to show the systematic relationship between differences in the degree to which factors may be substituted for one another and the shape of the production possibilities curve. Let us start with the very short run—for example, not longer than a year. Over such a period, capital is invested in specific types of plant, equipment, and tools which cannot be changed; labor is composed of categories of widely differing and often very specialized skills; and land—even in agricultural production—is combined with labor and capital in enterprises oriented to the production of specific kinds of crops. There is virtually no room for substitution between factors. A production possibilities curve would then be rectangular in shape, like M_1PF_1 in Figure 5.5. Output in each line of production would be dictated by the existing allocation of resources, with OM_1 of manufactures and OF_1 of foodstuffs produced. Any reduction in the output of either line of production would simply reduce total output, since factors could not be shifted from one line to the other.

If the time period were somewhat longer (say two or three years), some of the labor could be retrained and new entrants into the labor force could be directed into different activities, while some tools and equipment would

---

[6] By starting with complete specialization on food production (at OF) and reversing the procedure used above, we could show the reduction of food output by constant amounts yielding diminishing increments of manufactures.

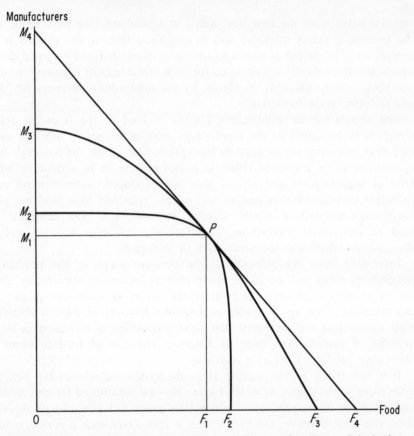

FIGURE 5.5   Production Possibilities Curves with Increasing Factor Substitution

wear out and depreciation reserves could be used to purchase different ones. The production possibilities curve would show some, though nqt much, flexibility, as M_2PF_2.

Over a period of time long enough to replace the major part of plant and equipment (say ten to twenty years), and to retrain and redirect the labor force, the possibility of factor substitution would be greatly enhanced. The production possibilities curve would take on a more gradual curvature, as in M_3PF_3. Substitutability is still imperfect, but it is much greater than in the short run. A straight line production possibilities curve (M_4PF_4) would reflect perfect substitutability between factors—an unrealistic but theoretically imaginable situation.

Production and Demand

Before we introduce international trade, it is important to consider how a country in isolation would allocate its production between a given set of alternatives, and for what reasons. When we were dealing with constant cost conditions, we saw that the slope of the production possibilities curve determined both the opportunity cost of one commodity in terms of the other, and the price or ratio at which the commodities would exchange. Demand was left to determine only how much of each commodity would be produced— that is, where the actual production point would lie.

Under conditions of increasing cost, the slope of the production possibilities curve is not constant, but varies throughout its length. The slope at any point (the tangent at that point) is the marginal rate of transformation, or the rate at which one commodity can be transformed into the other, given a very small shift of productive resources. It is the same as the relative opportunity cost at that point: the amount of wheat, for example, that can be obtained by giving up a unit of steel and transferring the released resources into wheat production. Since relative costs vary over the entire production possibilities curve, the relative price of the commodities will also vary over this range. Cost conditions therefore cannot alone determine what commodity price ratio will in fact rule. We must look to the forces of demand for an answer.

Let us assume, then, that the demand for steel and for wheat in Belgium

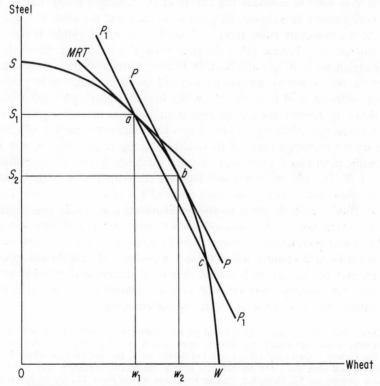

FIGURE 5.6   Price, Cost, and the Production Possibilities Curve

is such as to establish a price ratio of 2 steel = 1 wheat. This can be represented by the line P_1P_1 with that slope in Figure 5.6, intersecting the production possibilities curve at the points a and c. Assume that production is undertaken at the point a, with Ow_1 of wheat and Os_1 of steel being produced. The marginal rate of transformation, or relative cost, at this point is indicated by the line MRT tangent at a, with a 1 : 1 slope. For each unit of wheat given up, 1 unit of steel can be obtained. But in the market, 1 unit of wheat exchanges for 2 of steel. At this exchange ratio, it will be profitable to shift resources from the production of steel into the production of wheat. As this is done, the production point moves downward and to the right along the production possibilities curve until at point b, the MRT and the price line PP (drawn parallel to P_1P_1) coincide. Relative opportunity costs are now identical with relative prices, and the position is one of stable equilibrium. In general, the equilibrium position is represented by the point where the price line (determined by the relative strength of commodity demands) is tangent to the production possibilities curve.[7]

International Trade Under Conditions of Increasing Cost

It is now time to consider the effects of international trade. Let us begin with each country in isolation. Belgium is producing at the point P_b (in Figure 5.7) at a commodity price ratio of 2 steel = 1 wheat, while at the corresponding point in France (P_f), the price ratio is 1 steel = 2 wheat. Steel is relatively cheap in Belgium; wheat, in France. If trade is now opened up between the two countries, Belgian traders will find it profitable to buy wheat in France, offering steel in exchange, while French traders for similar reasons will desire to acquire the cheap steel from Belgium in exchange for wheat. The introduction of foreign demand into each country's market will tend to drive up the exchange value of its relatively cheap commodity. A new internationally determined price will become established, say at approximately $1S = 1\ W$. Belgian producers will increase the output of steel and diminish that of wheat until a new production point (P) is reached, at which the ratio of opportunity costs is equal to the international commodity price ratio. In France, production of the commodities will move toward greater specialization in wheat production, at point P' in France's diagram. The new production point in each country will represent a position of equilibrium, provided exports and imports are in balance—that is, if reciprocal demand is in equilibrium, each country being satisfied with the amount of imports it is getting in exchange for its exports at the ruling international price.

[7] This is true only under conditions of perfect competition, which have been assumed throughout. Other necessary conditions, upon which we shall not elaborate here, are that the factors (essentially labor) are indifferent as to the industry in which they are employed, and that there are no external economies or diseconomies. For a discussion of these points, see G. Haberler, "Some Problems in the Pure Theory of International Trade," *Economic Journal* (June, 1950).

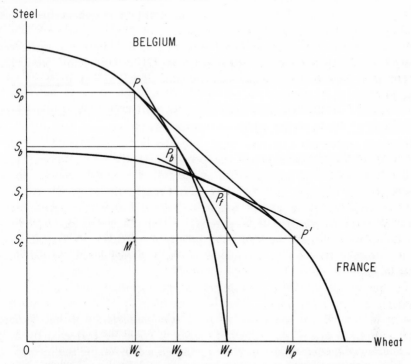

FIGURE 5.7   The Opening of Trade Between Two Countries

This condition of balance is shown in the diagram by the equality of each country's exports and imports at the ruling international price. Belgium produces Os_p of steel, of which she consumes Os_c and exports s_cs_p ($= MP$). France, in turn, produces Ow_p of wheat, consuming Ow_c and exporting w_cw_p ($= MP'$). Since Belgium's exports are France's imports, and vice versa, each country's exports and imports exactly balance at the price represented by the slope of PP'.

A table such as we used earlier provides the basis for determining the nature of the gains from trade.

	Belgium		France	
	Steel	Wheat	Steel	Wheat
Before Trade:				
Production	Os_b	Ow_b	Os_f	Ow_f
Consumption	Os_b	Ow_b	Os_f	Ow_f
After Trade:				
Production	Os_p	Ow_c	Os_c	Ow_p
Consumption	Os_c	$Ow_c + w_cw_p$	$Os_c + s_cs_p$	Ow_c
Exports	s_cs_p	––	––	w_cw_p
Imports	––	w_cw_p	s_cs_p	––

As a consequence of trade, Belgian consumption of wheat has nearly doubled, from Ow_b to Ow_p (home production of Ow_c plus imports $w_c w_p$), while consumption of steel has fallen from Os_b to Os_c. French consumption of steel, on the other hand, has expanded from Os_f to Os_p (home production of Os_c plus imports $s_c s_p$), while consumption of wheat has declined from Ow_f to Ow_c.

Consumers of the imported article are better off in each country, and consumers of the exported article are worse off. On balance, there must be gain, since consumers exercised their choice in a free market. The opportunity to obtain imports much cheaper than at the old domestic price evidently had a strong appeal—such as the call of a bargain counter to the wheat starved Belgians and the steel-short French. Before trade, the high price of steel in France and of wheat in Belgian had forced consumers of these products to constrict their purchases. The changed prices introduced by the opening of trade enabled them greatly to expand their consumption. In the process, they forced consumers of the exported article to cut down their buying.

To the extent to which consumers of the exported and the imported products are the same people, there is no problem of a shift in the distribution of welfare. But if consumers of these two products are distinct groups, such a problem arises. As suggested earlier, it could be corrected by a redistribution of income. This could be accomplished by taxing the incomes of import consumers and paying the proceeds to export consumers, or by placing a larger share of the costs of government on the shoulders of import consumers. These are only two of many possibilities.[8]

Partial Specialization

In our discussion of constant costs, we noted that trade would lead to complete specialization. This is not true under increasing costs, which is the usual situation. Each country continues to devote some part of its resources to home production of the good that is imported. Some producers can still compete with imports, since their relative costs are no higher than the international price ratio. Thus in Figure 5.7, at P' the opportunity cost of a unit of steel is one unit of wheat, and this is the going international exchange ratio. French steel producers whose opportunity costs are equal to or less than this ratio (at P' and to the right) will continue to compete with imported steel.

Stated in terms of resource costs, at P' a unit of steel can be produced for

---

[8] That greater welfare results from international trade and specialization can also be shown by the use of community indifference curves. There are, however, serious conceptual difficulties involved in the use of such curves; furthermore, they change in shape as the distribution of income is altered by the opening of international trade. Hence it seems preferable to avoid their use. For a good exposition of the indifference curve approach, consult C. P. Kindleberger, *International Economics*, 3rd ed., 1963, Ch. 6, or Delbert A. Snider, *An Introduction to International Economics*, rev. ed., 1963, Ch. 4.

the same resources that would be required to produce a unit of wheat. This is only half the (relative) resource cost that existed at P_f, before trade, when the resources needed to produce 1 unit of steel could produce 2 units of wheat. In moving from P_f to P', wheat costs have risen, since land is being used intensively and the factor mix is less suited to wheat production. The costlier steel output, on the other hand, has been eliminated; production has been concentrated in plants with the most efficient factor combinations. These plants can compete with Belgian imports.

The Meaning of Comparative Cost

You will recall that according to the classical theory of comparative cost, trade was shown to result in gain to each country when comparative labor costs were different in the two countries, or, alternatively, when each country had a comparative advantage in production. The classical writers made no serious attempt to explain why such a trade-creating situation existed, but attributed it to differences in national aptitudes that were much like the individual aptitudes that underlie specialization among different people within a single country. Such national aptitudes might be the result of a suitable climate (as of Portugal's for producing wine), of a social environment conducive to inventiveness and mechanical skill, or of rich soil or abundant capital that raised labor's productivity in agriculture or industry. These matters were rarely stated clearly, but were left to lurk in the shadows of theoretical discussion.

In the analysis just presented, we have dispensed with the limiting assumption that labor is the only factor of production. In its place, we have substituted the concept of a nation's total economic resources, consisting of land, labor, and capital, of which various subcategories could be distinguished. We have also allowed for the combination of these factors in varying proportions. Finally, for labor cost we have substituted opportunity cost—the alternative you forgo if you produce or consume one commodity rather than another.

According to this more modern approach, the basis for international trade is still comparative cost, only now it is comparative opportunity cost rather than comparative labor cost. If the opportunity cost of producing steel rather than wheat is lower in Belgium than in France, while the opposite is true of France, international trade will be profitable. But how do we explain such differences in opportunity costs? This crucial question still awaits an answer.

Probably the most satisfactory answer so far, and the most widely accepted, results from the work of two Swedish economists, Eli Heckscher and Bertil Ohlin. Heckscher made the pioneer effort in an article written in 1919 that set out the main lines of a modern theory of international trade.[9] Ohlin

---

[9] Eli Heckscher, "The Effect of Foreign Trade on the Distribution of Income," *Ekonomisk Tidskrift*, **XXI**, 1919. Reprinted in 1949 as Ch. 13 in *Readings in the Theory of International Trade*, Blakiston, Philadelphia.

expanded, elaborated, and systematized these ideas in a major treatise on the subject.[10]

Like any theory, which is a generalized statement of certain relations among complex phenomena, that of Heckscher and Olin inevitably indulges in oversimplification. It has recently been criticized for failing to deal satisfactorily with certain aspects of the subject, and we shall introduce some of these criticisms later. Yet the theory does give a reasoned explanation of the basis for international specialization and trade in terms that seem relevant and important.

What is the relation, you may well ask, between the opportunity cost theory just presented and the Heckscher-Ohlin theory? And why present two theories when one would do?

Essentially, the opportunity cost theory is a simplification of the general equilibrium approach used by Ohlin. It can be transformed into the latter, which is expressed in terms of money costs and money prices, by means of a series of relatively simple assumptions about product prices and factor prices.[11] Yet the opportunity cost doctrine has the merit not only of greater simplicity, but also of showing how our ideas have progressed without any sharp break with those of the classical economists.[12] Moreover, it draws attention more forcibly to the problem of factor substitution than does the more general theory. It also lends itself readily to diagrammatic representation, which can often be helpful as an expository device.

SELECTED REFERENCES

Caves, Richard E., *Trade and Economic Structure*. Cambridge, Mass.: Harvard University Press, 1960. Chapter II traces the development of the theory of international trade from the classical to the modern versions.

Haberler, Gottfried, *The Theory of International Trade*. London: Wm. Hodge & Co., Ltd., 1936. In Chapter XII, Professor Haberler develops his opportunity cost theory and shows how it can be transformed into a general equilibrium theory.

————, *A Survey of International Trade Theory*. Princeton, N.J.: International Finance Section, Princeton University, 1961. See Chapters I-III for a brief survey of the development of theory from classical times onward.

————, "Some Problems in the Pure Theory of International Trade," *Economic Journal* (June, 1950). This article expands on the presentation in Professor Haberler's book and discusses the implications of introducing certain market imperfections.

[10] Bertil Ohlin, *Interregional and International Trade*. Published in 1933 by Harvard University Press, Cambridge.

[11] Haberler himself shows how the transition to a general equilibrium form of statement is to be made. See Gottfried Haberler, *The Theory of International Trade*, pp. 180-82. Published 1936 by Wm. Hodge & Co., Ltd., London.

[12] I must confess that in earlier editions of this text I allowed my enthusiasm for the Heckscher-Ohlin approach to permit me to overemphasize its differences and to minimize the continuity of thought.

6

THE DETERMINANTS
OF MONEY COSTS AND PRICES
IN INTERNATIONAL TRADE

The task of this chapter is twofold: to provide a more satisfactory explanation of why comparative differences in costs come into being, and to express the theory of international trade in terms of money costs and prices, as is most of our thinking about the monetary economy we live in.

The Basis of Comparative Differences in Cost

When Adam Smith wrote about specialization and the division of labor, he gave as the reason for these phenomena the possession by individuals of natural or acquired aptitudes. Inherent human traits include intelligence, manual dexterity, an ear for music, or an eye for form; acquired aptitudes cover the acquisition of particular skills from extended training and practice. Either kind of aptitude gives its possessor an advantage, over those who lack it, in the performance of certain specialized tasks. He is more productive in this particular kind of work; therefore he can perform it more cheaply and earn a higher income. He specializes, to his own benefit and to that of society.

Many people have a variety of skills; they could turn in a superior performance in a number of occupations. When this is true, they tend to specialize in that occupation in which they have the greatest comparative advantage. Thus some executives are also excellent typists, better than those they employ in this capacity. Yet it is better that they concentrate on management if they have a comparatively greater advantage in that activity. It pays to specialize where specialization counts most.

Adam Smith extended the principle of the division of labor from individuals to nations, basing this extension upon "the natural advantages which one nation has over another." As we have seen, Ricardo and those who followed him perceived, as Adam Smith did not, that only a comparative advantage—not an absolute advantage—was needed to justify the international division of labor. None of them, however, made a serious effort to distinguish carefully just what elements constituted the "natural advantages" of a nation.

Just such a distinction lies at the foundation of the modern theory of international trade. Thus Ohlin notes that whereas individuals are differently endowed with certain natural or acquired traits, nations are differently endowed with the productive factors. Just as differences in personal endowments give rise to the division of labor among individuals, so differences in national endowments underlie the international division of labor. In some instances, as with individuals, differences in natural factor endowments may be absolute. Thus to produce copper ore a country must have copper deposits, which only a few countries possess; or to produce tropical crops, it must have a tropical climate. But most production and trade rests not on such sharp absolute differences, but on relative differences. All nations possess a labor force; all have some land; all have some capital. But they differ widely in their *relative* endowment with the various factors.

> Australia has more agricultural land, but less labour, capital, and mines than Great Britain; consequently Australia is better adapted to the production of goods which require great quantities of agricultural land, whereas Great Britain has an advantage in the production of goods requiring considerable quantities of other factors.[1]

It is thus in its relative endowment with the various factors of production that the natural advantage of a country consists.

In the light of these remarks, let us reconsider Figure 5.7. There was a substantial difference in shape of the production possibilities curves for France and Belgium. France's curve is long on the wheat axis, short on the steel axis, indicating a large output of wheat relative to Belgium when all the nation's resources are devoted to producing wheat, a relatively small output of steel if it concentrates on that product. France also had a lower comparative opportunity cost in the production of wheat; Belgium, in the production of steel. We can now explain these differences in comparative cost that made trade profitable. France must be better endowed than Belgium with land, the productive agent that is quantitatively most important in wheat production, while Belgium must possess capital, the dominant factor in steel production, in relative abundance. The possibility of producing the two commodities differs in the two countries because, given the differing factor requirements of these commodities, national factor endowments are different. Hence the production possibilities curves are quite dissimilar in shape. Opportunity cost ratios and price ratios will then be different, and the establishment of trade profitable.[2]

---

[1] Ohlin, *op. cit.*, p. 12.

[2] Try to establish a basis for trade between two countries with production possibilities curves of identical shape, reflecting identical factor endowments. Start by assuming different tastes in the two countries, so that the price lines in isolation are tangent at different points, reflecting different relative prices and a tendency toward specialization in opposite directions. The opening of international trade will establish a common price ratio, but the new price line will be tangent at the same relative point in each country's diagram. There will be no specialization and no trade, only a reshuffling of production and a new set of internationally determined demands and prices.

Having shown that geographical differences in the distribution of factors of production underlie comparative costs, we have provided that doctrine with a foundation similar to the one that forms the basis for individual specialization. But the theory of comparative cost, stated in terms of alternative production forgone, is a *real* cost theory. For some purposes, it is important to consider the real cost to society of obtaining a particular product. Thus the real cost of the missiles, missile sites, tracking systems, radar network, and other components of the American defense effort is the schools, hospitals, roads, houses, and industrial plants that could have been produced with the resources actually devoted to defense. Expressed in such terms rather than as an incomprehensibly large sum of money, the cost of the defense program becomes more vivid and more real.[3]

When it comes to the forces that lead a country to export certain products, while importing others, a real cost approach is less suitable. The problem is to explain the mechanism of international trade, not to compare different states of welfare. For this problem, the logical starting point is the immediate cause of international trade, which clearly is the existence of international differences in money prices and costs. Our task is to show how the natural advantages of different countries—their varying endowments with the factors of production—become translated into international price differences.

The Pricing Process in a Single Market

Our starting point is the single market, within which raw materials, finished products, and the factors of production (other than land) may be assumed to move with perfect freedom. Such a market might be national in scope if the nation were small, but in a large country such as the United States, it would be limited to a single region within which the condition of perfect mobility could be assumed to hold. To keep our model simple, we shall also assume perfect competition; that is, for the time being we set aside the problems of monopoly and large-scale production.[4]

In a free economy, resources are allocated and goods produced with a view to satisfying the demands of final consumers. We may appropriately begin

---

[3] The opportunity cost concept of real cost has nothing in common with the classical notion of real cost. To the classical and neoclassical economists, real cost was and is the effort or sacrifice of the labor required to produce a commodity, and the sacrifice involved in providing the necessary capital. Aside from the fact that the two kinds of sacrifice are of different kinds, hence incommensurable, and thus incapable of being added, the classical concept of real cost cannot encompass the cost of using land, since no human sacrifice is involved in its use. There is, however, a real cost to society of using land: the output forgone when it is applied to one purpose rather than to another.

[4] What distinguishes interregional and international trade from trade within a region is a significant immobility between regions or countries of the factors of production, as contrasted with their mobility within a region. Regional specialization and trade are just as much facts to be explained as international trade. But since the problems connected with international trade are, for various reasons, generally more interesting and more important, we shall center our attention on that area.

our brief review of the pricing process, then, with consumer demand, which authorizes and directs production.

The demand for goods and services derives from the wants of buyers, which may be taken as based on a given set of tastes, backed up by their incomes, which enable them to make their wants heard in the market. Demand for any particular commodity represents a willingness to pay a scale of prices for that commodity (the demand schedule); it depends upon the incomes of interested buyers and upon the price, not only the commodity in question, but also of all the various commodities included in their expenditure plans.

The precise point reached on each demand schedule—that is, the amount of each commodity actually consumed—depends on the terms on which that commodity is supplied. Here, two sets of conditions are relevant: the methods of production that are available to producers, and the prices they must pay for the various factors to be combined in the production process chosen. Technical conditions (governed by the application of past scientific discoveries) determine the processes of production available, each of which will call for a different combination of the productive agents. These may, and sometimes do, range all the way from highly capital-intensive processes or techniques to those that employ very little capital with large amounts of labor.[5] What particular process is chosen will depend on the relative prices of the factors employed.

Thus once factor prices are known, a specific production technique will be adopted for each commodity produced. This stipulates the amount of each kind of input (or factor) required to produce a given quantity of output. Total cost of this output will be the sum of all the factor payments: the wage of labor times the amount employed, plus the rent of land times the quantity used, plus the return on capital times the total invested, plus—finally—a charge for capital consumption, or depreciation. Total cost divided by output will give average unit cost, or total factor payments per unit of output. Since this cost must be covered if production is to continue, in equilibrium average unit cost will also be the price that consumers pay.

This does not mean that consumer demand plays no role in determining commodity prices, for if demands were different, the demand for the productive factors would be changed and their prices would be different. The demand for the factors of production is *derived* from the demand for commodities, being transmitted by entrepreneurs engaged in employing the productive factors as a means of satisfying consumers' demands. Entrepreneurs will tend to pay each factor the value of its marginal contribution to output; what this is in turn depends on how large a quantity of any factor is seeking employment. If a given factor, say labor, is scarce relative to the other factors, the last or marginal worker will make a substantial contribution to output.

[5] The proportions of land used will vary, too, especially when agricultural products are involved.

Entrepreneurs, each eager to obtain an adequate working force, will compete for labor's services, and wages will be high. If the labor force increases, through immigration or a high natural rate of population growth, while capital and land remain constant in amount, the employment of the additional workers will encounter diminishing returns; the marginal productivity of the augmented labor supply will decline, and with it labor's rate of pay.

With the determination of factor prices, we have closed the circle and are back at our starting point, the incomes of the individuals who own the factors. The pricing process in any region is a system of mutually determined general equilibrium, a set of causal relations of circular character, like the atom, the solar system, or a government which successfully reconciles the interests of conflicting groups.

The Interaction Between Different Price Systems

In each nation, the elements of the price system are the same. The chain of causation everywhere runs from individual incomes to demand for commodities to the determination (jointly with supply conditions) of commodity prices; then through the derived demand for productive factors to determine, together with available supplies thereof, the prices of these factors and thus individual incomes.

Although these elements of the price system are common to all free enterprise economies, the commodity prices established in any set of distinct national markets could differ, provided one or more of the price determining forces varied in magnitude in these markets.

It is here that the basis of a nation's natural advantage in production—its factor endowment—enters the picture. From the supply side, commodity prices are determined by costs of production. And costs of production are simply payments to the productive agents—that is, factor prices.[6] Factor prices, however, will differ from country to country with differences in factor endowment. In countries or regions with abundant land—such as Argentina, Australia, Canada, and the western United States—land will be cheap. Therefore commodities such as wheat or beef, which require relatively large amounts of land for their production, will be lower in price than in countries such as Great Britain or Belgium, where land is scarce and costly to use. In countries with abundant labor, such as India and Japan, wages are low; commodities such as jute, cotton textiles, ceramics, and bicycles, in whose production labor is a major component, will be relatively cheap.

[6] The contributions of any stage of production to the value of the goods or services it produces—the value added in manufacture, for example—can be attributed solely to the factors it employs in that stage. Its cost sheets will show, of course, payments other than the wages of labor, the interest on capital, and the rent of land employed in its distinctive productive activities—such payments, for example, as for raw materials, fuel, power, and insurance. But these payments represent value added at earlier stages of production, which can be broken down, ultimately, into payments to the factors.

We now have an explanation of international price differences and thus of international specialization and trade. Differences in factor endowments cause factor prices to differ, and these price differences will endure, since the factors are not free to move from one nation to another.[7] Since factor prices are the ultimate costs of production, costs and thus commodity prices will differ.

Note, however, that variation in factor endowment, although a necessary condition, is not a sufficient condition for international specialization and trade. *It is also essential that different combinations of the factors be required in production.* Another way of expressing this condition is to say that the production functions, which express the relations between inputs and outputs in the light of existing technical knowledge, must vary from commodity to commodity.

Thus what enables Australia to produce wheat cheaply is not just the fact that agricultural land is abundant and cheap there, but also that wheat requires for its production a relatively large amount of land as compared with the other factors. If in the production of every commodity, the factors were combined in the same proportions, the abundance and cheapness of any particular factor would count for naught; relative commodity prices would not differ among countries and there would be no basis for trade.[8]

Finally, we must admit that differences in national tastes and demands could furnish an independent cause of trade, or could nullify the effect of

[7] We shall assume, for the time being, that the factors are completely immobile internationally.

[8] To illustrate, let us suppose that to produce *any* commodity, land, labor, and capital must be combined in the proportions 10 : 6 : 2. Assume that in country A land is relatively abundant and hence cheap, while in B capital is the abundant and cheap factor, with labor in approximately the same relative supply in both countries. If we then assume that 10 units of land, 6 of labor, and 2 of capital are used in each country to produce pig iron, wheat, and aluminum, we could construct the following table of costs.

	Factor Require- ments	Factor Prices in: A	B	Cost of Production in: A Pig Iron	Wheat	Aluminum	B Pig Iron	Wheat	Aluminum
Land	10	1	5	10	10	10	50	50	50
Labor	6	2	2	12	12	12	12	12	12
Capital	2	5	1	10	10	10	2	2	2
Total cost of quantity produced:				32	32	32	64	64	64
Number of units produced:				1 ton	2 tons	4 tons	1 ton	2 tons	4 tons
Cost per unit:				32	16	8	64	32	16

The sum of the costs for each commodity is the total cost of producing the output yielded. Without any other stipulation, this must be assumed to be the same in each country. If we assume this output to be a ton of pig iron, 2 tons of wheat, and 4 tons of aluminum, the cost (and price) per ton will be as shown in the bottom row of figures. Clearly, relative prices are the same—each of B's prices is twice that in A. There is therefore no basis for trade in relative cheapness of production.

differences in factor endowment. Thus if two countries possessed the factors of production in identical proportions, but in one country the people were very fond of food while in the other they prized personal services of all kinds, land would be expensive in the first country, labor in the second. The latter might then export agricultural products to the former in exchange for products in which labor was the dominant component. Or, taking two countries with substantially different factor proportions, it is conceivable that the inhabitants of a nation richly endowed with land might have such a strong preference for food and other agricultural products as to make rents as high, in comparison with wages and the return on capital, as they were in a densely populated country with relatively little land. Yet either outcome is most improbable. Even regions that are in general quite similar are likely to have appreciable differences in factor supplies, while human demands for the services of the various factors usually differ far less than the supplies of these factors.

It is important to note that it is *relative* differences in factor supplies that are significant. Thus India, with an area of approximately a million and a quarter square miles, has *absolutely* more land than Argentina, with its 1,079,-000 square miles. But India's population is some 456 million, while that of Argentina is only 21 million; relative to its immense population, land in India is scarce and labor is abundant, while the reverse is true of Argentina. Expressed in per capita figures, available land in India amounts to 1.8 acres per capita, in Argentina to 34.5. No reliable estimate of capital supply in either country exists, but probably their relative supplies of capital are much closer together.

International Commodity Price Differences: Some Illustrations

In our modern explanation of international specialization and trade, two distinct sets of facts converge to give rise to international differences in commodity prices. On the one hand, national differences in factor endowment cause factor prices to differ. On the other hand, for technological reasons there is great variety in the way the factors are combined to produce different articles.

Automobiles, for example, are produced with immense quantities of capital, substantial amounts of labor, and very little land. They are a capital-intensive product. So are steel, machine tools, synthetic fibers, and refined petroleum products. Compared with these, fine watches, photographic and scientific equipment, and high-grade cutlery require the use of relatively large amounts of labor, especially of skilled labor. Even more conspicuously labor-intensive are hand-blown glass, musical instruments, lace, the finest types of rugs, and mink coats. Most agricultural products are, of course, land-intensive, though the relative use of land varies widely from one crop to another. The livestock industry, with its need for extensive grazing areas, very little labor or machinery, provides the most extreme example. Wheat cultivation is not too far behind in its relative use of land. At the other end of the scale is the cultivation of rice in the Orient, typified by the intensive application of labor to small areas of land, and with capital limited to simple implements and a team of bullocks or water buffalo.

If methods of production vary as to factor intensity from one commodity to another, while factor prices differ from country to country, then it is inevitable that international differences in commodity prices should appear.

To illustrate, let us begin with a simple two-country, two-commodity model. Assume that country A, like Argentina, possesses abundant land, a relatively small supply of labor, and little capital, while B, similar to Burma, is endowed with a relatively large labor supply, but has comparatively little land and very little capital. Factor prices such as the following would be consistent with these assumptions.

| | Factor Prices in: | | |
	A	B	
Land	$ 1	$ 20	(unit: 1 acre-year)
Labor	600	100	(unit: 1 man-year)
Capital	80	150	(unit: use of $1,000 for 1 year)

Land, being abundant in A, is cheap, but expensive in B, where it is comparatively scarce. Labor, B's abundant factor, is cheap there, but six times as costly in A, where it is relatively much scarcer. And capital, being less plentiful in B, is almost twice as dear there.

Introduce now two commodities, produced by contrasting methods. Beef and rice will do very well. Beef calls for the use of an extensive land area with only a small number of ranch hands, while rice is produced by a method in which land is economized and labor is applied in relatively large amounts. Suppose production requirements are as follows:

| | Quantity of Factors Required to Produce | |
| | Beef | Rice |
	(1 metric ton)	(1 metric ton)
Land	1,000	2
Labor	1	1
Capital	1	½

By combining these two tables, we can see what it would cost to produce beef and rice in each of our two countries.

Beef, the land-intensive product, costs $1.68 a kilogram or about 76 cents a pound to produce in A, where land, the factor weighing most heavily in costs, is abundant and cheap. In B, because land is scarce and expensive, the cost of beef is prohibitively high. Clearly, as between these two countries, A

	Factor Prices in:		Factor Require-	Beef Costs in:		Factor Require-	Rice Costs in:	
	A	B	ments	A	B	ments	A	B
Land	$ 1	$ 20	1,000	$1,000	$20,000	2	$ 2	$ 40
Labor	600	100	1	600	100	1	600	100
Capital	80	150	1	80	150	½	40	75
Cost of producing 1 metric ton:				$1,680	$20,250		$ 642	$ 215
Cost of producing 1 kilogram:				$ 1.68	$ 20.25		$0.64	$0.215
Cost of producing 1 pound:				$ 0.76	$ 9.20		$0.30	$0.10

would specialize in the production of beef. In rice, on the other hand, *B* achieves a low cost of 21½ cents a kilogram or about 10 cents a pound because labor, the factor contributing most heavily to costs, is cheap there. *A*'s costs, at approximately 30 cents a pound, are nearly three times as high, because even though land is cheaper, labor, the factor used most intensively, commands far higher wages. *B* would specialize in rice production and would even export it to *A* unless transportation charges and other costs of transfer exceeded some 20 cents a pound.

Methods of Production and Production Functions

Up to this point, we have tacitly assumed that, although methods of production differ from commodity to commodity, any single commodity is produced by a unique and invariant process. This process establishes rigid proportions for the combination of the factor inputs.

In fact, such extreme rigidity is unusual. Most commodities can be produced by two or more processes, each calling for a different set of factor proportions. There may be some degree of flexibility in the combination of the factors required by a given process. And at the opposite extreme from the single process, fixed-factor-proportions case would be the continuous production function, where the distinction between different processes of production becomes blurred because it is possible, by a smooth and gradual path, to vary the proportions in which the factors are combined.

These points can be given diagrammatic expression that should be helpful. In the figures that follow, the vertical axis represents units of capital and the horizontal axis represents units of labor. We are limited to the two-factor case, since we have only two axes in the horizontal plane. Units of output corresponding to various inputs of capital and labor are measured in the vertical direction and projected onto our diagrams like the contours representing elevation on a contour map.

Figure 6.1 illustrates a *production function* in which only one process is available; the proportionality of the factors is rigidly *fixed*. According to the left-hand diagram, 100 barrels a day of gasoline can be produced by combining 2 units of capital with ½ unit of labor (the units of each factor being defined in a meaningful and uniform manner). Or an output of 200 barrels

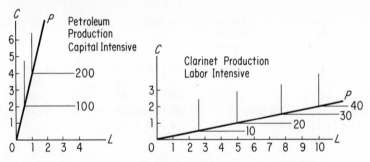

FIGURE 6.1 Fixed Production Functions: A Single Process

can be obtained by combining 4 units of capital with 1 of labor. There would be no use in varying the proportion of capital to labor. The application of more than 4 units of capital, together with 1 labor, would contribute nothing to output; the marginal productivity of capital would be zero. Likewise with labor: when 4 units of capital are employed, the use of more than 1 unit of labor will leave output unchanged.

In this instance, the production function (the equation expressing the relation between inputs of the factors and output of the product) consists of a single process—the combination of capital and labor in the proportions 4 : 1. It is represented by the ray OP, with the level of output measured from O along OP, as indicated by the distances between the rectangular production isoquants or equal product curves.[9]

The right-hand diagram of Figure 6.1 provides an illustration of a labor-intensive production function consisting of only one process. Here the proportions of capital and labor are rigidly fixed at 1 capital to 5 labor. Various levels of output corresponding to different levels of input of this fixed proportion are shown by the production isoquants. Again, the ray OP traces the path of the production function.

In Figure 6.2, we move on to a *production function consisting of two processes,* each rigid in its recipe for combining the factors. Rice is the commodity chosen, for in recent years the development of mechanical methods of planting and harvesting this crop has provided an alternative to the labor-intensive method practised for many years in Japan.[10] The mechanized process is represented by the production ray OP, according to which capital and labor are

[9] Try to think of the ray OP as being projected diagonally upward from the paper. Then the production surface would consist of two flat planes coming together at the ridge formed by OP. The optimum production points would all be on this ridge. Other points on the production surface, since they would involve the use of more capital or more labor than the corresponding ridge point, would be uneconomic.

[10] The Japanese method is the most labor-intensive form of the methods that have been practised in Asia for thousands of years. One could show this by introducing another ray or rays to represent these methods, but all these rays would be very close together because they represent basically similar methods.

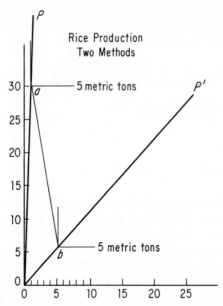

FIGURE 6.2   A Fixed Production Function: Two Processes

combined in the ratio of 30 capital to 1 labor. The ray *OP'* stands for the labor-intensive method, which combines 5 units of capital with 5 units of labor. Since rice can be produced by either process, or by some combination of the two, the entire production function—for a given level of output, say 5 metric tons—can be represented by the production isoquant formed by connecting the capital-intensive and the labor-intensive isoquants for this output by the diagonal line *ab*. The entire production function—for any level of output and any permissible combination of the factors—could be represented by the inclined surface between the production rays *OP* and *OP'*.

Instead of only one or two processes, or ways of combining the factors into an economical "factor mix," there could equally well be three, four, or even more. At the other extreme from the single process requiring fixed factor proportions would be the continuous production function, according to which the factor mix could be steadily altered by imperceptible degrees. This would represent an indefinitely large number of procesess, each differing from the next by (infinitesimally) small changes in the factor mix. Diagramatically, this case can be shown by smooth isoquants, as in Figure 6.3.

A given amount of the product in question, say 100 units, can be produced by combining a large amount of capital with very little labor, by combining much labor with a small quantity of capital, or by a whole (and continuous) range of alternative combinations. Note that in the left-hand diagram, the isoquants have considerable curvature in regions of high capital intensity, indicating a high degree of substitutability between the factors in this range.

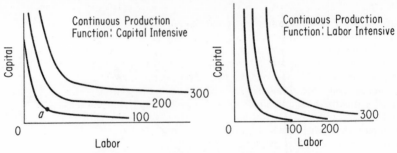

FIGURE 6.3   Continuous Production Functions

But as one moves along any isoquant toward greater labor intensity (as to the right of *a*), it becomes almost horizontal, reflecting a low degree of factor substitutability. Put differently, many alternative combinations of the factors are possible at relatively high levels of capital intensity, whereas before the proportion of labor to capital becomes at all high, such alternatives cease to exist. Curves of this type represent capital-intensive products. As we shall soon see, this means that whatever relative factor prices may be, the commodity will be produced by *relatively* capital-intensive methods (just as with such single-process production functions as in the left-hand part of Figure 6.1).

Opposite conditions are portrayed in the right-hand diagram, where the isoquants are elastic and factor substitutability is high for low capital-labor proportions, but rigid and with little possibility of factor substitution at relatively high capital-labor ratios.

Continuous, smooth isoquants like those of Figure 6.3 are generally used as the basis for theoretical discussions. This situation is not, however, one we are likely to meet very often in real life, where the alternatives practically available are apt to be rather small in number, though perhaps with some limited flexibility in the factor proportions in each factor mix or production process.

Dorfman has some interesting comments on this point. Writing about the smooth production isoquant, he states that it

> . . . very likely is valid for some kinds of production. But for most manufacturing industries, and indeed all production where elaborate machinery is used, it is open to serious objection. It is characteristic of most modern machinery that each kind of machine operates efficiently only over a narrow range of speeds and that the quantities of labor, power, materials and other factors which cooperate with the machine are dictated rather inflexibly by the machine's built-in characteristics. Furthermore, at any time there is available only a small number of different kinds of machinery for accomplishing a given task. . . . Earth may be moved by hand shovels, by steam or diesel shovels, or by bulldozers. Power shovels and bulldozers are built in only a small variety of models, each with inherent characteristics as to fuel con-

sumption per hour, number of operators and assistants required, cubic feet of earth moved per hour, etc. Printing type may be set by using hand-fonts, linotype machines or monotype machines. Again, each machine is available in only a few models and each has its own pace of operation, power and space requirements, and other essentially unalterable characteristics. . . . For many economic tasks the number of processes available is finite, and each process can be regarded as inflexible with regard to the ratios among factor inputs and process outputs. Factors cannot be substituted for each other except by changing the levels at which entire technical processes are used, because each process uses factors in fixed characteristic ratios.[11]

Factor Prices and Production Functions

A production function gives us the range of the technical processes that can be used to produce a commodity. It describes the alternative combinations of factor inputs made available to the producer by previous scientific discoveries and their application to industry by the engineer. Any of these alternatives will be technically feasible, but which will be *economical* will depend on the prices of the inputs—that is, on factor prices.

Let us draw an isoquant corresponding to a continuous production function (as in Figure 6.4) for, say, flashlight batteries, and by introducing factor

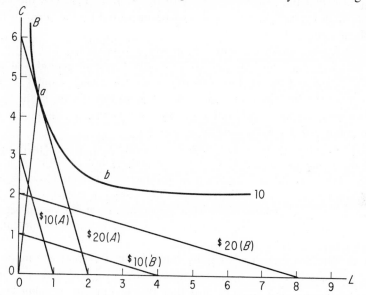

FIGURE 6.4   A Single Production Function with Different Factor Prices

prices, show how the specific factor combination actually used is determined. Suppose that in country *A* capital is plentiful and cheap, and that labor is

[11] Robert Dorfman, "Mathematical, or 'Linear,' Programming: a Nonmathematical Exposition," *American Economic Review*, **XLIII** (December, 1953), p. 803.

scarce and dear. Then a given sum spent on these factors in turn will command a relatively large amount of capital and a relatively small amount of labor. Let us assume that for $10 we can buy 1 unit of labor or 3 units of capital. A diagonal line drawn between the 3 unit point on the capital axis and the 1 unit point on the labor axis will then reflect this fact. A higher parallel line, say that connecting 6 capital and 2 labor, would indicate an expenditure of $20. The *slope* of these and other parallel lines tells us that 3 units of capital will exchange for 1 unit of labor, at a price of $3.33⅓ per unit of capital and $10 per unit of labor. Thus the slope of such lines indicates factor prices or exchange ratios; their distance from the origin indicates the amount of expenditure.

Given that the relative prices of capital and labor in country A are 1 : 3 (or 3.33⅓ : 10), then with this particular set of factor prices, the minimum cost of producing the output for which the isoquant in Figure 6.4 stands—10 units—will be given by the price-expenditure line that is tangent to the isoquant. For this expenditure (represented by the $20[A] line) is the least that will yield 10 batteries at these factor prices, while 10 units is the largest output obtainable for this expenditure. Unit cost of batteries will then be $2.

Note also that the point of tangency of the $20($A$) line with the isoquant is one of high capital intensity. This can be measured by the slope of the ray Oa, which is close to $6C : 1L$.

Consider, now, another country, B, in which a different set of factor prices rules. Suppose that with $10 you can buy only 1 unit of capital, but 4 units of labor (indicated by the line $10[B]). Labor is cheap, capital dear. The $20 expenditure line does not even come close to the 10-unit isoquant. Even a $30 expenditure line would fall a bit short of touching it. Therefore the unit cost in country B would be something over $3.

The prospective point of tangency for a country B price-expenditure line would occur at approximately b, where something not far from 2½ capital and 2½ labor would be combined in production. This is close to a 1 : 1 capital-labor ratio. It is, of course, much less capital-intensive than the point a. Thus the diagram demonstrates what we learned from our verbal argument: that a capital-intensive commodity can be produced more economically in a country where capital is relatively cheap.

Let us broaden our discussion by introducing a second commodity, one with a production function distinctly different from that for batteries. Suppose this to be onions, and suppose also that this commodity is labor-biased in production, or labor-intensive. This means that while capital can be substituted for labor over a considerable range, there are rather sharp limits to this process of substitution; above some rather low level of capital-intensity, capital cannot replace labor. More concretely, a given output of onions could be produced by large quantities of labor combined with nothing more than spades, or by somewhat less labor using hoes together with spades, or by still less labor combined with hand cultivators, and so on through an increasingly more complex variety of garden tools up to a combination embodying a gasoline-powered cultivator. At this stage, the proportion of labor would be much reduced, though the capital-to-labor ratio might still be low compared with that realized in other lines of production whose techniques permitted intensive use of capital. We shall assume that techniques permitting the introduction of a still larger proportion of capital in onion production are as yet undiscovered.

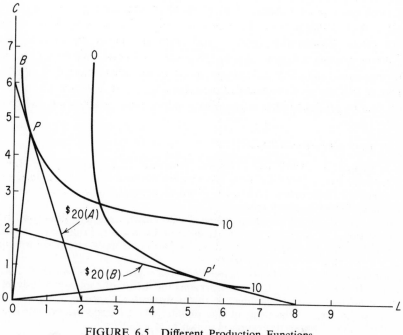

FIGURE 6.5   Different Production Functions

In Figure 6.5, we have reproduced the 10-unit isoquant for battery production, together with the price-expenditure lines for countries *A* and *B* corresponding to an outlay of $20. As before, *A* will produce batteries at a cost of $2 a unit. The isoquant *O* represents onion production at the level of output of 10 units.

Since in country *B* labor is cheap and capital is dear, its price-expenditure lines are relatively flat; the $20 line is tangent to the labor-intensive onion isoquant at *P'*. Thus *B* will be able to produce onions at a cost of $2 a unit (say a bushel). For *A*, on the other hand, the cost would be more than $3 a unit, since even an outlay of $30 on capital and labor, at *A*'s factor prices and using a more capital-intensive technique than that adopted by *B*, would not yield 10 units of onion output.

Thus so far as these two commodities are concerned, *A*, with abundant capital and scarce labor, would produce batteries at relatively low cost by means of a capital-intensive method, while *B*, with abundant and cheap labor, would devote its resources to producing onions by a labor-intensive technique.

Summarizing this section, we see that production functions, or the technical relationship between factor inputs and commodity outputs, determine the physical efficiency of different factor combinations. This relationship can be shown diagramatically in the form of production isoquants, or equal-product curves. Since any point on such an isoquant stands for the same output, each such point reflects equal physical or engineering efficiency. What point is most efficient from the economic point of view depends on relative factor prices. Commodities whose production techniques are biased toward the use of capital can generally be produced at lowest unit cost (and thus with maximum economic efficiency) in countries where capital is relatively abundant and cheap. Commodities biased toward labor intensity, on the other hand, can be produced most economically where labor is abundant and cheap.

SELECTED REFERENCES

Caves, Richard E., *Trade and Economic Structure*. Cambridge, Mass.: Harvard University Press, 1960. Contains an extended discussion of modern versions of the theory of international trade and of the theoretical problems that have arisen in the course of its development.

Haberler, G., *A Survey of International Trade Theory*, rev. ed. Princeton, N.J.: International Finance Section, Department of Economics, Princeton University, 1961. Chapter III reviews and evaluates Ohlin's and more recent contributions to the theory of international trade.

Kindleberger, Charles P., *International Economics*, 3rd ed. Homewood, Ill.: Richard D. Irwin, Inc., 1963. Chapter 5 presents the theory of comparative advantage in its different forms, including the factor proportions version. Chapter 6 contains an analysis of the demand side of international trade theory, introducing "offer" curves, whose derivation is shown in Appendix C.

Ohlin, Bertil, *Interregional and International Trade*. Cambridge, Mass. Harvard University Press, 1933. Part I contains the gist of the author's formulation of the general equilibrium theory of international trade. Appendix I presents a statement in mathematical form.

Robinson, Romney, "Factor Proportions and Comparative Advantage," *Quarterly Journal of Economics*, **LXX** (May–August, 1956). A trenchant criticism of the factor-proportions analysis.

Snider, Delbert A., *Introduction to International Economics*, rev. ed. Homewood, Ill.: Richard D. Irwin, Inc., 1963. Chapters 3 and 4 provide an excellent brief statement of the modern theory of international trade, including a brief introduction to the use of indifference curves.

7

MODIFICATIONS:
NONHOMOGENEOUS FACTORS;
TRANSPORT COSTS

Our presentation of the factor proportions theory of international trade has, up to this point, been conducted in terms of a much simplified model. Thus we have limited ourselves to the consideration of two countries, two factors, and two commodities. We have also assumed that the factors taken into account were homogeneous—that is, that all units of a given factor were identical in their productivity, so that units could be interchanged with no effect on output, and that the units in one country were of the same productivity or economic quality as those in another country. Moreover, these factors were assumed to be mobile within a single country, but internationally immobile. Production functions have been taken to be everywhere the same; that is, all the various processes encompassed by any given production function have been assumed to be open to adoption by producers in any country. And we have considered only production functions that, in mathematical language, are "homogeneous of the first degree," which implies constant returns to scale. Finally, we have operated under the assumption of perfect competition, and we have ignored the existence of transport costs.

This use of a highly simplified model was necessary to bring out clearly the essential features of the factor proportions theory: the fundamental role, first, of differing factor endowments and the relative differences in factor prices thus brought about, and second, of technically different ways of combining the factors (different production functions). International differences in commodity prices—the immediate determinant of what a country will export and what it will import—were seen ultimately to rest upon these two pillars: international differences in factor endowments and the existence of different production functions.

It is now time to relax the restrictions of our simplified model, and by so doing, to make our analysis of the forces governing international trade more realistic, but also more complex. Let us start by considering the assumption that all units of a given factor are everywhere identical.

Definition of Factors of Production

The need for the assumption of homogeneity of the factors should be obvious, for unless all units of a productive factor are everywhere identical in efficiency, we cannot explain commodity prices solely in terms of factor inputs and factor prices. Something else will have been introduced: the quality of the productive factor. If a given factor combination does not always yield the same output, then the latter (and therewith the cost and price of the commodity being produced) is determined not solely by the price and quantity of factor inputs alone, but also by their quality.

Now it is clear that the broad categories of factors with which we have been working—land, labor, and capital—are not in fact homogeneous. Land varies enormously as to fertility, as well as to the kinds of crops it can grow. Unskilled labor is incapable of performing the tasks undertaken with ease by skilled labor, while even a highly skilled laborer could not replace a trained medical technician.

We must take this diversity of quality into account. The most consistent way to do so would be to recognize the existence of a large number of qualitatively different factors, each carefully defined so that all the individual units included were identical in productivity. The needs of logical consistency, however, collide with the need for a generalized explanation. Were we meticulously to classify as a separate factor each area of land and each group of workers that differed in the slightest as to the output per unit or the charcter of the crop produced or function performed, we would end up with thousands of distinct factors of production. Since each production function includes as inputs only those factors actually used, for commodities which could be produced by a number of combinations of slightly different factors our explanation of international specialization would degenerate into specifying, for each instance of specialization, a particular, detailed production function. For commodities requiring a unique combination of factors, we would be reduced to specifying the presence of the needed factors.[1] But a theory is useful only insofar as it enables us to establish generalizations with respect to some underlying similarity of conditions. Clearly, the pursuit to the end of logical consistency in definition would mean the nemesis of theory, or useful generalization. Some workable compromise must be sought.

It may be possible to operate at different levels of generalization, to which different degrees of specification of the factors may be appropriate. Thus if we are interested in establishing a nation's comparative advantage only in terms of broad categories of commodities, as with the Ruhr area's specialization in coal, steel, and heavy industrial products, or if differences in factor endowments and hence in factor prices are large and thus of outstanding importance, as with Australia's specialization in wheat, we may be able to

---

[1] With respect to some products, such as minerals, we are forced to do this anyway. Thus nickel ore can be produced only where nickel deposits exist.

operate quite satisfactorily with the tripartite division of factors into land, labor, and capital. But if our concern is with specific commodities, or with countries whose factor endowments are similar, we must define factors more narrowly in order to eliminate the influence of qualitative differences.

In most situations, however, we should be able to attain reasonable accuracy with a relatively limited subdivision of the major factors into subgroups. Let us consider land.

Land, or Natural Resources

When we speak of the factor "land," what we have in mind is the contribution to production made by natural resources of any kind. Their varieties are obviously numerous. Most specialized of all are mineral deposits, and for the production of any mineral, availability of the relevant natural resource factor—deposits of the mineral in question—is uniquely necessary. The cooperation of labor and capital is also required, but a country without deposits of iron ore, nickel, or copper simply cannot produce these minerals.

Of all natural resources, minerals are the most unevenly distributed. Most of the world's nickel comes from Ontario, smaller amounts from New Caledonia and northern Finland. Copper is derived principally from Ontario, Chile, the Belgian Congo, and the United States. Iron ore is more widely distributed. Outstanding in this respect are the Soviet Union and the United States, though our best iron reserves are approaching exhaustion and we are having to rely increasingly upon imports from South America and Canada.

Forest resources, another highly specialized category, are also very unevenly distributed. Softwoods, such as the fir and spruce so important for building purposes, today come principally from British Columbia and the north-western United States, though vast, untapped stands exist in southern Alaska and Siberia. Most of the plywood to meet the ever-growing demand for paper is produced in Canada, the northern Scandinavian countries, and our southern states. Hardwoods, as yet of minor industrial importance, are available in vast quantities in Central America, the Amazon Valley, central Africa, and Malaya.

Fisheries are another widely dispersed natural resource, of which the most famous are the Dogger Bank of the North Sea, the Newfoundland Banks, and the salmon fisheries of the northwest Pacific region. The seas around Japan have for centuries contributed an important share of its people's diet and in more recent years of its exports.

Another specialized natural resource not to be overlooked is water power. Potentially best endowed in this regard are the U.S.S.R., India and Pakistan, the United States, western Europe, Canada, and China, in that order. Potential is one thing, however, accessibility another. Many of the finest power sites are so remote from markets as to render them unusable. This is particularly true of South America.

Agricultural land is the most abundant and ubiquitous of all resources, yet its amount in relation to the world's total land area is surprisingly small. Out of 52 million square miles in all, only 3.7 million, or about 7 per cent, are now cultivated. A somewhat larger area, 4.2 million square miles, now too dry or too swampy to be used, could be rendered arable by heavy expenditures on irrigation or drainage, while another 2.1 million square miles of pasture land could be cultivated. In all, not more than 20 per cent of the earth's land surface could be brought under crops; the rest is mountain, desert, hopelessly swampy, frigid, or suited only for grazing or forestry.

It is clear that from the point of view of accounting for international specialization, "agricultural land" is too broad a category to be very serviceable. Land areas differ tremendously with respect to fertility, character of terrain, and the three components of climate: insolation (exposure to the sun), humidity, and rainfall. Various combinations of these elements are suited to different kinds of crops. Depending upon the degree of refinement desired, a number of subfactors could be distinguished. A simple classification would certainly list the following:

1. The temperate, well-watered, and comparatively fertile areas that are the world's great grain-producing regions.
2. "Mediterranean" type lands—fertile, warm, but with relatively little rain and much sun (accounting for olives, citrus fruits, grapes, avocados).
3. The tropical lowlands (sugar, bananas, pineapple, cacao, coconuts).
4. The medium-altitude lands of the tropics, whose equable, warm climate especially suits them for growing tea and coffee.

These four categories of arable land, together with pasture (dairying) and grazing land (stock-raising), should be sufficient for broad generalizations. But in comparing costs of producing a given crop in different countries, qualitative differences within any one of these categories could be important. We would then either have to define subfactors within any such category more closely, or take qualitative differences directly into account. It seems preferable to avoid the loss of generality involved in the first alternative and to qualify the factor proportions analysis by allowing for differences in the quality of subfactors.

Labor

We can distinguish at least four labor subfactors:

1. Technical and managerial labor requires, in general, the highest degree of intelligence and the most prolonged training or experience. In this class are technicians of all kinds: engineers, architects, scientists, agronomists, plant superintendents and business managers, accountants, and professional people generally.
2. Skilled labor demands, in varying combinations, intelligence, manual dexterity, artistic talent, and other special qualities, usually together

with an apprenticeship of considerable duration. In this group are printers, plumbers, electricians, machinists, loom-fixers, draftsmen, commercial artists, and the like.

3. Semiskilled labor, though not divided from skilled labor by a sharp line, comprises those occupations in which skills and the human qualities that support them are less important. In this category fall such occupations as bus and truck drivers, tractor operators, loom operators, lumber workers, and most types of machine operatives.

4. Unskilled labor includes all those whose work requires little or no specialized skill. Here we find delivery men, janitors, sweepers, hand truckers, assembly line workers, and common labor generally.

Because the human attributes needed to perform the more exacting tasks are possessed by relatively few, and because lengthy training requires a financial outlay that relatively few can afford, we find the lower ranks of these noncompeting groups relatively crowded. Hence there is generally a fairly close correlation between the degree of skill and training and the level of pay, though exceptions are not hard to find. These groups are found in practically all countries; they are called noncompeting because although there is some movement from one group to another, it is slow and gradual and is mainly restricted to adjacent groups.

Capital

When labor and natural resources are combined with capital in a productive enterprise such as a factory, as many as four different kinds of labor may be required in proportions that vary with the kind of article being produced. The capital with which the labor works is likely to be equally or even more diverse. It includes buildings, machines, tools, and probably trucks, as well as typewriters and other types of office equipment. The capital, in other words, is in the form of extremely varied, concrete producers' goods. Each particular capital good—even the factory building—is suited to the performance of a specialized productive task; indeed, there is a good chance that some of the equipment was specially designed for this particular factory's operations. All units of a given type of capital good (except those specially designed), whether used in this or any other factory in the industry, are likely to be identical or at least closely similar.

Now if capital goods were "on all fours" with labor and natural resources, the tremendous specialization that characterizes these aids to production would require us to admit of a bewildering variety of capital subfactors. This would be true even if we were able to lump together all equipment performing a single type of operation, such as the dozens of kinds of lathes. As with labor, we would have noncompeting groups of capital goods, though instead of four, the number of such groups would be many times greater. Each of these types of capital goods would command a price for its services determined by its marginal productivity, as fixed by a supply which could be increased only slightly via competition from other analogous though distinct groups.

Capital goods differ from labor (and natural resources), however, in that they are wholly produced means of production. They are created by the investment of liquid or money capital in bringing about the cooperation of labor, natural resources, and previously existing capital goods to produce a machine or piece of equipment. This creation of capital goods can take place quite rapidly—even a large office building or a petroleum refinery can be constructed in a matter of two or three years at most. The return on one concrete investment, expressed as a percentage of its cost, consequently cannot long exceed (given competitive conditions) and return on any other type of investment.[2] There is a strong tendency toward equality of return to all concrete forms of investment, or toward a uniform supply price for capital.

What is this supply price a payment for? Let us consider first the supply price of natural resources or of labor. Each of these factors is an "original" means of production; it exists on its own, so to speak, and does not have to be produced.[3] If it is to be drawn into productive activity, it must be paid for its services. With capital goods, however, a payment is necessary, not to mobilize into productive activity something that already exists, but to get that something—a capital good—produced. To ensure the production of a capital good, as distinct from any other good, investment is essential. In the long run, investment can only occur if someone forgoes consumption, saves, and makes his savings available for investment.

Initially, savings are provided in the form of freely investible funds, or money capital, which later becomes embodied (through the employment of existing resources) in various kinds of concrete capital goods. Those who perform this function of supplying investible funds are unwilling to do so "for free," but exact a premium; when this premium is expressed as a percentage of the funds advanced, it becomes the familiar rate of interest. Payment of this premium is *possible* because indirect or roundabout methods of

---

[2] For the time it takes to increase the supply of a particular capital good, its return may exceed the normal, being, like the rent of land, determined by demand over against a (relatively) fixed supply. On the other hand, when the demand for an existing type of capital good contracts (as for office space or homes in a decaying section of a city), its return may fall below the normal for a relatively long period—as long as the life of this particular property. For these reasons, the short-period income from fixed capital assets is often characterized as a quasirent.

[3] This is not to deny that investment in natural resources or in labor may be necessary, in the one to make it operative, in the other to increase its productivity. An ore deposit cannot be exploited until a mine shaft is sunk, while skilled labor acquires its skill only as a result of a process of investment in education and training. The supply of these "original" means of production, however, differs essentially from that of capital goods. The supply of any natural resource is not freely producible, but is limited by nature's endowment, while the supply of any grade of labor is limited by the number of people in a population both able and willing to undergo the training essential to the acquisition of a given grade or skill or technical competence.

production, involving the use of capital goods to aid labor, are more productive than direct, noncapital-using methods. It is *necessary* to overcome the unwillingness of savers to divert resources from consumption to the production of capital goods.[4]

The rate of interest—the payment necessary to permit the use of roundabout methods—is determined in the .market for capital funds. These funds are in the first instance, as equivalent units of purchasing power, all alike. In the absence of complicating factors, they would receive a uniform return. But loans to different borrowers present different degrees of risk, depending on the creditworthiness of the borrower and whether the funds are invested in a safe or speculative venture. We must therefore distinguish between the pure rate of interest on riskless loans (that is, to responsible governments and perhaps large corporations with a top credit rating), and rates of interest that include varying premiums for risk. It is the former that we shall have in mind when we make international comparisons.

Since the supply of long-term capital is not completely homogeneous, but is differentiated according to the amount of risk attaching to different kinds of loans, logically we should classify capital into as many subfactors as there are degrees of risk. These are very numerous, however, ranging in an ascending scale from investments in the bonds of a financially sound government to outright speculations. We shall not be doing too great violence to the facts if we assume that, in the absence of contrary evidence, the relative supply of funds for investments of varying risks is the same in different countries. We can then treat capital *as if* it were homogeneous, and take the "pure" rate of interest in different countries as our measure of the relative abundance of capital. If, in any given country, there are no riskless investments, then it will be necessary to compare the return on investments with a similar degree of risk.

Where there is objective evidence indicating exceptional abundance or scarcity of funds for risky investments, this fact will have to be taken into account separately. Treatment of this problem requires careful judgment, however, for a tendency to shy away from risky investments in favor of the safer kinds (which appears to exist in some underdeveloped countries) may merely reflect an extremely high degree of risk. Although lenders might

---

[4] There would probably be *some* savings even at a zero rate of interest. The point is that these would be insufficient to satisfy the demand for capital (at a zero rate of interest) to be embodied in productive capital goods. *Additional* savings must be coaxed forth by offering a positive return.

Over short periods, the interest rate is not closely related to thrift, but is determined by the supply of liquid capital available. And the supply made available for active use, and the price or interest rate it can command, depends upon the attitude ("liquidity preference") of holders of idle balances. This attitude, however, is strongly influenced by what is felt to be a "normal" level of the interest rate. And this "normal" level is subject to determination by the long-run forces of productivity on the one hand, and the resistances to savings on the other.

be willing to advance funds for projects comparable in riskiness to ventures in other countries, unstable political conditions or the absence of basic investment in community facilities such as transport and power may make investment in manufacturing, for example, particularly hazardous.

Over the long run, the rate of interest as such, discounting risk, depends principally on the level of income, which is the source of savings, and on the savings habits of the public, together with the demand for investible funds as determined by the productivity of the roundabout method.[5] Since savings are made in the form of money, the supply of money capital can be augmented by the expansion of credit—that is, by banking policy. This, however, is essentially a short-run factor—in the long run, productivity and thrift assert themselves.

If we can treat capital as homogeneous, we need not concern ourselves about classifying it into subfactors. Unlike labor or natural resources, it can be regarded as a single, undifferentiated factor. Like these other factors, its relative supply or abundance in different countries varies. It is plentiful and cheap in countries with a large per capita income and a relatively high propensity to save, scarce and dear where incomes are low and/or the propensity to save is low.

It might be urged that we should regard short-term capital as a factor distinct from long-term capital. It does, indeed, generally receive a substantially lower return. Yet because the markets for short-term and long-term capital are interconnected, with a constant flow of funds between the two, the differential in returns tends to be fairly stable. This means that in countries where one kind is abundant, the other is almost certain to be, too. Thus for international comparisons, the distinction between short- and long-term capital is unimportant.

One further point: the immense variety of concrete capital goods is a technological fact. And since technology changes rather rapidly, so does the composition of the stock of capital goods, which are producible in relatively short order. The diversity of character of concrete capital goods is unrelated to the problem of the supply of capital, or what it is that requires a payment for its use. This diversity is a matter to be considered in connection with technology.

QUALITATIVE DIFFERENCES IN THE FACTORS

You will recall that the classical theory of international trade formulated its explanation in terms of the comparative effectiveness or efficiency of a

---

[5] There is an element of circularity here, since the level of current income is in part what it is because of the existing stock of capital goods, which are the result of past saving. The productivity of additional capital also depends on the size and existing stock of capital. At any point in time, however, this stock is a given datum.

single factor, labor. One of our objections to this theory was that the superior efficiency of labor in one country as compared to another might be largely due to the fact that it was combined with superior resources, greater amounts of capital, or better management. By taking these productive agents into account only indirectly—giving them, so to speak, only an off-stage part— the theory gave to a single factor an importance it does not possess in reality. It is, I believe, a strong point of the relative factor-supply approach that it avoids this fault by according each of the cooperating factors general equality of status. Then, by recognizing explicitly that factor combinations vary widely for different commodities, and that different countries are variously endowed with the different factors of production, it points the correct conclusion: that in some circumstances one factor, in others another, will be of preponderant importance in providing a cost advantage for a particular commodity in a particular country.

The shift in emphasis is from the *quality* of a single factor, labor, to the *quantity* of all the factors. This is a step in the right direction, since it expresses correctly, in terms of quantities of the cooperating factors, what were earlier taken to be qualitative attributes of labor.

Yet there is little reason to doubt the existence of significant qualitative differences in some, at least, of the factors or subfactors we have distinguished. Thus Chile's fertile central valley produces far more, acre for acre, than the poor and stony soil of Greece, although both would be classified as "Mediterranean" types of land. And as between two grain-producing regions, rich Kansas wheat land is far superior to the comparatively infertile land of central Montana.

Where, as with natural resources, differences in productivity are clear-cut and attributable to differences in the inherent quality of the resources compared, probably the best way of dealing with the problem is the direct one. Estimate the difference in efficiency when the resources are worked with equal amounts of the complementary factors, and multiply the more efficient resource by its coefficient of efficiency. Thus if Chile's central valley is three times as productive as land in Greece used to produce the same crops, under similar conditions with respect to the use of labor and capital, multiply the Chilean land supply by a coefficient of three. This means that, in terms of units of equal efficiency, Chile's supply of this kind of land is three times as large as the actual acreage.

Qualitative differences in labor raise more complex issues. Whereas differences in the productivity of a given category of natural resources may be attributed to the inherent quality of that particular resource, this is not true of labor. The inherent or inborn distinctions between individuals of various countries or races relate to such superficial characteristics as skin color, hair texture, bone structure, and other features that have little or nothing to do with productivity. Traits that are economically important, such as effective intelligence, industriousness, manual dexterity, or physical vigor, appear to be distributed about equally among large social groups. Where either the distribution of such traits or the degree of their development differs, these variations rest upon one of two bases.

Investment in Human Capital

Recent studies have shown that only a part (some two-thirds) of the rise in the gross national product of the United States over the past thirty years can be explained by the increase in the size of the labor force or by augmentation of the supply of physical capital with which it works.[6] Of the remainder, it is estimated that from two-fifths to three-fifths must be attributed to investment that has raised the literacy, the knowledge, the adaptability, and the skills of its labor force. This investment in human capital takes the form mainly of general and technical education, on-the-job training, apprenticeships, and individual efforts at self-improvement, but it also includes expenditures to facilitate movement of workers to better alternative employment and some undetermined portion of outlays on food and health that serve to increase physical vigor and well-being.

Such investment in human capital varies enormously from country to country. Can there be any doubt that where, as in the United States, a relatively large proportion of a high per capita income is devoted to this type of investment, the average productive efficiency of its population will be higher than where such investment is relatively smaller? Although the higher productivity is embodied in the labor force, which may therefore be termed qualitatively superior, the cause of this superiority is a relatively large investment in human capital. Therefore, rather than to say that United States labor is qualitatively superior, say, to European labor, it would be more accurate to say that United States labor is complemented by a larger supply of capital, in the particular form of "human capital." What we have here is not really a qualitative difference at all, but a relative difference in the employment of capital. Should a country enjoy a comparative advantage in consequence of its possession of a better educated or better trained labor force, this advantage should be attributed to its relative abundance of capital.

It may happen that a particular nation, whether or not its investment in human capital is relatively large, directs an unusually large proportion of that investment into particular channels. This occurred in Germany before World War I, when that country trained an extraordinarily large number of scientists—in particular, of chemists and chemical engineers. They may have been and probably were *better* trained than chemists elsewhere, but more importantly, the supply of this kind of labor was more abundant and relatively cheaper in Germany. This fact gave Germany a substantial comparative advantage in the chemical industry. Thus the main effect of extraordinarily

[6] Moses Abramovitz, "Economic Growth in the United States," *American Economic Review*, LII (September, 1962), Table 2, p. 766.

large investment in training a particular kind of labor is not to heighten its productivity relative to labor elsewhere, but to increase the country's endowment with this specific subfactor.

SOCIAL CONDITIONS OF PRODUCTION

One of the striking differences between nations, and one that is generally far less marked between different regions of the same country, lies in the realm of social habits, attitudes, and institutions. These features, which the anthropologist summarizes under the heading of culture, cover an immense range. They would include caste distinctions, racial or class prejudice, attitudes toward work in general and toward specific occupations in particular, religious convictions, arrangements with respect to land-holding, and the character of family relationships.

These environmental features, or social conditions of production, provide a second basis for qualitative differences in the labor force in various countries. They also have definite effects upon the relative supply of different kinds of labor.

Class Distinctions

Thus India's caste system divides the Hindu population into over a thousand occupational groups whose techniques are prescribed by tradition.[7] Mobility between groups is therefore negligible; the relative supply of any particular class of worker changes only very slowly. The traditional disdain among upper class Brahmans for material production or pursuit of gain has handicapped and continues to handicap the development of industrial leaders and of the technical and managerial staff so essential to industrial expansion. Similarly, where racial prejudice is strong, members of certain races may be denied access to preferred occupations. Thus in South Africa, skilled labor, of which there is a shortage, is the preserve of the white race; employment of Negroes is limited mainly to unskilled jobs in industry, to household service, and to agriculture. Though the lines are much less sharply drawn in the United States, racial discrimination is sufficient to push a disproportionate number of Negroes into semiskilled and unskilled occupations. Wages of groups thus swollen are depressed, while those of the higher categories are raised above the level that would be attained with fuller mobility.

Land Tenure Systems

Land tenure systems, or the laws and customs affecting land-holding, can strongly influence the character of a nation's agriculture. Where by primo-

[7] The caste system in India is undergoing rapid change, partly from deliberate pressure by the Government, partly from the needs of modern industry. Yet it is still strong enough to exert great influence upon industrial and agricultural organization and practices.

geniture (sole inheritance by the eldest son) or other means, the accumulation and maintenance of huge estates is encouraged, as in many countries of the Near East and Latin America, production of crops suited to large-scale agriculture with an established market is encouraged. The latifundia of Chile run to cattle and wheat; of Brazil, to coffee and cotton; of Iran, to sheep and wheat. Were the landholdings smaller, many different crops would doubtless be grown, especially fruits and vegetables for domestic consumption. Efficiency as well as the type of crops grown is also involved: large landholdings provide the owner a satisfactory income even when inefficiently cultivated; the land tends to be wastefully used, and there is little incentive to introduce improved methods or more plentiful crops. At the opposite end of the scale, extreme fragmentation of holdings, as in parts of India, Ceylon, and Mexico, can result in uneconomically small farms, dedicated to the inefficient production of subsistence crops.

Political Features

Unstable and corrupt governments, especially if their instability is accompanied by public disorder and if government policies are changeable and unpredictable, can exert a powerful influence on the direction and character of investment. Investments promising a quick return will be preferred to those requiring many years to yield their benefits, small-scale operations will be preferred to large, and capital will avoid normally risky investments. The results of these political considerations may be seen in the enduring preference among the peoples of the East for the embodiment of their savings in precious metals and jewels, and in the tendency in Latin American countries for a large proportion of investment to go into real estate and inventories of goods, or to move abroad into the securities of more stable countries. Such practices starve industry and other productive activities of the capital needed for their expansion and create an artificial scarcity of investible funds.

Among special laws that discriminate against particular kinds of business, especially against foreign enterprise, we should mention tax laws and those that require majority stock control by citizens of the country in which the business is located, or that prescribe the employment of a high proportion of its citizens.

"Climate of Productivity"

Similar in its all-pervasive character to a country's political structure is what has been called "the climate of productivity." This phrase sums up the attitudes of a people toward production—attitudes that are the result of the interaction of a wide range of complex and subtle forces. This "climate" appears to be most favorable in northern and western Europe, the United States, and the British Dominions settled and developed by British immigrants. These were the areas most deeply affected by the Renaissance and the Reformation, which led to the release of the spirit of inquiry, stress on individual freedom and the dignity of the individual, and emphasis on the virtues of thrift and work. The effects of this "climate" are apparent in the relative strength in these areas of competition as an economic force, of the willingness to innovate and to invest in productive enterprise, and of the social esteem accorded to economic success.[8] The deliberate efforts of the Japanese government in the late nineteenth century to foster the attitudes comprising the "climate of productivity" have enabled that nation to enjoy many of its beneficial results.

Poverty

Widespread poverty, though not an aspect of a nation's culture, but rather a result of that culture as it affects the utilization of resources, has a clear and obvious connection both with the supply of factors and with their efficiency. Capital originates in the savings of a community; if incomes are generally low, there is little surplus over living requirements; savings will be small and capital scarce and dear. Moreover, since entry into the ranks of technical and managerial labor generally necessitates a long period of training and education which few in a poor community can afford, such labor is also likely to be scarce and to command relatively high wages. Owing to the pressure to put children to work at the earliest opportunity, even the acquisition of skills may be beyond the reach of most. Unskilled occupations tend to be overcrowded and wages there especially low.

But this is not all. Poverty means crowded and unsanitary living conditions and an inadequate diet. From these follow undernourishment and a high incidence of contagious disease. Much time is lost from work, the worker lacks energy, and his productivity is low. Ignorance and illiteracy also usually accompany poverty; they too reduce the efficiency of labor.

If poverty places obstacles in the way of individual advancement, widespread educational opportunities help to overcome them. Countries that place a high value on education can, by making cheap and easy the acquisition of knowledge, both general and technical, minimize the barriers to advancement. The ready availability of educational opportunities in the United States certainly goes far toward explaining the relatively large numbers of skilled workers, managerial staff, and technicians in this country. The same is true of Germany.

TRANSPORT COSTS

Hitherto we have abstracted from transport costs, but they exist and must be reckoned with. Their introduction into our analysis requires us to make important qualifications, first with respect to prices in international trade, and second with respect to the location of industry.

[8] For an interesting discussion of the "climate of productivity," with special reference to the United States, see the chapter with this title in Graham Hutton, *We Too Can Prosper*. Published 1953 by George Allen & Unwin, Ltd., London.

General Effects on Prices and Trade

Transportation costs affect the prices of internationally traded goods in a broad general way, merely because of their existence. They prevent the complete equalization of prices that international trade would otherwise bring about. For commodities produced under conditions of constant costs, this would mean that all commodities would be either exported or imported. There would be no such thing as purely domestic production, except of services that have to be performed where they are consumed. The only justification for domestic production of an article not exported would exist in increasing cost industries, where at some point the rising costs of the principal supplier (exporter) would permit limited production in the importing country. This situation is portrayed in Figure 7.1.

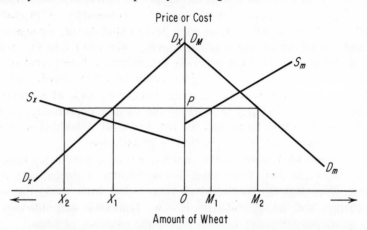

FIGURE 7.1   Specialization and Trade: No Transport Costs

In this diagram, price is shown on the vertical axis beginning at O, common to both countries. The demand and supply curves for the importing country (M) are shown in the right-hand side of the diagram, with quantities read from left to right starting with O. For the exporting country, X (left-hand side), quantities are read from O to the left. In isolation, each country would produce in the amount and at the price corresponding to the intersection of its individual demand and supply curves. With the opening of trade, and in the absence of transportation costs, X, whose supply curve starts at a lower point on the cost-price axis than that of M and remains lower for corresponding outputs, will export wheat to the importing country. Equilibrium will be established at the price OP (common to both markets), with exports (X_1X_2) equal to imports (M_1M_2). The price of wheat is now higher in X than it would have been in the absence of trade, since to satisfy the additional demand from the importing country, output has to be expanded at increasing cost. In M, of course, the price is lower.

Now let us introduce transport cost by adding to the cost of producing wheat a uniform charge per bushel for freight, insurance, and loading. To show this diagramatically, Figure 7.1 may be adjusted by raising the exporting country's entire half of the diagram by the amount of the transport cost. This is done in Figure 7.2, where the left side of the diagram is elevated

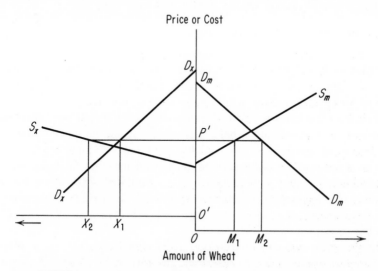

FIGURE 7.2 Specialization and Trade with Transport Costs

by the distance OO', the cost to the importing country of the transport services required. The price of wheat in M (OP') is now higher than the price in X ($O'P'$) by the amount of the transport costs (OO').

Note, however, that this does not mean that the price in M is raised by the amount of the transport costs. For as the price of wheat rises in M, demand contracts; total purchases in M (OM_2) are smaller than before. This reduction in purchases affects production in X. The distance $O'X_2$ is less than OX_2 in Figure 7.1; production has receded along the supply curve S_x to a lower point, where marginal cost ($O'P'$) is less than before (OP in Figure 7.1). The transport cost is added to an export price that is lower than before, so the price in M rises by less than the amount of transport costs.

With a reduced price in X, domestic consumption ($O'X_1$) is increased, while with the higher price in M, domestic output expands (OM_1 in Figure 7.2 is greater than OM_1 in Figure 7.1). Since M's domestic output is now greater, while total purchases are smaller, imports are also smaller. The new distance M_1M_2 (imports of M, equal to exports of X, X_1X_2) is less than the original distance M_1M_2.

Thus we see that the introduction of transport costs partially nullifies the price-equalizing effects of international trade; prices in the importing country are higher than in the exporting country by the amount of those costs. The volume of trade is, of course, also smaller. Only those goods that can bear the transport costs and still be cheaper than some part of domestic production in the importing country will be traded; all others will be produced locally. International specialization is therefore substantially lessened; with the "natural protection" afforded by transport costs, a wide range of wholly or partly home-produced articles comes into existence.

Differential Effects of Transport Costs

Treatment of transport costs would be comparatively simple if they were proportionate to weight or bulk and varied precisely with distance. Then only relatively light or compact goods would travel over great distances, while heavy or bulky commodities would move only a short distance, if at all. This would be the situation if the cost of transporting each article were independent of the cost of transporting others. Unfortunately for simplicity, this is not true. Transport services are unavoidably joint products: the same resources (such as a railway's roadbed, rolling stock, and terminal facilities) are used simultaneously to carry a wide variety of commodities. Most costs are therefore joint; it is impossible to attribute specifically to a single commodity any of the large overhead costs of transport, or more than a small proportion of operating costs.

With the great majority of transport costs jointly incurred, their allocation to the various commodities to determine the rate to be charged leaves enormous room for the exercise of discretion. It might seem logical to charge rates proportionate to weight and bulk, on the ground that heavy or bulky goods require more space and more fuel to transport. Such a policy, however, would result in serious underutilization of railways, barge lines, and ocean vessels. To ensure traffic sufficient to produce adequate revenue, rates on heavy and bulky articles must be kept relatively low. A disproportionate share of joint costs then has to be allocated to the lighter, more compact commodities, in particular to those of high value. This principle of charging "what the traffic will bear" is the one generally followed by shippers and by regulatory agencies, tempered by considerations of equity and of competition among shippers. Rates per ton-mile are thus generally low on bulky or heavy items with a low value per unit of weight—such as coal, lumber, iron ore, grains, and crude oil—and high on compact, highly fabricated, and valuable articles—such as cameras, watches, and jewelry.

Joint costs are also responsible for the phenomenon of low "back haul" rates. From every major shipping center, there radiates outward a network of rail, ship, plane, and truck lines. Each type of conveyance must make an outward and a return voyage. If the volume of traffic carried in each direction were normally about the same, freight rates on the outward and the inward journey would be approximately equal. But often over any given route, more tonnage is carried in one direction than the other. Without some specific inducement, such as especially low rates, trains or ships will have to make one voyage empty, or partially so. Their loads may be increased if transport charges are lowered. Hence the low rates on coal shipped from Cleveland or Erie to Duluth, as against the much higher rate on iron ore moving in the opposite direction.

A particularly interesting illustration is provided by the overseas shipments of dry cargo from London. Before 1930, the weight of outward freight, of which some four-fifths was coal, considerably exceeded the weight of inward freight and bore the major part of the joint costs of both voyages. The cumulative effects of a structural change in British trade made themselves felt at just this time. Because of growing depletion of the coal mines and the rising costs associated therewith, the British industry found itself unable to compete with other fuels in extra-European markets. In addition, the use of coal as a source of power had been declining since at least 1913. Between 1929 and 1931, while the weight of dry-cargo imports fell only 8 per cent, that of exports (predominantly coal) dropped 31 per cent. The major burden of costs shifted to the inward voyage; outward rates dropped sharply, while inward rates rose.[9]

Many other aspects of differential freight rates are of importance; we shall mention only one or two. There is of course the practice of quoting lower rates for the long haul than the short haul, which may result from the desire to stimulate increased traffic to outlying points, from the need to meet competition (as between rail and ship between Atlantic and Pacific coast ports of the United States), or simply because the long haul spreads some overhead costs thinner. And there is the advantage afforded by canal and river barges of exceptionally low rates on long-distance traffic as compared with rail or truck transport. Operating as compared with overhead costs are unusually low for barges; once goods are loaded, the cost of transporting them by barge is relatively little greater for a long than for a short journey. The opposite is true of trucks, while railways are in an intermediate position.

Transport Costs and Localization

If transport costs bore uniformly on all goods, they would raise delivered prices and reduce the value of trade, but would affect the location of industry only insofar as such costs exceeded international differences in production costs. As we have seen, however, transport charges vary widely from commodity to commodity and are not always proportionate to distance. Of particular importance is the fact that all commodities require raw materials for their production, and that freight rates are generally lower on raw materials

---

[9] Freight rates in May, 1931, to South America were 38 per cent lower than a year earlier, to India 20 per cent, while inward rates from these regions rose by 75 per cent and 34 per cent, respectively. All data for this illustration are taken from the interesting article by Carl Major Wright, "Convertibility and Triangular Trade as Safeguards Against Economic Depression," *Economic Journal*, **LXV** (September, 1955).

than on finished articles. Moreover, the manufacturing processes may by their very character eliminate much of the weight of the materials used or, on the other hand, they may add to the weight or bulk of the finished goods at a rather late stage of processing.

These complexities increase the difficulty of determining the most economical point at which to locate production, and they lend themselves poorly to generalization. Nonetheless, even though one can derive no broad, simple rule, yet one can arrange commodities into three groups in terms of where their processing will tend to take place. Commodities may be materials oriented, market oriented, or neutral in their orientation.[10]

MATERIALS-ORIENTED COMMODITIES   When the cost of transporting the raw material (or fuel) to the market exceeds the cost of transporting the finished good, the processing or finishing industry will tend to locate near the site of raw materials production. This will generally be the case if the raw material loses much weight in processing, for there is no sense in shipping waste matter to the point of manufacture. Thus lumber manufacture usually takes place near the timber stands—the bark, sawdust, and other waste are left behind, and only the finished lumber is shipped to the market. Vancouver, B. C., is an important lumber-milling center. Spruce trees are felled in the woods some hundreds of miles to the north, formed into huge rafts at tidewater, and towed (cheaply) to Vancouver. There an adequate supply of labor and external economies available in an industrial city provide excellent conditions for milling. The finished lumber is then loaded on ships and carried to markets all over the world.

Cotton ginning and baling (but not spinning and weaving), the extraction of cane and beet sugar and turpentine and rosin, vegetable canning, and pottery manufacture are further illustrations of materials-oriented processes. Aluminum refining requires immense quantities of electric power (the fuel factor). Hence the processing occurs not at the source of the raw material (bauxite) in Jamaica and British Guiana, but near the Grand Coulee Dam in the state of Washington, and in British Columbia.

Coal has immense drawing power, especially for the iron and steel and engineering industries, which are heavy users of this important fuel.[11] The

---

[10] By "materials" are meant the principal raw materials to be processed or the fuel required for processing operations. The production of raw materials (primary production) must, of course, occur where the essential natural resources are located.

[11] Coal rather than iron ore exerts a more compelling attractive power on the smelting process (manufacture of pig iron in blast furnaces), since the weight of coal used exceeds that of the iron ore, and the coal loses all its weight during the operations. (Formerly, many tons of coal were required for each ton of iron ore. As a result of many improvements, the ratio of coal to iron ore has been reduced to about 2:1 in the most modern blast furnaces.) Although other fuels are available, such as oil or electric or atomic power, they are unlikely to displace coal (in the form of coke) in the blasting process. The coke is more than a fuel: it is a deoxidizing agent as well. Its carbon unites with the oxygen in the iron ores to form carbon monoxide and carbon dioxide, gases that are carried away, leaving molten iron in the furnace.

greatest industrial area in western Europe arose in the coal deposits of the Ruhr—first iron and steel manufacture, drawing its ore from Lorraine and then northern Sweden, then industries fabricating heavy iron and steel products and needing coal for fuel as well as heavy steel sheets, rods, and bars as raw materials.

The steel industry of the Pittsburgh area got its start with the discovery of iron ore in the region about 1790. These deposits were near exhaustion by 1860, when the rich Superior ores of upper Michigan, later of Minnesota, were opened up. Because of the weight-losing feature of coal, the steel industry remained in the coal-producing Pittsburgh district, the ore being brought by boat from Duluth and Superior to lake ports such as Cleveland and Erie, and thence by rail. Rather than send the ore cars back empty, the rail companies offered low rates on return shipments of coal, so coal and iron ore began to meet at the lake shore, and steel mills were established in Gary, Cleveland, Erie, Toledo, Detroit, and other intermediate points. A similar combination of forces led to the establishment of the Bethlehem Steel Corporation's plant at Sparrow's Point, Maryland, and the U.S. Steel plant near Philadelphia: the nearness of Norfolk coke, low ocean freight rates on iron ore shipments (coming from Chile and Venezuela), and the proximity of the great eastern markets.

MARKET-ORIENTED COMMODITIES Just as weight-losing commodities tend to be attracted to the supply of raw materials or fuel, so commodities that gain weight or bulk in processing are attracted to the market.[12] Automobile assembly is of this character. Parts are made principally in Detroit or Flint, attracted originally by the availability of capital and enterprise and held there by ready accessibility of raw materials and fuel; but assembly in this area is only for nearby markets. To serve more distant markets (both domestic and foreign), unassembled parts, concentrated in small space, are shipped to widely scattered plants. Coca-cola extract is made in Atlanta; this is carried all over the world to local bottling companies, where carbonated water is added and the product bottled. Beer and ink, like soft drinks, are weight-adding products; they, too, tend to be produced near their market areas.

Also market-oriented are perishable commodities, such as bread and baked goods, flowers, ice, and fresh milk. Fresh vegetables in season are in this category, though competition from frozen foods shipped long distances is increasing.

Services, which must be rendered directly to the customer, must of course be produced in the market area. Laundries, dry-cleaning establishments, theaters, and gasoline filling stations are "industries" of this type.

---

[12] If the processing adds bulk rather than weight, this amounts to the same thing as adding weight, for the greater bulk displaces shipping space and will involve a higher freight charge than a smaller, more compact shipment. The same is true if the article in question breaks easily in shipment, since a given delivered amount will require more cargo space than a sturdier object.

NEUTRAL COMMODITIES   Some commodities, or more accurately, processes, are neutral or indifferent to the pull of supply or of the market, and hence may locate at either point (or occasionally at intermediate points). This will be true where transport costs are unimportant in relation to processing costs, or where there is little gain or loss in weight or bulk during processing. In the former category are matches, plastic novelties, photographic equipment, cigarette lighters, and other small metal objects; in the latter, cotton and woolen textiles, cement, boots and shoes, and furniture.

Where transport costs exert little influence, either because they are unimportant or because they exert a roughly equal pull toward materials and market, other elements will be decisive in determining industrial location. The relative supply and prices of factors tend to become dominant, just as they are in determining the location of crop production, lumbering, fisheries, and mining.

One cannot, however, rule out sheer accident as unimportant. A number of industries in which the availability of special types of skilled labor is vital can attribute their period of growth and expansion to the drawing power of a supply of specialized labor. But how did this particular kind of labor happen to be there in the first place? Where did the first skilled workers come from? They may have appeared simply as the result of gradual specialization in a center of large population, thus providing a specific illustration of the attraction of a large labor supply. Yet they may have migrated from some other center, settling where they did for capricious or at least noneconomic reasons.

Thus a small number of lens grinders from Germany migrated to Rochester, New York, in the first half of the nineteenth century, choosing this place to settle quite accidentally. With the outbreak of the Civil War, orders for telescope and binocular lenses poured in, requiring the training of additional workers and bringing prosperity and renown to Rochester. After the war, it was only natural that the photographic industry should locate in this city.

Or it may be that the man or men who conceive the idea of starting an industry happen to live in a particular place. Their natural attachment to their home town tends to keep them there, as well as the industry they establish. This attraction may be reenforced if the capital they need can only be obtained locally. The American automobile industry appears to have been initiated in Detroit for such personal reasons, for when it began, many other cities had equal advantages in most other respects.

Conclusion

It should be apparent that the introduction of transport costs modifies, but does not render inoperative, such basic forces determining regional or national specialization as factor endowment. In the extractive industries, natural resources inevitably exert the predominant influence. Neutral or footloose industries, which are very numerous, tend to locate where factor endowments are favorable.

As for market-oriented manufactures, we should note that it is in the larger market centers that the factors of greatest importance—labor and capital—are themselves located. In a broad way, the pull of transport costs and of factor endowment is in the same direction. But where final processing adds considerably to weight or bulk, transport costs may outweigh the advantages of factor endowment and cause the finishing processes to be undertaken at the site of the local market.

It is in the processing as contrasted with the extraction of raw materials that the role of transport costs is greatest. Only infrequently are the factor supplies essential to such activities as copper smelting, power production, saw-milling, or sugar-refining available in abundance where the raw materials are produced. In spite of this, the saving in transport costs from locating basic processing facilities at the raw material source may be so great as to induce movements of capital, management, and even labor to that source, just as do rich raw material sites themselves.

SELECTED REFERENCES

Anstey, Vera, *The Economic Development of India*. London: Longmans, Green & Co., 1952. Contains illustrations of the effects of caste and social organization on production (see especially pp. 46-64).

Caves, Richard E., *Trade and Economic Structure*. Cambridge, Mass.: Harvard University Press, 1960. Chapter IV discusses factor supplies.

Lösch, August, *The Economics of Location*. New Haven, Conn.: Yale University Press, 1954. An attempt to formulate a general equilibrium theory of location.

Isard, Walter, *Location and Space-Economy*. New York: The Technology Press & John Wiley & Sons, 1956. An up-to-date statement of location theory.

Hoover, Edgar M., *The Location of Economic Activity*. New York: McGraw-Hill Book Co., 1948. A comprehensive discussion of transfer costs and other factors affecting the location of industry.

Ohlin, Bertil, *Interregional and International Trade*. Cambridge, Mass.: Harvard University Press, 1933. Chapter X contains a fairly extended discussion of transport costs and problems of localization, with illustrations.

Zinkin, Maurice, *Economic Development for Free Asia*. Oxford: Blackwell, 1956. The first few chapters contain many illustrations of the social conditions of production typical of the countries of Southeast Asia.

8

ECONOMIES OF SCALE, EXTERNAL ECONOMIES, MONOPOLY

One of the assumptions that has served to simplify our model is that all production functions are linear and homogeneous. In plainer language, this means that all operations are small-scale, and that any increase in output is proportionate to the increase in input of all the factors. In other words, there are no economies to be obtained from increasing the scale of operations of a firm. This is contrary to the well-known facts of large-scale production: in some industries, an increase in the scale of operations leads to a more than proportionate increase in output, with resulting lower unit costs.

ECONOMIES OF SCALE

A principal reason for economies of scale is the technical superiority of certain indivisible units of capital goods. Use of a machine or piece of equipment requiring a large investment may permit an enormous saving in labor time. Consider, for example, the case of a corporation confronted with the technical problem of calculating the critical shaft speed for a steam generator. When attacked by clerical labor using ordinary office calculating machines, solution of this problem required three man-months of labor. When punch-card machines were substituted for calculators, the task could be accomplished in forty hours. But when the work was done with three different versions of a modern automatic electronic computer, the time required was reduced, respectively, to one hour, fifteen minutes, and fifteen seconds.[1]

Modern industry abounds in illustrations of the great productivity of techniques relying upon the use of expensive and indivisible capital equipment. Thus a pair of modern dual-drum concrete paving machines operating together can lay a mile of concrete highway 8 inches thick in a single ten-hour day, a speed twenty or more times that attainable by manual methods.

[1] Cited in Robert H. Gregory and Richard L. Van Horn, *Automatic Data Processing Systems*. Published 1963 by Wadsworth Publishing Co., Belmont, Calif.

The drawing press used in up-to-date automobile plants can stamp out of steel sheets some twenty automobile fenders an hour. A modern punch press can punch holes in half-inch thick steel at the rate of approximately thirty a minute; in one-eighth-inch steel, it reaches a speed of 120 strokes a minute.

Equipment of these types is indivisible in the sense that it is impossible to retain the technical efficiency of the large unit by building a smaller unit costing only a fraction as much. Thus a punch press comes only in a large size; a small press cannot exert the necessary pressure. For small-scale operations, an electric drill would be substituted.

Large-scale economies are not limited, however, to those related to the use of costly and indivisible units of equipment. Specialized labor, as well as specialized machines, becomes economical as the scale of production increases. Inventories of finished goods and of materials, which are necessary because of unpredictable variations in demand and output, need not vary proportionately with output, but only with its square root. Partly because inventories can be smaller, but also because large firms make bulk shipments, storing, handling, and shipping charges decline as the scale of operations increases. Some activities not directly related to current operations, such as research, planning, and public relations, increase in cost less rapidly than output.

Economies dependent on a large volume of output imply that this output can be sold at a price sufficient to cover costs. If the market is small, this will be impossible. This suggests that a large country, especially one with high per capita incomes, will be a more fruitful field for the development of large-scale industry than will a smaller, poorer country. It is not surprising that the United States is conspicuous for its use of large-scale production methods, nor that, with the growth in wealth and incomes in the European Common Market and the reduction of barriers to trade among its members, large-scale industries there are expanding and multiplying.

This is not to say, however, that a small country is denied any possibility of enjoying economies of scale. Many small nations provide a market of sufficient size to justify the establishment in some industries of at least one optimum-scale firm. But this limitation in the number of firms that can operate efficiently and profitably entails the obvious danger of monopolistic domination of markets.

EXTERNAL ECONOMIES

Closely related to, but distinct from, economies of scale, which are internal to the individual plant, are external economies. These arise from the growth of a single industry and from the spread of industry over many areas of production. A very few of these external economies are technological or real in nature: the *efficiency* of one firm or industry is increased by the activity of other firms or industries. The most commonly cited illustration is the emergence, as the number of firms in an industry increases, of a trained supply of labor. When this stage is reached, the individual firm can readily draw upon this pool of qualified labor, instead of having to make do with untrained and inefficient workers, with clear benefits in terms of efficiency and output. Closely related to this external economy is the development of managerial talent as an accompaniment to industrial expansion.

Growth in the size of an industry or an entire economy also leads to the spread of existing technological knowledge and to its development through use. Methods of production are thereby improved and efficiency increased.[2]

Most external economies, however, are pecuniary rather than technological in character. They affect not the efficiency of the resources a firm or industry uses, but their price. Both types of economy, however, lower the costs of the beneficiaries.

Major sources of pecuniary external economies are the possibility of intra-industry specialization as the industry expands, or of certain suppliers developing economies of scale. Thus as the output of a given industry or group of industries grows, it becomes profitable for various specialized suppliers to begin operations. Credit facilities, formerly lacking, may develop, providing more adequate funds more economically. A normal progression is from money lenders to commercial banks, to savings banks and building and loan associations, and finally to mortgage banks and investment banks. The automobile industry has benefited greatly from the concentration in economical large-scale plants serving the entire industry of the production of carburetors, speedometers, generators, and numerous other parts.

EXTERNAL AND INTERNAL ECONOMIES AND INTERNATIONAL TRADE

The existence of internal economies introduces an important new element into the theory of international trade: it provides a basis for international specialization *additional* to differences in factor endowments. Imagine two countries with factor proportions so similar that no specialization or trade can develop. If each country's market is sufficiently large to ensure economies of scale in certain industries, then the establishment of large-scale plants in one or more such industries in each country (provided the industries are not the same ones) will result in specialization and trade.

In what particular industries large-scale methods are first introduced in any country will mainly depend upon the size of markets for specific commodities. Once an industry realizes economies of scale, however, it is in a favorable position to maintain its lead. It has the advantage of a headstart

[2] Bela Balassa, *The Theory of Economic Integration*, p. 46. Published 1961 by Richard D. Irwin, Inc., Homewood, Ill.

on potential rivals. Moreover, as it expands, its initial advantage is likely to be reenforced by the realization of external economies.

A considerable part of the trade in manufactures of western European countries probably rests on this foundation. Illustrations might include Belgium's large exports of plate glass, Denmark's trade in marine engines, and Britain's in electrical equipment. Germany's advantage in the chemical industry, though initially it may have been due to an abundance of specialized labor, was certainly reenforced by the early introduction of large-scale production techniques.

The appearance of external economies may also operate to give a country a comparative advantage where it had none before. Suppose a country to be producing a commodity to supply its domestic market, with neither exports nor imports present. As the country grows in population and wealth, the market for this product expands. At some point, external economies (real or pecuniary, it does not matter which) may well arise. When they do, the cost of producing this item will fall. If the industry was just holding its own with foreign competitors earlier, it will now enter the ranks of exporters. There would appear to be good grounds for believing that with the rapid growth in the size of markets in the United States during the nineteenth and twentieth centuries, the emergence of external economies over a wide area has contributed importantly both to the rise in per capita incomes and to the strengthening of many export industries. In this process, the relation between internal and external economies has been close: to a considerable extent the external economies of one industry have resulted from the ability of its suppliers to introduce efficient large-scale methods.

THE ROLE OF ENTREPRENEURSHIP

Up to this point, we have said relatively little about the entrepreneur and his role in production. Yet as the person (or group of persons) who brings capital, labor, and resources together, fashions them into a productive organization, and faces the risks of an uncertain world, he occupies a strategic position. So long as our model is a purely competitive one, this oversight is not too important. For an economy in which all firms are small-scale, as they must be under conditions of pure competition, the implicit assumption that entrepreneurial ability is distributed about equally among different populations is a reasonable first approximation.

This assumption, though it may be acceptable with respect to nations with a similar social environment, can hardly be applied to countries of widely differing culture. The historical development of western Europe was such as to stimulate the growth of qualities essential to successful entrepreneurship, whereas in most other parts of the world—Southeast Asia, the Near East, Africa, and Latin America—prevalent institutions were inimical thereto.

Societies organized on feudal lines place a high value on land ownership and management, but see little merit in business activities. The submission to authority that is stressed in the traditional societies of Asia inhibits innovation, while the extended family, with its highly developed set of mutual rights and responsibilities, discourages individual striving for advancement and material success. In these circumstances, it is hardly surprising that entrepreneurial ability has been in short supply outside of Europe and countries settled by Europeans. Even before large-scale methods of production became important, relative differences in the supply of the entrepreneurial factor gave European nations an advantage where entrepreneurship counted most—in manufacturing.

But this advantage has been compounded with the growing importance of large-scale industry, simply because with increase in scale has come an increase in complexity. Functions that in the small-scale plant of yesteryear could be performed by a knowledgeable jack-of-all-trades now require the services of highly trained experts: production engineers, accountants, advertising and sales specialists, technicians in research and development. Most important is the coordination of all these diverse activities into a smoothly operating, unified organization.

> *Organisation-building ability* is probably the most critical skill needed for industrial development on a large scale. The organisation-builder must be able to harness the new ideas of different innovators to the rest of the organisation. He must be able at the same time to select and develop persons who can properly manage and control a labor force. His task is to stimulatè initiative and enthusiasm in the accomplishment of the objectives of the organisation. . . . [This] suggests that organisation is more than a summation of the particular abilities of certain individuals. It is more than the statistical aggregate of managerial personnel. Organisation connotes a constellation of functions, the persons and abilities necessary to perform these functions, plus the integration of persons and functions in a common undertaking.[3]

Administrative talent, or organization-building ability, would certainly seem to be crucial to the success of a large business, once established. It would therefore also be vitally important to the emergence and expansion of large-scale firms. Even with the presence of potential economies of scale, and of abundant capital to build a plant incorporating them, a large firm would fail unless its diverse activities were effectively coordinated, as many stockholders have discovered to their sorrow.

The early preeminence of the United States in large-scale industry can probably be explained in part by the initial advantage of an extensive market, favorable to the adoption of large-scale methods, and in part to the provision to an increasing extent of experience and training in coordinating and inte-

---

[3] Frederick Harbison, "Entrepreneurial Organisation as a Factor in Economic Development," *Quarterly Journal of Economics* (August, 1956) p. 367.

grating the activities of large firms. Before large-scale techniques were widely adopted elsewhere, the United States had acquired a substantial executive group skilled in this demanding type of administration. Other nations— notably the Common Market countries, Britain, and Japan—are now catching up in this respect as, with the growth of regional or world markets and with the advance of technology, internal and external economies become more widespread.

ECONOMIES, MANAGEMENT, AND INTERNATIONAL TRADE

How can internal and external economies, together with the element of management, best be fitted into the analysis of international trade? We have suggested that large-scale methods will be instituted, and economies of scale realized, in regions or countries where the demand for individual commodities is sufficient to justify the establishment of at least one optimum-size plant. Once internal economies have been captured, such an industry has a cost advantage over potential competitors. This cost advantage may endure for some time, especially if the economies attained by large-scale operations are reenforced by external economies, which tend to accompany the expansion of an individual industry and of industry in general. External economies can also be generated by the provision of social overhead capital in such forms as railroads, an interconnecting highway network, power plants, and a good educational system that includes, especially, facilities for technical and vocational training.

A large and prosperous country acts as a sort of magnet in attracting large-scale industry. It affords a large number of markets of sufficient size to furnish economies of scale; a wide range of large-scale plants therefore tend to become established. Numerous industries of this type in turn generate external economies that help lower costs still further. Moreover, such a country is certain to be well-supplied with social overhead capital, another source of external economies.

We have noted that a high level of managerial skill is vitally important to the success of large-scale enterprise. Clearly, a nation that possesses many large-scale industries will enjoy a real external economy in the form of a relatively abundant supply of executives who have acquired their training and experience in these very industries. Moreover, given an abundance of high-level administrators, not only will the expansion of large-scale industry be supported, but the productivity of labor will be increased. Managerial talent, when plentiful, need not spread itself thin, but can see to it that the labor force is well-selected, properly trained, suitably motivated, and supplied with appropriate tools and equipment.[4]

[4] "An essential management function is the selection, training, and development of the persons comprising the labor force. Most, though not all, skills of manual labor and

We have seen that the possibility of taking advantage of economies of scale may give a country a comparative advantage. Such an advantage is additional to the kind provided by a country's relative factor endowment, but not independent of its endowment, for economies of scale imply large investment and a high use of capital relative to labor. Where capital is scarce and dear, any potential economies of scale might well be more than offset by the costliness of capital. This is not certain, however. The gains from the use of large-scale methods in some industries apparently are great enough to outweigh the high cost of capital and even a paucity of managerial ability.[5]

How enduring is the advantage derived from economies of scale, reenforced by external economies? The advantage enjoyed by the pioneering large firms tends to be retained, partly owing to the benefits of a headstart, partly because of the accumulation of experience and knowledge. If the management remains alert and aggressive, and especially if it devotes sufficient attention to research and development to keep abreast of technological change, a firm or an industry may retain its preeminence for a long period. It will, however, very likely have to share its market with newcomers who get their start as local markets expand abroad, perhaps aided by infant industry protection or by the natural protection afforded by transport costs.

DEGREES OF COMPETITION

With the introduction of economies of scale and large-scale production, we have departed widely from our assumption of perfect competition. In the competitive model, producers are so numerous that none can affect price by variations in his output. Each individual small firm can dispose of any attainable output at the ruling market price, which means that each such firm confronts an infinitely elastic demand at the going price. Average revenue (or price), which is the return from *each* unit sold, is constant and therefore equal to marginal revenue, or the return from the *last* unit sold. In equilib-

---

even clerical employees are acquired on the job. Another management function is to provide the incentives for work. To these functions we can add many more which directly affect the productivity of labor: proper lay-out of machinery and processes, work study, breakdown of jobs in order to economize on use of critical skills, safety programs, systems for appraising performance and discovering talent, and many other related techniques. Such techniques of 'scientific management,' however, are expensive. They require the employment of specialized personnel and investment of time on the part of members of the line organization. Even more important, they require relatively high levels of education, experience and training among the members of the line organization." [Harbison, *op. cit.*, p. 372.] Harbison gives evidence to support his contention that "the organization which employs labor is probably the principal factor—the dominant factor—in determining labor productivity with constant technology."

[5] This conclusion is very tentative. Although capital-intensive, large-scale plants have been introduced in countries where both capital and management are scarce, many—perhaps most—such plants can survive only because of ample protection.

rium each firm will expand output up to the point where marginal cost equals marginal revenue, but not beyond, since marginal cost would then be higher than marginal revenue. Although in the short run marginal cost could exceed average cost, in the long run competition would ensure that each firm produced at the optimum point where its marginal cost was equal to its minimum average unit cost. If the supplies of all the factors needed in the industry were unlimited, this minimum average cost would remain constant. But if some factor (a natural resource, or entrepreneurship) were in scarce supply, diminishing returns to the use of that factor would operate, and minimum average cost would rise.

We have noted that, if economies of scale are to be realized, large-scale production units must be established. But when the output of each firm in relation to its market is large, price will be affected by changes in its output, and the industry will no longer be competitive in character. Such an industry tends to be dominated by a relatively few large firms. Moreover, if internal economies accompanied each increase in the scale of a firm's output, it would not be long before production was concentrated in the hands of a single giant firm.

Although there appears to be a limit to the extent to which economies of scale can be realized in any industry, and thus to the degree to which production becomes concentrated, yet in a small country (as we have already noted) the market may be large enough to justify the existence of only a single producer. Local monopoly of this sort seems to be fairly common, especially in the underdeveloped countries; but instances of complete monopoly are rare in large markets, and even these are subject to the competition of fairly close substitutes.[6] In the United States, one thinks of aluminum metal before World War II, when the Aluminum Company of America was the sole producer. In the international field, the outstanding illustration is the de Beers' diamond syndicate.

Perfect competition is also exceptional. Most illustrations that come to mind are in agriculture. Wheat, corn, wool, cotton, and many other crops meet the requirements quite well when the government does not intervene; producers are very numerous, and the product (or at least any given grade) is homogeneous. In most lines of industry, however, firms operate under conditions of imperfect competition, somewhere between perfect monopoly and perfect competition.

Preceding chapters have established the relative factor endowment of different countries as the principal ultimate determinant of international specialization. Differences in such endowments become translated into relative commodity price differences through the operation of a competitive price system. But if industry is imperfectly competitive or monopolistic,

---

[6] "Natural" monopolies, such as railways and other public utilities, are an exception, but these are generally recognized as such, and subjected to government regulation.

differences in factor supplies may not be reflected in commodity prices as they are when perfect competition is assumed to operate. International specialization might be quite different. We must undertake at least a brief examination of price determination under these alternative conditions.

Monopoly

At the other extreme from perfect competition is perfect monopoly. Here there is a single producer responsible for the entire output of a homogeneous product: the monopolist *is* the industry. Therefore the demand curve for the firm and the industry are one and the same. Although the product of the monopolist may confront competition from substitutes (as steel must compete in industrial uses with aluminum and other light metals, plastics, lumber, and fibreboard), there are no *close* substitutes. A typical monopoly situation is illustrated by Figure 8.1. The marginal and average cost curves are similar to those for a competitive firm, reflecting average costs that diminish until the point of optimum plant utilization is reached, with marginal costs crossing average costs at this minimum point.

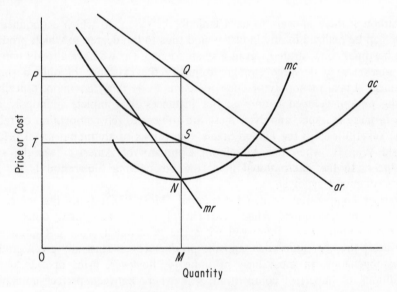

FIGURE 8.1   Monopoly Price

The differences from the competitive firm's position show up in the average and marginal revenue curves. The demand, or average revenue, for the output of the firm is no longer horizontal: it has a negative slope, with an elasticity determined by the tastes of the buyers of the product. Since the monopolist is the sole producer, variations in his output will affect price. When the sale of additional output lowers price ($= ar$), not only is the average return on each unit sold reduced, but the revenue yielded by the additional unit or units sold (*mr*) falls even more. This net addition to receipts is not the (reduced) price times the additional quantity sold, but that product *less* the reduction in receipts on all units *previously* sold. Thus the marginal revenue curve lies at all points below the average revenue curve.

If the monopolist follows the principle of maximizing profits, he will determine his most profitable output in the same manner as the individual firm in a competitive industry. He produces that output at which marginal cost equals marginal revenue. This is the output *OM*, at which marginal cost and marginal revenue are both equal to *MN*. The price at which this output can be sold is *OP* (= *MQ*), and monopoly profits are equal to *PQST*. At any smaller output, marginal cost would be less than marginal revenue; by increasing output, the monopolist would add less to costs than he added to revenue. If he increased output beyond *OM*, he would add more to costs than he added to revenue.

Imperfect Competition

The degree to which, in actual practice, elements of competition and monopoly are intermingled varies widely. Some industries include a very large number of firms, each with very little power to affect price, while others consist of only a handful of sellers, each capable of exerting a great influence on price.[7] In between lies a host of intermediate cases.

Thus, in the United States and in other countries with a sizeable market, producers of textiles, women's dresses, and plastic manufactures, and the printing and the fruit and vegetable canning industries, should be placed at the competitive end of the scale, where the number of firms is quite large and competition is keen. Somewhat removed from this end of the scale would come producers of men's suits and coats, shoes, cement, paper, and machine tools. "Competition among the few" would characterize aluminum, steel, automobiles, industrial chemicals, ethical drugs, petroleum refining, heavy electrical equipment, and banana imports. With the declining relative number of producers that is the basis of this rough classification, there corresponds a rising volume of investment in plant and equipment, a feature that increases the difficulty new firms have in entering the ranks of the "monopolistic competitors."

---

[7] It should be noted that a very strict definition of an industry would include only a group of firms selling in a single market area, within which, if competition were perfect, a single uniform price would rule. This would confine an "industry" to a single geographical region, and exclude those firms separated from this market by distance and the necessity of incurring transport costs. This is rather unrealistic, since all firms must incur transport costs, even for goods sold in the city where they are produced. We shall consider an industry to include all sellers of a given product who do in fact compete effectively for sales in a given area, which of course will vary in size from industry to industry.

If the products of individual firms in one of these imperfectly competitive industries were completely undifferentiated, it would be very difficult to maintain a price above the competitive level and to earn monopoly profits. This would be especially true if the number of firms were large, or even sizeable. For with a homogeneous product, customers would have no reason to show preference to one firm over another. Price would be the only consideration, and all firms would have to adopt the same price tag.[8] Even with oligopoly (a very small number of competitors), unless there is collusion in the form of an agreement, either tacit or explicit, maintenance of a price close to the monopoly level is very difficult—the threat of a price war is always present. "Competition among the few," when the product of the industry is homogeneous, tends to be unstable, periods of high prices alternating with periods of cut-throat competition.

It is for reasons such as these that we find firms in practically every industry making strenuous efforts to differentiate their product, for each producer wants to ensure for himself a good level of profit, and there are only two ways in which he can do so, short of collusion. First, he can approach the problem from the supply side and attempt to reduce his costs below those of his competitors. If the industry is already reasonably efficient, this is difficult; in any event, others can and will imitate him. Eventually, the general level of costs of the entire industry will be lower and will be reflected in a lower price, with profits no greater than the competitive norm.

Second, the individual firm can try to differentiate its product favorably in the minds of the consumers. To the degree to which it is successful, competing products become imperfect substitutes for that of the differentiating firm. In other words, it insulates its market from competition to some extent, and the demand curve for its product ceases to be horizontal and acquires some downward slope. (In non-technical terms, this means that this firm can charge a higher price without losing all its sales.)

To differentiate its product, our firm can adopt one or both of two strategies. (1) It can improve the quality of its product, or if this is too difficult, it can appear to do so by changing its shape, appearance, or packaging. But any differential advantage established by such means is also subject to erosion by imitation. Hence (2) it is common to resort to sales strategy. A firm employs salesmen and buys advertising space to impress upon the minds of its customers the real or trumped-up advantages of its product. Sales efforts are expensive, and will of course raise the firm's cost curve. But they may pay off, by raising the demand curve more than the cost curve.

Again, success breeds imitation. If one firm by these devices manages to expand its sales at the expense of its competitors, they are almost certain to follow suit. But if all the members of an industry engage in competitive

---

[8] If entry into the industry were difficult, the price might remain above the competitive level for some time. All firms, however, would receive the same price.

selling and advertising, each will partly offset the efforts of the others. Individual demand curves move downward. Where ease of entry is great, the end result is not very different from that of perfect competition. Quality and sales competition will push individual demand curves downward and to the left until each is tangent or almost tangent to the average cost curve of the individual producer. Price will be equal to or only slightly above average cost, though (because the average revenue curve is downward sloping) a bit above the minimum point, with profits little if any greater than competitive returns. (See Figure 8.2.)

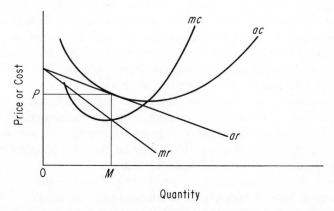

FIGURE 8.2   Monopolistic Competition with Intensive Quality and Sales Competition

Where the number of competitors is small, owing to economies of scale, and especially where the realization of such economies requires heavy investment and thus keeps numbers small, successful product differentiation may make it possible for firms to charge prices well above the competitive level. If each firm pursued only the short-run goal of profit maximization, high prices would be the outcome.

Longer-run considerations, however, may and often do lead producers in such an industry to adopt a policy of moderation, charging a price not much higher than would exist under competition. Profits are then positive, but not huge. Each producer might be concerned lest high prices and high profits attract new competitors into his field, or elicit the unwanted attentions of government attorneys. Rapid technological progress in the economy as a whole, ensuring the frequent appearance of fairly close substitute goods, helps to reenforce this tendency toward moderation.

There is another aspect of technological progress that should be allowed for. A partially insulated market and the higher profits that go with it may establish the sort of financially secure base needed if the firm is to engage in active research, improve its product, and lower its costs. Paradoxically, an element of monopoly can be the prerequisite of more effective competition in the longer run. If this is true, then although at any moment in time successful product differentiation, achieved by not too strenuous sales competition, results in a price that is substantially higher than the competitive level, in the long run the price can be brought even lower than had the industry been marked by intense competition.

The Temptation of Collusion

Although there are many reasons for doubting that, even under conditions of imperfect competition, price or profits will differ much from those established under pure competition, there is no guarantee of such a happy outcome. A small number of competitors selling highly differentiated products may not be deterred from exerting their monopoly power—their government may not be hostile to monopoly, or perhaps the high initial investment necessary to establish a new business may effectively limit new entrants. Their fear of stirring up competition from existing firms may be eliminated by an agreement to hold competition within defined bounds.

The temptation to reach such an agreement is especially great in an industry producing a standardized product with few natural differentiating characteristics, such as sheet metal, industrial chemicals, or raw materials. For them the regulation of competition may be the only practicable means of avoiding recurring and destructive price wars.

Effective collusion (agreement to avoid competition) is the surest means to the universal goal of high profits. Understandably, therefore, it is widely practiced, both on the national and the international level. We shall therefore conclude our discussion of imperfect competition by considering briefly some of the typical ways in which it is deliberately organized.

CARTELS

Agreement to restrict competition, whether formal or informal, explicit or merely tacit understandings, may be classed together under the general term, "cartels." Since explicit agreements are both more definite and more capable of enforcement than looser arrangements, cartel members commonly are linked in some form of organized association.

The purpose of cartels is to ensure members higher profits than would be possible without agreement;[9] their means, one device or another to limit competition.

Scope of Cartels

According to each of several estimates of the international importance of cartels, something between a third and a half of world trade was subject

[9] In self defense, members of cartels sometimes plead that their objective is merely "stable profits." It is safe to say, however, that these stable profits are invariably higher than they would be even under stable but truly competitive conditions.

to some degree of cartel control during the inter-war period.[10] A very large number of commodities falls within this range, including both important raw materials such as the principal metals and minerals, and a long list of manufactured goods, of which the more important have been chemicals and dye-stuffs, pharmaceutical products, and electrical equipment.

Means of Control

Although in some instances, prices to be charged by members have been fixed by a cartel, real power to control prices rests upon limitation of output. Price policy therefore has more often been applied to effect discrimination in different markets (see below) or among different classes of buyers, or to eliminate competition through an actual or threatened price war. To restrict output, thus indirectly but effectively raising price, cartels have commonly imposed quotas on members, enforcing their observation by a system of penalties and bounties for overproduction or underproduction. Since patents give the exclusive right to manufacture the patented object, agreements limiting the amount to be produced by licensees have been widely used.

Allocation of markets has also been a favorite cartel device. Each member of an international cartel (often itself a national cartel) agrees to keep out of markets cherished by another member in exchange for a similar agreement on the part of other members.

Owing to the emergence in Britain and to the establishment in the European Common Market of a policy unfriendly to monopoly, the area of cartels is probably smaller than before the war. Of particular importance has been the substitution of public for private control over the production and sale of European coal and steel, with the inauguration in 1950 of the European Coal and Steel Community (see Chapter 27). In the United States, a number of antimonopoly suits by the government have effectively damped the urge toward collusion. Only in Japan has there been a resurgence of monopolistic organization, with the government approving and even sponsoring such activities.

Price Discrimination

When a firm has a monopoly of its product in its own domestic market, it is in a position to charge one price in that market, a different one in one or more foreign markets. This is due to the fact that these markets are separated from one another by transportation costs, and possibly also by tariffs

---

[10] Machlup estimated the figure to be "at least 32 per cent." Mason gives 42 per cent as a "minimum estimate" for the share of world trade "cartelized or influenced by loosely knit associations or conferences." [Fritz Machlup, "The Nature of the International Cartel Problem," in Corwin D. Edwards and others, *A Cartel Policy for the United Nations*, Columbia University Press, New York, 1945, p. 11; Edward S. Mason, *Controlling World Trade*, McGraw-Hill Book Co., New York, 1946, p. 26n.] Postwar estimates are not to my knowledge available.

or differences in tastes, customs, and business practices. If the commodity in question is sold at a lower price in a foreign market, it cannot—within the limits set by the cost of reentering the high-priced domestic market—be reexported at a profit. On the other hand, if the price is lower in the domestic market, the monopolist's control of production there gives him control also of exports to the foreign market.

Price discrimination will be profitable provided the elasticity of demand in the two markets is different. For if the monopolist sells at the same price (f.o.b. plant) in the two markets, the marginal revenue in the market with an inelastic demand will be less than the marginal revenue in the market with an elastic demand. Total revenue will be increased if he shifts some sales from the market in which marginal revenue is low into the market in which it is high. It will pay to continue thus shifting sales until marginal revenue in both markets is equal; at this point of maximum profits, marginal revenue will be equal to marginal cost for the entire output.

The argument can be visualized in a diagram (Figure 8.3). A and B represent two separate markets with the vertical axis (average and marginal revenue) in common, but with distinct horizontal (quantity) axes, amounts of the commodity being read from 0 to the right for B, to the left for A.

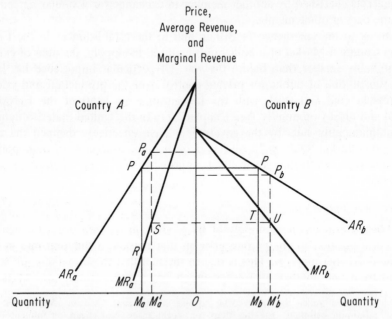

FIGURE 8.3   Discriminatory Pricing in Two Markets

If the same price, P, is charged in both markets, marginal revenue will be lower in A, where the demand is relatively inelastic, than in B, where it is comparatively elastic. By shifting a part of the output sold in A (M_aM_a', equal to M_bM_b') to B's market, marginal revenue in A is raised from R to S, while the price is increased from P to P_a. In B marginal revenue is lowered from T to U, price from P to P_b.

Either A or B could be the home market, with the other the foreign market. If A is the home market, where the seller has his original monopoly, demand may be more elastic abroad (as in B of the diagram) because of the presence of some competition, though of differentiated products, or because of the character of buyer's tastes. (In the extreme case of perfect competition abroad, our seller would sell at the competitive price there and charge a monopoly price at home.) On the other hand, if B is the home (monopoly) market, a more inelastic demand in the foreign market (A) would have to be accounted for in terms of differences in tastes or of the availability of fewer indirectly competitive substitutes.

EFFECTS OF MONOPOLISTIC PRACTICES

Whenever producers can wield effective monopoly power, whether as a result of collusion or merely because competitors are few and entry is difficult, price is generally higher and output smaller than it would be under competition. The allocation of resources is therefore different from what it would be in a competitive system, and socially less desirable.

We have seen that in a freely competitive market, price and cost are equal for each commodity, with price equal to both marginal and minimum average cost. Costs just cover the prices paid for the services of the various factors needed to produce a unit of each commodity, while the factors receive an equal return in all uses.

Allocation of Resources

Resources are therefore allocated in the most efficient manner possible.[11] If more resources were devoted to any use, costs would rise while the price fell, and consumers would be paying for the commodity less than the services of the factors were worth in other uses. Allocation of fewer resources to any use would lower marginal cost and raise price; consumers would be paying a premium over the value of factor services.

Optimum results are ensured by the existence of perfectly competitive conditions, when price, and average·revenue and marginal revenue of the individual producer, are all equal. He maximizes his returns by producing an output at which marginal cost is equal to marginal revenue and thus to price. With perfect mobility of the factors, the price of each will be the same in all uses, and equal to the value of its marginal product.

---

[11] There is the possible exception of the monopoly or oligopoly that is "well-behaved" in the long run, and that uses its financially secure position to engage in research, improve its product, and reduce its costs.

When some degree of monopoly is present, whether because producers are few in numbers, because they collaborate, or because they differentiate their product, price tends to exceed marginal cost. This will be so if producers exercise their monopoly power by limiting output to the amount that equates marginal cost and marginal revenue. For under monopoly conditions, the individual firm's demand or average revenue curve is no longer infinitely elastic, but is negatively inclined, and average revenue exceeds marginal revenue.

But if price exceeds marginal cost, it follows that resources are allocated uneconomically. For if marginal cost is equal to the value of the services of the factors, then the consumer is paying the monopolist more than the value of the resources used in production. If additional resources were devoted to producing the monopoly product, the satisfaction of consumers— which is the goal of production—could be increased. Moreover, with the restricted output produced by the monopoly, average costs are above their minimum level, indicating that resources are being used inefficiently. With increased output, not only would consumer satisfaction be increased, but, with average unit costs lowered, resources would be used more efficiently.

Where monopoly is deliberately enforced by collusion among producers, the inefficient use of resources is likely to be magnified. This is so because to make a collusive agreement effective, it is usually necessary to include a number of high-cost, inefficient producers. Their output is not needed; if production were concentrated in the most efficient plants, their resources could be transferred to other, more productive uses. But to obtain their consent to the agreement, it is essential to allot them some part of the output.

Price Discrimination

When a monopolist exports part of his output, he may practice price discrimination between his home and his foreign market. The price will be lower in the foreign market if its demand is more elastic than demand in the home market, either because of differences in tastes or because the monopolist has to meet competition abroad. Price will be lower at home if home demand is more elastic. *Total* resources used will be the same whether uniform or different prices are charged; on this score, there is no advantage or disadvantage in price discrimination. The parties discriminated against will naturally resent the discrimination. If we regard home and foreign buyers as equally important, however, there is no reason to prefer flat pricing to discrimination.

Effects on Trade

Even when confined to a single country, a monopoly tends to diminish the volume of international trade. This follows from the fact that monopoly depresses the earnings of the factors by restricting job opportunities in the monopoly area, thus causing overcrowding elsewhere. With reduced incomes, they have less to spend on everything, including imports.

When a monopolist in one country sells abroad at a higher price, the volume of trade is still further reduced. On the other hand, if he discriminates against the home buyer, his exports may be larger than they would be under pure competition.

The reduction of international trade is clearest when several markets are controlled by an international cartel, and these markets are allocated among the members. Potential international trade is then simply stopped at its source.

Adaptation to Change

Also to be noted is the tendency of monopoly to increase the rigidity of prices and to decrease the mobility of resources as compared with competition. At least in the short run, there is less flexibility of costs in the face of changing conditions, and unless a monopolist (or a group operating as a monopoly) is alert to his long-run interest in improving processes and lowering costs, costs may be rigid in the long run too. This consequence can be important when changed international conditions require an expansion of exports and an increase in productive efficiency.

PUBLIC POLICY TOWARD MONOPOLY

There are three ways in which governments can respond to monopoly, whether it extends across international boundaries or is confined to a government's own territory. They can leave it alone; they can attempt to destroy it; or they can regulate it.

Something can be said in favor of each policy. Spokesmen for international cartels contend that they stabilize prices, prevent destructive, cut-throat competition, and stimulate technical improvement through the exchange of information and patents. If this and nothing else were true, laissez faire would be the correct policy.

Such a view of cartels is highly idealized, and is unsupported by the facts. Prices are certainly raised by cartels, usually to a level sufficient to permit operation of the least efficient plants. Since this stimulates the competition of outsiders, as well as increased production by the more efficient cartel members, the history of many cartels has been a period of high prices followed by a collapse to a low level. Rather than preventing cut-throat competition, restrictive agreements have encouraged its use, or the threat of its use, to eliminate potential competition. Cartels are designed, moreover, not to avoid cut-throat competition, but to eliminate *all* competition. As for technical advance, exchange of patents has more often than not been accompanied by restrictions on their use; and with some justice, cartels have been accused of suppressing new inventions rather than encouraging their adoption.

Prohibition of monopoly, though it has more to recommend it as an abstract proposition, is too undiscriminating. It fails to distinguish between monopoly, or more accurately, oligopoly, that rests on economies of scale and that which depends on collusion. If all oligopoly positions were destroyed, say by limiting any single firm to a small percentage of its industry's output, important economies of scale might be lost. So far as this is true, a policy of prohibition would be self-defeating, for it would bring about a more uneconomic allocation of resources, the very feature of monopoly to which objection can legitimately be made.

As we saw earlier, collusion is the surest means to output below and price above the competitive level. This suggests regulation or prohibition of collusive practices, rather than prohibition of monopoly or oligopoly, as a preferable policy. Practices to be banned would include the establishment of production or sales quotas, price fixing, allocation of markets, or restrictive patent agreements. The problem, however, is to achieve international agreement on such a program. The attitude of different governments toward monopolistic practices differs widely; attempts to reach agreement in the past have brought these differences sharply to the fore. Although agreement to prohibit such practices as those mentioned above was reached in the proposal to establish an International Trade Organization (see Chapter 29), enforcement was to have been left to each country. At this level, the basic difference in attitudes would probably have reasserted itself.

SELECTED REFERENCES

Edwards, Corwin D., *Economic and Political Aspects of International Cartels.* Washington, D.C.: Committee Print No. 1, Senate Subcommittee on War Mobilization of the Committee on Military Affairs, 78th Congress, 2nd Session, 1944. This study contains an unusually large number of illustrations of cartel practices.

Hexner, Ervin, *International Cartels.* Chapel Hill, N.C.: University of North Carolina Press, 1945. An excellent, full-scale discussion of the cartel problem.

Linder, Staffan Burestam, *An Essay on Trade and Transformation.* New York: John Wiley & Sons; Stockholm: Almquist & Wiksell, 1961. This book came to my attention too late to incorporate its argument in the text of this chapter. It complements the argument on p. 126ff. very neatly, in that it stresses, as an explanation of specialization among the industrial countries with rather similar factor endowments, the role of similar demands in causing the emergence of specific industries.

Machlup, Fritz, *The Political Economy of Monopoly.* Baltimore: The Johns Hopkins Press, 1952. Chapters 4 and 5 provide an especially detailed, descriptive discussion of the type of business practices used to enforce monopoly.

Marsh, Donald B., *World Trade and Investment.* New York: Harcourt, Brace & Co., 1951. Chapter 21, in which monopoly and imperfect competition are treated with special reference to their impact on international trade, is excellent.

Mason, Edward S., *Controlling World Trade*. New York: McGraw-Hill Book Co., 1946. Chapter I provides an excellent brief statement of the issues raised by cartels. Part II is devoted to a discussion of the attempt to regulate trade by intergovernmental commodity agreements.

Samuelson, Paul A., *Economics*, 5th ed. New York: McGraw-Hill Book Co., 1961. Chapter 25 gives a good brief review of imperfect competition.

Schumpeter, Joseph A., *Capitalism, Socialism,* and *Democracy,* 3rd ed. New York: Harper & Bros., 1950. Chapters VII and VIII have an especially interesting discussion of monopolistic practices as a protection against the blasts of competition and as giving rise to a "process of creative destruction" that constantly revolutionizes the economic structure.

Stocking, George W. and Myron W. Watkins, *Cartels or Competition?* New York: Twentieth Century Fund, 1948. This is another full-scale discussion of the cartel problem.

9

DYNAMIC ASPECTS
OF INTERNATIONAL TRADE

Our discussion of international trade theory so far has been conducted mainly in terms of static assumptions. This is particularly true with respect to the factor endowment of nations. We have shown that if various countries start out with different endowments of the various factors, they will tend to specialize in types of production that require intensive use of their abundant factors.

Such specialization also requires, we may recall, the further assumption that internal mobility of labor, capital, and enterprise is substantially greater than their mobility between countries. Otherwise, national boundaries would be irrelevant to the location of productive activities; the movable factors would converge on the most fertile farm lands and the richest mineral deposits, leaving the less productive regions of the earth virtually uninhabited. Manufactures of all kinds would spring up in each of the fertile agricultural regions, creating a number of nearly self-sufficient industrial-agricultural centers. About the only basis for trade and specialization would be the uneven distribution of the richer mineral deposits, which would attract extractive and materials-oriented industries.

It is now time to take into account the possibility that factor endowments are not fixed once for all, but may change, either from causes that are internal to a particular economy or as a consequence of quite substantial international movements of the factors. Let us start with internal forces affecting a nation's supply of the productive factors.

Changing Factor Endowment: Internal Causes

None of a country's factors is unalterably fixed in supply. Its labor force can, of course, be augmented by the growth of population. When the natural rate of increase suddenly rises, as it has in recent years in many underdeveloped countries as a consequence of improved public health services, the first impact is on the proportion of children and young people in the popula-

[144]

tion. Only later, as these groups mature, is there a large increase in the work force.

Through the process of saving and capital accumulation, a nation's capital supply is enhanced. The rate of increase may be quite steady, depending on ingrained habits of thrift combined with a slowly rising national income, or it may spurt upward because of institutional change that makes saving safer and more attractive, or (as in western Europe since the war) because of a sharp increase in productivity and national income. Changes in the distribution of income in favor of groups with a high marginal propensity to save will produce a like result.

Even natural resources can be increased by exploration and discovery, or depleted through exhaustion. We need only mention the discovery of oil in Venezuela in the early years of this century and the disappearance of the superior iron ore deposits in the United States. The former created the basis for Venezuela's single great export industry; the latter transformed the United States from a condition of self-sufficiency in iron ore to one of growing dependence on imports.

From the point of view of international trade and specialization, what matters is not the indisputable fact that factor supplies can increase or decrease; this would be of no importance if the *relative* supplies of the different nations remained as before. What is important is the possibility that the relative factor endowment of nations may change.

That this possibility is a reality is demonstrated by the experience of many nations, of which we give some illustrations in the next chapter. To anticipate, we may point out that the United States during the nineteenth century became transformed from a nation in which land was abundant and labor and capital relatively scarce into one in which capital was the abundant factor. (Not all of this change was due to purely internal forces; an important contribution to both the supply of capital and the size of the labor force came from abroad. This aspect of the problem will be considered in the next section.)

The effect of such changes in a nation's relative factor endowment should be obvious. The principal basis for its specialization and the character of its trade is altered. Instead of producing and exporting primary products, it shifts gradually to the production and export of manufactures. Though it may still retain a comparative advantage in some of its earlier exports, these tend to diminish in importance or even disappear.

In diagrammatic terms, the country's production possibilities curve undergoes an alteration in shape. If the two axes are primary products and manufactures, respectively, at first the curve is biased toward the former, since the output of primary products is large relative to that of manufactures. As the factor proportions alter, so does the shape of the curve. After a process of gradual change, the curve becomes biased toward manufactures; their output is eventually relatively greater than that of primary products.

What we have been describing is an aspect of economic growth, an objective—including particularly the accumulation of capital and greater industrialization—ardently pursued by the underdeveloped nations of the world. We shall consider this problem of structural change in a broader setting in Chapter 27.

FACTOR MOVEMENTS AND FACTOR ENDOWMENTS

The Premise of International Immobility

At the beginning of this chapter, we noted that one of the basic assumptions of the theory of international trade is that the mobility of the factors of production is much greater within a country than between countries. It is now time to consider the validity and importance of this assumption.

Over thirty years ago, Professor John H. Williams attacked this premise in a well-known article.[1] He contended that international mobility of the factors was far greater than had been supposed, often being greater *between* countries than *within* a single one. If taken properly into account, this international factor mobility could contribute greatly to the explanation of international specialization and trade. In particular, he suggested that the very economic backwardness of underdeveloped countries minimized the internal mobility of labor and capital; these factors, particularly capital, moved more freely from the advanced to the underdeveloped countries, rather than within the latter.

> This is part of the explanation of great cosmopolitan seacoast cities, foreign trading centers, nearer to Europe in their economic and cultural contacts and characteristics than to their own interiors, and relying upon Europe for finance, transport, and management; of the presence of large-scale foreign enterprise, mainly in the extractive industries; of the existence of problems of immigration or emigration, in countries and continents otherwise comparatively primitive, "pre-economic," to use Bagehot's phrase.[2]

A good illustration of the importance of Professor Williams' critique for the theory of international trade is provided by a recent application of his argument to the development of the "export economies"—those nations that acquired industries producing and exporting primary products.[3] These industries did not arise because of the attractive power of a specially suitable

[1] John H. Williams, "The Theory of International Trade Reconsidered," *Economic Journal*, XXLIX (1929); reprinted in *Readings in the Theory of International Trade*. Published by The Blakiston Co., 1949.

[2] *Ibid.*, p. 261.

[3] Jonathan V. Levin, *The Export Economies, Their Pattern of Development in Historical Perspective*. Published 1960 by Harvard University Press, Cambridge, Mass.

factor endowment. Before their emergence, the future primary exporting nations were traditional, subsistence economies, having comparatively little contact with the outside world and, if not content with things as they were, at least apathetic toward change. Their entry into international trade was thrust upon them quite suddenly by an invasion of foreign entrepreneurs, who brought with them the necessary capital, managerial talent, technical labor, and (according to Levin) even the major part of the common labor essential to establish a thriving primary export industry. Generally, the only needed factor available in these countries was some natural resource—a rich mineral deposit or fertile or well-located tropical land.[4]

Thus Levin shows how, in the 1840's, the prospective profits to be made from exploiting the rich guano deposits on the Chincha Islands off the coast of Peru attracted British capital and enterprise. Since money incentives had little appeal for the Peruvian Indian, the management was forced to import Chinese coolie labor under contract.[5] Burma's rice industry before the war depended heavily on seasonal Indian labor, Chettyar money-lenders, and British rice millers.[6] Besides these two industries, Levin cites the sugar industry of Queensland, the banana industry of Central America, Ceylonese tea plantations, the rubber industry of Malaya, and various but less important primary products in South Africa, East Central Africa, and the South Sea Islands as being based on local natural resources financed and managed by foreign enterprise and capital and actually worked principally by imported labor. To this fairly impressive list could be added—as depending upon foreign capital, enterprise, and certain kinds of technical or skilled labor—such industries as petroleum extraction in the Middle East, Sumatra, and Venezuela; Chilean copper mines and nitrate works; and Mexico's mineral industries. There are many more, all depending not upon the initial presence within the exporting economy of all the required factors, but upon foreign sources of supply for their capital, their management, and to some extent their labor.

To the extent that international trade rests on this foundation, it would seem to constitute an important class of exceptions to the orthodox theory, for the latter asserts that a country specializes according to its relative supplies of the productive factors *before* trade. But here we have an important group of industries whose very origin depends not upon the prior endowment of a nation with appropriate factors, but upon their migration from abroad. Given a rich mineral deposit, or rich or well-located tropical land, the prospective high return obtainable—essentially rent—leads some entrepreneurs to assemble and organize the other required factors into an enterprise to exploit

---

[4] *Ibid.*, pp. 4-5.
[5] *Ibid.*, Ch. 11.
[6] *Ibid.*, pp. 206-12.

the resource. Such is the basis on which rest, according to this view, a substantial number of primary exporting industries.

Professor Williams put the matter even more broadly, contending that there is

> . . . an impressive and ever increasing array of basic industries which have expanded in disregard of political frontiers. They represent in some cases the projection by one country into others of its capital, technique, special knowledge along the lines of an industry and its market, as against the obvious alternative of home employment in other lines. They represent, in other cases, an international assembling of capital and management for world enterprises ramifying into many countries. (They represent, in some cases, the response of industries to tariffs and patent laws, providing one class of cases in which impediments to the flow of goods produce a flow of productive factors.) They suggest very strikingly an organic interconnection of international trade, movement of productive factors, transport, and market organization.[7]

Dynamics versus Statics Again

It is true that the factor proportions theory explains a nation's specialization and trade by its pretrade endowment with factors specially suited to the production of specific goods, but as we have already noted, this is a static type of analysis. We have shown that a country's factor endowment can change radically from internal causes, and that the character of its industries and its trade will alter accordingly. As the illustrations just cited demonstrate, a country's factor endowment can also change from external causes. If it possesses only a rich natural resource, the prospective returns from exploiting it may attract the complementary factors. If we take a dynamic view of a nation's factor endowment, fact and theory can be reconciled.

To solve the problem in this way, however, presents a logical difficulty, for we are relying upon international movements of the productive factors for an explanation of certain kinds of international specialization. But factor movements of such scope would seem to be ruled out by the traditional assumption of low international factor mobility. We are brought face to face with the contradiction between this assumption and factor movements of the kind described.

International Factor Mobility Reconsidered

It seems to me that the best way to meet this problem is to concede the criticism and amend the assumption. International factor movements *are* larger than theory previsaged. In general, however, they seem to require at least the expectation of returns higher than those that can be obtained from their employment at home. Given such favorable expectations (as in the extraction of petroleum), capital, enterprise, and technical and skilled labor

---

[7] Williams, *op. cit.*, p. 263. The sentence in parentheses is a footnote in the original.

will respond to the lure.[8] This amounts to qualifying the assumption as to factor mobility, which could now be restated as follows: There are obstacles to international mobility, so that for equal returns, factors will tend to stay home. But given a sufficient differential in the return to capital, labor, or enterprise, any or all of these factors will migrate abroad.

We can go even further. The task of international trade theory is to explain international specialization. For much commodity production, the factor proportions theory serves reasonably well. International trade, however, includes services as well as goods; specialization in their provision should be accounted for by the theory of international trade, too.

Specialization in the rendering of certain important services—notably shipping, marketing, advertising, insurance, management, and banking—has become highly developed during the course of the past two centuries. We shall have more to say about this in Chapter 11. For the moment, let us note that with the growth of both domestic and international trade, members of the London business community acquired great skill in the grading and classification of commodities, in the evaluation of market prospects, in the assessment of customer's credit-worthiness, in the estimation of risk, and in the performance of all the manifold tasks connected with buying, selling, and transporting goods and in financing these transactions. As the volume of trade grew, the degree of specialization in the performance of these functions increased apace; so too did the pool of knowledge essential for informed action. This knowledge and these skills enabled London to become, early in the nineteenth century, the purveyor to the world of the services of shipping, marketing, insurance, and banking.

Banking services were at first limited mainly to the provision of short-term credit to finance the international movement of goods. The combination of experience, knowledge, and reputation, however, together with the attraction to London of small and large sums of savings, permitted certain firms to undertake investment banking on an international scale. Relying on their reputation to attract capital, these firms used their skill and knowledge to overcome the obstacles to its international movement. Where returns to international investment were sufficiently high, they discovered these attractive opportunities and engineered a flow of capital.

New York experienced a development similar to that of London, though considerably later. Until after World War I, New York was almost exclusively a *national* commercial and financial center. Thereafter, with the growing importance of the United States in world affairs, it came to rival London on

[8] A freer flow of capital and management from advanced to underdeveloped countries, especially as in the nineteenth century from Britain to Hong Kong, Shanghai, Singapore, and other "cosmopolitan" centers, seems susceptible to a simple explanation. These overseas cosmopolitan centers were, in fact, extensions of the homeland, subject to British law and administered by British civil servants. Factor movements between Britain and these ports were more intranational than international in character.

the international scene. Moreover, especially since the end of World War I, the pull of New York and London as financial and marketing centers has attracted to them the head offices of many large corporations, so that they have become great pools of managerial talent. To the services of shipping, insurance, trading, and banking has been added that of management, which is provided either in the form of consultation, or in the direct export of managerial staff to branch plants and subsidiaries abroad or to foreign firms under management contracts.

There is in reality not so much difference in the character of goods production and the rendering of services as the traditional distinction between the two would suggest. For interregional or international specialization in the production of commodities is in specific activities, not necessarily (though it may be) in the whole range of activities required to produce a completed good. Thus some regions specialize in the extraction of raw materials, perhaps even undertaking some of the processing activities, as smelting copper ore into blister copper. Other regions may engage in the intermediate activities of turning the crude or processed raw materials into semimanufactured articles which they then export. Examples are yarns of cotton, wool, rayon, and nylon; textiles made of these yarns; pig iron and semifinished steel products; lumber, paper pulp, and so on. Still other regions import such semimanufactured goods and perform the finishing activities. They make textiles out of imported yarns; shirts, dresses, or suits out of imported textiles; automobiles or machine tools or hardware out of steel-mill products; furniture from imported lumber; newsprint or other paper products from imported pulp. Each region undertakes only one or a few of all the various activities necessary to produce a finished article. It may, of course, if it possesses all the necessary factor supplies and their prices are competitive, engage in all the relevant activities.

The activities involved in providing services differ in no essential respect from those undertaken during a given stage of commodity production—for example, raw material extraction, refining, or finishing. The factors of production are combined in proportions determined by the technical production function. In the case of services—such as insurance, marketing, or banking—the proportion of certain specialized types of labor is very high; that of capital or natural resources is low. Rather than causing a visible transformation of materials, the utility created or the service rendered is intangible. Both types of economic activity, however, consist in the performance of useful and valued services.

A real distinction between commodity-connected services and intangible services arises when the latter include the export of a factor—as when the banking services entail the export of capital, or when managerial services require the actual migration of personnel. Those rendering the service and exporting the factor have become experts (specialists) in performing the technical tasks associated with their work, such as overcoming or coping with the obstacles to international factor movements. Such services occupy a legitimate place in a comprehensive theory of international trade.

FACTOR REVERSAL

Another challenge to the factor-proportions version of international trade theory must now be reckoned with. It, too, will be seen to have dynamic implications.

In recent years, a number of writers have converged in criticizing the theory on the ground that it must assume a special kind of production function.[9] To ensure specialization in accordance with factor endowment, it is charged, each production function must be biased toward intensive use of one or the other of the two factors in question, say capital or labor. In diagrammatic terms, one could say that its isoquants must be decidedly asymmetrical in shape relative to the capital and labor axes, as in Figure 9.1(a). For only then will it be true that, for any set of factor prices in a country, one commodity will always be capital intensive; the other, labor intensive. Thus, in Figure 9.1(a), with relative factor prices as represented by the parallel price lines $k_1 l_1$ and $k_1' l_1'$, the production point for commodity *1*, at *a*, is more capital intensive than the production point for commodity *2* at *b*. This would be true for any other set of factor prices chosen, such as those represented by the dashed lines $k_2 l_2$ and $k_2' l_2'$. Again, the production point for commodity *1*, at *a'*, is more capital-intensive than the production point for commodity *2*, at *b'*.

But production functions of this decidedly biased and asymmetrical type are by no means the only kinds conceivable. They could also be such as to yield isoquants that were symmetrical with respect to the axes, as in Figure 9.1(b)[10]. Two such isoquants, for two distinct commodities, could then be found that were tangent at a single point, as at *T*.

But notice what this implies. If, with relative factor prices as represented by the lines $k_1 l_1$ and $k_1' l_1'$, a country (*A*) undertakes the production of both commodities, commodity *1* will be produced by a relatively more capital-intensive technique (at *a*) than commodity *2* (at *b*). This would be true for any set of factor price lines tangent to the two isoquants above and to

[9] See, among others, Romney Robinson, "Factor Proportions and Comparative Advantage," *Quarterly Journal of Economics,* LXX (May-August, 1956); Ronald Jones, "Factor Proportions and the Heckscher-Ohlin Theorem," *Review of Economic Studies,* XXIV (1956-57); K. Lancaster, "The Heckscher-Ohlin Trade Model," *Economica,* 24, 1957; B. S. Minhas, "The Homohypallagic Production Function, Factor-Intensity Reversals, and the Heckscher-Ohlin Theorem," *Journal of Political Economy* (April, 1962).

[10] Production functions yielding symmetrical isoquants are not the only type that give the results under discussion, but they serve well to illustrate the point. (See Minhas, *op. cit.*)

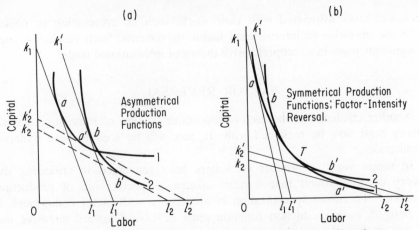

FIGURE 9.1   Asymmetrical and Symmetrical Production Functions

the left of the point T. Below T, however, with production functions giving symmetrical isoquants, there occurs the phenomenon that has come to be known as factor reversal. Thus with factor prices in another country, B, as represented by the price lines k_2l_2 and $k_2'l_2'$, commodity 2, not commodity 1, will be produced by the more capital-intensive technique.

Neither commodity is now uniquely or continuously capital intensive, regardless of relative factor prices. For any set of factor prices establishing production points above T, commodity 1 will be capital intensive and commodity 2 will be labor intensive, but for factor prices establishing production points below T, the factor intensity of the two commodities is reversed. The country with abundant capital (A) might export the commodity (1) that, at A's factor prices, is capital-intensive. But the country with abundant labor (B) might export the commodity (2) that, at B's factor prices, is also capital-intensive. Or the opposite might be true. In either event, while one country exported the product stressing its abundant factor, the other could export the product stressing its scarce factor. For any pair of commodities exhibiting factor reversal, a country's factor endowment need not determine its specialization. Even if the phenomenon of factor reversal were rather uncommon, the predictability permitted by the factor proportions theory would be seriously compromised.

Another consequence of certain production functions of the type that give rise to factor reversal should also be noted. If these yielded isoquants symmetrical with respect to both axes (rectangular hyperbolas with origin at zero), then differing factor endowments would provide no basis for specialization.[11] Each of several countries, with wide variations in their factor endowments, could produce a given commodity at a similar cost.

---

[11] Isoquants could be symmetrical, though not relative to both axes (i.e., rectangular hyperbolas with origin above or to the right of zero). These would not have the consequence under discussion.

To illustrate, suppose the line k_1l_1 in Figure 9.1(b) to represent both the relative prices of capital and labor and a given total expenditure on these factors in a country in which capital is abundant and cheap and in which labor is scarce and dear. This country (A), in producing commodity *1*, would adopt the capital-intensive process represented by point *a*. Suppose now that the price line k_2l_2 represents relative factor prices in country B, where capital is dear and labor is cheap, and that it also represents the same total expenditure as k_1l_1. Country B could then produce commodity *1* at the same cost as country A, adopting the labor-intensive process indicated by the point *a'*. Other countries, too, with factor endowments intermediate between those of A and B, might be able to produce this commodity at a similar cost, using techniques intermediate in factor intensity to *a* and *a'*.

It is quite possible, even probable, that production functions yielding iso-quants of this form exist, alongside of others that are strongly capital-biased or labor-biased. This might explain the ability of different countries, producing a given commodity by widely differing processes, to compete in the sale of that commodity in international markets. Rice is an outstanding illustration, but there are many others. Thus there is competition between bicycles produced in western Europe by a relatively capital-intensive process and those produced in India with considerably greater use of labor and much less of capital; between sewing machines of Indian and Japanese origin and those produced (with more capital and less labor) in Europe and the United States; between Japanese and American toys; and between sandals produced in Hong Kong and the United States.

Does all this mean that the factor endowments of nations have little to do with international trade—that the factor-proportions theory is not now and never has been a tenable explanation of international specialization? I believe that if we consider changes that have occurred in production functions over the past two centuries or so, we can throw some light on this question.

PRODUCTION FUNCTIONS IN HISTORICAL PERSPECTIVE

Until the latter part of the eighteenth century, what we now call manufactured goods were produced everywhere by handicraft, or labor-intensive, processes. The Industrial Revolution constituted, from the technological point of view, a violent change in production functions, principally in manufactures and in transport. New, capital-intensive processes of producing commodities hitherto made exclusively by hand were introduced, capable—at the factor prices ruling in England and western Europe—of turning out manufactures at substantially lower, even catastrophically lower, costs. The new manufacturing industries first wiped out many lines of handicraft production in western Europe. During the nineteenth century, as British textiles (to take a single example) invaded the markets of the East, they gradually destroyed the hand-loom production of cotton textiles. Locksmiths, scribes, candlemakers, and many other artisans saw their occupations disappear with the influx from the West of cheaper factory-made goods or of modern substitutes such as the typewriter, the kerosene lamp, and the flashlight. Others, like braziers and potters, found their markets constricted to specialized products in the face of imports of cheap metal pots and pans. Everywhere in the world, mechanical methods of production came to dominate in manufactures.

In terms of the character of the production function, what had been a labor-biased function had become capital-biased instead. This can be illustrated by Figure 9.2(a). The rectangular fixed-proportions isoquant marked HH' stands for a given output of the commodity in question, say cotton textiles, produced by handicraft techniques. This output can be produced, at the factor prices ruling in India, for example, for the expenditure represented by $k_1 l_1$ (whose slope reflects relative factor prices in India). So long as other methods were unknown, this labor-biased isoquant reflected the existing production function.

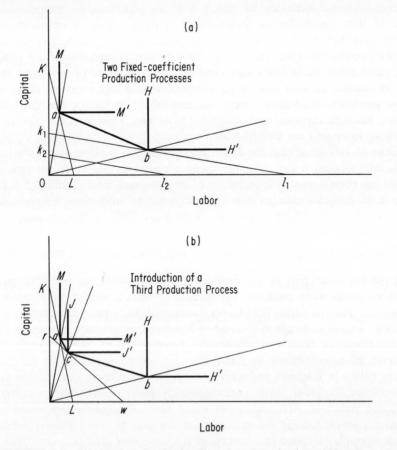

FIGURE 9.2 Changes in a Production Function: Introduction of New Processes

With the Industrial Revolution, however, the capital-intensive method represented by the rectangular isoquant *MM'* (with output the same as for *HH'*) became a reality. At the relative factor prices current in England, this output could be produced for an expenditure *KL*. If we assume this expenditure to be half that represented by k_1l_1 (that is, equal to k_2l_2, which reflects the purchase of half as much capital or labor as with the outlay k_1l_1), unit cost of producing textiles by process *MM'* would be half the unit cost by process *HH'*, and handicraft production would sooner or later be forced to stop. The entire production function, embodying all *known* processes, would now be represented by the discontinuous line *MabH'*; but at existing relative factor prices, actual production would only be undertaken by the factory method, *MM'*.

Let us now follow historical developments one step further. Late in the nineteenth century, Japan (where capital was costlier than in England and western Europe but cheaper than in India, and where labor was also intermediate in price) adapted capital-intensive techniques to her factor endowment, and introduced into the production function the technique represented by *JJ'* in Figure 9.2(b). This uses somewhat more labor than Western producers, but rather less capital, too. If *rw* (whose slope indicates relative factor prices in Japan) represents the same total outlay as *KL*, Japan can now compete with the West in the production of textiles. The discontinuous isoquant *MacbH'* stands for the entire production function, though actual production takes place only according to processes *MM'* and *JJ'*.

The spread of modern technology from one industry to another over the past hundred years has resulted in the dominance in manufacturing of highly mechanized (that is, capital-intensive) techniques. Industrial production functions are capital-biased. At existing relative factor prices, these capital-intensive processes alone are economically efficient; handicraft methods require such an inordinate amount of labor to reach a given output (as *HH'* in Figure 9.1(b) that even with very cheap labor they cannot compete. (Witness, for example, the Indian government's efforts to rejuvenate the hand-loom cotton industry by a generous subsidy program.)

In agricultural and raw materials production, at least until comparatively recently, conditions have been the opposite of those in manufacturing. Many of the basic staple foods and raw materials (such as sugar, tea, coffee, rice, rubber, and cotton) have been produced mainly by labor-intensive techniques. Their production, therefore, has tended to locate in countries where (given a comparable land endowment) labor is abundant and capital is relatively scarce. Exports of these and other primary commodities have, indeed, been the principal means available to these countries to pay for their imports of manufactures.

Increasingly, however, this picture is being altered. Capital-intensive techniques, applied to rice production, have made the United States a formidable competitor of Burma and Thailand in the world's rice markets. Improved techniques (including not only mechanization of production, but also the extensive use of fertilizers and pesticides) applied to such temperate-zone crops as wheat, corn, and soya beans have so increased productivity that, were it not for the use of artificial price supports, supplies from the United States, Canada, and Australia, produced by far fewer farmers using highly capital-intensive techniques, could dominate world markets. And while natural rubber is still a labor-intensive product, types of synthetic rubber are now being produced, by highly capital-intensive processes and at comparable cost, that are nearly identical in their relevant characteristics with the natural product.

Although the alteration of production functions to include highly efficient capital-intensive processes has not gone so far in the production of foodstuffs and raw materials as in manufactures, it does pose a serious threat to countries that depend on exports of such commodities to earn foreign exchange. Each such development, be it the introduction of a new synthetic substitute or a more efficient process for producing foodstuffs, diminishes the range of exports available to these countries. Changes of this kind that have occurred in the fairly recent past have already intensified the pressure of these countries for international agreements to support the prices of, and guarantee markets for, their products. They have also helped generate a strong sentiment in these countries for the stimulation of industries producing import substitutes—a sentiment that tends naturally to be excessive and that certainly needs no outside support.[12]

A natural and sensible reaction (from the viewpoint of primary producing countries) to the emergence of new capital-intensive processes that intensify the competition for their exports is to seek to offset this competition by perfecting methods of production that are especially suited to their factor proportions. This means seeking through applied research to devise more productive labor-intensive processes. It would be equally logical to seek a similar solution to the problem of producing substitutes for manufactured imports, where at present the capital-intensive methods of the industrial countries tend to be copied with little change.

If these steps should be taken, the results for the structure of world production and trade would be interesting. Something approaching the theoretical situation where production isoquants are symmetrical with respect to the substitution of capital and labor would apply over an appreciable range of commodities. Over this range, the basis of a comparative difference in costs or of comparative advantage would vanish. Many countries would then produce the same goods at similar costs, though by different processes. The geographical distribution of industry would also become more uniform, and there would tend to be less specialization and less trade.

As yet, the production of identical products by divergent processes appears

---

[12] These and related matters are more fully discussed in Chapter 27.

to be the exception rather than the rule, although the exceptions are undoubtedly becoming more numerous. Most commodities still tend to be most efficiently produced by a process that makes heavy demands on some particular factor, be it capital, skilled or technical labor, or a specific type of land. So long as this continues to be true, the factor-proportions theory provides a valid and useful explanation of international trade.

Simple Models vs. Reality

All this discussion, however, and that having to do with the related phenomenon of factor reversal, has been conducted in terms of the severe abstractions of a two-factor model. The real world is far more complex. At the most general level, we must always reckon with at least the three factors: land, labor, and capital. And the more detailed our analysis, the larger is the number of specific factors we must take into account.

The introduction of more than two factors enormously dilutes the significance of factor reversal. Even the meaning of that concept becomes dubious once we have three factors, let alone a larger number. As for the possibility of the emergence, with technological change, of production functions permitting the realization of equal costs by two or more dissimilar techniques, the presence of several factors would appear to cut both ways. On the one hand, the possibility of there being a number of equal cost combinations is increased. On the other hand, the larger the number of factors, the greater is there a chance of there being offsetting, or more than offsetting, differences in factor prices.

Factor proportions are still the most fundamental element in explaining international specialization. For the costs of any stage of processing a commodity are the payments to the factors of production. Given production functions that are biased in their factor requirements, a country will specialize in those productive activities that require relatively large amounts of its abundant and cheap factors. Sometimes alternative techniques may exist that allow nations with differing endowments to compete in the production of certain commodities. Or the cost advantage arising from favorable factor prices may be offset by the pull toward the market or toward the site of raw material production. As between countries with similar factor endowments, realization of economies of scale may provide the basis for the establishment of specialized production, which becomes reenforced if external economies also appear. Even in this area, however, abundance of certain factors, notably capital and alert and aggressive entrepreneurship, are likely to play an important role. We should not discount the importance of factor proportions.

ARE PRODUCTION FUNCTIONS EVERYWHERE THE SAME?

Another of the assumptions on which our analysis of international trade has been based is that any given production function is the same everywhere. More specifically, this means that of the entire range of technical processes encompassed within a production function, any country is free to choose that particular process best suited to its factor endowment.

In a static model for which the technical conditions of production remain constant, this assumption is valid. Except for a few well-guarded industrial secrets, and processes that can be patented, any production technique is open to exploitation by any potential user; it will be exploited provided only that factor proportions and factor prices are suited to the particular technique. In the longer run, there are no industrial secrets, and even patents expire.

In a dynamic world, however, and especially in one whose technology is constantly changing, it is normal for one country to get a headstart in the development of new techniques in a specific industry or even in a substantial number of industries. By continuous creative adaptation and improvement, the innovating industry may retain its lead for a considerable time; or the lead may soon pass to another country, where energetic competitors adapt and improve upon the original innovation.

Thus Germany was the first nation to develop a modern mass-production chemical industry, based on capital-intensive processes and centered on the production of aniline dyes. Firmly established in the late nineteenth century, this industry kept its lead until after the first World War. Wartime demands gave a great stimulus to certain branches of the chemical industry in the United States and in Great Britain. Other branches, notably dyestuffs, aided by the wartime seizure of German patents and by protective duties, sprang into being in the United States in the 1920's. Further growth in both these countries came from continued investment in research and from improved facilities for the training of chemists and chemical engineers. By the late 1920's, I. G. Farben, the giant chemical combine of Germany, found itself faced with formidable rivals in Du Pont of the United States and Imperial Chemical Industries of Great Britain.

As was suggested in the last section of this chapter, rapid changes in technology appear to be most frequently associated with the development of capital-intensive processes. But the industries in which such major innovations are being made alters from time to time. With the progress of technological innovation, industries that experienced earlier advance and that at one time were the most capital-intensive of all become outranked in the relative use of capital by newer lines of production. The older industries now become candidates for adoption by newer countries, where acquisition of the needed skills together with capital accumulation have prepared the way.

The cotton textile industry has followed this pattern conspicuously. Originating in England, mechanical techniques of production passed to the continent of Europe and the United States during the nineteenth century, though England retained its preeminence. After World War I, however, Japan increasingly took the lead in this branch of manufactures, which compared to newer industries such as automobiles, rayon, radios, and other durable consumer goods became relatively labor-intensive. Since then, more and more of the underdeveloped countries, such as India, Egypt, and many others, where low wages tend to give them a comparative advantage, have become important producers of textiles. As Kindleberger has remarked, this seems to be an industry on which developing countries "cut their development teeth," an important reason being that its factor requirements are fairly well suited to the endowments of such countries. Other industries that have moved down the scale of capital intensity as newer industries have grown up or as old ones have undergone a metamorphosis are the manufacture of bicycles, plastics, tires, flashlight batteries, and ceramics.

In sum, the forces described here generate a recurrent—or more accurately, a continuous—disturbance of static equilibrium. Technological innovation introduces new techniques, predominantly capital intensive in character, into production functions. The new methods—most frequently originating in countries where capital is relatively abundant—give the nation where they originate a cost advantage that may be enduring or only short-lived, depending upon whether the initial technological advance is sustained or passes to energetic competitors elsewhere. In the course of time, industries in which technology becomes relatively stabilized tend, by the very progress of technology in other areas, to decline in rank as to capital intensity. They are displaced in importance in the industrial countries by the growing, innovating industries and become candidates for adoption in the newer, developing countries where the social and economic conditions essential to their success are improving.

SELECTED REFERENCES

Caves, Richard E., *Trade and Economic Structure.* Cambridge, Mass.: Harvard University Press, 1960. Contains an extended discussion of modern versions of the theory of international trade and of the theoretical problems that have arisen in the course of its development.

Haberler, G., *A Survey of International Trade Theory.* Princeton, N.J.: International Finance Section, Princeton University, 1961. Chapter III discusses a number of recent theoretical developments.

Johnson, Harry G., *International Trade and Economic Growth,* London: George Allen & Unwin Ltd., 1958. Chapter 1, "Factor Endowments, International Trade and Factor Prices," constitutes an excellent statement of the issues with respect to factor reversal and related matters.

Kindleberger, Charles P., *International Economics,* 3rd ed. Homewood, Ill.: Richard D. Irwin, Inc., 1963. Chapter 7, on the dynamic basis of trade, discusses changes in tastes, technology, and factor endowments, with a considerable difference in emphasis from that adopted here.

Levin, Jonathan V., *The Export Economies, Their Pattern of Development in Historical Perspective.* Cambridge, Mass.: Harvard University Press, 1960.

Williams, John H., "The Theory of International Trade Reconsidered," *Economic Journal,* 1929; reprinted in *Readings in the Theory of International Trade.* A landmark in the literature, well worth consulting.

I0

SOME EFFECTS OF TRADE

RECAPITULATION

Our effort to expose to view the foundations upon which international trade and specialization rest is now complete. We have seen that the most basic of these is the relative endowment of the different countries with the productive factors, taken together with the alternative methods of combining these factors that are at any time available. Considering these elements alone, each country would specialize upon those products best suited to its factor endowment, which means those using little of its scarce factors and drawing heavily upon the cheap and abundant ones. Its export industries might undertake all the stages of producing a given product, from the extraction of raw materials through the intermediate stages and the final stages as well, or they might undertake only one or two of these stages. In determining which productive services each country can carry out most economically, allowance must be made for any qualitative differences in its factors. Cheapness or dearness might be offset by qualitative inferiority or superiority, which we saw could be explained principally in terms of the social conditions under which production takes place.

For most of its exports, there would be competitors—either from countries with comparable factor endowments or from countries with endowments suited to a different production technique. All productive services adapted to a country's factor supply and price situation and therefore producible at relatively low cost would be exported. The only exceptions would be those tied to the local market by such considerations as perishability, the need for personal service, and the like. All other commodities would be imported, although part of home consumption might be met from local production, if a commodity were subject to conditions of increasing cost.

Transport costs alter this picture in important respects. By raising the delivered price of a country's exports, they reduce the volume sold, and if they exceed the difference in production costs between the home country and a potential market, they rule out trade altogether. Beyond this, they may determine (with respect to industries that process raw materials or foodstuffs) whether that industry locates at the source of supply or near the market. It will tend to be materials-oriented if the cost of transporting the raw material to the market exceeds that of transporting the finished product, it will tend to be market-oriented if the opposite is true.

Where there is some degree of effective monopoly, prices will be raised above the competitive level. This tends, as with any cause that raises price (such as transport costs), to diminish the volume of trade. The income effects of monopoly, which will only be serious if it is extensive, work in the same direction. Trade may also be reduced directly, as when an international cartel allocates markets among its members. It is doubtful, however, if imperfect competition, whose most restrictive form is the collusive agreement, must be regarded as a major obstacle to international trade.[1]

This group of principles should enable us to explain the composition of a country's exports, to account for the pattern of world trade, and even to determine why a particular industry is located as it is or whether a particular industry is likely to be an economical proposition for a given country. A working model based on these principles makes no allowance for interference with its operation, in the form of government subsidies, tariffs, special tax favors, and the like. In any detailed analysis such distorting factors would, of course, have to be taken fully into account.

Our concern up to this point has been with the forces underlying international trade and with the nature of trade, which we have seen to be essentially the exchange of the products of specialized resources. It is time now to consider how trade affects the people who engage in it—how and why they benefit from it, how the incomes of different groups are influenced, and what kinds of relationships are established between nations that trade with one another. We shall begin with the gains from trade.

THE GAINS FROM TRADE

Specialization Means a Larger Income

Trade in its essentials is a very simple thing: it is merely an exchange of one kind of goods for another. Yet it is one of the most important of man's social inventions, for it freed the isolated individual from the need to produce all his own requirements. Assured that by trade these could be met, each such individual could specialize, to the great enlargement of the total income of the group.

Specialization can occur under various conditions. It may be regulated

---

[1] Thus Mason advances as his opinion that "the injury inflicted by tariffs on domestic competition and American foreign trade has been several times greater than the effect of cartels." Edward S. Mason, *Controlling World Trade*, p. 28. Published 1946 by McGraw-Hill Book Co., New York.

by tradition, as during the Middle Ages; it may be controlled by the state, as during the Mercantilist period; or it may develop spontaneously in accordance with the choice of individuals. It can be shown that it yields the best economic results under a free price system; that is, a system where the mobility of both labor and capital is unfettered and where producers are effectively competitive.[2] For such a system results in a single uniform price for each commodity that is the minimum the competing producers can charge and stay in business. Faced with a list of minimum prices, consumers can allocate their expenditures until each dollar spent yields the same satisfaction; since nothing further can be gained by shifting expenditure from one use to another, consumers' satisfaction is maximized. The price of each factor will also be uniform in all its various uses; this makes the return to each factor a maximum. If labor, for example, could earn more in some occupations than others, its movements from the poorly paid to the better paid jobs would lower wages in the latter and raise them in the former, thus improving the earnings of labor as a whole. Moreover, equalization of each factor's returns would mean that it was being put to the most important uses, as measured by the free choice of consumers. In summary, we can say that a free price system leads to the most efficient use of a community's resources—that is, to the highest possible income.

International Trade Extends Specialization

International trade is simply the extension of trade beyond the boundaries of a nation. It therefore extends the range of specialization and the gains derivable therefrom. Just as local trade enables advantage to be taken of the special aptitudes of individuals, so international trade makes it possible for each country to draw upon the special aptitudes of other countries and to utilize its own resources more efficiently. A region poor in land, where land-using products are consequently scarce and costly, though unable to import land to aid its labor, can import the products of land-rich areas, while the latter, with relatively little labor or capital, can obtain by exchange products requiring large amounts of these factors. Each region benefits in

---

[2] The assumptions of perfect competition and mobility imply full knowledge of alternatives by buyers and sellers of commodities and of the factors, the absence of important costs of moving from one occupation to another, and prompt but not excessive response to price changes. These are strong assumptions, and the conclusions of this brief summary would have to be considerably qualified in practice, since it is clear that these assumptions are by no means fully realized. Yet it seems worth while to set up this strong case as the ideal which a reasonably efficient price system will approximate.

The above is not meant to imply that socialism need be inefficient. But if it is to be efficient, its managers must act like perfect competitors—they must follow the rule of equalizing the value of each factor's marginal product and its price. This is essential to maximize output and minimize cost. On this point see Oskar Lange & Fred M. Taylor, *On the Economic Theory of Socialism* (edited by Bejamin E. Lippincott), University of Minnesota Press, 1938; and Abba P. Lerner, *The Economics of Control.* Published 1944 by Macmillan, New York.

so far as trade enables it to obtain at low cost commodities that it could produce only at higher cost.

From the viewpoint of the people of the world as a whole and of any single country in it, both as consumers and as the owners of factors of production, international trade thus permits a better allocation of resources. Some countries have the right factor combination for the low-cost production of tropical agricultural products; others can produce grains and meats cheaply; and still others, special types of manufactured goods. With international trade and specialization, a wide range of commodities can therefore be made available at lower prices to everyone. Consumers' money incomes will stretch farther, and satisfaction can be increased.

Instead of being used unproductively in home production for home use, the factors can be transferred to more efficient uses where their marginal return is higher. Instead of using its relatively abundant labor to raise high-cost wheat on scarce land, Britain combines it to better effect with capital in the production of manufactures. Rather than lying idle, the prairies of Canada and Australia are put to work growing the wheat Britain needs.

Note that this means that Britain indirectly uses the abundant land of Canada and Australia, while they are enabled to use the relatively abundant labor and capital of Great Britain. Similarly, India and other countries that lack capital in effect obtain the use of the abundant capital of the United States by importing capital-intensive products, while the United States supplements its short labor supply by obtaining labor-intensive goods from India.

Measuring Gain

The concrete gain of any country from international trade may now be expressed as follows: imports, which if produced at home would require an uneconomical and costly use of resources, can be obtained more cheaply abroad. A given quantity of import goods can therefore be acquired for a smaller outlay of resources if those resources are used to produce exports and these are exchanged for the imports. Or, a given expenditure of resources will yield more import goods if devoted to export production than if used to produce the import goods directly.

To compute the gain from trade for any country would involve immense labor, even if it were possible to estimate with any accuracy what its imports would have cost had the country produced them itself instead of buying them from a cheaper foreign source.

Terms of Trade

A method widely used to estimate not the total gain from trade at any moment, but the trend of the gains from trade, does so by measuring changes in the barter or commodity terms of trade. These measure the *relation* between the prices a country gets for its exports and the prices it pays for its imports. If, as compared with this relation in a given or base year, its export prices rise or its import prices fall, its commodity terms of trade are said to have improved. If, on the other hand, the prices of its exports decline or the prices of its imports rise, its terms of trade are said to have worsened.

To make such comparisons, index numbers are used. For the base year, an average of a country's export prices is computed, with each commodity in the average weighted according to its importance in total trade. For a later year, a similar average is computed; it will reflect the average change in export prices. The same procedure is followed for imports. The change in the country's terms of trade can then be measured by obtaining a ratio of the change in export prices to the change in import prices.

$$T_c = \frac{P_{x_1}}{P_{xo}} \bigg/ \frac{P_{m_1}}{P_{mo}}$$

In this expression T_c stands for the commodity terms of trade, the subscripts x and m for exports and imports respectively, and the subscripts 1 and 0 for the given year and the base year.

Thus, taking 1937 as the base year and expressing both British export and import prices for that year as 100, we find that in 1956 the index of export prices had risen to 339, that for import prices to 385. The terms of trade, consequently, had changed as follows:

$$T_c = \frac{339}{100} \bigg/ \frac{385}{100} = 88$$

Since Britain's import prices had risen more than its export prices, the terms of trade had deteriorated, by 12 per cent as compared with 1937. This can be interpreted as meaning either that for a *given* amount of exports, Britain could obtain 12 per cent less imports, or that to purchase a *given* amount of imports, Britain had to give up 13.6 per cent more exports.

Although changes in the commodity terms of trade by themselves indicate the direction of movement of the gains from trade, their implication may be seriously modified by accompanying change of other kinds. We must reckon with at least three offsetting elements: changes in the character of the statistical data themselves, changes in the volume of trade, and changes in productivity.

1. Index numbers of export and import prices often make no allowance for variations in the quality of the goods traded, or for changes in the composition of goods entering into international trade. Unless specifically corrected, a barter terms-of-trade index shows only what has happened to the relative

prices of exports and imports that were traded in a certain base year. Yet changes in the quality of goods can be enormous, while new goods are constantly entering the ranks of traded commodities.

This point is particularly important in connection with recent discussions of the terms of trade of primary producing countries. Thus a United Nations' publication shows that according to the price indexes used, the terms of trade between primary products and finished industrial goods deteriorated substantially (from 100 to 64) between 1876–80 and 1936–38. This proves, it is claimed, that only 64 per cent as large a volume of manufactured goods could be purchased with a given amount of primary products at the end of this period as at the beginning.[3]

Besides other defects, this interpretation of the statistical results completely ignores the fact that while the primary exports of 1938 were substantially the same as primary exports in 1875, manufactured imports had improved tremendously in quality.[4] Consider the nylon stockings of today as constrasted with the cotton stockings of 1875, or the mercury vapor lamp as compared with the kerosene lamp. Moreover, many commodities, such as the automobile, the television set, and the radio, were unknown in 1875 and hence cannot be given any weight in index numbers covering such a long span of years.

Because changes in the quality and the composition of exports or imports are constantly taking place, the conventional conclusion drawn from variations in an index of the commodity terms of trade must be limited to short periods. Even then, the evidence must be treated with care. As for long periods—for example, more than ten years—any statement about changing terms of trade will in all likelihood have to be highly qualified.

2. Subject to the forgoing qualification, a fall in the commodity terms of trade implies that a *given* quantity of exports will buy a smaller quantity of imports than formerly. Suppose, however, that the volume of exports has simultaneously risen, perhaps as a consequence of their lower prices. The exporting country's "capacity to import" may remain unchanged or even improve, despite the poorer terms on which it trades.

Such changes in the volume of trade can be taken into account by an index of the *income terms of trade*, which is simply the commodity or barter terms multiplied by an index of the change in export volume: $T_y = T_c(Q_{x1}/Q_{x0})$. Thus between 1950 and 1960, Colombia's commodity terms

[3] United Nations, Economic Commission for Latin America, *The Economic Development of Latin America and Its Principal Problems* (E/CN.12/89/Rev. 1. 1950). Table I.

[4] For a discussion of the issues at stake, see J. Viner, *International Trade and Economic Development*, pp. 143-44. Published 1952 by The Free Press, Glencoe, Ill.; also P. T. Ellsworth, "The Terms of Trade Between Primary Producing and Industrial Countries," *Inter-American Economic Affairs*, X (Summer, 1956); Theodore Morgan, "The Long-Run Terms of Trade Between Agriculture and Manufacturing," *Economic Development and Cultural Change* (October, 1959).

of trade fell from 100 to 91, but the volume of her exports rose from 100 to 128. Had her exports remained constant, in 1960 they would have purchased nine per cent less imports than in 1950. But owing to the increased export volume, the country was actually able to import, in 1960, 17 per cent more than in 1950 (91 × 128/100 = 117). Although each unit of exports would command a smaller quantity of imports than before, the country's capacity to import had improved. The income terms of trade, it should be noted, carry no implication of gain or loss from trade. They do, however, indicate any change in a country's ability to pay for its imports with its exports, which may be very important.

3. A movement in the commodity terms of trade may be partly or wholly offset by a change in the efficiency with which exports are produced. Thus suppose that, while a country's import prices on the average remain constant, the costs and prices of its exports fall ten per cent because of an increase in productivity. An index of the commodity terms of trade would then indicate that these had worsened by the percentage decline in costs. There would be no real worsening of the country's position, however, for although a given value of exports can now command ten per cent less imports, the exports required to obtain the imports can be produced for a correspondingly reduced expenditure of resources. The real cost of imports, in terms of resources used, is unchanged.

An index of the *single factoral terms of trade* could take such a change in productivity into account. Simply multiply the commodity terms of trade by an index of the change in physical productivity in the export industries: $T_f = T_c(R_1/R_2)$. Use of this measure of changes in the terms of trade is limited by the difficulties in obtaining the data necessary to compute an index of productivity. Very rough approximations may have to be used, amounting to little more than "guesstimates," but the point is important and should always be borne in mind.[5]

Different Cost Conditions

We know that commodities may be supplied under conditions of increasing, decreasing, or constant cost. Does the gain from trade in any way depend upon which of these conditions holds good? We have seen that if the imports are produced at constant or decreasing cost, production in the importing country will cease. But if conditions of increasing cost hold, some home production may continue. Imports will be limited to that volume for which marginal cost is equal to the marginal cost of domestic supplies of the good. The intramarginal gain is still there.

[5] For a fuller discussion of the terms of trade and additional ways of measuring changes, see J. Viner, *Studies in the Theory of International Trade,* pp. 558-70. Published 1937 by Harper & Brothers, New York. See also Gerald M. Meier, *International Trade and Development,* Chapter 3. Published 1963 by Harper & Row, New York.

Holland, for example, imports some of its grain, though it raises some itself. Were that country unable to procure wheat, rye, and other grains from abroad, the resources now used to produce the exports exchanged for grain would have to be shifted onto its scanty agricultural land, marginal costs would rise sharply, and the additional grain obtained would be far less than current imports.

But what if a country's exports are also produced at increasing cost? Then if it withdraws from international trade, it can reduce production of these commodities to the smaller amount required for home consumption, and their marginal cost will be substantially lower. Is it not possible that the loss from higher-priced export goods, some of which are consumed at home, will offset the gain from lower-priced imports?

The answer is "no." For remember that exports embody large amounts of a country's abundant factors, while its imports contain large quantities of factors that are scarce at home. To produce domestic substitutes for imports would increase the demand for scarce factors and drive up costs sharply. Producing export-type goods with which to buy imports would increase demand primarily for factors that are abundant and costs would rise more moderately. Resources can be more efficiently used to produce exports than to produce substitutes for imports.

EFFECTS OF TRADE ON FACTOR PRICES

Seeking profitable employment of their energies and their capital, individual businessmen, firms, and farmers undertake, in each country, the production of a wide variety of goods and services. If they exercise good judgment, they take into account as best they can the competitive situation they are likely to face, the cost of materials, the availability and wages of the kinds of labor they will need, and the availability and cost of capital and suitable land. These bases of each decision to produce or not to produce are determined, in an economy linked to others by the ties of trade, by such forces as the strength of demands in the various economies, relative factor supplies, alternative production methods, economies of scale, and transport costs. Under the guidance of these forces, an immense number of individual decisions to invest capital and employ labor results in the emergence, in each country, of many different industries, some producing for a sheltered home market, others sending their goods to the far corners of the world.

Prices of Traded Goods

Concerning goods that cross national borders, these sell everywhere at the same price, after allowing for costs of transport and other obstacles to trade. (The existence of monopoly, of course, may lead to price discrimination in different markets.) The effect of international trade, in other words, is to equalize prices which, in the absence of such trade, would differ very substantially.

Factor Price Equalization

International trade does more than equalize the prices of traded goods. It also exerts a strong influence toward equalizing the prices of the factors that make these goods. For the corollary of one country's specialization on its cheap-factor products is the concentration of world demand for that factor's services on the abundant supply available in that country and in others similarly situated. Similarly, the demand of this country for its scarce and expensive factors is shifted to other countries, where they are abundant and cheap. As a consequence of this reshuffling of demands, the price of each country's abundant factors tends to rise; of its scarce factors, to fall. Factor prices throughout the world therefore tend to become more uniform and equal.

To illustrate: Canada possesses abundant and relatively cheap land suited to producing wheat. Its production costs are low and it exports large quantities. The demand in more populous nations for this land-intensive product and therefore for the services of land is focused upon Canada (and also upon Australia, Argentina, and the prairie states of the United States). Land rents in Canada are, in consequence, higher than they would be had Britain and other western European countries been forced to depend for their wheat supplies upon their own scanty agricultural land; rents are correspondingly lower in the latter.

Need for Factor Mobility

Complete factor price equalization throughout the world, and, therewith the most efficient use of its factors, could be attained only if the factors were fully mobile. Although natural resources cannot move to achieve this result, it would be closely approximated if capital and labor could be freely redistributed. Then, infertile regions of the earth would be deserted, and food production would be concentrated in the most fertile regions, together with most of the population and most of the industry. Each of these settled areas would be comparatively self-sufficient, requiring imports only of such special products as minerals, lumber, and fish, coming from those scattered small centers of economic activity where the relevant natural resources were located. Wages would be the same for comparable skills in China, India, the United States, and Europe, and the entire world would share a common rate of interest.

Obstacles to Factor Price Equalization

Although international trade works in the same direction as international mobility of the factors—toward equalizing factor returns everywhere—for a number of reasons it cannot achieve the complete equalization that mobility would bring. For one thing, transport and other costs of trading prevent the equalization of commodity prices that would be necessary were factor returns also to be equalized.

Second, where there is great inequality of factor endowments, the concentration of the world's demand for specific factors upon those regions where they are most abundant is not sufficiently powerful to offset the initial great disparity in supply. To illustrate, it is inconceivable that even if the rest of the world bought all its labor-intensive goods from such areas as China and India, this would suffice to raise wages in the latter and lower them in the former until they were equal. Countries in which labor is the scarce factor can shift only *part* of their demand for labor onto countries in which labor is abundant, since the demand for the factors is a joint demand. *Some* labor must always be combined with capital and natural resources.

Third, the equalizing effect of the channeling of world demands toward abundant factor supplies is reduced when alternative methods of production can be used. When a capital-intensive process was developed for producing rice, for example, part of the demand hitherto directed especially toward the labor of Burma and Thailand was shifted toward U.S. capital.[6]

Injury to a Scarce Factor

In spite of these obstacles to complete equalization of factor prices, international trade unquestionably works in this direction. Any country's abundant factor receives a higher return, and its scarce factor receives a lower return, than it would in the absence of such trade. From the point of view of the entire world supply of the factors, the average reward of each is raised. Yet from the national point of view, a country's scarce factor is injured.

In a country where labor is the scarce factor, this effect of international trade might be socially important, and justify, in terms of a desirable distribution of income, the protection of labor-intensive industries.[7] Its practical significance, however, is doubtful. The entire argument is based upon the static assumption that the supply of each factor is fixed and unchanging. In the

---

[6] Theoretically, if any country specialized *completely* on a certain product, this alone would be sufficient to prevent factor price equalization, since it would eliminate contact between the ratio of commodity exchange and the ratios of factor reward. Practically, this case is unimportant, since the argument rests on the assumption of two countries and two commodities, with one or both countries devoting all its resources to specialized production. With the numerous lines of production actually open to any country, complete specialization on one or even a few becomes almost inconceivable.

We leave to one side the effect of factor reversal, on the ground that in a world of many factors, its role would be dubious. In a two-factor world, of course, the phenomenon of factor reversal means that insofar as any countries export the products of their scarce factors, factor price differences tend to be increased.

[7] For a statement of the theoretical basis for such protection, see p. 228.

real world, this is not true; factor supplies can and do change. If capital is the abundant factor, the growth of trade will cause its return to rise. Moreover, as we have already shown in the last section, even though the real income of one factor may decline, that of the entire community will be raised by international trade. With a larger total income, and with capital receiving an increased reward, it is probable that savings will increase. Over a period of years, labor would then stand to gain by having a larger total complement of capital to assist it in production. Nor should we overlook the possibility that an expanding supply of capital, by holding down the interest rate, will encourage the growth of capital-intensive industries, a development that is likely to stimulate technological advance, to the benefit of all elements in the community, including labor.

Even if none of these things happens, the disadvantage to which scarce labor is subjected may be counteracted by a deliberate act of government policy. Taxes may be levied on those who gain because of trade, and the proceeds distributed to labor, either directly or as a supplement to wages, or by the socially more acceptable method of financing social security, recreation facilities, or simply a larger share of ordinary government operations.

FACTOR ENDOWMENTS AND THE PATTERN OF TRADE

If the model of international trade we summarized at the beginning of this chapter really works, we should be able to show that trade actually does proceed in accordance with its principles. There should be some sort of system in the trading relations of the world, with the flow of goods dominated by international disparity in endowments with the major categories of factors—land, labor, and capital. We should expect to see a large volume of exports of agricultural products moving from land-rich countries in exchange for the manufactures, handicrafts, and other goods produced in countries where capital or labor is abundant. Within this broad schema, of course, there would be many cross currents. For as we know, the division of the productive factors into three main categories is only valid as a first approximation; in a more detailed account we have to consider at least three or four different kinds of labor and several kinds of agricultural land, in addition to specific types of natural resources such as mineral deposits.

Factor Endowment and Specialization: 1870–1890

To obtain the broad view here in question, let us look first at the much simpler world of the 1870's and 1880's, just after the expansion of railways had opened up the major grain-producing or Great Plains regions (Argentina, Australia, Canada, Russia, and the United States). At that time the more important trading nations of the world could have been grouped into four main regions in accordance with the test of relative factor supply. In the tropics, particularly in the parts for which trade was of considerable importance (India, Ceylon, and the Dutch East Indies), population was relatively dense, capital very scarce, and land, as compared with the other regions, in moderate supply. In the United Kingdom, transformed by the Industrial Revolution into the world's premier manufacturing nation, capital was far more abundant than elsewhere, land scarce, and labor in an intermediate position. Continental Europe, with a dense population, was behind the United Kingdom in the accumulation of capital and in industrial development, but like it in the possession of a relatively small area of usable land. In the Great Plains area, of course, land was the most abundant factor, capital in short supply, and labor only moderately abundant. Thus the relative factor supply structure in these major trading regions looked approximately like this:

Relative Factor Supply	Tropics	Great Plains Regions	Continental Europe	United Kingdom
Ample	Labor	Land	Labor	Capital
Moderate	Land	Labor	Capital	Labor
Scarce	Capital	Capital	Land	Land

Now consider the main features of trade in this period. The records are inadequate to permit us to state with any precision the direction or size of net export or import balances, but they are perfectly clear as to the character of the goods exchanged between the various regions. The United Kingdom was the great exporter of manufactures to the rest of the world. These ranged from light consumer goods such as cotton and wool textiles, pottery, notions, and hardware to heavy capital goods such as railway rails and rolling stock, stationary engines, pumps, and mining equipment.

The Great Plains regions, of course, supplied the United Kingdom and Continental Europe principally with meats, wheat, wool, and (from the United States alone) cotton. Except in the United States, even the production of manufactures for local use was in its infancy, and although the United States exported some specialized manufactured goods, they totaled only a little more than one-tenth of all its exports.

The tropics, with labor as the abundant factor, exported such labor-intensive agricultural products as rice, raw silk, tea, cocoa, coffee, and spices and fine handicrafts such as lacquer ware, silk fabrics, and fine cotton goods.

Continental Europe stood in a position intermediate between industrial Britain and the predominantly agricultural areas. Production of wheat, in the face of competition from the prairies overseas, declined (except in Russia), and farmers increasingly turned to more labor-intensive commodities—in particular, butter and cheese, eggs, ham and bacon, perfumes, and temperate and subtropical varieties of fruits. Lumber exports also grew in importance, and manufactures, especially those demanding close attention by skilled labor (watches, jewelry, fine leather goods, lace), expanded steadily.

These results may be portrayed in tabular form:

Type of Product	Tropics	Great Plains Regions	Continental Europe	United Kingdom
Labor-intensive	Tropical agricultural products; handicrafts		Dairy products; skilled labor manufactures	
Land-intensive		Grains, meats wool, cotton		
Capital-intensive				Light and heavy manufactures

Changes in Relative Factor Endowment

During the generation between 1890 and the 1920's the relatively simple factor-supply structure of the 1870's and 1880's changed appreciably. There were large international movements of labor and capital, and internal growth through capital accumulation and the increase of population was substantial.

The most striking case is that of the United States. Between 1880 and 1914, the international movement of population totaled approximately 40 million, of whom most came from Europe. Over half proceeded to the United States, meeting the demand for labor for its expanding factories and farms without, however, changing the status of labor as the relatively scarce factor. Since productivity continued to be high and rising as North America's natural resources were exploited, and entrepreneurs reaped large gains therefrom without hindrance from progressive income taxes, capital accumulation was rapid. By the 1920's, it would appear to have become relatively more abundant even than the land factor, at least in the Northeast.

The Great Plains regions shared in the growth of population from European immigration, and benefited also from large capital movements, principally from the United Kingdom, as well as from rapid domestic accumulation. Land remained the abundant factor, but a more rapid rise in the supply of capital than of population enabled it to displace labor as the factor in moderate supply.

In the Tropics, the benefits of trade were largely taken out in the form of population increases, while in spite of sizeable investment of European funds, the general poverty kept the supply of capital relatively scanty.

In Europe, large-scale emigration held down the growth of population, while at the same time its increasing industrialization and urbanization slowed down the birth rate in the more advanced countries. Population continued to increase, though less rapidly than formerly. Meanwhile, the profits from its expanding industry, especially prominent in Germany, Belgium, France, Switzerland, and Sweden, were invested in this very expansion. As capital accumulated, it ceased to be the scarce factor and became at least moderately abundant.

By the 1920's the relative position of the major trading regions of the world with respect to factor supplies appears to have assumed the following pattern:

Relative Factor Supply	Tropics	United States	Great Plains	Continental Europe	United Kingdom
Ample	Labor	Capital	Land	Labor	Capital
Moderate	Land	Land	Capital	Capital	Labor
Scarce	Capital	Labor	Labor	Land	Land

Factor Endowments, Pre-World War II

This conclusion is supported by such data as are available. These include fairly reliable estimates of agricultural land and of the working population and very rough estimates of the value of capital stock in five major regions of the world. The land and capital figures for each region were divided by those for the working population, thus converting them into the amount of land and capital per worker. These data are shown in columns (1) and (3) of Table 10.1. The working population is given a value of 1 in each region (column 2), since the figure for land and capital is relative to each region's working population.

Table 10.1. RELATIVE SUPPLIES OF CAPITAL, LABOR, AND LAND IN MAJOR REGIONS, 1935-38

Region	(1) Capital Per Worker	(2) Working Population	(3) Land Per Worker
United Kingdom	5,024	1	0.94
Western Europe	2,500	1	1.08
United States	4,365	1	9.0
Great Plains	4,290	1	43.9
Tropics	510	1	4.57

NOTE: The data on capital were derived from Colin Clark, *The Economics of 1960* (London: Macmillan, 1942), p. 80, and are expressed in "International units," defined as the amount of goods and services that could be purchased for $1.00 in the United States over the average of the decade 1925-34. Figures for working populations used in the computations are from the same source. The data on agricultural land are based on materials in Food and Agriculture Organization of the United Nations, *Yearbook of Food and Agricultural Statistics,* 1952, Vol. VI, Part I (Rome, Italy), pp. 3-7. Both arable and pasture land are included; they are expressed in hectares.

The capital data relate to the years 1935-38; those for the working population are for the same period. The figures for land are for the year 1951. Since land areas changed inappreciably between 1937 and 1951, the various data may be regarded as closely comparable. The same countries are included in each region for all three factors compared. They are: Western Europe—Germany-Austria, France, Belgium-Luxembourg, Italy, Switzerland, the Netherlands, Sweden, Norway, Denmark, and Czechoslovakia; Great Plains—Argentina, Uruguay, Australia, Canada, New Zealand; Tropics—India, Pakistan, South Asia, Africa, and Oceania other than Australia and New Zealand.

To determine which factor is relatively the most abundant and which the scarcest in each region, we must look at the figures for the three factors in each region in relation to their values in all the other regions. Doing this, we see that in the United Kingdom, capital has the highest value for any region, land the lowest, clearly indicating that these are the abundant and the scarce factors in the U.K., with labor in the intermediate position. The data for the Great Plains stand out equally sharply; its figure for land is the highest of all, that for capital is relatively large. Land is abundant; capital is in relatively moderate supply; labor is relatively the least abundant.

In the United States, capital and land are both abundant relatively to the other regions. But the capital figure is higher than the average of 3,336 for all regions, while the land figure is below the average (11.9), though exceeded only by that for the Great Plains. The abundant factor is capital, labor the scarce one, with land in between.

As for Western Europe, both capital and land show values that are below the average. That for land, however, is relatively much lower. Land is the scarce factor, capital is in moderate supply, and labor (with a value that *relative* to the others is highest) is the abundant factor. Similar reasoning shows that in the Tropics, labor is relatively abundant, capital scarce, while land falls in between.

World Trade in the Inter-War Period

Consider now the trade between these areas. Empirical studies have shown that, as of 1928, it fell into a well-defined multilateral pattern, illustrated by the following diagram.[8] The arrows point in the direction of net export balances of merchandise trade, whose values in millions of dollars

---

[8] The original study is *The Network of World Trade* (League of Nations, 1942). The detailed data of this study are summarized and discussed in Folke Hilgerdt, "The Case for Multilateral Trade," *American Economic Review,* XXXIII, No. 1, Pt. 2 Supplement (March, 1943). The diagram used here is the modified one in the article by Karl-Erik Hansson, "A General Theory of the System of Multilateral Trade," *American Economic Review,* XLII, No. 1 (March, 1952). I have also used Hansson's simplified method of stating relative factor-supply structures.

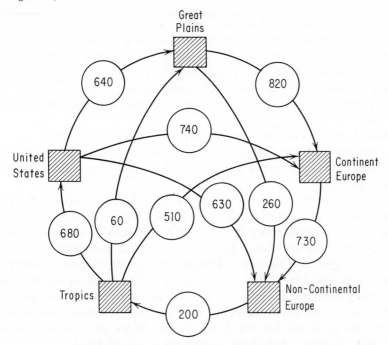

FIGURE 10.1   The System of Multilateral Trade

are inscribed in the circles. The countries represented in the diagram in 1928 accounted for nine-tenths of total world trade.[9]

The Tropics had a large export balance with the United States, reflecting heavy U.S. purchases of tropical produce (coffee, tea, rubber, fruits, vegetable oils) and minerals (petroleum, copper, manganese). Based on relative abundance of labor and of tropical land (as well as specific mineral deposits), these exports provided a large proportion of the raw materials needed by American industry and of highly specific consumption requirements.

Next, the capital-rich United States economy complemented the land-rich economies of the Great Plains by shipping large quantities of tractors and other agricultural machinery, automobiles, and industrial goods generally— some $640 million worth more than its imports of wool, leather, meat and minerals.

The Great Plains region, in turn, exported a large net balance of its

[9] The Great Plains include, besides the four countries in Table 10.1, Paraguay and South Africa. Continental Europe comprises all continental European countries except the U.S.S.R., and is thus more inclusive than the region, "Western Europe," used in that table. Non-Continental Europe is the United Kingdom plus Ireland and Iceland and a few small islands. The Tropics is much more representative than the table, since it is limited to truly tropical countries, whereas in Table 10.1 many countries are included that are not in the tropics.

land-intensive products—principally wool, grains, and meat—to Continental Europe. This region, though its factor structure resembles that of non-Continental Europe (substantially the U.K.), nonetheless exported to the latter, on balance, more specialized manufactures than it received, as well as large amounts of such relatively labor-intensive commodities as dairy products, bacon, eggs, and wines, together with lumber and wood-pulp from the northern European forests.

Finally, non-Continental Europe, like the United States, drew upon the land and labor of the Tropics for many raw materials and consumption items, but unlike the United States, exported a still larger value of manufactured goods.

In addition to the direct movement of trade balances around the circle, which if equal in amount would permit each region to cancel its import balance to the preceding member by its export balance to the next, large net balances ran from the United States direct to both European regions, and from the Tropics to Continental Europe. Settlement of these balances and of the gap in the circular flow caused by the relatively small export balance from non-Continental Europe to the Tropics was made possible by an opposite movement of service items, such as freight charges, insurance, and interest and dividends for which the United States and the Tropics were indebted to Europe. (U.S. loans, especially to Germany, were also important at this time.)

Taking the pattern of trade shown by the diagram together with the factor-supply structure indicated by the table, we see that theoretical expectations based on the latter are borne out by the actual movement of trade. The major trading regions of the world complemented one another in terms of factor supplies, and their trade corresponded fairly well to factor endowments in broad terms of the three main categories. A more detailed account, of course, would have to use a narrower classification, and consider as well other relevant determinants of trade such as transport costs, economies of scale, monopolistic restrictions, and government policies as embodied in tariffs, subsidies, and the like.

SELECTED REFERENCES

Hansson, Karl-Erik, "A General Theory of the System of Multilateral Trade," *American Economic Review*, **XLII** (1952). Well worth consulting for a more elaborate statement of the application of the theory of international trade to the system of world trade.

Hilgerdt, Folke, "The Case for Multilateral Trade," *American Economic Review*, **XXXIII**, Supplement (1943). A pragmatic and well-documented formulation.

Kindleberger, Charles P., *International Economics*, 3rd ed. Homewood, Ill.: Richard D. Irwin, Inc., 1963. Chapter 16, "The Case for Free Multilateral Trade," has an excellent though brief discussion of the price system in relation both to efficiency and to general welfare considerations.

Leontief, W. W., "The Use of Indifference Curves in the Analysis of Foreign Trade," American Economic Association, *Readings in the Theory of International Trade*. Philadelphia: The Blakiston Co., 1949, chapter 10. Shows how indifference curves may be applied to international trade, and in particular, how the gain from trade may be demonstrated by this method.

Meade, James E., *Problems of Economic Union*. London: Geo. Allen & Unwin, Ltd., 1953. Pp. 56-72 contain a brief statement of the factor-price equalization argument, and of the principal obstacles to its operation. A less difficult version than Samuelson's.

Samuelson, Paul A., "The Gains from International Trade," American Economic Association, *Readings in the Theory of International Trade*. Philadelphia: The Blakiston Co., 1949, Chapter 11. This is the definitive proof of the gain from trade, expressed in mathematical language and in terms of the general equilibrium theory.

———, "International Trade and the Equalisation of Factor Prices," *Economic Journal*, **LVIII** (1948); **LIX** (1949). These two articles provide the fullest discussion of the tendency toward factor-price equalisation.

Scitovsky, Tibor, "A Reconsideration of the Theory of Tariffs," *Readings in the Theory of International Trade*, chapter 16. Provides an advanced though non-mathematical discussion of the gains from trade and of the possible use of tariffs by a single country to maximize its advantage.

Viner, Jacob, *Studies in the Theory of International Trade*. New York: Harper & Brothers, 1937. Chapters VIII and IX contain an exhaustive discussion of the issues and the literature of the gains from trade, in the setting of a real costs approach to international trade theory.

PART III

Internationalism and Its Rival

II

THE GROWTH OF AN
INTERNATIONAL ECONOMY

The body of theory whose study we have just completed explains the bases on which international trade rests and indicates in what ways nations can benefit from the specialization trade makes possible. In pointing to these gains, the theory serves as a policy prescription that has found wide, though not universal, acceptance. As a model that describes reality, however, it can be valid only if a number of critical assumptions are at least approximated in practice.

The more important of these are that capital and labor shall be highly mobile within a single country, substantially less so between countries; and that production and merchandising shall be effectively competitive. But for competition to be effective, buyers and sellers must be able to communicate readily with one another. This implies that trade shall be free, especially of direct quantitative restrictions, and that currencies shall be at least partially convertible into one another, for without convertibility contact between national markets is lost.

Europe in 1815

Conditions in the real world of the early nineteenth century were far different from those postulated in the theoretical model. Only in Great Britain and Holland was it comparatively easy for capital and labor to seek out those industries or occupations in which returns were highest, owing to the fact that in these countries alone had thoroughgoing national unification been achieved. Internal barriers to trade were nonexistent. The feudal order was a thing of the past; in Holland a good canal system, and in England canals, coastal shipping, and recently improved roads quickened the movements of goods and people. Men of commerce had long dominated the political and economic affairs of the Netherlands. In Great Britain, energetic and enterprising businessmen had already revolutionized the production of iron and cotton textiles and were spreading the new techniques over an

[181]

ever-widening range of industry. Although the landed aristocracy still dominated Parliament, the political influence of the business class was steadily increasing. British agriculture, too, had but recently undergone a revolutionary change in technology and provided a prosperous and efficient model for others to copy.

On the Continent, on the other hand, local tariffs, dues, and tolls impeded commerce, even in countries as united as France. Germany and Italy were still divided into petty kingdoms and principalities. ("Germany" consisted of some 300 independent territories, each with its own customs and currency system, and using a bewildering variety of weights and measures.) The feudal system, binding the peasant to the land and concentrating its ownership in the hands of a favored few, had only recently been demolished in France; over most of the rest of Europe, it retained a shaky dominance. Capital was scarce and the enterprise to use it even scarcer.

As for international trade, the complex Mercantilist structure of tariffs, prohibitions, bounties, and shipping regulations continued unimpaired. Even in Britain, the Navigation Acts were still in force, and what Adam Smith said in 1776 could have been repeated in 1815 with little change.

During the nineteenth century all this changed. Northwestern Europe became industrialized; its agriculture was improved; people and investment funds flowed from Britain, France and Germany to the Americas and other regions new and old; and the Mercantilist structure was thoroughly dismantled. From about 1860 until the outbreak of the first World War, one could say that the world of fact reasonably approximated the world of our theoretical model. It will be the task of this chapter to trace the main changes that occurred and to sketch the principal features of the international economy they brought into being.

Three aspects of change in the nineteenth century will be stressed. First, there is the rise of Great Britain to a position of economic and political pre-eminence, and the accompanying emergence of London as the world's economic nerve center. Second is the rapid economic growth of western Europe and then of the overseas regions settled by Europeans. And finally, there is the demolition of the surviving remnants of Mercantilism, the restrictions on foreign trade. These strands of history were, of course, closely interwoven; it is possible to distinguish them only for purposes of analysis. Together they produced the institutions and the forces that constituted a truly international economy.

THE RISE OF BRITAIN

Industry

During the sixty years between 1815 and 1875, the Industrial Revolution continued its work of transforming the predominantly agrarian economy of Britain into the workshop of the world. The weaving of cotton textiles, still a hand-loom operation at the turn of the century, gradually gave way to machinery. By 1875 the hand-loom was extinct. A few years later the woolen industry, too, succumbed to mechanization. With this technical progress, costs fell, and British textiles, even with expanding output in Europe and the United States, dominated markets from Shanghai to Buenos Aires. Iron had become liberated from its dependence on charcoal and was now processed with coke from the rich British coalfields; it found expanding uses as new machines were perfected and took over more and more operations. From less than a quarter of a million tons in 1800, pig-iron production expanded fifty times in the next seventy-five years. By 1875, Great Britain accounted for more than all the rest of the world put together. The factory system, with its clanking machines, its soot and smoke, its sprawling slums, but also with its cheaper and more abundant stream of cottons, woolens, glass, pottery, leather goods, and the tools and machines to make them, attracted more and more workers from farms and fields. City dwellers, from a mere 31 per cent in 1801, came by 1871 to comprise 61 per cent of the population. Though rivals were emerging, they presented as yet no serious challenge. Britain stood out alone as the world's sole industrial nation.

It was the displacement of manual by mechanical operations in industry after industry that mainly accounted for the phenomenal growth in the output of coal and iron, the dominant materials of the age. No other product of the nineteenth century even began to compare with machines as a consumer of iron and steel. And the greatest pressure on these resources came when the steam engine acquired mobility by land and sea with the appearance of the locomotive and the steamship. These early nineteenth century inventions[1] not only required iron and steel to build them and coal to drive them; far larger quantities of iron and steel were needed for rails, wheels, carriages, and miscellaneous gear, and later (especially after 1850) in the construction of ships.

Transportation

Although the railway and the steamship gave a tremendous impetus to the growth of the iron and steel industry, their real importance lay in their true function—that of providing rapid, reliable, and cheap transport of goods and people. Within a quarter century after the first short line opened in 1825, Great Britain had acquired its main trunk lines. The dray, the carriage, and the canal boat became, instead of the sole means of transport, supplements to the railroad—supplements of ever declining importance. By 1880, some 18 thousand miles of lines crisscrossed the country with a dense network.

Though the steamship antedated the railway as a new form of transport by some twenty years, technical problems delayed its extended use by several

---

[1] Although preceded by earlier experimental models, the first successful steamboat was Robert Fulton's *Clermont* (1807), and the first successful locomotive, George Stephenson's *Rocket* (1825).

decades. Not until 1865 did steamships become quantitatively important; they then comprised some 15 per cent of total British shipping tonnage. In the meantime, greatly increased numbers of sailing vessels served the needs of expanding world trade. British ships and sailors maintained and extended their earlier lead; by 1850, about 60 per cent of world shipping tonnage was of British registry. Toward the end of the century, when steamer tonnage far exceeded that of sailing vessels, Britain's share of the world's merchant fleet reached a peak of 73 per cent.

Trade

As her railways ensured speedy and cheap delivery of raw materials to processors and of finished goods to shipping ports, as her expanding fleet furnished ready means of carrying her industrial products to overseas markets and of bringing back raw materials and foodstuffs of every kind, Britain's trade mounted ever higher. Exports tripled in the first half of the nineteenth century, and almost tripled again in the second half. Imports grew even more rapidly, reflecting the country's increased dependence on foreign raw materials and foods; they expanded nearly fivefold by 1850, and trebled again by 1900. Textiles and textile products continually exceeded all other exports; in the early 1880's they accounted for just over half the value of total exports. Taken together, coal, and iron and steel and their products comprised another quarter. The remaining exports were scattered among a wide variety of industries.

As Britain's population moved into the cities and as the nation specialized increasingly in the production of manufactures, her dependence on foreign farms, plantations, and mines grew constantly. At the end of the Napoleonic Wars, the country was still largely self-sufficient as to foods; as for raw materials, it needed no foreign wool nor iron ore, but had to import all its cotton and most of its timber. With the needs of her growing population (15 million in 1800, 44 million in 1900) constantly rising, and with her expanding exports, Britain rapidly lost most of her relative independence. By the close of the century, close to 60 per cent of the wheat and flour consumed in the country came from overseas. Imports of meat began in the seventies; with the introduction of refrigeration after 1876, cheap Argentine beef and Australian mutton steadily displaced the products of local slaughterhouses. To ever-growing imports of cotton and timber were added wool from Australia, which with later supplies from Uruguay and South Africa eventually furnished practically all of this fiber. After 1860, imports of rich Spanish iron ores began to supplement those of native origin; by 1885 imports amounted to almost a quarter of domestic ore production. In addition to these most basic imports, purchases of innumerable other products— hemp, jute, and flax; tin, copper, lead, and nickel; tea, coffee, and cocoa— also reflected the growing specialization of Britain and of her suppliers.

Specialized Market Facilities

An interesting and important result of expanding imports of highly specialized products was the emergence one after another of specialized marketing facilities. Some of these were of long standing, such as the markets for spices and sugar, in which specialized dealers and brokers had carried on an active import and reexport business since at least Elizabethan times. After 1846, with the steady increase in wheat imports that followed the repeal of the Corn Laws, specialized trading in this and other grains coming from Russia centered in the Baltic Coffee House in London, long a rendez-vous for general traders. Simultaneously, Liverpool began to develop specialized facilities for dealings in imports from America. With the flood of cheap American wheat after 1870, when railways opened up the western States, Liverpool came to outrank London as a market. Liverpool, as the port nearest the cotton manufacturing towns, also became the outstanding cotton market, with organized exchanges dealing in both "spot" and "future" transactions in standardized grades. London had long been the country's chief market for transactions in wool; as imports outdistanced domestic production in importance, it became the great distributing center for the world.

The London Money Market

Of all the specialized markets that developed in Great Britain as that nation rose to a position of commercial and industrial preeminence, none was as important in its contribution to the country's leadership as the London money market; for it was the gradual perfection of London's banking and financial facilities that made the pound sterling a true world currency, and the entire world a sterling area.

London had for centuries been the commercial and financial metropolis of the kingdom. By the end of the Napoleonic Wars, its banking business was conducted by over 800 private, unincorporated banks, the sixty strongest being located in London, the rest scattered throughout the country. To finance the stream of commodities moving to London for local use, for re-distribution to other parts of the nation, or for export, provincial traders and manufacturers drew bills of exchange on their London customers, ordering them to pay the sum due to some city bank. These bills they dis-counted with a local country bank, from which they received the amount owed less a discount. The country bank then forwarded these bills of ex-change to the London bank of its choice, which either held the bill for collection, say thirty or sixty days later, or rediscounted it immediately for cash itself or with some other bank with funds to invest. Immediately or later, the country bank acquired deposits in London to compensate it for its pay-ments to local clients.

Simultaneously, goods moved from London to the provinces. For these, provincial buyers had to make payment in London. They did so by purchasing bills of exchange drawn on its London correspondent by a local bank. These ordered the former to pay the sum specified to the London merchant. In this way the deposits built up in London by county banks were constantly being depleted. Buyers and sellers in the provinces paid their bills to and received payment from local banks; their opposites in London received or paid London funds. Little gold or currency had to move in either direction, the great bulk of transactions being cleared against one another.

BILL BROKERS AND DEALERS   If this mechanism was to work efficiently, someone had to stand ready to discount the large numbers of country bills of exchange constantly being drawn, ordinarily not for immediate but only for a later payment. As the volume of this business increased, specialized agencies arose to put up the money, or to find someone who would. The first to appear, just as the struggle with Napoleon ended, was the bill broker. For some time, he was just what his name implies—a financial go-between, seeking out the bills of country merchants and bankers, locating banks with surplus funds, and persuading the latter to invest in the bills in his care. For his trouble and his knowledge, he exacted a small commission.

About 50 years later, the bill broker began to give way to the dealer. The bill dealer was himself a principal, not just an agent. Using sizeable funds of his own or borrowing for short periods at the big London banks, he took up bills on his own account. Still later came the so-called discount house, which was simply the dealer writ large; it had more capital of its own; it took deposits from the public and paid interest on them; and it did a greater volume of business.

ACCEPTANCE HOUSES   The acceptance function, the second task to be taken over by a highly specialized group, was from the latter part of the eighteenth or the early part of the nineteenth century performed by various leading London mercantile firms. Because of the great knowledge they acquired as to the credit-worthiness of an immense number of merchants and manufacturers with whom they did business, they could afford to underwrite, as it were, the bills of exchange of reliable individuals and firms whose names were less well known than theirs. This they did by simply writing "accepted," together with their signature, across the face of a bill. For this act, which amounted to guaranteeing the bill, they received a small commission. The effect was that:

> In plain English the man with second-class credit paid a commission to the possessor of first-class credit and thereby secured an improvement in the discount terms which was equal to an amount far in excess of the small commission paid for the accommodation.[2]

[2] Ellis T. Powell, *The Evolution of the Money Market*, p. 374. Copyright 1915 by the Financial News, London.

As the volume of their business increased, and as England waxed wealthier and began to invest in the securities of foreign governments and railways, some of the more prominent of these trading firms dropped their mercantile transactions and specialized in the business of acceptance and of security issues. Because of their foreign connections and because of the phenomenal growth of British foreign trade, the bulk of their acceptance business had to do with international transactions. Down to about 1850, these great acceptance and issue houses also had a near monopoly of the foreign exchange business—that is, the purchase and sale of bills and drafts running in terms of foreign currencies. Later, they began to leave this part of their operations to be carried out by a new class of financial institutions, the branches of foreign banks that appeared in London after the Franco-Prussian War.

At the same time that some of these more important houses were turning their attention increasingly to the issue of securities, others, together with newcomers, specialized entirely in the acceptance business. By the end of the nineteenth century, the function of accepting, as well as that of discounting, was very largely in the hands of highly specialized firms and companies. Some part of each type of business, however, was undertaken by the commercial banks, particularly by the branches of foreign and colonial banks that came to London after 1870.

THE BANK OF ENGLAND Occupying a central position in this banking system was the Bank of England. Privately owned, its directors insisted on regarding it as in no essential different from any other private bank. Nonetheless, it had even by the end of the eighteenth century come to perform certain of the functions typical of a central bank: (1) it carried on all of the banking business of the government, and during the Napoleonic Wars had been its financial right hand; (2) it maintained the only gold reserve of importance in the kingdom; and (3) it kept in the form of deposits a large part of the reserves of all other London banks.

Nowadays it is a commonly accepted duty of a central bank to provide commercial banks with additional reserves in time of need by rediscounting certain types of commercial paper. This duty the Bank of England came to accept only grudgingly and reluctantly. In a whole series of early crises, when extraordinary demands for currency or gold caused a drain on the reserves of the commercial banks, refusal of the Bank to play the role of "lender of last resort" forced the government to take the initiative. It did so either (as in 1793 and 1811) by advancing Exchequer bills to merchants against the security of goods, or (as in 1847 and 1857) by promising the Bank legislation indemnifying it for issuing its notes liberally, in excess of the legal limit.

Finally, in 1866 the Bank on its own initiative lent freely to meet the demands upon it, and in a letter to the Chancellor of the Exchequer, laid the facts before him. His reply authorized free lending to stem the crisis. Following this action, there was considerable dispute as to the wisdom of the Bank's accepting the duty of acting as "lender of last resort." The issue was finally settled by the publication of Bagehot's *Lombard Street*, whose

> lucid common sense . . . was itself decisive. Since then the responsibilities of the Banking Department as the lender of last resort have been unequivocably recognised.[3]

SUMMARY We are now in a position to see the London money market as a whole and to examine its operation. The London banks, including the branches of foreign and colonial banks, furnished the principal source of funds for financing the short-term requirements of industry and commerce. This was supplemented to some extent by the capital of bill dealers and discount houses and by money deposited by the public with the latter. The ultimate borrowers of these funds were traders and manufacturers in London, in various parts of the United Kingdom, and—increasingly as the nineteenth century wore on—exporters and importers all over the globe. British borrowers obtained part of their short-term working capital by direct loans from one or more of the London or country banks; the rest they raised by offering their bills of exchange on the discount market, which furnished practically all the funds supplied to foreigners. Bills coming on the discount market, if from a well-known and established firm, whether domestic or foreign, would either be discounted directly by a bill dealer or a discount house, or parceled out among the banks by the bill brokers. If the borrowing firm was not outstanding, it had its credits validated by one of the specialized acceptance houses before placing it on the discount market.

In normal times the supply of funds lent at short-term by the banks to their clients, together with those available in the discount market, was adequate to finance smoothly the conduct of Britain's domestic and foreign trade, as well as a large part of the foreign trade of the rest of the world. All the loans and bills discounted ran for short periods of time, usually from sixty to ninety days, and since some were coming due every day, there was a steady stream of repayments and issuance of new credits. The entire resources of the London money market were therefore a gigantic revolving fund, constantly being depleted and as constantly, replenished.

Of course the demands varied from time to time in relation to the supply of funds available; these changes were reflected in movements of the discount rate. When the demands became exceptionally large, or when the capacity of the London banks to make advances was strained by having to draw upon their reserves to ship gold abroad or to meet unusually heavy internal needs for currency, it became necessary for the market to have recourse to the Bank of England. Then the discount houses, rather than the banks, obtained the additional reserves necessary to avoid a disastrous contraction of credit.

We have already referred to the fact that dealings in foreign exchange

---

[3] R. G. Hawtrey, *The Art of Central Banking*, p. 126. Copyright 1932 by Longmans, Green & Co., London.

proper—that is, the purchase and sale of bills of exchange drawn in foreign currencies—came to be concentrated in the hands of foreign banks. The volume of this business was never large in London before World War I. British exports were in demand everywhere; the pound sterling was as good as gold and more convenient; and British exporters and importers preferred to draw and to be drawn upon in pounds sterling. Hence sterling bills of exchange were used to finance the exports and imports of the United Kingdom, and those of a large part of the rest of the world as well.

The volume of sterling bills constantly coming into the London money market was immense. They arose, as we have seen, out of the financial requirements both of purely domestic economic activities and of foreign trade, including in the latter remittances for shipments which never saw English shores. The reasons for this worldwide preference for the pound sterling as a medium of international payments were numerous. In part it was Great Britain's paramount position as exporter of manufactured goods and importer of raw materials and foodstuffs and her equally great preeminence as international investor. In part, also, it was the stable value of the pound sterling in terms of gold, resulting from the rigorous adherence to the gold standard from 1821 until 1914. But certainly of great importance was the high standing of the British acceptance houses and the assurance that any bill receiving their endorsement could be readily discounted, at the world's most favorable rates, on the London discount market. As Powell expressed the matter:

> The effect of this system, from the point of view of our national economy, is that we are able to take toll of a vast aggregate of foreign trade in which we have no direct concern whatever, by lending our acceptances to finance it. A draft on New York or Berlin may be imagined as negotiable in Canton against shipments of silk to New York itself; but if the silk exporter is to get the best rate for his drafts, he will see that they are drawn on London.[4]

From the operation of these compelling forces, London became the world's great financial center, furnishing short-term credits to foreign as well as to British importers, to overseas borrowers needing funds to meet a temporary excess of foreign claims over foreign credits, and providing, through the capital-raising activity of the security-issuing houses, sterling loans for foreign long-term capital requirements.

WESTERN EUROPE CATCHES UP

With a lag of several decades, western Europe went through a phase of development similar to Britain's, though with certain important differences.

Agriculture

Before appreciable progress could be made, the feudal landholding system had to be abandoned. The Revolution had freed the peasant in France. His

[4] Powell, *op. cit.,* p. 375.

inbred conservatism remained, however, and it required both official prodding and the competition brought by the railway to persuade him to adopt new crops and new methods. In Prussia, the defeat at Jena in 1806 forced the large landholders to recognize the need for reform. Emancipation edicts followed, which, by freeing the serfs and permitting land transfers and choice of occupations, created the mobility essential for progress. Similar reforms spread to other parts of western Europe.

Improvements in agriculture now became possible. Leadership in some countries, notably Prussia, came from the more progressive landowners, who saw in the modernized large-scale commercial farms of England a model to emulate. With population increasing and the towns and cities growing, markets were good, and new crops—especially potatoes, sugar beets, and linseed —afforded good returns and required a break with old methods. Government sponsorship of change helped, both in France and Germany; agricultural societies were formed, new techniques and new machinery demonstrated, and competitive exhibits organized. After 1840, the expansion of the railway network added the stimulus of intensified competition to force the abandonment of antiquated methods and the less profitable crops.

Industry

European industry in 1815 remained almost completely in the handicraft stage. Its progress thereafter varied widely. Change was negligible in Italy and Spain until late in the century. In France, for a variety of reasons, it lagged badly until about 1860, when railway mileage was substantial. Advance came sooner and was most rapid in Germany and Belgium.

German industrialization exhibited a sharp contrast with that of Britain. There was no revolution in thought or attitudes such as occurred in England between the fifteenth and nineteenth centuries. Prussia, the dominant state, carried down into modern times a spirit of medieval submission to authority and of looking to the state for leadership. From the very first, the state took an active part in fostering the growth of industry, both from choice and from necessity.

In 1816, a staff member of the Prussian Department of Commerce, Industry, and Public Works established the Industrial Institute (*Gewerbeinstitut*), which began training engineers and machine builders in 1821. Both Prussia and other German States sent industrial spies to England, where they used various stratagems to evade the numerous British laws (repealed in 1842) restricting the export of machines, models, and blueprints. Prussia also displayed a keen interest in and careful attention to education, with special solicitude for the teaching of science.

Lack of a numerous class of enterprising businessmen concerned with manufacture, as well as a shortage of capital, also handicapped industrial development on the Continent. As additional remedies for these deficiencies,

Prussia granted a number of subsidies to industry, admitted imports of machinery duty free, and encouraged the migration of skilled British workers and engineers. After the formation in 1834 of the German Customs Union (*Zollverein*), which brought the German states behind a single tariff, new industries were sheltered by protective duties. The Prussian State took an active part in the planning and construction of railways. Their stimulating effect became especially important after 1860, when Germany possessed nearly seven thousand miles of track.

Any account of the early stages of industrialization on the Continent would have to give an important place to the aid provided by British capital, labor, and enterprise. It was less in Germany than elsewhere, but even here British workers and engineers installed machinery and demonstrated its operation in the cotton, woolen and jute industries, in machine manufacture, gas works, mines, and railways. In France and Belgium, most of the early railways were built by British engineers and navvies, manned by British engine drivers, and financed in part by British capital. Many industrial plants, too, owed their origin or their modernization to British skills and capital.

By 1870, the leading nations of western Europe had gone through the first stages of the Industrial Revolution. They had a well-developed railway system; factory methods of production were well-entrenched in the textile industries; and modern engineering establishments were producing most of their own requirements of machinery. They still lagged far behind Great Britain, however. Measured by the output of pig-iron, the most important industrial raw material, Britain was far out in front, with over 6 million tons. Germany produced a little less than a quarter of this amount (1.4 million tons), with France somewhat behind with 1.2 million tons. Britain also stood far ahead in manufactures, with almost a third of world production. The United States was coming to the fore, accounting for about a fifth; Germany was responsible for some 13 per cent; France, for about 10 per cent.

ECONOMIC DEVELOPMENTS OVERSEAS

Many volumes have been written about the economic development of the United States, Canada, Australia, Argentina—the "regions of recent settlement" outside Europe. It would be impossible to deal in brief scope with this phenomenon—to trace the effect of differing government policies, the relative importance of specific natural resources, and the exertions by which the citizens of these areas peopled the empty spaces, built cities, and founded and developed important industries. We shall, therefore, limit ourselves to an account of the international contributions to overseas growth—the tremendous migration of labor and capital of the nineteenth century—and to some of the more important social conditions surrounding that growth.

Overseas Investment

British capital not only helped to get the Industrial Revolution under way in Europe, but it also aided greatly in inaugurating the process of economic development overseas. Here its main contribution was to provide what has come to be called *social overhead capital*—the facilities without which specific industries and even agriculture cannot function efficiently, but which they are incapable of furnishing themselves: railways, roads, harbor works, power plants, telephone and telegraph systems. Of total British foreign investment of some $18.5 billion outstanding in 1913, 40 per cent was in railways, 5 per cent in other utilities, and 30 per cent in loans to governments, most of which probably went into one form or another of social overhead capital. This is three-fourths of the total. The rest was scattered in mining, finance, manufacturing, and plantations. Moreover, about two-thirds of all British overseas investment went to the newly settled lands; only a quarter was directed to the tropical or semi-tropical economies with large populations and widely differing cultures. Europe obtained the rest, mainly before 1870.

British capital began to move abroad in sizeable amounts soon after the Napoleonic Wars. By 1850, it amounted to £200 million, most in western Europe and the United States, and the larger part in railways. During the next twenty-five years, the destination of Britain's surplus funds remained the same; the rate of flow increased. Between 1875 and 1913, Canada and the Empire came to the fore, though the United States and Latin America also received substantial amounts. At the end of this period, nearly $9 billion was invested in the Empire (principally in the great Dominions), while the United States and Latin America shared some $7.5 billion almost equally.

Beginning with the second half of the nineteenth century, France and Germany also became foreign lenders. Both countries at first invested mainly in Europe; political considerations strongly influenced the direction of their loans. Thus France, with strong diplomatic ties with Russia, lent heavily to the Russian government. Germany, to counter Russian expansion, concentrated on southeastern Europe. Later investments of both countries helped finance overseas development. France directed large sums to Latin America and the French Empire; Germany, to Latin America and the United States. By 1914, French investments abroad totaled approximately $9 billion, of which about 60 per cent was in Europe. Germany had lent some $6 billion, half of it to European borrowers, and a sixth each to the United States and Latin America.[5]

Results of Investments

Although some of the funds invested came from governments, the great bulk derived from private savings. The decisions that directed them to their

---

[5] Figures from William Ashworth, *A Short History of the International Economy 1850-1950*, p. 173. Copyright 1952 by Longmans, Green & Co., London.

destinations were made by individuals, banks, and business firms. Frequently these decisions were strongly influenced by fanciful misrepresentation by the banks that distributed the securities. With few exceptions, however, their motivation was gain. Investors expected a higher return than they could get at home. By and large, in spite of numerous defaults, they do not appear to have been disappointed. On comparable home and foreign investments (government bonds, or railway securities, for example), British investors did rather better on their foreign ventures.[6] Frenchmen came off worse; any advantage on the side of foreign investments was very small, for French banks gave bad advice, and the native caution of the French investor was outweighed by his credulity.

The most important gains from the international investment were not those received by the investors themselves, but those accruing to the entire community, both at home and abroad. In the lending countries, export industries enjoyed larger markets and bigger orders; their expansion permitted them to achieve economies of scale. Investments in foreign mines, plantations, and means of transport assured the industrial countries of needed supplies of raw materials and foodstuffs; they also, especially those in railways and shipping, made them cheaper. In the borrowing countries, foreign investment provided the social overhead capital so necessary for economic growth. It opened up new regions, thus making possible the combination in more effective proportions of labor and hitherto unexploited resources, while freeing domestic capital to provide such direct aids to labor as farm implements and machinery, factory equipment, and all the array of producers' goods so badly needed in a growing economy.

People on the Move

One of the outstanding features of nineteenth-century investment was that it was accompanied by, even correlated with, a large migration of labor. Between 1820 and 1930, gross migration amounted to 62 million people, some three-fourths of it occurring in the half century before World War I. Europe contributed much the greater part of these immigrants. Until 1890, most of them came from Ireland, Germany, and the Scandinavian countries; thereafter southeastern Europe, especially Italy, supplied the majority. The United States exerted the greatest drawing power; it attracted over three-fifths. Another fifth went in about equal proportions to Canada and to Australia, New Zealand, and South Africa, while Argentina and Brazil between them claimed most of the remainder.

---

[6] Excluding about one-tenth of total British investments between 1870-1880 in government bonds on which losses from defaults outweighed gains from interest payments, returns from foreign government bonds exceeded those on British consols by amounts ranging from 0.7 per cent to 10.7 per cent. The differentials on railways stocks and bonds were comparable. Figures are from A. K. Cairncross, *Home and Foreign Investment, 1870-1913,* pp. 229-30. Published 1953 by Cambridge University Press, New York.

In the earlier stages, the immigrants moved from relatively unproductive farms in the old countries to more productive agricultural employment in the newer countries, or they provided the labor to open mines and build railways. Later, an increasing proportion went into industry; in the United States, the steel industry, the women's dress industry, and the building industry took large numbers.

With a few exceptions, factors—both labor and capital—moved from areas where they were abundant and cheap to regions where they were scarce and dear. (It will be recalled that the movement of goods, which may be regarded as a substitute for factor movements, is similar in character.) In the nineteenth century, too, the migration of labor and capital was complementary; both entered the new countries together, to be combined with the relatively rich, virgin resources of the new lands in proportions that were more productive than those formerly attainable either there or in the old countries. Economic growth resulted—the appearance of new industries, better communications, the settlement of empty plains, the emergence of new towns, and all with rising per capita incomes—probably at a faster rate than ever before witnessed.

Conditions Favorable to Development

One aspect of the economic development of western Europe and of the regions of recent settlement overseas merits special attention. This is the *social environment* in which that development took place. Feudalism had been destroyed early, either before or on the threshold of the great economic changes of the nineteenth century. With the elimination of the relatively rigid social relations of feudalism, the class structure became fluid, ensuring the social mobility and the freedom to exploit resources so essential to the new industrial society. (The contrast is sharp between the rate of economic development in Latin America, where a feudal land tenure system and social structure were imported by the Spanish and Portuguese, and in the United States, Canada, and Australasia.)

More positively, western Europe and the regions settled mainly in the nineteenth century by its emigrants possessed a set of institutions uniquely favorable to rapid economic growth. High on the list is a tradition of orderly government and all that implies: the supremacy of the law and a corresponding willingness to abide by the decisions of courts, respect for prescribed methods of transferring political power between contending parties, and a reasonably efficient and honest bureaucracy. Given this tradition, changes in government could be peaceful; continuity and stability were assured; and transactions involving the government could be guided by reason and common sense.

Western Europe also acquired (as a result of the stimulus to secular and scientific interests given by the Renaissance, of the emphasis on individual efforts generated during the Reformation, and of the vigorous political, economic, and philosophical disputes of the eighteenth century Age of En-lightenment) a high respect for the role of the individual, for the experimental approach, and for the material rewards of effort. The importance of these considerations for the successful operation of a private enterprise system are clear.

Finally, the prior accumulation of capital in England, the creation in London of an international capital-market open to European borrowers, and its later widening to include western Europe itself, provided financial re-sources vital to rapid overseas development. The tradition of order and stability carried overseas by the settlers in turn guaranteed their access to these sources of capital.

TRADE IS MADE FREE

An efficiently functioning international economy would have been impos-sible without the third of the great changes of the nineteenth century—the release of trade from its burden of Mercantilist restrictions. Here, as in the growth of industry and the creation of an international market for goods and capital, Britain led the way. We have repeatedly called attention to the in-creasing numbers and wealth of the English manufacturing and mercantile class, whose desire for economic freedom resulted in the gradual repeal or nullification of various domestic regulations of Mercantilism. After the Napoleonic Wars they were ready for an attack on its still intact foreign ramparts. Both their interests in, and their ideas on, foreign trade had been altered by recent or current developments.

The Need for Wider Markets

Although the long years of war with France had intensified rather than relaxed the regulation of trade, they had also speeded the growth of Britain's newer industries—cotton, iron and steel and coal, and engineering. After Waterloo, though their position was unchallenged abroad, their markets were in a state of collapse. The government stopped buying firearms, cannon, and naval vessels. Supplies of uniforms, blankets, and tents were no longer needed. Nor was Continental Europe, for years overrun by marauding armies, likely for some time to be a heavy buyer of British goods. Concern for mar-kets, therefore, led merchants and manufacturers to look more favorably on measures to increase the freedom of trade.

Changing Ideas

At the same time that sagging sales aroused an interest in broader markets, ideological weapons useful in the coming fight against trade barriers were being sharpened. Adam Smith had made a good beginning with his exposure of the absurdities of Mercantilism and his limited demonstration of the gains from trade. Now Ricardo, himself a businessman and a recognized spokesman for business groups, strengthened the argument for the liberalization of trade with his famous doctrine of comparative costs. Followers in England and France, and popularizers too, soon took it up, clarified it, and developed a well-reasoned case for free trade. This became part of the standard intellectual equipment of liberal statesmen and crusading reformers. One of the former, Huskisson, brought some order into the chaotic jumble of Britain's Mercantilist and wartime duties, paring down the most exorbitant, substituting moderate tariffs for import prohibitions, and abolishing bounties. The Corn Laws, the core of British protectionism, remained sacred so long as an archaic distribution of Parliamentary seats gave unqualified political control to the landed gentry.

The Reform Bill of 1832 abolished at a stroke the numerous rotten or pocket boroughs that permitted many great landowners to appoint members of Parliament, and at the same time enfranchised half the middle class. Though still far from representative, Parliament reflected more accurately the views of the governed. Its reform furnished an essential ingredient for repeal of the Corn Laws.

Repeal of the Corn Laws

Sir Robert Peel (Prime Minister, 1841-46), who became the great parliamentary leader of the free trade movement, began the dismantling of protection by obtaining adoption of the income tax. This provided assured revenues hitherto derived from a mass of duties on exports of manufactures and imports of raw materials, which with the support of the manufacturing class were now dropped or greatly reduced. On the issue of agricultural protection, however, he at first sided with his party. But a rising tide of opposition to the Corn Laws outside Parliament, together with eloquent representation of the free trade interest within, finally caused him to desert it.

The opposition was the work of the Anti-Corn Law League, an organization of manufacturers founded in 1839 to promote repeal. The prospect of cheaper bread had a strong appeal to the laborer, whether on the farm or in the factory, while the manufacturer saw in cheaper food, according to the Ricardian theory of the day, the possibility of lower money wages and higher profits. Backed with plenty of money, organized with extraordinary efficiency, and supported with the eloquence of Richard Cobden and John Bright, the League

accomplished the miracle of uniting capital and labour. It combined argument and emotion, bringing both to perfection in meetings that began with Cobden and ended with Bright. It appealed equally to self-interest and to humanity. In an age when political literature was limited in quantity and inferior in quality, the League, in 1843 alone, distributed nine million carefully argued tracts by means of a staff of eight hundred persons. In an age when public meetings were rare, when finance and government were regarded as mysteries appertaining to the political families and to well-born civil servants, the League lecturers taught political economy, and criticised the year's budget, to vast audiences of merchants and clerks, artisans and navvies, farmers and agricultural labourers.[7]

Within Parliament, Cobden's lucid economic arguments, combined with Peel's own study of the facts, finally converted the Prime Minister to free trade. In 1845 he seized the opportunity afforded by the Irish potato blight to suspend the Corn Laws. Popular opposition to their restoration was so strong that in 1846 repeal was inevitable.

The Spread of Freer Trade

In ensuing years, Great Britain completed her movement toward free trade, and other countries followed her lead. In 1860, Parliament removed all but 60 of 400 articles from the dutiable list; gradually even these fell by the wayside and the British market became and remained open to imports without restriction until 1914. France, under the leadership of the liberal emperor Napoleon III, replaced her highly protective tariff with a very moderate one in a series of international negotiations beginning with the Cobden-Chevalier Treaty of 1860. After 1850, Holland and Belgium adopted distinctly liberal tariffs. Even the United States, which had pursued a protective policy since 1816, substantially moderated its duties in the tariff of 1857. And during the 1860's the German *Zollverein*, whose original mild tariff of 1834 had been raised thereafter, succumbed to free trade pressures and lowered its duties from protective to purely revenue levels.

In addition to their liberality, two features of these mid-nineteenth century tariffs that were to endure until after 1914 are well worth noting. These were their stability and their generality. Even though rates of duty tended to move upward again after 1870, tariffs changed very gradually, usually being left in force for a decade or more. By reducing the risks and increasing the calculability of trade, this feature facilitated its steady expansion. And by the insertion into commercial treaties of the now famous "most-favored-nation" clause, which extended to all treaty partners concessions granted in each treaty, the benefits of tariff reductions were generalized throughout the world.

Stimulated by its release from restrictions, international trade grew apace. Rough estimates, which are all that are available, suggest that its value doubled between 1830 and 1850. In the next thirty years world trade at least trebled and may have nearly quadrupled. From being a relatively unimportant adjunct of domestic activity, foreign trade loomed increasingly large where it did not dominate economic life altogether. Australia, New Zealand, Argentina, and Uruguay became specialists in the production of wheat, wool,

[7] G. M. Trevelyan, *British History in the Nineteenth Century*, p. 270. Copyright 1922 by Longmans, Green & Co., London.

and meat. Britain, their principal market, permitted its agriculture to go through a sharp phase of contraction while the nation concentrated its energies on specialized manufactures. In the face of cheap supplies of western wheat, Denmark transformed its economy from a grain-growing and exporting basis to one that imported grain and exported bacon, ham, eggs, and dairy products. All over the globe, specialization matched the growth of trade.

AN INTERNATIONAL ECONOMY

With the adoption of the gold standard in the early 1870's by all the important countries of Europe and by several Latin American nations, currencies became firmly linked at stable exchange rates and were made fully convertible.[8] The expanding needs of the rising industrial countries for imported raw materials and foodstuffs and for markets for their manufactures could be met by purchases from one group, sales to another, the balances being cleared through a complex multilateral network centering in London. There the highly developed and efficient money market attracted funds from all over the world and made them available to finance the major part of world trade and an important share of the capital requirements of growing national economies.

Disturbances and consequent adjustments were inevitable. Yet because it was an era of rapid growth, the disturbances could be assimilated without too great dislocation. For such as remained, the gold standard provided an effective mechanism of adjustment which, though it tended toward deflation, was politically acceptable and therefore allowed to work.

Although socialist doctrines—both "utopian" and Marxist—had their adherents, neither they nor any other rival seriously challenged the combination of industrial capitalism and political democracy that spread throughout the western nations. Reliance could be and was placed upon market forces to regulate production, the flow of raw materials and finished goods, the movement of capital and even, in large part, of labor. By the late nineteenth century, an international economy not too unlike the theoretical model actually existed.

[For Selected References, see end of Chapter 12.]

[8] The United States had legally established the gold standard in 1873, after being on a paper currency basis since 1861. Specie payments, however, were not resumed until 1879.

12

THE REVIVAL OF NATIONALISM

From the vantage point of the mid-twentieth century, there can be no doubt that the nineteenth, or more accurately the hundred years between the Napoleonic Wars and World War I (1814-1914), constituted a unique period in many respects. From our own focus of interest, it stands out as the century during which deliberate governmental regulation of trade gave way to regulation by market forces. Nations became free to specialize in production according to the dictates of relative costs, and did so. A large and constantly growing volume of international trade linked the various regions of the world into a smoothly functioning, integrated economy of global scope. The developments that brought this about began soon after 1815 and reached a crescendo in the fifties and sixties in the free trade movement.

By the early 1870's, the liberalizing forces reached their peak of accomplishment. From then on, though far from spent, they had to fight a rearguard action against a rising tide of nationalism. Though most of the gains remained intact, events of the late nineteenth and early twentieth century established a trend which foreshadowed the future. These include a revival of nationalism with its anticosmopolitan policies, and a great shift in the balance of economic power. This chapter will examine these developments.

THE CHALLENGE TO BRITAIN'S LEADERSHIP

The Rise of Germany

At the time Germany achieved political union in the Empire (1871), she was no better than a poor third in economic weight, whether this be measured in manufacturing production, the output of iron and steel, or the volume of trade. But within forty years, she outdistanced the United Kingdom, became the strongest European power, and made a bid for world domination!

Germany's rapid economic growth began immediately after the Franco-Prussian War and the attainment of political unity. With a strong central government replacing the numerous small and ineffectual principalities, a coordination of hitherto independent and sometimes conflicting policies became possible. The billion dollar indemnity from France enabled Germany to adopt the gold standard; the acquisition of Alsace-Lorraine, with its textile mills and iron ore deposits, provided additional resources for expansion. Coal and iron production, which had increased slowly until now, rose sharply. Between 1870 and 1900, the output of both minerals grew fivefold. Still behind at the turn of the century, in the next decade Germany rushed forward, surpassing Britain in the production of pig-iron and coal and outranking her in her share of world manufacturing output.

Nor was Germany's growth exclusively internal. Her exports grew steadily, but more slowly than industrial production up to 1900, then increased sharply. In 1872 they totaled $500 million; in 1900, $1,132 million; and in 1913, $2,494 million. The principal export items were manufactures—hardware, chemicals, cotton textiles, beet sugar, and one major mineral, coal—while the leading imports were raw materials and foods—grain, wool, cotton, and timber.

Because of the similarity of Germany's exports to those of Britain, their expansion depended partly upon the ability of German producers to undersell the British. Germany's advance unquestionably introduced a strong element of direct competition. But these exports were by no means wholly competitive. There was considerable specialization within products; Germany concentrated on the coarser textiles, Great Britain on the finer grades; German producers made principally cheap watches and clocks, the British (and later the Swiss) the more expensive types. Some German goods, too, were relatively noncompetitive, even being exported to England; among these were chemicals and electrical equipment. Moreover, in eastern Europe, Germany found a market to which British exporters had paid little attention and in which she had the advantage of location. The increase of her exports in this area, especially, represented a net increase in world trade rather than a loss to Britain.

Lulled into complacency by their long enjoyment of an unchallenged position, the commercial interests of Britain were stunned when confronted, in the eighties and nineties, by German and to a lesser degree by French, Belgian, Swiss, and Austrian rivalry. British goods had always been superior. They had required little pushing. If they were not precisely suited to the foreigner's needs, then the foreigner had had to adapt himself to what was available!

To get a foothold in foreign markets in the face of British dominance, the German trader exploited his rival's every weakness. He adapted products to his customers' wishes; he packaged his wares attractively; he took pains with even the smallest orders, hoping that larger ones might follow. His representatives abroad became more numerous than the British, and unlike the latter, learned the local language and often married local girls and took root in the community. Cash on demand, or at the most, sixty to ninety days' credit, was sound British practice. But the upstart Germans did not hesitate to give six to nine months or even longer.

These new, unpleasant facts aroused acute alarm, notably in the mid-eighties and mid-nineties, years of severe depression. But as world trade recovered, it became apparent that although British manufactures had lost ground in some markets, especially on the Continent, the development of new, together with the growth of old, provided more than an offset. Expansion overseas required steadily increasing imports, while exploitation of the mass market for cheap textiles in Asia furnished a new outlet. The net result of the new competition was not, as some had feared, England's collapse as an industrial power. British traders had to work harder and producers had to relinquish some lines of production to new, low-cost rivals, and to specialize where their resources and skills counted most.[1] Channels of trade altered, some diminishing, some swelling. And with the emergence of Germany and other western European nations as important producers of manufactures, an increasing proportion of trade took the form of an exchange of manufactured specialties—German electrical and mining machinery for English agricultural and textile machines, coarse grades of textiles for finer, dyestuffs for heavy industrial chemicals.

The United States

The economic progress of Germany was far exceeded by that of the United States. The contrast was but natural, considering the fact that the transition from a predominantly agrarian to a modern industrial nation took place in a country of continental size, possessing immense resources of land, minerals, power, and timber. Rapid development of these resources was assured by their very richness, which gave the profit-seeking businessman the prospect of high returns; by the prevalence, as in England, of an individualist philosophy; by the rapid growth of population; and by the relatively high level of incomes attributable to a favorable ratio of population to resources.

The high proportion of resources to population, or the relative scarcity of labor, together with the rapid growth of population, played a most important role in the speedy development of American industry. With abundant fertile land available almost for the asking down to the end of the nineteenth century, farming offered rich rewards for the enterprising and provided a growing market for products of industry. Continued expansion of this market was assured by the phenomenal growth of population, which nearly doubled between 1870 and 1900.

Not only did the high productivity of American agriculture furnish a large

---

[1] Some branches of British industry met sharp German competition in the home market, notably sugar refining, chemicals, iron and steel, and cotton and woolen textiles. Exports of woolen fabrics declined absolutely, from 324 million yards per annum in 1870 to 174 million in 1909-13.

and growing market for industry among the farming population, but also by offering an attractive alternative to work in mine or mill it forced the payment of high wages in industry. And because of the basically democratic character of the American people, they were ready to spend their high per capita earnings on mass-produced goods. Thus the tendency toward the production of standardized commodities with a broad, mass market received a strong impetus from the nature of the buying public.[2]

The economies attainable when industry can concentrate upon the production of large quantities of identical goods were partly responsible for the rapidly increasing efficiency of American industry. Probably of equal importance was the high level of wages caused by the scarcity of labor. This forced manufacturers to adopt labor-saving devices, the invention of which has been a unique feature of "Yankee ingenuity."[3] Thus necessity compelled the use and stimulated the development of the most advanced technology of any of the industrial nations.

The presence of mass markets and the need for labor-saving machinery made their effects evident early. Before 1850, guns and pistols were manufactured from interchangeable parts. After the Civil War, this system was applied to sewing machines and to clocks and watches, agricultural machinery, the typewriter, and the bicycle. The machine tool industry, located first in the eastern States, later spreading to Ohio, furnished the technical basis for the precision manufacture of interchangeable parts.

In spite of the early introduction of mass-production methods, American industry remained until the very end of the nineteenth century well behind British, though advancing rapidly. The figures for both pig-iron production

---

[2] This explanation of the prominence of mass-production industries in the United States is advanced by Erwin Rothbarth in a brilliant and suggestive article, "Causes of the Superior Efficiency of U.S.A. Industry as Compared with British Industry," *Economic Journal,* LVI (1946), p. 383. By way of contrast with the United States he cites the United Kingdom, where "there remains an aristocracy and a middle class impregnated with aristocratic ideas, who reject mass-produced articles and insist on articles with individual character." (P. 386.)

We may add to what Rothbarth says, that in addition to the relative abundance of land, our comparatively enlightened land policy (as embodied in the Homestead Act of 1862), by making land accessible to would-be-buyers, "put purchasing power in the hands of those . . . ready to buy large quantities of standardised goods." Had the concentration of land-holdings been permitted on a wide scale, as in many Latin American countries, great extremes of income distribution such as characterize those nations might have resulted here as well.

[3] "The American display of machinery at the Vienna International Exhibition of 1873 was, according to the contemporary reporter, 'the richest in new forms of apparatus, and contained by far the most striking examples of the special adaptation of machines to peculiar varieties of work, and of what is commonly described as "labor-saving machinery." ' . . . As an English observer noted in 1885: 'The tools and processes which we are inclined to consider unusual are the commonplaces of American shops, and the determination to do nothing by hand which can be done by machinery is the chief characteristic.' " Samuel Rezneck, "Mass Production Since the War Between the States," in *The Growth of the American Economy* (edited by Harold Williamson), p. 502. Copyright 1944 by Prentice-Hall, Inc., Englewood Cliffs, N.J.

and for share of manufacturing production reflect this fact. (See Tables 12.1 and 12.2.) In 1870, U.S. output of iron was just over a quarter of British. It is doubtful if manufactures at this date amounted to more than half the production of the U.K.[4] By 1900, the United States ranked first as a producer of pig iron and of coal. It also apparently was the premier manufacturing nation. By 1913, there was no question as to relative position. U.S. output of pig iron was as large as that of the United Kingdom, Germany, and France together, while its share of world manufactures (35.8 per cent) was only slightly less than that of these three industrial nations (36.1 per cent). In other words, just before the outbreak of World War I, the United States had replaced Britain as the world's principal industrial power.

Table 12.1. PIG-IRON PRODUCTION IN LEADING COUNTRIES
(in millions of metric tons)

	Great Britain	United States	Germany	France	Russia
1870	6.1	1.7	1.4	1.2	0.4
1900	9.1	14.0	7.6	2.7	2.9
1910	10.2	27.7	13.1	4.0	3.0
1920	8.2	37.5	6.4	3.3	0.1
1930	6.3	32.3	9.7	10.0	5.0
1940	8.4	43.0	21.0	4.6	15.5

SOURCE: W. Nelson Peach and Walter Krause, *Basic Data of the American Economy*, p. 59. Copyright 1948 by Richard D. Irwin, Inc., Chicago. Reproduced from *The Metal Industry During 1941* (edited by G. A. Roush); published by McGraw-Hill Book Co., New York.

Table 12.2. PERCENTAGE DISTRIBUTION OF THE WORLD'S MANUFACTURING PRODUCTION

	U.S.	Germany	U.K.	France	Russia	Italy	Belgium	Sweden	Japan
1870	23.3	13.2	31.8	10.3	3.7	2.4	2.9	0.4	——
1896/1900	30.1	16.6	19.5	7.1	5.0	2.7	2.2	1.1	0.6
1913	35.8	15.7	14.0	6.4	5.0	3.1	2.1	1.0	1.2
1926/29	42.2	11.6	9.4	6.6	4.3	3.3	1.9	1.0	2.5
1936/38	32.2	10.7	9.2	4.5	18.5	2.7	1.3	1.3	3.5

SOURCE: League of Nations, *Industrialization and Foreign Trade*, p. 13.

[4] While Table 12.2 shows the U.S. in 1870 as accounting for 23.3 per cent of world manufacturing production, as against the U.K.'s 31.8 per cent, the figure for the U.S. is almost certainly too high. It includes a large proportion of articles produced by handicraft and neighborhood "industries." In addition, prices were very low in 1870, and there is no indication that this factor is taken into account. Even the 1900 figure for the U.S. is probably too high, owing to the fact that almost a fourth of total manufactures were of the handicraft variety.

A large growth in our foreign trade accompanied our phenomenal expansion. Just after the Civil War, United States exports barely exceeded $300 million (1866-70 average). A few years before the outbreak of World War I, they were nearly six times as large, or $1,750 million (1906-10 average). Despite their growth, however, our exports were much more complementary to, than competitive with, British production. As late as 1910, nearly three-fourths consisted of crude materials and foods, manufactured foods (of which flour is by far the most important), and semimanufactures, and only about a quarter (26.7 per cent) of finished manufactures. Moreover, although our exports exhibited rapid growth, they remained a relatively small proportion of our total production. In 1870, exports were seven per cent of gross national product; in 1913, eight per cent.

We were so busy developing a continent and satisfying the needs of our immense free-trade area that the development of export markets, except as an outlet for the abounding production of our farms, forests, and mines, was comparatively unimportant. As our production of manufactures grew, we became, it is true, more capable of taking care of our requirements of finished goods. This is reflected in the decline in imports of finished manufactures from over 40 per cent in 1866-70 to just under 25 per cent in 1906-10. In spite of this trend toward industrial self-sufficiency, reenforced by rising tariff rates, our total imports increased so rapidly—from $408 million to $1,345 million—that imports of finished manufactures doubled in the period under review. Europe, moreover, remained by far our greatest market and our principal source of imports. In 1870, that continent (including the United Kingdom as a major customer) took 80 per cent of our exports; in 1910 the figure was still 65 per cent. As for imports, we obtained 55 per cent of these from Europe in 1870; by 1910, its share had dropped only to 52 per cent.

Britain's Position in 1913

Although the economic growth of Germany and the United States had vital implications for power politics, as the events of 1914-18 were to show, it made little difference to the average citizen of the British Isles. Real wages increased steadily throughout the last half of the nineteenth century, owing to the fact that money wages either rose more rapidly than prices, or fell less rapidly. From 1901 to 1914, the rise of real wages was reversed; they fell an average of 0.7 per cent per annum during this period. Prices were now rising rather rapidly, and especially the prices of raw materials and foods. Yet even then, hours of labor continued to be shortened, and the extension of social services worked to labor's advantage. According to another estimate, which covers not only labor but all gainfully employed, real income continued to rise right up to 1913, though less rapidly than during the last half of the nineteenth century.[5]

The British balance of payments had been under no strain from 1870 onward. Not only was a large and somewhat irregular growing excess of imports over exports paid for out of the earnings of British foreign investments, the merchant marine, and insurance and banking establishments, but there was also a substantial surplus available each year for additional investment overseas. For the period 1873-96, it is true, investment turned more toward internal improvements, and the rate of foreign lending declined. It increased again, however, after 1900, and by 1913, British total foreign investment stood close to £4,000 million, yielding an annual income of £210 million. At the close of our period, the balance of payments surplus was larger than ever before, and still growing.

There was, in short, nothing unsound about Britain's position on the eve of World War I. Though forced, by the fact of world economic expansion, to share markets with relative newcomers, she herself benefited from this expansion. Some adjustments to competition had been necessary, but the industries that had been the backbone of her own development were still growing and were still the world's largest exporters. Real income per head of the population had been rising for two generations and was exceeded only moderately by that of the United States and Canada. A huge stake in foreign investment yielded a substantial annual revenue. Together with large earnings from services, this enabled the country to import each year far more than it exported, and in addition to export a large sum of capital.

NATIONALISM AND PROTECTIONISM

The rivalry for markets that arose in the eighties and nineties reflected the attainment of maturity by continental industry and its consequent release from British tutelage. Since this successful industrial development had been achieved during an era of relatively low tariffs, one might have expected the liberal attitude toward trade to persist. Indeed, in view of the challenge to Britain's exports and the invasion even of her domestic market, a revival of protectionist sentiment in the United Kingdom would have been understandable. And though there was such a revival, it never acquired sufficient strength to alter Britain's commitment to free trade. On the contrary, it was on the Continent that a rising spirit of nationalism took root, one of whose

[5] From 1850 to 1873, when prices and wages were both rising, the annual increase in real wages, after allowing for unemployment, was 1.3 per cent. From 1873 to 1900, the annual increase averaged 1.85 per cent. (W. W. Rostow, *British Economy of the Nineteenth Century,* Chapter IV). The data for the period after 1900 show that income per head of the occupied population, in constant prices, stood at £175.8 in 1894-1903; by 1913 it was £195.4, or 11 per cent higher. (Colin Clark, *The Conditions of Economic Progress,* 1940 edition, p. 83.)

fruits was a renewed campaign for protection which reversed the earlier downward trend of tariffs.

The resurgence of nationalism appears to have been partly the perverse outcome of liberal doctrine and partly the aftermath of wars. Liberalism, the dominant political philosophy of the nineteenth century, stressed the supremacy of the individual and the natural harmony of individual and social interests under a regime of free competition. It took the existence of national states for granted—they were the necessary agency for eliminating obstructions to economic and political freedom and for establishing the minimum rules of a free society. But if the individual was to be free, he must not only be free from excessive government intervention, his freedom implied also freedom from foreign oppression. National self-determination was an essential ingredient in the liberal system of thought.

Enforcement of the doctrine of self-determination by local leaders resulted in the formation, by peoples who were by and large homogeneous as to language and culture, of several new nations. Greece, with British aid, threw off Turkish rule in 1829. Belgium became an independent nation in 1830. In the 1850's, Garibaldi led the Italian people against their Austrian oppressors, and with the help of French troops and British diplomacy, Italy achieved national unity in 1860. Self-determination had little to do with the creation of the German Empire, which was more the result of the assertion of Prussian military hegemony, yet the Empire did bring together peoples who were linguistically and culturally similar.

When a new nation is born, it tends to assert its new-found nationality. This is especially true when it is large and powerful and when its birth is attended by military struggle. Germany and Italy provide good examples. One of the characteristic forms of nationalist self-assertion is the imposition of protective duties on imports. In the revival of nationalism in the mid-nineteenth century we have a force providing at least a predisposition toward protection.

History also records that protection is a legacy of war and a common expression of national rivalry. We have already noted the growing rivalry of the eighties and nineties; as for war, there was the Crimean War, the bitter struggle between the Northern and Southern States of the American Union, and conflict between France and Prussia. All these influences together were surely enough to generate a reaction against the earlier, liberal trade policies.

What actually set the protectionist movement under way was, however, none of these broad political factors, but two specific economic developments of the 1870's. One was the invasion of the Continent by cheap American and Russian grain, made accessible by the activities of railway builders. The other was the depression of 1873-79, the longest and deepest period of stagnant trade the world had yet experienced. Peasants and manufacturers alike were full of lamentations; their clamor for relief gave the initial stimulus to protection.

Another influence was at work over the whole latter half of the nineteenth century. To meet rising expenditures on armaments, education, public health, and social insurance, greater revenues became necessary. And since customs duties provided, during the nineteenth century, the larger part of the revenue of many nations, it was natural to turn the screw a bit tighter.

Once the swing to protection started, the deeper force of nationalism supported and maintained it. There is also a tendency for a rise in duties to continue, as vested interests grow and gather political strength. They also tend to spread over an ever wider range of commodities, since it is difficult to deny to others what has already been granted to some. The operation of these forces is illustrated in the history of tariff policy from 1870 to 1913.

Tariff Policy to 1913

Even in the face of serious depression, German tariffs continued to fall in the 1870's. Duties on grain had been abolished in 1865; those on iron and on shipbuilding materials followed in 1873; and the tariff on iron manufactures was to go in 1877. Despite the pressure of distressed farmers and worried industrialists, Bismarck resisted; the iron duties were dropped according to schedule. His need for funds, however, helped win him over. In the tariff of 1880, moderate duties were imposed on various iron products, while grains and a number of other items received considerably more protection. Further upward revision of the iron and food duties occurred in 1902, when rising tariffs elsewhere and the lapse of various treaties which had frozen German duties furnished the motive and the opportunity. Even then, though the tariff on grains was highly protective, that on manufactures averaged only a rather modest 25 per cent.

In France, inability of agricultural and industrial groups interested in protection to unite promptly postponed for two decades any action to reverse the low duty treaties of the 1860's. Not until 1892, when these groups controlled Parliament, was tariff revision undertaken, but when it came, it was thorough. Duties on agricultural products were set at new high levels, and those on manufactures were raised to an average of about 34 per cent. Another increase came in 1910, when protection was also extended to many newly developed products, among them chemicals and electrical and rubber goods.

For the beginning of that policy of protection always associated with the Republican party in the United States, we have to go back to the eve of the Civil War. Victory in the elections of 1859 brought them to power on a platform calling for the encouragement of industrial development by tariff protection. The tariff of 1861 embodied this principle; it repealed the low duties of 1857 (24 per cent on most imports, with maximum rates of 30 per cent) and restored these current in 1846, when most dutiable articles paid 30 per cent, a few 40 per cent, and brandy and spirits, alone, a maximum of

100 per cent. Rising financial requirements of the Union government led to further increases and extensions until 1864, when rates averaged 47 per cent, a record level. After a brief lowering of duties by a flat 5 per cent in the 1880's, owing to a constant surplus in government revenues, the tariff was hiked twice in rapid succession, in 1890 (average rate of duties, 50 per cent) and in 1897 (average rate of 57 per cent).[6]

Some idea of the intellectual level of tariff discussion of these times may be gained from the following excerpt from the Republican platform of 1896, which wrapped the tariff in the American flag and propounded most of the conventional arguments in its support:

> We renew and emphasize our allegiance to the policy of protection as the bulwark of American industrial independence and the foundation of American development and prosperity. This true American policy taxes foreign products and encourages home industry; it puts the burden of revenue on foreign goods; it secures the American market for the American producer; it upholds the American standard of wages for the American workingman; it puts the factory by the side of the farm, and makes the American farmer less dependent on foreign demand and price; it diffuses general thrift, and founds the strength of all on the strength of each.[7]

No further change of general importance in the U.S. tariff occured until 1913, when the new Democratic administration, the first since 1892-96, undertook in the Underwood Tariff a thoroughgoing revision. Over 100 items, including sugar and wool, were added to the free list; rates on nearly 1,000 classifications were reduced, and relatively few were raised; the ratio of duties to dutiable imports fell to the extremely low average of 16 per cent. Unfortunately, this new tariff had little opportunity to be tested; within a year, war broke out in Europe.

With the sole exception of Great Britain and the Netherlands, European countries generally followed the lead of Germany and France by adopting protective tariffs. Russia even preceded them. Before 1868, the Russian tariff had been comparatively moderate, aiming chiefly at revenue. That year, however, marked the introduction of a deliberate policy of protection. Recurrent and substantial increases in the duties from then until 1914 gave her one of the highest, if not the highest, tariffs in the world.

Upon the unification of Italy in 1860, the moderate tariff of Sardinia became the law of the new kingdom. Parliament adopted a policy of industrial protection in 1878, extending the program to agriculture in the following year. In 1887, rates were raised to a high level and remained in effect until

---

[6] These percentages are very approximate, owing to the difficulty of estimating the ratio of duties to dutiable imports when some rates effectively prohibit imports. Nonetheless, they probably give a fairly accurate impression of the upward trend.

[7] Cited in Asher Isaacs, *International Trade: Tariff and Commercial Policies*, pp. 207-8. Published by Richard D. Irwin, Homewood, Ill., 1948. See also Ch. 13 in this book for a discussion of these arguments.

after the war. Switzerland first embarked upon a policy of mild protection in 1891, then stepped the rates up sharply fifteen years later.

Though increasing foreign competition stimulated the rise of strong internal opposition to Britain's liberal trade policy, its practical effect was to divide the Conservative party and to unite the free trade forces. In the election of 1906 the Liberals enjoyed an overwhelming victory, and little more was heard of protection as a general alternative to free trade until the economic collapse of the 1930's.

IMPERIALIST EXPANSION, 1880-1913

Just as during the liberal era governments showed an antipathy toward protection, so too they exhibited at least a passive attitude toward colonies. There was little interest in subjugating native peoples and thus extending the dominion of the metropolitan countries. If the practice of governments thus coincided with the liberal doctrine of self-determination, it is doubtful if this resulted from deliberate intent. More likely, it was the consequence of preoccupation with internal problems of growth and development, as well as recent experience with colonies. Thus in Britain, the value of colonies was seriously questioned, partly as a reaction perhaps to the rebellion of her American possessions, partly because larger and more accessible markets for her rising production were available in Europe and abroad. To England's experience of 1776, buttressed by claims for and achievement of self-government by Canada and Australasia, was added that of Spain and Portugal, which between 1810 and 1825 witnessed the loss of all but shreds of their former empires. Even Bismarck as late as 1868 regarded the advantages of colonies as illusory. Small wonder then that "colonies were looked upon as an antiquated encumbrance from the past."[8] France alone sought overseas possessions, acquiring Algiers in 1830 and parts of Indo-China and Somaliland in 1862.

All this changed suddenly. Beginning in the 1880's a wave of colony grabbing began that continued right down to the outbreak of war in 1914. Its principal results were the division of Africa among the European powers, the spread of Britain's dominion over Burma and Malaya, the extension of France's Indo-Chinese empire over an area half again as large as the mother country, and the economic, if not the political, partition of China. The Americas were exempt from this land-grabbing fever—apart from the earlier, ill-fated attempt of Louis Napoleon to conquer Mexico—because of the Monroe Doctrine, the presence of the British fleet, and the growing strength of the United States.

How shall we explain this burst of imperialist expansion? Although it was

[8] L. C. A. Knowles, *The Industrial and Commercial Revolutions in Great Britain During the Nineteenth Century*, p. 321. Published 1922 by Routledge, London.

a manifestation of the intensified national rivalry of the late nineteenth century, it can no more be explained by nationalism than can protection. Nationalism is a pervading sentiment that is conducive to certain types of action, but it contains no mechanism capable of generating change. It may provide the intellectual climate needed for change, but it is not itself a moving force.

It would appear that the planting of national flags in alien territory was closely related to the industrial growth of the metropolitan countries. This growth created a voracious appetite for raw materials—for copper, tin, manganese; for sisal, hemp, and jute; for ivory, teak and mahogany; for palm oil, copra, and rubber. Demand for these and other raw materials was high and rising; traditional sources of supply were inadequate, and new ones needed to be opened up.[9] Traders on the spot at the source of raw materials could make handsome profits—profits that were enhanced by the superior knowledge and sophistication enjoyed by the trader in his dealings with primitive people.

But to obtain the raw materials on which his profits depended, together with sales to the native population of cotton cloth, liquor, beads, and trinkets, the trader required trading ports with an assured food supply, protection for his own and his employees' lives, and safe conduct for his goods to and from the interior. And when, as with rubber, cacao, tea, and palm oil, careful cultivation of crops in large plantations became necessary, substantial funds had to be invested.

All this implied a reasonably stable and effective government, capable of keeping the peace, of disciplining outlaw and criminal elements, and of providing assurances against the destruction or expropriation of property. Since backward and warring tribes could provide none of this, the trader had to do it himself. Very often the first political penetration of an area came about in this way, as an additional function of private enterprise in primitive surroundings. Later, as traders of rival nationalities threatened to invade his preserves, he appealed to his government. Supported by the industrial interests to which he ministered, and reenforced by the pervading sense of national rivalry, his appeals seldom fell on deaf ears. The "white man's burden" was accepted; and like protection, once started, land-grabbing tended to continue of its own weight, since unappropriated territory probably contained resources of value that someone else might get first. This sequence of events could be observed

---

[9] Although the London prices, both of finished manufactures and of raw materials and foodstuffs, followed a downward trend from 1875 to about 1900, there is considerable evidence to show that at the source, primary products prices remained constant or even rose. They fell in London owing principally to the large reduction in transportation costs brought about by the extension of railways, the substitution of steam for sailing vessels, and improvements in warehousing and handling facilities. See P. T. Ellsworth, "The Terms of Trade Between Primary Producing and Industrial Countries," *Inter-American Economic Affairs*, 10, No. 1 (Summer, 1956).

in many parts of the world, but nowhere more clearly or consistently than in Africa.

The Partition of Africa

Africa stood alone as a comparatively empty, vast, and defenseless area, and it was in Africa that the new imperialism found its main outlet. Before 1875, nearly nine-tenths of this continent was a primitive wilderness. The Ottoman Empire controlled, after a fashion, a fringe along the Mediterrean coast including Egypt, with the French-conquered territory of Algeria to the west. At the extreme southern tip, Great Britain had acquired the Cape Colony (1806) and Natal (1843). Apart from these substantial European and Turkish possessions, there was no trace of foreign domination except for scattered and largely forgotten trading posts established long before by the Spanish, Portuguese, French and British along the west coast and by the Portuguese and French on the east.

The new imperialism began, strangely, as an international venture. After Stanley's exploration of central Africa brought news of its wealth in 1878, Leopold II of Belgium formed an international company that sent Stanley back into the Congo basin to stake out claims and establish trading posts. In 1885, the company transformed itself into the Congo Free State, with Leopold as its private sovereign and business manager. Later, in 1908, after mounting indignation over the brutal methods of exploitation used in the ivory, rubber, and slave trades, it was taken over by Belgium.

Simultaneously with Stanley's activities, the French got busy. De Brazza pushed inland from the French coastal settlement at Gabon, preceded Stanley's arrival at a point which later became Brazzaville, and established claims that were rapidly enlarged into French Equatorial Africa.

On the heels of de Brazza's and Stanley's exploits, rivalry between French, English, and German trading companies began in and around the basin of the Niger, which lies at the base of the west African bulge. The Germans also, with the support of Bismarck, now converted to imperialism, made a start in carving out German Southwest Africa, far down the coast next to Cape Colony. Typical methods were to buy small tracts or to make treaties (containing unintelligible text but accompanied by appropriate gifts) with native chiefs, and then to set up trading and missionary posts. Later the areas were extended by a wider network of "treaties" or by outright conquest; railways were built; and direct rule over large territories became a reality.

The partition of east Africa occurred simultaneously with that of the west, and by identical methods. Cecil Rhodes built an empire in Rhodesia and Bechuanaland, while other Englishmen were busy acquiring British East Africa and British Somaliland. Germany absorbed Tanganyika, France picked a quarrel with the native queen of Madagascar and added this huge island to its domain. Even the Italians entered the race, to gain their slice of Somaliland, together with Eritrea.

Meanwhile Britain, after a period of joint supervision of Egypt's finances with France, had taken control of the country in the process of putting down a nationalistic revolt (1882). Using dubious Egyptian claims to the Sudan as a legal basis, Lord Kitchener pushed up the valley of the Nile, conquering the native dervishes as he went, until he reached Fashoda in 1898. There he met a Captain Marchand, who, after a two-year trek across the jungle from the French Congo, had hoisted the French flag. A diplomatic wrangle in London and Paris settled the question of sovereignty in favor of the British; the Sudan became nominally an Anglo-Egyptian condominium, and the British were well on their way to establishing their rule over a solid belt of territory from Cape to Cairo. Thus after two decades of exploring, land purchase or conquest, and economic assimilation, all Africa except Abyssinia and the Negro Republic of Liberia had fallen under foreign rule.

Imperialism in the Far East

French imperialism, checked at Fashoda, found more scope in the Orient. The acquisition in 1862 of Cochin-China, at the tip of the Indo-Chinese peninsula, had only whetted France's appetite. By intervention to avenge the murder of (non-French) Christians, by conquest, and by war with China, the French during the decade of surging imperialism extended their rule over all of what came to comprise Indo-China. After an ultimatum to the King of Burma (demanding revocation of trading rights granted the French), followed by invasion, British India annexed Burma in its entirety (1886).

At the end of the 1880's the era of imperialistic land grabbing was almost at a close. There was little unpopulated or weakly held territory not already under the dominion of one or another of the major powers, except in China. It was to China that the scene of imperialistic rivalry shifted in the nineties.

Both China and Japan had been forcibly opened to commerce between 1840 and 1880. And even though Britain, as a result of the Opium War (1839-42), had obtained Hong Kong, as well as five "treaty ports" where traders were to be free to reside and do business under their own laws, the rights so acquired were not to be exclusively British, but were to be enjoyed equally by other nations. The liberal principles of trade, not imperialistic exclusiveness, became the rule.

It was Japan, rapidly modernizing on western lines, which in 1894 began the race for foreign domination of the mainland. Rivalry in Korea between Japanese and Chinese factions unleashed the Sino-Japanese War, which resulted in Korean "independence" under Japanese tutelage, and the cession to Japan of Formosa and various smaller islands. Fearing Japan's expansion, Russia, joined by France and Germany, intervened to prevent her taking south Manchuria. For their "friendship," and at their urging, China granted important concessions. The battle for concessions was on, and with the concessions came economic penetration and trade dominance as the preludes to possible territorial partition.

Thus matters stood when in 1904 Japan challenged the presence of Russian troops in Manchuria. The success of the well-trained Japanese troops in the war which followed gave Japan bases in Port Arthur and Dairen, together with important railway and mining rights hitherto held by Russia.

After the Russo-Japanese war, the parceling out of the earth had about come to an end. Only a few changes occurred before the frictions bred of imperialism broke out in World War I.

Dollar Diplomacy

Somewhat belatedly, the United States also became caught up in the wave of nationalist expansion. During our war with Spain, military strategy had dictated the seizure of the Philippine Islands. Since there was danger that they might fall into Germany's hands, since they had great economic and strategic value, and since there was also the "white man's burden" to consider, it was decided to keep them. In the same year, 1898, sugar interests in the Hawaiian Islands fomented a rebellion, established a Hawaiian Republic, and succeeded in getting it adopted by the United States as a territory. Hawaiian sugar thereby became a domestic American product, with duty-free entry to the mainland.

Barring these two episodes, our imperialist phase involved no acquisition of foreign real estate, but what came to be called "dollar diplomacy"—intervention in the affairs of our near neighbors in support of previous commercial or financial penetration. Thus in Mexico a struggle between British and American oil interests for control of the Mexican oil fields brought their governments to their support, with each backing a rival Mexican political group. The outcome was not too happy for either of the big powers, however, since the Mexican constitution of 1917 vested all subsoil rights in the Mexican people, and furnished the legal basis for Mexico's expropriation, in 1938, of all foreign oil holdings. A similar conflict between British and American oil interests in Costa Rica led to United States support of a rebellion which established in power a regime that recognized American oil concessions and canceled British ones.

Threatened losses to American bondholders led to direct armed intervention in the Caribbean republics. In 1905, our government insisted that the Dominican Republic appoint an American receiver-general to collect customs and to allocate to American and foreign bondholders the amounts necessary for interest payments. Political interference followed a few years later and culminated in 1916 in armed intervention and the establishment of an American military dictatorship, which lasted until 1924. In Haiti, other means of imposing an unwelcome treaty having been unsuccessful, American armed forces in 1915 took over administration of the country.

Strategic rather than commercial or financial interests lay behind our armed support of the Panamanian "revolution" of 1903, which pried Panama loose from Colombia and gave us a perpetual lease of the Canal Zone. In Nicaragua, strategic and financial interests merged in American support, by loans and by armed intervention, of a rebellion (1909) friendly to our purposes. In the end, a treaty gave to our government the right to build a canal and a naval base; it also gave, to American bankers, control over Nicaragua's finances, banking, and railways.

SELECTED REFERENCES

Ashworth, William, *A Short History of the International Economy*. London: Longmans Green & Co., 1952. An excellent brief study of the spread of the Industrial Revolution during the past century, of the emergence of an international economy, and of the course of international economic relations since 1914.

Bagehot, Walter, *Lombard Street,* 14th ed. London: Murray, 1915. A nineteenth century work which had great influence on the formation of central banking policy.

Buchanan, Norman S. and Howard S. Ellis, *Approaches to Economic Development*. New York: Twentieth Century Fund, 1955. Chapters 7 and 8 contain a good, brief account of the expansion of the western economy.

Clapham, J. H., *An Economic History of Modern Britain*, Vol. II. New York: Macmillan, 1932. A standard work on the subject.

Feis, Herbert, *Europe the World's Banker 1870-1914*. New Haven, Conn.: Yale University Press, 1930. The best single source for data on international investment in this period.

Henderson, W. O., *Britain and Industrial Europe, 1750-1870*. Liverpool: Liverpool University Press, 1954. Contains much illustrative material on Britain's role in the industrial expansion of Europe.

Jones, G. P. and A. G. Pool, *A Hundred Years of Economic Development in Great Britain*. London: Gerald Duckworth & Co., 1940. An interesting and readable account of Britain's economic growth in the nineteenth century.

Knowles, L. C. A., *The Industrial and Commercial Revolutions in Great Britain in the 19th Century*. London: Routledge & Kegan Paul, 1922. Noteworthy for its emphasis on the role played by transportation in Britain's development.

13

THE TARIFF ISSUE

We have now analyzed the forces that determine international specialization and trade, and have traced the emergence of a highly integrated international economy which gave wide scope to those forces. Our next major task will be to consider the various ways in which the operation of the international economy may be disturbed and the manner in which such a disturbance is assimilated or adjusted.

Before we commence this study, however, let us consider the grounds on which free international trade is opposed. We have noted that the era of thoroughgoing liberal trade was brief, being succeeded by a gradual swing toward protective tariffs between 1870 and 1914. The initiation of this change can be accounted for by the sharp increase in European grain imports during the lean years of the eighties and nineties, reinforced by the rising spirit of nationalism. But the spread of protection required action by national legislatures. To obtain the necessary changes in laws, protagonists of protection had to prepare and argue their case.

First we must distinguish between tariffs for revenue and for protective purposes and indicate the more important effects resulting from the imposition of a tariff.

EFFECTS OF A TARIFF

Protection or Revenue?

Duties on imports may be imposed with a view to raising revenue, or to give protection to producers of the commodity taxed.[1] But unless a protec-

---

[1] In this chapter our sole concern will be with import duties. Other kinds of duties are also levied: transit duties and export duties. Transit duties are imposed on goods traversing a country en route from the country of origin to the country of consignment. They were of considerable moment before the early part of the nineteenth century, but are no longer important. Export duties are of greater significance, and are used principally by primary producing countries either to raise revenue or to stimulate domestic processing of the primary products (that is, as a protective measure). To conserve space, we shall omit any further discussion of these duties.

tive duty is so high as to exclude all imports, it is bound to have some revenue effect.

Is there such a thing as a tariff providing revenue, but no protection? The best candidate is a tariff on imports of a commodity not produced in the country at all. But even such a tariff does give some protection by diverting demand to other products. It appears that the intent of legislators provides no clear criterion for distinguishing between duties for revenue and duties for protection.

It is best to leave the matter as follows: A duty is purely protective only if it is so high as to prohibit all imports of the taxed commodity. And a duty can be made to have no net protective effects if domestic production of the commodity subject to duty also has imposed on it a domestic excise tax equal to the import duty. All duties lower than prohibitive and unaccompanied by equivalent excise duties have both revenue and protective effects.

Let us examine the impact of a customs duty and see how its influence is spread.[2] In Figure 13.1, SS is the supply curve of domestic producers of

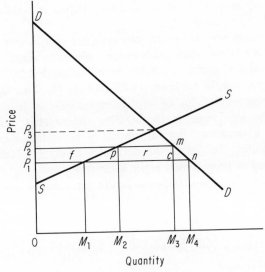

FIGURE 13.1   Effects of a Tariff

a commodity (their long-run average cost curve), DD the domestic demand curve. In the absence of a tariff, foreign competition sets the price at P_1. (Factor prices in some other country or countries are assumed to be more suited to the optimum production function for this commodity, since imports

[2] The analysis which follows is similar to, though it differs in some respects from, that used by Kindleberger in his *International Economics* (Homewood, Ill., Richard D. Irwin, Inc., 1963.)

are available at a lower cost than can be attained except on a relatively small amount of domestic production.) Domestic production is OM_1, while imports amount to M_1M_4.

A duty equal to P_1P_2 is now levied on imports of this commodity. To simplify the argument, let us assume that the foreign price of this article remains unchanged. The price in the domestic market now rises to P_2. At this price, domestic output expands from M_1 to M_2, while consumption shrinks from M_4 to M_3. Imports decline from a total of M_1M_4 to the smaller amount M_2M_3.

Revenue Effect

Since not all imports are excluded (to be prohibitive, the duty would have to be equal to P_1P_3), there is a revenue effect; the government collects customs revenue equal to the duty times the volume of imports. This is reflected in the rectangular area r.

Protective Effect

In terms of domestic production alone, the protective effect may be seen in the expansion of output from M_1 to M_2. This is made possible by the fact that the higher price, P_2, enables producers to cover their rising marginal costs on the larger output. The wherewithal to do this comes from that part of producers' increased receipts represented by the triangular area p, which measures the purely protective effect of the duty. It is that part of increased receipts necessary to pay for the increasingly inefficient use of factors to obtain the additional output M_1M_2.

Transfer Effect

The remaining portion of the larger producers' receipts, measured by the area t, is a surplus over costs on all but the last unit of output produced. It is an economic rent extracted by producers from consumers of the commodity, and represents a mere transfer of income. This can be called the transfer effect of the duty. (Kindleberger calls it the redistribution effect.)

If we assume that resources were fully employed before the imposition of the duty, the protective effect measures the loss to the country from the uneconomic reallocation of its productive resources. Before the duty was introduced, these were employed in other lines of production, where they earned the going rates of return. They earn no more in their new, protected employment, so they gain nothing, whereas the country loses from their more costly, less efficient use.[3]

[3] To attract resources (e.g., labor) from their old employment into the protected industry, however, they may have to be offered higher pay. If so, then since their remuneration is a cost to producers, its increase will be reflected in a more steeply rising cost curve. Their increased earnings are a partial offset to the loss to the community due to rising costs.

Consumption Effect

Let us look at matters from the viewpoint of consumers of the protected commodity. Before the imposition of the duty, their total satisfaction from consumption is measured by the area under the demand curve to the left of the vertical line M_4n. The cost of obtaining this satisfaction, on the other hand, is measured by the price paid times the amount consumed, or by the rectangular area OP_1nM_4. On all units consumed other than the marginal one (at n), they obtained a consumers' surplus measured by the triangular area between P_1n and the demand curve.

After the duty is imposed, total consumers' satisfaction is measured by the area under the demand curve to the left of the vertical line M_3m. The cost of obtaining it is consumers' outlay, or the area OP_2mM_3. Consumers' surplus is now the area between P_2m and the demand curve. Since this is smaller than the previous consumers' surplus (by the area P_1P_2mn), consumers have suffered a net loss in satisfaction as the result of protection.

Partially offsetting the loss to consumers is the revenue received by the government (r) and the surplus transferred to producers (t). The net loss to the community as a whole is measured by the two triangular areas, p (less efficient use of resources) and c (loss to consumers not offset or otherwise accounted for).

The loss of consumers' satisfaction is not imaginary, but very real, though it may not be consciously realized by consumers who are not aware of the existence of particular customs duties. It is the difference between the enjoyment consumers would get from having the use of a larger quantity of Swiss watches, for example, at a lower price, and the enjoyment they actually get from a smaller quantity bought at a higher price.

Tariffs and Prices

In all the forgoing discussion, we adhered to the assumption that the introduction of an import duty would have no effect on the foreign price of the import, and that hence the price in the protected market would rise by the full amount of the duty. This may occur, or price may not rise at all, or it may rise by less than the amount of the duty.

The price in the protected market will rise by the full amount of the duty only if the commodity is produced abroad at constant cost. Then imports come in at an unchanged price at the customs house; to this the duty must be added to get the domestic price.

No change in price will occur if the commodity taxed is exported from the country imposing the duty. The price at home will then be (barring discriminating monopoly) the world price less cost of transport. If, after protection, the home price should rise, domestic sales would be increased at the expense of exports until the home and foreign prices were brought into line again.

Whenever foreign production of the taxed import takes place under conditions of increasing cost—and in the long run, this is probably the typical case—the reduction in sales of foreign producers will force a contraction of production, and with it a decline of cost to a lower level. To a new, lower, landed price of imports the duty is added. The price in the protected market is higher than the foreign price by the amount of the duty, but not higher than the *old* pretariff price by this amount, owing to the decline in foreign costs.

FREE TRADE VERSUS PROTECTION

The case for free trade is very simple. It consists in the fact that, if trade is free, goods and services can be obtained at lower cost abroad than if domestic substitutes are produced in their stead. By producing exports and exchanging these for imports, fewer resources are required than if the imported goods were produced at home. If this were not true, the goods would not be imported, but would be obtained from home producers, as are those commodities that *are* produced more economically at home.

In other words, free trade permits full advantage to be taken of the possibilities of geographical specialization. Some countries have endowments of the factors that enable them to achieve economical production of one group of commodities; others are suitably endowed for the production of another group. Left alone, each country will specialize in producing those goods for which its factor endowment best suits it, and will exchange these specialties for those of other countries, to the mutual benefit of all.

The gain to any country from free trade can be expressed in terms of increased real income. By using a given amount of resources to produce imports, or import substitutes, a certain quantity of these goods can be obtained. But this quantity will be larger, and national income correspondingly greater, if the same resources are first used to produce exports, which are then exchanged for the cheaper foreign imports.

Protection wipes out, or at least reduces, the gains from trade. As our analysis has shown, its net effects are two in number: (1) It causes resources to be shifted from a more efficient to a less efficient use; (2) By raising the price of goods and services, it restricts the consumer's freedom of choice, arbitrarily forcing him to reduce his consumption of things of which, with uninhibited choice, he would prefer to buy more.

The case for free trade has never been successfully refuted, nor even has an intellectually acceptable argument for long-run, enduring protection, based on economic considerations, ever been devised, though much ingenuity has gone into the attempt. The arguments for protection that do have validity are either short-run or noneconomic in character, or require the realization of very special conditions. Yet most of the arguments advanced by protectionists are unqualified, asserted with great conviction, and what is more important, are widely believed.

Professor Viner concludes:

The contrast is striking between the almost undisputed sway which the protectionist doctrine has over the minds of statesmen and its almost complete failure to receive credentials of intellectual respectability from the economists. The routine arguments of the protectionist politician differ somewhat in quality from country to country. In my own country they are often magnificent achievements of sustained and impressive oratory, capturing their audiences in spite of—or perhaps because of—the absence of any visible means of intellectual support. . . . They are fairly adequately disposed of in any one of a large number of elementary textbooks, and what importance they have is due mainly to the fact that the general public does not read economic textbooks.[4]

SERIOUS ARGUMENTS FOR PROTECTION

Infant Industry

Protection can be an effective means of stimulating the development of an industry that is well suited to a country but which finds it impossible to get started unless it is sheltered for a time from the blast of competition from established foreign producers. The only advantage possessed by the foreign industry is that of an early start; in all other respects—especially suitability of factor prices to the combination required, availability of raw materials, and nearness to market—the two are on a par. This means that established producers, because of their early beginning, have been able to acquire internal and external economies not available to the potential producer in another country. These economies would develop gradually if the potential producer were given the temporary shelter of a tariff, and the newcomer would become equally or more efficient than his older competitors, since he suffers from no other disadvantage.

Suppose, for example, a new producer finds his domestic market preempted by existing foreign firms. He would have to start on a small and uneconomic scale, and could not possibly meet the low costs of his competitors. But with the shelter furnished by protection, he could expand gradually until, having attained optimum size, he could confront them on an even footing. In more technical terms, growth, as the years go by, permits the new producer to acquire internal economies of scale which are unattainable in the infant stage of development.

External economies, or those economies that accompany the growth not of a single plant but of an entire industry, are also at stake. As more domestic firms enter the field, the labor force grows and becomes able to supply specialized workers to fill vacancies on short notice; service and repair establishments arise to provide their specific contributions; research may be taken over by a special agency, and so on. All these developments help to bring

[4] Jacob Viner, *International Economics,* Ch. 6, "The Tariff Question and the Economist," p. 109. Published 1951 by The Free Press, Glencoe, Ill.

costs down and to hasten the day when the infant industry becomes mature and capable of standing on its own feet.

A moment's reflection will show that this argument in no way conflicts with the goal of the free trader: maximum international specialization on the basis of relative national advantage. Its proponents correctly believe that this result may not always be achieved without intervention. At bottom, intervention is justified because one of the assumptions on which the free trade case rests—perfect competition—is not realized in practice. Imperfections in competition, in the form of unequal access to internal and external economies, make temporary protection necessary to equalize competitive conditions.

But notice that the infant industry case is definitely circumscribed. Protection is only warranted if the industry in question is clearly suited to the country's factor endowment, market prospects, and facilities for obtaining raw materials, so that it can reasonably be expected one day to stand on its own feet. Moreover, the grant of protection should be for a limited period only; the day of the industry's maturity should be foreseeable in the reasonably near future.

In the practical application of infant-industry protection, these limitations are seldom observed. Infants are selected for nurture without the careful exercise of parental judgment necessary to determine their chances of survival. "Infant industry" becomes a slogan to justify promiscuous protection without regard to merit. When the indiscriminately chosen infants fail to become vigorous adults, the protection that keeps them unhealthily alive is rarely removed. Their anemia may even be treated to fresh doses of protection.

Before leaving this topic, notice that when infant-industry protection is applied to several industries at once, the argument acquires added force—always assuming that due care was used in choosing the recipients of aid. For to the external economies that arise with the growth of a *single* industry are added others of a broader character, such as accompany a country's total industrial expansion. Roads are improved, railways constructed, power plants erected, and technical and engineering training provided—facilities which are needed by all industries, but many of which cannot be economically justified until a certain stage of development is attained or within sight. These are what Friedrich List, a German economist of the early nineteenth century, had in mind when he wrote:

> Manufactories and manufactures are the mothers and children of municipal liberty, of intelligence, of the arts and sciences, of internal and external commerce, of navigation and improvements in transport, of civilisation and political power. They are the chief means of liberating agriculture from its chains, and of elevating it to a commercial character. . . . If restrictions on the importation of raw products hinder . . . the utilisation of the natural resources

and powers of a State, restrictions on the importation of manufactured goods, on the contrary, call into life and activity (in the case of a populous country already far advanced in agriculture and civilisation) a mass of natural powers; indeed, without doubt, the greater half of all natural powers, which in the merely agricultural State lie idle and dead for ever.[5]

Diversification of Industry

Among the battery of protectionist arguments, one that has frequently been prominent urges the diversification of industry as a goal. A highly interdependent international economic system, made up of individual nations specializing upon a rather narrow range of exports and depending upon others for a much wider range of imports, is very unstable. Its members are subject to the recurrent shock of worldwide depression and to serious economic disruption in the event of war or of major industrial change. These disturbances could be avoided or minimized, it is held, if the nation deliberately set out, through protection, to create a more balanced and self-sufficient economy. Insulated from these outside disturbances, the country would gain more in the long run from greater stability than it would lose from the higher cost of its protected production.

The argument has a strong popular appeal. Everyone prefers a "balanced" to an "unbalanced" economy, safety to danger; and national pride is stirred by the thought of being economically independent. Moreover, there is no denying the fact that between World War I and World War II the international economy was very unstable, and that these wars, by cutting off markets and sources of supply for many years, seriously disrupted the economies of many countries. These effects fell with particular harshness upon the more specialized producers of foodstuffs and raw materials, such as Australia, Argentina, Mexico, and Chile, where they strengthened the case for diversification of industry.

But let us be clear about the nature of this argument. It applies only to highly specialized economies, in practice especially those which export a narrow range of primary products and which depend upon imports for most of their supplies of manufactured goods. If diversification in these conditions is to be warranted, it should provide, without excessive cost, substantial insulation against depression and wars.

Thus qualified, the argument has little to recommend it. Highly specialized economies export from a fourth to a third or more of their national incomes. Their dependence on imports is equally great. Sufficient independence to give effective insulation against international shock would probably require that these proportions be brought down to around five per cent, close to the figure for the United States. To do so would mean such a huge reallocation of resources and such a wholesale denial of the benefits of international

[5] Friedrich List, *The National System of Political Economy*, pp. 115, 175. Copyright 1922 by Longmans, Green & Co., London.

trade as to make the goal prohibitively costly. It would be much more sensible to rely on infant industry protection, legitimately applied, to achieve —together with conscious efforts at economic development—a greater degree of industrialization, and to meet the problems of war and depression in other ways. (As a matter of fact, the war years, though they brought serious disturbance to primary producing countries, also brought great prosperity and rapid economic advance.)

Maintenance of Employment

During periods of severe unemployment, as in the 1930's, much use has been made of the argument that protection can furnish an effective remedy. By reducing imports, a tariff stimulates employment directly in the import-competing industries; from this focus, the employment-creating effect spreads to other industries in ever-widening though diminishing waves. Investment in facilities for producing substitutes for imports may also result, setting in motion a second force to increase employment.

Taken by itself, the argument is valid. Whether it is the best means of dealing with the problem, however, is questionable. First, it may not be very effective. If one country reduces its imports by a newly imposed tariff, the exports of its trading partners are thereby reduced in like amount. A decline in employment is set in motion abroad; as employment and incomes fall there, less is spent on imports, which are our country's exports. Even though this foreign repercussion is likely to be of smaller magnitude than our country's initial reduction of its imports, it may well constitute a substantial offset. Second, our country's exports are almost certain to be reduced, directly and drastically, by retaliation on the part of other countries. A country attempting to increase employment at home by means of a tariff is in effect exporting its unemployment. This sort of beggar-my-neighbor policy is sure to arouse resentment and prompt counter measures abroad. Finally, the stimulation of employment by a tariff involves a permanent reallocation of resources for what may be at best a temporary gain. The remedy is a costly one.

An alternative is to use monetary and fiscal policy to relieve unemployment. If successful, the accompanying rise in income will bring with it an increase in imports, which may lead to a deficit in the balance of payments and a loss of international reserves. A good deal depends upon whether the unemployment is purely local or is part of a worldwide phenomenon. If the former, and income and employment are merely restored to a preexisting level, there need be no ensuing balance of payments difficulties. If the latter, and other countries also adopt expansionary monetary and fiscal policies, incomes and imports of the several countries will rise together and no country need lose reserves. Even if our country has to go it alone, it would be preferable to combine an internal policy of expansion with direct quantitative restrictions on imports. For then imports may remain constant, any tendency to increase with rising incomes being held in check by quotas, whereas a tariff alone depresses imports and makes economic conditions worse abroad. Moreover, there is a better chance that direct restrictions can later be removed, especially if they are adopted for the specific purpose of safeguarding the balance of payments. Tariffs, once imposed, are very difficult to dislodge.

Improving the Terms of Trade

Some economists have urged the use of tariffs to take advantage of their tendency to force down prices in the exporting country. If this occurs, the tariff-raising country gains from obtaining its imports on better terms: a given amount of exports will exchange for a larger amount of imports than formerly.

As we have seen, the degree to which the landed price of imports will fall depends upon the conditions under which they are supplied. If their supply in the country of origin is highly elastic (approaching infinity, or constant cost), a tariff on imports will cause their prices to decline little or not at all. Only if their supply is inelastic (steeply rising costs) will a reduction in imports push their costs down appreciably.[6]

There is, moreover, no assurance that there is any net gain at all. We must remember the two certain adverse effects of a tariff: its diversion of resources to a more uneconomic use, and the loss in satisfaction it imposes on consumers. These offsets to any gain from lower-priced imports must be taken into account. When they are, if there is any benefit to the country as a whole, it is likely to be very small.

Nations being sensitive to the action of others in tariff matters, we must reckon with the possibility of retaliation. If other nations retaliate, and the prices of our country's exports fall, its terms of trade (the ratio of its export prices to its import prices) revert to or approximate their previous position. Even the fancied gain—which ignores the offsets to which we have called attention—is lost. Nothing remains but the reduction in consumers' satisfaction and the worsened allocation of resources.

Tariffs for Bargaining

A country which already has a tariff can, and frequently does, use it as a means of bargaining to obtain from other countries lower duties on its exports. The trade-agreements program of the United States amounted in effect to using our tariff as just such an instrument of bargaining; it consisted essentially in a swapping of duty reductions.

Such a course is not open to a free-trade country or one with only a revenue tariff. It is therefore sometimes argued that adoption of protective duties would benefit the country by giving it a lever with which to pry open

---

[6] Moreover, if *foreign* demand for these goods is elastic, any decline in their price will be checked by expanding purchases abroad.

foreign markets for its goods. There is some merit in this argument, but only for a free-trade or very low-tariff country. And there is the offsetting disadvantage that duties introduced for bargaining purposes cannot fail to create vested interests which will oppose the use of the tariff for the purpose originally intended. Indeed, the bargaining lever, instead of being used to gain tariff concessions from foreign powers, may be employed by others to extract additional protection from the home government.

Antidumping

The tariffs of many nations contain special provisions against "dumping," a practice which arouses the indignation, real or feigned, of producers in the market where dumping occurs.

What is "dumping"? Contrary to a widespread impression, dumping is not selling abroad below costs of production. It means instead *sales in a foreign market at a price below that received in the home market,* after allowing for transportation charges, duties, and all other costs of transfer. Discrimination between the home and foreign price is the essential mark of dumping. Thus, sales abroad below cost of production would not constitute dumping *unless* the foreign were lower than the domestic price.

The problem is complicated by the existence of different kinds of dumping. It may be *persistent,* continuing indefinitely because the exporter is in a position to practice discriminating monopoly (see Chapter 8). Selling in two separate markets, if the elasticity of demand is greater in the foreign than in the (monopolized) home market, he will gain by selling at a lower price abroad. Such dumping may continue indefinitely. On the other hand, dumping may be *intermittent* rather than continuous, with price-cutting undertaken for the purpose of destroying foreign competition.

From the point of view of the country in which the dumping occurs, it is clear that intermittent dumping can be most disturbing, even ruinous, to local firms. The gains of consumers are at best purely transitory, while the effects on business can be lasting. If care is taken to define dumping precisely, and not simply as selling below costs, antidumping duties can be justified. Such duties appear to have worked reasonably well in the United States and Canada.

Persistent dumping, on the other hand, is no different in its effects from sales by a low-cost foreign producer. Year in and year out, buyers get their supplies at low cost; competing producers, if there are any, can adjust to a stable situation. There is no special case for protection because of dumping; if a case can be established, it must rest on other grounds.

National Defense

Protection of certain industries is often supported by appeal to the needs of national defense. If the products of a particular industry are essential to military strength, it is argued, then, if that industry cannot survive without protection, it should by all means be maintained by protective duties. The desirability or necessity of providing for the national defense involves ends, such as security, power, or even the survival of the nation, that lie outside the scope of economics.

Notice, however, that nowadays, when war is total, practically any industry necessary for the operation of an economy is essential to the national defense. Hence the argument implies that military security can be guaranteed only by establishing nearly complete self-sufficiency. *Complete* self-sufficiency is a goal impossible to any nation. It can be substantially realized only by the United States and the Soviet Union.

Even near self-sufficiency, moreover, would for most nations require massive protection. But protection means inefficiency, and inefficiency is certainly no aid to defense!

If "essential industries" are defined very narrowly, to include only those engaged in producing technical military goods, such as optical instruments, radar equipment, explosives, and airplanes, then we should remember that there are less expensive ways than protection to ensure their survival. The industries in question may be carried on by the government as part of a national defense program, or they may be supported by bounties from the public treasury. The former alternative means that they would be included with other ordnance works, supplying the needs of the government. The requirements of the public for optical instruments, and so forth, would continue to be met by imports or by such domestic private enterprise as might exist without protection. Alternatively, bounties might be held down to a level only just adequate to provide for military needs, or expanded to support industries supplying the entire population.

Either of these alternatives would be superior to protection on grounds of justice (and possibly of cost as well), since the benefit of possessing an industry essential to the national defense accrues to the entire population, and it should therefore be paid for out of general taxation rather than supported by the consumers, as it would be under a protective policy.

NONSENSE ARGUMENTS FOR PROTECTION

All the protectionist arguments so far considered are relatively sophisticated. So far as any is valid, it is so only under narrowly circumscribed conditions. To deal with the situations toward which some of them are directed, clearly superior alternatives are at hand. Being sophisticated, none of these arguments is popular (barring perhaps that for national defense) except the infant-industry argument, whose very popularization has brought its corruption. It is a striking fact that the arguments for protection that carry the greatest political weight contain the least economic sense.

The case for protection one commonly encounters is loaded, not with rational argument, but with appeals to prejudice and to vested interests.

This is especially true where the retention or increase of existing protection is at stake, rather than the introduction of new duties; for when an inefficient industry is threatened with more intense foreign competition, either from the removal of duties or the worsening of its competitive position, a good many people are likely to be at least temporarily hurt. Their probable injury is exaggerated; the sympathies of their fellow citizens are invoked; and consideration of the national, as opposed to special, interest is ignored. Bear these things in mind as you examine the arguments that follow.

The Pauper Labor Argument

Everyone knows that wages in different countries vary tremendously. The average level in the United States for example, is about twice as high as in Great Britain, approximately 3 or 4 times that of Italy, and perhaps 6 or 7 times the average Japanese wage. With only these facts to go on, it is natural to conclude that the products of "pauper labor" can undersell those of high-wage labor. The tariff is extolled as "protecting the American standard of living" or "sheltering the American worker from the competition of pauper labor."

In contending that a high-wage country cannot compete with a low-wage country, this view is patent nonsense. It is possible to advance it seriously only if one is completely ignorant of both the principles and the facts of international trade. As for the facts, every day, year in and year out, the products of high-wage American labor are sold abroad in competition with goods made by low-paid workers. High wages are clearly no bar to low-cost production, at least in many important lines.

These facts, and the fallacy in the pauper labor argument, can only be explained by an appeal to the principles underlying international trade. There are two reasons why high-wage labor can without difficulty compete with low-wage labor. One is that labor is not the only factor of production. It is always combined with capital and natural resources. But the proportions in which the different factors are combined varies enormously from one product to another. And we know that the prices of the factors differ greatly between countries. Hence commodities embodying much capital can be produced at low cost in countries where capital is cheap; land-intensive products will be cheap in countries abundantly endowed with land, whereas labor-intensive commodities will be cheap where wages are low.

Low-wage countries, in other words, have an advantage over high-wage countries *only* with respect to commodities whose production requires the combination of much labor with relatively little capital or land—that is, where the wage bill is the preponderant element in costs. It is senseless for a high-wage country to try to compete in the production of such commodities, but it is equally senseless to contend, as the pauper labor argument does that a high-wage country is at a disadvantage in *all* lines of production.

There is, however, an additional element of fallacy to deal with. Even if labor *were* the only factor, a high-wage country could still meet the competition of a low-wage country wherever its relative productivity was higher than its relative wages. To take a simple case, suppose wages in A are three times as high as in B, but that in the manufacture of shoes its labor is three times as efficient as B's. It could then produce shoes at the same cost. If its ratio of efficiency were higher than its ratio of wages, say 4 or 5 to 1, its costs would be lower than B's.

The causes of such superior efficiency could be better management, better fed or better educated labor, access to a more advanced technology, or any of the social conditions of production which give rise to qualitative differences in the labor of different countries. These causes of efficiency would explain labor's higher average wages in A. Wherever they operated with particular force, A's labor efficiency would be relatively high, its costs relatively low. In industries in which A was less than three times as efficient as B, the latter country would have a cost advantage.

Taken together, differing factor combinations and conditions affecting labor efficiency go far toward explaining the ability of a high-wage country such as the United States to meet the competition of low-wage countries. It cannot compete, of course, where labor dominates the factor combination unless its labor is disproportionately productive. But the pauper labor argument makes no such qualifications. It is a sweeping generalization, and as such, wrong.

A QUALIFICATION   In one respect, and one only, is there any merit in the pauper labor argument. This is in its contention that a tariff can support the level of wages in a country. It can do so, however, only for a country in which labor is the scarce factor. The reason for this is highly sophisticated, and certainly was never comprehended by those who advanced the pauper labor argument.[7]

Imagine a country in which capital is abundant and labor is scarce, and whose commercial policy is one of free trade, so that it specializes on capital-intensive products, say automobiles. If it now introduces a tariff on relatively labor-intensive goods, say textiles, the automobile industry will contract, releasing both capital and labor, while the textile industry will expand.

But as labor moves out of the automobile industry into textiles, it is accompanied by a larger complement of capital than is currently being used in the textile industry. If the released capital is to be employed, the return on capital must fall. This encourages its more liberal use in the textile industry, with the result that the marginal product of labor and the real wage

---

[7] The argument presented here was developed by and is taken from the well-known article "Protection and Real Wages" by W. F. Stolper and Paul A. Samuelson in the *Review of Economic Studies*, IX (November, 1941) and reprinted in *Readings in the Theory of International Trade*, published 1949 by The Blakiston Co., Philadelphia.

of labor rise in that industry. But the decline in the return to capital will also encourage the substitution of capital for labor in the shrunken automobile industry. There, too, since labor is now combined with relatively more capital than formerly, the marginal product and the real wage of labor rise.

With no change in the country's total supplies of capital and labor, protection effects a rise in wages. The apparent paradox results from the fact that, although *total* capital and *total* labor are unchanged in amount, the *proportion* of capital to labor in each industry is raised.

Though valid and interesting, this argument has little practical importance as a basis for protection, even for a country such as the United States, where labor is the scarce factor. The argument is purely static: it makes no allowance for such dynamic considerations as the possible effect of a decline in the return to capital on its rate of accumulation and thus on the total supply of capital and its proportion to labor in the long run. A relatively high return to capital in the short run might, through its effects on capital accumulation, provide higher wages in the long run. Moreover, labor could also benefit from the stimulus to the introduction of technological innovations provided by a higher level of saving and investment.

Protection of the Home Market

An argument sometimes encountered claims that if a country's manufactures are protected, this will expand the market for agricultural products by increasing the purchasing power of industrial workers.

> Agriculture derives large benefits not only directly from the protective duties levied on competitive farm products of foreign origin but also, indirectly, from the increase in the purchasing power of the American workmen employed in industries similarly protected.[8]

The implication, of course, is that there will be a net expansion of the market for agricultural products. But if the purchasing power of industrial workers is increased because more are employed, the purchasing power of foreign customers will be reduced, since domestic manufactures replace imports. A domestic market is substituted for a foreign market. This is no gain to the farmer, and he suffers a certain loss in the higher prices he will have to pay for protected manufactures.

Keeping Money at Home

One of the crudest protectionist fallacies is well expressed in the form of a remark falsely attributed to Abraham Lincoln: "I do not know much about the tariff, but I know this much, when we buy manufactured goods abroad we get the goods and the foreigner gets the money. When we buy the manufactured goods at home we get both the goods and the money."

[8] Cited in Asher Isaacs, *International Trade: Tariff and Commercial Policies,* p. 229. Copyright 1948 by Richard D. Irwin, Inc., Homewood, Ill.

Except for its occasional currency, this argument scarcely deserves consideration. The classically appropriate comment has been made by Beveridge: "It has no merits; the only sensible words in it are the first eight words."[9] The view represents, of course, the crassest form of mercantilism, with its emphasis upon money as a form of wealth. It is only necessary to point out that in international trade goods pay for goods, and that international money (gold) moves only to perform the function of adjusting disturbances to trade. Our money—that is, the money our our country—will not be useful to the foreigner unless he spends it in our country!

Equalizing Costs of Production

Proponents of protection often contend that a truly "scientific" tariff is one which equalizes costs of production at home and abroad. This principle of cost equalization is not, properly speaking, an argument for protection; it is rather a way of dressing up the case to make it more palatable.

> The doctrine has an engaging appearance of fairness. It seems to say, no favors, no undue rates. Offset the higher expenses of the American producer, put him in a position to meet the foreign competitor without being under a disadvantage, and then let the best man win. Conditions being thus equalised, the competition will become a fair one. Protected producers will get only the profit to which they are reasonably entitled and the domestic consumers are secured against prices which are unreasonable.[10]

The doctrine's apparent fairness is only skin deep. To appreciate this, one needs only to realize that a tariff is essentially discriminatory. It picks out for special advantage at the cost of the public precisely the least efficient of a country's industries. By keeping out imports, this protection reduces foreign markets for the country's most efficient (export) industries, and so injures them. Legislation that discriminates in favor of inefficient producers, against efficient ones, and against the general body of consumers, can hardly be given high marks for common sense, let alone for fairness.

If there were such a thing as a "scientific" tariff, it should provide an unambiguous set of criteria for determining what commodities to protect and how far protection should be extended in each case. Apply this test to the principle of equalizing costs of production. Should any producers who want to establish an uneconomic industry, or who have already established such an industry, be granted sufficient protection to meet foreign competition even if this requires a duty of 100 per cent—or 1,000 per cent? If not, where shall the line be drawn? Shall cost equalization apply only to the most efficient 10 per cent of firms in the industry, to 90 percent, or to all, in-

---

[9] Sir William Beveridge, *Tariffs: The Case Examined*, p. 27. Copyright 1931 by Longmans, Green & Co., London, where the quotation above is also cited.

[10] In the course of criticizing the argument, F. W. Taussig, *Free Trade, The Tariff, and Reciprocity*, p. 134. Copyright 1920 by the Macmillan Company, New York.

cluding the least efficient? Where shall we draw the line? Where *can* the line be drawn except between those who have the political power to exact discriminatory treatment and those who do not?

Upon closer inspection, therefore, this "scientific" principle of tariff-making turns out to be a completely unscientific and irrational appeal to national prejudice against the foreigner. Its disarming character, and its lack of any criteria for limiting protection, are its most dangerous features.

SELECTED REFERENCES

Beveridge, Sir William, *Tariffs: The Case Examined*, 2nd ed. New York: Long-mans, Green & Co., 1932. Still one of the best general discussions of the tariff in all its aspects.

Isaacs, Asher, *International Trade: Tariffs and Commercial Policies*. Homewood, Ill.: Richard D. Irwin, Inc., 1948. A detailed study of tariffs, with much useful illustrative material.

Kindleberger, Charles P., *International Economics*. Homewood, Ill.: Richard D. Irwin, Inc., 1963. Chapter 10 has a somewhat fuller discussion of tariffs to improve the terms of trade, to increase employment, and to redistribute income in favor of the scarce factor than is given here.

Lloyd, Lewis E., *The Case for Protection*. New York: Devin-Adair Co., 1955. A frankly partisan book, which tries to make protection seem in the national interest.

Scitovsky, Tibor, "A Reconsideration of the Theory of Tariffs," American Economic Association, *Readings in the Theory of International Trade*. Philadelphia: The Blakiston Co., 1949, Ch. 16. Besides its discussion of the gains from trade (Ch. 9), this article contains an exhaustive analysis of the terms-of-trade argument and of retaliation, with some interesting closing comments on infant-industry protection.

Stolper, Wolfgang F. and Paul A. Samuelson, "Protection and Real Wages," American Economic Association, *Readings in the Theory of International Trade*. Philadelphia: The Blakiston Co., 1949, Ch. 15. Shows that a country's scarce factor's return is raised, both relatively and absolutely, by protection.

Taussig, Frank W., *Some Aspects of the Tariff Question*, 3rd ed. Cambridge, Mass.: Harvard University Press, 1931. Examines the growth of the protected sugar, steel, and textile industries in the United States to determine the role played by the tariff in their development.

PART IV

The Balance of Payments and Its Adjustment

14

NATIONAL INCOME AND THE
BALANCE OF PAYMENTS

Our main concern in preceding chapters has been with different possible ways of allocating the world's resources, on the assumption that these resources were fully employed. We found that in general the best results for all concerned would be attained under free trade, when resources would be allocated according to the relative advantage different nations possessed in the production of the various commodities. Only a few narrowly specified exceptions to this general principle could be admitted.

The advantage of a nation in production and trade was seen to depend on its relative endowment with the productive agents and on the possible development of internal and external economies of production. As modified by the natural protection afforded by transportation costs and by the artificial protection of its tariff laws, these elements determined what commodities the country exported and imported.

We have also seen how, during the nineteenth century, there developed a complex pattern of specialization and trade. In such a world, if there were no international movements of capital and if demands were stable, the operation of reciprocal demands would soon establish a situation where each nation's exports and imports balanced one another. Its international receipts and payments, or its balance of payments, would achieve a stable equilibrium.

In fact, however, demands are not fixed, but change with changing tastes and with the progress of technology. Moreover, capital movements do occur in response to variations in the profitability of investment. Nor does national income, and with it aggregate and specific demands, remain constant; as we know, income changes progressively as growth occurs and spasmodically as cyclical fluctuations take place. For all these reasons, a nation's international balance of receipts and payments is unlikely for long to remain in a state of stable equilibrium; it is almost certain to be subjected to frequent disturbances. The question arises: how does a nation adjust to these disturbances, small or large? Particularly if it suffers a large and persistent excess of international payments over receipts, by what means can equilibrium be restored to its international accounts?

This section of the text is devoted to answering these important questions. We shall see how international accounts are kept and what they do and do not reveal, by what mechanisms equilibrium may be restored to a balance of payments that has been seriously disturbed, and consider what policy alternatives are open to governments. Since a country's balance of payments reflects all of its economic transactions with the outside world, these are bound to be strongly influenced by changes in the level of its income and aggregate demand. Therefore we shall first examine systematically the relations between a country's income and its balance of payments.

Whereas in our earlier discussion of the bases for international specialization and trade we assumed resources to be fully employed, but allowed prices to vary, we shall now make the opposite assumption: that prices are constant. So long as this is true, there must be idle resources that will be called into employment with an increase in money expenditure. Money income and real income will move together, up to the point where resources are fully employed. Then, of course, any further expansion of money expenditure would raise prices, putting us outside the bounds of our model. This assumption of constant prices is unrealistic, but it is useful. It enables us to isolate for examination what we are interested in—the relations between national income and the balance of payments. Later we shall have to take into account the fact that both prices and income vary together.

GROSS NATIONAL PRODUCT

An economy's productive activity can be represented in a number of ways. Basic among these is the concept of *gross national product* (*GNP*). This measures, in money terms, the gross value of the final product of an economy's productive activity over a specified period, normally a year. The productive activity of an economy is directed toward providing consumers' goods and services, which yield current satisfaction to producers and their dependents, and also toward maintaining and augmenting the community's stock of capital goods. Final product, in other words, is of two kinds: goods (and services) destined for *consumption*, and goods which go to maintain or to increase the capital stock, or *gross investment*.

Final product is specified so as to exclude intermediate goods and thus to avoid double counting. For example, the value of the output of the shoe industry includes the value of the leather purchased and thus the contributions to final output of the producers of hides, and of tanners. These must not be counted separately, since the value added at each stage in production is included in the value of final product. Alternatively, the contribution of each stage of production may be counted separately, including the final stage, provided only the "value added" at each stage is included in reaching the total.

Gross value of final product is specified to warn that part of current invest-ment is for the replacement of capital goods that are worn out or become obsolete in the course of producing current income. That is, the investment component of *GNP* includes the production of capital goods that add nothing to the nation's stock of wealth, but merely maintain it by replacing the portion that becomes worn out and is discarded.

THE NATIONAL INCOME EQUATIONS

National product or income is a circular flow. The impetus that generates this flow comes from the expenditure of consumers and investors, which con-stitutes orders to produce. When production is undertaken in response to these orders, the purchases of investors and consumers become the sales of producers—that is, the expenditures of the investors and consumers become the receipts of the producers. These are simply different ways of looking at the same thing: the *production* side of national income. There is a flow of goods and services into the hands of buyers, and an opposite flow of money ex-penditures into the coffers of producers.

National income or product can also be regarded from the side of *distribu-tion.* The money proceeds from the sale of output are passed on by the pro-ductive sector to individuals for the services in production of their labor, their capital, and their land. In addition to these factor payments, the income resulting from sales is also distributed to individuals in the form of business transfer payments and to government in the form of indirect taxes and cor-porate taxes.[1] Income thus distributed is now available for expenditure; when spent by its recipients, it comes back to producers again to complete the cir-cular flow.

We are now in a position to show this circular flow of income in convenient equation form. Starting with expenditures on *GNP* as the force motivating production, we note that in a closed economy these consist of purchases by consumers, purchases by investors, and purchases by the government for both current consumption and investment. We can express this in a simple equa-tion:[2]

$$GNP = C + I_g + G_c + G_i.$$

In an economy with foreign trade, we would have to add merchandise ex-ports and various services performed for foreigners. But if we introduced only this addition, our equation would reflect not gross national product, or the total value of goods and services produced by the economy, but gross pur-

---

[1] Personal income taxes and property taxes are not included here, since they are levied on individuals *after* income from production has been distributed.

[2] G_c represents government consumption outlay, devoted to the purchase of the services of government employees and of currently used supplies such as stationery, uniforms and food for the armed forces, and so forth. G_i is government investment, as in buildings, power plants, and so forth. The subscript g for investment calls attention to the fact that investment is gross.

chases from the productive sector. Yet each category of goods purchased includes an import component. Many stores sell finished imported goods, while even exports may include imported raw materials. To express gross national product for an open economy, then, we must *add* exports of goods and services and *subtract* similar imports. Our equation now becomes

$$GNP = C + I_g + G_c + G_i + X - M.$$

Now consider gross national product from the point of view of its distribution rather than from that of its production. Most of the *GNP* will be allocated to individuals as factor payments: wages (W), interest (i), rent (R), and profits (P). In addition, there may be business transfers; for simplicity, we omit them here. Also, there are sure to be taxes (T), both indirect and on corporate profits. Moreover, business enterprises are unlikely to distribute all their profits to stockholders; they normally withhold or save some part (S). Finally, a sufficient sum must be set aside to provide for the replacement of that part of previously existing capital equipment and plant that was used up in the course of producing the national output. In practice, this allowance is made by charging off an estimated amount for depreciation (D).[3] We can now state in equation form how *GNP* is allocated to distributed income, taxes, corporate saving, and depreciation:

$$GNP = W + i + R + P + T + S + D.$$

Since *GNP* produced and *GNP* distributed are simply two aspects of the same thing, we can express this equality in the equation

$$C + I_g + G_c + G_i + X - M = GNP = W + i + R + P + T + S + D.$$

NATIONAL ACCOUNTS

Our major immediate task is to show how a nation's productive activities, as reflected in its gross national product, are related to its foreign transactions, which are pictured in its balance of payments. In a general way, of course, the connection is obvious. Part of national product is generated by those employed in producing exports, while some part of national income is always spent on imports. Such obvious relationships, however, do not carry us very far, for foreign transactions are of many kinds, and the points of contact between one economy and the rest of the world are numerous and complex. It is desirable to express the more important economic relations between one nation and the rest of the world as precisely and clearly as possible. To attain this clarity and precision, it is helpful to introduce a set of national accounts which reflect the activities and transactions of the different sectors of the economy.[4]

[3] This is only an approximation to the actual decline in the value of plant and equipment. In lieu of anything better, it is generally used.

[4] The method of presentation used here is an adaptation of that used by Jaroslav Vanek in Chapter 2 of his *International Trade: Theory and Policy* (Richard D. Irwin, Inc., Homewood, Ill., 1962). I have combined the consolidation of national accounts with the national income equations.

The Gross National Product and Income Account (IA_p)

Let us start with the gross national product and income account, which presents, in somewhat more detailed form, the same information contained in the equation for *GNP*. The two sides of such an account correspond exactly to the two sides of the *GNP* equation. One side shows the sources of national income in the production resulting from the expenditures of consumers, investors, the government, and foreigners; or, alternatively, this output of goods and services is regarded as sales to these various buyers. The other side shows how the income resulting from this production is distributed among those whose contributions of labor, capital, or other resources made it possible. The gross national product and income account pictures the activities of all the economic units of a nation—of the corporations, small enterprises, farmers, professional people, and even the government—so far as they contribute to or share in the annual output of goods and services. It is the account of the *productive sector* of the economy.

The accompanying gross national product and income account is a close approximation to those of the United States in the mid-1950's. To avoid un-

Table 14.1. GROSS NATIONAL INCOME AND PRODUCT ACCOUNT (IA_p)
(Billions of Dollars)

	Income Distributed (Drs.)			Product (Crs.)		
	Wages and salaries:			Sales to consumers	230	C
W_p	Of private employees	175		Sales to government:		
	Of government			On current account	75	G_c*
	employees	35		On capital account	5	G_i
i_p	Interest	12		Sales to producers on		
	Income of unincorporated			capital account and		
	enterprises:			accumulation of fixed		I_g
W_p	Wages	24		assets	50	
R	Rent	10		Inventory accumulation	2	
i_p	Interest	5		Merchandise exports	17	X
P	Profits	15		Shipping &		
t_p	Business transfer payments	1		tourism	3	
	Corporate profits:			Interest, dividends, &		F_p
P	Dividends	18		other income from		
S_p	Undistributed profits	8.5		foreigners	3.5	
T_p	Corporation profits tax	20		Minus:		
D	Depreciation allowances	23		Merchandise imports	—10	M
T_i	Indirect taxes	30		Shipping services &		
				tourism	—5	
	Minus:			Interest, dividends, &		F_p'
i_g	Government interest &			other income pay-		
	subsidies	—7		ments to foreigners	—1	
		369.5			369.5	

* Includes services furnished by consumers' sector (i.e., services of government employees).

necessary complexity, detail has been suppressed; all figures have been rounded, and some altered; but the net result substantially represents the facts of that period.

On the right-hand side are shown the sources of income in the production and sale of the various categories of goods and services. Each entry is followed by a symbol corresponding to one you have already encountered in the equation for GNP.[5] Note that gross investment (I_g) consists of two parts: capital goods sold to producers or accumulated by those who produced them (as in the case of a blast furnace erected for its own use by a steel company), and additions to inventories. As we noted when discussing the GNP equation, the value of imports and of other services rendered by foreigners must be deducted from gross product, since those imports and foreign services entered as components into that product.

Turning now to the allocation of income side, we find the familiar factor shares, with wages (W_p) coming from corporations, government, and unincorporated enterprises (farmers, professional people, and other self-employed).[6] Interest earned on capital used in production (i_p) is found in two places: (1) under a general entry for capital provided by corporations, and (2) for that provided by the rest of the economy, under unincorporated enterprises. But government interest (i_g), together with government subsidies, is entered as a subtraction. This is because government interest paid to producers and individuals is not counted on the product or sources side, on the ground that most government interest payments are for the unproductive use of capital in the conduct of wars. Yet this interest *is* included in income allocated. Therefore its subtraction is necessary so as not to have income allocated exceed income produced.[7]

Although the total for corporate profits is $69.5 billion, it is divided up in the account according to its distribution: $18 billion as dividends (P), $8.5 billion as corporate savings or undistributed profits (S_p), $20 billion paid to the government as corporate income taxes (T_p), and $23 billion as depreciation allowances (D). The latter, like corporate savings, represents a part of income produced that is not disbursed, but is set aside. The need for this is

[5] There are a few new ones. Thus F_p stands for receipts from foreigners for various services, as distinct from merchandise exports (X). We use the primed letter F_p' to stand for similar payments for services rendered by them.

[6] Usually the income of unincorporated enterprises is shown as farm, rental, professional, and other income, since the manner in which it is reported does not permit its presentation according to factor shares. Here this income is arbitrarily distributed among those shares so as to avoid complicating the GNP equation presently to be used with an unnecessarily large number of symbols.

[7] Government subsidies likewise are not included on the sources side, since they do not enter into the market value of goods and services sold. (A subsidy permits a product to be sold at a lower price than would otherwise be possible.) But subsidies, like government interest, are paid to individuals and firms, and must therefore be deducted from the allocations side to preserve the equality of income generated and income distributed.

clear. Some of the capital equipment used in the process of producing the national output will wear out or become obsolete. If the economy's productive capacity is to be preserved, a part of the income produced must be reserved for replacement of this equipment.

There is one final entry that needs to be mentioned: business transfer payments (t_p). A part of the national income resulting from production is not paid out in factor shares, but is distributed in the form of charitable contributions, Christmas bonuses to employees, cash prizes, and the like.

To conclude this section, we can now express the product and income account as an equation similar to, but more elaborate than, the one you have already encountered:

$$W_p + i_p + R + P - i_g + S_p + D + T_p + T_i = GNP$$
$$= C + G_c + G_i + I_g + (X + F_p) - (M + F_p').$$

The Personal Income and Outlay Account (IAₑ)

Besides their activities as producers, which are recorded in the production statement or *GNP* account, individuals also act in their capacity as consumers and heads of households. In so doing, they not only carry out transactions with the productive sector which are recorded in the *GNP* account from its point of view, but they also conduct transactions with one another, with the government, and with foreigners. To have a complete view of a nation's economic activity, therefore, we must have accounts that show the activity of individuals as consumers, of the government as an important segment of the economy, and of all sectors in their relations with foreigners.

The introduction of these accounts is also necessary to preserve an appropriate balance in all the economy's transactions. Every transaction has two sides; what is a receipt to one economic entity is a payment to some other. Therefore if all transactions are to be fully accounted for, for each payment we must show a corresponding receipt, and vice versa. In accounting language, for every debit, there must be a corresponding credit. To show the payments that are the counterparts of the receipts in the account of the productive sector, and the payments that are the counterparts of its receipts, we must introduce accounts reflecting the current activities of the household sector and the government sector, and (somewhat later) an account that records transactions with foreigners. First, let us look at the personal income and outlay account corresponding to the gross national product and income account we have already inspected—as shown in Table 14.2.

The first five lettered entries on the side of income receipts (credits)—W_p, R, i_p, P, and t_p—appeared in the *GNP* account as disbursements or debits. Here they represent the corresponding receipts of private individuals in their role as heads of households and consumers. These individuals also receive income from the government in the form of transfer payments (t_g): old

Table 14.2. PERSONAL INCOME AND OUTLAY ACCOUNT (IA_c)

	Outlay *(Debits)*			Income *(Credits)*		
C	Consumer expenditures	230		Wages & salaries:		
	Tax payments by individuals:			From corporations	175	⎤
	⎡ Income taxes	40		From government	35	⎟ W_p
T_c	⎨ Property taxes	3		From unincorporated		⎟
	⎣ Social insurance contributions	8		enterprises	24	⎦
F_c'	Transfer payments to abroad	1		Rent	10	R
S	Savings	25		Interest	17	i_p
				Profits:		
				Dividends from		⎤
				corporations	17	⎟ P
				From unincorporated		⎟
				enterprise	15	⎦
				Business transfer payments	1	t_p
				Transfer payments from		
				government	12	t_g
		307			307	

age pensions, unemployment compensation, veterans' bonuses, and the like. Although these payments add to the income of individuals, they are not derived from productive activity and therefore are shown here rather than in the account of the productive sector. They are mere transfer payments; the government uses part of the taxes it collects to make them.

To see how the private sector used its income of $307 billion, we look to the outlay or debit side of the account. Consumers' expenditures of $230 billion are the counterpart of the sales of these goods by the productive sector. Income and property taxes, together with social security contributions, add up to $51 billion of taxes (T_c) paid by individuals, while they remitted $1 billion (F_c') to relatives and friends or charitable institutions abroad. Finally, what they did not spend, they saved (S_c); as we shall see shortly, this is transferred to the private sector's capital account.

Just as we were able to express the equality of both sides of the *GNP* account in an equation, so we can express the private sector's income statement in a similar equation:

$$C + T_c + S_c + F_c' = W_p + R + i_p + P + t_p + t_g.$$

The Government Receipts and Outlay Account (IA_g)

The government constitutes the third and final element of the economy. We can explain its current transactions very briefly (Table 14.3).

The first three sources of government receipts are the counterparts of the taxes paid by individuals (T_c). Corporation taxes (T_p) and indirect taxes (T_i), here receipts, were payments in IA_p. The remaining item consists of a small amount of interest and transfer payments by foreign governments (F_g).

Table 14.3. GOVERNMENT RECEIPTS AND OUTLAY ACCOUNT (IA_g)

	Outlay (Debits)		Receipts (Credits)		
G_c	Government expenditure on current goods and services	75	Individual income taxes	20	T_c
i_g	Government interest and subsidies	7	Social insurance contributions	8	
			Property taxes	3	
t_g	Transfer payments to individuals	12	Corporation profits tax	20	T_p
F_g'	Transfer payments to foreigners	6	Indirect taxes	30	T_i
S_g	Surplus	1.5	Interest and transfer payments from foreign governments	0.5	F_g
		101.5		101.5	

Of the outlays of government from its income, we have already encountered the first three items. Current government expenditures on goods and services (G_c) corresponds to sales to government on current account in the productive sector's account. Government interest and subsidies (i_g) was shown in IA_p as a *deduction* from income distributed, since this income is not a payment for productive services; here the payment is entered. Transfer payments to individuals (t_g) appears in IA_c as a receipt. The government transferred $6 billion to foreigners (F_g'), mainly as foreign aid. Finally, since government's receipts exceed its outlays, there is a small surplus (S_g) to go into the capital account.

Expressing the equality of the government sector's outlays and receipts in equation form, we have:

$$G_c + i_g + t_g + S_g + F_g' = T_c + T_p + T_i + F_g.$$

CONSOLIDATION OF THE INCOME ACCOUNTS

Now that we have the income statements or current accounts of the three sectors of the economy before us, we can consolidate or merge them. When the accounts of two corporations are consolidated upon the conclusion of a merger, all transactions formerly carried out between the corporations become a purely internal matter and disappear from the accounts. Only transactions with firms and individuals external to the new corporation will be recorded. So with an income statement for the entire economy regarded as a unit: all that we are left with is transactions with foreigners and certain non-current transactions that relate not to current receipts or payments of income nor to the sale or purchase of goods and services for current use, but to the creation of capital assets or the establishment of claims on those assets.

The operation of consolidating the income accounts can be handily shown with the aid of the equations expressing the equality of gross national income and gross national product, of personal outlays and receipts, and of government outlays and receipts. All we need do is set these equations down one after the other and perform the algebraic operation of addition. Identical items on opposite sides of any two equations will cancel out, as will plus and minus items on the same side.

$$IA_p \quad W_p + i_p + R + P - i_g + S_p + D + T_p + T_i + t_p$$
$$+ \qquad\qquad\qquad = C + G_c + G_i + I_g + X + F_p - (M + F_p')$$
$$IA_c \quad C + T_c + S_c + F_c'$$
$$+ \qquad\qquad\qquad = W_p + R + i_p + P + t_p + t_g$$
$$IA_g \quad G_c + i_g + t_g + S_g + F_g'$$
$$\| \qquad\qquad\qquad = T_c + T_p + T_i + F_g$$
$$IA \quad (S_p + S_c + S_g) + D + (F_p' + F_c' + F_g') + M$$
$$\qquad\qquad\qquad = I_g + G_i + X + F_p + F_g$$

The final equation for the consolidated income account of the entire economy shows only what is left after all current transactions between the different sectors of the economy have been eliminated, namely: current transactions with foreigners, and capital transactions within the economy. For convenience, let us regroup the elements in this last equation in a manner that brings related items together:

$$(S_p + S_c + S_g)$$
$$= (I_g - D) + G_i + (X - M) + (F_p + F_g) - (F_p' + F_c' + F_g')$$

Now we can condense this equation into a simpler form. Since $(S_p + S_c + S_g)$ comprises net domestic saving, substitute the single letter S for this expression. Also, $(I_g - D) + G_i$ is net domestic investment, for which we shall use the symbol I_d. The remainder of the equation stands for the balance of current foreign trade and services, or the balance of payments on current account. Let us add current receipts from foreigners $(F_p + F_g)$ to exports, and current foreign payments $(F_p' + F_c' + F_g')$ to imports, so that X and M now represent total current receipts from foreigners and total current payments to foreigners. We can now restate the equation in the much simpler form:

$$S = I_d + X - M.$$

This equation states that a community's net savings are equal to net domestic investment plus the net balance of current foreign receipts and payments. It is a relationship that we shall find of considerable interest later on.

THE CAPITAL ACCOUNTS

Most of the transactions recorded in the accounts so far considered have to do with strictly *current* activities—those relating to the sale or purchase of goods and services that enter into the current year's consumption or to the payment or receipt of the current year's money incomes. There were a number of transactions, however—those reflecting the activities of investment and saving —that made no direct contribution to the current satisfaction of consumers' wants, or did not augment current money incomes. Instead, they served to maintain or to increase the community's stock of wealth. They added to its capital assets, and, as we shall see, established claims or liabilities against them. To record these changes in the community's assets and liabilities, we need a separate set of accounts, the capital accounts.[8] These accounts record both the changes in the assets or liabilities of a sector that result from the year's activities of saving and investing, and changes effected by independent financial transactions undertaken during that period. To understand these capital accounts, it will help if you regard such an account as the independent custodian of the assets and liabilities it records. Think of the capital account of the productive sector, for example, as holding the assets of that sector as a custodian distinct from the sector itself. The claims of the sector, and of others outside the sector, against these assets it records among liabilities. Following the practice used in the current or income accounts, debits reflect things acquired through purchase (assets bought, or liabilities reduced, as through the payment of maturing debt). Credits, on the other hand, show things given up by the custodian capital account: claims on assets issued to creditors or to the productive sector itself, or assets sold.

The Capital Account of the Productive Sector (KA_p)

Starting with the capital account of the productive sector, we note as debit entries the assets produced by that sector and recorded in the gross national

Table 14.4. CAPITAL ACCOUNT OF THE PRODUCTIVE SECTOR (KA_p)

	Assets (Debits)		Liabilities (Credits)		
I_g {	Plant and equipment	50	Net worth:		
	Inventory accumulation	2	Undistributed profits	8.5	S_p
B_{gp}	Domestic government securities	4	Depreciation	23	D
B_c	Private loans	3	Common & preferred stock	20	O_c
$\bar{F}_p'$ {	Investment in foreign assets	1.5	Long-term debt (private)	3 ⎱	
	Foreign bank deposits	0.5	Short-term debt:	⎰ L_c	
			Private	2 ⎰	
			Foreign	1.5	$\bar{F}_p$
			Demand deposits:		
			Private	2	m_c
			Government	0.5	m_g
			Foreign	0.5	$\bar{F}_p$
		61		61	

[8] A complete capital account shows *all* the assets and liabilities held or owned at a given instant, together with changes that have occurred during the income period. Here, however, we are interested only in the *changes* that take place; that is all the capital accounts will show.

product account and equation as credits: plant and equipment (50), and inventory accumulation (2). These goods were produced by the productive sector but were not sold to consumers for current use; they were sold to, or retained by, firms in the productive sector and were *not* consumed. Therefore they constitute an addition to assets, or investment (I_g). This addition to the assets of the productive sector is recorded by entering their value on the assets side of the custodian capital account.

During the period to which the accounts relate, a number of other assets—government securities, evidences of private debt, and foreign assets and bank deposits—were also acquired, for a total increase in assets or $61 billion. How was this substantial increase made possible?

To a relatively moderate extent, the decisions of corporation directors not to pay out to individuals all the net income received was responsible. They withheld $8.5 billion of corporate earnings, which were invested in certain of the assets acquired. Thereby they established a claim against the increased assets of the productive sector, a claim that is recorded in the custodian capital account on the liabilities side.

A part of corporate receipts was also set aside (not paid out) as depreciation reserves; these funds, too, were invested in one asset or another. Such assets can later be converted into cash, to be used to replace worn-out plant and equipment. This refusal to spend is also a form of (gross) saving, and gives the productive sector a claim (23) against the increase in assets.

Another $20 billion came from the private sector. Individuals purchased new issues of stock in corporations to this value (O_c), and thereby established a claim on the productive sector's assets.

Finally, the productive sector borrowed from the private sector (domestic long-term and short-term debt, $5 billion) and from foreigners ($1.5 billion), while banks "borrowed" in effect by increasing their demand liabilities (demand deposits) to the private and public sectors and to foreigners by $3 billion. These financial or capital transactions, as opposed to current transactions, gave rise to liabilities or claims against the assets whose acquisition by the productive sector they made possible.

Just as we were able to translate the current accounts into equations, we can also do so with the capital accounts. Using the symbols given alongside the entries in KA_p, but summing into a single symbol entries of similar character, the capital equation for the productive sector is

$$I_g + B_{gp} + B_c + \bar{F}_p' = S_p + D + O_c + L_c + \bar{F}_p + m_c + m_g.$$

The Capital Account of the Private Sector (KA_c)

Individuals in the private sector acquired assets worth $28 billion in a number of ways: they bought government securities (B_{gc}, $1 billion); they acquired demand deposits (m_c, $2 billion), they made loans to the productive sector (L_c, $5 billion); and they purchased stock in corporations (O_c, $20 billion).

Table 14.5. CAPITAL ACCOUNT OF THE PRIVATE SECTOR (KA_c)

	Assets (Debits)		Liabilities (Credits)		
B_{gc}	Purchase of government securities	1	Saving	25	S_c
m_c	Demand deposits	2	Borrowing from banks, etc.	3	B_c
	Loans to business:				
L_c {	Short-term	2			
	Long-term	3			
O_c	Purchase of stock	20			
		28		28	

The funds with which they acquired these assets came from their savings (S_c, $25 billion), and from money they borrowed from the productive sector (B_c, $3 billion). Note that the savings of $25 billion, which reflect the fact that individuals spent this much less than their incomes, is the only transaction in the capital account derived from any current account. All the other entries represent purely capital transactions having no direct relation to current activities.

Now we can summarize the private sector's capital transactions in an equation:

$$B_{gc} + m_c + L_c + O_c = S_c + B_c$$

The Capital Account of the Government Sector (KA_g)

Like both the other sectors of the economy, the government added appreciably to its assets. The first debit entry shows the physical assets it acquired through the purchase of current output of the productive sector (G_i, $5 billion). In addition, it lent $3 billion to foreign governments ($\bar{F}_g'$) and it acquired cash balances in banks (m_g).

Table 14.6. CAPITAL ACCOUNT OF THE GOVERNMENT SECTOR (KA_g)

	Assets (Debits)		Liabilities (Credits)		
G_i	Purchases of capital goods	5	Surplus	1.5	S_g
$\bar{F}_g'$	Long-term loans to foreign govts.	3	New government debt	5	$B_{gp,c}$
m_g	Demand deposits	0.5	Foreign debt repayment	1	} $\bar{F}_g$
			Sales of gold abroad	1	
		8.5		8.5	

To obtain these assets, it derived funds from its budget surplus (S_g, $1.5 billion); it borrowed from both the productive and the private sector ($B_{gp,c}$, $5); foreign governments repaid past debts of $1 billion, and the Treasury sold $1 billion of gold abroad.

Expressing these capital transactions of the government in equation form, we have

$$G_i + m_g + \bar{F}_g' = S_g + B_{gp,c} + \bar{F}_g.$$

CONSOLIDATION OF THE CAPITAL ACCOUNTS

Earlier we consolidated or merged the income accounts to obtain a statement showing only the *net* current transactions of the entire economy. All transactions between the different sectors of the economy canceled out, leaving us with nothing but current transactions related to the capital accounts and current transactions with foreigners. Now we can perform a similar operation on the capital accounts. Copying each sector's capital equation and adding them, we get:

$$KA_p \quad I_g + B_c + B_{gp} + \bar{F}_p' = S_p + D + O_c + L_c + \bar{F}_p + m_c + m_g$$
$$+$$
$$KA_c \quad B_{gc} + O_c + L_c + m_c = S_c + B_c$$
$$+$$
$$KA_g \quad G_i + \bar{F}_g' + m_g = S_g + B_{g,pc} + \bar{F}_g$$
$$\|$$
$$KA \quad I_g + G_i + \bar{F}_p' + \bar{F}_g' = S_p + S_c + S_g + D + \bar{F}_p + \bar{F}_g$$

All capital transactions between the different sectors of the economy cancel out. We are left with two types of transactions: (1) those that reflect *net* changes in assets or liabilities resulting from the current activities of investing and saving, which were carried over from the income statements, and (2) *net* capital transactions with foreigners. This outcome can be more clearly shown if we rearrange terms so as to get related categories of transactions together:

$$(I_g - D + G_i) + (\bar{F}_p' + \bar{F}_g') - (\bar{F}_p + \bar{F}_g) = (S_p + S_c + S_g).$$

This revision of the consolidated capital equation expresses a significant economic fact: the net savings of the economy are equal in magnitude to net domestic investment and net capital transactions with foreigners. Since net capital transactions with foreigners *are* net foreign investment (I_f), we can state this equation in the simple form:[9]

$$I_d + I_f = S.$$

That is, the net savings of a community are equal to total net investment, which is the sum of net domestic investment and net foreign investment.

CONSOLIDATION OF TOTAL SECTORAL ACCOUNTS: THE BALANCE OF INTERNATIONAL PAYMENTS

Let us take one further step. Add together or consolidate the net results of current activities (the consolidated income statement) and of capital trans-

[9] Capital transactions with foreigners consist of buying and selling foreign assets, lending ("purchasing" claims on foreigners), and borrowing ("selling" claims on oneself to foreigners). If the purchase of foreign assets (possibly of securities) and of claims exceeds sales of assets and of claims, there is a net outward movement of capital funds, which is net foreign investment. This may not be identical in all ways with domestic investment, but for our purposes, this is immaterial.

actions (the consolidated capital account). To save ourselves labor, we shall use the simplified forms of the consolidated income and capital equations:

$$IA \qquad S = I_d + X - M$$
$$+$$
$$KA \qquad I_d + I_f = S$$
$$\|$$
$$BP \qquad I_f = X - M.$$

Or, expressing foreign investment in its original form, as capital transactions:

$$\bar{F}' - \bar{F} = X - M.$$

What we are left with here is simply *all* foreign transactions of the economy, both capital transactions and current transactions.[10] This is what we would expect, since the process of consolidation eliminates all transactions that are common to the accounts being consolidated.

All foreign transactions of an economy are simply its balance of payments. So this final equation is an expression of the balance of payments of our economy. Stated more exactly, *a country's balance of international payments is a summary statement, or account, of all the transactions of its residents with the residents of the rest of the world.*

Being an account of a certain set of transactions, the balance of payments is essentially the same in nature as any of the accounts whose acquaintance we have already made, say that of the current activities of the productive sector of the economy.[11] On one side it records transactions giving rise to receipts (credits); on the other, transactions giving rise to payments (debits). If it is a complete record, everything must be accounted for. All receipts are either spent or set aside for some purpose. This means that both sides of the balance of payments account must balance; debits must equal credits.

Our balance of payments equation, however, is not in the right form to express this accounting necessity. Each side of the equation is a mixture of receipts and expenditure items. Exports are sources of receipts to the economy concerned (credits); imports are sources of payments (debits). So, too, with the capital transactions: $\bar{F}'$ stands for assets purchased or liabilities paid off (payments or debits); $\bar{F}$ stands for borrowing undertaken or assets sold (receipts or credits). We must rearrange the terms of our equation so as to get all debits on one side and all credits on the other:

$$\bar{F}' + M = \bar{F} + X.$$

[10] Had we used the expanded, rather than the condensed, forms of the consolidated income and capital equations, the end result of their consolidation would have been the following more elaborate equation:

$$(\bar{F}_p' + \bar{F}_g') - (\bar{F}_p + \bar{F}_g) = (X - M) + (F_p + F_g) - (F_p' + F_c' + F_g').$$

[11] It differs from these accounts, however, in one respect. It merges together current and capital transactions, whereas for each sector of the economy, its current transactions were recorded in one account, its capital transactions in another.

This says that debits equal credits, and that the account balances, as any complete account must.

A NATION'S INTERNATIONAL ACCOUNT:
THE BALANCE OF INTERNATIONAL PAYMENTS

Now we are ready to construct the balance of payments account. Simply enter all items giving rise to receipts from foreigners as credits, and enter all items giving rise to payments to foreigners as debits. These items can be picked out of the six accounts we have already recorded. Following the usual practice, we shall separate current from capital transactions. Unilateral transfers such as foreign aid, which are in the nature of gifts as distinct from loans, together with noncommercial receipts of the government from abroad, are distinguished from other, more normal entries in the current account by appending them to it (Table 14.7).

Table 14.7. THE BALANCE OF INTERNATIONAL PAYMENTS

Payments (Debits)   Receipts (Credits)

CURRENT ACCOUNT

M	Merchandise imports	10	Merchandising exports	17	X
F_p'	Shipping services and tourism	5	Shipping services and tourism	3	F_p
	Interest, dividends, and other income payments to foreigners	1	Interest, dividends, and other income from foreigners	3.5	
		16		23.5	
F_c'	Transfer payments, personal	1	Interest & transfer payments to govt. by foreigners	0.5	F_g
F_g'	Foreign aid	6			
	(Net credit balance	1)			

CAPITAL ACCOUNT

	Private:		Private		
$\bar{F}_p'$	Investment in foreign assets	1.5	Short-term foreign debt	1.5	$\bar{F}_p$
	Foreign bank deposits	0.5	Foreign-held bank deposits	0.5	
	Government:		Government:		
$\bar{F}_g'$	Long-term loans to foreign governments	3	Foreign debt repayment	1	$\bar{F}_g$
			Sales of gold	1	
			(Net debit balance	1)	
		28		28	

Now let us check our equation, $S = I_d + I_f$. Savings are the sum of S_p, S_c, and S_g, or $8.5 + 25 + 1.5$ for a total of 35. Net domestic investment is $I_g - D + G_i$, or $52 - 23 + 5 = 34$. Savings exceed domestic investment by the amount of foreign investment.

Looking at this balance of payments, you will see that the total of export items in the current account (credits) exceeds the total of import items (debits) by $1 billion. You can also see that in the capital account there is a debit balance of the same amount. This is the result of the fact that capital claims established against foreigners exceed claims established against our country by $1 billion.[12] Thus net capital transactions with foreigners are equal to the excess of export items over import items, or the surplus in the current account. $I_f = X - M$, which is as it should be.

CONCLUSION

Let us remind ourselves that all the millions of transactions carried out in the productive sector of a nation's economy, and in the private and government sectors as well, are independent transactions. They reflect the decisions of consumers to buy assorted consumers' goods, both domestic and imported; of investors to invest in specific kinds of plant, equipment, and tools; and of foreigners to purchase the nation's export commodities. They also reflect the decisions of business firms and individuals to respond to these expenditures by producing the desired goods and services; of individuals to remit charitable contributions abroad; of the government to make social security and other transfer payments in accordance with established laws; and many others. These innumerable decisions result in the creation and distribution of income and in the acquisition or disposal of various kinds of assets and liabilities.

Despite the fact that these decisions and the transactions to which they lead are largely unrelated, it turned out that when all the *current* transactions (more accurately, the accounts in which they are recorded) were consolidated, so that all complementary transactions canceled out, we were left with only those current transactions (1) that effected a change in assets or liabilities, through the process of saving and investment, and (2) that were carried out with foreigners. Moreover, this consolidation brought to light an important conclusion: a nation's net savings must be equal in amount to its net domestic investment and its net current transactions with foreigners.

Again, by consolidating all capital transactions of all sectors, we saw that the community's net savings must be equal to net domestic investment plus net *capital* transactions with foreigners. By finally merging the community's consolidated income account and its consolidated capital account, we ended up with nothing but the sum total of all transactions with the rest of the world, or the country's balance of international payments. Like any account, both sides had to balance. Moreover, the net balance in the current section of this international account was equal to the net balance in the capital section, as it had to be.

---

[12] "Sales of gold" are included on the credit side of the capital account, since gold is an internationally recognized means of payment. By exporting gold, our country is parting with a capital asset.

SELECTED REFERENCES

Ackley, Gardner, *Macroeconomic Theory*. New York: Macmillan, 1961. Chapters II and III discuss the concepts of national income and national product, and provide a good introduction to the structure of national accounts.

Ruggles, Richard and Nancy D. Ruggles, *National Income Accounts and Income Analysis*. New York: McGraw-Hill, 1956. A thorough and lucid exposition of national accounting methods.

$I\int$

CHANGES IN GROSS NATIONAL PRODUCT AND THE FOREIGN TRADE MULTIPLIER

CHANGES IN GROSS NATIONAL PRODUCT

Having established certain important relationships between a nation's gross national product and its balance of payments, we are now ready to consider how *changes* in national income or product affect the balance of payments, and how conversely, changes in exports or imports, which are components of the balance of payments, affect gross national product.

A change in any income-generating component (C, I, G, or X) will affect *GNP* unless it is offset by an equal and opposite change in another sector. Thus if investment increases by $10 billion, *GNP*—which includes investment—will rise by that amount unless at the same time either C, G, or X decreases.

The "Multiplier" Effect

It is most unlikely that a change in one component will be offset by an opposite change elsewhere; as a general rule, a change in one element will be reinforced by a similar movement in another part of the economy.[1] The reason for this is to be found in the repercussions of the initial change. If there is some slack in an economy in the form of unemployment, a $10 billion increase in investment outlays will put some people back to work—construction workers, employees in machine tool plants, and others normally engaged in the production of capital goods. They will spend some part of their new incomes, and this expenditure will put still more people back to work supplying their wants. The additional incomes of these latter workers will have the same effect, and em-

[1] One exception should be noted that at times may be important. If business men are frightened by government spending, then an increase in government outlays may, through its effects on business confidence, induce an offsetting (partial or complete) decline in private investment.

ployment and income will go on increasing in ever diminishing amounts, very much like the series of wavelets set off by throwing a stone into a still pool.

An opposite sequence of repercussions would follow from an initial decline in investment: reduced employment and income in the capital goods industries, reduced expenditure by those now unemployed, an induced fall in employment and income in the trades supplying their wants, and so on.

The total effect on national income and product of such a change (positive or negative) in investment depends on what proportion of the initial increase in incomes is passed on by its recipients in the form of consumption expenditure, what part leaks away into savings, tax payments, and imports. The relations between investment, consumption, and income will follow the pattern described unless, as they change, variations are induced in the other components of income—government outlay and exports. It seems reasonable to regard these components as substantially independent. Government decisions as to expenditure are made by a different group of men acting independently of the businessmen who decide to increase investment, or of the consumers who decide to increase their expenditure. As to exports, changes in these result from decisions made by foreign businessmen, consumers, and governments, which are external or exogenous to the economy in question.[2]

For the discussion that follows, a notion of income somewhat more appropriate than gross national product is net national product or income, which we shall refer to as national income, and for which we shall use the symbol Y. This differs from GNP only in that depreciation is subtracted from both national product and income distributed. Investment is now net investment, for which we shall use the symbol I.

Derivation of the Multiplier

Whether national income rises by twice the initial increase ($\triangle I$), or by more or less, depends, as we have said, on the *proportion* of the rise in income that is allocated to domestic expenditure on consumer goods. Economists have adopted a technical term for this: they call it the *marginal propensity to consume*; that is, the proportion of any increase in income that is spent on consumer goods, or $\triangle C/\triangle Y$. Since this concept refers to expenditure on consumer goods in general, whether foreign or domestic in origin—and thus includes expenditure on imports—let us first give it a workout in a simple model of a closed economy (one without foreign trade). This enables us to avoid the complication raised by imports, which can easily be introduced later.

We shall assume the marginal propensity to consume is ½, meaning that

---

[2] Later we shall see that the increase in imports resulting from the increase in incomes in our economy stimulates a rise in employment and income abroad. Since some part of this larger foreign income will be spent on imports, which are our economy's exports, there will be a minor secondary repercussion on its income. But this is a refinement we can postpone for the moment.

one-half of any increase in income is allocated to the purchase of consumer goods, and the other half to savings and taxes. If investment increases by 10, the total effect on income and ñational product can be shown by Table 15.1, in which each column represents one of the successive stages or waves of diminishing increments of income, each row an income payment period. (The latter may be defined as the average time required for a dollar of income to flow from the hands of one recipient into the hands of the next. A number of estimates place this period for the United States at about three months.)[3]

Table 15.1. THE PROPAGATION OF INCOME: A SINGLE INJECTION OF INVESTMENT

Income Payment Period	I	C_1	C_2	C_3	C_4
1	10				
2		5			
3			2.5		
4				1.25	
5					0.625

During the interval of, say, fifteen months for which this table gives definite figures, the total increase in income is equal to the sum of all the increments shown:

$$10 + 5 + 2.5 + 1.25 + 0.625 = 19.375.$$

This can also be expressed in the form:

$$10 (1 + 1/2 + 1/2^2 + 1/2^3 + 1/2^4) = 19.375.$$

At each stage after the first, you will note that the original increment in investment, ΔI, is multiplied by an increasing power of the marginal propensity to consume ($\Delta C/\Delta Y$, or for brevity, c), which we have assumed to be ½, but which could conceivably have any value between 0 and 1. Formulated in general terms, the total effect on income of an initial increase in investment, over an indefinite number (n) of income payment periods, can be expressed in the following equation:

$$\Delta Y = \Delta I (1 + c + c^2 + c^3 + c^4 \cdots + c^n).$$

[3] For his own and several other estimates, see Fritz Machlup, "Period Analysis and Multiplier Theory," *Quarterly Journal of Economics,* **LIV** (1939); reprinted in American Economic Association, *Readings in Business Cycle Theory,* pp. 213-15. Published 1949 by The Blakiston Co., Philadelphia.

The expression in parentheses may be reduced by mathematical manipulation to the following much simpler form:[4] $\dfrac{1}{1-c}$

This is known as the "multiplier" (k) for a closed economy. From it we can tell immediately by how much income will be increased as a result of an initial change in any one of its components, such as I. For the current example, it is:

$$\Delta Y = \Delta I \cdot \frac{1}{1-c} = 10 \cdot \frac{1}{1-\frac{1}{2}} = 10 \cdot 2 = 20.$$

This means that with $c = \frac{1}{2}$, over an indefinite (infinite) period of time, any increase in I will cause Y to increase by twice that amount. Far the greater part of this effect will be felt, however, within a fairly short time. In our table, which covers only some 15 months, 19.375 out of a total increase of 20 will have been experienced; this is 96.875 per cent. If we lengthened our table to two years, the total effect would be 19.921875, which is 99.61 per cent of the ultimate total of 20. For practical purposes, therefore, we can ignore the very small changes that occur after eight or ten income periods.

Any Multiplicand Will Do

An expansion of income need not start with an increase in investment. It could equally well be initiated by a change in any other sector of income—in C, G, or X. A spontaneous increase is most likely to occur either in investment, because of a change in businessmen's estimates of the future; in government outlays, as when it is decided to expand public works to combat a depression; or in exports, following a reduction in foreign tariffs, or increased expenditure abroad out of rising incomes. These components of national income are more subject to independent change than is consumption, which is dependent upon, or a function of, income—rather than independently determined.

Changes in the volatile components of national income may be down as well as up. Thus a decline of exports can inaugurate a multiplied contraction of income. The mechanism is the same as for expansion, but in reverse.

---

[4] The derivation of the multiplier, k, or $\dfrac{1}{1-c}$, is as follows:

$$k = 1 + c + c^2 + \ldots \ldots c^n$$
$$kc = c + c^2 + c^3 + \ldots \ldots c^{n+1}$$
$$k - kc = 1 - c^{n+1}$$
$$k(1-c) = 1 - c^{n+1}$$
$$k = \frac{1 - c^{n+1}}{1-c}$$

When n is infinite,

$$k = \frac{1}{1-c}$$

A Continuing Multiplicand

In our illustration, we have introduced only a single, once-for-all injection of increased investment, occurring in the first of our three-month income periods. We have seen that (with $c = \frac{1}{2}$) the total increase in income is twice the initial increment of investment, but that this effect is distributed over time, and that it gradually wears off and disappears. Suppose, however—and this is more realistic—that whatever change in the investment climate caused businessmen to expand their investment outlays leads them to maintain this increased investment. Our table would then appear as shown in Table 15.2.

Table 15.2. THE PROPAGATION OF INCOME: A CONTINUING
INJECTION OF INVESTMENT

Income Payment Period	I	C_1	C_2	C_3	C_4	C_6	C_6	C_n
1	10							
2	10	5						
3	10	5	2.5					
4	10	5	2.5	1.25				
5	10	5	2.5	1.25	0.625			
.								
.								
n	10	5	2.5	1.25	0.625	0.3125	0.15625	 0

National income rises steadily in each period. By the fifth (after 15 months), it is higher than its starting level by 19.375; eventually its rise will reach the limit of 20 and remain there as long as investment stays at its new higher level.

The Import Leakage

We are now ready to take into account the leakage into imports and apply our analysis to an open economy. The required alteration is very simple. If the marginal propensity to consume includes, as it is usually taken to do, expenditure on imported goods as well as on domestic goods, in arriving at a value for the multiplier we must correct it for the expenditure that spills over into imports. We do this by introducing a further concept, the *marginal propensity to import*—that is, the proportion of any increase in income spent on imports.

Thus suppose that, continuing our illustration with a marginal propensity to consume of $\frac{1}{2}$, the marginal propensity to import (m) is $\frac{1}{4}$. Then out of every $10 of additional income, $5 will leak off into savings and taxes, $5 will be spent on consumer goods. But if the marginal propensity to import is $\frac{1}{4}$, $2.50 out of the $10, or half the sum spent on consumer goods, will be directed toward the purchase of imports. The series of increments of income will be, not $10 + 5 + 2.5 + 1.25 + 0.625$, etc., as in Table 15.1, but $10 + 2.5 + 0.625 + 0.15625$ etc.

The total increase in income will be substantially less than when there was no leakage into imports. How much less? This depends upon the multiplier. For the closed economy, it was $\dfrac{1}{1-c}$, which with $c = \frac{1}{2}$ gave a value of 2. But we must now diminish c by the value of m, the proportion of increased income directed toward imports, so our multiplier becomes: $\dfrac{1}{1-(c-m)}$. Removing the parentheses, this is $\dfrac{1}{1-c+m}$.

With $c = \frac{1}{2}$ and $m = \frac{1}{4}$, the multiplier takes the value of

$$\frac{1}{1-\frac{1}{2}+\frac{1}{4}} = \frac{1}{\frac{3}{4}} = \frac{4}{3} = 1.33.$$

For each dollar of investment injected into the economy, national income will increase by a total of $1.33. Or take the values, $c = \frac{2}{3}$, $m = \frac{1}{3}$. Then the multiplier is

$$\frac{1}{1-\frac{2}{3}+\frac{1}{3}} = \frac{1}{\frac{2}{3}} = \frac{3}{2} = 1.5.$$

With $c = \frac{3}{4}$, $m = \frac{1}{8}$, we get

$$\frac{1}{1-\frac{6}{8}+\frac{1}{8}} = \frac{1}{\frac{3}{8}} = \frac{8}{3} = 2.67.$$

A large value of the marginal propensity to consume will increase the multiplier; a large value of the marginal propensity to import will diminish it. That part of increased income which is spent on domestic goods goes on generating a further rise in income, while that part which leaks abroad has no such (direct) effect.

Simplification of the Multiplier

The formula for the multiplier can be still further simplified. We do this by substituting for $1 - c$, the symbol "s." Since $1 - c$ represents the difference between a dollar of income and what is spent on consumption, or that part of a dollar of income that is diverted into domestic leakages (savings and taxes), we can say that s stands for these domestic leakages. The multiplier now becomes: $\dfrac{1}{s+m}$, of which the denominator may be said to stand for the sum of the leakages.

OPERATION OF THE MULTIPLIER

A Simple Model

To show how the multiplier operates, diagrams are most useful. Let us take a simple situation first, then move on to the more complex. In Figure 15.1(a), national income is measured on the horizontal axis, investment and saving on the vertical axis. Investment decisions are assumed to depend on expectations

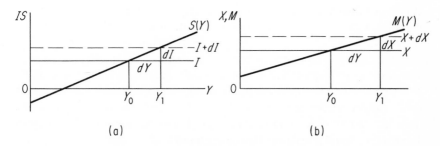

FIGURE 15.1   (a) The Investment Multiplier, and (b) The Foreign Trade Multiplier with No Saving

as to future profitability, and thus to be independent of the level of current income. Therefore initial investment is shown as a horizontal line of a given height or amount. Savings, on the other hand, depend on, or are a function of, income. Total savings of the community are therefore shown as a positively inclined line, starting with negative savings, or dissavings, at low levels of income and rising as income rises. Income of Y_0 is a position of equilibrium, since investment equals savings.

Now suppose that investment expectations improve; investment is increased by dI to the position $I + dI$. A process of income expansion such as that shown in Table 15.2 will be inaugurated. Over a period of time, Y will rise from Y_0 to Y_1. Savings, too, will increase along the $S(Y)$ line, which expresses the dependence of saving on income. At the income level Y_1, equilibrium will be established, since only at that point are saving and investment equal ($S = I + dI$). At any higher level of income, savings would exceed investment, operating to depress income, while at any lower level of income, investment would exceed savings and stimulate a further rise of income.

In all this, where is the multiplier? Note that $S(Y)$ is the *total* saving function; any point on this line (measured on the vertical axis) gives the total savings for the corresponding level of income. $S(Y)$ therefore expresses the community's *average* propensity to save. The *marginal* propensity to save (s), on the other hand, is the *increment* of saving that accompanies an *increment* of income. In the diagram, this is the slope of the $S(Y)$ line. But between the income levels Y_0 and Y_1, this slope s is dI/dY. The multiplier, $1/s$, is the reciprocal of the slope of $S(Y)$, or dY/dI. This last expression also corresponds to the meaning of the multiplier: it is the amount by which income increases for a given increase in investment or in any other multiplicand.

Now turn to another simple case, an open economy, but one without saving or investment—Figure 15.1(b). Exports, like investment, are taken to be independent of national income, since they depend on the decisions of foreigners. Imports, however, are functionally related to income. The line $M(Y)$ expresses the community's *average* propensity to import. As with savings, the *marginal* propensity to import (m) is the slope of this line.

We start with an equilibrium level of income (Y_o), where $X = M$. If exports are now increased, income will rise to Y_1, while imports move up along the $M(Y)$ line until they are again equal to exports ($X + dX$), when a new equilibrium is established. The multiplier, dY/dX, now has the value of $1/m$.

It is worth noting at this point that the absence of any saving is what makes possible an increase in imports exactly equal to the increase in exports. When savings are introduced, as in our next model, part of the increased income leaks into this channel instead of just into imports.

A More Realistic Model

Now let us consider an open economy, with exports and imports, in which investment and saving are also present. Figure 15.2(a) illustrates this case.

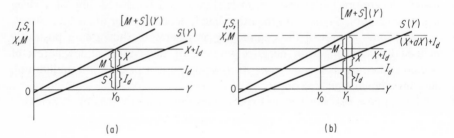

FIGURE 15.2 The Foreign Trade Multiplier

Government expenditures and taxes are omitted, simply to avoid complicating the diagrams; their inclusion would in no way affect our results.

As before, investment (I_d, to designate net *domestic* investment) and exports are independent of income, with the I_d line representing the expenditure upon which investors have decided. The line $X + I_d$ shows the sum of investment and exports, so that the value of exports is represented by the vertical distance between I_d and $X + I_d$. The community's average propensity to save is shown, as before, by the $S(Y)$ line. The combined average propensity to save and to import are represented by the $[M + S](Y)$ line, so the average propensity to import is equal to the distance between this and the $S(Y)$ line. At the income level Y_o, equilibrium prevails, with domestic investment equal to savings and exports equal to imports.

Now suppose that, owing to a lowering of tariff barriers abroad or to a rise in foreign incomes, exports increase. The line standing for investment and exports combined $(X + I_d)$ shifts upward to a new position represented by the dashed line $(X + dX) + I_d$ in Figure 15.2(b). Income rises to Y_1. The multiplier, defined as the increment in income accompanying the increment of exports, is dY/dX. In terms of the diagram, this is the horizontal distance on the $X + I_d$ line equal to the distance Y_0Y_1 $(= dY)$, relative to the vertical distance dX. Now this ratio dY/dX is the reciprocal of the slope $(m + s)$ of the $[M + S](Y)$ line, or $1/m + s$, which is the multiplier as we derived it earlier.

Equilibrium in National Income

Note that whereas at the initial equilibrium level of income (Y_0) domestic investment was equal to savings and exports were equal to imports, these relations no longer hold when income is Y_1. Now, as may be seen from the bracketed distances in Figure 15.2(b), exports exceed imports and savings exceed investment. Nonetheless, $I_d + X = S + M$.

Now recall the conclusions reached at the end of the last chapter. From the operating accounts of an economy, we were able to establish that the community's net savings are equal to net domestic investment plus the balance of current foreign transactions: $S = I_d + X - M$. This is identical with the equation we have just derived from the diagram. It expresses the condition for equilibrium of national income in an open economy. But we also saw in Chapter 14 that $I_f = X - M$, and that $S = I_d + I_f$. Rephrased, the condition for income equilibrium is that savings equal *total* investment. For both an open and a closed economy, the conditions for stability of income are the same; the only difference is that in the former, part of the investment may be foreign rather than domestic.

Income Propagation

Suppose that the initial stimulus to a rise in income was an increase in investment rather than in exports. Although the path of expansion is similar, there will be a marked effect on incomes abroad. To show a rise in investment diagrammatically, it is more convenient to have the investment line on top; therefore in Figure 15.3 we reverse the position of exports and investment, and of the propensities to save and to import.

As before, income rises from Y_0 to Y_1. But since imports are an increasing function of income, imports are now higher. One country's imports, however, are the exports of other countries. So in the rest of the world, a multiplicand will now operate to raise income. How large this effect will be will depend upon foreign propensities to save and to invest.

The main point is that through the multiplier mechanism, a rise in income in one country is transmitted abroad. When the initial change occurs in an

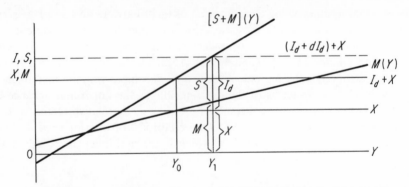

FIGURE 15.3   The Foreign Trade Multiplier: A Change in Investment

economically important country such as the United States, the effects on other countries can be substantial. Prosperity—or, as in 1929-30, depression—can be propagated on an international scale.

As before, when income reaches the stable position Y_1, the equilibrium condition is satisfied: $S + M = I_d + X$. But in this instance I_d, S, and M have all increased, while exports remain constant.[5] Also, instead of savings being greater than domestic investment, they are smaller. Equality of the two sides of the equation is preserved by the increase in imports. But what about foreign investment ($I_f = X - M$)? Since imports are now larger than exports, foreign investment is negative. This means that foreigners are supplementing our country's savings with some of their own; it is foreign savings that make possible the excess of imports.

FOREIGN REPERCUSSIONS

Our formal presentation of the multiplier has reckoned only with the changes in expenditure occurring within the borders of a single country. But we have just noted that a change in the income of 'one country is transmitted abroad through the induced change in its imports. If income in the United States rises, its imports will also rise, and stimulate an increase in income in the rest of the world. But if incomes abroad increase, imports there will rise, too, and some of these imports will come from the United States, further reinforcing the rise in its income. We must take this foreign repercussion, or "play-back" effect, into account. To do so, we need merely alter the formula for the multiplier.

Since the circumstances under which the multiplier operates may vary, the formula to be used will likewise differ. I shall merely present, without showing

[5] Because of the induced rise in incomes abroad, exports will indeed increase somewhat. This will be taken into account in the next section.

their derivation, foreign-trade multipliers for two sets of conditions.[6] First, when the stimulus to increased income—the multiplicand—comes from a rise in exports accompanied by an equal decline in expenditures abroad on home consumption, the multiplier with foreign repercussions is

$$k = \frac{1}{s_a + m_a + m_b \left(\dfrac{s_a}{s_b}\right)}.$$

The subscript a refers to the country whose exports and income increase; b, to the rest of the world; while s and m have the now familiar meaning of domestic and foreign leakages.

Second, when the multiplicand is derived from an autonomous increase in spending by consumers, investors, or the government in country A, or an increase in imports by country B from country A financed, say, by an expansion of credit, the foreign trade multiplier will have a larger value. It will be

$$k = \frac{1 + \dfrac{m_b}{s_b}}{s_a + m_a + m_b \left(\dfrac{s_a}{s_b}\right)}$$

A Word of Caution

We must beware of using the marginal propensities to consume and to import too mechanically, and in particular of assuming that their values remain constant regardless of circumstances. Statistical data for the United States covering the period from the early 1920's to World War II, for example, give a marginal propensity to consume of approximately 0.8. This value, however, is an average for some twenty years. *Within* this period, the marginal propensity to consume fluctuated widely; it was much lower in the early years of the great depression of the thirties, when fear of unemployment afflicted those who were still employed, and higher in the late twenties, when business was buoyant and optimism ruled unchecked. The propensity to import, too, varies with circumstances. It will be high as an economy approaches full employment, when the possible increase in domestic output is small and any sizeable additional purchases must be made abroad. It will also tend to be high if the investment which stimulates a rise in income is predominantly in inventories, in which imported raw materials bulk relatively large, as contrasted with invest-

---

[6] Those interested in the derivation of the multipliers, and in particular, in the general formula that covers all cases, should consult Kindleberger, *International Economics* (1963 edition), Appendix E, or Jaroslav Vanek, *International Trade: Theory and Economic Policy*, Ch. 7. (See Selected References at end of chapter.)

ment in building, which uses mainly domestic materials. The multiplier, the marginal propensity to consume, and the marginal propensity to import are all useful analytical tools, but unlike the tools of a craftsman, their size can change without our being aware of it. Practitioners making use of them in a concrete situation must recognize this possibility and always take it into account.

Finally, although the multiplier analysis can always be applied to a contraction of income, it is only valid for an expansion if there is room to expand. That is, if there is to occur a rise in real incomes as contrasted with money income and prices, there must be a reasonable amount of slack in the economy, in the form of unemployed resources. If there is not, then any force, such as increased exports or a rise in investment, which tends to raise income and employment, will merely cause an inflationary rise in prices. For then, total expenditures will exceed the value at current prices of the productive resources available, which is how we define an inflationary situation. As was pointed out at the beginning of the last chapter, by explicitly assuming constant prices, we implicitly assume the presence of unemployed resources.

SELECTED REFERENCES

Kindleberger, Charles P., *International Economics*, 3rd ed. Homewood, Ill.: Richard D. Irwin, Inc., 1963. Chapter 10 has a somewhat more elaborate presentation of the multiplier than is given here, with numerous illustrations; and Appendix E has derivations of the various forms of the multiplier.

Machlup, Fritz, *International Trade and the National Income Multiplier*. Philadelphia: The Blakiston Co., 1943. This is still the most thorough and detailed discussion of the multiplier and its relation to foreign trade that is available. It takes into account many points omitted in this chapter for the sake of brevity.

Meade, James E., *The Balance of Payments*. New York: Oxford University Press, 1951. Part II describes in detail the income and price effects of changes in domestic expenditures.

Polak, J. J., "The Foreign Trade Multiplier"; Haberler, G., "Comment"; Polak and Haberler, "A Restatement," *American Economic Review*, XXXVII (1947). This discussion is chiefly concerned with the question of the suitable multiplicand to use when a change in exports causes national income to change.

Vanek, Jaroslav, *International Trade: Theory and Economic Policy*. Homewood, Ill.: Richard D. Irwin, Inc., 1962. Part I deals with the balance of payments and the national income accounts; Part II, Chapter 7, gives a mathematical formulation of the foreign trade multiplier.

16

THE BALANCE OF
INTERNATIONAL PAYMENTS

We have already acquired some acquaintance with that important concept, a country's balance of international payments. In Chapter 14 we established that it comprises all of a country's transactions with foreigners, both current transactions of exporting and importing goods and services, and financial transactions—such as the purchase and sale of foreign assets and borrowing from, and lending to, foreigners. We also saw that since a balance of payments is a complete account of all the transactions between one economic unit and the rest of the world, it must always balance.

To establish these facts about a balance of payments is only a beginning. Since it is a revealing and useful document, it is necessary to learn a good deal more about the nature of the items that comprise it and how they are related to one another and to the balance of payments as a whole.

Purposes

Comparison of a pair of balances of payments covering a given period shows changes in the country's trading position—that is, in the relative movement of exports and imports. Such information could clearly be significant for the determination of trade and commercial policies. The effect of such changes on employment and production will also be relevant to monetary and fiscal policy. So will variations in the country's holdings of international reserves of gold and foreign exchange. Also revealed will be any alteration in the country's net position as a lender or borrower, with implications for future income or outgo on this account.

THE BALANCE OF PAYMENTS ON CURRENT ACCOUNT

Let us begin our more detailed study of the balance of payments with the current account. The following schedule lists, with explanatory notes, the types of transactions distinguished in the current account of the balances of payments published by the International Monetary Fund.

Components of Balance of Payments on
Current Account of Country A

DEBITS (PAYMENTS)

Merchandise imports (all goods imported from foreign sources).

Foreign travel (goods sold and services rendered to normal residents of A who are temporarily residing or traveling abroad).

Transportation (passenger or freight services rendered to residents of A by international carriers).

Insurance (premiums on insurance policies issued to residents of A by companies domiciled abroad, and indemnities on insurance policies issued to foreigners by companies domiciled in A).

Investment income (interest and dividends on securities of or property in A owned by residents of other countries).

Government (purchases of goods or services from foreigners by A's diplomatic or military establishments abroad, and any other government outlays abroad).

Miscellaneous (payments on account of motion picture royalties, telephone and telegraph service, management, engineers' and contractors' fees, etc.).

CREDITS (RECEIPTS)

Merchandise exports (all goods shipped to foreign destinations).

Foreign travel (goods sold and services rendered to foreigners travelling in or temporarily residing in A).

Transportation (passenger or freight services rendered to foreigners by firms in A engaged in the international carrying trade).

Investment income (interest and dividends on foreign securities or property owned by residents of A).

Insurance (premiums on insurance policies issued to foreigners by companies domiciled in A, and indemnities on insurance policies issued to residents of A by companies domiciled abroad).

Government (sales of goods or services to foreign diplomatic or military establishments in A, and other sales of goods or services to foreign governments).

Miscellaneous (earnings abroad on account of motion picture royalties, telephone, telegraph service, management, engineers' and contractors' fees, etc.).

Of this sizeable group of components, merchandise exports and imports are normally by far the largest, accounting in most cases for two-thirds or more of the total. For some countries, foreign travel or tourism bulks relatively large. This is especially true of the United States, for which it is a net payment or debit item, and for Mexico and the nations of western Europe, for which it constitutes a source of income. In recent years, government expenditure for military purposes has run to a figure in the neighborhood of $3 billion for the United States.

Investment income is included in the current account since it is associated with a service: the use of one's capital. It gives rise to a payment for the country that has borrowed or in which foreigners own income-earning property; it is a source of receipts to a lending or investing country.

Since transactions are carried out by individuals, corporations, or governments, and not by an abstraction such as a country, it is truly correct to speak of transactions between residents of one country and residents of another. For brevity, however, we shall continue to refer to the transactions of a "country" or a "nation," always meaning thereby some legal person or entity that is a resident of the country in question.

In most instances, it is perfectly obvious who is a resident of a given country and who is not. But there are some complications. A tourist is regarded as a resident of his home country, and his expenditures abroad are treated as international payments of that country, no different, essentially, from imports of goods and services. But a person living abroad more than some arbitrary period defined by the laws of his country is considered a foreign resident; his transactions are treated just like those of nationals of the country in which he resides.

Foreign subsidiaries of a parent corporation located, say, in the United States are regarded as residents of the foreign country, even though wholly owned by the parent company. For they are incorporated under the laws of the country where they are located, which makes them (legally) residents. Transactions between the parent and the subsidiary are therefore foreign transactions, and enter the balance of payments of each country involved. Any dealings between the subsidiary and other residents of the country where it is located are purely internal.

Branch offices are regarded as an outpost of the parent company; transactions between them are domestic, while those with firms and individuals where the branch office is situated are international. A nation's embassies, consulates, and military establishments abroad are similar. International organizations such as the International Monetary Fund and the World Bank are "foreign" regardless of location, whereas their employees are not. Thus transactions between the United States and these two institutions, housed in Washington, D.C., appear as international transactions in the balance of payments of the United States.

Balance-of-Payments Accounting

A matter that needs some further clarification is the manner in which a balance of payments is constructed. In principle, a balance of payments is built up according to the rules of double-entry bookkeeping. Its most fundamental rule is that every business transaction has two sides, both of which must be recorded. This simply reflects the economic principle underlying all business dealings: you pay for what you get; or, one never gets something for nothing. (Gifts present a special problem, to be considered shortly.)

As we have already suggested, it is a convention of bookkeeping to charge, or debit, the owner of an account for everything he gets, and to credit him for everything he gives up. Thus if a merchant sells goods worth $100 and is paid in cash, his account would look like this:

Dr.	Merchant's Account	Cr.
Cash	$100 Merchandise	$100

He is credited for the merchandise with which he has parted, and he is debited for the cash he got in exchange.

These rules apply to a country's balance of payments on current account, just as to any other account. Let us try them on a hypothetical balance of payments, in which we shall condense all the service items listed above into a single entry for the sake of simplicity. We shall assume that the country is one, like Venezuela, whose residents transact their foreign business mainly through New York banks, and that they pay for what they buy and are paid for what they sell with bank deposits in that city. Assume that the country imports goods to the value of $1,800 million, exports goods worth $2,300 million, that it renders services (shipping, foreign travel, and so forth) amounting to $200 million and receives services from others totaling $300 million. The country's balance of payments on current account would then appear as shown in Table 16.1.

Table 16.1

Dr.		Balance of Payments on Current Account of Country A		Cr.
	(million)			(million)
Increase in New York balances	$2,300	Merchandise exports		$2,300
Merchandise imports	1,800	Decrease in New York balances		1,800
Increase in New York balances	200	Services		200
Services	300	Decrease in New York balances		300
	$4,600			$4,600

The account balances, since each item is entered on both the debit and the credit side. The entries are few, since each condenses numerous individual transactions into an aggregate. (In practice, the "service" entries should be shown in at least the detail we used in our classification.) But we can usefully carry condensation one step further. To a large extent, the payments into and out of New York banks offset one another. In-payments total $2,500 million; out-payments, $2,100 million. Since both kinds of payments refer to the same thing, deposits in New York banks, it will suffice if we subtract the smaller item from both sides and show only the net change.

A's international account would then take the form shown in Table 16.2.

Table 16.2

Dr.		Balance of Payments on Current Account of Country A		Cr.
	(million)			(million)
Merchandise imports	$1,800	Merchandise exports		$2,300
Services	300	Services		200
Net increase in New York balances	400			
	$2,500			$2,500

FOREIGN BALANCES IN GENERAL Had country *A* conducted part of its international business through London, or other financial centers, some of its in-payments for export items and of its out-payments for import items might have been made in pounds sterling or other currencies. Bank deposits in London, owned by banks in *A*, would then have been increased or diminished. Unless for some special reason it was desired to distinguish these from New York deposits, the balancing financial entry, or surplus in the current account would then be called by a more general name, such as "Net increase in foreign balances." (This, and all the items in the balance of payments, can be expressed in terms of dollars or of the country's own currency. For our purposes, it is immaterial.)

Foreign-Owned Domestic Balances

Suppose *A* itself, like France or Switzerland, possessed an international financial center of some importance. Then it is likely that parts of its transactions would have been settled in its own currency. This creates a difference, about which it is well to be clear. Imports of goods and services for which payment was made in *A*'s currency would require importers in *A* to add to deposits held in *A*'s banks by foreign banks. Exports similarly handled would require a transfer from those deposits to *A*'s exporters, and thus a reduction of foreign-owned deposits. Whereas with transactions carried out through foreign financial centers, exports would increase *A*'s foreign assets (bank deposits held abroad) and imports would *diminish* them; with transactions carried out in *A*'s currency—through banks in its financial center—exports would *diminish A*'s foreign *liabilities* (foreign-owned deposits in *A*'s banks) and imports would increase them.

Transactions carried out in foreign currencies and in a country's own currency are usually distinguished in the balance of payments. Thus suppose that of *A*'s exports of goods and services, $200 million had been paid for in its own currency, and of its imports, $100 million. This would have left a net reduction in the liability of *A*'s banks to foreigners to be recorded. The increase in *A*'s foreign balances would have been that much smaller, and its current account would take the form shown in Table 16.3.

Table 16.3

Dr.	Balance of Payments on Current Account of Country A		Cr.
	(million)		(million)
Merchandise imports	$1,800	Merchandise exports	$2,300
Services	300	Services	200
Net increase in foreign balances	300		
Net decrease in balances due abroad	100		
	———		———
	$2,500		$2,500

Accounting for Donations

Donations differ from ordinary business transactions, such as are included in the current account, in that they do not reflect an exchange of goods or services for money (or perhaps for goods, as in barter transactions, or for evidences of debt, as when exports are financed by long-term credits). Donations involve no *quid pro quo*. A person or a government transfers commodities or services or money to some other person or government, but receives nothing in exchange. Yet since in any system of accounts, all transactions must be accounted for, if any items have been given away, it is necessary that that fact be recorded. The method of doing so is to make an entry indicating the character of the gift on the side of the account opposite to the entry for the thing given or received. This not only "accounts" for the gift, but also preserves balance in the accounts.

Thus suppose that a wealthy individual gives his daughter, on her marriage, a house and lot. This would be shown in his personal account as follows:

Dr.	Account of Mr. Wellfixed	Cr.
Gift to daughter $35,000		Real estate $35,000

This records the fact that (1) Mr. Wellfixed has parted with real estate valued at $35,000, and that (2) he has received no cash or other *quid pro quo*, but instead has made a gift of this property.

The category of donations in a nation's balance of payments includes a wide variety of transactions: military aid, economic aid, technical assistance, immigrants' remittances, charitable contributions of churches or organizations such as CARE, and also such compulsory donations as reparations and indemnities. Frequently the term "unilateral transfers" is applied to these transactions to indicate their one-sided character.

Such transfers are recorded in a country's balance of payments in the manner already indicated. If the country has furnished military or capital equipment to another nation on an aid basis, those goods will be entered among its exports on the credit side, and an offsetting entry will be made on the debit side, to indicate that no payment was received for them, but that they were gifts. Thus suppose that of country A's exports of $2,300 million, $100 million were machinery and equipment, donated as economic aid to under-developed countries. This would reduce by a like amount the net receipts from exports and would require a debit entry to record the fact that a donation had been made. A's balance of payments would be altered to appear as shown in Table 16.4.

Where the donation consists, not of goods or services, as in the preceding illustration, but of money, as is the case with immigrants' remittances and some government transfers, the transaction is treated in the same way. Thus, if A's donations had all been made by private individuals or organizations, the only

Table 16.4

Dr.		Balance of Payments on Current Account of Country A	Cr.
	(million)		(million)
Merchandise imports	$1,800	Merchandise exports	$2,300
Services	300	Services	200
Net increase in foreign balances	200		
Net decrease in balances due abroad	100		
Donations:			
Official	100		
	$2,500		$2,500

change in the balance of payments would be that the donations would be entitled "Private" instead of "Official." If all of these gifts consisted of remittances of foreign deposits to relatives or charitable organizations abroad, the entry would record the fact that $100 million of the $400 million surplus in the current account, which otherwise would improve *A*'s short-term capital position by this amount, had been purchased by residents of *A* for transfer to foreigners.

Estimates versus Accounts

If governments kept a set of accounts covering international transactions, with every transaction recorded, construction of a balance of payments would be a simple matter of closing the account books. At the end of the accounting period (normally a year), a summary of the accounts—the balance of international payments—would show the total flow through each type of account giving rise to receipts (such as exports and services rendered to foreigners), and through each type of account giving rise to payments (such as imports, services from foreigners, and so on). But the account or accounts in which actual receipts and payments were recorded—bank balances at home or abroad—would show only the net change.

But no such set of accounts is kept. Instead, an attempt is made to estimate each individual debit or credit item, by methods of varying degrees of accuracy. For merchandise exports and imports, the figures are usually quite accurate, since reports are made to the customs authorities as goods enter or leave a country. All other items, however, have to be estimated. Thus many countries estimate foreign travel expenditures of their own residents by generalizing from a sample survey based on questionnaires filled out by returning tourists. An estimate of the receipts from foreign travelers in the country can be derived from statements by entering and departing travelers as to their initial and final holdings of domestic and foreign moneys, or from reports required of banks as to the value of travelers' checks cashed. A country's banks can also be required to report changes in foreign-held balances, in balances they hold abroad, and other transactions under their surveillance. Obviously there are many possibilities of error in these estimates. It is very unlikely that the two sides of any balance of payments will in fact be equal. This makes it necessary to include a balancing entry for "errors and omissions."

Despite the inevitable errors, a nation's international account can be discussed and analyzed as if it were a true double-entry record, for the facts it records are an approximation to what an accounting summary would show, and can be treated in the same manner. Sometimes we may have clues as to the source to which errors and omissions should be attributed. Since short-term capital transactions are the most difficult to ascertain, when reported evidence indicates these are large, failure to count them all is likely to be responsible for the major part of "errors and omissions."

THE CAPITAL ACCOUNT

Consider again country A's balance of payments on current account as we left it in Table 16.4. Exports of goods and services of $2,500 million exceeded similar import items, plus official donations, by $300 million. This resulted in an increase in foreign balances of $200 million and a reduction in balances due abroad of $100 million.

The rise in foreign balances is an increase in A's holdings of liquid foreign assets, while the fall in balances due abroad is a reduction in short-term liabilities to foreigners. Assets and liabilities, however, are part of a country's capital. What are these items doing in A's current account? Since they reflect changes in the country's capital position, they clearly belong in the capital account. Let us transfer them to their proper position. Now A's balance of payments takes on the form shown in Table 16.5.

Table 16.5

Dr.	Balance of Payments of A		Cr.
	Current Account		
	(million)		(million)
Merchandise imports	$1,800	Merchandise exports	$2,300
Services	300	Services	200
Donations:			
Official	100		
	2,200		2,500
	Capital Account		
Short-term capital (net change)	300		
	$2,500		$2,500

Besides moving the capital items down into the capital account, we have merged them into a single entry, relabeled "Short-term Capital." The net change it specifies consists of a \$200 million increase in short-term foreign assets and a \$100 million decrease in short-term foreign liabilities.

The Balance on Current Account and Foreign Investment

Since A's receipts from her export items exceed payments for import items and donations, A is said to have a *surplus* on current account. (An excess in the opposite direction, of import over export items, is of course a deficit.) As we learned in Chapter 14, the difference between a country's exports and imports, interpreted broadly to include all current account components, is its international investment: $I_f = X - M$. Here we see that A's surplus on current account is the basis for an improvement of its (short-term) capital position *vis-a-vis* the rest of the world, or for positive international investment.

Consider also that total savings equal total investment, domestic and foreign: $S = I_d + I_f$. We are also familiar with this equation in a slightly different form: $S - I_d = X - M$. This tells us that when a country is engaging in international investment, savings must exceed domestic investment. Part of total savings go into, or finance, domestic investment, while the excess over this amount, in the instance before us, is devoted to acquiring foreign balances, domestic balances formerly held by foreigners, or—another possibility—gold. Foreign investment of this type is clearly a *consequence* of the country's balance of payments position; it is involuntary or induced rather than autonomous.

It is quite possible, however, that conditions may be such as to make voluntary foreign investment attractive.[1] If yields on comparable investments are higher abroad than at home, investors in A will undertake to purchase foreign securities or other earning assets. The excess of A's savings over its domestic investment will be directed into acquiring these securities instead of into holding such short-term liquid assets as foreign balances or gold. Suppose that this condition is fulfilled, and that investors in A voluntarily seek to invest \$250 million in foreign stocks and bonds. This portion of A's total saving is now directed into long-term foreign investment. Accordingly, the capital account in A's balance of payments would now consist of two entries:

Short-term capital (net change)   50
Long-term capital   250

It is still true that A's foreign investment is identical in amount with its surplus on current account; $I_f = X - M$. The question suggests itself, does the size of a nation's current account surplus set an absolute limit on the amount it can invest abroad during a given balance of payments period? The answer is "Yes," provided we preface "foreign investment" with the qualifying adjective "net."

Thus suppose that, during the period to which A's balance of payments

[1] In Chapter 19, we shall see that the persistence for some time of a surplus in a nation's balance of payments on current account does set in motion forces that make for foreign investment.

refs (a single year), the yield on foreign securities is so attractive that investors in *A* wish to invest, not $250 million, but $500 million. The surplus in *A*'s current account provides short-term foreign assets that can be used to acquire long-term investments, but only to the amount of $300 million. How can *A*'s investors acquire another $200 million for the purchase of the desired foreign securities? Their only means is to purchase, with domestic money, foreign balances acquired in the past by their own banks and still in their possession,[2] or to buy and export gold. Or, if foreign banks are willing, they may exchange bank balances in *A* directly for the desired securities. Table 16.6 shows how *A*'s balance of payments might look upon the completion of these transactions.

Table 16.6

Dr.	Balance of Payments of A		Cr.
	Current Account		
	(million)		(million)
Merchandise imports	$1,800	Merchandise exports	$2,300
Services	300	Services	200
Donations:			
Official	100		
	2,200		2,500
	Capital Account		
Long-term capital	500	Short-term capital (official)	150
		Gold exports	50
	2,700		2,700

But the acquisition of foreign securities in this fashion involves only the exchange of an existing short-term foreign asset for a long-term asset, or the creation of a short-term foreign liability in exchange for a long-term foreign asset. There is no *net* change in the country's total foreign assets and liabilities; its *net* foreign investment has not increased by a single dollar. A country can invest abroad *net* only an amount equal to its balance of payments surplus on current account.

A country with an excess of imports over exports of goods and services is said to have a *deficit* in its balance of payments on current account. Clearly, for such a country, say *A*, foreign investment is negative. Referring again to the equation: $S - I_d = X - M$, its domestic investment must exceed domestic savings. Foreigners are investing in the country. They may do so involuntarily, acquiring additional bank balances or gold, or reducing their short-term lia-

---

[2] Since private banks make a practice of maintaining only minimum balances of foreign deposits, it is most likely that "official" foreign funds will have to be acquired from *A*'s central bank. Central banks often maintain large holdings of foreign deposits, or can readily obtain them.

bilities to A, or they may convert these short-term assets voluntarily into long-term investments.

A Matter of Terminology

When long-term foreign investment occurs, the investing nation exchanges currently or previously acquired foreign balances or gold, or deposits in its own banks, for stocks, bonds, or physical capital of long-term or indefinite maturity. It will therefore be importing securities or other claims on foreign assets. An appropriate entry in its balance of payments would be a debit in the capital account to "security imports," which has the advantage of referring specifically to what is being imported and thus has to be paid for. The corresponding credit is to foreign balances or gold (decreased) or to foreign-owned domestic balances (increased). Since we have already characterized these balances as short-term capital, what occurs in this kind of transaction is that long-term assets of the investing country are increased, its short-term assets decreased (or short-term liabilities increased).

Although debiting "security imports" would be an appropriate way of entering a long-term loan or investment, it is not the usual way. Many writers prefer to use the term "long-term capital export." This has the advantage of calling attention to the direction of the capital flow, but it tends to be confusing, since exports of commodities entitle the exporter to receive a payment, whereas exports of capital require the exporter to make a payment. The International Monetary Fund uses the neutral term "long-term capital" as a general heading, then lists under this the different kinds of international capital transactions. If the country in question is lending or investing abroad—exporting capital—the entries appear on the debit side of its balance of payments. If the transactions involve borrowing, or importing capital in any manner, they of course appear as a credit.

Types of Long-Term Investment

There are three main types of long-term investment: direct investment, portfolio investment, and amortization. Direct investment includes the acquisition of stocks or bonds of firms abroad in which the investors own a controlling interest, as well as real estate or physical assets which become the property of such firms. Portfolio investment covers all other stocks and bonds, such as the obligations of governments or the securities of firms in which the investor does not have a controlling interest. Amortization refers to the repurchase or retirement of securities previously sold to foreigners. As with direct or portfolio investment, there is an import of securities and an export of capital by the investors; the securities imported, however, are not foreign issues, but domestic issues previously sold abroad and now being retired.

One special type of direct investment deserves attention. Suppose a firm in the United States exports equipment for installation in a branch plant abroad. These goods will be recorded in the U.S. balance of payments among exports;

this implies that the exporting firm is entitled to receive a payment. It receives no such payment, however. Instead, it increases the value of its assets abroad. This should be shown as a debit entry under direct investment.

Short-Term Capital Movements

We have already encountered short-term capital movements in the net increase or decrease in a country's short-term capital position resulting from a surplus or deficit in the current account.[3] But short-term capital movements are also undertaken for their own sake, or autonomously, just as are long-term capital movements.

Three types of short-term capital transactions may be distinguished in terms of the motives that cause them: (1) An individual may be stimulated to purchase foreign short-term securities (treasury bills, commercial bills, bankers' acceptances) because he can earn a higher return on them than he can on similar short-term investments at home. Such capital transactions may be said to be income-motivated. (2) Anticipated changes in the international value of a particular country's currency (that is, changes in the exchange rates on this currency) may lead some people to seek gain from buying it when they think it is cheap, or selling it when they believe it to be dear. Such transactions are speculative in nature. (3) Fear of war, of political instability, or of inflation may lead the residents of a country, or foreigners holding assets in that country, to seek to liquidate fixed assets and to transfer these and other liquid assets abroad. Such transactions are fear-motivated.

Short-Term Capital Movements and the Balance of Payments

Whatever the motive underlying a short-term capital movement, the effect on a country's balance of payments is the same. If residents of France, for example, acquire short-term assets in the United States (Treasury bills, or perhaps just dollar deposits), the purchase of these assets will be entered in France's balance of payments as a debit to short-term capital, to indicate what has been acquired. (This is the Fund's practice; some would call the debit entry "short-term capital export.") The corresponding payment made will be a credit in the balance of payments; it will consist of a reduction in French-owned deposits in New York or an increase in foreign-owned deposits in Paris. Thus, the end result of an autonomous short-term capital movement would appear to be a mere swapping of one kind of short-term foreign asset for another, or possibly of a foreign asset for a domestic liability to foreigners.

---

[3] Actually, every transaction in the current account, or for that matter, any transaction, involves a short-term capital movement if it is currently settled, or paid for. This is because the means by which transactions are settled is bank deposits, either foreign or domestic, and bank deposits are a liability of the bank in which they are held, an asset to the person who holds them. Since the greater part of payments and receipts resulting from current account transactions offset one another, our attention was focused upon the net receipts or net payments, which reflect the net change in the country's short-term capital position.

There is more to it than this, however. Who owns the foreign assets can be important, and short-term capital movements may cause changes in the ownership of those assets that will be to a country's disadvantage. To clarify this point, let us again introduce A's balance of payments into the discussion.

As we last left it, A's capital account showed that the country's residents were investing abroad on long term $500 million, this investment being financed to the extent of $300 million by the short-term foreign funds made available by A's excess of exports over imports, and to the extent of $200 million by "official" funds made available by the central bank and by gold exports.

Suppose now that, owing to the fact that short-term interest rates in some foreign financial center (say B) are above the level current in A, A's commercial banks decide to lend $50 million in that money market. They will purchase foreign balances from the central bank with a check drawn against their reserve deposit, then invest the B funds so acquired in treasury bills or other suitable short-term assets.

The effect on A's balance of payments is nil; there has been a transfer of ownership of foreign short-term assets from the central bank to commercial banks; that is all. Since in most countries today the commercial banks engaging in foreign transactions are subject to the control of the monetary authorities, this change in ownership is seldom important. That the foreign assets are now in the form of B's treasury bills instead of bank deposits is of little moment, for such bills are almost as liquid as deposits.

It is different if the export of capital is undertaken, not by banks, but by private persons; for then, foreign balances hitherto under the control of the monetary authorities pass into the hands of individuals over whom they have no control. Those balances cease to be part of the country's international reserves (see below) and thus available to the authorities in case of need.

Commercial banks are by all odds the most important exporters and importers of short-term capital to take advantage of interest-rate differentials. Short-term capital movements by private individuals are far more likely to be speculative or fear-motivated. If they are so small that they do not seriously deplete the central bank's holdings of foreign balances, they can be ignored. If large, they may raise serious problems.

Assume, for example, that serious inflation got under way in A during the year to which our balance of payments refers, and that as a consequence a flight of capital develops. Individuals and firms in A want to transfer $500 million of domestic funds into balances in foreign centers that are free of inflation. To do so, they surrender domestic currency and deposits to their commercial banks, which—if they adhere to the practice of maintaining only working balances abroad—will have to obtain the desired foreign balances from the central bank. If A's international transactions are free of controls, that institution will provide the desired balances to the extent of its ability. But suppose that, after the transfer of $150 million in official balances recorded in Table 16.6, it has only $300 million in foreign deposits available. It surrenders these, and to supply the remaining $200 million, must withdraw gold from its reserves and ship it abroad, where it is deposited. These deposits, too, are turned over to the persons who are exporting capital. A's balance of payments is changed as shown in Table 16.7.

Table 16.7

Dr.		*Balance of Payments of A*	Cr.
		Current Account	
	(million)		(million)
Merchandise imports	$1,800	Merchandise exports	$2,300
Services	300	Services	200
Donations:			
Official	100		
	2,200		2,500
		Capital Account	
Short-term capital (private)	500	Short-term capital (official)	450
Long-term capital	500	Gold exports	250
	$3,200		$3,200

Private individuals have transmitted short-term capital of $500 million, as is shown by the debit entry of this amount. It represents the foreign balances acquired by these individuals. The former entry, "Short-term capital (official), $150 million," on the credit side, has been increased by $300 million, reflecting a transfer of the central bank's previously held foreign assets to private individuals in A. Gold exports are $200 million larger than before. Since they require a payment of this amount to residents of A, they are added to the credit side. The payment is $200 million more of foreign balances; it appears as part of the $500 million of the debit to private short-term capital.

This large fear-motivated movement of capital has two important consequences: it seriously reduces the country's international reserves, and it changes a balance of payments with a moderate deficit to one with a very large deficit. Both these topics require further examination. Let us begin by explaining more fully the meaning of a deficit and a surplus in a country's balance of payments.

DEFICIT, SURPLUS, AND RESERVES

Meaning of Deficit and Surplus

We first encountered these terms when discussing the current account of the balance of payments. A surplus in the current account was said to arise when receipts from exports of goods and services exceeded payments for similar items. Similarly, a deficit was taken to mean an excess of such payments over corresponding receipts.

To make these concepts unambiguous when applied to the balance of payments as a whole, *it is well to emphasize the distinction we have already introduced, between transactions that are undertaken for their own sake,* for the profit they entail or the satisfaction they give (autonomous transactions) *and those that result from these* (induced transactions). Thus, referring again to the current account, exports and imports of goods and services are undertaken for the sake of the profit to be made—they are autonomous transactions. When they differ, there is an induced increase or decrease in foreign balances—a short-term capital movement—that is *not* undertaken for its own sake, but which results from the relative size of exports or imports.

Of the other balance-of-payments transactions considered, donations are voluntary and deliberate in character. So too are long-term capital movements, whether exports or imports. Short-term capital movements motivated by the desire to earn a higher return, to make a speculative gain, or to get one's capital into a safer place must also be classed as autonomous or made for their own sake.

This leaves, in the illustration before us, only gold movements and official short-term capital movements. These clearly are the result of the other transactions. *A*'s central bank reduced its foreign balances, not from any decision of its own, but because of the pressure on the balance of payments. It exported gold, too, in response to the balance of payments situation.

We conclude that *a deficit appears in a balance of payments when autonomous transactions requiring payments exceed autonomous transactions involving receipts.* By the same token, a surplus exists when autonomous transactions giving rise to receipts exceed autonomous transactions requiring payments.

International Reserves

The *induced* transactions, in our illustration, were movements of reserves. This is always the case. International reserves serve the purpose of filling in a gap in a balance of payments. And we can measure the size of a surplus or a deficit by the volume of reserve movements. This makes it necessary to be clear as to what constitutes such a movement. The following descriptive list uses the concept of reserve movements developed by the International Monetary Fund.[4]

[4] Since we are concerned here with international reserves as they are used to finance a deficit or a surplus in a country's balance of payments, it is appropriate to limit ourselves to defining reserve movements rather than the total of international reserves in a country's possession at any time. This approach also avoids the need for an elaboration of such distinctions as that between a country's total gold holdings and the portion required by law to be held as a currency reserve, and that between total short-term liabilities to foreigners and the actual or probable use of them in financing balance of payments deficits or surpluses. For a discussion of these problems, see International Monetary Fund, *Balance of Payments Yearbook 1938-1946-1947* (Washington, D. C., 1949), pp. 4-23.

Components of International Reserve Movements

Monetary gold. Only movements of gold into or out of the holdings of the monetary authorities (treasury, central bank, or exchange stabilization fund) are counted. Shipments of gold by producers (for example, South African mines) or to manufacturers, or movements into or out of private hoards, are classed as ordinary commodity exports and imports.

Foreign currency or bank deposits held by the monetary authorities, or by commercial banks subject to their control (official holdings).

Short-term foreign claims, officially held, which can be readily liquidated at a stable price (such as treasury bills and bank acceptances). Both this item and foreign bank deposits are reserves in the fullest sense if they are in convertible currencies. When they are in currencies subject to limited transferability their reserve quality is of course impaired.

Domestic bank deposits held by foreign monetary authorities and banks.

Domestic short-term claims, similarly held. These two items are the counterpart of foreign reserves; changes in them serve to finance a deficit or surplus.

Sale of long-term securities officially held (including any requisitioned from private owners by the government). Purchases would not appear here, since purchase of long-term securities would merely represent a shift of foreign assets of low yield into a higher yielding form.

Use of International Monetary Fund resources.

The Financing of Deficits and Surpluses

The method by which a deficit or surplus in the balance of payments is financed varies with the kind of currency and exchange system in force.

Under the international gold standard of pre-1914 days, deficits or surpluses and the means of financing them appeared simultaneously. The financing was automatic, and took the form both of gold and of capital movements. Commercial banks maintained convenient working balances of foreign deposits, which they allowed to vary very little. When the United States, for example, had a surplus in its international account, and the United Kingdom a deficit, bank balances accumulated in London to the credit of New York banks. Ordinarily the latter would convert these into gold for import into the United States.[5] This gold movement financed the U.S. surplus, and at least part of the U.K. deficit.

On such occasions, the Bank of England frequently took action to check the outflow of gold by raising its discount rate, thus forcing up market rates. At the higher level of interest rates in London, New York banks found it profitable to leave their accumulating balances there, and lend them in the market. An American export of short-term capital (import of British short-term obligations) replaced the gold flow. From the viewpoint of the United States, this capital movement was undertaken for its own sake, to earn a higher return. As an additional autonomous item in the U.S. balance of payments, it reduced or perhaps eliminated the surplus needing to be financed. From the viewpoint of

---

[5] The actual procedure was more indirect than this, but came to the same thing. It is explained in Chapter 19.

the United Kingdom, however, there can be no doubt that the import of capital was deliberately engineered as a preferred alternative to gold exports as a means of financing the deficit. Britain's short-term borrowing was undertaken not for its own sake, but because the deficit had to be financed.

A second and very different situation with regard to unbalanced international payments arises when exchange rates are free to fluctuate, instead of being held steady through the linkage of currencies to gold. For then, any tendency toward an excess of autonomous receipts over payments, with a consequent accumulation of foreign balances, would be counteracted by a fall in the value of foreign currencies. Imports are cheapened; exports become more expensive to foreign buyers; and the surplus simply disappears. No compensatory financing is needed.

Another kind of situation arises when, as in much of the world today, governments exercise effective controls over international payments. They do so through quantitative restrictions on imports, together with controls over the uses to which foreign receipts may be put. Nations equipped with such regulatory apparatus can, within broad limits, have a deficit as small as their control authorities wish to make it. Whatever deficit arises is then deliberately planned; it is the task of the monetary authorities to determine how it is to be financed. Their action, which is called "compensatory official financing," involves choosing between the different kinds of reserve movements to be permitted—for example, drawing upon foreign balances, liquidating officially held foreign assets, exporting gold, or acquiring a drawing right from the International Monetary Fund. Compensatory official financing may also include, in addition to use of various components of international reserves, loans specifically arranged for the purpose of meeting a deficit in a country's balance of payments. The Anglo-American loan of 1946 was of this character; so were most of the loans of the Export-Import Bank and of the International Bank to European governments after the last war, as well as a large proportion of American aid to Europe.

WHAT A BALANCE OF PAYMENTS SHOWS

As we noted at the beginning of this chapter, a balance of payments is an extremely useful aid to economic analysis, for by examining it, we can learn much about the strength or weakness of a country's international position. Particularly revealing is a series of balances of payments for successive years, or a pair of statements at the beginning and end of an interval of time during which important changes have occurred; by comparing these statements we can perceive in some detail both the character and the magnitude of the change. Even though the balance of payments itself may not tell us *why* the change took place, examination of its components may suggest where we can obtain further information as to the causes (Table 16.8).

Table 16.8. BALANCE OF INTERNATIONAL PAYMENTS OF
THE UNITED STATES, 1955

Debit		Current Transactions	Credit
Merchandise imports	$11,516	Merchandise exports	$14,264
Foreign Travel	1,155	Foreign travel	645
Transportation	1,202	Transportation	1,336
Investment income	512	Investment income	2,512
Government	3,190	Government	333
Insurance & miscellaneous	489	Insurance & miscellaneous	825
Sub-total	18,064	Sub-total	19,915
(Net credit balance on current transactions	1,851)		
Donations:			
Private	456		
Official	1,865		
		(Net debit balance before capital transactions	470)

Capital and Monetary Gold

Short-term capital	537	Short-term capital	560
Long-term capital	918	Long-term capital	873
		Monetary gold	41
		Errors and omissions	451
Total	$21,840	Total	$21,840

SOURCE: International Monetary Fund, *Balance of Payments Yearbook*, February, 1957. In addition to the above, goods and services totaling $2,134 million were transferred under military aid programs.

Looking at the United States balance of payments for 1955, we see that exports of goods and services substantially exceeded similar imports, providing an apparent surplus on current transactions of $1,851 million. This surplus was fictitious, however, since not only were exports and services of this amount provided to foreigners without payment (principally as military aid), but an additional net sum of $470 million was turned over as a donation.

This amount, plus an autonomous debit of $45 million for net long-term capital movements (U.S. investment abroad, $918 million, less sales of U.S. government bonds and other securities to foreigners, $873 million), or $515 million in all, had somehow to be covered by compensatory financing. Relatively little of this financing is actually accounted for: $23 million from net short-term capital movement,[6] and $41 million from gold exports. All the rest —$451 million—is unexplained; it shows up in "errors and omissions." This is in all likelihood to be traced mainly to unreported changes in short-term

---

[6] Short-term capital credits or imports of $560 million were principally in the form of an increase in the liabilities of U.S. banks to foreigners, while short-term capital debits or exports of $537 million represented mainly increases in U.S. balances in foreign banks.

capital items, since these are the most subject to error, although a considerable part of the error may be scattered among the other elements of the balance of payments.

In spite of the current account and over-all deficit in the U.S. balance of payments for 1955, that nation's position was, to say the least, comfortable. It was able to donate the entire surplus from current transactions and to finance an additional half billion dollars in gifts mainly, it would seem, by changes in bank balances at home and abroad.

Contrast with the comfortable U.S. balance of payments that of France in 1947 (Table 16.9). At that time France desperately needed imports of many

Table 16.9. BALANCE OF PAYMENTS OF FRANCE
(FRANC AREA), 1947

Debit	Current Transactions		Credit
Merchandise imports	$2,497	Merchandise exports	$1,093
Foreign travel	51	Foreign travel	57
Transportation	427	Transportation	104
Investment income	68	Investment income	148
Government	48	Government	2
Insurance & miscellaneous	159	Insurance & miscellaneous	158
Sub-total	3,249	Sub-total	1,562
		(Net debit balance, goods	
		and services	1,687)

Movement of Capital and Monetary Gold			
Private:		Private:	
		Short-term capital	81
Long-term capital	15	Long-term capital	5
Government & banking institutions:		Government & banking institutions:	
		Short-term capital	744
Long-term capital	361	Long-term capital	794
		Monetary gold	438
		Errors and omissions	1
Total	$3,625	Total	$3,625

Source: International Monetary Fund, *Balance of Payments Yearbook, 1938-1946-1947*. As presented here, the data have been rearranged and consolidated to a minor extent.

kinds to keep her economy going. On the other hand, her ability to produce exports was at low ebb, owing to the destruction and disorganization caused by World War II. These facts are reflected in a total for imports almost two-and-a-half times as great as the value of exports, which in large part accounts for the deficit in current transactions of $1,687 million.

To obtain France's total deficit, we add to this the private and public long-term capital exports of $376 million, and subtract the $86 million of private capital imports, for a net addition of $290 million. Together with the deficit on current account, this makes the over-all deficit $1,977 million. To meet this deficit, France was forced to borrow heavily and to export gold. The large ($794 million) debt item under "Long-term capital" reflects, in the main, loans to France by the Export-Import Bank of the United States and by the International Bank for Reconstruction and Development, made for the purpose of financing France's deficit. Official short-term borrowing (net) of $744 million is accounted for principally by French borrowing from the International Monetary Fund and by a reduction of foreign balances.

Contrast France's international position in 1954 with this unfavorable state of affairs (Table 16.10). Imports have increased only moderately over 1947,

Table 16.10. BALANCE OF PAYMENTS OF FRANCE
(FRANC AREA), 1954

Debit		Current Transactions	Credit
Merchandise imports	$2,724	Merchandise exports	$2,545
Foreign travel	121	Foreign travel	182
Transportation	211	Transportation	137
Investment income	146	Investment income	121
Government	65	Government	582
Insurance & miscellaneous	310	Insurance & miscellaneous	261
Sub-total	3,577	Sub-total	3,828
(Net credit balance, goods and services	251)		
Donations	10	Donations	509
(Net balance, current transactions	750)		

		Capital and Monetary Gold	
Private, short-term capital	121	Private, long-term capital	55
Official & banking institutions:			
Short-term capital	581		
Long-term capital	136		
Monetary gold	6	Errors and omissions	39
Total	$4,431	Total	$4,431

SOURCE: International Monetary Fund, *Balance of Payments Yearbook*, Vol. 6, 1953-54.

while exports have expanded almost two-and-a-half times. Foreign travel in France has recovered, providing net earnings of $61 million; transportation charges have been cut in half; and income from this source has risen slightly. Only "insurance and miscellaneous" and payments on investment income have moved unfavorably. Moreover, France is earning $582 million from foreign government expenditures in the country, chiefly U.S. outlays on military projects and military equipment.

As a result of these favorable changes, in 1954, France's goods and services account shows a surplus of $251 million instead of a deficit of $1,687 million. When to this is added $509 million of donations (chiefly U.S. economic aid, but also including a special grant of $89 million from the European Payments Union), there is a surplus on current transactions of $750 million.

France used this credit balance for investment abroad; this took the form of repayment of long-term loans to the United States, the United Kingdom, and Canada; repayment of a large short-term debt to the European Payments Union; and the acquisition of foreign balances and the reduction of franc balances in the hands of foreigners. Everything considered, France's balance of payments in 1954 was in good shape, even though most of the loan repayments undertaken depended in large part on donations of a half-billion dollars.

WHAT A BALANCE OF PAYMENTS DOES NOT SHOW

Effects of Controls

As the preceding illustrations demonstrate, a country's balance of payments can be highly informative. It shows clearly whether it is paying its way internationally on its current transactions, so to speak, or whether to balance its imports of goods and services it is being forced to borrow abroad heavily or to export large amounts of gold. But it may not always reveal whether a country is having difficulty in balancing its imports and exports. For example, imports may be subject to artificial controls. Then a country's balance of payments might show current transactions in substantial balance, with no increase in its international indebtedness. Yet it might be maintaining an apparently satisfactory position only by the imposition of rigorous restrictions on its imports. To analyze and understand a situation such as this, it is necessary to go behind the balance of payments and acquire information as to its trade policy and how it affects its international payments.

Lack of Detail

For many analytical purposes, balances of payments, as published, provide insufficient detail. Thus merchandise trade, both exports and imports, is shown in aggregate form; there is no breakdown as to types of commodities or as to origin or destination of the goods-movements. Yet often such information can be revealing. Changes in the composition of a country's exports may stem from a deep-seated change in its economic structure, or they may simply reflect a shift in commercial policy. It is important to trace such changes, and to know what lies behind them. To obtain a commodity classification of a country's trade, one has to go to the detailed trade figures published by many nations. These must also be consulted if one needs to know a good deal about origins and destinations of trade, although the IMF *Balance of Payments Yearbook* publishes supplementary balances of payments giving a breakdown of all transactions by major areas. When currencies are inconvertible, as most of them were from about 1931 until the end of 1958, whether a country sells to the United States or to Argentina or Egypt may be just as important as whether it has a credit or a debit balance on current account.

The Balance of International Indebtedness

One thing a balance of payments does not show, and that it may be important to know, is a country's over-all balance of indebtedness. This is the total of its investments in securities and property in other countries, less the total of such investments by foreigners in the country in question. Such information can be useful for estimating a country's net earnings from overseas investment income or for calculating what liquid funds it could raise in a crisis, as on the outbreak of war. Together with known investment income, it provides a check on the average yield on the country's foreign investments. Such information has to be obtained through a separate inquiry or inventory of foreign long-term assets and liabilities. We cannot expect to get it from the balance of payments, since that includes, on the one hand, that part of the gross national product derived from net sales abroad, and on the other hand, *changes* in the country's foreign assets and liabilities, both short-term and long-term.

SELECTED REFERENCES

Badger, Donald G., "The Balance of Payments: A Tool of Analysis," *IMF Staff Papers*, Vol. II, No. 1 (September, 1951). A detailed discussion of the International Monetary Fund's method of presenting balances of payments, together with a reply to Machlup's criticism (see below) of the concept of compensatory official financing.

"The Adequacy of Monetary Reserves," *IMF Staff Papers*, Vol. III, No. 2 (October, 1953). A discussion of the meaning of international reserves and the concept of adequacy.

International Monetary Fund, *Balance of Payments Manual*. Washington, D. C.: The Fund, 1950. Detailed instructions for preparing balance of payments statements.

International Monetary Fund, *Balance of Payments Yearbook 1938-1946-1947*. Washington, D. C.: The Fund, 1949. In addition to the balances of payments of member countries, this number of the yearbook contains an extended discussion of the concepts underlying the Fund's presentation of balance of payments data. For later data, see the annual volumes.

Machlup, Fritz, "Three Concepts of the Balance of Payments and the So-Called Dollar Shortage," *Economic Journal*, LX (March, 1950). Draws a careful distinction between a market balance, a program balance, and an accounting balance of payments, on the basis of which the concept of compensatory official financing is criticized.

"Oskaloosa vs. the U.S.," *Fortune* (April, 1938). An interesting application of the concept of a balance of payments to the trade and financial relations of this Iowa town.

U.S. Department of Commerce, *Balance of Payments of the United States, 1949-1951*. Contains a detailed discussion of the methods used in balance of payments accounting, how the data are collected, the sources of data, and how data are arranged in the Department's presentation.

17

FOREIGN EXCHANGE

One of the features that distinguishes international trade from trade within a country is that each nation has its own currency and its own banking system. Prices in each country are reckoned in the country's own currency units—in dollars, pounds, francs, marks, lire, pesos, rupees, and so on. To the inhabitants of one country, the currencies of others are usually almost as unfamiliar as their languages.

Within a single country, its currency moves freely. Purchasing power can be transferred over considerable distances through the use of checks on a local bank, and the great bulk of these payments are cleared against one another, assisted either by relationships established between banks in different parts of the country or by the central bank acting as a clearing agency.

It is the necessity of making payments at a distance *and* in different currencies that raises the problem of foreign exchange. Exporters, as they sell their goods abroad, acquire claims in an alien currency. But since they must pay wages and other costs in their own national money, they need a means of exchanging the foreign money for their own. Importers confront the same problem—they must pay for goods from foreign lands, but they have only local currency to do it with.

THE FOREIGN EXCHANGE MARKET

It is the foreign exchange market that in any country provides the needed facilities. This is not a place, like a produce market, where buyers and sellers confront one another face to face. The people who participate in it have highly specialized jobs in the foreign departments of banks, or in the offices of brokers or dealers, and they are in constant touch with one another by telephone. Because communication is so easy, all dealers quote the same price for each currency, which is the test of a unified market.

Dealings, of course, are in foreign currencies. Into the foreign exchange market comes a supply of all the currencies on which a country has claims—from exporters, borrowers who are selling domestic securities abroad, sellers of services, and at times, speculators. The demand comes from those having to make foreign payments—importers, buyers of services or foreign securities, and perhaps speculators as well. Either in the market of the particular country or in some related foreign exchange market abroad, depending upon the specific method used to finance an international transaction, both sides of the country's balance of payments meet in day-to-day purchases and sales of foreign exchange.

Different Exchange Rate Quotations

As the accompanying table (taken from *The Wall Street Journal*) shows, a number of different rates are quoted on a single currency in the same market on the same day. This scarcely corresponds to our concept of a market as

Sterling Exchange Rates
(Wednesday, June 12, 1963)

Cables	2.8008
30-day Futures	2.7994
90-day Futures	2.7968
Switch or security	2.7910

giving rise to a single price for a given item, or of an exchange rate as the price of a specific currency.

There is no inconsistency, however, for the various exchange rates, though all are dollar prices of sterling, are for different kinds of sterling. The cable rate is for sterling to be made available immediately in London, and is the highest in price. The 30-day and 90-day rates are for sterling to be delivered at later dates. Each is slightly below the next highest rate, reflecting mainly the discount rate in London. Whoever buys sterling to be made available in London, for example, only after 30 days, cannot expect to get his funds there immediately unless someone makes an advance, for which he will charge the going rate of discount. The buyer of sterling therefore pays a lower rate the more distant the date of delivery.

Switch or security sterling, the cheapest of all, is quite a different kind, one which is subject to certain controls, in contrast to "free" sterling, to which the other rates apply.

THE MECHANISM OF FOREIGN PAYMENTS

Two components are required to transfer purchasing power across national boundaries and from one currency to another. One is an instrument, the bill of exchange (or its more speedy counterpart, the telegraphic transfer); the other is an institution, the bank, of which one is needed in both the paying and the receiving country. The way in which these two operate to effect international transfers can be most clearly presented by an illustration.

Financing Exports

SIGHT BILLS   Suppose a Colombian coffee exporter has entered into a contract with a New York importer to deliver a shipment of coffee worth, at the price agreed upon, $100,000, payment to be made upon arrival of the shipment in New York. The coffee is put aboard ship, and the exporter receives from the shipping company a bill of lading, which carries title to the shipment, as well as documents certifying its insurance and clearance through customs. If the exporter can afford to wait the two weeks or so it takes the coffee to reach New York, he will delay until just before it is to arrive, and then—in accord with arrangements made when the deal was settled—draw a bill of exchange on the New York importer. This is an order by the "drawer" (the exporter) on the "drawee" (the importer) to pay a "payee" (a New York bank) $100,000 at sight—that is, on presentation of the bill. Since the exporter has no use for dollars, but wants pesos with which to buy coffee from growers and to pay his other expenses, he takes this bill of exchange to a local bank with a foreign department and obtains immediate payment.[1] He receives the value of the bill in pesos at the current rate of exchange for dollar-sight-bills. This will be the same as, or very close to, the rate for cable transfers, since in these days of fast airmail service, the bank purchasing a sight bill will have the use of its money in the foreign financial center within a very short time. Assuming the sight rate of exchange is seven pesos per dollar, the exporter's receipts will be 700,000 pesos.

The Colombian bank mails the bill of exchange, together with the bill of lading and other documents relevant to the shipment, to a bank in New York with which it has "correspondent" relations. Presumably this is one of the large banks with a foreign department, say the Guaranty Trust Company. It will present the bill of exchange to the importer, who pays its face value with a check on his own bank and receives the bill of lading, with which he can obtain the coffee at dockside.

Observe now the results of this financial transaction. The exporter has obtained payment in pesos. The Colombian bank has paid out 700,000 pesos, either in currency or in the form of a checking deposit in the exporter's name. In either case, the supply of money in Colombia is increased by this amount, just as it would be had the bank made a new loan. To compensate this reduction in its assets or increase in its liabilities, the bank now has a deposit of equivalent value in New York.

TIME BILLS   Had the exporter wanted his payment as soon as the coffee was put aboard ship in Baranquilla, or had the New York importer needed

---

[1] The bank is protected in such a purchase by the fact that, so long as the importer has not guaranteed payment of the bill by accepting it, the drawer remains primarily liable. Sometimes an advance guarantee is provided by the importer's bank, in the form of an "authority to purchase" issued to the exporter's bank.

time to dispose of the coffee before making payment, an extension of credit for a more or less extended period would have been involved. Assuming that the bill of exchange is drawn as of the date of shipment and is not to be collected for sixty days, it would be a "time" bill instead of a "sight" bill. The exporter would sell it, as before, to his bank, but at the lower rate for 60-day bills, say 6.96 pesos per dollar, which would yield the exporter a total of 696,000 pesos.

The Colombian bank would now forward the bill to its New York correspondent bank, which would present it to the importer for "acceptance." The bill now becomes a *commercial acceptance*; depending upon instructions from the Colombian bank, the New York bank will either discount it in the money market or hold it until maturity. If the former, the Colombian bank would obtain the discounted value of the bill, which it had paid the exporter. The credit to carry the transaction is then provided by the money market. Had it ordered the bill held the Colombian bank would provide the credit and earn the discount, since it advanced only the discounted value of the bill and would obtain its face value upon payment. At the end of sixty days, of course, the bill would be presented to the importer for payment.

But, in all probability, since there is no ready market for commercial acceptances in New York, a *bankers' acceptance* would have been used instead. In this instance, the American coffee importer would have arranged for his bank to issue a letter of credit. This instrument authorizes the Colombian exporter to draw a bill on this bank—say the Chase Manhattan Bank—for the sum specified. Upon receipt of this letter of credit, he would draw such a bill and cash it in the usual fashion. His bank would mail it to its correspondent, the Guaranty Trust Company, which would present it to the Chase Manhattan Bank for acceptance and then either hold it until maturity, if the Colombian bank elected to earn the interest, or discount it in the New York money market. At the end of sixty days, it would be presented by its holder for payment, the funds necessary for this purpose having been turned over to the Chase Manhattan Bank by the importer.

Financing Imports

To pay for an import into Colombia, the importer would initiate action, just as the Colombian exporter did in the preceding transaction, for the good reason that New York is a great international financial center with whose banks those of many other countries maintain correspondent relations and in which they keep substantial dollar balances.

SIGHT DRAFTS   Consider a Colombian importer who has bought a $100,000 shipment of machine tools from an American manufacturer. The shipment has arrived and the arrangement is that the importer is to pay on delivery. He goes to his bank (let us suppose it is the same one used by the coffee exporter) and purchases a sight bill of exchange (a sight draft) on the drawee (Guaranty

Trust Company) to pay the payee (the American exporter of machine tools) the sum specified. The importer pays for the draft with cash or a check in pesos, mails it to the exporter in the United States, who presents it to the Guaranty Trust Company for payment.

The results of this transaction are plain to see. The importer has received the goods and paid for them in the money of his country, while the exporter has received payment in dollars. The Colombian bank's assets in New York have diminished; its cash holdings have increased; or its demand deposits have diminished. A contraction of the supply of money in Colombia has therefore occurred, since either currency has been retired from circulation or checking deposits have been extinguished. Finally, purchasing power has been transferred over a great distance and from one currency to another. This is made possible by the practice of Colombian banks of keeping deposits in New York, which are augmented by Colombian exports and diminished by Colombian imports.

TIME PAYMENTS Our import illustration, involving a cash payment on delivery of the goods, is the simplest type of transaction. But suppose the importer had wanted sixty days in which to dispose of the machine tools before settling his bill. The necessary extension of credit could have been arranged in any one of a number of ways. One of the simplest would be for the American exporter to sell the shipment on *"open book account"*—thereby undertaking to wait perhaps sixty days or more before expecting the importer to purchase and remit a draft. This method would only be used, however, if the seller was well-acquainted with the buyer and if the latter had a first-class credit rating.

A more common procedure would involve the use of a *dollar export bill.* Here the importer would arrange through his bank to have its New York correspondent, the Guaranty Trust Company, issue a letter of credit to the American exporter, authorizing him to draw a *dollar* bill of exchange upon it for the $100,000. This would order the Guaranty Trust Company to pay this sum at the end of sixty days to the bearer—that is, whoever held it at that time. The machine tool exporter, located, let us say, in Cleveland, would discount it at his local bank and obtain immediate payment, while the Cleveland bank would send it to its correspondent in New York and have it accepted by the Guaranty Trust Company. The bill has now become a bankers' acceptance, and would probably be rediscounted in the money market, the proceeds being deposited to the credit of the Cleveland bank with its New York correspondent. Just before the sixty days expired, the Colombian importer, according to terms prescribed when the letter of credit was arranged, would purchase a dollar sight draft in favor of the Guaranty Trust Company for $100 thousand. This would be mailed to New York and would transfer to the Guaranty Trust Company this amount of the Colombian bank's deposit with it. Even more simply, the funds could be transferred by telegraph.

The economic results of this more complicated transaction would be precisely the same as those of our first and simpler one, which involved the purchase by the Colombian importer of a sight draft on New York. Only the details differ.

THE ROLE OF INTERNATIONAL FINANCIAL CENTERS

Practically every country in the world has economic transactions of one kind or another with many other countries. If each country's banks maintained correspondent relations with banks in each and every country with which its residents did business, the number of such correspondents and hence the number of separate foreign balances to be kept would be unconscionably large. Such complexity is made unnecessary by the concentration of international payments in a small number of financial centers.

Two such—London and New York—are of outstanding importance. British Commonwealth countries, and a number of others comprising the sterling area or more or less closely linked with it, use London as their principal financial and clearing center. Their banks maintain balances there and finance most of their transactions with the rest of the world through bills of exchange drawn in favor of or against these balances, in a manner identical or similar to those of our Colombian-U.S. illustrations. New York, on the other hand, is the established clearing center for the countries of the so-called dollar bloc—those bordering on the Caribbean, Canada, the Philippine Republic, and Japan.

These two currency areas are by no means sealed off from one another; the banks of most countries maintain balances in both New York and London, using the one center or the other as the occasion demands. In addition, a number of other cities—Paris, Berne, Rome, Cologne, Amsterdam, and Tokyo, to mention the more important ones—also perform similar clearing and financing functions, though on a smaller scale.

For any group of nations whose banks have balances in a center such as New York, it is a simple matter to carry out their transactions, not only with the United States, but also with one another, in dollars. Thus Brazil can export to Greece and receive payment in dollars, while paying for its imports from that country in the same currency. Both Brazilian and Greek exporters, under letters of credit issued by correspondents of their banks in New York, draw bankers' acceptances on these New York banks, discount them at their local banks, which then have them rediscounted when they reach New York. When the time comes for the respective importers in each country to pay, each buys a sight draft or a cable transfer from his local bank, and therewith transfers Brazilian- or Greek-owned dollars in New York to the banks in that city which have to meet the acceptances as they come due. The Brazilian and Greek exporters receive payment in cruzeiros and drachmas respectively; the importers pay in these currencies; and so far as the exports of the two countries offset one another, they are cleared in dollars in New York. So far as Brazilian-Greek trade is concerned, that country whose exports are larger will wind up at the end of a given period with an increased dollar balance, the other with a diminished one.

Why London and New York?

The reason why London and New York are such important centers, financing and clearing a large proportion of the trade of many countries, is that they provide abundant and expert banking facilities, together with ample funds from their respective money markets for the discounting of bills of exchange at low rates of interest. We saw in Chapter 11 that during the nineteenth century, a variety of specialized brokers, dealers, and bankers arose in London who were ready to provide, or to find the funds for discounting, an ever-increasing volume of commercial or bankers' acceptances. Funds in this money market were so plentiful that discount rates ruled generally lower than anywhere else in the world. No wonder that importers, who have to pay the cost of carrying their transactions, preferred to have bills drawn on London, where the cost of the needed credit was low.

Not until after the establishment of the Federal Reserve System in 1915 and the growth of a market for bankers' acceptances that its existence aided, did New York become an important international financial center. With the growth of the United States as a trading and investing nation, and as a reserve-currency country, it has since come to rival London.

Even though the great bulk of dealings involving New York or London is carried out in dollars or pounds sterling, this does not mean that, even in these centers, other currencies are never used. A part of the trade with such countries as France and Italy, for example, is transacted in francs and lire, and there is always a demand for the currencies of a large number of countries for the remittance of dividends and charitable contributions. A demand for dollars arises in these countries from similar needs. Hence, New York and London banks maintain balances in a large number of countries, often in branches of the great metropolitan banks, and stand ready to discount or sell bills of exchange, buy or sell telegraphic transfers, on these balances.

FOREIGN EXCHANGE RATES

In our discussion of the foreign exchange market and its operation, we have taken the rate of exchange between two currencies as given, since the method of its determination, or even fluctuations in that rate, did not immediately concern us. It is now time to consider these matters.

Importance of Exchange Rates

The rate at which a country's currency exchanges for those of other countries measures its external value. It provides a direct link between the domestic prices of commodities and productive factors and their prices in the rest of the world. With prices at home and abroad at a given level, a low set of rates of exchange (low prices, in home currency, of foreign currencies) will hamper exports and stimulate imports, and thereby tend to bring about a deficit in the balance of payments. On the other hand, high exchange rates will stimulate exports and restrict imports, thus tending to bring about a balance-of-payments surplus.

This central role of exchange rates in determining a country's ability to export can be illustrated as follows: We choose a list of commodities produced both in the United States and in the United Kingdom; we arbitrarily take as the *unit* of each of these commodities the *amount that costs $1 to produce in the United States*. This cost of a given amount of each commodity in the U.S. appears as column one in Table 17.1. Column two shows the (assumed) cost of producing the same amounts of each of these products in the United Kingdom in shillings and pence. Whereas the price of each commodity is the same ($1) in the U.S., because we chose an amount that cost $1 to produce, the prices vary widely in the United Kingdom, ranging from a minimum of 4 shillings for margarine to a maximum of 10 shillings for tin cans.

Table 17.1. PRICES AND EXCHANGE RATES

	(1)	(2)	(3)	(4)	(5)
			Cost in the United Kingdom		
Commodity	Cost in	In shillings		in dollars	
	U.S. in $	and pence	@£1=$5	@£1=$4	@£1=$2.80
Margarine	$1	4/—	$1.00	$0.80	$0.56
Wool cloth	1	4/3	1.06	0.85	0.60
Cotton cloth	1	4/8	1.16	0.93	0.65
Cigarettes	1	5/—	1.25	1.00	0.70
Linoleum	1	5/6	1.38	1.10	0.77
Paper	1	6/—	1.50	1.20	0.84
Glass bottles	1	7/—	1.75	1.40	0.98
Radio tubes	1	8/—	2.00	1.60	1.12
Pig iron	1	9/—	2.25	1.80	1.26
Tin cans	1	10/—	2.50	2.00	1.40

These relative price differences reflect, of course, differences in factor prices and in the proportions in which the factors are combined, as well as differing economies of scale. Since wages in the United States average approximately 2½ times as high as in the United Kingdom, while costs of using capital are possibly slightly lower in the United States, commodities at the top of the list— relatively cheap in the U.K.—comprise relatively labor-intensive products, those at the bottom of the list—relatively cheap in the U.S.—are capital-intensive, as well as prone to economies of scale.

The various British prices are then converted into dollars and cents at three different rates of exchange. Column three shows the prices British producers would have to charge American and other foreign buyers at a rate of exchange of £1 = $5. Columns four and five show the very different prices corresponding to rates of exchange of £1 = $4 and £1 = $2.80.[2]

If the pound had a value or rate of exchange as high as $5, the United Kingdom could sell in competition with the United States, ignoring transport costs, only the first commodity in the list, margarine.[3] In all the others, the United States would be able to undersell British products. The volume and value of British exports would be very small, while without serious restrictions on imports, their value would far exceed that of exports. The United Kingdom would confront a serious imbalance in its international payments.

At a rate of exchange of £1 = $2.80, on the other hand, the U.K. could undersell the U.S. in all but the last three commodities. This would ensure large exports, while imports would be much reduced. Instead of a deficit in its balance of payments, the U.K. might well enjoy a large surplus. With an intermediate exchange rate of $4 to the pound, the United Kingdom could undersell the United States in the first three products and compete on an even basis with respect to the fourth, while the U.S. could underbid British producers on the other six commodities.

From this illustration, it is easy to see that the rate at which a country's currency is quoted on foreign exchange markets is a matter of crucial importance. Since it is by means of the exchange rate that home prices are translated into foreign prices, and vice versa, the exchange rate occupies a key position with respect to a country's international transactions. Close attention to how exchange rates are determined and what causes them to vary is therefore warranted. The next chapter is devoted to a discussion of these problems.

Some Technicalities

An exchange rate is normally defined as the price, in domestic currency, of a unit of foreign currency. It might equally well be defined as the price, in a foreign currency, of a unit of domestic currency. For an exchange rate is simply the value or price of one currency in terms of another, and it makes no difference in which currency the price ratio is expressed. The British continue to follow their traditional practice of quoting exchange rates on all currencies as the price of the pound in terms of foreign currency units. In New York, as in most other financial centers, the opposite practice is followed:

---

[2] For those not familiar with British monetary units, there are 20 shillings to the pound, 12 pence to each shilling. Thus at an exchange rate of £1 = $5, a shilling would be worth 1/20 of $5, or 25¢, and a penny 1/12 of 25¢ or approximately 2¢. At £1 = $4, 1 shilling = 20¢, 1 d. (pence) = 1.67¢; at £1 = $2.80, 1 shilling = 14¢, 1 d. = 1.167¢.

[3] If the value of the pound in dollars was high, its value in other currencies of given dollar values would also be high. Therefore we can ignore price comparisons with other countries, which would be similar in nature, though the list of commodities compared would presumably be different.

foreign currencies are expressed in terms of domestic currency. The rate on the pound has since 1949 been slightly above or below $2.80. The dollar/franc rate (for the French franc) has since 1958 been around $0.2041.

Which form of quotation is used is unimportant. What *is* important is that you be conscious, in any particular instance, of just which way this relationship is expressed and from which country's point of view it is being regarded. This is of particular significance when changes in a rate of exchange are involved. Thus a fall in the dollar/franc rate from $0.2041 to $0.2032 would represent depreciation of the franc, appreciation of the dollar. In Paris, a simultaneous rise in the franc/dollar rate from 4.90 frs./$ to 4.92 would reflect the same facts.

It is this two-sided relationship between currencies that is the source of much confusion with respect to foreign exchange problems. To minimize difficulties, always make sure you know (1) in which currency, domestic or foreign, an exchange rate is expressed, and (2) from which country's point of view the rate or a change in it, is being considered.

Arbitrage

When foreign exchange markets are free from or subject to only very limited controls, the rate of exchange between two currencies in one of the markets must be the same in the other market. Thus if the pound is quoted at $2.80 in New York, it must also stand at $2.80 in London. For if dealers were free to buy or sell dollars and pounds without limit, then if the rate were $2.80 in New York and $2.85 in London, they would acquire pounds with dollars in New York at the lower rate, sell these pounds for dollars in London at the higher rate, and make 5¢ profit on each pound bought and sold. The increased demand for pounds in New York would raise the rate there, while the additional supply of pounds sold against dollars in London would lower it, and the two rates would converge. They could differ only by the very small cost (which is low per pound because transactions would be in large sums) of carrying out these operations, which are known as "arbitrage."

But arbitrage is not limited to operations in two currencies, or to two-point arbitrage. Three-point (and even wider) arbitrage is also common when currencies are free. Thus suppose the dollar/sterling rate is $2.80, the franc/dollar rate is 4.90 francs per dollar, and the cross rate between the pound and the franc is 13.97 francs per pound. Arbitragers will buy pounds with dollars, convert each pound into francs in London, and then sell the francs thus obtained for dollars in New York. For an investment of $2.80 they will obtain $2.85 (13.97/4.9 = 2.85). Assume, to simplify the arithmetic, that the dollar/sterling and the franc/dollar rates remain unchanged. Then arbitraging will continue until the value of the franc in pounds is consistent with its value in dollars. This will be when the franc/pound rate is 13.72 francs per pound. Continuing purchases of francs in London would drive up the value of the franc, which means lowering the number of francs obtainable for a pound. The result of arbitraging is to link the three exchange markets virtually into one, and to bring into being consistent cross rates. To the extent to which foreign exchange markets are free, arbitraging of this kind unifies all the markets of the world.

When the purchase and sale of foreign exchange are subject to effective and tight control, arbitrage becomes impossible. Exchange controls usually require the surrender to the authorities of all foreign currencies acquired by residents, and limit purchases thereof to specific approved purposes. If, in our illustration, France had such controls, arbitragers would be unable to buy francs with pounds at the cheap franc/sterling rate. This would effectively block the operation of selling francs at the relatively higher franc/dollar rate. The rate between the franc and the pound could then be inconsistent with the dollar/sterling and the dollar/franc rates. Such "disorderly" cross rates are a common accompaniment of exchange controls.

FORWARD FOREIGN EXCHANGE

The Risk of Exchange Rate Fluctuations

Individuals or firms engaged in the export business make their profit from the spread between their buying price and their selling price, like any other trader. If they are manufacturers, the necessary profit comes out of the markup over costs. But if the exporter carries on his business in terms of a foreign currency (that is, if he normally finances a shipment by drawing an export bill in a foreign currency), a fall in its value occurring between the time he contracts the shipment and undertakes to obtain payment could wipe out or seriously reduce his profits as a trader. Risks arising from exchange rate fluctuations are at a minimum under gold standard conditions, but they can be very serious in the case of fluctuating exchange rates. These risks can be avoided by the trader, and he can concentrate on his normal functions and the risks attendant thereto, if there exists a market for forward foreign exchange, where the exporter can obtain an advance assurance of a guaranteed price for the foreign exchange he will have at his disposal at a later date.

To illustrate, suppose that a French exporter of wine to the United States knows in the late spring that he will be shipping wine to buyers in this country in the autumn, and about how much. If he can obtain a contract from his bank to accept, say ninety days later, a stipulated amount of dollars, at an exchange rate specified in advance, he will thereby avoid all risk of fluctuations in the franc/dollar rate of exchange. The existence of a forward exchange market enables him to "hedge" against the risk that the sum of dollars for which he has contracted to deliver the wine will yield him a reduced sum in francs, owing to a fall in the franc/dollar rate of exchange. The bank, of course, will take over the risk, but as we shall see, it has at its disposal means of offsetting this risk or of passing it along to someone else.

Similarly with the importer: After placing his orders with foreign exporters, he knows he is going to have to buy foreign exchange in the near future, say in sixty or ninety days. He too can avoid a possible increased cost of imports resulting from a rise in the exchange rate if he can hedge by obtaining a contract from his bank to deliver foreign exchange when he needs it, at a rate specified in advance.

Thus suppose a French importer of tobacco places an order for a shipment of $10,000 with an American exporter, shipment to be made in ninety days, payment to be by sight draft upon arrival. If the importer thinks it possible that dollars may cost him more in francs at that time than when he places the order, he will welcome the opportunity to buy $10,000 forward from his bank.

Of course, both exporter and importer might gain, rather than lose, if the exchange rate moved favorably. In the case of the exporter, a rise in the franc/dollar rate would net him more francs and a profit larger than his normal trading profit. With the importer, a fall in the franc/dollar rate would put him ahead. But the point to be stressed is that if there is uncertainty as to the probable movement of the exchange rate, there is a risk of loss over and above the normal trading risks. So far as a foreign trader concentrates upon his purely trading activities, he will shift this risk to someone else. Only if he wishes to speculate on the future of the exchange rate will he fail so to shift this risk.

The Role of Banks in the Forward Exchange Market

The bank that undertakes to provide forward exchange to importers will at the same time be contracting to purchase forward exchange from exporters. So far as any bank succeeds in matching forward purchases and sales, it avoids "taking a position" and assumes no risk. Both its buying and selling rates are known to it in advance, and they will differ only by an amount sufficient to assure the bank of a commission on its dealings. Whether they are above or below the spot rate at the time the forward contracts mature is immaterial, since the purchases of exchange provide the means for deliveries on sales.

There is, however, no particular reason to expect that the needs of exporters and importers for forward exchange will exactly coincide at any one point in time. If a bank undertook to deliver forward exchange in amounts greater than its purchases, this would result in its taking an uncovered position. But this would mean that the bank was speculating on the course of the foreign exchanges, and normally banks do not engage in speculation, but confine themselves, so far as they are foreign exchange dealers, to the normal activities of dealers, making their profit (like exporters and importers) on the spread between the buying and selling prices of the commodity in which they trade. A bank can, however, avoid taking an uncovered forward position by adjusting its spot position with the future in mind.

Thus suppose that a French bank has contracted to sell 90-day forward exchange to importers in excess of its purchases from exporters. At the end of this period, it will have to make available more foreign exchange, say dollars, than is coming to it from the execution of exporters' forward contracts. Foreseeing this situation, it can, at the time of making the forward contracts, supplement its dollar resources by buying 90-day bills currently coming on the market. When these mature in New York, they will provide the dollars needed to meet the excess forward sales. Alternatively, the bank can buy spot dollar exchange (currently available sight drafts) from exporters, or it may be able to purchase additional dollar balances from banks which have surplus dollar resources. Adoption of these latter alternatives will mean holding dollars in New York for ninety days. If the supply of 90-day bills, sight drafts, and exchange available from other banks is inadequate, the bank may simply refuse to make additional forward commitments. There remains only one alternative —the purchase by the bank of additional forward exchange from speculators, who, since they are speculators, are willing to take an open position. This alternative, however, is present only with respect to a limited number of currencies—those in which the volume of trading is sufficient to create a market of proportions such as to attract the activity of speculative dealers.

The Forward Market and International Capital Movements

When banks buy spot exchange and hold it until needed to meet forward commitments, they pay out domestic currency. On such investments of their funds, they lose interest which they might earn by making loans. But the foreign currency acquired can be lent out in the foreign money market. Thus the French banks we have used in our illustrations will forgo interest on the francs they pay out for spot dollars, but these dollars can be lent in New York. The difference in interest rates in the two money markets will be an important element in determining whether the forward rate is at a premium or a discount relative to the spot rate.

Let us suppose that the short-term rate of interest in Paris is one percent; in New York, two per cent. If at the time of entering into forward contracts, the spot and forward exchange rates are the same (say 4.90 francs per dollar), then the covering of any excess forward commitments to French importers by spot purchases of dollars will yield one per cent per annum extra income for ninety days. Banks will then compete in selling dollars forward, and in buying spot dollars too. Competition in the sale of forward dollars will drive down the forward rate, while the spot rate will be forced up. A discount on forward exchange relative to spot exchange will tend to arise. These opposite price movements, resulting in an increased cost of dollars to transfer to New York and a decreased yield from their sale when they are brought back to France, will tend to eliminate the gain from lending in New York, leaving only a commission available to the banks.

Purchases of spot exchange of this kind, which result in the transfer of funds from one market to another, are undertaken not only to provide cover for (or a hedge against) excess sales of forward exchange, but also on their own account. When interest rates abroad are higher than at home, banks will want to lend overseas. A forward exchange market provides the mechanism by which they can do it without risk.

From the point of view of the French lender, a spot purchase of dollars must be covered by a simultaneous sale of dollars forward. Otherwise, the return of dollars to France at a later date—implicit in the fact that these are *short-term* loans—will involve an exchange loss if francs appreciate—that is, if a given dollar loan yields at maturity less francs than it cost. The possibility of appreciation will always exist under inconvertible paper currency conditions, and it will be present under the gold standard if at the time the foreign loan is made the spot rate is above the gold import point, which is as low as this rate can fall under gold standard conditions. In the absence of a forward market, short-term foreign lending will be hazardous except when, under gold standard conditions, the spot rate stands at, or very close to, the gold import point for the lending country.

How small a fluctuation in the exchange rate may convert a gain in interest into a loss is shown by the following example. In accord with the tendency in

Purchase of spot sterling @ $2.81/£:	£100,000	= $281,000
Excess interest @ 1% for 90 days:	250	
Sale of sterling at end of 90 days @ $2.80/£:	£100,250	= $280,700
Loss:		$ 300

recent years, it is assumed that the short-term rate of interest in London exceeds that in New York by one per cent, that a 90-day loan of £100,000 is made by a U.S. bank when the spot rate is $2.81 per pound, and that when the loan expires the spot rate has fallen to $2.80/£. Instead of earning a net return from the higher interest rate in London, the New York bank suffers a small loss of $300.

Since the excess interest obtainable in London is one-fourth per cent of the principal, a decline of the exchange rate by this percentage will exactly wipe out the gain from the interest differential. With a forward market, the discount on the forward rate would have to be something less than one-fourth per cent ($0.0068 with the spot rate at $2.81/£) for the New York bank to earn even a small commission.

When lending operations were profitable for New York, they would be duplicated by simultaneous borrowing operations in London. London banks would sell spot dollars for pounds, and lend these out in London. Spot dollars would be available either from (1) existing balances of London banks in New York or (2) balances in New York established by drawing 90-day drafts on New York banks. Repayment of borrowed balances would be necessary at the end of ninety days. To avoid exchange loss on this operation, London banks would have to purchase forward dollars simultaneously with the sale of the borrowed balances. Therefore in London the forward rate on dollars would rise; the spot rate would fall; and forward *dollars* would go to a premium.

If, on the other hand, the interest rate were higher in New York than in London, then pounds would be converted into dollars, to be lent in the New York money market. United States banks would sell sterling bills (and cables) against their London balances, and would borrow pounds. To borrow, they would draw long sterling drafts, which would be accepted by London banks, and discounted in the London money market. Against the sterling balances so established in favor of New York banks, the latter would then sell spot sterling exchange, lending the dollar proceeds in New York. To avoid exchange loss when these loans matured, they would have to buy forward sterling simultaneously.

Competition to sell spot sterling would depress the spot rate, while the increased demand for forward sterling would put the forward rate at a premium. Competition to buy forward sterling would stop when, after allowing for a commission on spot sales of exchange by the banks, the premium on forward sterling was equal to the excess earnings in New York.

With respect to the relationship between forward and spot rates, we can say that, in the absence of speculation, the forward rate will tend to be at a discount from the spot rate on a given country if interest rates there are higher, and at a premium if interest rates in that country are lower.

Speculation

In addition to exporters wanting to hedge against exchange loss by selling forward exchange and importers wanting to buy forward exchange for similar purposes, together with banks desiring to earn commissions or to take advantage of interest rate differentials, there may be other important buyers and sellers of forward exchange: the speculators. As we have already seen, these individuals take an open position. If they anticipate a fall in the future spot rate for a specific currency, they will enter into contracts to sell forward exchange at a rate slightly higher than their estimate of the future spot rate. If, on the other hand, they anticipate a rise in the future spot rate, they will contract to buy forward exchange at a rate slightly lower than their estimate of the future spot rate. They hope to gain from gambling on the future level of the spot rate.

Thus a French speculator who anticipates that the franc will appreciate, or that the franc price of dollars will fall, will sell forward dollars. When, say ninety days later, he has to deliver, he will make a speculative profit if he can buy spot dollars with which to fulfill his forward contract at a rate below that specified in this contract.

Suppose, for example, that speculators at a given date are optimistic or "bullish" with respect to the franc, "bearish" with respect to the dollar.

Assume the spot rate at that date is 4.90 francs/dollar, and that competition to sell forward dollars has driven the forward rate to 4.88 francs/dollar. An individual speculator sells $100,000 forward; that is, he undertakes to deliver this sum in dollars, ninety days later, for a total sum in his own currency of 488,000 francs. If the spot rate at that time is 4.87 francs/dollar, he will purchase the dollars to meet his forward contract for a total outlay of 487,000 francs, clearing a thousand francs profit on the deal. If the spot rate were then above 4.88 francs/dollar, he would of course lose on his speculation.

So far as the forward rate of exchange is determined by the activities of speculators, the fact that the dollar stands at a discount in Paris does not mean that no speculators will be willing to buy, rather than sell, forward dollars at this rate. One of the characteristics of a speculative market is that there is usually a division of opinion among speculators. In the illustration we have just given, those who were "bullish" with respect to the dollar would be buyers rather than sellers of forward dollars. They would gain if, when their forward contracts came due, the spot rate stood above 4.88 francs/dollar. The fact that, on the initial date, dollars were at a discount reflects a preponderance of "bearish" opinion relative to the dollar, not unanimity.

Had speculators been preponderantly "bullish" instead of "bearish" relative to the dollar, total forward purchases would exceed forward sales, and competition to buy dollars forward would drive the rate to a premium, say to 4.91 francs/dollar. If, at the delivery date, the spot rate were 4.92, the "bulls" would make a profit; the minority of "bears" would lose.

Influence of Speculation on the Spot Rate

When the opinion of speculators with respect to the future value of foreign currencies is strongly "bearish" (or "bullish" with respect to their own), they will on balance *sell* forward exchange, thus depressing the forward rate. Those who buy from them, principally banks and foreign exchange dealers, *not* being speculators, will have to cover their purchases by spot sales. The increased volume of spot offerings will push down the spot rate, thus reflecting *in the present* the opinion of speculators as to the *future* course of exchange rates. (The forward rate will, however, remain at a discount, owing to the continued pressure of speculation.)

On the other hand, if speculators are preponderantly "bullish" with respect to foreign currencies ("bearish" with respect to their own), they will on balance *buy* forward exchange, thus driving the rate up. Those who sell to them, to cover their position, will have to buy spot exchange. This forces up the spot rate, again reflecting *in the present* fears or hopes about the *future*.

If "bull" speculators have difficulty in buying forward exchange, the premium over spot rates will tend to be substantial. As the premium rises, however, it becomes more attractive for banks to buy spot exchange, transfer their funds abroad, and by simultaneously selling this exchange forward, to ensure the return of their funds at a profit.

To illustrate, suppose the spot rate in Paris is 4.90 francs/dollar, the forward rate 4.93, and to eliminate capital movements induced by interest rate differentials, let us assume interest rates in New York and Paris are identical. A Paris bank can then transfer $100,000 to New York by purchasing spot exchange at a cost of 490,000 francs, lend the proceeds out there, and by simultaneously selling these dollars forward to a speculator, be sure of obtaining from its loan a total sum of 493,000 francs. By undertaking such an exchange arbitrage,[4] the bank gains 3,000 francs.

A large premium on forward dollars would indicate lack of confidence in the future of the franc. This would be the first manifestation of such pessimism, stemming from the competition of speculators to buy forward dollars. By making capital movements profitable, however, it would induce (1) additional supplies of forward dollars to match the speculators' desire to buy and (2) additional purchases of spot exchange to transfer funds abroad. The additional supplies of forward exchange would tend to moderate the rise in the forward rate, while the additional demand for spot exchange would tend to force the spot rate up, thus reflecting in the present the lack of confidence in the future of the country's currency.

It is clear that when forward dollars are at a sufficient premium in Paris to induce exchange arbitrage, or capital movements of this type, banks will gain regardless of whether, when their loans mature, the spot rate is above or below the rate specified in their forward contracts. For they buy dollars at a specific (spot) rate, and sell them at a higher (forward) rate. Speculators, in such a situation, will gain only if, when they acquire dollars from their prior forward contracts, the spot rate is *above* the rate specified in these contracts. Then they will gain by selling dollars acquired at, say, 4.90 francs/dollar for a price of 4.91 or 4.92 francs.

Moreover, it should also be noted that a speculative capital movement may be profitable even though interest rates are *higher* in the lending market than in the borrowing market. This will be true provided the gain from buying spot exchange at one rate and selling the proceeds forward at a higher rate (exchange arbitrage) exceeds the loss from transferring funds from a market where the interest rate is high to one where it is low.

SELECTED REFERENCES

Crump, Norman, *The ABC of the Foreign Exchanges*. London: Macmillan & Co., Ltd., 1951. An excellent, simple discussion of the mechanism of international payments.

---

[4] That is, the simultaneous purchase and sale of dollars in different markets, to take advantage of exchange rate, rather than interest rate, differentials.

Export and Import Procedures. New York: Morgan Guaranty Trust Co., July, 1962. This provides a simple explanation of various types of foreign exchange transactions.

Holmes, Alan R., *The New York Foreign Exchange Market*. New York: Federal Reserve Bank of New York, March, 1959. Gives a clear picture of the organization and operation of this major foreign exchange market.

Southard, Frank A., Jr., *Foreign Exchange Practice and Policy*. New York: McGraw-Hill Book Co., Inc., 1940. Still one of the best accounts of the mechanism of foreign payments. Chapter IV has an illuminating discussion of various types of credit management.

18

FOREIGN EXCHANGE RATES
IN FREE MARKETS

From our numerous references to the demand and supply of foreign exchange, the foreign exchange market, and the exchange rate as the price of one currency in terms of another, it should be apparent that the determination of an exchange rate is a pricing problem, to which the usual demand and supply analysis presumably applies.

Many Rates of Exchange

That analysis applies, however, with some differences. One is that whereas in a commodity market there is a single price for a given grade of a commodity, in the foreign exchange market there is no one price for foreign exchange of a certain kind (for example, spot or cable transfers). Instead, there are as many prices as there are currencies traded. Yet just as a country's balance of payments includes all its transactions with the rest of the world, so its foreign exchange market brings together all its demands for foreign currencies and all its supplies of those currencies. These are merged in a common market.

Which of the numerous rates of exchange are we to take as reflecting the interaction of the forces of demand and supply? Actually, if a free market exists, the problem is not serious. We can take the rate on any currency as representative of all the rest, for arbitrage operations keep the rates on different currencies in line. If the price of one rises or falls, the prices of all the others must move in the same direction and in the same proportion.

Balance of Payments and the Foreign Exchange Market

The parallelism between a country's balance of payments and its foreign exchange market extends beyond the fact that each encompasses a total of that country's relations with the rest of the world. This total to which each concept refers is the same—it is all of a nation's economic transactions with all other nations. Yet there is a difference. A balance of payments refers to all such transactions as *actually occurred* during a given period, at whatever exchange rate or rates ruled during that interval. It is a record of accomplished fact.

The demand and supply that meet in the foreign exchange market, on the other hand, tell us what a country's autonomous payments and receipts *would be* at each of a whole series of exchange rates. Demand and supply of foreign exchange are schedules that interact to determine the exchange rate, and therewith the transactions actually undertaken. If these market forces can be taken to have remained comparatively constant over a given balance-of-payments period, say a year, then we can say with reasonable accuracy that the actual payments and receipts recorded reflect the size of market demand and market supply at the ruling exchange rate.

Another distinction, too, must be noted. A balance of payments is complete; it shows not only the autonomous payments and receipts, but also the amount and sources of compensatory financing. The demand and supply of foreign exchange, however, include only the autonomous transactions—the imports of goods, services, and securities that would be undertaken and the exports of similar items that would be forthcoming at each of a series of exchange rates. Under stable conditions, therefore, a deficit or surplus in the balance of payments indicates the amount by which the demand for exchange exceeds the supply of exchange, or vice versa, at the ruling rate.

Composite Demand and Supply

A second difference between commodity markets and foreign exchange markets results from the fact that the demand and supply of a commodity are homogeneous, whereas the corresponding foreign exchange schedules are composite. The demand, say, for cotton reflects the wants of buyers for a single commodity with distinctive characteristics. The demand for foreign exchange, it has just been suggested, is a mixture of many different demands—for many types of commodities, for a great variety of services, for a wide range of securities. The supply of foreign exchange is similarly composite.

If the components of demand and supply in the foreign exchange market differ so radically from those that operate in commodity markets, how can we be sure they will not produce different results? Is there not a danger that foreign exchange rates are inherently unstable—in the sense that a rise or fall, once started, will go unchecked? Commodity prices tend to vary widely only when demand and supply conditions themselves change substantially. Even then, the resultant price changes are generally self-limiting. A rise in price calls forth additional supplies, which bring the rise to a halt; a price decline stimulates additional purchases, which check any further fall.

Stable and Unstable Markets

A market is said to be stable when at any price above the one at which demand and supply are equal and the market is cleared, supply exceeds demand, and when at any lower price demand exceeds supply. These conditions are generally met in commodity markets. But if, at prices above the one that clears the market, demand is greater than supply, any rise in price above the "equilibrium" level will continue without limit, since demand exceeds supply by ever-increasing amounts. Similarly, if below this "equilibrium" price supply is greater than demand, a drop in price will go on unchecked because of the depressing effect of an increasing excess of supply.

It is possible that foreign exchange markets tend to behave in this unstable fashion. Certainly there have been periods of wild fluctuations in exchange rates, notably just after the first World War, when the German mark, the Austrian crown, and the Russian rouble, after violent gyrations, ended by losing virtually all their value. One of our tasks will be to determine whether the peculiar composition of the demand and supply of foreign exchange predisposes exchange rates toward excessive fluctuations, or whether this is true only under exceptional circumstances.

Crucial Role of Exchange Rates

We observed in the last chapter that because changes in exchange rates alter the scale of relative prices between countries, exchange rates play a role of crucial importance in international trade. Because a rise in the price of foreign currencies raises the prices of a nation's imports and permits it to lower the foreign prices of its exports, thus retarding the former and stimulating the latter, variations in a nation's exchange rates afford a potential means of eliminating a deficit in its balance of payments without recourse to costly compensatory financing. This is a further reason for discovering how exchange rates are determined.

In this chapter we shall explore this topic. In doing so, we shall consider only the case of a country confronting a balance-of-payments deficit, for only such a country has a real problem. A country enjoying a surplus accumulates foreign balances and gold; it is under no strain to find such means of compensatory financing. Hence our analysis will be confined, with only incidental exceptions, to the effects of exchange depreciation. To determine the impact of appreciation, or a decline in exchange rates, you need only reverse both the analysis and the conclusions. The following chapter will apply our findings to the solution of balance-of-payments problems, and contrast the very different solution provided under the gold standard with the use for this purpose of exchange-rate variations. Finally, we shall consider a third alternative: combating a balance of payments disequilibrium with direct controls.

If exchange rates are to be effective in altering international price relationships, they must be free to move. This obviously implies the absence of controls over the purchase and sale of foreign exchange. But exchange rates cannot move freely if currencies are anchored to a common standard, such as gold. We shall therefore assume not only uncontrolled exchange markets, but also independent currencies. That is, each country's monetary authority determines the supply of its currency and thus the level of internal prices in accordance with a policy independently arrived at.

A Deficit Reflects the Foreign Exchange Situation

We noted previously that the demand and supply of foreign exchange include only the autonomous transactions in a nation's balance of payments. If this is true, then over a period during which demand and supply conditions remain stable, a deficit in the balance of payments indicates the amount by which the demand for foreign exchange exceeds the supply at the ruling rate of exchange. For a deficit *is* the difference between autonomous receipts and autonomous payments, and the supply of exchange actually delivered during the period in question corresponds to these receipts, the demand for exchange to these payments.

Thus when a country has a balance-of-payments deficit, this gives the location of one point on both the foreign exchange demand and supply curves, namely, the demand for, and supply of, exchange at the ruling rate. Of what the demand and supply would be at higher or lower rates, the country's monetary authorities have no indication. This depends upon the relative steepness of these curves, or their elasticity.

Relevance of Foreign Exchange Elasticities

If these monetary authorities are contemplating exchange depreciation, or a rise in exchange rates, as a means of eliminating the deficit, the elasticities of demand and supply of foreign exchange are of vital importance. An illustration will clarify this point.

Figure 18.1 portrays an imagined situation in France's foreign exchange market. The franc/dollar rate is taken as representative of all exchange rates, and the total amount of foreign exchange demanded and supplied is expressed in dollars. We assume that the demand and supply of foreign exchange have been reasonably stable over the past several months. During this period, autonomous balance-of-payments receipts from exports of goods, services, and long-term securities amounted to $400 million. Corresponding payments were $700 million. The resulting deficit we may assume was financed by exports of gold, reduction of official foreign balances, and short-term official borrowing abroad. By such means alone, in the absence of controls, would it be possible to maintain the exchange rate stable at five francs/dollar.

From our knowledge of the value of autonomous payments and receipts and of the ruling exchange rate, we obtain one point on the foreign exchange demand curve, at *M*, and one on the supply curve, at *X*. What the position of these curves is at other rates of exchange, we have no idea, since transactions have been effected only at the ruling rate of five francs/dollar.

If the monetary authorities have good reason to believe that for the fore-

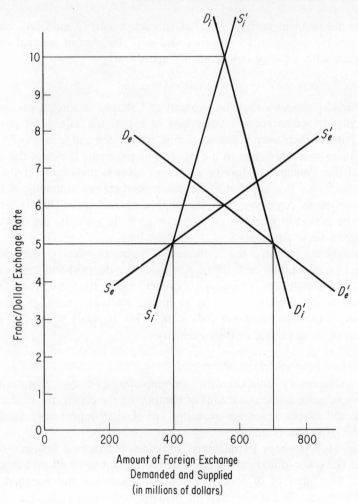

FIGURE 18.1   Adjustment via Free Exchange Rates

seeable future, underlying conditions will continue about the same, they can expect the current deficit to be repeated. To avoid the need for further compensatory financing, they are considering whether it may not be advisable to let the exchange rate rise. But by how much is it likely to go up? A moderate rise, say of 20 or even 30 per cent, might not create serious problems, whereas depreciation of 50 or 100 per cent might be unsupportable.[1]

Two possibilities are illustrated in the diagram, where we have drawn two sets of demand and supply curves, one (D_eD_e' and S_eS_e') relatively elastic,

---

[1] We shall postpone consideration of the problems raised by exchange depreciation until Chapter 20, concentrating in this upon what factors determine how severe it is likely to be.

the other (D_iD_i' and S_iS_i') relatively inelastic. If demand and supply were as elastic, or as responsive to an increase in the exchange rate, as the first pair, the supply of exchange would expand and the demand contract quite rapidly, clearing the market at a rate of exchange of six francs/dollar—representing an appreciation of the dollar in terms of francs of 20 per cent, a depreciation of the franc of 16⅔ per cent.

If, however, demand and supply were as inelastic as the second set of curves (D_iD_i' and S_iS_i'), the exchange rate would have to rise to 10 francs/dollar before an equilibrium position was reached. This involves a 100 per cent appreciation of the dollar in francs, or a 50 per cent depreciation of the franc.

Clearly, it is important for the monetary authorities of a country for which depreciation is being contemplated to have some idea, even if only approximate, of how far depreciation is likely to have to go before the deficit is eliminated. The purpose of what follows is to explore this problem.

THE DEMAND FOR FOREIGN EXCHANGE FOR GOODS AND SERVICES

Since the demand and supply of foreign exchange are made up of quite different components that react differently, as we shall see, to changes in the exchange rate, it is necessary to consider these components separately. We shall begin with goods and services, leaving capital movements for later consideration. Moreover, we shall also take the point of view of the short-run, meaning by this a period long enough for producers to adjust output to changed demands, but not so long as to permit any change in productive capacity.

Elasticity of Demand for Imports

Let us continue our illustration and suppose that the French franc is allowed to depreciate. The franc price of dollars rises, and if we may assume for the time being that the dollar price of France's imports remains constant, their price in francs will increase in direct proportion to the rise in the exchange rate. What will determine whether the demand for foreign exchange is elastic or inelastic, and thus whether this side of the market contributes much or little toward eliminating the deficit? Clearly, this elasticity will directly reflect the elasticity of demand for imports, since we are considering the demand for foreign exchange (that is, dollars) with which to acquire these goods and services.

So far as concerns imports, none of which is produced in France, the demand for goods in general of the kind imported and the demand for imports proper will be identical; their elasticities are therefore also the same. The demand for foreign exchange will mirror the demand for imports. The only difference is that the demand for foreign exchange is expressed in rates of exchange and amounts of foreign exchange, whereas the demand for imports is stated in terms of import prices and quantities of the goods (or services) demanded.

Supply of Import-Competing Goods

If, however, goods that compete with imports are produced in France, a distinction must be drawn between the demand for goods such as are imported (or import-type goods, for short) and the demand for imports. The former demand is directed toward, and can be satisfied by, supplies from French or from foreign producers; the latter is directed toward imports alone.

The demand for import-type goods, being the general demand for a particular good, say shoes, has an elasticity, or responsiveness of sales to price, determined by the tastes of consumers, just as with any other commodity. The *demand for imports* of shoes, on the other hand, will be *more elastic* than the demand for shoes in general, since as the price of imported shoes is reduced (increased), competing domestic producers will contract (expand) their output in the face of the intensified (reduced) competition. Sales of imported shoes increase as their price is reduced, not only because of the normal inclination of buyers to purchase more at lower prices, but also because the higher cost portion of competing domestic production is eliminated, leaving a larger share of the market to be taken over by imports.

These reactions are shown in Figure 18.2. DD' is the demand (say in France) for some commodity such as shoes. C_hC_h' is the short-run supply curve of domestic producers. If for the sake of simplifying our argument we leave aside costs of transport, then at a price of P_n or above, home producers can supply the entire market. If imports can be landed only at a higher price, they cannot compete. If, owing to a reduction in foreign costs or to appreciation of the franc (a lower franc price for the dollar), the import price is lowered, imports will begin to enter the country. The highest cost portion of French production will be discontinued. Successive reductions of the import price will cause more and more competing French supplies to be displaced, until at a price of P_a, they disappear completely. The demand for imports, as distinct from the demand for the goods imported (DD') is represented, within the price range of P_nP_a, by the curve D_mD_m'. Below P_a, imports supply the entire market; the demand for imports becomes the same as the demand for the commodity in question.

Elasticity of Demand for Foreign Exchange

Having established this peculiarity of a country's demand for imports when import-competing goods are available, we can continue our discussion of the demand for foreign exchange. This will be a carbon copy, so to speak, of

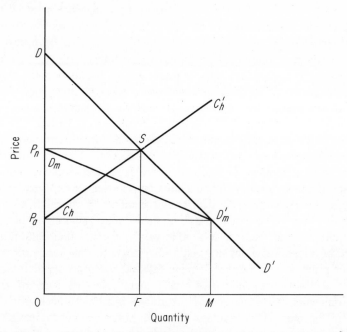

FIGURE 18.2   Elasticity of Demand for Import-type Goods and for Imports

the demand for imports, with only the difference that rates of exchange are substituted for prices and amounts of foreign exchange for quantities of imports.

How elastic a given country's demand for imports (and thus for foreign exchange) is, depends (1) on the elasticity of demand for import-type goods, (2) on the proportion of imports that encounter local competition, and (3) on the rapidity with which such local competition withdraws (expands) when confronted with declining (rising) import prices (the elasticity of supply of import-competing goods).

The elasticity of demand for imports, and thus of the demand for foreign exchange, will naturally be high in a country whose imports are principally luxuries, for whose imports there are many domestic substitutes, and whose import-competing production expands and contracts rapidly in response to price changes. Contrariwise, this elasticity will be low where imports are mainly necessities, where few domestic substitutes are produced, and where these substitutes are relatively fixed in supply.

Elasticity of Supply of Imports

Somewhat less important, though certainly to be included in a complete account, are conditions in the country where the imports are produced. To enable us to concentrate on what happens in the importing country when its currency depreciates, we have assumed up to now that the price of imports remains constant in their country of origin. We have assumed constant costs, or infinite elasticity of supply. This condition is likely to be approximated in the short run in periods of depression, when many resources lie idle. And then it is likely to apply most fully to goods whose production is continuous, such as manufactures.[2] In these circumstances, what we have said about the elasticity of demand for foreign exchange requires little modification.

Even under conditions of full or near-full employment, prices of manufactured goods in the exporting center are likely to change little or not at all, if, because of depreciation, foreign demand is reduced. This curious result is due to the fact that most manufactures are produced under conditions of highly imperfect competition. When plants are working at capacity, producers seldom raise their prices to the full extent justified by the high level of demand. Unless wages and other costs are rising, they accumulate backlogs of orders, while keeping their prices relatively constant, thus rationing their customers by means of a waiting list rather than by the competitive device of a higher price. And if foreign demand falls off owing to depreciation, these producers need not lower their price—they merely see their backlog of orders dwindle somewhat. With respect to a country's manufactured imports, one is not wide of the mark if he assumes that with either severe depression or full employment in their country of origin, prices there will remain comparatively stable. Depreciation of the importing country's currency then will be reflected in a parallel rise in the prices of manufactured imports.

Agricultural products, which become available only intermittently, at the end of the growing season, tend to react differently to depreciation of an importer's currency. Between one season and the next, the supply is fixed. If sales in the import market decline as a result of depreciation there, unsold stock will accumulate. To maintain sales and dispose of the supply, the price in the producing country must be lowered sufficiently to keep the price in the depreciating country constant.[3]

Thus if the franc depreciates, the price of imported tobacco will rise, French imports will decline, and stocks in the supplying country (say the United States) will accumulate. To prevent this, growers in the United States will have to reduce the dollar price enough to offset the rise in the franc/dollar exchange rate. This will leave the price of tobacco in France unchanged, and French buyers will maintain their purchases.

But if Frenchmen buy the same amount of this import at the same price,

---

[2] A wide range of behavior in different industries is possible. Hence generalization is dangerous. But resistance to price cuts is likely to be especially great when production has fallen to a low level.

[3] This conclusion is valid only if there are free markets for farm products. When, as in many countries today, price support schemes are in force, the outcome is more like that suggested in the preceding paragraphs.

their outlay in dollar exchange will remain constant. What does this mean? When total outlay on a commodity is constant at all prices, we say the elasticity of demand is unity. Here, with the rate of exchange rising, outlay on foreign exchange stays the same. The elasticity of demand for *foreign exchange*, in these circumstances, has a value of 1. The elasticity of demand for *imports*, whether high or low, has no opportunity to make itself felt, since with the price of imports constant, it is simply not brought into play.

Thus, so far as concerns the conditions under which a country's imports are supplied, we have two extremes: (1) when the exporter's price remains constant and the price in the importing country's currency rises with the exchange rate and (2) the opposite, when the price in the importing country's currency remains constant, while the exporter reduces the price in his currency. When the first condition holds good, the demand for foreign exchange has an elasticity identical with that of the demand for imports. Under the second condition, the elasticity of demand for foreign exchange is unity, regardless of what the elasticity of import demand may be.

Intermediate cases, where import prices rise, though not in proportion to the exchange rate, are not hard to imagine. They will occur when the elasticity of supply of imports is neither zero nor infinite. This will be true when, for example, as producers of French imports respond to reduced sales in France by contracting output, they encounter decreasing unit costs. With manufactures, this will be most likely when capacity is neither stretched to its limit, with orders backed up, nor seriously underutilized. With agricultural products, it will be over periods longer than a single growing season.

Foreign Demand for a Country's Imports

Until now, we have ignored the fact that the imports of a given country, such as France, are sold in other parts of the world, too. If the prices of French imports remain constant abroad, this foreign demand will not be called into play and can be ignored. But if those prices are depressed as a result of France's declining purchases, foreign buyers will increase their purchases. This will support foreign prices. The price-maintaining effect of foreign demand will, of course, be greater the more elastic is this foreign demand.

SUPPLY OF FOREIGN EXCHANGE FROM GOODS AND SERVICES

We now turn to the supply side of the foreign exchange market, and consider the supply of foreign exchange derived from the export of goods and services. Our task is made easier now that we have covered the demand side, for most of what we shall have to say about the supply side is analogous in character.

Foreign Exchange Supply, and Demand for Exports

The supply of foreign exchange, or the amount of foreign exchange that will be forthcoming at different rates of exchange, is simply the foreign demand for a country's exports seen in reverse. A rise in the franc/dollar exchange rate, if the franc price of a given export remains constant, will permit a lowering of its foreign price and thus stimulate increased sales abroad.

Consider a French export costing 5 francs to produce, say an inexpensive pair of gloves. At an exchange rate of 5 frs./$, these would sell for $1 in the American market (and at equivalent prices in other currency markets). At 6 frs./$, to realize his 5 francs, the exporter would need to charge the American buyer only $0.833. At the rate of 7.5 frs./$, the price abroad could be further reduced to $0.67; at ten frs./$, to $0.50; and so on.

Other things equal, the volume of exports and therewith the supply of foreign exchange will expand more rapidly the more elastic is foreign demand. To obtain a benchmark to which we can refer, let us first assume an elasticity of demand for exports of 1. In Table 18.1, which assumes an export whose home price remains constant at 5 francs, franc/dollar rates are shown for 50-franc intervals, and in column three, the price which would have to be charged in the American market, at each exchange rate, to yield 5 francs.

Table 18.1. DEMAND FOR EXPORTS AND SUPPLY
OF FOREIGN EXCHANGE

(1) Price of Export in Francs	(2) Franc-Dollar Exchange Rate	(3) Price of Export in $ (1 ÷ 2)	(4) Quantity of Export Demanded (Elas. = 1)	(5) Amount of Foreign Exchange Supplied (3 × 4)	(6) Quantity of Export Demanded (Elas. = 2)	(7) Amount of Foreign Exchange Supplied (3 × 6)
5	10	$0.50	2,000	$1,000	3,000	$1,500
5	9	0.555	1,802	1,000	2,604	1,445
5	8	0.625	1,600	1,000	2,200	1,375
5	7	0.714	1,401	1,000	1,802	1,287
5	6	0.833	1,200	1,000	1,400	1,166
5	5	1.00	1,000	1,000	1,000	1,000
5	4	1.25	800	1,000	600	750
5	3	1.67	600	1,000	200	334

Column four gives the quantity of exports that will be demanded if, over the range of American prices listed, the elasticity of demand is 1. This requires that price times quantity, or total outlay, shall be constant.[4] But note what this means from the point of view of the supply of foreign exchange: If total outlay in the United States on our export remains constant, the supply

---

[4] The quantities demanded are inaccurate to the extent that the introduction of decimals was avoided. Therefore price times quantity does not quite meet the test of constancy.

of foreign exchange will also be a constant. When such a supply is represented graphically, it takes the form, as in Figure 18.3, of a vertical straight line (S_1S_1'). Such a curve is said to have an elasticity of zero. Thus when the foreign elasticity of demand for our exports is unity, the elasticity of supply of foreign exchange is zero.

An elasticity of demand greater than unity exists when the quantity demanded increases more than in proportion to the decrease of price. Column six introduces figures appropriate to such an elasticity of demand for exports. But this means that as price falls, total outlay will increase. Column seven

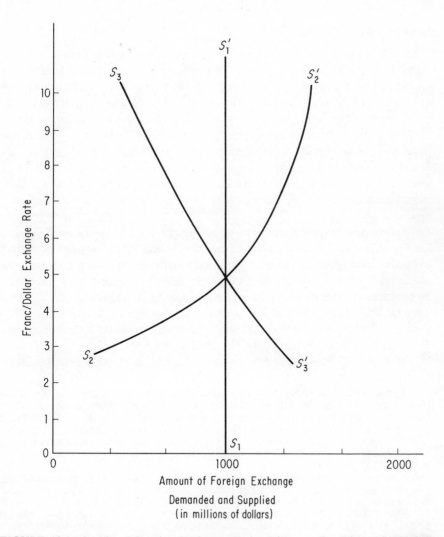

FIGURE 18.3   Supply of Foreign Exchange Under Different Conditions of Elasticity

shows the total expenditure in the United States on the export in question corresponding to the prices of column three and the quantities of column six; this is the same thing as the supply of foreign exchange derived from this export. Portrayed graphically (curve S_2S_2' of Figure 18.3), this gives a supply curve of positive inclination. To an elasticity of demand for exports greater than unity, there corresponds a positively inclined supply curve of foreign exchange. A similar process of reasoning could easily show that when the foreign elasticity of demand for exports is less than unity, the corresponding supply curve of foreign exchange will be negatively inclined (S_3S_3' of Figure 18.3).[5]

Supply of Export-Competing Goods

Just as in the case of demand for foreign exchange we had to take account, along with the elasticity of demand for imports, of elasticity of supply of import-competing goods, so in dealing with the supply of foreign exchange we must allow for the competition exporters are almost sure to meet abroad. That is, we must reckon with the elasticity of supply of export-competing goods.

Since a rising franc/dollar exchange rate induces a decline in the dollar price of French exports, sales abroad will expand more rapidly just to the extent to which French price competition causes foreign competitors to contract output and to retire from the field. And the rapidity with which their output contracts is simply the elasticity of supply of these export-competing products.

The outcome may be stated in terms of the effect on the elasticity of demand for the exporting country's (say France's) exports. This demand is distinct from the more general demand for goods such as are being exported. Its elasticity depends upon the commodity elasticity of demand for such goods, as modified by the elasticity of supply of export-competing goods. Since a single nation (particularly if it is a small one) is almost certain to meet extensive competition for its exports, this modification is likely to be substantial. Even though the underlying elasticity of demand for export-type goods may be less than unity, the displacement of foreign production from export markets

---

[5] There is a limit, however, to the negative inclination of such a curve. It cannot rise (from right to left), as the exchange rate rises, so slowly as to reflect a declining yield in francs (rate of exchange times supply forthcoming at each rate). For this would imply, as the quantity of exports increased, that they were being sold at a constantly diminishing price in francs. But this cannot be. For the pressure to expand output as exports increase will put pressure on productive resources. In the short run, this is almost certain to result in rising costs and prices.

If a supply of foreign exchange reflecting a declining franc-yield is an impossibility, this means that the limit to the negative inclination of the foreign exchange supply curve is that which represents a constant franc-yield. But this corresponds to an elasticity of -1. Therefore this is the most adverse supply of foreign exchange conceivable—from the point of view of the exporting country, and so far as this supply is derived from exports of goods and services.

may well be great enough to transform a negatively inclined supply curve of foreign exchange into a positively inclined one.[6]

A Range of Export Goods

This conclusion is reenforced when we consider not merely the goods that were already on an export basis at a given rate of exchange, but also those additional commodities that become exportable as a currency depreciates. The range of such commodities may be very sizeable; it is particularly likely to be so for a large and diversified economy. Therefore even though the elasticity of demand for a country's existing exports might be only moderate, perhaps no more than unity, when this factor is taken into account, there is a strong presumption that it will be greater than unity, and that as a consequence the aggregate supply curve of foreign exchange will be positively inclined.

Elasticity of Supply of Exports

So much for the forces operating abroad to determine exports. But we must also reckon with domestic factors—the ease or difficulty with which the output of exports can be expanded, and the extent to which domestic customers reduce their purchases and release goods for export as their prices rise. These forces determine whether the home prices of exports remain constant, as we have assumed up to this point, or whether, and to what degree, they will be raised.

Distinguishing, as before, between manufactured and agricultural products, it would seem that, as to the former, much will depend upon the state of employment and the effectiveness of competition in the exporting country. With many resources idle, output can be increased with little, if any, increase in cost and price. Supply is infinitely elastic, or close to it; export prices in the home market will remain constant or rise very little; in foreign markets they will fall in proportion to the home currency's depreciation, or only a little less. The supply of foreign exchange will reflect the foreign elasticity of demand, either exactly or approximately.

With full employment, any decline in the foreign price of exports as a result of depreciation will cause export orders to pile up. If manufacturers of exports react competitively, they will tend to raise their prices in domestic currency to all customers approximately in proportion to the rise in the exchange rate. Under conditions of imperfect competition, producers would stand to gain most by keeping prices charged domestic buyers constant, and by also maintaining constant prices (in terms of foreign currencies) in export

[6] With only minor changes, Figure 18.2 could be transformed to portray the demand for exports. *DD'* would represent the demand for goods such as are exported (export-type goods), $C_hC'_h$ (perhaps relabeled $C_fC'_f$) foreign production of export competing goods, and $D_mD'_m$ (relabeled $D_xD'_x$) the demand for French exports within the price range P_aP_n.

markets. Total sales would then remain unchanged, but the yield in domestic currency from foreign sales would rise in proportion to the rise in the exchange rate. Thus under both sets of conditions, prices and sales abroad would remain unchanged, and total foreign outlay on the depreciating country's exports would be constant. This gives an unvarying supply of foreign exchange, with elasticity zero.

Over a period of no more than a year, the same conclusion would apply to agricultural products, unless there were large accumulated stocks whose release would moderate the price increase. Over a period of more than a year, increased supplies of agricultural commodities could presumably be made available, though probably only at some increase in cost. This would also tend to be true of manufactures when some, but not excessive, idle resources were present. Such intermediate conditions would, of course, give intermediate results. With some increase in export prices, but less than in proportion to the rise in the exchange rate, prices paid by foreign buyers would decline somewhat. The elasticity of demand would not be called fully into play, and the supply of foreign exchange would have an elasticity between zero (with a constant foreign price) and that reflecting the elasticity of demand for exports (with a constant home price).

With pressure from increasing foreign sales tending to raise prices, domestic demand for exports would act as a safety valve, releasing goods for export as prices rose and thus moderating this rise. This moderating influence would be more powerful, the more elastic were these domestic demands.

Summary

There is a symmetry in the forces determining the demand and supply of foreign exchange. This symmetry helps one remember them. Four elasticities are involved on each side of the market, and of these, two are domestic in origin and two are foreign.

THE DEMAND FOR FOREIGN EXCHANGE   The domestic determinants of the demand for foreign exchange are the demand for import-type goods and the supply of import-competing goods. Their interaction determines the demand for imports, whose elasticity will vary *directly* with the elasticity of each of these determinants.

The two foreign elasticities involved are the elasticity of supply of imports and the elasticity of demand abroad for these goods. Together they determine whether the foreign price of imports will remain constant in the face of declining imports in the depreciating country, or whether that price will fall, and how much. If the foreign price of imports stays the same, price in the importing country will follow the rate of exchange and the elasticity of import demand will determine the demand for foreign exchange. If the foreign price of imports falls sufficiently (in proportion to the exchange rate), price in the import market will remain unchanged, total outlay on imports will be constant, and the elasticity of demand for foreign exchange will be unity. Intermediate price changes abroad will produce intermediate results.

THE SUPPLY OF FOREIGN EXCHANGE   The supply of foreign exchange derives from the demand for the depreciating country's exports. Underlying this demand are the demand for export-type goods (goods such as our country exports) and the supply of export-competing goods. Their interaction determines the demand for exports, whose elasticity will vary directly with the elasticity of each of these determinants.

The two domestic elasticities are the elasticity of supply of exports and the elasticity of home demand for these goods. Together they determine whether the home price of exports remains constant as the exchange rate rises, or whether the home price goes up, and how much. If this price stays unchanged, the foreign price of exports will vary with the exchange rate, and the elasticity of demand for our country's exports will be fully reflected in the supply of exchange. If the home price of exports rises in proportion to the exchange rate, the foreign price will remain constant, foreign outlay on our country's exports will not change, and the elasticity of supply of foreign exchange will be zero. Intermediate price changes will produce intermediate results.

INTERACTION OF THE DEMAND FOR AND SUPPLY OF FOREIGN EXCHANGE

Having terminated our examination of the forces determining the elasticity of demand for and supply of exchange, so far at least as these are dependent on imports and exports of goods and services, we are now in a position to give an answer to two questions raised early in this chapter: (1) Are elasticities in the foreign exchange market likely to be sufficiently large so that a deficit in a country's balance of payments can be eliminated by a moderate depreciation, or will it have to be excessive?[7] (2) Is the foreign exchange market, so far as it depends on exports and imports, likely to be stable?

With respect to the first question, our analysis entitles us to be fairly optimistic, with the reservation that some countries may be subject to an especially adverse combination of circumstances. In general, however, the foreign exchange elasticities should be sufficiently great to make it possible to eliminate a "reasonable" deficit by a depreciation that is not excessive.

The Demand Side of the Market

1. In the first place, the demand for foreign exchange is certain to be negatively inclined, since it directly reflects the demand for imports. This

---

[7] Clearly, the size of the deficit is related to the amount of depreciation needed to correct it. An enormous deficit would require far more depreciation for its elimination than a moderate one. A reasonable statement of the problem is whether foreign exchange elasticities are sufficiently large to make depreciation a feasible remedy for situations that are not so abnormal as to require desperate measures.

being a demand for commodities (and services), it obeys the normal rule that a lowering of price will induce increased purchases. If the demand for foreign exchange is of this kind, depreciation will always contribute something to the elimination of a deficit, since as the exchange rate rises, less foreign currency is demanded.

2. Barring an unfavorable combination of circumstances, we can expect the demand for imports to be quite elastic. Even if the demand for import-type goods is inelastic, the presence of home-produced substitutes guarantees that the demand for imports proper will have a much higher elasticity.

If this elasticity is to be felt fully, however, prices in the exporting center must remain constant, so that import prices will vary with the rate of exchange. Our study suggests that, after account is taken of the price-moderating effect of foreign demand for a country's imports, manufactured products, at least, are not likely to vary greatly in price, whatever the level of employment. This is the more true, the smaller the market of the depreciating country.

Agricultural prices are subject to greater short-run variations. The price of a major crop, however, is unlikely to change much in response to some decline in the demand of a single customer, unless it is a very large one. But the demand for agricultural products is typically less than unity. Hence if farm products count heavily in a country's imports, this could greatly reduce the average elasticity of import demand.

3. The aggregate demand for imports is not a demand for an array of commodities fixed once and for all. As the exchange rate rises, and import prices consequently go up, more and more domestic producers, who at lower exchange rates could not meet foreign competition, become able to do so. One after another, additional imports are pushed out of the market by new domestic competition. This gives to the aggregate demand for imports an elasticity greater than that for any single import or for any fixed group.

4. As the time period under consideration is lengthened, import demand is certain to be more elastic than in the short run we have had in mind. Over a longer period, more and more import substitutes will appear on the market, for it takes time to make plans and assemble productive resources into a going concern. Moreover, as time passes and the depreciation sticks, potential producers become reassured and determine to enter the field.

For all these reasons, it appears very likely that the demand for imports will normally have a rather high elasticity, especially if manufactures bulk large among imports. This elasticity will be enhanced if the economy is well-diversified, with a wide range of import-competing production. And it will be increased with the passage of time.

The Supply Side of the Market

Although the supply of foreign exchange is simply the demand for exports turned around, it will contribute nothing—in the event of depreciation—to the elimination of a deficit unless the export demand has an elasticity greater than unity. For with that value, foreign outlay, which *is* the supply of exchange, remains constant at all rates of exchange. This gives a vertical exchange supply curve—elasticity is zero. With depreciation, although demand (autonomous payments) contracts, supply (autonomous receipts) stays unchanged.

Considerations analogous to those underlying demand, however, suggest that often, at least, we can expect something better than this rather unsatisfactory outcome.

1. There is even more reason than in the case of imports to expect export demand to have a relatively high elasticity, probably greater than unity. A single country facing the rest of the world is almost certain to find its exports encountering substantial competition from foreign suppliers. As depreciation permits our country to lower its prices abroad, it displaces some competing suppliers and commands a larger share of the market. This is true even of as large a country as the United States; it is even more true of smaller countries whose exports are but a small proportion of world consumption.

2. Moreover, as the exchange rate rises (our country's currency depreciates), the range of domestic commodities able to enter into export competition constantly widens.

The combined operation of these two factors should in most cases be sufficient to give the demand for exports, as distinct from the demand abroad for goods such as our country exports (export-type goods), an elasticity greater than one. This would mean a supply curve of foreign exchange that was positively inclined.

3. Were we to consider a period longer than the short-run, with its assumption of a fixed amount of productive resources, then just as with imports, the supply of foreign exchange would, without doubt, expand still more rapidly. With more time, the supply of exports can be adjusted to demand; exporters can develop their market connections; and foreign competitors can complete their adjustment to the new competitive situation.

Thus there is a good prospect that the demand for a single country's exports will be quite elastic (greater than unity), so that the supply curve of foreign exchange will be positively inclined. With depreciation, the expansion in the supply of exchange will contribute its share to bridging the gap in the balance of payments. This auspicious outcome is the more likely, the larger is the share of manufactures in a country's exports; for being generally in more elastic supply than agricultural products, substantial price increases are less probable. A diversified list of exports and potential exports is also an advantage, as is the presence abroad of a wide range of competing products. A country with one or two commodities dominating its exports, on the other hand, is at a disadvantage, a disadvantage that will be increased if that country is also the chief supplier, as Brazil with its coffee.

It should be clear that although general considerations support the view that for most countries exchange market elasticities are fairly high, there are many special combinations of circumstances that could produce a very different result. In any concrete situation, detailed analysis is essential to sound judgment.

Market Stability

The answer to our second question, whether the foreign exchange market—so far as it depends on exports and imports of goods and services—is likely to be stable, is now fairly obvious. The demand for a country's exports must be quite inelastic for its foreign exchange supply curve to have a negative inclination. As for imports, unless they are predominantly necessities, and encounter little competition from substitutes, there is small likelihood that the demand curve for foreign exchange will be steeper than the supply curve, so that above their point of intersection the former will lie above and to the right of the latter. Unless this especially unfavorable combination of circumstances is encountered, the foreign exchange market will be stable.[8]

CAPITAL MOVEMENTS AND THE FOREIGN EXCHANGES

In addition to transactions involving the purchase or sale of goods and services, those arising from the desire to effect international transfers of capital may be quantitatively important in a country's balance of payments and in its foreign exchange market. It is necessary to consider them separately, since the demand and supply of foreign exchange to which they give rise respond differently to variations in the exchange rate.

Capital movements can be classified in various ways. For our purposes, it is important to distinguish between those undertaken for investment purposes—for the sake of the interest or dividends to be gained; and those whose motivation is speculative, where the object of the transfer is to gain from appreciation in the capital value of the investment. Fear-motivated flights of capital in search of a safe haven are a special category. The usual distinction between short-term and long-term investments is of secondary interest only.

Transfers for Investment Purposes

International transfers of capital to take advantage of an attractive yield may be invested in stocks, bonds, and physical assets such as manufacturing

---

[8] This special relation of the two curves can be expressed in terms of the elasticities of demand for exports and imports. Instability will exist when the sum of the elasticity of demand for imports and of the elasticity of demand for exports is less than 1 ($n_m + n_x < 1$). (This is known as the Marshall-Lerner condition. See, for example, Abba P. Lerner, *The Economics of Control*, pp. 377-79.)

This theorem, however, assumes that, initially, exports and imports are equal. If imports exceed exports to begin with, as when a country is running a deficit, the critical value is not 1, but less than 1. The theorem also assumes that the elasticity of supply of exports and imports is infinite. Lower values of these elasticities would be more favorable if n_m and n_x (the demand elasticities) are both small.

plant, all of which are long-term in character, or in such short-term securities as bills, notes, and acceptances. Such movements, it is clear, may, from the point of view of any country, be in either direction; they may give rise to a demand for or a supply of foreign exchange.

Let us consider, first, investment by the residents of a particular country, say the United States, in the stocks, bonds, and similar assets of other countries. Funds must be transferred from the United States to the foreigners who are offering these assets for sale; hence the process of investment brings into the foreign exchange market a demand for foreign currencies, say pounds sterling. How is this demand expressed? Stocks of corporations, physical assets, and short-term securities are always priced in the currency of the country where they are issued or where they exist. Earnings from such assets will be payable in the same currency. Bonds, however, may be issued with principal and interest stipulated in the issuing country's currency or in the currency of some other country, usually that of the principal buyers.

When the principal and interest of bonds are expressed in the issuing country's currency, let us say sterling, a decline in the dollar/sterling exchange rate cheapens the bond to the American buyer. Taken by itself, this should make additional purchases attractive. But a lower price of sterling, if it is expected to be enduring, also lowers the dollar return on the investment equally. This cancels the effect of a lower purchase price.[9] The sums invested abroad would depend upon the relative attractiveness of foreign as opposed to domestic investments; the exchange rate would be irrelevant. A fixed amount of sterling, depending upon investment considerations alone, would be demanded for the purpose of transferring capital abroad. The investment demand for sterling would be a vertical straight line (elasticity zero); added to the demand derived from transactions in goods and services, it would give a total demand curve for foreign exchange a fixed distance to the right of the former.

Suppose, however, as sometimes occurs, the principal and interest of bonds are expressed in the buying country's currency (dollar bonds). Here the exchange rate is irrelevant from the very beginning. U.S. investors would determine, on the basis of the attractiveness of the various foreign investments, how many dollars they wished to invest in any given period. This sum in dollars would be offered for sterling whatever the exchange rate. (Extreme depreciation of sterling might arouse fears as to the ability of the security issuers to service and repay the debt, and thus reduce the sum invested. This is equally true when securities are issued in terms of sterling.) Here we have total outlay in dollars on foreign exchange constant. The demand for foreign exchange for investment purposes has an elasticity of unity. The total demand for sterling would lie to the right of the transactions demand by an ever-increasing amount.

Sales of U.S. securities or property to foreigners for investment purposes

[9] If the lower exchange rate is expected to be only temporary, speculative considerations take over; all sterling holdings would become attractive for speculative purchase.

give rise to a supply of foreign exchange. Stocks, physical assets, and short-term securities, always priced in the issuing country's currency, may be considered together with bonds whose principal and interest are quoted in dollars. As with goods and services, the supply of foreign exchange arising from the sale abroad of U.S. assets will depend upon the foreign demand. This will be determined by investment considerations alone, since depreciation or appreciation of the dollar will affect principal and yield in the same direction and to the same degree. Foreigners will demand the fixed quantity of dollars so determined, whatever the exchange rate. Translated into a supply of exchange in the United States, this would mean that at a high dollar-sterling rate, a relatively small amount of sterling bills would need to be drawn to yield a given sum in dollars, and that at lower rates, the sum to be drawn in sterling would increase in inverse proportion to the fall in the exchange rate. (One million dollars would require only £200,000 to be drawn at $5/£; at $2/£, £500,000 would be necessary.) This is a supply of foreign exchange with a negative elasticity of 1, which would be added to the supply from goods and services transactions.

Should the United States issue bonds with principal and interest payable in sterling, the foreign investment in sterling would be that amount determined by investment considerations. This gives a fixed supply of sterling, to be added to the supply from merchandise transactions to get the total supply of foreign exchange.

At this point, we may add that all types of gifts and one-sided payments such as reparations would give rise to a demand for or supply of foreign exchange corresponding precisely to the above analysis. For although donations are not undertaken to earn an income, like transfers of investment capital the criteria on which they are based bear no relation to the exchange rate.

Capital Flight

At times of great political and economic insecurity, owners of capital are likely to want to transfer their funds abroad for safety. Although once they have transferred them, they will doubtless sooner or later invest them in earning assets, considerations of income have nothing to do with the original capital movement. It is motivated by fear; the owners of capital sought for it a safer haven. During the disturbed years before World War II, huge amounts of capital were exported from Europe for this reason. Estimates place the amount coming to the United States alone, between 1935 and 1939, at well over $5 billion.

When fear spurs people to send their wealth abroad, the dearness or cheapness of the currency into which they are converting is of little moment. The demand for foreign exchange in the exporting centers tends toward zero elasticity; in the receiving country, the corresponding supply will have a negative elasticity of 1.

Speculative Capital Movements

International transfers of capital with the aim of profiting from an increase in the value of the principal, rather than to earn an income, may be like rifle shots, directed at specific long-term assets, or like the scattered discharge of a shotgun, directed at foreign assets in general. Purchase for appreciation of a particular long-term foreign asset, such as the stock of a corporation, would not be undertaken unless the buyer were reasonably certain that the exchange rate would remain stable, or that it would appreciate; for currency depreciation could wipe out any gain from the appreciation of an asset.

Thus suppose that an investor in the United States purchases a British stock at £100 a share, in the expectation that it will rise in value 10 per cent in the following year. If at the time he makes this purchase the exchange rate is $2.80/£, he will pay $280 for each share. At the end of a year, the stock has appreciated, as expected, to a value of £110. If now the pound has depreciated to $2.50, the sale of the security will yield only $275, for a net loss of $5 a share. On the assumption, therefore, that any change in the exchange rate will be upward, the foreign exchange demanded would be a fixed amount at all rates—whatever amount was justified by the prospects of appreciation of the particular foreign assets involved. For similar inward capital movements, since the demand abroad would be for a fixed amount of dollars, for example, the supply of foreign exchange reflecting this foreign demand would have a negative elasticity of 1.

The most common object of international speculation, however, is not particular foreign assets, but holdings of some country's currency. It is the shotgun case. Such speculation will be stabilizing if the anticipations of speculators are, on balance, correct. It will be destabilizing if their judgment of future events is incorrect, so that speculation is "perverse."

Speculation should normally be stabilizing when a drop in the price of a particular currency is accidental and temporary. Speculative sentiment, anticipating a reversal of the forces causing depreciation, will on balance be "bullish." Demand from this source will support the exchange rate, effecting a prompter return to normal.

Suppose, however, that the forces affecting the exchange rate are more permanent. Demand for the exports of the country in question (say the United Kingdom) may have declined, or a rise in its export costs may have caused it to lose foreign markets to competitors. There is a deficit in Britain's balance of payments, and depreciation of the pound appears unavoidable. Any such depreciation will be greater over a period of a few months than over a longer period of a year or two, during which exports can be expanded, import substitution can develop, and buyers can become acquainted with the new set of price relations. If the initial rate of exchange is $2.80, elimination of the deficit might in the short run require that the pound depreciate to $2.20. But given more time for the adjustments to be worked out, over the longer run balance might be restored at a $2.50 rate.

In the absence of speculation, the rate would first drop to $2.20, then gradually recover. But if speculators enter the market, they will sell sterling, both spot and forward. This will hasten the depreciation, but as the rate falls below $2.50, foreseeing the recovery of the rate to that level, they will cease selling spot exchange and may start buying, and they will sell forward at rates substantially above $2.20/£. Both actions support the value of sterling, which may fall no further than $2.35 or $2.40/£. Thus if speculators exercise correct foresight, their activity tends to be stabilizing.

Perverse speculation, with destabilizing effects, will result if speculators anticipate events incorrectly. If they are impressed only by the fact of the initial depreciation of sterling, and fail to foresee its later recovery, they will tend to become overly pessimistic. They will dump any holdings of spot sterling they may have, and will sell forward at greatly depressed rates. With this speculative pressure added to normal forces inducing depreciation, the pound may sink to $2.00 or even lower. In this instance, speculation is a destabilizing element.

Instead of being overpessimistic at the start, speculators might err on the side of overoptimism, supporting the pound at close to its initial value. Upon later recognizing their mistake, they would remove their support and swing to the opposite extreme, depressing the exchange rate below the short-run "equilibrium" figure of $2.20/£.

Both types of perverse and destabilizing speculation are possible. That they are probable, however, is open to question. If speculators are to stay in business, they must make money; but if they often make mistakes of the kind just indicated, or on a grand scale, they will go broke. Under a regime of fluctuating exchange rates, to which the present discussion is most relevant, speculators could surely be expected to learn from experience—to become expert in evaluating the forces affecting the value of a country's currency. The professionals in stock and commodity markets have acquired expertness and find their occupation profitable; why should not exchange speculators, too? As they did so, their actions would become well-informed and would tend to exert a stabilizing effect on exchange rates.

SELECTED REFERENCES

Friedman, Milton, "The Case for Flexible Exchange Rates," in *Essays in Positive Economics*, pp. 157-203. Chicago: University of Chicago Press, 1953. Compares different systems of international payments; includes an interesting discussion of speculation.

Haberler, Gottfried, "The Market for Foreign Exchange and the Stability of the Balance of Payments," *Kyklos*, **III** (1949). Discusses the derivation of demand and supply curves for foreign exchange, *a priori* considerations relating to their elasticity, and their relation to a deficit.

Machlup, Fritz, "The Theory of Foreign Exchanges," Chapter 5 of *Readings in the Theory of International Trade*. Philadelphia: The Blakiston Co., 1949. A lucid presentation of the theory of foreign exchange.

————, "Elasticity Pessimism in International Trade," *Economia Internazionale*, III (February, 1950). A vigorous criticism of the pessimism reflected in measures of demand elasticities in international trade.

Meade, J. E., *The Balance of Payments*. New York: Oxford University Press, 1951. Chapter XVI provides a more detailed discussion of speculation than that given here.

Metzler, L. A., "The Theory of International Trade," Chapter 6 of *A Survey of Contemporary Economics*, ed. Howard S. Ellis. Philadelphia: The Blakiston Co., 1948. Section III is devoted to fluctuating exchange rates, with particular emphasis on the stability condition.

Sohmen, Egon, *Flexible Exchange Rates: Theory and Controversy*. Chicago: The University of Chicago Press, 1961. See Chapter I for a strong presentation of the case for stability in the foreign exchange market; see Chapter III for a good discussion of speculation; and see Chapter IV on the forward exchange markets.

19

DISEQUILIBRIA IN THE BALANCE OF PAYMENTS AND THEIR ADJUSTMENT

DIFFERENT KINDS OF BALANCE

A balance of payments must always balance. This is required by the rule of accounting, that debits must always equal credits. Such an accounting balance can plainly be realized—*must* be realized—under any conceivable circumstances: with exports rising or falling, with capital moving into or fleeing from a country, with prices fluctuating or stable. No country, therefore, need concern itself with whether its balance of payments balances—this is unavoidable.

A country must, however, concern itself with *how* this balance is achieved. It may be attained easily and without effort; if so, there is no cause for worry. On the other hand, the balance may be realized only under conditions of severe strain. To ease the strain, strong remedial measures may be necessary.

An Analogy

Consider the balance of payments of an individual. Each has a balance of payments with the rest of the world; it consists simply of his total receipts and expenditures. So long as one's income equals his outgo, he is in a stable position that can continue indefinitely; his balance of payments is in equilibrium. But let him begin to spend more than he earns, and he will have to draw on his savings or run into debt. His payments and his receipts still balance, in an accounting sense, but his changed situation cannot continue indefinitely. Sooner or later he will exhaust his savings; sooner or later his creditors will refuse to extend further loans. Then he will have to make a radical adjustment, either increasing his earning power or cutting his spending down to his income.

Similarly with a nation: so long as it lives within its international means, all is well. Its balance of payments is not only in accounting balance, but in equilibrium too. But let the expenditures its residents wish to make abroad exceed the expenditures foreigners choose to direct toward this country, and it will have to draw on its international reserves to meet the resultant deficit.

This condition of disequilibrium cannot continue; the drain on reserves must be checked before they are exhausted. Some kind of adjustment is necessary.[1]

Rephrasing the foregoing statement in more technical terms, we can say that a country's reserves will not change if its autonomous receipts equal its autonomous payments. Autonomous transactions on both sides of the international account include *all* transactions undertaken for their own sake—not only imports and exports of goods and services, but inward or outward movements of capital as well.

Balance of Payments Equilibrium

Beyond indicating that disequilibrium is present in a country's balance of payments when it is forced to draw upon its international reserves, which implies as a corollary that equilibrium exists when reserves do not change, we have done little to clarify these concepts. In other words, we have given one important criterion of equilibrium—absence of changes in international reserves—but have not explained the concept itself. Let us now turn to this problem.

What must be true if equality of autonomous receipts and payments, once established, is to continue? The answer to this question will specify the conditions of stable balance-of-payments equilibrium.

Consider first a country's exports of goods and services. These will tend to remain constant when the forces that determine them are in a stable relationship with one another. Summarily, this means that the supply of exports is adjusted to the demand for them at stable prices. More specifically, the prices of the productive factors and the amounts of them used to produce exports have achieved stable adjustment to the wants of consumers at existing levels of income. Similarly, imports will be stable when the forces determining their supply are adjusted to consumers' demands. When a stable adjustment of all these interrelated forces is reached, there will be no tendency for exports or imports to increase, nor for resources to move from one industry to another.

In a static world, we would have to concern ourselves with nothing but

---

[1] If a nation's current international receipts exceed its current payments, it will develop a surplus in its balance of payments, marked by an inflow of gold and foreign exchange. This is a condition favorable for the country immediately concerned, yet it does not reflect equilibrium. It too must be corrected, if only because a surplus in one country's balance of payments implies a deficit in those of some of its trading partners. Much depends, of course, upon the relative size of the surplus country. We shall focus upon the problems of deficit countries, however, for that is where the real difficulties lie.

exports and imports of goods and services. There would be no capital movements, because there would be no saving and no investment. But in the real world there is growth: population expands, people save, and these savings are invested in increasing a community's capital resources. And there are movements of capital from countries where accumulation is relatively rapid and returns to capital comparatively low, toward regions where capital is less abundant and its earning power (after allowing for risk) is greater. Given the differential in the return to capital in various parts of the earth, a steady flow of capital will reflect balance between the desire of investors for a higher return, and the retarding effect of such obstacles as ignorance of investment opportunities, differences in laws and customs, the greater difficulty of supervising foreign investments, and a natural fear of the unknown.

Growth would, of course, mean changes in exports and imports, as well as capital movements. Stability in a country's balance of payments could be preserved by small but continuing adjustments through changes in factor prices, in volume of output, in the allocation of resources, and in the rate of capital flow.

The world we live in, however, does not behave in this smooth and orderly fashion. Change takes place, not only slowly and gradually, but often violently and unexpectedly. When such changes affect a country's exports, its imports, or its lending or borrowing, equilibrium in its balance of payments is disturbed. A deficit or a surplus develops. Adjustment becomes imperative for a deficit country, and this adjustment must be reasonably prompt. We shall consider two alternative methods by which a nation can adjust to disturbances in its balance of payments later in this chapter. But first let us see what kinds of disturbance are likely to be encountered.

DISTURBANCES OF EQUILIBRIUM IN THE BALANCE OF PAYMENTS

Our discussion of balance of payments equilibrium enables us to say, with some suppression of detail, that a country's exports depend upon three things: (1) the total volume of purchasing power available to foreigners for expenditure on all conceivable items, including this country's exports; (2) the particular kinds of commodities and services wanted by foreigners, as determined by their tastes; and (3) the prices at which goods such as our country's exports and substitutes therefor are available. Similarly, a country's imports depend upon: (1) the total purchasing power its residents can command; (2) their specific desires or tastes: and (3) the prices of imports and possible domestic substitutes.

In sum, any change in the level of income, at home or abroad, tends to affect imports or exports, since it alters total expenditures in one place or the other. And any change in demand or supply conditions, either at home or abroad, will influence the volume of specific imports and exports, and through these, their aggregate value. Long-term capital movements depend principally upon international differences in the return to capital. As new opportunities for investment appear in some countries, they raise the relative rate of return there. Similarly, returns may decline relatively or even absolutely where capital accumulates faster than new investment outlets appear. Such changes will cause the direction and rate of flow of capital to vary.

One important source of disturbance to a country's balance of payments thus resides in income changes. The rest may be classified as structural changes, if we define "economic structure" as the way in which the parts of a country's economy are put together and how they are related to the external world. A structural change thus implies an alteration in some specific sector of a nation's economy; its effect on the balance of payments will generally be limited to one or a few of its component items. By way of contrast, income changes affect exports or imports in their totality, though not necessarily in equal degree throughout their entire range.

Short-Run Disturbances

We can simplify our analysis by eliminating some causes of disequilibrium as relatively unimportant. To begin with, a distinction can be made with respect to the duration of disequilibria. Some are short-run in character, lasting only for a few months or perhaps a year or so. Such are purely seasonal disturbances, commonly encountered by agricultural-exporting countries.

Thus Australian wool floods the market between November and March. During this period, Australia's exports greatly exceed her imports and foreign balances accumulate rapidly. In subsequent months, there is an excess of imports, and foreign balances are drawn upon. Since this is a recurring pattern, it poses no problem. The sensible way of meeting the deficits between April and October is to draw upon international reserves, since their prompt replenishment is assured.

A crop failure, leading either to reduced exports or increased imports, is more serious. But it is usually a temporary disturbance, to be succeeded by a return to normal. A nation, like an individual, can justifiably draw on its reserves when confronted with such unusual and short-run emergencies.

We shall pay little attention to phenomena of this kind, and consider only situations which continue or threaten to continue for some time and thus tend to exhaust or reduce to the danger point a country's international reserves.

Changes in Money Income

Let us first consider changes in money income as a cause of balance-of-payments difficulties. Two types of income variation need to be distinguished: those that occur independently in one or more countries, and those that are linked together through the international progagation of the business cycle.

An independent change in income in a given country may be inflationary or deflationary. Only the former need concern us here, since a decline in national income (deflation) will cause imports to decline and thus lead to a surplus in the balance of payments.

Inflation is present when the total demand for goods and services exceeds, at current prices, total domestic output plus any normal long-term capital inflow. Usually, inflation will be accompanied and made possible by a flood of money, newly created by the banking system or the government. But inflation may also occur when increased spending is financed by dishoarding of existing money. Inflation is usually accompanied by, and its existence is proved by, a rising price level. Eventually, there will be some changes in the pattern of relative prices. Relative price changes may fail to appear, however, if the inflation is mild or if price controls suppress significant price increases.

Any inflation tends to bring about a deficit in the balance of payments, for increased expenditures are bound to affect exports and imports. The seriousness of the resultant deficit depends very largely on the degree to which a country is involved in international trade. If, like the United States, it is comparatively self-sufficient, rising demands may be largely concentrated on home goods. A country whose exports and imports are a large proportion of national income, on the other hand—such as the United Kingdom, Belgium, or Norway—will feel the international impact of excess demand more promptly; it will quickly develop a serious balance-of-payments deficit.

When an inflation is serious, to the direct impact on exports and imports of increased expenditure must be added its indirect effect through its influence on internal prices. Home goods are likely to rise first and most. Increased costs of living stimulate wage demands. As wages rise, the cost of producing exports goes up too, reenforced by higher prices for home-produced raw materials and other components of exports. Exporters will find sales abroad diminishing, the more so if competing products are available from many sources. They may even be forced to contract output. Imports, in the meantime, will have become increasingly attractive substitutes for domestic goods.

The immediate causes of the higher spending of inflation, whether mild or severe, vary widely. There may be a war, which results in enormous outlays on military equipment and troops. Inflation can result, as in western Europe after World War II, from an attempt by government to maintain both consumption and investment at levels beyond the reach of the country's resources. It will come about, as in many underdeveloped countries, if the country undertakes a rate of investment in excess of domestic saving and normal capital inflow. Or it may simply be the consequence of a lax or ineffectual central bank, unable or unwilling to resist the demands of consumers or producers for expanded credit. Whatever the cause, the results are the same: excess of demand over available production, rising imports, falling exports, and a continuing balance-of-payments deficit.

THE BUSINESS CYCLE AND THE BALANCE OF PAYMENTS   In all the instances so far considered, disequilibrium in a country's international accounts resulted from an absolute rise in that country's money income, independently of what was happening elsewhere. But similar difficulties may arise even though incomes in all countries rise or fall together, due to a common cause, provided these variations in national incomes are not synchronized. If all nations entered the phase of prosperity together, though each would find its imports increasing, its exports (which are the imports of others) would keep in step. Similarly in depression: each country's imports and exports would keep pace with one another. In fact, however, such perfect correspondence in timing does not exist. A depression, for example, generally gets under way first in one country, then is transmitted abroad in the manner shown in Chapter 15.

If all of the hundred or so nations of the world were of equal economic importance, this phenomenon would cause little trouble.[2] For a decline (or rise) in the income of a sector of the world economy with a weight of only about 1 per cent would be spread so thinly as to have little effect. But when a few nations are of outstanding importance, the situation is very different.

This has been particularly true since the United States became the economic giant it is today. Various estimates indicate that the U.S. comprises, economically speaking, some 40 per cent of the entire free world. Small wonder then that when, between 1929 and 1932, our national income fell by half, and our imports and foreign investments by even more, our trading partners faced balance-of-payments deficits of huge proportions. Their levels of income, employment, and production were dragged down by the decline in ours, which was bad enough. But added to this was a severe balance-of-payments problem, brought about mainly because their income contraction lagged behind ours, so that their imports fell less promptly and drastically than their exports.

Cyclical disequilibrium in a country's balance of payments may be either aggravated or moderated by differences in national propensities to import. It will be aggravated if the country has a lower marginal propensity to import than the average of its trading partners, for then its imports will decline less than its exports during depression, independently of any income lag, while during prosperity they will rise by a smaller proportion. It would be unwise to generalize on the basis of this point, however, since we know relatively little about variations in the propensity to import during the different phases of the business cycle, except that they are probably very substantial.

Structural Changes

A structural change can originate at home or abroad, and on the demand or on the supply side. Thus a *domestic change in supply conditions* occurs

---

[2] Such an assumption of the equal importance of nations underlies much reasoning about international trade. It is well to be on guard against it, especially when it comes to applying theoretical analysis to practical problems.

when the depletion of a natural resource raises an industry's costs, or when an invention or improved processes give rise to a new production function permitting a lowering of costs or the introduction of a new product. An illustration of the former is the gradual exhaustion of the better coal seams in Great Britain, which in spite of improved mining methods has raised costs. Combined with the difficulty of attracting sufficient labor to the mines, this has caused a shift in the country's status from a net coal-exporting to a net importing basis. New products and improved processes are legion. We need mention only nylon, dacron, and other synthetic fibers, which have affected especially the world market for silk; synthetic nitrates; synthetic rubber; and transistors to replace radio tubes. Among noteworthy new processes are the use of mechanical cotton pickers, of mechanical handling equipment, and the introduction of "automation" in the manufacture of automobile engines.

A *domestic change in demand* occurs when tastes alter, either in favor of or adversely for a domestic industry, with a consequent shrinkage or expansion of imports. The shift in the diet of the United States and other Western nations, as the standard of living has risen, from cereals and toward meat and dairy products may be mentioned.

The conversion of ocean shipping from coal- to oil-fuel engines brought a *shift in world demand* that contributed to declining British coal exports. The development and spreading use of nylon in the United States reduced that country's demand for imports of silk; the reverse side of the coin was its effect on Japanese exports.

Any of these changes in demand and supply conditions, whether they originate at home or abroad, affect a country's economic structure in relation to that of the rest of the world and therewith its balance of payments. If many such changes occur at once, the relative prices of its exports and its imports as a whole may be affected. We then get a change in its *terms of trade*. If a country's imports consist predominantly of raw materials and foodstuffs, while its exports are principally manufactured goods, a rapid increase in world population and in manufactures, set against scarce supplies of minerals and more intense cultivation of land, could raise the prices of its imports relatively to its exports. The resultant worsened terms of trade would require it to export larger quantities of manufactures to obtain the same volume of raw materials and food imports, thus presenting it with a serious problem of adjustment.

In addition to structural change resting on altered demand and supply relations, we must consider *variations in the rate of international capital flow*. The discovery of important new resources in a country that has been importing no or little capital is likely, by raising the expected returns from investment, to stimulate the inward movement of capital. Venezuela is a good example; first came oil, which led to huge investments by some of the world's leading oil producers during and since the 1920's. More recently the uncovering of large deposits of rich iron ore has induced heavy investment by Bethlehem and U.S. Steel. Discovery of new resources may play a less striking role, as when a gradual growth of a country's population and wealth create a market and cause its resources to be developed to the point where investment becomes attractive to foreigners. The United States attracted foreign investment in this fashion during much of the nineteenth century. So has Canada, both before World War I and since World War II, and more recently, the nations of the European Common Market.

A rise in the inflow of international capital from an established level to a new, higher one has a direct impact on a country's balance of payments. The export of securities expands, perhaps suddenly, creating an international surplus to which the country must become adjusted. In the investing or lending country or countries, adjustment is required to the deficit caused by the importation of securities.

A *special case* of structural change traceable to altered debtor-creditor relations is that exemplified by Britain's loss of overseas earning assets during World War II and the subsequent incurring of heavy international indebtedness. Britain's international investment income shrank sharply for a time; this and the need to liquidate outstanding debts (notably the so-called "blocked sterling balances") added to the strain on a balance of payments which for other reasons already constituted a grave problem.

Finally, we should note a particularly puzzling kind of structural disequilibrium, what Kindleberger calls *"structural disequilibrium at the factor level."*[3] This is typified by an inappropriate relation between factor prices and their relative supplies. As an illustration, Kindleberger cites postwar Italy, where wages, though low relative to most other countries of western Europe, were high relative to Italy's endowment with labor, while interest rates appear to have been low relative to the amount of capital available. Too much production used capital-intensive methods, too little was carried on by labor-intensive methods, with the result that there was a constant shortage of capital alongside of chronic unemployment of labor. In the absence of a readjustment of factor prices more in line with factor endowment, or vice versa, any attempt to employ labor more fully was almost certain to lead—through the consequent rise in income and imports—to an open balance-of-payments disequilibrium. In the meantime, it was concealed or disguised by being transformed into an unemployment problem. More recently this underlying cause of disequilibrium appears to have been at least partially resolved by a sharp rise in labor productivity in Italy (see Tables 25.3 and 25.4). Buoyant conditions of demand in Europe also helped.

[3] C. P. Kindleberger, *International Economics*, 2nd ed. Published 1958 by Richard D. Irwin, Inc., Homewood, Ill. See pp. 461-69 for a more extended discussion, in particular of the "dual economy" problem, when factor prices differ substantially between the developed and undeveloped sectors of an economy.

THE ADJUSTMENT OF BALANCE OF PAYMENTS
DISEQUILIBRIUM

Ever since the dawn of modern times, constant change—at least in western Europe and the countries settled by Europeans—has been a leading characteristic of the economic order. More recently, the profound stirring in the hitherto relatively stagnant, undeveloped areas of the world has shaken them loose from their traditional patterns and introduced a dynamism hitherto lacking. The changes are of the types we have been examining—in incomes, either of the inflationary or cyclical variety, and in economic structures.

Whatever the cause of a specific alteration in income or structure, in an "open economy" (one linked to the rest of the world by trade and by factor movements), it is bound to affect international receipts and payments. It will generate balance-of-payments surpluses in some, deficits in others.

When such a disequilibrium is enduring, especially if it involves a deficit, it must somehow be halted. Something must give, and bring to an end the loss of international reserves a deficit imposes. But what? Are there any alternatives, and if so, which entails the least difficulties? These are the questions to which we must now turn.

A clue is provided by commodity markets. In these, a disturbance of an equilibrium position, owing say to an increase in demand, leads—through the operation of the price mechanism—to a new position of equilibrium. Now we know that the various national economies are related through the prices of goods and factors and the exchange rates which link those prices together. The possibility suggests itself that a process of adjustment analogous to that in a commodity market may be set in motion—that a change in demand or supply may lead, through its effect upon the relevant prices, to a restoration of equilibrium.

Other "natural" or automatic adjustments are suggested by our study of national income, where we saw that a rise in exports generates an expansion of income and therewith a parallel, but smaller, change in imports. We already have at our command a considerable analytical equipment with which to tackle problems of this kind. Our task now is to use it appropriately.

Any country has a choice as to how its own currency shall be related to those of other nations. It can adopt a completely independent currency system, determining the internal value or purchasing power of its money by its own monetary policy, while allowing its external value in terms of other currencies to be settled by the free interaction of demand and supply upon the foreign exchange markets. No attempt is made to influence exchange rates—they are permitted to fluctuate freely.

Or one nation may join others in establishing a fixed relationship between the different national currencies. This is accomplished by expressing each cur-

rency in terms of some objective standard, such as gold. If each co
a price, in national currency, at which it will buy and sell gold with
then exchange rates between the various gold standard currencies
at the relative gold value of each pair of currencies. As we shall see, ن اon
of such an international system implies the sacrifice of monetary autonomy.

Finally, a country may try to obtain the best of both worlds, and so enjoy
both independence of monetary policy and stable exchange rates. It can do
so by establishing direct controls over the demand and supply of foreign
exchange.

We shall examine the process of adjustment to a balance of payments disturbance under each of these different systems. What the cause may be is of
secondary importance to the operation of the adjustment mechanism. Later
on, we shall consider whether different methods of adjustment are appropriate
or inappropriate to specific types of disturbance.

INTERDEPENDENT CURRENCIES: THE GOLD STANDARD AS TYPICAL

When exchange rates are fixed, either because the value of each currency
is linked to some common standard of value such as gold or because of strong
official support, the monetary systems of the different countries are *interdependent*. The nature of and reasons for this interdependence can be seen most
readily if we examine how a system of fixed exchange rates operates. For this
purpose, let us take the gold standard as the outstanding representative of a
fixed exchange rate or interdependent currency system.

Consider the gold standard as it was supposed to function during its heyday,
in the half century or so before 1914. Each country adhering to the gold standard established as its monetary unit a gold coin containing an amount of gold
specified by law. Thus the standard monetary unit in Great Britain was the
gold sovereign or pound containing 113.0016 grains of pure gold. The U.S.
dollar, in turn, contained 23.22 grains. With both currencies tied to gold, there
existed a basic exchange rate, or "mint par" of exchange, that expressed their
relative gold content. This was $4.87 to the pound ($4.86656, to be more
exact).

Gold coins constituted only part of the money supply, circulating alongside
a larger amount of paper currency and demand deposits. But the ultimate reserves of each gold standard country consisted of gold, held (as in Britain,
France, and Germany) by the central bank, or (as in the United States) by the
individual commercial banks. For convenience in carrying out international
transactions, banks in most countries maintained sterling balances in London
which were allowed to vary somewhat with minor variations in the balance of
payments. But any substantial disturbance tended to bring about a movement
of gold.

Exchange rates under the gold standard could fluctuate only within the narrow range set by the costs of shipping gold, which between New York and London amounted to approximately 3 cents per pound sterling in either direction. Thus the dollar/sterling rate was subject to an upper limit set by the "gold export point" at \$4.90/£, and to a lower limit established by the "gold import point" at \$4.84/£.

To see how the gold standard mechanism operated, let us consider a hypothetical example. Assume that the United States carries out all its international transactions in terms of the pound sterling. Its balance of payments is in equilibrium, with autonomous receipts and autonomous payments in balance at £10 million, and the exchange rate at par, \$4.87 to the pound. Demand for and supply of foreign exchange are as represented by the curves D_f and S_f in Figure 19.1.[4]

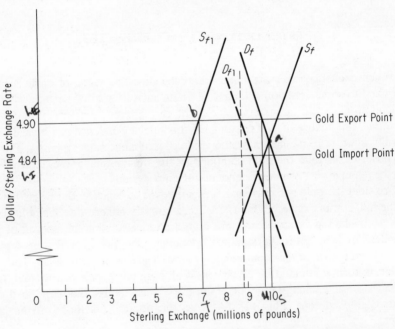

FIGURE 19.1   Exchange Rates Under the Gold Standard

Now suppose that exports of the United States decline (owing perhaps to an increase in tariffs abroad, more intense competition in U.S. export markets, or a business recession abroad). The supply of foreign exchange shifts to the left, to the new position S_{f1}. The rate of exchange rises to the gold export point, \$4.90/£. With the shrinkage of exports, the supply of foreign exchange now

---

[4] The vertical axis, representing the dollar/sterling exchange rate, is broken to permit enlargement of the scale in the neighborhood of par.

amounts to only £7 million. There is no shift in the demand for foreign exchange; but at the slightly higher exchange rate, purchases decline a bit, to £9.7 million. The U.S. balance of payments shows a deficit of £2.7 million.

To finance the deficit, some £2.7 million of gold now moves out of the country. The flow may be moderated if the sterling deposits normally held by New York banks are above the minimum convenience level. They could draw and sell sterling bills to the amount by which they were willing to permit their sterling deposits to decline.

We can now readily see the monetary effect of an adverse shift in a country's balance of payments. After the decline in U.S. exports, banks in the country will be discounting bills of exchange brought to them by exporters and others with claims on foreigners to the amount of £7 million. By this action they *add* $34.3 million (4.90 × 7) to the supply of domestic money. Simultaneously, they sell bills of exchange to importers and others with foreign payments to make to the value of $47.53 million (4.90 × 9.5), thereby causing the domestic money supply to *diminish* by this amount. There is thus a *net diminution* in the U.S. money supply of $13.23 million. Corresponding to this decline in the domestic money supply, there is an equivalent loss of gold (£2.7 million), perhaps offset to some small extent by a decline in sterling deposits. This is the compensatory finance necessary to balance the difference between autonomous receipts of £7 million and autonomous payments of £9.7 million.

Thus changes in the U.S. balance of payments bring in their wake a change, not only in the nation's international reserve position, but also in the domestic money supply. The gold standard links together the monetary systems of its members—it creates a condition of monetary interdependence. This effect can be counteracted, as we shall see, but only at the cost of also counteracting the effectiveness of the adjustment mechanism, to which we now turn.

Adjustment: the Price Effect

In the period before 1914, central banks showed little interest in using their powers to stabilize employment and prices. Instead, discount policy was geared to protection of the country's reserves and thereby to maintenance of currency convertibility. Facing a deficit and a consequent loss of gold, central banks reacted by raising their discount rates.[5] This set in motion a chain of consequences expressed in a classic statement by a British Parliamentary committee in the closing days of the first World War:

> . . . the raising of the Bank's discount rate and the steps taken to make it effective in the market necessarily led to a general rise of interest rates and a restriction of credit. New enterprises were therefore postponed and the de-

[5] Before the establishment of the Federal Reserve System in 1915, the large commercial banks in the United States held the bulk of the nation's gold reserves; they reacted to reserve changes in the same manner as central banks elsewhere.

mand for constructional materials and other capital goods was lessened. The consequent slackening of employment also diminished the demand for consumable goods, while holders of stocks of commodities carried largely with borrowed money, being confronted with an increase of interest charges, if not with actual difficulty in renewing loans, and with the prospect of falling prices, tended to press their goods on a weak market. The result was a decline in general prices in the home market which, by checking imports and stimulating exports, corrected the adverse trade balance which was the primary cause of the difficulty.[6]

In this and other typical formulations of the gold standard mechanism of adjustment, stress is laid on the role of price changes. There is little advance over the traditional price-specie-flow mechanism. A deficit causes a country to lose gold; its central bank raises discount rates and tightens credit; commodity stocks are liquidated; orders decline; prices fall; exports are stimulated and imports retarded; and the deficit is eliminated.

In actual fact, price changes do not appear generally to have been of sufficient magnitude to perform the task of adjustment.[7] With the development by Keynes of the analysis of the determinants of national income, attention was directed to elements mentioned (but glossed over) in the Cunliffe Committee Report. This led to a reinterpretation of the gold standard mechanism, with increased emphasis on the role of income changes. Let us introduce this explanatory element into our examination of how the nineteenth century gold standard was supposed to work.

Adjustment: the Income Effect

Consider the consequences of the contraction in the money supply caused by an adverse disturbance to the balance of payments. Where will its impact be felt? In the export industries, of course; they are selling fewer goods abroad. In our illustrative example, their total receipts in domestic money have fallen from \$48.7 million to \$34.3 million, or by \$14.4 million. There is a fall in income equivalent to the reduction in the value of exports.

But the decline in income does not stop here; we must reckon with the multiplier. Allowing for foreign repercussions, this is:

$$\frac{1}{s_a + m_a + m_b \cdot \dfrac{s_a}{s_b}}$$

[6] *Interim Report of the Committee on Currency and Foreign Exchanges after the War* (Cunliffe Committee), reprinted in *British Banking Statutes and Reports, 1832-1928*, Vol. II (edited by T. E. Gregory), pp. 336-37. Copyright 1929 by the Oxford University Press, New York.

[7] Thus Professor Taussig commented on the "surprising exactness and speed" with which merchandise movements adjusted to balance of payments disturbances, on the failure of the requisite price changes to appear, and on the "surprisingly little transfer" of gold. F. W. Taussig, *International Trade*, pp. 239, 261. Published 1927 by Macmillan, New York.

where the subscript *a* refers to the U.S., the subscript *b* to the rest of the world. Assuming the values: $s_a = 0.2$, $s_b = 0.2$, $m_a = 0.15$, and $m_b = 0.25$, the multiplier has a value of $10/6$, or 1.67. The ultimate decline in income will be 1.67 times the decline in exports, or $24 million. Assuming that the reduction of exports lasts for some time, income will remain at this lowered level just so long as the deficit persists.

But with the decline in income, this deficit will not remain unchanged. With a marginal propensity to import of 0.15, a decline in income of $24 million will cause imports to fall by $3.6 million.[8] After the multiplier and the propensity to import have done their work, a new situation emerges in the foreign exchange market. The sterling value of imports has fallen by approximately £0.73 million (the dollar value of the decline in imports, $3.6 million, divided by the rate of exchange, $4.90). Diagrammatically, this can be shown (see Figure 18.1) by a shift to the left of the demand curve for foreign exchange such that at $4.90 per pound, £8.77 million of imports are demanded (D_{f1}). If exports are unchanged, this means that the balance-of-payments deficit has been correspondingly reduced—from £2.7 million to £1.77 million.

To the corrective effect of income changes should be added the contribution, if any, of price changes. To the degree to which these occurred, and depending upon the elasticity of demand for exports and imports, the demand for foreign exchange would shift a little further to the left, the supply curve somewhat to the right.

Induced Short-Term Capital Movements

Under a regime of fixed exchange rates such as the gold standard, relatively small variations in a nation's international receipts and payments could cause large changes in its reserves. Many economists have thought that the fact that gold movements were comparatively small must be attributed to the presence of offsetting short-term capital movements.

According to the accepted principles of the gold standard, when gold began to flow out of a country's reserves, the central bank would have to take protective action by raising its discount rate. In the country or countries receiving the gold, the banks would lower their interest charges. Thus a difference in national levels of short-term interest rates would appear. Once this difference exceeded a certain minimum (about ½ per cent), it became profitable for banks in the country where interest rates were relatively high to borrow abroad. In terms of our illustration, U.S. banks would, by prior arrangement, draw sterling bankers' acceptances on correspondent banks in London. They would then have these discounted in the London money market, thereby acquiring sterling deposits. Against these deposits they could then sell bills of exchange

---

[8] This will, of course, take time. Except for a very small residue, the effects of the multiplier will work themselves out in 1½ to 2 years.

to U.S. importers for dollars which could then be lent out in the New York money market at the higher interest rate ruling there.

By this procedure, short-term obligations of New York banks (sterling bankers' acceptances) took the place of an outflow of gold reserves. Thus the impact of a balance-of-payments disturbance on the country's reserves was cushioned and the severity of measures to restrict credit was moderated. Without this possibility of borrowing foreign exchange to satisfy the excess demand, reserve losses would have been much greater. To protect its reserves, essential to the maintenance of currency convertibility, much greater reliance would need to have been placed on restricting credit, contracting business activity, and forcing down prices. Instead of putting an immediate and heavy burden on the long-run mechanism of adjustment, this mechanism could be given more time to work out its effects.

Fact versus Fiction

A steady accumulation of evidence suggests that the gold standard of the late nineteenth century did not in fact perform as it was thought to.[9] Price and income changes, it appears, did not play the main equilibrating role called for by the established theory of the gold standard.

We have already noted that gold flows and price changes were surprisingly small. But even with respect to those gold movements that did occur, the monetary authorities often failed to follow the supposed "rules of the game"—to contract credit when gold flowed out and to expand credit when gold moved in. Instead, central banks frequently countered a loss of gold by a policy of "neutralization." When a gold outflow reduced the reserve deposits of commercial banks at the central bank, the latter offset this decline by a purchase of securities on the open market. Or it would offset an increase in the reserve deposits of commercial banks by a sale of securities. With the reserve position of commercial banks unaffected, interest rates also remained unaltered. Thus monetary contraction or expansion, the prime element in adjustment according to the theory of the gold standard, was not allowed to occur.[10] Yet deficits

---

[9] Among the studies that contributed importantly to this conclusion should be included: W. Edwards Beach, *British International Gold Movements and Banking Policy, 1881-1913* (Harvard University Press, Cambridge, 1935); Arthur I. Bloomfield, *Monetary Policy Under the International Gold Standard, 1880-1914* (Federal Reserve Bank of New York, 1959); W. Adams Brown, *The International Gold Standard Reinterpreted, 1914-1934* (National Bureau of Economic Research, New York, 1940); Oscar Morgenstern, *International Financial Transactions and Business Cycles* (Princeton University Press, Princeton, N.J., 1959); R. S. Sayres, *Bank of England Operations, 1890-1914* (P. S. King & Son, Ltd., London, 1936); John A. Stovel, *Canada in the World Economy* (Harvard University Press, Cambridge, 1959); C. H. Walker, "The Working of the Prewar Gold Standard," *Review of Economic Studies*, Vol. I (1934); P. B. Whale, "The Working of the Prewar Gold Standard," *Economica*, Vol. IV *ns* (1937); H. D. White, *The French International Accounts, 1880-1913* (Harvard University Press, Cambridge, 1933).

[10] Thus Bloomfield (*op. cit.*, p. 31) found that for five out of eleven central banks, "discount rates and reserve ratios did *not* characteristically move in opposite directions."

and surpluses in international payments did not persist indefinitely, but were somehow eliminated comparatively promptly to preserve or restore equilibrium.

An Alternative Interpretation

To explain the smooth adjustment that seems to have taken place, a much more important role must be given to long-term capital movements. Rather than acting as a disturbing element calling into operation an adjustment mechanism, as traditional gold standard theory has tended to treat them, these capital movements appear to have been a crucial part of this mechanism. They replaced gold flows by providing needed foreign exchange; they thereby gave time for adjustment to proceed more deliberately; and they sometimes contributed importantly to final adjustment. Let us elaborate.

An outstanding feature of the world economy of the late nineteenth century was the close integration of the more advanced nations. Nowhere was this integration more striking than in the financial realm. London was the unquestioned leader in finance; British banks had correspondent relationships with banks all over the world; and many important foreign banks had branches in London. Capital markets in New York, Paris, Rome, and other centers were closely linked to London; the flow of capital was unrestricted, and it was quickly responsive to changing opportunities for profit. There existed something approaching a world capital market, centered in London. Moreover, confidence in the maintenance of currency convertibility into gold at fixed rates strengthened and supported the close financial relationships.

Given this institutional environment, commercial banks, other financial agencies, security dealers, and private investors normally held substantial amounts of international securities, especially of reputable British firms and of the British government.[11] When a disturbance generated a deficit in some country's balance of payments, its banks could (and frequently did) liquidate some of these international assets. The sale of these securities provided the sterling necessary to finance the deficit, with no need to draw upon reserves. If there was an initial loss of reserves accompanied by a rise in discount rates, the liquidation of these securities would be reenforced, since it increased the relative attractiveness of investment in the deficit country. And once a suffi-

---

Moreover (p. 50), for all eleven banks, "changes in international and domestic assets were more often in the *opposite* than in the same direction." (60 per cent of observations.) That is, when a central bank's international assets (e.g., gold or foreign balances) declined, its domestic assets (holdings of government securities) would increase, reflecting offsetting operations. Gold standard theory, on the other hand, would require that as a central bank's international assets or reserves declined, it should enforce credit contraction by selling securities and thus also reducing its holdings of domestic assets.

[11] Evidence is lacking as to how large commercial bank holdings of such assets were. Holdings of other members of the financial centers are known to have been substantial, and international security transactions are also known to have been large. While admittedly the suggestion made here is hypothetical, it is only partly so, for security liquidation by *some* members of the financial community did frequently occur.

cient differential in interest rates became established, short-term capital movements could be counted on to supplement such shifts in long-term international asset holdings.

Thus compensatory movements of capital replaced international reserve movements, reducing the need for credit restriction and allowing more time for underlying adjustments to occur. Sometimes, when a disturbance was relatively mild, there might be a good chance of another offsetting disturbance making further adjustment unnecessary. If the disturbance were more severe, the continuance of moderate pressure on credit, prices, and incomes could over time correct the maladjustment gradually. It remained true, however, that one important potential cause of disturbance—divergent national credit policies—could not operate so long as central banks made the safeguarding of reserves and maintenance of gold convertibility the ultimate criterion of action.[12] For credit policy so oriented is corrective, not disruptive.

Finally, capital movements not only provided breathing space, but also played an important adjusting role with respect to such important kinds of disturbance as differing rates of national growth or national differences in the timing of the business cycle. Thus Canada experienced rapid economic expansion in the period from 1900 to 1913, with investment and income rising rapidly. This induced a sharp increase in imports. But instead of this generating a gold outflow, British and American investors, attracted by the promising investment opportunities, directed a rising stream of capital into Canada's mines, railways, and industries. The adjustment that would have been called for, in the absence of this capital movement, was made unnecessary by its presence. A steady flow of foreign funds financed Canada's growing imports, even including a modest amount of gold to support the expansion of credit.[13]

Besides the high mobility of capital, there was also a much freer international movement of labor than since 1914. Barriers to immigration were few; indeed, migrants were sought out for the developing areas of the world. Their movement contributed to the growth of the developing areas, thereby helping to attract the adjusting flow of capital. Insofar as labor migrated from countries suffering from relative contraction, its movement also helped reduce unemployment, maintain labor productivity, and reduce the need for imports, thus assisting the realization of both internal and external equilibrium.

The Gold Standard After 1914

Since the first World War, a broad-based gold standard has existed for only two brief periods: 1925-31, and since 1958. During both periods, the features

[12] Although the link between gold movements and discount rate changes was less close than had been supposed, Bloomfield (*op. cit.*, p. 32) cautions that central banks did watch reserves closely and did act decisively when convertibility was threatened.

[13] This account of Canada's experience is based on John Stovel's analysis in his *Canada in the World Economy*. See, especially, Chapter XVI.

that made the gold standard operate so smoothly before 1914 have been absent. Financial markets have been far less closely linked. New York outranks London as a financial center, and Paris, Rome, Basle, Frankfurt, and Tokyo now play a relatively much more important and a much more independent role. Official limitations on capital movements have characterized the entire post-1914 period, and though greatly reduced in scope, still exist. Unofficial impediments to the flow of capital have also grown up, although they are being gradually overcome: inadequate marking facilities, ignorance, the regulations of supervisory bodies, and local patriotism. International investment is to a far greater degree *direct*, embodying control over the object of investment, rather than *portfolio*, where securities are held for their own sake.

Tight immigration restrictions have minimized the international mobility of labor, while the stability of exchange rates is no longer taken for granted. The fifty years since 1914 have seen many periods of unstable rates and numerous devaluations.

In the absence of the conditions that made the gold standard work smoothly before 1914, it could only operate—if allowed to do so—in the harsh manner ascribed to it by traditional gold standard theory. That theory served much better as an explanation of the gold standard mechanism after 1914 than it did for the period to which it supposedly applied. Serious misgivings arose, however, as to the suitability of such a mechanism to the conditions of the twentieth century. For these conditions included the emergence as goals of national policy (first), price stability, then full employment, and (more recently) satisfactory economic growth. None of these goals is consistent with an international adjustment mechanism that corrects deficits by deflationary means, and surpluses by inflationary means.

The outcome was prompt and frequent interference with the operation of the restored gold standard. Rather than adopt a restrictive credit policy when confronted with a loss of international reserves, central banks have become even more inclined than earlier to neutralize this loss. In the surplus country, the goal of price stability requires the sterilization of the gold inflow. Offsetting of reserve losses or gains, of course, checks the process of adjustment. If, in addition, a nation experiencing a balance-of-payments deficit goes even further and pursues the goal of full employment by expanding credit and increasing government expenditures, the adjustment mechanism may be completely counteracted and the international payments deficit perpetuated.[14]

Conclusion

There can be no doubt that the gold standard can furnish an effective international adjustment mechanism. This mechanism can operate smoothly—with

---

[14] Cautious efforts in this direction in the United States in the period 1958-62 appear to have been partly responsible for the persistence of the large balance-of-payments deficit.

a minimum of disturbing effects on prices, incomes, and employment—if the environment is propitious, as it was before 1914. (It could also operate smoothly if prices and wages were highly flexible, but they are not.) Without such a favorable environment, it can still perform the task of eliminating international deficits and surpluses, though only with substantial variations in incomes and prices, and even then, only if national monetary and fiscal policies are subordinated to balance-of-payments requirements. Without that subordination, any maladjustment will be perpetuated, not eliminated.

Continued allegiance to the gold standard has presented the nations of the western world with a recurring dilemma. They have chosen an international currency system that cannot work if monetary and fiscal policies are independently determined, yet they insist that each nation shall be free to decide these policies for itself. Clearly, the question arises: what sort of international monetary system *is* consistent with the pursuit of such important national goals as full employment, economic growth, and price stability? We shall examine some of the alternatives, investigate the attempt since the last war to reach a compromise solution, and later (Chapter 27) study the leading current proposals for reform of the international monetary system.

Capital Transfer Under the Gold Standard

Since international transfers of capital have received special attention in the literature, a short digression on this topic may be justified.

IN THEORY   According to the traditional gold standard analysis, an international transfer of capital is, in its effect on a nation's balance of payments, no different from any other kind of disturbance. A burst of long-term international lending, or the remission of tribute or reparation, increases the payments a country has to make, just as does an increase in its imports. What happens after the inauguration of such a capital movement depends mainly upon the source of the funds used to make the new payments.

If these funds come from savings that would otherwise have financed domestic investment, the consequent decline of home investment will set in motion a multiple contraction of income. Additional investment abroad, made possible by the foreign loan, takes place and raises income there by some multiple. Imports of the lending country contract; its exports expand; and a substantial part of the loan is transmitted in the form of goods. Price effects accompanying the income changes work toward the same end. If the initial loss of reserves induces credit contraction, to the initial fall in income and prices inaugurated by the decline of investment will be added a secondary fall in income and prices. The entire loan may be transferred in the form of an excess of exports over imports. That is, the foreign exchange derived from the excess of exports is purchased by the buyers of foreign securities and turned over to the sellers in the borrowing country.

IN PRACTICE   Long-term international capital movements are not normally a source of balance of payments disturbance, as the forgoing account
assumes, but are a *consequence* of a country's balance of payments position.
A country enjoying a surplus in its balance of payments will see its reserves
of gold and foreign exchange rising. In itself, a surplus implies that the country's savings are in excess of its domestic investment; this excess is being invested in gold and foreign balances. The increase in the latter will raise the
liquidity of that country's banks, and will tend to induce a decline in short-term
interest rates. It now becomes attractive for investors to place their surplus
funds in short-term earning assets abroad. If the balance of payments surplus
continues, long-term security yields in the country are also likely to decline,
leading investors to look abroad for profitable outlets for their funds. What
started as investment of excess savings over domestic investment in a balance
of payments surplus becomes gradually transformed into long-term foreign
investment (see page 398).

Now both a surplus in one country's balance of payments and more attractive long-term investment outlets abroad will tend to coexist when, during
the recovery phase of the business cycle, that country's recovery lags somewhat
behind recovery in other nations. For a lag in recovery means that expansion
is faster elsewhere; this in turn ensures both a balance of payments surplus to
the laggard and better investment prospects abroad.

Indeed, the historical record shows that foreign investment, like domestic
investment, tends to follow a cyclical pattern, typically getting under way during recovery, rising to a peak during prosperity, and falling sharply, even ceasing altogether, during recession and depression. Domestic investment and
foreign investment grow together. International investment is not a rival inhibiting home investment, but is its companion. The lending country need not
suffer unemployment and depression, as required by the usual gold standard
analysis of a capital transfer, but may enjoy rising business activity in company
with the borrower.

Given only that expansion is more rapid in the capital-receiving country,
the investing country's initial balance of payments surplus could readily be
enlarged, permitting a rising volume of net foreign investment. For then
additional sums put at the borrower's disposal would either be spent on imports of capital goods or be used for investment in physical assets, in which
case income and therewith imports would be increased. In either event, the
lending or investing country would tend to see its exports rise, increasing its
balance of payments surplus and thus its net transfer of capital.

When, as increasingly in recent years, long-term international loans are
made by relatively rich, developed countries to relatively poor, less developed
ones, the need for any transfer mechanism largely vanishes. The appetite of
the underdeveloped countries for capital goods to carry out their development
plans, and for other essential imports, is so voracious that the loans are spent

as soon as they become available.[15] Indeed, the principal danger is that these countries may undertake to invest in their development sums considerably in excess of domestic savings and foreign loans and aid, with internal inflation and balance-of-payments deficits as consequences. Instead of the lending country suffering a loss of reserves, it is the borrower who is more likely to do so.

When international lending is not eased by simultaneous expansion in the lending and borrowing countries, or by the spending proclivities of the borrower, the theoretical transfer mechanism may be needed. Sometimes, as with German reparations payments in the 1920's, it may not be easy to get it started (see Chapter 23). Or, as with the United States in the years after 1958, the export of capital may add to existing balance-of-payments strain. Or an outflow of capital may be more than a country's balance of payments can stand, and may lead to the introduction of exchange controls. If the mechanism is allowed to operate, however, it can effect a sizeable international transfer of capital along the lines described by the traditional theory.

[15] If the borrowing country is free to spend the loan proceeds where it wishes (i.e., if the loan is "untied"), funds advanced by the lending country may get into the hands of other nations supplying imports to the borrower. Should these nations choose to hold part of the funds thus acquired (either as balances in the lending country or in the form of gold) rather than spend them on imports from the lender, to this extent the latter has failed to make a net international transfer of capital of the amount intended.

(For Selected References, see end of Chapter 20.)

20

BALANCE-OF-PAYMENTS ADJUSTMENT: ADDITIONAL METHODS

ADJUSTMENT WHEN CURRENCIES ARE INDEPENDENT AND EXCHANGE RATES FREE TO FLUCTUATE

Meaning of an Independent Currency

We have seen that when exchange rates are fixed, disturbances to a country's balance of payments result in compensatory financing. A deficit must somehow be financed; normally, this is accomplished by a reduction in the country's international reserves—by a gold flow or some other form of compensatory financing. Barring an offsetting inward movement of capital or deliberate action by the monetary authorities, the money supply declines by the excess in the purchase of foreign exchange by importers over the sale of foreign exchange by exporters.

When foreign exchange rates are free to fluctuate, however, with the monetary authorities taking no steps to stabilize these rates, currencies are independent. *Disturbances to a nation's balance of payments have no direct effect on its money supply.* This can be made clear by an illustration.

Let us take Germany as our country, and let the mark/dollar exchange rate represent foreign exchange relations between Germany and the rest of the world. These will exclude capital movements, so that transactions are confined to trade in goods and services. We start from an equilibrium position, with the demand for and supply of foreign exchange as represented in Figure 20.1, (D_m and S_x) effecting a balance of international payments and receipts at a rate of exchange of 4 marks per dollar. At this rate exports are equal in value to imports, in terms either of dollars or marks. (The dollar value of each is $100 million; the mark value is 4×100 or 400 million marks.)

Now suppose that, as in our earlier illustration, the country for some reason experiences a decline in its exports. The supply of foreign exchange shifts to

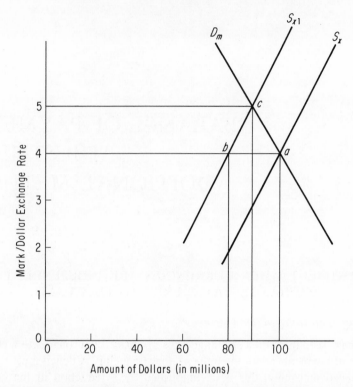

FIGURE 20.1   Adjustment with Flexible Exchange Rates: Inelastic Demand

the left, to the new position S_{x1}. If nothing else happened, the value of exports (in dollars) would fall to $80 million, while imports remained unchanged at $100 million. A gap or deficit of $20 million in the balance of payments would emerge.

Adjustment Through Depreciation

Since the exchange rate is free to move, however, it will rise to 5 mks./$, at which demand and the new supply schedule are in equilibrium. At this new rate, since imports are now more costly in domestic currency, certain buyers of dollars withdraw from the market—there is a movement along the demand curve from a to c. Similarly, Germany's exports are now cheaper abroad, so there will be a partial recovery of exports, shown by a movement along the new supply curve from b to c. Exports and imports are brought to equality at the 5 mks./$ exchange rate (at $90 million), and the potential deficit in the balance of payments is prevented from appearing. The change in the exchange rate, or currency depreciation, performs the entire task of adjusting to the disturbance in the balance of payments. The degree of this depreciation depends, as we saw in Chapter 18, on the elasticities underlying the demand and supply of foreign exchange.

With depreciation bringing Germany's purchases and sales of foreign exchange into balance at the 5 mks./$ rate, no change will take place in Germany's money supply. At the initial exchange rate of 4 mks./$, exporters added $4 \times 100 = 400$ million marks to the money supply from the sale of their bills of exchange to commercial banks. Simultaneously, importers took an equivalent amount of money out of circulation by their purchase of bills of exchange. At the new rate of exchange and the new equilibrium position, the destruction of domestic money again matches the creation of money, though at a higher total figure (5×90 m. $= 450$ m.).

Nor will there be any net change in the German aggregate demand and hence in national income and output. The total value of exports in terms of marks is greater than before by 50 million marks, despite the decline in demand, because the dollar has *appreciated* by 25 per cent. Assuming that German exports are produced under conditions of constant cost, their prices in Germany remain the same. Abroad, they can be shaved by 20 per cent. Foreigners respond by increasing their purchases. Instead of spending only $80 million, as they had intended, by the price cuts they are enticed into spending $90 million. But at 5 mks./$, in Germany this yields 450 million marks, 50 million marks more than before the initial decline in demand. With export prices unchanged, the volume of exports, employment in the export industries, and income paid out by them will be larger, too. Depreciation has caused an increment of output (dX) of 50 million marks to appear in the export sector, which will tend to raise income still further by means of the multiplier.[1]

At the same time that national income generated in the export sector has increased as a result of depreciation, however, national expenditure on imports has increased in equal amount. Simultaneously with the rise in exports of 50 million, an identical sum will be diverted from expenditure on domestic goods and services (C, I, or G). There will be a decrement in output in the domestic sector ($-dC$, for example) that will offset the increment dX in the export sector.[2] Only if the increased outlay on imports is partially or wholly at the expense of saving will there be any net increase of money income, real income, or employment.

It should be noted, however, that although there need not be (and under

[1] Had we assumed rising costs of production of exports in Germany (elasticity of supply less than infinite), any price cuts abroad would have had to be smaller, and the consequent rise in purchases smaller, too. At the limit, with German elasticity of supply = 0, *German* prices would have been cut, foreign prices would have remained unchanged, and foreign expenditure on German exports would be constant. In general, the extent of price reductions abroad, and thus the stimulus to increased sales (given the foreign elasticity of demand), will vary directly with export elasticity of supply.

[2] The exact outcome will depend on supply elasticities in the two sectors. Contraction in the domestic sector will offset the expansion in the export sector in terms of output and employment as well as in terms of value in the event that these elasticities are equal.

the assumption of equal supply elasticities in the two sectors, will not be) any change in income or output, there is likely to be a decline in real income due to the terms of trade effect of depreciation. In the simplest case, with the elasticity of supply of both imports and exports infinite, the domestic price of exports will remain unchanged, while the domestic price of imports will rise in proportion to the exchange rate. Thus the terms of trade turn against Germany. A larger volume of exports is required to pay for a reduced quantity of imports. There is therefore a decline in real income in the sense of consumers' satisfaction, though there is no change in aggregate output. In general, import prices in a country will rise more than export prices, and the terms of trade will turn against it, unless the elasticity of supply of imports is less than the elasticity of supply of exports.

Suppose, however, that the demand for foreign exchange had been more elastic, as in Figure 20.2. To effect the same degree of depreciation as before

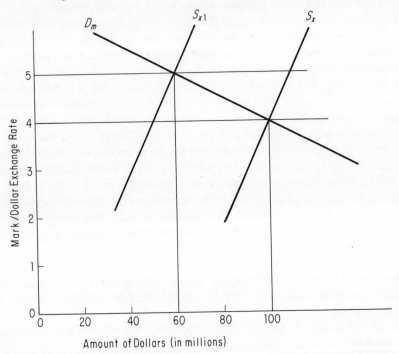

FIGURE 20.2   Adjustment with Flexible Exchange Rates: Elastic Demand

(to 5 mks./$), a greater shift of the supply curve would be required, as in the diagram. The foreign value of exports falls from $100 million to $60 million, their domestic value from 400 million to 300 million marks. The domestic value of export production is now 100 million marks *less* than before the disturbance; if export prices are unchanged, output and employment in the export sector are also lower. Taken by itself, this decline in export production ($-dX$) would cause income to contract still further.[3]

But since we have assumed an elastic demand for imports, their total value and expenditure on them likewise declines by 100 million marks. Unless consumers decide to save some part of this money formerly spent on imports, it will be diverted to the purchase of domestic substitutes. Therefore output and employment rise in the domestic sector, providing an increment (say dC) that offsets the decline in the export industries. As in the former illustration, income, output, and employment remain constant.

Since, as before, import prices have risen relative to export prices, the terms of trade will have turned against Germany. A unit of exports will now buy a smaller quantity of imports. Although aggregate income is unchanged, the enjoyment derived from it declines.

Both the situations considered are identical in one respect: the adjustment of the balance of payments disturbance through exchange depreciation need have no effect on aggregate demand and thus on national income produced. They differ in that when the demand for foreign exchange is inelastic, export production expands while the diversion of expenditure to imports causes production of domestic goods to decline; when, on the other hand, the demand for foreign exchange is elastic, both the value and the volume of exports shrinks, while the reduced value of imports signals a shift of expenditure to import substitutes and expanded production in that sector. This is just what we would expect from the analysis presented in Chapter 18. There we saw that the elasticity of demand for imports (and thus the demand for foreign exchange) depends not only on the elasticity of demand for import-type goods, but also on the presence of actual and potential import substitutes and on their elasticity of supply (see Figure 18.2). An inelastic demand for foreign exchange thus suggests the absence of such substitutes, while an elastic demand suggests ample possibilities of import substitution under conditions of relatively elastic supply.

One further point is worth noting: the initial degree of depreciation necessary to adjust a balance of payments disturbance will likely be more than that needed after some time has passed. As our earlier study of elasticities showed, it takes time for exporters to expand output and to extend market connections; similarly, consumers of substitutes for imports require time to discover them, and producers to improve their marketing facilities and to increase production. Some time—a year or two—after a given disturbance, the elasticities determining the shape of the foreign exchange curves should in-

---

[3] The outcome would be similar if—instead of shifting the S_x curve sufficiently, in the face of the more elastic demand, to cause the exchange rate to rise to 5 mks./$—we had shifted it by the same amount as in Figure 20.1. Then the exchange rate would have risen only to about 4.5 mks./$, with foreign expenditure on German exports at approximately $80 million. This would yield German exporters, in marks, only 4.5×80 million $= 360$ million marks—again, less than the 400 million of export sales with which we began.

crease, thereby increasing the elasticity and diminishing the steepness of those curves. This will cause the equilibrium exchange rate to fall below the initial or impact level.

Internal Effects of Depreciation

Certain indirect effects of the inevitable changes in price relationships must now be taken into account. The *direct* enect of higher import prices, and of possibly higher (domestic) export prices too, upon the home demand for imports and the foreign demand for exports, has already been reckoned with in arriving at determinate values for the elasticity of the foreign exchange curves. But if imported raw materials are used in producing exports, their costs will be raised. Moreover, if imports enter significantly into the cost of living, demands for wage increases are almost certain to be heard. If such increases are granted, export costs will be further raised. And if wages increase, expenditures on imports will almost certainly be greater.

To reflect the worsened conditions under which exports are supplied, the supply curve of foreign exchange (S_{x1}) would have to be raised somewhat above the position shown in the diagram. With larger imports, so too would the demand curve (D_m). Depreciation of the mark would be slightly greater than originally shown, but unless these price changes set off a wage-price spiral of inflation, the foreign exchange market and the balance of payments should come to rest at a somewhat higher rate of exchange.

Need for Monetary Restraint

Clearly, a policy of monetary restraint would be needed to offset the inflationary tendencies. If the supply of credit were held constant, employers would be unable to finance wage increases and would have to refuse them, possibly at the cost of strikes. Furthermore, at the expense of some actual contraction of credit and diminution of income, even the adverse effect on the balance of payments of higher prices of imports used to produce exports could be counteracted, for any reduction of income would cause the demand for imports to fall.

The need for a restrictive monetary policy to offset the adverse, indirect price effects of currency depreciation depends, of course, upon how much export prices are raised. A study by staff members of the International Monetary Fund[4] indicates that this rise is only 5 to 6 per cent of the amount of the depreciation under conditions of depression. If the depreciation were 20 per cent, the rise in export prices would be insignificant—only about 1 per cent; with a 50 per cent depreciation, it would still be only 2½ to 3 per cent. With

---

[4] See J. J. Polak and T. C. Chang, "Effect of Exchange Depreciation on a Country's Export Price Level," *Staff Papers*, Vol. I, No. 1 (1950-51), International Monetary Fund, Washington, D. C. The results of this study are rather inconclusive with respect to conditions of prosperity, owing partly to the small number of case studies and to the admixture of other price-raising forces in the main example (France, 1936-37).

prosperity, however, the rise of export prices appears to be much greater—30 per cent or more of the amount of depreciation. This means a rise of export prices of 6 per cent or more if the depreciation is 20 per cent, of 15 per cent or more if it is 50 per cent.

The danger is negligible if depreciation occurs when the economy is depressed, but under conditions of prosperity it could be serious, especially if the depreciation is substantial. Clearly, if depreciation is to be relied upon as a means of adjusting to an adverse change in the balance of payments, and if it occurs during a period of prosperity, a policy of monetary restraint will be in order. But that is precisely the time when it will do the least harm to the economy. It is also clear that at such a time the extent of the depreciation should be minimized.

Capital Transfer with Flexible Exchange Rates

To balance the discussion of the gold standard, let us consider how a transfer of capital is effected under conditions of flexible exchange rates. Let us suppose that a country, say Germany, begins a phase of lending abroad. To begin with, we shall assume that this foreign lending is at the expense of domestic investment.

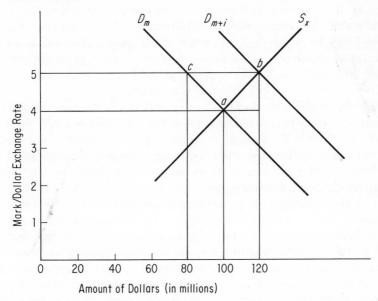

FIGURE 20.3 Capital Transfer Under Flexible Exchange Rates

Start, as in Figure 20.3, from a position of equilibrium in the balance of payments and the foreign exchange market, with demand for (D_m) and supply of (S_x) foreign exchange arising out of current transactions equal to one another at 4 marks/$. Now German investors undertake to purchase securities worth $40 million during a given balance of payments period, say a year. The demand for foreign exchange to pay for these securities, added to the normal demand for imports of goods and services, shifts the demand curve from D_m to D_{m+i}.

The exchange rate now rises to 5 mks./$. The supply of foreign exchange derived from exports expands from $100 million to $120 million, reflecting a movement along the supply curve from a to b. Import prices in home currency rise; the demand for import exchange shrinks from $100 million to $80 million. The excess of the supply of foreign exchange over the demand provides the $40 million needed to transfer the German investment abroad.

As for income and employment, this would tend to decrease because of the decline in domestic investment of 200 million marks ($= $40 million) in favor of foreign investment. But this income-depressing force would be offset by the rise in exports caused by depreciation. In the simplest case, with the domestic price of German exports constant, the rise in their value (200 million marks, from 4×100 to 5×120) would be accompanied by an equivalent rise in their volume and in export employment. This increment of income from exports (dX) would then just offset the decrement $(- dI)$ on the side of investment. If, however, export prices rose because of relatively full employment in that sector, total employment would diminish, at least for a time. But profits would likely be higher in that sector, stimulating investment in increased capacity, which would cause some of the idled workers in the industries producing investment goods to be reemployed. And as export capacity rose, more workers could be employed in export production.[5]

Were the foreign investment to be financed, not at the expense of domestic investment, but by the use of idle funds or the expansion of credit, there would then be no offset to the increase in exports. Income would rise, provided there were sufficient slack in the economy, in proportion to the multiplier. Under conditions of full employment, the income-generating forces would, of course, be largely dissipated in rising prices.

In our examination of the gold standard mechanism, we saw that the transfer of capital could be greatly facilitated if, at the time of transfer, expansionary forces were at work in the borrowing country. The same is true under fluctuating exchange rates. Expansion in the borrowing country will tend to cause its currency to depreciate, that of the lending country to appreciate. Capital transfer by the lender would then require little if any depreciation; this would depend on the relative strength of the expansionary forces in the borrowing country and the size of the capital movement.

---

[5] Industries formerly unable to compete in export markets would be able to do so after exchange depreciation. Shortage of capacity would limit this possibility at first, and prices would rise, just as in established export industries. But given time, with increased capacity prices might be reduced toward their original level, permitting additional exports to be realized.

THE EQUILIBRIUM RATE OF EXCHANGE

Our study of how, with freely fluctuating exchange rates, a disturbance to a country's balance of payments is adjusted has shown that equilibrium between autonomous international receipts and payments is restored by a rise in the exchange rate. Since the new rate establishes a new equilibrium in the balance of payments, it may appropriately be called an equilibrium rate. Are we, then, to mean by an equilibrium rate of exchange whatever rate exists when autonomous international receipts and payments are in balance?

What the Term Means

On a superficial level, the equilibrium rate may be described as the one that clears a nation's foreign exchange market, thereby bringing its autonomous international transactions into balance and restoring equilibrium in the balance of payments. Since this outcome requires a balanced relationship between a country's factor and commodity prices, its income, and its demands, and prices, incomes, and demands in the rest of the world, an equilibrium rate of exchange may be defined, in a more fundamental sense, as one that establishes this kind of balance.

An equilibrium rate will remain the same only so long as these underlying determinants are unchanged. Thus, if a given country's factor prices are altered, commodity prices will be different; so will the distribution of income. With changed commodity prices and a new distribution of income, expenditures at home and abroad will be affected; shifts will occur in the demand and supply of exchange; and balance-of-payments equilibrium will require a different exchange rate. Changes in real or money income in any part of the world will have similar consequences.

When Is an Exchange Rate an Equilibrium Rate?

How are we to tell when an equilibrium exchange rate, so defined, is realized? Is the absence of a deficit (or surplus) in the balance of payments an adequate test? Must this balance be attained every day, every month, every year? What is the relevant time period?

THE TIME PERIOD   Let us consider the last question first. To what time period should an equilibrium rate of exchange refer? Changes in demand occur almost continually; price changes are frequent; and national incomes vary somewhat even from month to month.

Strict logic would seem to require, in a free exchange market, an equilibrium exchange rate varying almost from day to day. No country, however, would permit such instability. If stabilizing speculation did not counteract casual and seasonal disturbances, the monetary authorities would use the country's international reserves for this purpose. This implies, of course, that complete monetary independence, with completely free rates, would not be tolerated.

Suppose we take a year as the minimum period to which an equilibrium exchange rate is to refer, on the ground that a period of this length eliminates from consideration seasonal and casual disturbances. Then some specific rate should preserve international balance over that interval. Reserves will ebb and flow within this period in response to short-term fluctuations. But there should be no appreciable net change in a country's international reserves if the exchange rate is at the appropriate level. Over periods longer than a year, the equilibrium rate would vary with changes in prices, incomes, and demands.[6]

RESTRICTIVE MEASURES   Restrictions on trade or payments can eliminate a deficit just as effectively as the establishment of an equilibrium rate of exchange. They are a substitute for an appropriate change in the exchange rate (or in internal prices and incomes). The mere fact that a country has no deficit in its balance of payments is therefore no proof that its exchange rate is at the equilibrium level. Were we to restore the restrictions to their predeficit condition, the reappearance of a deficit would clearly show that the controlled rate was not an equilibrium rate.

UNEMPLOYMENT   Finally, we know that deflation is an effective means of eliminating a deficit. With mass unemployment and a low national income, an economy might balance its international payments; with full employment, that same economy would have to depreciate its currency to preserve balance-of-payments equilibrium. Thus different levels of employment are consistent with balance-of-payments equilibrium only at differing exchange rates.

Taking this fact into account, which of several exchange rates are we to regard as the equilibrium rate—only the one that will establish balance-of-payments equilibrium at full employment? Since full employment, or something closely approaching it, is a universal goal of national policy today, the answer has to be "yes." A country whose (autonomous) payments balanced only because of heavy unemployment would then be said to have an overvalued rate.

> Great Britain in the years 1925-1930 affords a good illustration of this point. There was little sign of disequilibrium in the British balance of payments, yet the pound was rightly regarded as overvalued. There was practically no net change in the British gold reserve during that period. . . . If we apply our definition of the equilibrium rate literally, the pound cannot be said to have been overvalued. The British balance of payments was kept in equilibrium, however, only at the cost of depressed conditions at home compared with conditions in the outside world.[7]

CONCLUSION   To conclude, we have three criteria of an equilibrium rate of exchange: (1) It refers to a period of at least a year; during that period there

[6] Nurkse has suggested that a period of five to ten years, sufficiently long to include a complete business cycle, is the appropriate period of reference for an equilibrium rate. But maintenance of a stable rate over such a long period, in the face of a major cyclical swing, would require the use of international reserves on a scale unattainable by most countries. See Ragnar Nurkse, "Conditions of International Monetary Equilibrium," *Essays in International Finance*, No. 4, Spring, 1945 (International Finance Section, Princeton University); reprinted in *Readings in the Theory of International Trade*.

[7] *Ibid.*, pp. 6-7.

must be no major change in international reserves. (2) Balance-of-payments equilibrium must be achieved without introducing new or intensifying old restrictions on trade. (3) This equilibrium must not require the existence of a significant volume of unemployment.

Purchasing Power Par

An attempt was made, after the first World War, to develop a concept of the equilibrium rate of exchange that would permit its measurement by readily available data. This concept is known as "purchasing power par." It holds that the equilibrium rate is one that equalizes the purchasing power of two currencies, and that the actual rate, if free to move, will approximate this rate.

Thus if in a given year, as compared with a base year when balance of payments equilibrium prevailed, prices in the United States have trebled, while in the United Kingdom they have risen only 50 per cent, the new equilibrium rate of exchange between the dollar and the pound will be double the old rate. Assuming that in the base year the exchange rate was $4 a pound, the purchasing power rate for the later year will be

$$\$4 \times \frac{300}{150} = \$8.$$

Rigorously interpreted, the purchasing power par doctrine assumes that relative commodity prices are the sole determinant of international transactions. We know this is not true. We have encountered many causes of balance-of-payments disequilibrium besides changes in commodity prices. We need only mention variations in the rate of flow of capital, in service payments, and in the level of real income.

Nonetheless, purchasing power par may be a useful first approximation to an equilibrium rate for periods dominated by price changes. To get a more accurate evaluation, one would then have to take into account concurrent changes in tastes, techniques, capital movements, and real income.

OBJECTIONS TO DEPRECIATION AND DEFLATION

The forgoing analysis has shown that adjustment to a balance-of-payments disequilibrium may be reached by either one of two distinct paths.

If a country maintains a completely independent currency, taking no steps to finance a deficit by drawing upon foreign balances and allowing exchange rates to be determined exclusively by market forces, the balance of payments will be adjusted (in the absence of destabilizing speculation) through a rise in exchange rates. No important change in national income need occur.

At the other extreme stands the case of an interdependent currency. Here the entire initial deficit is financed by sacrificing foreign balances or gold reserves; the exchange rate is not allowed to vary, but is held constant. In the course of time, the deficit is eliminated by the effect upon imports of the induced decline in income, reenforced by the effect upon both imports and exports of the accompanying decline of prices. The mechanism may be still further intensified by a multiple contraction of credit or by credit restriction deliberately imposed by the central bank.

Each of these methods of adjustment has aroused strong opposition. Exclusive reliance on variations in exchange rates encounters the objection that it implies, in practice, constantly fluctuating rates. An orderly, once-and-for-all shift from one equilibrium rate to another is held to be, in a world of constant change in demand and supply conditions, and in levels of income, highly improbable, a purely theoretical expectation based on unreal assumptions. Given the ever-varying conditions of the real world, exchange rates would fluctuate incessantly, increasing the risks of trading and therefore penalizing the conduct of trade. Even though well-organized forward exchange markets, by providing facilities for hedging, could greatly reduce this risk, it is contended— with some reason—that they could never encompass all trade and that they could not eliminate the risk entirely. Moreover, with fluctuating exchange rates, speculation is sure to appear, and when a currency is under pressure and there is no foreseeable limit to its depreciation, speculation is likely to be a destabilizing force. Finally, there is the fear that currency depreciation, through its effects on internal prices, may set off a spiral of inflation. For all these reasons, with the notable exception of Canada from 1950 to 1962, no country has for long tolerated completely free exchange rates.

Opposition to the income-and-price method of adjustment typified by the gold standard has been even more vigorous. If this adjustment mechanism is allowed to operate, it eliminates a balance of payments, or external disequilibrium, by replacing external with internal disequilibrium in the form of income deflation, unemployment, and reduced production. The cure, it is held, is worse than the disease.

To combat the deflationary effects of a decline in foreign exchange or gold reserves, many central banks in the 1920's adopted a policy of neutralizing or sterilizing these movements. When a balance-of-payments deficit caused a contraction of deposits and a loss of bank reserves, this was offset by the purchase by the central bank of open-market securities. Thereby bank reserves were replenished, leaving the credit base, at least, relatively unaffected. A similar offsetting of gold inflows was effected through the open-market sale of securities. By this practice, a country's money supply and, to a degree, its national income, were insulated from influences originating in the balance of payments.

A COMPROMISE SOLUTION: CONTROLLED DEPRECIATION AND DEVALUATION

A compromise solution to the problem of international adjustment was sought in the 1930's in attempts to combine both methods of adjustment in a workable mixture.

Controlled Depreciation

One such effort places principal reliance upon exchange rate variations. But these are either held within certain limits or else depreciation is allowed to take place only in a gradual and controlled manner. An instrument to achieve this end is needed; most countries found it in a fund specifically set up for the purpose of exchange stabilization.[8] These *exchange stabilization funds* smoothed out seasonal and speculative fluctuations in exchange rates by buying foreign currencies when these rates fell and selling them when they rose. Rate movements due to the more basic forces of demand and supply of exchange for goods, services, and long-term capital transfers were moderated, even sometimes offset, in a similar manner. The various funds also to a large degree insulated the domestic money supply against change by the manner of their operation.

Thus the British Exchange Equalization Account, when the balance of payments was under pressure and the pound tended to depreciate, supported the pound by exchanging gold in its possession for foreign exchange, which it supplied to satisfy the excess demand for foreign exchange at the existing rate. It received pounds sterling from importers and speculators.

If it hoarded these pounds, the effect was, of course, deflationary. But the Account usually turned them over to the money market through the purchase of short-term Treasury bills. Thus the domestic supply of money remained constant; all that happened was a change of ownership.[9] Only to the extent that changes in the supply of money and in national income were consistent with the objectives of monetary policy were they allowed to occur.

Britain used this technique exclusively from June, 1932, until early 1940, after which it was combined with exchange controls. From about the end of the first year of the prewar experience, fluctuations in the crucial dollar/sterling rate were held within a range of only slightly over 10 per cent. France's record was similar, though over a shorter period. Between November, 1933, and September, 1936, the franc/dollar rate remained within approximately the same range.

Devaluation

A second compromise between stable exchange rates and freely fluctuating rates has been worked out gradually, coming to prominence since World War II when it was officially embodied in the charter of the International Monetary Fund. This is devaluation of a currency that is under pressure, from its overvalued level to a lower level that, it is hoped, will restore equilibrium. A

---

[8] As, for example, Belgium, Canada, France, the Netherlands, Switzerland, the United Kingdom, and the United States.

[9] This is subject to some qualification so far as the Exchange Equalization Account transactions were with banks rather than with the public or nonbanking institutions.

sharp and definitive downward revision of a currency's value is substituted for gradual and controlled, but somewhat indefinite, depreciation.

To correct a balance-of-payments disequilibrium, devaluation relies upon the stimulus to exports and the check to imports characteristic of currency depreciation (rising exchange rates). It avoids the deflationary contraction of income typical of adjustment when exchange rates are fixed. But since devaluation would only be used to combat a severe disequilibrium, it is to be presumed that changes in exchange rates would be infrequent. Thus it combines the merits of the relatively easier adjustment process of fluctuating rates and of stability of exchange rates over considerable periods.

As with freely fluctuating and flexible rates, the effectiveness of devaluation depends, in the first instance, at least, upon the elasticity of the demand and supply of foreign exchange. If, for special reasons, these are very low, devaluation either would not restore equilibrium at all, or would have to be excessive. As we have suggested, however, it seems reasonable to expect that, for any single country, these elasticities are likely to be substantial, especially if sufficient time is allowed for the full effect of revised price relationships to register.

Income Effects of Devaluation

We saw that when exchange rates are free to fluctuate, depreciation need have no appreciable effect on total national income, since expansion in, say, the export sector will be offset in whole or in part by a contraction in the domestic sector.

The outcome will normally be different, however, when a country devalues its currency. For the decision to devalue is made to correct a preexisting deficit in the balance of payments that has continued for some time. This means that when corrective action is taken, we start with imports in excess of exports. Devaluation now brings exports and imports into equality. For this to occur, if the domestic value of both increases, that of exports must increase *more than* the domestic value of imports. Hence there is bound to be a net increase in income.

In terms of the national income equation
$$Y = C + I + G + (X - M),$$
we start (before devaluation) with M greater than X; the net contribution of $(X - M)$ to national income is negative. Devaluation now causes the value of M in domestic money to rise. The value of X must rise still more if it is to be brought to equality with M, whereas with fluctuating exchange rates, the two were equal to begin with and remained equal after depreciation had taken place. In other words, in the case of devaluation, there is an increment of income that is not offset by the effects of a decrement of income elsewhere in the economy. We may add that if, as the total value of exports rises, export prices remain constant (or rise less than in proportion to the exchange rate), there will be an increase in real income as well as in money income.

This income effect of devaluation must be reckoned with in judging the efficacy of devaluation as a balance-of-payments corrective. For with increased income, imports will rise. A deficit will reappear. It is even possible that the increase in income and in imports will be so great as nearly to swamp the price and elasticity effects of devaluation, with the end result that the deficit is almost as large as before.

How great the "reversal effect" of induced income changes will be will depend, first, on the rise in income and thus on the multiplier, and second, on the marginal propensity to import. This effect has been neatly expressed in a reversal coefficient stated in terms of the marginal propensity to save and the marginal propensity to import.[10] If, before devaluation, the economy is less than fully employed, then with reasonably normal values of s and m, the income reversal effect will offset the price effect to only a limited degree. If, however, the economy is fully employed, money income, but not real income, will increase; domestic prices will rise; and expenditure will be shunted onto imports and exports, greatly raising the value of m. Under inflationary conditions, the marginal propensity to save will tend to be very low, possibly even negative. Though the multiplier will be small, most or all of the increase in income will be spent on imports or on exportables. Any favorable influence on the balance of payments from the price effect of devaluation will then be largely swamped by the income effect.

As a remedy for balance of payments disequilibrium, therefore, devaluation is least likely to be successful when an economy is fully employed. If, despite this, a country chose at such a time to devalue its currency to combat an adverse balance of payments, it would be imperative simultaneously to pursue a vigorous internal policy of deflation. Without such a policy, internal inflation would be added to a worsened external payments situation.

[10] S. Alexander, "Effects of a Devaluation: A Simplified Synthesis of Elasticities and Absorption Approaches," *American Economic Review*, Vol. **XLIX** (March, 1959). If the initial improvement in the balance of payments resulting from the price effects of devaluation is E_f, the reversal effect can be expressed as

$$\frac{1}{1 + \dfrac{m_1}{s_1} + \dfrac{m_2}{s_2}}$$

where s and m have the usual meanings, the subscript "1" refers to the devaluing country and "2" to the rest of the world. The net improvement in the balance of payments will then be

$$\frac{E_f}{1 + \dfrac{m_1}{s_1} + \dfrac{m_2}{s_2}}$$

Since Alexander's analysis starts with the balance of payments in equilibrium, this result has to be modified somewhat if one starts from a deficit position.

Speculation and Devaluation

Adoption of devaluation as an official policy carries the implication that it will be used infrequently. For relatively long periods, therefore, a country's currency would be pegged at a fixed exchange rate. This combination of fixed rates with occasional revaluation has been named the "adjustable peg" system. Like most compromises, it has certain disadvantages of its own. Perhaps the most serious disadvantage of the adjustable peg system is the sure profit it guarantees speculators when a change in the peg appears imminent.

So long as speculators were confident that a currency would be maintained at its pegged rate, they would be willing to support that currency. This would be true when it was not overvalued, and the country's balance of payments was in substantial equilibrium. Then, with an upper limit to exchange rate fluctuations, established either by attachment of the currency to gold or by strong official support, speculators could gain by selling foreign currencies when demand for them was strong, confident that they could be repurchased later at a lower price.

But let the currency become overvalued, with serious balance of payments pressures making themselves felt, then speculators would have every motive to move against the pegged and overvalued currency. For they could purchase unlimited amounts of foreign currencies at the fixed rate (so long as official support continued) with the certainty that eventually, when devaluation became necessary, they could sell these currencies at a higher rate. Such speculation would simply add to the pressure on the balance of payments and hasten the exhaustion of the country's reserves. While not destabilizing in the sense of being perverse, or going contrary to reasonable expectations, it is against the national interest and serves only to enrich the speculators.

To avoid an unnecessary loss of reserves and providing speculators with a windfall gain, devaluation should be undertaken promptly once the need for it becomes apparent. This, of course, poses a difficult problem of timing for a country's monetary authorities; it also explains the strong official denials that always precede a currency devaluation.

Conclusion

Despite the danger of inducing unwanted speculation, devaluation can be an effective remedy for the balance-of-payments difficulties of a single country. This is particularly true when the cause of its difficulties is a previous overvaluation of its currency.

Devaluation must be used with caution. It is almost certain to be ineffective if applied at a time of full employment unless accompanied by restrictive monetary and fiscal policies. Even when some slack in the economy favors its use, monetary restraint is imperative to check the expansion of income and the rise in prices sure to be set in motion. Since devaluation affects the trade of other countries adversely, however, there is a danger—especially when many countries suffer from balance-of-payments problems—that devaluation may become competitive. This possibility suggests the need for international consultation and agreement, a topic we shall explore more fully when we consider the provisions of the International Monetary Fund (see Chapter 26).

SELECTED REFERENCES

Alexander, Sidney S., "Effects of Devaluation on a Trade Balance," *IMF Staff Papers*, Vol. V. (April, 1952). An extension of the income analysis that stresses the favorable effect of devaluation as consisting in its reduction of absorption (real expenditure), which permits the release of goods for export.

————, "Effects of a Devaluation: A Simplified Synthesis of Elasticities and Absorption Approaches," *American Economic Review*, **XLIX** (March, 1959). Reconciles the price and income effects of devaluation by introducing a "reversal factor."

Bloomfield, Arthur I., *Monetary Policy Under the International Gold Standard, 1880-1914*. New York: Federal Reserve Bank of New York, 1959. Reinterprets the working of the gold standard in the light of further evidence.

Kindleberger, Charles P., *International Economics*, 3rd ed. Homewood, Ill.: Richard D. Irwin, Inc.,.1963. Part VI provides an extended and relatively advanced discussion of cyclical, secular, and structural disequilibrium and of the means of adjustment.

Lary, Hal B., *The United States in the World Economy*. Washington, D. C.: Government Printing Office, 1943. Still one of the best treatments of the U.S. balance of payments during the interwar period.

League of Nations, *International Currency Experience* (1944). The interwar experience with international monetary relations. Chapters IV and V are especially relevant to these chapters.

Meade, James E., *The Balance of Payments*. New York: Oxford University Press, 1951. A book of broad scope, with its central concern the means of realizing both internal and external balance.

Whale, P. B., "The Working of the Prewar Gold Standard," *Economica*, **IV** (1937). An enlightening discussion of the gold standard before 1914.

21

EXCHANGE CONTROL

CONVERTIBILITY AND ADJUSTMENT

A common feature shared by the two major methods of adjustment we have examined, flexible exchange rates and the gold standard, is that neither of them involves any direct interference with the operation of market forces. Purchases can be made in the cheapest market and sales in the dearest, or where they are most badly needed. Moreover, international payments can be made in any currency, in any amounts, and for any purpose. Thus whether adjustment is through fluctuating exchange rates or stable rates with deflation (or some combination of the two), currencies remain fully convertible. Any intervention, as when a government supports the value of its currency by sales of foreign exchange, is indirect, affecting the results of market forces, but leaving those forces themselves free to function in their normal manner.

Exchange control, the remaining alternative means of dealing with balance of payments difficulties, differs radically in that in essence it disregards market forces and substitutes for them the arbitrary decisions of government officials. Imports and other international payments are no longer determined solely by international price comparisons, but also by considerations of national need. Not only is government intervention direct rather than indirect, but since the core of exchange control is a set of restrictions on international payments, convertibility is also sacrificed.

LEADING FEATURES OF EXCHANGE CONTROL

A full-fledged system of exchange control aims at establishing complete government domination over the foreign exchange market. All receipts from exports and other sources must be surrendered to the control authorities. To ensure against evasion, export licenses, which certify the delivery of foreign exchange to these authorities, must be presented to customs officials before shipment is permitted. The available supply of foreign exchange is then allocated to the various competing buyers according to the criterion of relative

[368]

national importance. Capital exports are frequently banned, and interest and amortization payments are severely limited. Imports of goods essential to the functioning of the economy, such as basic foodstuffs, petroleum products, and raw materials of industry, receive relatively liberal rations of exchange, while luxuries and nonessentials fare poorly.

Not all systems of exchange control are so rigorous. If the balance-of-payments pressure is not severe, and especially if it derives mainly from the export of capital, the controls may involve no more than general supervision of applications for foreign exchange, together with informal limitations of certain categories of demand. For example, at the time Great Britain departed from the gold standard in 1931, it banned capital exports but set up no government control apparatus. It left the enforcement of this prohibition to the commercial banks.

Such mild forms of exchange control have generally been shortlived; they have been removed with the disappearance of the difficulties that brought them into being. Where the balance-of-payments pressure has continued, and especially when it has been severe, limited restrictions have given way to comprehensive and rigorous controls.

WHY EXCHANGE CONTROL?

Why should a country faced with a deficit in its balance of payments not rely upon the automatic mechanism of fluctuating exchange rates or of deflation, or upon some compromise between the two? Why should it, instead, sacrifice both convertibility of its currency and reliance upon the self-regulating forces of the market, and erect a cumbersome bureaucracy to enforce arbitrary judgments? There must be powerful reasons to explain the great popularity of exchange controls, which for many years after World War II were in one form or another all but universal, and even before the war were used by many European and most Latin American countries.

Defects of Automatic Methods

The answers to these questions are to be found in defects, real or fancied, in the automatic methods of adjustment, and in the superior effectiveness of exchange control for coming to grips with certain types of disturbances.

As we have already noted, the gold standard, the archetype of the system of fixed exchange rates, requires in the deficit country a decline of income and employment, accompanied by a contraction in the supply of money and by falling prices. This is a severe discipline, submission to which implies—unless the disturbance and the consequent adjustment are relatively mild—a degree of fortitude and an ability to ignore outraged opinion that no democratic government possesses.

Freely fluctuating exchange rates, by restoring an equilibrium relation between internal and external prices, afford a solution that avoids disturbance of the deficit country's economy. But many fear that fluctuating rates will set off destabilizing capital movements and thus induce excessive depreciation. Even in the absence of speculation, depreciation may have to be excessive for the exceptional country whose demand and supply of foreign exchange are both of fairly low elasticity. Finally, some countries have bitter memories of depreciation accompanied by inflation, and wrongly attribute causation to the former. For them, even devaluation or flexible but controlled exchange rates are remedies to be shunned.

Exchange Control as a Check to Capital Exports

Such rational or irrational objections to the available alternatives go far to explain the adoption of exchange control. But in addition, exchange control possesses one positive advantage. This is its special effectiveness for dealing with capital movements. Many exchange control systems of the 1930's originated because of this specific advantage, notably those of Germany, Denmark, and Argentina, among others.

If the government acquires an effective monopoly over the foreign exchange market, it can eliminate capital movements simply by refusing to make foreign exchange available for such transfers. In the event that the incentive to export capital is strong, measures supplementary to the basic technique of rationing will be necessary. The requirement that all foreign exchange be surrendered to the control authorities can be evaded by under-billing exports or over-billing imports. An export shipment, in fact worth $10 thousand, may be billed to the foreign importer at $8 thousand, with the understanding that the difference will be paid into a foreign bank account in the exporter's name. Or, by prior agreement an exporter abroad bills the domestic importer at an excessive value; on the basis of his invoice the importer obtains the foreign exchange and pays the exporter, who deposits the excess in the importer's foreign bank account. To block these methods of exporting capital requires a constant study of markets by commodity experts and the checking of invoices against this information.

How effectively can fluctuating exchange rates discourage capital exports? Although the cost of acquiring foreign currencies rises with depreciation, this rise is no serious deterrent to capital in search of a safe haven. Price is no object when safety of one's principal is in question.

With stable rates, on the other hand, the only check to the capital export comes from a relative increase in interest rates in the deficit country. This may attract an equilibrating or stabilizing movement of capital if the country's balance-of-payments problem is not severe and if confidence in the maintenance of the exchange rate (that is, the gold standard) is consequently high. But if the pressure of international payments is intense, a rise in discount rates may simply generate uncertainty, thereby stimulating what it was aimed to prevent. If a fear-motivated capital flight is already under way, even large differences of interest rates will be of small consequence.

As a means of checking a flight of capital, exchange control is clearly superior to either fluctuating exchange rates or the deterrent of high discount rates.

In general, exchange control deals with balance-of-payments disequilibrium by suppressing the deficit that is a symptom, not the basic trouble. When the deficit is due to capital flight, suppressing the deficit does not cure the underlying cause: political or economic uncertainty, fear of war, or expected devaluation. In all other situations, also, exchange control fails to come to grips with basic causes.

Even so, it may be the only possible choice for some countries, especially if their reserves are inadequate to support a fixed exchange rate while deflation takes hold or if the factors underlying their demand and supply of foreign exchange are exceptionally adverse. In such circumstances, exchange control can be justified as a temporary measure, to gain time while other steps are taken to restore equilibrium.

THE LOGIC OF RESTRICTIONISM

Once exchange controls are introduced, they are apt, especially under conditions of widespread balance-of-payments strain, to set up a train of increasing restrictions. As we shall see, trade is forced ever more into bilateral channels; more and more countries are drawn into the system of controls; and convertibility of currencies becomes increasingly limited. If no check is interposed, these developments are likely to continue until exchange control becomes practically universal—the world market is fragmented into a number of isolated regions among which the kinds of things traded are determined by availability of supplies without much regard to comparative cost, and the volume of trade is shrunk down to a minimum.

Insulation Removes Restraints

What sets this logic of restrictionism into operation is the insulation that exchange control gives an economy against outside forces. The external deficit that led to the imposition of controls has been removed; the balance of payments is in a strait jacket; and any loss of reserves can be checked or eliminated. The country has acquired freedom of action with respect to internal policies that might affect the balance of payments.

No government is apt to delay very long using this newly found freedom, usually in a way that increases the supply of money and credit. Monetary and fiscal disciplines are difficult and unpopular, and there are many attractive national goals—maintenance of full employment, economic development, postwar reconstruction, raising the standard of living—whose pursuit inevitably leads along the path of monetary expansion. Some countries will follow this primrose path reluctantly and slowly, some rapidly.

Overvaluation

Let us assume that the initial disequilibrium that forced the introduction of exchange control in one or a number of countries was due to capital flight. Current accounts—the trade and service items—were in equilibrium—which means that costs, prices, and incomes in the different countries were also in equilibrium at the existing level of exchange rates. Even so, if easy-spending monetary and fiscal policies are followed, prices and incomes in the insulated countries will rise. Exports are overpriced abroad and tend to shrink; imports are underpriced at home and tend to expand. Imports rise the more because people's money incomes have risen. Currencies become *overvalued* at the controlled rates. Controls over imports are now necessary.

Producers of goods competing with imports (whose types and quantities are now determined by administrative decision rather than by international price comparisons) have less incentive to keep a close watch on costs, since the threat of foreign competition has been removed. Moreover, with rising money incomes, pressure from the demand side also tends to raise their prices. And restriction of imports is itself directly inflationary: with quantitative limits on their supply, imports rise in price. Overvaluation of the currency becomes ever greater unless offset by deflationary measures.

Bilateral Channeling of Trade

A country in this position almost inevitably is forced to search for new outlets for its exports and for new sources of imports. The accustomed markets, so far as they are in countries with convertible currencies, become increasingly constricted. Because of its overvalued currency, its exports are overpriced, and its imports are cheap, attractive, but insufficient. If some other countries have introduced exchange controls, they are probably in the same fix. What is more natural than that two or more such countries should get together? All have a common interest in augmenting both imports and exports; all that is required is some device making it unnecessary to pay in scarce, convertible currencies.

Out of such shared difficulties and interests have arisen various forms of bilateral trading arrangements, the essence of which is agreement to accept one another's inconvertible currencies in payment for exports and to use them to acquire imports. (We shall examine some of these arrangements in more detail shortly.)

If only one country adopts controls, its currency becomes inconvertible by the very fact that use of that currency is restricted. This inconvertibility is nondiscriminatory, however; restrictions apply equally to the purchase of any other currency. But with the spread of exchange control and of its inevitable companion, bilateral trading arrangements, restrictions quickly become discriminatory. Applications for foreign exchange are granted readily if the currency desired is that of a bilateral trading partner, where balances can be easily acquired. But if it is a free or convertible currency, applications are rigidly restricted. The world becomes divided into "hard" and "soft" currency areas, one with convertible currencies, the other regulating convertibility with varying degrees of discrimination.

This division of the world encourages the further spread of exchange controls; for a country still adhering to convertibility finds that although its balance of payments, as a total, is in over-all balance, it has a surplus with the soft currency bloc, a deficit with the hard currency area. To deal with the latter, depreciation or deflation would be appropriate, but either policy would tend to increase its surplus in inconvertible currencies. The country needs to reduce exports to, and increase imports from, the soft currency area—and the reverse with respect to the hard currency countries. It may find that to do this it is obliged to introduce exchange controls itself.

BILATERAL TRADING ARRANGEMENTS

Private Compensation

Among the earliest forms of bilateral trade were barter deals undertaken by private firms. These were common in the 1930's; although largely superseded by more formal arrangements, they continued to be used after the war. Thus in the early thirties, German coal producers arranged for the export to Brazil of nine million marks worth of coal, obtaining in exchange an equal value of coffee. German fertilizer was similarly exchanged for Egyptian cotton.

Somewhat more complicated arrangements, having the advantage of releasing the exporter from also performing the unaccustomed functions of an importer, involved an export and import firm in *each* country. Agreement had to be reached on what commodities would be exported, in what quantities, and at what values. Upon receipt of the goods, the importer in each country paid the exporters *in the importing country's currency,* and the transaction was completed.

All such arrangements require the approval of the exchange control authorities, even though they avoid the need to apply for an allocation of foreign exchange. Not only are exports and imports both subject to license; it is also the duty of the authorities to see that exports that can, in spite of difficulties, be sold for scarce, free currencies are not needlessly diverted from these markets. Hence it has generally been necessary for firms engaging in such deals to show that their exports were "'additional"—that is, that except for some special arrangement, they could not be sold. This tends to give weight in this type of trade to relatively unimportant or fringe items in the exports of each partner.

Private compensation requires that the individual exports and imports of each transaction offset each other. This puts upon the exporter wishing to consummate such a deal the responsibility of ascertaining what imports are acceptable both to the exchange control authorities and to buyers in his country. Even when a fellow countryman among importers is drawn into the arrangement, it is still necessary for the two parties to find one another. To overcome such difficulties, specialized brokers emerged before the war in Germany and other countries, devoting their energies to uncovering possibilities of mutually advantageous and permissible trade, and to finding and bringing together potentially interested parties.

Clearing Agreements

A more satisfactory solution to these problems was found with the development of *exchange clearing,* which broadens and generalizes the offsetting procedure. Each country enters into an agreement to establish, usually in its central bank, an account through which all payments for imports and exports shall be cleared.[1]

Argentina and Italy in 1952 entered into a five-year agreement of this type. For all imports from Italy into Argentina, payments by importers had to be made into the Argentine clearing account in pesos. Similarly, Italians importing Argentine goods made payments into the Italian clearing account in lire. Exporters in each country were in turn paid in local currency from the balances deposited by importers.

Such an arrangement eliminates the need for applications for import licenses, for checking the prices of exports and imports to prevent overvaluation or undervaluation, and thus greatly reduces the amount of red tape. So long as exports and imports are equal in value, clearance is complete and there is no problem of keeping the account in balance.

Since precise equality is not to be expected, some provision to meet such a divergence is necessary. The commonest method is to establish a "swing" credit of a fixed amount. Thus in the Italian-Argentine agreement, exports could exceed imports in either direction by as much as $100 million. Any further excess had to be settled in gold or dollars. Another device is to alter the exchange rate applied to the clearing transactions, which is always specified in the agreement. Since it is an arbitrarily determined rate, it may overvalue one of the currencies and thus be responsible for the trade imbalance. Before the war, Germany deliberately used its superior bargaining power vis-à-vis the Balkan nations to force their acceptance of an overvalued rate for the mark. This gave it advantageous terms of trade and led also to the accumulation of large mark balances, which it was willing to liquidate only by exporting relatively unwanted commodities. Hence the large Balkan imports of aspirin and harmonicas.

---

[1] Some clearing agreements are limited to certain categories of commodities, the rest of the trade being carried out in the normal manner.

Without a "swing" limit to the net excess of trade in either direction, not only might large unusable balances accumulate, but the monetary effects in each country could be serious. In the country with an excess of imports, substantial net payments of local currency would be made into the clearing account, thus retiring money from circulation. As with any excess of imports over exports, this is deflationary. In the country whose exports exceeded its imports, in-payments by importers would be insufficient to compensate the exporters. If the central bank were willing to advance credit to pay them, the money supply would be increased immediately by this amount, and ultimately, after these central bank funds had been deposited with commercial banks, perhaps by the full amount made possible by reserve requirements. Without such advances, the exporters would have to wait for payment until their turn came, which would dampen their enthusiasm to export.

Payments Agreements

Another type of bilateral arrangement, somewhat wider in scope than the clearing agreement, is the *payments agreement*. It is no different from the clearing agreement in principle or in mechanism, but simply extends clearing facilities to additional categories of payments. The most important of these is outstanding debts, although the various service transactions, including the service of debt, are usually included.

Countries that build up substantial credits in exchange control countries, either prior to the introduction of controls, as a result of the operation of a bilateral accord, or simply because of the rashness of exporters, acquire a frozen asset. A payments agreement provides the means to thaw it, by prescribing that a certain per cent of payments for imports into the creditor country's clearing account shall be earmarked for the liquidation of accumulated debt. The creditor country need exercise no control over imports from the debtor, since only if imports exceed exports can accumulated debt be paid off. The debtor country, on the other hand, must hold imports from the creditor down sufficiently so that the agreed proportion of the value of its exports actually becomes applied to debt retirement.

Since World War II, most bilateral agreements have been of this broader type, including provisions not only for the settlement of debt, but also for payments for shipping charges, debt service, tourism, and the whole range of service items. With the gradual liberalization of trade, strictly bilateral accords gave way more and more to arrangements that permitted a considerable degree of multilateral clearing, as in the European Payments Union (see page 445).

DISORDERLY CROSS RATES

In addition to causing a bilateral channeling of trade, exchange control tends to disturb the orderly relationship between exchange rates, replacing it with disorder.

So long as currencies are convertible, the whole system of interrelated exchange rates between different currencies must remain consistent. Any tendency, for example, for the cross rate between the franc and the pound to diverge from the rate between the dollar and the pound and between the franc and the dollar will be promptly corrected by the activity of exchange arbitragers.[2] With the introduction of exchange control and inconvertibility, exchange arbitrage—the simultaneous purchase and sale of exchange in different markets—becomes impossible. Since the rate on any currency is arbitrary—being set by the authorities and maintained by quantitative restrictions—then, unless consistent cross rates are consciously sought, they will generally become disorderly or disparate. This is particularly true if a country has a deficit with one trading partner, a surplus with another, for then it will be tempted to depreciate its currency vis-à-vis the first and appreciate it vis-à-vis the second.

To take an illustration from the period just after World War II, suppose, with the dollar/pound rate at $2.80, the rates on the dollar and the pound in French francs were consistent, at 350 frs./$ and 980 frs./£ respectively. Encountering a deficit in its balance of payments with the United States and a surplus with the United Kingdom, the French exchange control authorities now depreciate the franc against the dollar to a 400-franc rate, appreciate it relative to the pound to 960 francs. The corresponding cross rate is $2.60 per pound (960/400 = 2.60), inconsistent or disparate as compared with the actual cross rate of $2.80 per pound.

This inconsistency provides an opportunity for Americans (or perhaps the nations of other countries) to purchase sterling cheaply. At a 400 frs./$ rate, they could buy 960 francs for $2.60, and with these francs acquire £1 —a saving of 20¢ over the rate on sterling in New York. Even though the British exchange control authorities permitted sterling so obtained to be used only for goods shipped to France, these could be transshipped to the United States, or the destination could be changed after they have left a British port.

Situations of this kind arose frequently in the years after World War II, and were the basis for official protests against the establishment of inconsistent exchange rates which led to the emergence of disorderly cross rates.

MULTIPLE EXCHANGE RATES

In our discussion of exchange control, we have repeatedly stressed how an overvalued exchange rate depresses exports and requires the strict regulation of imports. In the search for relief from this constriction of trade, Germany in the 1930's originated and developed to a high degree the bilateral arrangements which soon became widespread.

[2] See page 297.

Another device serving the same purpose—*multiple exchange rates*—also originated in Germany in the early thirties. Its effectiveness in opening up hitherto closed markets, together with other advantages that appeared as time went on, led to its rapid extension, especially in Latin America. In the years immediately after the war, some twenty-odd countries used multiple exchange rates in one form or another.

Dual Rate Systems

The simplest, though not historically the earliest, of multiple exchange rate systems is one employing only two rates, an official rate (usually an overvalued one) for permitted transactions, and a free rate for all others. Ordinarily the official rate is confined, on the supply side, to exports capable of holding their markets even at an overvalued rate. These are typically commodities in which the country's position as a supplier is strong, even semi-monopolistic, as with Brazil in coffee or Chile in copper. Part or all of the foreign exchange from these exports must be surrendered at the official rate. Under Thailand's postwar exchange control system, for example, 100 per cent of rice proceeds had to be turned over to the government; for rubber, the surrender quota was 20 per cent; and for tin it was, successively, 50, 40, and 20 per cent.

On the demand side, imports of basic necessities alone are usually permitted at the official rate. If the list of these commodities is narrowly restricted and if sufficient foreign exchange is allotted to satisfy demand at the import price plus the normal importer's profit, their prices can be held down. If, however, the exchange made available is insufficient, low prices can only be maintained in the face of shortages with supplementary price controls. Otherwise, importers will charge prices high enough to ration the scarce supplies and will gain a windfall profit.

All transactions other than those permitted at the official rate take place at the free rate. These include exports needing encouragement, nonessential and luxury imports, and usually all invisibles as well as capital exports and imports. With a truly free rate, the competition of these various demands and supplies establishes a rate that clears these transactions. There is, it should be noted, a possibility that this competition may drive the rate up to the point where costly luxuries are imported at the expense of semiessentials needed by the lower and middle income groups. This is especially true where, as in some underdeveloped countries, income distribution is highly uneven, with a large share in the hands of the wealthier classes.

If the free rate fluctuates violently, the government may attempt to stabilize it by entering the market as a buyer or seller. To avoid the need for this, or to limit depreciation thought to be excessive, it may limit the transactions allowed at the free rate. This is almost certain to lead to the emergence of a "black" market, where deals excluded from other markets are transacted.

Because they are difficult to detect, these transactions are usually confined to such invisible items as tourists' expenditures, remission of profits, and transfers of capital.

Fixed Multiple Rates

Complex multiple exchange rate systems emerged from the trial-and-error procedure of prewar days, when many countries were seeking relief from the restrictiveness of an overvalued official rate buttressed by exchange controls and import licensing. Unwilling to devalue their currencies at a single stroke, they tried a piecemeal approach, establishing a number of distinct exchange rates, one for each of several categories of transactions. The lowest rates were commonly applied to exports in the strongest competitive position, or perhaps to only part of them, and to imports of the greatest importance to the economy. On the ascending scale of higher rates, the position of any export depended upon the degree to which it was felt necessary to stimulate it, of any import, upon its relative unimportance. The highest of all rates usually applied to invisibles, including capital transfers.

Effects of Multiple Rates

Take the average of all the various exchange rates used by a given country as a base for comparison. Those below the average overvalue the currency. They have the effect of a tax on exports and a subsidy on imports. Higher than average rates, on the other hand, undervalue the currency. They resemble a subsidy on exports and a tax on imports.[3]

Overvaluation (low exchange rates) tends to discourage the use of a country's more productive resources, both in export and in import-competing lines. With respect to exports, only the strongest export producers—that is, those whose resources have the greatest international advantage—are able to sell at these low rates. The subsidy to imports provided by low rates of exchange discourages domestic production of substitutes that could easily compete at the average rate.[4] On the other hand, undervaluation (higher than

[3] Unless we can assume that, under a free exchange rate system, the average of multiple rates would be the equilibrium rate, there is a difficulty here. If, as has sometimes appeared to be the case, the equilibrium rate would approximate the highest of the multiple rates in effect, then *all* lower rates would provide varying subsidies to imports and impose taxes of varying severity on exports. Since it is impossible to generalize *a priori* with respect to where in a range of multiple rates a free equilibrium rate would lie, and difficult even to estimate such a rate in a concrete situation, we adopt the average rate merely as a provisional and convenient bench mark.

[4] The scheduling of imports of essential foodstuffs at subsidy rates greatly handicapped Chile's agriculture. From being a net exporter of agricultural products in the 1930's, by the late 1940's the country had become a net importer. Although this shift was partly due to growing domestic demand for agricultural products not suited to Chile, it was aggravated by rising imports of such commodities as wheat and meat, whose production was made unprofitable by the low export and import exchange rates applied to these products.

average rates) encourages the use of inefficient resources, through the sub-
sidization of marginal exports and the protection of inefficient import-
competing industries.

In addition to these protective and subsidy effects, there is also a revenue
effect if the supply of exchange at the lower rates exceeds sales to importers
at these rates. For then the government can make a profit by selling this
surplus of cheaply bought exchange at higher rates. A common device for
ensuring such a revenue to the government is to establish an appreciable spread
between the buying and selling rates in any given category.

EVALUATION OF MULTIPLE EXCHANGE RATES

Administrative Simplification

Multiple exchange rates are in essence a form of partial devaluation. Consequently, foreign exchange is less scarce than it would be with a single but
overvalued rate. Imports not permitted at a low, overvalued rate can be
obtained, but only at some higher rate and at higher prices. Rationing by
price thus replaces rationing by quantitative restrictions. The whole complex
apparatus of quantitative control can be dismantled.

This reintroduction of rationing by price greatly reduces the area of administrative decision—the need for determining the amount of each commodity
to be imported, the source from which it may be obtained, and which importer is to get the business. The huge bureaucratic staff required to carry
out such detailed regulations can be heavily pruned, to the substantial benefit
of the government budget.

Since the efficiency of the control apparatus depends upon the honesty
and ability of the administrators, elimination of quantitative restrictions is a
particularly great boon to a country lacking a first-rate civil service. Incompetence compounds errors in judgment, serious enough in the best of circumstances, and corruption means that exports and imports will be determined
largely on the basis of graft and favoritism.

Complexity and Uncertainty

Despite these advantages over exchange control with no devaluation whatever, multiple exchange rates have their own shortcomings. They introduce
an additional element of complexity, and if either the rates themselves or the
transactions permitted at each rate are frequently changed, as has often been
true, further uncertainty is created. Further, unless positive action is taken
to prevent it, disorderly cross rates are very likely to emerge.

Inefficient Use of Resources

The increased ease of importing and the stimulus to favored exports are,
of course, a gain to the country adopting multiple rates. Against this must

be set the inefficient use of resources resulting from the combination of taxes and subsidies implicit in such a system. This effect can be quite serious;[5] it is, moreover, haphazard, in that the various subsidies and penalties are not determined with reference to prospects of long-run industrial efficiency, but by balance-of-payments considerations.

Discriminatory Effects on Competitors

Also to be taken into account is the effect of multiple exchange rates on other countries. Particularly important in this respect is the fact that when a subsidy rate is introduced for exports, it applies only to a limited number of exports, and thus concentrates its impact upon a few competing countries. This is rightly regarded as a form of unfair competition, which is aggravated by resort to further changes in such rates. With uniform, over-all depreciation, on the other hand, the impact on competitors is spread "as broadly as the diversity of the economy of the depreciating economy permits."[6]

EXCHANGE CONTROL IN REVIEW

Reviewing the system of exchange control as a method of safeguarding a country against an adverse balance of payments, we find it to have serious consequences for the economy immediately affected. When the system becomes widespread, as both before and after the last war, the world economy as a whole becomes disrupted.

Due to the insulation it provides against outside forces, the nation practicing exchange control is free to adopt policies with an inflationary bias which tend to convert an equilibrium exchange rate into an overvalued rate, or to increase any initial degree of overvaluation. There is a strong temptation to use this freedom, since nation-centered objectives normally have a stronger political appeal than more cosmopolitan goals.

When exchange controls and overvaluation extend to a number of countries, trade is gradually forced into bilateral channels, to ensure markets for overpriced exports and adequate supplies of scarce imports. Because countries with overvalued currencies are eager to obtain imports if they can pay for them with their own inconvertible money but are reluctant to draw upon scarce free exchange, convertibility of the controlled currencies becomes not

---

[5] Thus, not only Chilean agriculture, but that of Peru and Ecuador (and doubtless of other countries as well) suffered serious contraction after World War II because of the penalty rates on certain foodstuffs. Before Peru introduced multiple rates, domestic production of meat was sufficient for home consumption; with imports of meat permitted at the (low) official rate, home production fell to less than half of total consumption. Ecuador had a similar experience with wheat flour. E. M. Bernstein, "Some Economic Aspects of Multiple Exchange Rates," *International Monetary Fund Staff Papers*, Vol. 1, No. 2 (September, 1950), p. 230.

[6] *Ibid.*, p. 234.

only limited but also discriminatory. Soft currencies are made available with relative liberality; hard currency allocations are severely restricted.

With the spread of bilateralism and the consequent destruction of a truly international trading system, the gains from trade, both for the uncontrolled and the controlled regions, are greatly reduced. Goods can no longer be bought freely where they are most efficiently and cheaply produced, nor can they be sold where the need is greatest and prices are consequently highest. Ability to buy, as always, is determined by ability to sell. Exports priced in overvalued currencies have limited access to free markets; disproportionate amounts must be exchanged for the similarly overpriced exports of other nations that have hedged themselves in with restrictions.

With trade determined in considerable part not by comparative costs, but by availability of means of payment, the allocation of resources becomes more and more uneconomic. Export industries come into being or are expanded, not because they are efficient, but because their markets are sheltered. Quantitative restrictions on imports give effective protection to high-cost substitutes.

To the reduction in the gains from trade must be added the direct cost of supporting a sizeable bureaucracy and the more intangible, indirect costs of errors in judgment, magnified manyfold if the administrators are incompetent and corrupt.

Resort to multiple exchange rates can mitigate some of these deficiencies. Multiple rates are, however, only a partial solution to devaluation, and introduce uncertainties and distortions of their own.

A country facing a balance-of-payments disequilibrium and forced to choose between depreciation, deflation, and exchange controls should weigh carefully the desirable and undesirable consequences of each. Exchange control furnishes no solution to the problem. It deals only with the deficit, not its causes, and it exacerbates those causes, tending to create a more basic disequilibrium.

Unless restrictions can be kept moderate or are to be used as a temporary stopgap while other, more fundamental adjustments are made, resort to exchange control is likely to be a costly and disappointing choice

SELECTED REFERENCES

Bernstein, E. M., "Some Economic Aspects of Multiple Exchange Rates," *IMF Staff Papers*, Vol. I, No. 2 (1950). A brief theoretical discussion of the effects of multiple exchange rates.

Bloomfield, Arthur I., *Speculative and Flight Movements of Capital in Postwar International Finance*. Princeton, N. J.: Princeton University Press, 1954. In addition to much factual material, this book considers methods of avoiding exchange controls and possible means of dealing with capital flight.

Chalmers, Henry, *World Trade Policies*. Berkeley, Calif.: University of California Press, 1953. A continuing account of events in the field of international commercial policy in the form of a collection of current articles.

de Looper, Johan H. C., "Current Usage of Payments Agreements and Trade Agreements," *IMF Staff Papers*, Vol. IV, No. 3 (August, 1955). An extended discussion of the main features, effects, and problems of trade and payments agreements.

Ellis, Howard S., *Exchange Control in Central Europe*. Cambridge, Mass.: Harvard University Press, 1941. Examines the operation of control schemes in the 1930's.

League of Nations, *International Currency Experience* (1944). Chapter VII deals with exchange control.

Meade, James E., *The Balance of Payments*. New York: Oxford University Press, 1951. Part V contains a good discussion of direct controls, both financial and commercial.

Mikesell, Raymond F., *Foreign Exchange in the Postwar World*. New York: Twentieth Century Fund, 1954. The best source for a general discussion of the postwar system of controlled trade and payments, with much illustrative material.

22

CHOOSING THE BEST
WAY OUT

In the last two chapters we saw that a nation confronted with a serious disequilibrium in its balance of payments can resort to any one of three distinct methods of dealing with it. (1) It can allow exchange rates to fluctuate freely, relying upon the resultant changed relationship between the prices of exports, imports, and domestic goods to eliminate the deficit. (2) It can maintain stable exchange rates, permitting the decrease in exports or the increase in imports that brought about the deficit to induce a decline in income and in domestic prices; if these changes are insufficient to restore equilibrium, they can be reenforced by a contraction of the supply of money, either deliberately engineered by the central banking authorities or caused by the effect of reserve losses upon a fractional reserve banking system. (3) Or it can subject the foreign exchange market to controls, limiting exchange allocations to the supplies made available to the control authorities.

These alternatives are not mutually exclusive, but can be combined in various ways. We have noted how flexible exchange rates and devaluation may combine, in different degrees, reliance upon rate changes and upon internal deflation to effect adjustment. Exchange control need not imply refusal to devalue in some degree, either piecemeal or at one stroke. Moreover, internal economic policies may, as we shall see, be used to supplement these adjustment mechanisms.

THE PROBLEM OF CHOICE

A country confronting a balance-of-payments problem has a choice among alternatives. Which should it choose? What criteria should determine its choice? Does it make any difference what caused the disturbance, or is the cause irrelevant? These are the questions to which we must now address ourselves.

The criterion for the determination of *any* economic policy should be the

[383]

attainment of maximum results at minimum cost. In our particular setting, this criterion means elimination of the balance-of-payments deficit with the least disruption of the national economy. As will soon become apparent, success in treating the disease of balance-of-payments disequilibrium depends in large measure upon the nature of its cause.

Our analysis of the various methods of adjustment up to this point has focused entirely upon mechanisms; the cause of the initial disturbance has been assumed to be irrelevant. We must now discard this assumption. A deficit is a deficit, whether caused by internal inflation or by more intense competition with a country's exports. But to restore equilibrium with the least friction requires a quite different kind of treatment for each situation.

DIAGNOSIS

We might now proceed to prescribe, for each major type of disturbance, the appropriate remedy. But diagnosis, as in medicine, comes first. We have, it is true, described the main causes of balance-of-payments disequilibrium, and have classified them according as they are due to income changes or structural changes. But how is one to recognize them in practice?

The policy-determining official, who must choose the measures to be adopted, confronts a going economy in all its complexity. A balance-of-payments deficit stands out clear and obvious in statistical data readily available in most countries today. But what lies behind it? Is it due to price disparities caused by past inflation, to rising costs in his country's principal export industries, to technological change abroad, to depression in a major export market, or perhaps—and most likely—to a mixture of these and possibly other causes? The government official, with an important decision to make, must answer this question as best he can. The answer is not clear and self-evident, but is buried in the mass of statistics that he and his staff have to work with. These relate to income, employment, prices, bank credit, industrial and agricultural production, inventories, construction activity, exports, imports, capital movements, and many other economic phenomena. Here is a real problem of diagnosis—of knowing what symptoms to look for and where to find them. Some clues to the solution of these problems can be given.

Income Changes

Easiest of all the possible causes of balance of payments disequilibrium to identify is *rampant inflation*. It will stand out clearly in rising prices, expanding currency and bank credit, and government budget deficits; in over-full employment and in shortages of labor and raw materials. Chile from 1932 to 1959 is a good illustration. It had either an actual balance-of-payments deficit or a potential one, held in check by rigorous exchange controls and moderated from time to time by piecemeal devaluation. In this period, currency and bank deposits expanded at annual rates ranging from a minimum of six per cent to a maximum of 70 per cent. Prices roughly kept in step with the money supply, rising at annual rates that averaged about 25 per cent. Though other causes played a role in Chile's balance-of-payments difficulties, inflation was far the most important.

Mild inflation is less easy to spot. There is almost certain to be less than the normal frictional unemployment—that is, employment is over-full. Aggregate demand exceeds supply available from production at current prices, but the pressure on prices may not be severe enough to overcome rigidities, or controls may suppress their tendency to rise. Credit expansion may be negligible, the excess demand being financed by past accumulations of cash, as in the United States immediately after World War II.

> Nevertheless, with full employment the existence of a balance of payments deficit is a clear indication of current inflation. When a country absorbs in consumption and investment more than its own output and any ordinary capital inflow, without offsetting unemployment, aggregate demand must be excessive to the extent of the balance-of-payments deficit.[1]

During a mild inflation, investment would tend to be high in relation to income as compared with previous, noninflationary periods. So would the whole range of imports, while exports in general would be relatively low. Reports of materials and labor shortages should also provide confirmatory evidence.

A balance of payments deficit may be due, not to current inflation, but to *price-cost disparities* caused by a preceding period of inflation. If inflation is serious and continues for some time, a country's costs and prices are almost certain to be raised substantially in relation to those of other countries. Prices of domestic commodities, in particular, are likely to be especially out of line, since they are not restrained by competition with foreign producers. Clearly, a comparison of the relative trend in the recent past of prices and wages at home and in other countries is called for. A deficit resulting from a price-cost disparity is likely to be characterized by large imports and small exports relative to the size of national income. There is likely to be substantial unemployment because of the price disadvantage suffered by both export and important-competing industries.

Cyclical disequilibrium in the balance of payments would be reflected, in the early stages, by a sudden drop in exports, while imports, income, and employment remained relatively unchanged. Data for the country or countries where the depression originated should show declining income and

---

[1] E. M. Bernstein, "Strategic Factors in Balance of Payments Adjustment," *International Monetary Fund Staff Papers*, Vol. V, No. 2. August, 1956, p. 158. Much of this chapter is heavily indebted to Dr. Bernstein's analysis.

imports. As the depression spread, deficit countries would also experience rising unemployment and declining income.

Structural Changes

Structural changes causing balance-of-payments disequilibrium are of many different kinds. Those due to *altered demand or supply conditions* would share the common trait of affecting specific exports or imports, so it is primarily detailed trade data that the analyst would want to examine. If particular exports had declined, this might be due to a shift in foreign demand, to a worsened competitive position of domestic exporters, or to an improved position of foreign competitors. Inquiry should be directed to discovering whether trade barriers abroad had been increased, whether there had been a change in tastes, or whether foreign competitors had introduced new processes lowering costs or improved or totally new products. If exports remained substantially unchanged but certain imports were abnormally large, inquiry should center upon such possibilities as a shift in domestic tastes, improved efficiency and lower costs of suppliers of imports, or the introduction of new types of imported goods.

To illustrate the points at issue here, we may cite a Tariff Commission study requested by President Eisenhower in 1955. The briar pipe industry had experienced declining sales, which it (and the Tariff Commission in an earlier report) ascribed to rising foreign competition. The requested study showed that the major cause of the industry's difficulties lay not in the competition of imports but in the changing habits of smokers, who were turning steadily away from pipe smoking to cigarettes. A similar study of the difficulties of the felt-hat industry showed the villain to be, not the foreign producer, but the American male: he was determined to go bareheaded.

Changed debtor-creditor relationships are another type of structural change that can cause a balance-of-payments deficit. These could include an upsurge in long-term lending, a sudden decline in long-term borrowing, flight movements of capital, or the loss of overseas earning assets. For a country with good balance-of-payments statistics, these changes would be evident in the data for capital movements or, for the last-named case, in declining yields from past overseas investments. In the absence of such statistics, inquiries of banks doing a foreign business should provide some corroborative evidence.

TREATMENT

In the practice of medicine, treatment of symptoms is rarely effective in eliminating the disease that causes them. The case is no different in economics. A balance-of-payments deficit is simply the manifestation of some deeper malady. The deficit can be suppressed by direct controls, but unless corrective measures attack its causes, it will break out again with their removal. *To be effective, remedies must be specific.*

Inflation

The truth of this is most easily seen with a deficit caused by inflation, whether severe or mild. To free exchange rates to rise or to devalue the currency would be useless or worse if the inflation itself were to go unchecked. The continuing excess demand would merely generate a recurring deficit, requiring for its correction a steadily rising free rate or new doses of devaluation. Moreover, either form of depreciation would aggravate the inflation by stimulating exports and checking imports.

The appropriate remedy is clearly deflation, at least to the extent necessary to destroy the excess demand: maintain fixed exchange rates, and allow the pressure of the deficit upon income to do its work. With moderate inflation, unaccompanied by any appreciable rise of prices, little if any positive deflation would be necessary. With severe inflation, accompanied by a marked rise in the price level, reliance upon deflation would require a substantial decline of income and prices.

Since, in the social context of the mid-twentieth century, deflation would be sure to encounter stiff political opposition, the checking of inflation ("disinflation") might well represent the limit to the use of this classical remedy. To restore balanced price relationships, devaluation would now be appropriate, accompanied by sufficient restraints on credit to prevent a reemergence of the inflationary trend. Devaluation and credit restraint would also be suited to an existing price-cost disparity left over from previous inflation.

Cyclical Disequilibrium

Cyclical disequilibrium in the balance of payments is more difficult to cope with. The deficit has been caused by declining exports, traceable to a depression originating abroad. Under the gold standard, the decline in exports and the loss of reserves would be followed by income and price deflation. Eventually the balance-of-payments disequilibrium would be corrected, but at the cost of severe depression.

Devaluation may appear to offer a less costly remedy, but with a worldwide decline in incomes, demands tend to become inelastic, especially for commodities whose consumption is readily postponable. In the face of inelastic and shrinking demand, devaluation, unless very substantial, is unlikely to stimulate exports or check imports appreciably. Moreover, so far as it does retard imports, the depression is aggravated in other countries. Retaliation is almost certain.

As we indicated earlier, the solution much to be preferred in this situation is *the concerted adoption of expansionary monetary and fiscal policies,* especially in the economically more important countries. If, whether by agreement or by accident, the larger countries simultaneously generate a recovery of income and employment, their imports will increase, spreading the impulse toward expansion throughout the world. The exports of each will increase as income and imports rise in the other countries following an expansionary program. Although, in these countries, imports are likely to exceed exports, as the major trading nations their reserves are also likely to be relatively large; these can be drawn upon to support the program of expansion. As recovery spreads, balance-of-payments deficits will gradually be eliminated and equilibrium restored.

In view of the political importance of preventing unemployment, it may not be too optimistic to hope that, even without international agreement, the onset of depression would today be promptly countered by vigorous monetary and fiscal action. Although to foresee the complete elimination of depressions would be utopian, their duration and severity should be greatly moderated. Domestic expansionary measures together with use of their international reserves might well enable the major countries to weather the storm at tolerable cost.

If this hope is not realized—and lack of international reserves by one or more of the larger countries might frustrate it—neither deflation nor devaluation have anything to offer. The prescription for any country facing depression abroad, with declining exports and income, remains internal expansion—but accompanied by exchange and trade controls to suppress the deficit and avoid exhaustion of its reserves. It is all the better if these controls discriminate against imports from the country where the depression originated, for then its spread can be minimized. Moreover, the pressure of such discrimination may, by intensifying the depression at its focus of infection, help force the adoption of an expansionary policy.

Structural Disequilibrium

A change in specific demand or supply conditions affects only one or a few exports or imports. The affected country has either lost an advantage in the production of exports or its disadvantage in some import-competing industry has increased, with the consequence of a deficit in its balance of payments. What is clearly called for here is not general deflation, nor even necessarily a change in the relative prices of the whole range of exports and imports, but a shift of resources into a new export line or into the production of additional import substitutes.

A good deal depends upon the degree to which the economy in question is specialized. If it is already well-diversified, the easiest solution may well be a moderate amount of devaluation to effect an across-the-board stimulus to exports and import substitutes, accompanied by a policy of credit restraint to inhibit inflation. If, however, the economy has been heavily dependent upon one or a very few exports—such as Chile on copper and nitrates, Malaya on rubber and tin, or Ceylon on tea and coconuts—and its exports have lost out to new products or to a more efficient competitor, devaluation is unlikely to be of much help. This is even more true if there are few domestic substitutes for imports. There is little in the way of domestic industry, either on the export or the import-competing side, to stir into action; the whole burden of the devaluation falls on the shoulders of the consumer of imports.

A country in this situation desperately needs to reallocate its unemployed resources to the most productive remaining uses. Use of all the techniques of economic development is suggested. These include government aid, both financial and technical, to promising industries; appeal to international agencies for similar help; carefully chosen infant-industry protection; possibly a measure of devaluation once progress is under way; and quite probably the introduction of exchange controls to safeguard the country's reserves while the internal changes are taking place.

Conclusion

This chapter should have made clear the relevance, both to the diagnosis of a country's problems and to the choice of a suitable remedy, of economic analysis. Theory has a real task to perform. It is a tool needed to isolate the causes of difficulties, to determine what policies can be used to combat them, and to judge which is appropriate. Without analysis, facts alone are refractory and meaningless. With it, they become orderly, tractable, and significant.

SELECTED REFERENCES

Bernstein, E. M., "Strategic Factors in Balance of Payments Adjustment," *IMF Staff Papers*, Vol. V, No. 8 (August, 1956). A fine example of the application of economic analysis to balance-of-payments problems.

Haberler, Gottfried, "Some Factors Affecting the Future of International Trade and International Economic Policy," in *Economic Reconstruction*, ed. S. E. Harris. New York: McGraw-Hill Book Co., 1945. Reproduced in *Readings in the Theory of International Trade*.

Kindleberger, Charles P., *International Economics*, 3rd ed. Homewood, Ill.: Richard D. Irwin, Inc., 1963. Chapter 29, on the "Means of Equilibrium," compares the different remedies, and stresses the contribution of competition, mobility, high income elasticity, etc., to their efficacy.

League of Nations, *International Currency Experience* (1944). Chapter IX contains a review of adjustment methods in the light of interwar experience.

Meade, James E., *The Balance of Payments*. New York: Oxford University Press, 1951. See Chapters IX, X, XV, and XXIV for a comparison of the different methods of adjustment.

Polak, J. J., "Exchange Depreciation and International Monetary Stability," *Review of Economics and Statistics*, XXIX (August, 1947). Urges devaluation as especially suited to income and price disequilibriums, but as quite unsuited for dealing with structural disequilibrium.

PART V

Toward Collapse of the
International Economy

23

STRUCTURAL WEAKENING OF THE WORLD ECONOMY

THE WORLD ECONOMY OF 1913

The hundred years between the Napoleonic wars and the war of 1914-18 witnessed the creation of a true world economy, with most of its member nations closely integrated through a highly developed network of trade and finance. The numerous facilities essential to the operation of this complex system of interrelated markets were centered in London, but their influence was spread throughout the globe by means of branch offices, correspondents, and contractual relationships. These facilities included specialized export and import firms, commodity brokers, commercial banks and investment banks, acceptance and discount houses, insurance companies, shipping lines, and a worldwide system of telegraphic communications.

Specialization of national production, based on widely varying factor endowments, was intense. Although tariffs to some extent obstructed trade and retarded specialization, their effect was not too serious, for they were changed infrequently and only a few were high. Because each of the various kinds of specialized production was concentrated in a very few geographic localities, multilateral trade was essential. Fortunately, since all the principal and many of the less important countries were on the gold standard, there existed the universal convertibility of currencies so necessary for the operation of a multilateral trading system.

This was not a static world, but one of rapid change. Technology advanced with great speed, bringing into existence new methods of production and totally new products. Heavy migration of labor and large movements of capital progressively altered relative factor endowments, the very foundation of international trade. Nor were these movements themselves constant—they ebbed and flowed and changed their direction without warning. Intermittently, too, the channels of trade were interrupted and diverted by changes in the commercial policy of nations.

All these phenomena introduced disturbances of varying severity, to which the balance of payments of each nation affected had somehow to become adjusted. The means to that adjustment was furnished by the automatic mechanism of the gold standard, which operated smoothly because the institutional environment—notably the close relations between London and other financial centers—was favorable. Through its operation, the many and recurring changes were assimilated with a remarkable smoothness and lack of friction.

FORCES OF DISINTEGRATION

This happy combination of economic institutions, market forces, and harmonious climate of opinion was rudely shattered after 1914. The balance of power in Europe, carefully nurtured by a century of British diplomacy, ended abruptly with the challenge of German expansionism. Four years of bitter war, with entire nations in arms, wrought terrible destruction and loss of life.

Despite all the damage and disruption, within a few years the worst of Europe's wounds had healed. Production recovered to prewar levels and then began, after a brief interruption, a steady climb. A deep nostalgia for the past bred a sincere attempt to reconstruct the international framework. The gold standard was restored; the wartime restrictions on trade were abandoned; trade connections were reestablished; and a new agency—the League of Nations— was created to ease international tensions and to facilitate agreed solutions for common problems.

For a time, success appeared within reach. The middle and later twenties were years of great prosperity; production and trade advanced steadily and standards of living improved. Yet the international structure on which all this rested had been greatly weakened in ways little appreciated at the time, ways that made the world economy less resilient and less capable of smooth adjustment to further change. Moreover, that structure was subjected to a series of disturbances far greater than any it had hitherto been forced to face. Even before the great upheaval of a second World War, the impact of these developments destroyed the highly articulated but feebler successor to the world economic system of the late nineteenth and early twentieth centuries.

This chapter depicts the sources of weakness in the international economy of the interwar years, indicates the structural and other changes to which adjustment had somehow to be made, and shows how failure to meet this challenge brought about collapse.

A WEAKENED INTERNATIONAL STRUCTURE

Monetary Developments After the First World War

The pressures of war had caused most of the belligerents and many of the neutral nations to abandon the gold standard. Although the sharpness and extent of the break varied from one country to another, free movements of gold ceased during the war and for some years after it. Thus the close link between national price systems was broken, and prices in different countries were free to move independently. Inflation went to varying lengths, depending upon the balance of payments situation confronting each nation and the fiscal policies it followed. It was most intense in Germany, Russia, and Austria-Hungary, where currencies became, within a few years after the war, virtually worthless and had to be replaced by new issues. In France, wholesale prices rose to more than eight times the 1913 level; in Italy, the rise was about sevenfold. Even the United Kingdom and the United States witnessed a postwar peak of prices of 330 and 272, respectively.

To bring some order into this chaotic situation was one of the first postwar concerns. Except where currencies had become virtually worthless, the earlier long attachment to the gold standard bred a strong desire for its restoration. Its abandonment during and after the war was generally regarded as but a temporary break with the past.

If gold was again to be the base, there arose immediately the question of what the metallic content of each currency should be, and thus the level of exchange parities. The United States, which during the war had modified its attachment to the gold standard only to the extent of requiring licenses for the export of gold, merely abolished this requirement in 1919 and returned to gold at the old parity. With ample gold reserves, it could do so. Germany and Austria scrapped their worthless currencies and adopted new ones—the Reichsmark, with the prewar gold parity relative to the dollar of 23.8 cents, and the schilling, with the relatively high parity of about 14 cents. Rigorous controls over the supply of money in both countries kept the internal value of these new currencies in line with their external or gold value, while international loans provided the reserves needed to meet adverse swings in the balance of payments. Many countries, however, had to make do with their existing but badly depreciated currencies. For them to have restored the relatively high prewar gold parities would have meant exchange rates that seriously overvalued their currencies. It would have required ruinous deflation to bring down internal costs and prices sufficiently to effect an appropriate balance between exports and imports. The only alternative for these countries was to devalue their currencies in terms of gold—to bring their external value into line with the existing and depreciated internal value. Some nations— notably the United Kingdom—stood in an intermediate position, with prices and costs high in relation to 1913, but not so much higher than in the United States that the gap could not be eliminated by moderate deflation.

Restoration of the Gold Standard

Great Britain, the center of the prewar gold standard, approached the problem of restoration gradually, yet with its course set in advance. The British decision rested on a report (in 1918) of the famous Cunliffe Committee, which assumed that the gold standard still existed in Great Britain, that its continuance was imperative, and advocated its restoration "without delay."

The Committee's recommendations were followed, however, only slowly and tentatively. Exchange restrictions were removed gradually; the Bank of England pursued a cautious deflationary policy; and British prices became more closely aligned with prices in the United States. As a result, the dollar/sterling exchange rate recovered from a low of $3.18 in early 1920 to $4.36 two years later. An embargo on the placement of foreign loans in Britain, and American credits of $300 million, gave sufficient support to the pound to permit Parliament in 1925 to put the currency back on gold at the prewar parity of $4.866.

At this time the index of wholesale prices in the United Kingdom stood at 159, in the United States at 155 (1913 = 100), a fairly close correspondence. But because the wholesale index is heavily weighted with the prices of internationally traded commodities (which must meet foreign competition and therefore cannot differ much across national boundaries), it failed to reflect adequately the fact that British costs remained relatively high. Restoration of the old parity is generally conceded to have overvalued the pound by at least 10 per cent and to have subjected the island's economy for the next seven years to continuous deflationary pressure. Because prices and costs were quite rigid, they failed to decline appreciably. Instead, Britain suffered from chronic unemployment, which throughout the twenties never fell below the figure of a million.

Between 1925 and 1928, more than forty countries returned to gold, some at their prewar parity, others at a devalued level. Switzerland and the Netherlands were among the former group; France and Italy, on the other hand, where even postwar deflation left prices far higher than in 1913, cut the gold content of their currencies by approximately four-fifths and three-quarters, respectively. By the end of 1928, an extensive international currency system based on gold had been recreated.

Hopes and Expectations

With the reconstruction of a broadly inclusive international gold standard, that prewar pillar of stability and cohesion, it was widely assumed that the most essential aspect of reconstruction had now been achieved. The world, it was felt, could look forward once more to the attainment of a stable international equilibrium, subject of course to temporary disturbances or even to changes of a deeper, more enduring character, but sufficiently limited or gradual so as to permit adjustment by the old familiar processes. It is hardly surprising that statesmen, weary of the burden of unaccustomed problems, should have regarded with relief the restoration of an automatically functioning mechanism. That mechanism, it was believed, would take from their shoulders the responsibility for thought and for difficult decisions.

As it turned out, their hopes rested in large part on illusion. They had, they thought, reconstructed a well-understood and efficient piece of machinery. They overlooked the fact that parts of this machinery beyond their control had changed in ways that seriously hampered its operation. They could not foresee the excessive burdens to which it would be subjected.

Formal Changes in the Gold Standard

The gold standard established in 1925-28 differed somewhat from that of 1914. To alleviate an impending shortage of gold, its coinage had been generally discontinued, except in the United States, and assets in the form of balances in gold-standard countries were permitted to count as reserves of a country's central bank. These changes, known as the gold bullion system and the gold exchange system, were comparatively unimportant. Under the former, currencies were convertible into gold bullion rather than coins, and vice versa, at a fixed price; under the gold exchange system, local currencies could be used to acquire the currencies of gold-standard countries. Gold exports and imports were unrestricted.

It was in the basic or vital, rather than in the purely formal or external, characteristics of the system that serious change had taken place. The prewar efficiency of the gold standard had depended upon the centralization of international transactions in London and upon adherence to well-established rules of international conduct. These essential foundations had been eroded.

Prewar Features of the Gold Standard

Before the war, the gold standard had centered in London. By the simple process of adding to and subtracting from the sterling balances owned by the banks of practically every nation, the great bulk of international transactions was *cleared*. The London market also played the role of a world central bank. When other countries suffered an adverse balance of payments, the London market advanced short-term loans that supplemented their dwindling gold reserves. When Britain lost gold, the London market borrowed from the entire world. These short-term capital movements were supplemented by changes in the ownership of outstanding long-term securities. With gold movements in part replaced by capital movements, the extent of the accompanying contraction or expansion of credit was moderated. If the underlying disturbance proved short-lived, this was all to the good; if, however, a fundamental readjustment were needed, London's lending or borrowing interposed no obstacle, but merely gave more time for deep-seated forces to assert themselves.

Finally, London had for long been the principal source of long-term investment abroad. From their experience in this exacting business, her bankers developed a high degree of skill and judgment. Moreover, the well-organized London investment market was very sensitive to international influences. When exports exceeded imports, foreign balances were transferred to British ownership and gold moved in, easing the money market. For a time, short-term foreign lending might absorb part of the additional funds now available. But the scope of such lending is limited; if the balance-of-payments surplus continued, the lending would come to a halt, with a resumption of gold movements and a further easing of the money market. The continuance of easy credit conditions would now stimulate long-term foreign lending. An inward movement of foreign securities replaced the flow of gold, and the purchasing power put at the disposal of foreigners supported and made possible the continuance of the large volume of exports. International investment thus played an essential part in, and greatly facilitated, the adjustment mechanism.[1]

Substantive Change: Divided Responsibility

Because of events transpiring during and after the war, these substantive aspects of the gold standard had undergone radical change. The Federal Reserve System, established in 1915, gave the United States a central banking structure that stabilized the hitherto erratic money markets, as well as an acceptance market which soon came to rival that of London. The growing importance of this country as a source of supplies, both during and after the war, supported this market and also made increasingly necessary the maintenance of substantial dollar balances in New York. Though negligible in 1914, these balances as early as 1926 amounted to nearly $1.5 billion. Moreover, the New York Stock Exchange at no time imposed restrictions on trading in foreign securities, while the United Kingdom at various intervals had to place an embargo on foreign issues. This fact, together with the availability of credit for long-term borrowing in New York, brought additional deposits and a large and growing business of distributing securities.

Two heads may be better than one, but two clearing centers certainly are not; for the efficiency of a clearing center is in direct proportion to its centralization of transactions. When there is more than one, after the transactions are cleared in each center, those between the centers must be offset. More foreign balances must be maintained, and more labor devoted to the clearing function.

Two *financial centers*, on the other hand, can strengthen the international economy if they work in harmony, not at cross purposes. The additional resources, both short-term and long-term, that the rise of New York made available, were all to the good, the more so since London's ability to finance foreign investment was declining. On the debit side, however, must be set the inexperience of New York bankers and the greater sensitiveness of its money market to domestic and speculative forces than to the pressures of a changing balance of payments. It is to be expected that the financial center of a nation continental in extent and comparatively self-sufficient in production, whose

---

[1] This account is confirmed by direct evidence. "In London interviews granted the writer it was repeatedly stated by investment bankers that before the war they never concerned themselves with the position of the balance of payments, but that when money was knocking around, looking for employment, they felt that to be a good time for bringing forward foreign issues." William Adams Brown, Jr., *The International Gold Standard Reinterpreted*, p. 55. Copyright 1940 by the National Bureau of Economic Research, New York.

foreign trade is a small fraction of its total turnover, should be relatively un-affected by surpluses and deficits in its international accounts. Less predictable was the dominating influence in New York of the rate of interest on stock market loans (the call loan rate), responding to speculative influences rather than to movements of trade.

In such a money market, if active speculation drives up the call loan rate, commercial interest rates, including that on acceptances, will also rise, for competition for funds is pervasive. If at the same time there exists a surplus in the U.S. balance of payments (which means deficits in those of other countries), short-term international lending by New York would be appro-priate to the international needs. Yet a contrary inward movement of funds may take place, attracted by the high return on stock market loans. Precisely this combination of circumstances arose during the 1920's. The stock market boom made it impossible for New York to perform its function of short-term international lender.

Despite this contradiction, the United States did engage in substantial *long-term* foreign lending. Yet these loans (totaling nearly $5 billion between 1922 and 1928) were not closely related to the state of our balance of payments, but to inflationary forces within the country. Moreover, the inexperience of New York bankers had unfortunate results: excessive attention to the immedi-ate gains from bankers' commissions rather than to the underlying soundness of the loans themselves. Hence, there were many loans to dubious borrowers, and for unproductive purposes. Financing of foreign investments also tended to be sporadic rather than steady.

Most important of all, however, the disappearance of the close integration of the world's capital markets eliminated the rapid shifts in long-term securities that had contributed so much to the smooth operation of the prewar gold standard. For that standard to work after the war, much greater reliance would have to be placed on the contraction and expansion of credit.

Changes in Goals

Before the war, the maintenance of a currency's convertibility had been the ultimate criterion of monetary policy in the leading countries, and the condition of a nation's reserves had been the main guide to action. In the favorable environment of the late nineteenth century, the monetary authorities seldom had to use their powers vigorously, but they took decisive action in accord with this criterion when necessary.

All this changed after the war. Each nation insisted on determining its supply of money independently; the state of its reserves became a secondary consid-eration. Inward movements of the metal were neutralized by central bank sales of securities to the market: the additions to commercial bank reserves from abroad were offset by domestic withdrawals. Losses of reserves due to a gold outflow were similarly replaced by central bank funds devoted to the purchase of open-market securities. Thus, between 1920 and 1924, the Federal Reserve authorities offset a considerable part of the large gold receipts of these years, attributing their action to the need (1) to maintain sound credit conditions (*domestic* stability), and (2) to ensure that this gold would be available for export again when the need arose.[2] The Bank of England, too, after 1925, followed a systematic policy of gold neutralization by varying its security holdings inversely with gold movements—a policy whose net effect was deflationary. Although, in view of all the circumstances, and especially in view of *domestic* conditions in both countries, these actions may have been wise, they clearly went counter to traditional gold standard practice.

Many reasons underlay this substitution of national goals for reliance on the automatic operation of an international monetary system. Among them was a growing concern for internal economic stability, induced by increasing industrialization and urbanization, which subjected more and more people to the hazards of unemployment. The advance of economic knowledge also played a role. Confronted with the monetary disturbances of the war and postwar years, economists had studied these phenomena intensively; out of their studies came greater understanding and increased powers of control. In particular, schemes for the stabilization of prices and therewith of economic activity through central bank action acquired a wide following. Furthermore, the means to make these schemes effective increased apace. Central banks, formerly confined to a few countries, now arose all over Europe, in several Latin American nations, and in Australia and South Africa.

The Changing Climate of Opinion

The trend toward independent national action in monetary affairs was only an eddy in a much broader current. Especially since World War I, but starting much earlier, there has been an unmistakable movement toward increasing government intervention in economic life. This was an inevitable reaction against some of the unfortunate consequences of laissez faire.

Economic freedom brought striking increases in productivity and therewith in standards of living. It released the energies of business men to amass capital, to form new enterprises, and to adopt new techniques, and thus to expand output at a phenomenal rate. But it also enabled the strong and well-informed to take advantage of the weak and ignorant. The result was long hours of labor, widespread employment of children, dangerous working conditions, insecurity, and filthy slums. These consequences had not been foreseen by the early supporters of laissez faire, for they assumed all participants in economic activities to be equal—equal in bargaining power, in knowledge of

---

[2] The gold came from countries that were off the gold standard, and whose trade was still disorganized; its movement was therefore regarded as abnormal. For an official explanation of the policy of neutralization, see the *Tenth Annual Report of the Federal Reserve Board* (1923), pp. 20-22.

their interests, in capacity to distinguish good wares from bad, and equal, too, in available alternatives as to occupation, place of work, or housing. Since this necessary equality was patently absent, individual and social interest failed to coincide. The actual situation was aptly suggested by an oft-quoted parody of the mid-nineteenth century: " 'Every man for himself and God for all of us,' as the elephant said when he danced among the chickens."[3]

The response to the antisocial effects of industrial change in a framework of individualism varied widely. Some thoughtful and sensitive people, such as the Tory humanitarians in Great Britain, introduced specific reforms for particular evils such as child labor and long hours of work. Others rejected the individualist philosophy in its entirety and sought to formulate a new and more adequate social theory. These included utopian socialists such as Robert Owen in England and Saint-Simon and Fourier in France, Christian Socialists such as Charles Kingsley, and most important of all, Marx and Engels and their followers.

With the spread of industry and with it the growth of cities and an urban working class, the numbers subjected to the hazards of unemployment, industrial accidents, a weak bargaining position, and slum living constantly rose. There developed a basis of mass support for reforms directed toward these deficiencies and for the new collectivist ideas. Political parties broadened their appeal by introducing reform measures; trade unions organized the workers for more effective bargaining; and socialist and labor parties emerged to promote their political interests. Legislatures enacted laws to regulate public utilities, to outlaw child labor, to regulate the conditions of work, and to protect the consumer. Generally somewhat later to appear were the various forms of social insurance: workmen's compensation, old-age insurance, unemployment insurance, and finally, health insurance. Also to be included under the heading of social legislation are slum clearance and public housing and our old acquaintance, central banks, established to permit the more effective control of credit.

These new laws all had two things in common: they aimed at improving conditions of life in modern industrial society, and to accomplish this, they required more intervention by the state in the operation of the economy. The role of the state took on ever-increasing importance. In changing social conditions and the response made to them, there existed a solid foundation for an ever-larger exercise of national authority.

Economic Nationalism

Reenforcing this trend toward independent national action were the forces of nationalism bred of economic rivalry. We have shown how they led, after about 1870, to rising tariffs and to colonial expansion. After the first World

---

[3] Attributed to Charles Dickens by W. Jethro Brown, *The Underlying Principles of Modern Legislation*. New York: E. P. Dutton & Co., 1915.

War, economic nationalism was reenforced, quite naturally by the inflammatory effects of war itself, artificially by the creation of Poland and the Baltic
states and of the succession states of the Austro-Hungarian Empire. Moreover,
during the war, in belligerent and nonbelligerent nations alike, new industries
arose or old ones expanded to replace supplies cut off by the war. With the
war's end, motives of security and of self-interest combined to exact protection
against the original and more economical centers of production.

Thus, free-trade Britain continued duties established in wartime on certain
luxuries and inaugurated the "Key Industries" duties (with rates of 33⅓ and
50 per cent) on a number of militarily important items. The United States
abandoned the policy of low duties embodied in the Underwood Tariff of
1913, and in 1922 enacted a new high tariff. In Japan, India, Australia, and
Latin America, the disappearance of European competition for four years in
many lines of industry called forth local production. Some of these war infants
died a natural death as trade was reopened, but many clamored for and obtained protection.

Resurgent economic nationalism not only raised barriers to trade, but it
also interfered with the international movement of labor. The United States,
though it remained the principal destination of immigrants, restricted immigration sharply, and in 1924 introduced quotas based on national origin.
These quotas favored immigrants from northern Europe, and discriminated
against those from southern Europe and the Orient where population pressure
was greatest. The total numbers entering the United States, which had averaged
880,000 a year in the decade ending with 1910, fell to an annual average of
411,000 in the 1920's.

All the developments to which we have drawn attention in the last few
pages—the rise of New York as a second and less experienced world financial
center, the national determination of monetary policy, the increased role of the
state in economic affairs, and the resurgence of economic nationalism—weakened the delicately balanced international economic system, making it more
rigid and less sensitive to changes calling for adjustment. Our next task is to
examine the increased burden this mechanism was called upon to meet.

THE BURDEN OF STRUCTURAL CHANGE

War Debts and Reparation

Prewar capital movements, at least since the Franco-Prussian war, had been
the result of the free choice of individual investors, and were mainly in response
to the attraction of a more promising yield. Though they varied from year to
year, and altered their direction as time passed, these shifts were seldom
violent. Between each lender and borrower, too, the current of lending generally began slowly, rose gradually to a peak, and then tapered off, thus giving

time for balances of payments to adjust to the flow of capital, or itself contributing effectively to that adjustment.

The situation was very different after 1918, for the war left a heavy legacy of international debt. At the end of the paying line was Germany, saddled (in 1921) with a reparation burden of $33 billion, most of which was to be paid to Great Britain and France. Italy, France, and Belgium were in debt to one another and to Britain. All of these countries, together with several others, owed the United States at the time of the armistice a principal sum of a little over $7 billion.

For the chain of payments to move smoothly all along the line, two requirements had to be met: large sums in marks had to be extracted annually from the German people, and these sums had to be transferred regularly into other currencies—ultimately a large proportion into dollars.

The first of these problems was one of taxable capacity—an internal problem. The capacity of Germany to pay reparation from this point of view would amount to the difference between the maximum taxable capacity of the country and the minimum needs of government. In the late twenties, German taxes were 25 per cent of the national income, while reparation obligations comprised 10 per cent of these taxes, or 2.5 per cent of the national income. Though heavy, the burden would not appear to have been insuperable.

The transfer problem was more complex and difficult. After the sums in money had been raised in Germany, they had to be remitted to the reparation recipients. Over any but a brief period of time and for relatively small amounts, such international transfers could only be made in the form of goods and services. Under the restored gold standard, it was essential to set in motion an expansion of incomes and a rise of prices in the creditor countries, a decline of incomes and prices in Germany, sufficient to cause Germany's exports to exceed its imports by the amount of annual reparation to be transferred.

To some extent, the extraction of additional taxes from the German people helped set this mechanism in operation. By reducing their personal consumption, this taxation released goods, or the factors to produce goods, for export, and also caused some diminution of imports. In addition, however, an expansion of incomes and spending was needed in the creditor countries. This could have been started had Germany been able to make a sizeable transfer of funds. Had the receiving governments then spent these sums on reconstruction, in addition to similar expenditures out of domestic resources, a rise in incomes would have resulted. Imports would also increase, to the direct or indirect benefit of German exports.

The catch was that Germany had insufficient reserves of gold or foreign exchange with which to make the needed initial transfers of purchasing power. Moreover, the Dawes Plan protected Germany against any serious loss of international reserves, and also prohibited any devaluation of the newly stabilized mark as a means of making her exports more attractive. The essentials for setting the transfer mechanism in motion were therefore lacking.[4]

The problem of war debts and reparation continued to plague both creditors and debtors throughout the twenties and early thirties. Although the British government owed the United States only about half as much as was due it from its allies, at the peace conference in 1919 it unsuccessfully urged the cancellation of all war debts. Three years later, the British offered to scale down payments from their debtors to what they in turn had to pay the United States. But the American government met these overtures with stubborn resistance, and steadily refused to concede the existence of any connection between allied war debts and German reparation. Its attitude was tersely expressed in President Coolidge's famous dictum: "They hired the money, didn't they?"

Not until 1927, some three years after the Dawes Plan arranged a settlement of German reparation, did all the countries involved finally reach agreement on the amounts owed and the terms of payment.[5] Capital sums were scaled down considerably, and annual payments were to be spread over a period of 62 years. At least, some degree of certainty replaced the earlier bickering and confusion. Yet the former European belligerents were left with a burden of payments reflecting a debt not based on productive assets, but representing a sheer dead weight.

International Investment

International investment revived after the war; by the end of the decade, the United States, the United Kingdom, and France had each lent substantial sums. Between 1919 and 1929, the United States invested abroad approximately $7 billion, France about $600 million, while Britain restored her foreign investments, which had fallen about a quarter, to the prewar level of some $19 billion.

Although this international lending of the twenties provided foreign exchange needed by many countries, it was not as large in proportion to income as in prewar days, nor directed to as productive uses. Instead of going mainly into railways, public utilities, and other capital equipment to increase the

---

[4] The fullest discussion of the German transfer problem is to be found in the controversy between Keynes and Ohlin, which appeared in 1929. Keynes stressed the need for a fall in German costs and prices to make her exports more attractive—the classical aspects of the adjustment mechanism—while Ohlin emphasized the effect upon international demands of initial transfers of purchasing power. But as Keynes finally pointed out in a reply, the means of starting the transfer of purchasing power was lacking. "If Germany was in a position to export large quantities of gold or if foreign balances in Germany were acceptable to foreign Central Banks as a substitute for gold in their reserves, then it would be a different matter." (J. M. Keynes, "Mr. Keynes's Views on the Transfer Problem: III, a Reply," *Economic Journal*, XXXIX (1929), pp. 404-8.) The two original articles, though not the subsequent discussion, have been reprinted in *Readings in the Theory of International Trade*.

[5] No settlement was ever reached between the U.S.S.R. and its major creditors, owing to the Soviet unwillingness to assume debts incurred by the Czarist government.

output of the relatively undeveloped areas, a major share went to European national and municipal governments, notably in Germany, where it was used for building and other public works. Though serviceable, these investments did little to increase productivity, nor did they yield a salable output which could earn foreign exchange with which to meet interest payments. Moreover, particularly after 1925, to these long-term investments was added a large volume of short-term lending, much of which was actually used to finance long-term projects. These short-term loans created an unstable situation, in which the danger of default was serious.

In one important respect, international lending of the 1920's created an illusion of soundness and stability that simply did not exist. Some countries used the proceeds of new loans to pay the interest on past loans. It was only in this way that Germany, which borrowed almost three times as much abroad as it paid in reparation, was able to transfer the required payments. These, in turn, enabled European governments to meet their war debt payments to the United States.

The Changing Structure of Industry and Trade

The postwar years also witnessed a change in the relative industrial strength of different countries that both imposed an additional burden of adjustment and rendered the international economy less capable of meeting that burden. These developments were the consequence partly of the war and the economic disruption that followed in its wake, partly of differences in long-term trends of economic growth.

Industry in the European belligerents, faced with the implacable demands of war, had to convert from the production of peacetime goods to the manufacture of munitions and military supplies. Exports naturally suffered, in the case of Britain declining to about half the prewar volume. Even this reduced volume was more precarious and uncertain, being subjected to constant interruption by Germany's unrestricted submarine warfare. After the conflict ended, to the difficulty of restoring broken trade connections were added the uncertainties caused by inflation and by the losses in shipping.

In this interval of some eight years or more, many countries began themselves to produce goods no longer available, or available only intermittently and uncertainly, from Europe. We have already noted this development; suffice it to say that it was very widespread. Another alternative was to place orders with neutral suppliers, especially those outside the area of combat. Japan benefited particularly from such sales; her output of manufactures doubled between 1913 and 1921-25. This was not a total loss to European countries, since the economic growth of their customers meant higher incomes and a greater ability to import than before. But if this opportunity was to be met, it required rapid adaption of supplies to the new types of goods for which demand was increasing.

Pressure on Britain

The effects of industrial expansion abroad were felt with particular severity in Britain. Japanese and Indian production of cotton piece goods increasingly displaced British sales in Far Eastern markets. By 1937, these were less than 10 per cent of the 1913 figure. Like cotton, the woolen textile industry lost heavily to protected domestic industries in foreign markets, and to a lesser extent to rising Japanese competition. Exports of woolen tissues fell from 219 million square yards in 1913 to 156 million in 1929. In the same interval, coal exports declined almost 20 per cent. This industry faced additional competition from newly opened mines in Russia, China, India, and South Africa at the same time that fuel conservation and the use of petroleum and hydroelectric power were reducing the demand. The iron and steel industry barely held its own; to do so, it was forced to concentrate more and more on finished products, where its disadvantage was least, while pig iron lost ground to the new, larger plants in Germany and the United States.[6]

Faced with declining demand for her traditional staples and with many markets lost to new competitors, Britain clearly had to undertake a major shift of resources. This she did with considerable success—even though hampered by an overvalued currency and the restrictive credit policy this implied. While output of cotton and woolen textiles and of coal were lower in 1930 than before the war, a rapid expansion took place in the production of motor cars and motorcycles, electrical machinery and equipment, and chemicals. Exports of these and other products replaced coal and textiles, with the result that in 1929 the total value of exports was some 15 per cent greater than in 1913.

Even so, Britain—and to a lesser degree, other European countries as well —lost ground relatively. Between 1913 and 1929, the total value of world exports increased by two-thirds. The British increase of only 15 per cent is small by comparison; so is that of Belgium, of 22 per cent. Germany fared somewhat better, with her exports rising 33 per cent. France almost held her own with a 50 per cent increase. In contrast with Europe, Canada, Japan, and the United States forged ahead. Canada's exports multiplied three-and-a-half times between 1913 and 1929, Japan's increased threefold, and those of the United States doubled. Expressed in terms of percentages for continents, the distribution of world exports had changed as follows:

    1913: North America, 15.8; Europe, 50.9; Asia, 12.5; Other, 20.8
    1929: North America, 19.5; Europe, 47.4; Asia, 14.9; Other, 18.2

Although Europe remained the world's greatest exporting region, it was losing ground. Moreover, the changes that occurred in the twenties were, as we shall see, only the beginning of a continuing trend.

---

[6] Data in this paragraph from Alfred E. Kahn, *Great Britain and the World Economy*, Ch. VI. Copyright 1946 by the Columbia University Press, New York.

Increasing Dominance of the U.S.

A particularly interesting and important feature of the industrial change going on in the world was the increasingly important position occupied by the United States. We have already noted that in the interval 1870-1913, that country came to surpass Great Britain as a manufacturing power, its share of world manufactures rising from 23 to almost 36 per cent, while Britain's declined from nearly 32 to only 14 per cent. (Germany's share of manufacturing output also rose from a little over 13 to just under 16 per cent.) This phenomenal increase reflected the rapid economic growth of a young country; its roots are to be found in a steady natural increase in population, supplemented by a large volume of immigration, and in a high rate of capital accumulation and investment. Between growing numbers and rising incomes, more and more opportunities for the domestic production of manufactured goods appeared and were exploited.

Immigration and the natural increase in the population added less to growth in the 1920's than formerly, although total population increased from 106 to 123 million during the decade. Investment, that dynamic factor in economic expansion, continued at an extremely high level. Gross capital formation averaged 20 per cent of gross national product from 1919 to 1929. Technology, most visible in new and improved products, also continued its advance. Thus, it is not surprising to find that industrial production simultaneously rose by 51 per cent. This was the period when the automobile industry grew from infancy to adulthood, carrying with it petroleum extraction and refining and tire production. This decade also saw the output of electrical equipment and of the power to drive it more than double. This rate of industrial growth was unmatched by any other country, although Canada, Japan, and South Africa, each starting from a much smaller base, came close.

As a result, the United States increased its lead as a producer of manufactures still further. In 1926-29, it accounted for 42.2 per cent of the world total, as against 11.6 per cent for Germany and 9.4 per cent for the United Kingdom. Other estimates tell a similar story: of the consumption by the fifteen most important commercial nations of the nine principal raw materials and foodstuffs, the United States accounted for 39 per cent. Its national income was equal to that of twenty-three other nations, including its most important rivals. When we add to these facts that in the twenties the U.S. became the world's first exporter and its principal investor, though still second to Great Britain as an importer, its dominant position is striking.

The meaning of these facts is clear. As the world's outstanding manufacturing power, its largest creditor, and one of its two largest traders, the economic health and the economic policies of the United States were of the greatest significance to the suppliers, customers, and debtors of that country.

Ready access to the U.S. market, stable U.S. income and employment, and a steady flow of U.S. lending were not only important but vital. Sudden changes in the U.S. tariff, capriciousness in its lending, or instability in its business could disrupt economic life in most of the rest of the world. Its position of leadership, so suddenly achieved, imposed responsibilities. These, unfortunately, the nation was not prepared to assume.

Agricultural Overproduction

If the expansion of industry in various new lands created an unbalanced situation, even greater instability resulted from the growth of agricultural production. The 1914 war greatly increased the demand for many raw materials, as well as for some foodstuffs, while it removed from production or from contact with world markets important sources of supply, especially of wheat and sugar. Consequently, production in accessible regions bounded upward. With the return of peace, supplies from older producing areas gradually reappeared. But the newer producers did not retire from the field. The result was an accumulation of stocks, downward pressure on prices, and agricultural discontent.

Producers of rubber, wheat, sugar, and coffee attempted to deal with the situation by establishing various types of control schemes. Although details of these projects varied, they all shared one common weakness: the controls could be made effective over only a portion, though usually a major share, of the producers. Each scheme foundered because it made expansion profitable outside the area under control. Thus, rubber restriction applied only to Malaya: additional plantings in the Netherlands East Indies brought its ruin. Coffee control was limited to Brazil, but production in Colombia, Venezuela, and other regions increased rapidly. Cane sugar producers tried restriction, but beet sugar output, aided by tariffs and subsidies, continued to rise.

Thus, at the end of the 1920's, overproduction of important agricultural products, and of such raw materials as timber, copper, and nitrates, as well, both contributed to world instability and presented a problem of structural disequilibrium that would take years to correct.

The World Situation: 1929

Reviewing the developments of the decade 1919-29, we may put on the credit side the re-creation, after the disruptive effects of World War I, of a working international system. Though the world's monetary arrangements were less effective than formerly, they were still truly international in character. Currencies practically everywhere were convertible into one another at stable exchange rates, thus making possible the continued existence of a truly open or multilateral trading system. It is true that tariffs were considerably higher than in prewar days and that, therefore, less advantage was taken of the possibilities of international specialization. Yet trade was large and growing, and it continued, with minor exceptions, to be free of those particularly repressive barriers, direct quantitative controls. International lending was once again providing, in large volume, badly needed foreign exchange.

Yet the painfully reconstructed international economy labored under great difficulties. The new gold standard was less efficient than the old, and the goal of currency convertibility into gold had been discarded in favor of nationally more congenial, but internationally more questionable, practices. The same forces that had led nations to assert greater monetary independence —the increasing role of government and the rising tide of economic nationalism—also led to greater self-assertion in policies concerned with employment, taxation, trade, and immigration. A huge dead weight of war debts and reparation had somehow to be collected and fitted into balances of payments, and although the large volume of international lending contributed to the momentary solution of this problem, it did relatively little to increase the capacity of debtors to service these loans. Major shifts in the location of industry required a vigorous response in the older countries: though this adjustment had begun, it was proceeding at a rather sluggish pace. The increasing dominance of the United States forced. it into a position of leadership for which its isolationist tradition equipped it most inadequately. And to the structural changes in industry were added serious maladjustments in important sectors of agriculture.

It is possible that, given time, even the weakened international structure could have carried through the necessary adjustments and that some difficulties would have yielded to sensible negotiations—if only a reasonably high level of world demand had been maintained. The gradual and piecemeal changes that normally occur, involving the transfer of labor and capital from unprofitable to profitable lines of production, would have had a chance to operate.

Such a gradual solution of its problems, however, was denied the world by the outbreak of the worst depression in history. Even the most profitable industries became unprofitable. There was nowhere for surplus resources in the overexpanded industries to go, no incentive to build up new fields of employment, and no opportunity for lending to improve by continued experience.

(For Selected References, see end of Chapter 24.)

24

FORCES OF DISINTEGRATION

Beginning with 1929, new difficulties piled on top of old. The precariously balanced international economy collapsed under their weight.

THE GREAT DEPRESSION OF THE 1930's

Its Origin and Spread

The great depression of the 1930's throws a strong light upon the dominant economic position of the United States, and reenforces the view that economic conditions in this country go a long way toward determining the level of activity in the rest of the world. There can be little doubt that the major forces that transformed the prosperity and optimism of 1929 into the unemployment and pessimism of 1932 had their origin in the United States, and that declining activity and demand here spread outwards in all directions until they encompassed most of the globe.

Although it is true that a downturn in economic activity got under way in half a dozen of the less developed countries (and in Germany) at various points in time between late 1927 and the middle of 1929, their collective economic weight was not sufficient to spark a worldwide collapse. It was not until the downturn of industrial activity in the United States in July, 1929, followed by the stock market collapse in October, and therewith the puncturing of the bubble of overoptimism, that conditions became rapidly worse in ever-widening circles.

The main support of generally prosperous conditions over most of the world had been a high level of income, employment, and production in the United States, dating from 1922. Underlying and making possible this eight-year stretch of prosperity was an investment boom of record proportions. Investment, the dynamic factor in any modern economy, attained unprecedented heights. Besides this large and continuing investment, induced principally by the rapid growth of industries related to the automobile and to the use of electric power, the country enjoyed its greatest building boom in history.

What brought this era of good times to an end? There can be little doubt as to the principal factors responsible for the onset of depression, even though any brief explanation is bound to involve serious oversimplification. It was simply that major fields of investment, whose activity primed that of the whole economy, had become saturated. The capacity of the automobile industry to produce cars, by 1929, far exceeded its ability to sell them. The tire industry, too, was overbuilt. Many other producers of durable goods faced a similar situation, and encountered serious sales resistance early in 1929. Investment in additional plant and equipment to produce still more of all these goods was not needed and was unlikely to be needed until demand had caught up with existing capacity.

Ever since the beginning of 1928, residential construction had been falling off sharply; it was clear that the supply of houses and apartment buildings, whose numbers the building boom had immensely augmented, was adequate to meet even a growing demand for some time to come.

The decline in activity was swift, especially after the shock to confidence administered by the stock market collapse. With only brief interruptions, investment, industrial production, employment, and national income plummeted downward for three disastrous years. Investment, the key to industrial activity, virtually ceased. In real terms, the gross national product shrank by one-third; in current prices, by nearly half. Industrial production fell to less than half the 1929 level, and that of durable manufactures, reflecting both industrial goods and consumer goods such as automobiles whose consumption could be long postponed, to less than a fourth.

The collapse of the huge American economy reacted swiftly and violently upon other countries. As our income declined, so did our outlay on imports. Indeed, as Figure 24.1 shows, the quantity of our imports went down almost precisely in accord with our income. Over the entire period covered by the chart, there is a close correspondence between physical imports and the level of industrial production, understandable because two-thirds of United States imports consist of primary products and semimanufactures used in industry.

In terms of purchasing power directed toward foreign countries, our outlay on imports fell from $4.4 billion in 1929 to $1.3 billion in 1932. This meant reduced activity in the export industries of our trading partners, and by the well-known mechanism of the multiplier, a decline in their incomes and levels of employment. But this was not all. Payments by the United States for service transactions were cut almost in half—from just under $2 billion in 1929 to $1 billion in 1932. Even more important, American long-term lending not only ceased entirely, but turned into an import of capital (mainly a repatriation of American funds). Long-term foreign loans by the United States averaged $978 million from 1927 to 1929; in 1932, there was an inflow of $251 million of long-term funds from abroad.

Taken together, the amount of dollars spent or invested abroad by Americans

Indexes of Physical Volume (1929-100)

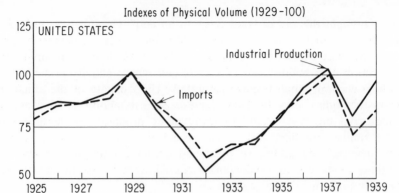

FIGURE 24.1 Industrial Production and Imports of the United States, 1925-39 [Reproduced from Hal B. Lary and associates, *The United States in the World Economy,* Economic Series No. 23, U.S. Department of Commerce, Washington D. C., 1943. p. 8.]

dropped from a level of about $7,400,000,000 for the 3 years 1927 to 1929 to a mere $2,400,000,000 in 1932 and 1933—a reduction of 68 per cent over a span of only 3 years.[1]

This in itself was a terrific shock to the economies of other countries. Added to the difficulties already encountered by agricultural producing nations, it sufficed to pull the entire world (outside the insulated and planned Russian economy) down with us.

The Smoot-Hawley Tariff of 1930

To the depressing effect on world trade of a sharp decline in our national income there was added, in June, 1930, a substantial increase in our tariff.

Discussion of tariff revision had been underway in Congress for some time. It started as a means of providing relief to agriculture, many branches of which, because of declining prices, did not share fully in the general prosperity of the 1920's. The general argument seemed to be that since industry was prosperous, and industry had protection, therefore agriculture would be made prosperous if it were granted protection. Quite aside from the fact that the prosperity of industry depended mainly upon the high level of investment and the high level of production induced thereby, and hardly at all on protection, this naive argument overlooked the fact that many of the farm products (wheat, cotton, tobacco, lard) for which protection was being urged were export commodities, which customs duties could not possibly protect.

Limitation of the tariff revision to agricultural commodities proved, as was to be expected, impossible. The temptation for senators and congressmen from industrial regions to use the technique of vote-trading or log-rolling to

[1] Hal B. Lary and associates, *The United States in the World Economy,* p. 173, Economic Series No. 23, U.S. Department of Commerce, Washington, D. C., 1943. This excellent study is also the source of the data cited above.

obtain increases on products of interest to powerful constituents was too great. So the range of commodities considered broadened from a few to 25,000; the end result was an increase in over 800 rates, covering a wide variety of both agricultural and industrial goods.

This gratuitous and totally uncalled-for raising of our already high tariff produced nothing but unfortunate results. It evoked widespread protests, and precipitated prompt tariff increases in a dozen nations, notably of duties on products of particular importance to the United States.

How much the Smoot-Hawley Tariff reduced our imports is impossible to judge, though there is no doubt that it had an appreciable effect. At least as serious was that it nullified completely efforts of the League of Nations, in progress since 1927, to halt the upward trend of tariffs, and instead accelerated that movement.

Why Not Insulation?

With the shrinkage in United States imports and foreign lending, in each of a large number of countries there set in a decline of production and employment. Reenforced by the operation of the multiplier, their incomes and imports fell sharply, spreading depression in ever-widening circles. Because of the lag between the initial decline in their exports and the induced fall in their imports, these countries experienced an adverse shift in their balances of payments that caused a large outflow of gold. To the primary deflation of income due to falling exports there was added a secondary deflation in response to the contraction of reserves.

With the wisdom of hindsight, we might now recommend as a preferred policy for these countries the prompt introduction of exchange control, coupled with discriminatory restrictions on imports aimed at the source of depression. These external measures should have been combined with increased government outlays to sustain income and employment. Removal of the import restrictions could then have been made conditional upon the adoption by the United States of similar expansionary policies.

There are many reasons why such action was impossible at the time. It was a type of policy that would have required international agreement, and this agreement would have been impossible to achieve. Moreover, devotion to the principles of laissez faire was still too strong. In spite of the enlargement of the area of state action, no government as yet accepted responsibility for the level of economic activity and employment. At most, it was felt that government should attempt, through central banking policy, to check booms and to moderate depressions. The very fact that no depression comparable in severity to that of 1929-33 had been experienced in the memory of living man tended to reenforce this view, as also did the rapidity of recovery from the postwar slump of 1920-21 and the success attending the use of monetary policy in the twenties.

Finally, there existed as yet no general agreement, even among economists, as to the principal causes of the business cycle or as to means of combating it. It was the great depression of the thirties that directed attention forcibly to the problem, and led to the development of the modern theory of employment and income, with its stress on anticyclical fiscal policy.

Varying Reactions

Instead of acting together to insulate the depression and counteract its effects, each nation was left to face its mounting difficulties as best it could. One alternative was to adhere to the gold standard and allow the deflationary forces to tighten their grip, while perhaps restricting imports by higher tariffs. Another was to abandon the gold standard and permit the currency to depreciate. Still a third was to subject the balance of payments to direct control, either by quantitative restrictions on imports or by outright exchange control.

Each nation's response varied with its financial strength, its dependence on foreign loans, and the degree of its attachment to the gold standard. The countries of western Europe without exception chose fixed exchange rates plus deflation. They allowed their balances of payments to deteriorate, their gold reserves to shrink, and the level of economic activity to contract.[2] This solution proved impossible for certain primary producing countries whose export prices had been under severe pressure and which were hard hit by the decline in foreign lending. Thus even before the end of 1929, Argentina, Brazil, Paraguay, and Uruguay all depreciated their currencies. Australia, New Zealand, Bolivia, and Venezuela followed them in 1930. Only Turkey and Iran introduced exchange controls.

By the spring of 1931, it looked as though deflation, even if a painful method of readjustment, was doing its work. The gold standard was still intact in western Europe and the United States. Exchange depreciation had not spread beyond the original nine countries, nor had controls been extended. There were even some hopeful signs on the horizon: in the early months of 1931, industrial production recovered slightly in Germany and the United States. Money rates were low even in Germany, and credit was easy in all the principal centers. There was some prospect that recovery might finally take hold.

The International Financial Crisis of 1931

The hesitant optimism of the spring of 1931 was shattered by the outbreak of an international financial panic. It began, not in a major financial center,

---

[2] Contrary to the general trend, France throughout 1928 to 1932 added heavily to its gold holdings. This may be explained largely in terms of the calling back to France of overseas balances, the liquidation of French security holdings, and the attraction to France of foreign short-term capital in search of a safe haven. Germany's imports declined more rapidly than its exports, thus giving rise to a surplus in its current international account which made possible the continuance of reparation payments and the service of foreign debt.

but in little Austria. A revaluation of the assets of the Credit-Anstalt, the largest commercial bank in Vienna, showed that they had depreciated to the point where the bank was technically insolvent. This revelation led immediately to the withdrawal of foreign short-term credits. A "standstill" agreement with creditors, followed by restrictions on withdrawals, stopped the run on Austria, but did nothing to stem the anxiety that lay behind it.

Worried creditors shifted their withdrawals to Germany, which was a net short-term debtor (see page 405) to the amount of 5 billion marks (over a billion dollars). Although a one-year moratorium on reparation payments, initiated by President Hoover, caused withdrawals to slacken, it did not end them. An important German bank failed early in July, the run intensified, and by the end of the month nearly three billion marks of short-term funds had been transferred abroad. Rather than see the gold and foreign exchange reserves of the Reichsbank exhausted, the government introduced exchange control by a series of decrees, a step followed by eleven other countries in eastern and northern Europe before the year ended.

Germany's choice of exchange control was dictated by the fact that the public had been schooled to believe that exchange depreciation would lead to extreme inflation. Also, exchange control was especially suited to blocking capital flight. The traditional weapon—a high discount rate—had proven its ineffectiveness, for the Reichsbank had raised it to 15 per cent without producing the slightest effect.

Britain Abandons Gold

Capital withdrawal now shifted to England. It was known that British bankers had lent heavily to Germany and other central European countries and that now these credits were tightly frozen. On the other hand, foreigners had claims on London totaling £560 million. Adding to the uncertainty of Britain's position was the probability of a large government deficit, as well as the steady worsening of the country's balance of payments.

Foreign withdrawals mounted rapidly. Despite advances of £130 million from the Bank of France and the Federal Reserve System, these and more were soon paid out. With further credits unavailable, on September 21, Parliament suspended the Bank's obligation to sell gold.

During the crisis, Bank Rate had been raised only to 4½ per cent. Critics claimed that had a rate of 8 to 10 per cent been established, the run on London might well have been halted. This argument is nonsense. What are earnings of 10 per cent against a possible loss of 30 or 40 per cent of one's capital? In the circumstances of 1931, a Bank Rate of 10 per cent would far more likely have been interpreted as a sign of weakness than as the exercise of a bygone power "to pull gold from the earth."

With the abandonment of gold, sterling exchange rates were freed to reflect the country's weak balance-of-payments position. Gradually, sterling depreciated, reaching a point 30 per cent below the old parity in December.

Within five months, the pound began to rise again. In June, 1932, with the establishment of the Exchange Equalization Account, Britain inaugurated a period of flexible, rather than freely fluctuating, exchange rates. The Account, or stabilization fund, received certain foreign assets from the Bank of England, together with £150 million in Treasury bills (in 1933 increased by £200 million) which it could sell in the market for sterling, using the proceeds for the purchase of gold or foreign exchange. By alternately buying and selling foreign currencies, it could keep fluctuations of the pound within bounds, subject to a limit on support imposed by previous accumulations of gold and foreign exchange.

Formation of Currency Blocs

In abandoning gold, Britain carried with her a large number of countries which, because Britain was their major market and London their reserve center, could not afford to see sterling depreciate against their currencies. They too left the gold standard, tied the value of their currencies more or less closely to the pound, and continued to keep the major part of their international reserves in the form of sterling assets. Here we have the beginnings of a formally organized sterling area.[3] London, as the principal reserve center of the members, also performed most of their clearing, although until the outbreak of war, their currencies remained on the whole freely convertible. Each member kept the value of its currency stable in terms of the pound by official purchases and sales of sterling; and the British Exchange Equalization Account moderated fluctuations of the pound against the dollar and other gold currencies. Stability of the pound was also enhanced by an informal but very effective control of foreign lending by the Treasury, which confined capital exports to sterling area members.

After the depreciation of sterling and the formation of the sterling area, only five countries remained solidly on the gold standard. These were the United States, France, Switzerland, Belgium, and the Netherlands.

Most other nations adopted some form of exchange control, whereupon their currencies immediately became inconvertible. The European members of the exchange control bloc kept their exchange rates stable at the old gold parities, while others, especially in South America, allowed their currencies to depreciate heavily, then held the new exchange rates absolutely or relatively fixed.

Disintegration of the World Trading System

The introduction of exchange control and inconvertibility over a rather large area set in motion the tendency toward the bilateral channeling of trade

---

[3] With later additions to the membership, the prewar sterling area included all British Commonwealth countries except Canada, plus the Baltic nations, Egypt, Eire, Iraq, Palestine, Portugal, the Scandinavian countries, and Thailand.

to which we drew attention in Chapter 21. Depreciation by the sterling area and by certain countries outside it (notably Japan) reenforced this tendency, especially among the nations that used exchange controls to maintain unchanged the nominal gold value of their currencies. For quite independently of monetary developments within these nations, their currencies now became overvalued relative to those that had depreciated. Their exports were depressed, their imports stimulated. Controls had therefore to be tightened, and alternative markets for exports and sources of imports sought by means of bilateral trading arrangements.

The members of the gold bloc were, of course, similarly affected. As their balances of payments became increasingly adverse, they attempted to check rising imports by raising tariffs or by introducing quantitative restrictions. France, in particular, relied heavily upon import quotas, a form of trade restriction that sets a fixed limit to the amount of imports of different categories permitted to enter the country.

Even Great Britain, in spite of the relief from the pressure of falling world prices afforded by depreciation, embraced protection. Earlier duties, imposed during and immediately after the war, had been limited in scope. In 1931 and 1932, the Conservative Party, now dominant in a coalition government and since the onset of the depression strongly committed to a protective policy, pushed through a comprehensive tariff. Duties ranged from 20 per cent on a wide variety of manufactures to 30 per cent on many luxuries and to 33⅓ per cent on the products of "key" industries.

For a long time the Conservative Party had cherished the ambition of uniting the Empire more firmly by a system of *Imperial Preference*. Since the new tariff did not apply to Commonwealth countries, a basis now existed for the negotiation of mutual concessions. The Ottawa Conference of 1932 was called to explore the possibilities.

Being mainly an exporter of manufactured goods, Britain wanted freer access to dominion markets for these products. But the Dominions were keenly interested in developing further their growing manufactures. These objectives appeared irreconcilable. They could only be realized, in part, if the Dominions raised the duties on foreign goods, while leaving them more moderate, though still protective, on British goods. In general, this is what they did. For her part, Britain maintained a number of existing preferences and imposed new "Ottawa" duties on foreign supplies of certain products of particular interest to the Dominions. Thus, after Ottawa, Commonwealth tariffs were higher against the foreigner.

We can summarize the effects of the international financial crisis by saying that it led, first, to the breakdown of the international currency system and its replacement by three fairly distinct blocs, consisting of five countries still on the gold standard, a much larger group with fluctuating but convertible currencies, and another large group subject to exchange controls. Second, largely because of the effects of this division, but partly for extraneous reasons, the world trading system itself began to disintegrate as tariffs multiplied and climbed, as quantitative restrictions spread, and as trade became increasingly diverted into bilateral channels.

World Economic Conference: 1932

By the summer of 1932, the opinion was widespread that general and lasting recovery required measures to combat the breakdown of international trade and finance, and that such measures could only be undertaken through intergovernmental cooperation. Plans were laid for a World Economic Conference to be held in June, 1933. A Preparatory Commission of Experts worked out an elaborate draft agenda dealing with tariffs, quantitative trade restrictions, agreements on raw materials and foodstuffs, and a wide variety of monetary problems, including, particularly, currency stabilization. It was hoped that by restoring stable currency conditions, the revival of international trade would be facilitated, through "making it possible to abolish measures of exchange control and remove transfer difficulties." Shortly after the Conference had convened in London, however, and before it could achieve any concrete results, these hopes were dashed by the destabilization of the American dollar.

Devaluation of the Dollar

Deflation in the United States had been especially severe. Between 1929 and 1932, wholesale prices fell 32 per cent, while the national income was cut in half. As prices fell, the banks liquidated commercial loans rapidly. Total loans of all banks had by the end of 1932 been contracted by 42 per cent. Real estate loans, however, shrank only 10 per cent. As property values declined, the security behind this paper evaporated, and more and more banks were forced to close their doors. Some 5,100, about a third of the total, did so between 1930 and 1932.

As the weak position of the banks became more apparent, a wave of currency and gold hoarding got under way, rising to panic proportions early in 1933. President Roosevelt declared a national banking "holiday" on March 16. At the same time he imposed an embargo on gold and silver exports except under license from the Treasury. A month later, the President announced that our departure from the gold standard would continue indefinitely. Simultaneously, Congress passed legislation permitting him to lower the gold content of the dollar by 50 per cent. The dollar was left to fluctuate uncertainly.

The reason for this drastic step had nothing to do with our balance of payments, which was stronger than that of any other country, but reflected our obsession with the credit and price squeeze. Some of President Roosevelt's advisers held the naive view that if the price of gold were raised, commodity prices would automatically rise in direct proportion. Won over to their position, he was determined to put their policy into effect. Therefore he rejected a specific proposal of the World Economic Conference aimed at exchange stabilization; the Conference dragged on in futule discussion for some three weeks more, but accomplished little.

For a time, depreciation of the dollar and rising prices went hand in hand. At first, speculators, anticipating further government action, bid up foreign currencies. Then the Reconstruction Finance Corporation used its newly acquired authority to buy gold, gradually raising its price. By July, a weighted average of exchange rates had risen 32 per cent over the February level, export prices had climbed 33 per cent, import prices 27 per cent, and purely domestic prices 12 per cent.

The rise of export prices was considerably more than theoretical considerations would appear to justify, for in the existing conditions of depression, the supply of exports was very elastic. Moreover, a large proportion of U.S. exports being consumed at home, any appreciable increase in their dollar price would reduce home purchases and divert production abroad.[4] As for U.S. imports, these are predominantly raw materials and crude foodstuffs whose supply is inelastic in the short run. And the huge U.S. market is highly important to their producers. For both these reasons, foreign suppliers of our imports would tend to cut their prices as the dollar depreciated, thus leaving prices in the United States relatively unchanged.

The apparent contradiction between theoretical expectations and what actually happened can be explained by other contemporary developments. The National Industrial Recovery Act of 1933 prohibited price cuts and set floors under wages and raised them. In anticipation of higher wages, manufacturers expanded output halfway to the 1929 level. Agricultural legislation paid farmers to reduce output, generating speculative buying of farm products. In these purely domestic events, not in exchange depreciation, is to be found the main explanation of the rise of export prices. Reenforcing the rise of export prices and stimulating an increase in the price of U.S. imports was a temporary improvement in the world situation, accompanied by an upward movement of the wholesale price level in several important countries.

During the next several months, the picture changed. Between July, 1933, and February, 1934, export prices rose only two points, to 135. Import prices climbed a bit more, from 127 to 131, while the average of exchange rates went on up from 132 to 146. Without any firm support, the earlier expansion ceased and turned into a slump. Industrial production, income,

[4] Since the United States is a large country, exporting only a small part of its production, increased foreign sales resulting from lowered foreign prices would add relatively little to total demand. Also, the large U.S. economy contributed a relatively large proportion to the total world supply of many goods; any increase in its exports would therefore tend to have a seriously depressing effect on prices abroad. (For a review of the various factors involved, see Chapter 18.)

and consumption fell. Foreign prices stopped rising and moved downward, probably in part reflecting the deflationary influence of exchange depreciation in this country.

It is difficult to justify the depreciation of the dollar by the results. This policy served badly the price-raising objective of the administration. Nor is that objective itself above criticism, for it represented a treatment of a symptom rather than the cause, which was the collapse of private investment expenditure. Later recovery measures relied much more heavily upon government outlays to replace this shrunken component of income, and were more successful.

In any event, on January 31, 1934, our experiment with currency depreciation came to an end when the price of gold was fixed at $35 an ounce, as compared with the predepreciation price of $20.67. The dollar was now definitely devalued relative to gold and gold-standard currencies by approximately 41 per cent.

THE RESULTS OF EXCHANGE DEPRECIATION

Effects on Trade and Production

Devaluation of the dollar, added to the depreciation of sterling and related currencies, intensified deflation in the remaining gold-standard countries and increased the pressure on the balances of payments of those with overvalued currencies supported by exchange controls. As the ability of the gold countries to resist devaluation became more doubtful, a speculative flight of capital developed, reenforced by growing fears of war. With the dollar stabilized, most of these funds sought safety in the United States. Between 1934 and 1936, the inward flow of gold, closely paralleling the inflow of capital, surpassed $4 billion, almost half of this amount coming from the reserves of the gold-standard nations.

At first these countries responded by raising tariffs and tightening quantitative restrictions on trade. Then, early in 1935, Belgium devalued her currency 28 per cent; Switzerland, France, and the Netherlands followed in September, 1936, with devaluations of approximately 30, 25, and 19 per cent, respectively. France, with gold losses continuing, found herself unable to hold the fort. Two further downward readjustments of the franc were succeeded, in 1938, by abandonment of gold altogether and stabilization of the franc in terms of sterling. Germany and other exchange control countries in eastern Europe and South America stiffened their controls, and to stimulate exports, began to experiment with multiple exchange rates.

Although world industrial production mounted steadily from 1933, reaching at the end of 1936 a level 20 per cent above 1929, world trade recovered but haltingly. In December, 1936, it was still 10 per cent below 1929, reflecting the intensification of restrictions in both the gold standard and exchange control areas.

Partially offsetting these adverse developments was the stimulus exchange depreciation and abandonment of gold gave to internal expansion. By releasing countries following this policy from the fear of losing reserves, it permitted them to introduce more liberal credit and fiscal policies. Early in 1932, the Bank of England lowered Bank Rate from 6 to 2 per cent and added to commercial bank reserves by open-market security purchases. Sweden also adopted a cheap-money policy and stepped up government expenditures. In these and other sterling-area countries that took similar steps, industrial production recovered rapidly, by 1936 reaching levels substantially above the previous peak of 1929. Rising production and incomes in these countries also brought an increase in their trade, especially with one another.[5]

Insulation against outside forces permitted a comparable internal expansion where exchange controls were in force, as in Germany, though these same controls held the advance of trade in check. But in those nations that still adhered to gold, economic recovery was but slight; 1936 production levels remained well below those of 1929.

THE WORLD ECONOMY PRIOR TO WORLD WAR II

Although the trend toward higher tariffs, the wider use of quantitative restrictions, and the intensification of exchange controls continued after 1932, thus tending further toward the disintegration of the world economy, the picture just before the outbreak of the second World War was not one of unrelieved gloom.

Exchange-Rate Equilibrium Approached

While three distinct currency areas still existed, the period of recurring devaluation and exchange-rate instability was at an end. Since final devaluation of the dollar, the dollar/sterling rate had varied within a range of approximately three per cent ($4.90 to $5.05), and some sixteen other currencies were pegged to sterling. Exchange rates, except on the controlled currencies, had approached equilibrium levels, and even those subject to controls were being brought more in line with reality by the fractional depreciation that goes with the introduction of multiple exchange rates.

The Trade Agreements Program

Even in the field of trade policy, a modest program of tariff liberalization got under way. Sponsored by Cordell Hull, the U.S. Secretary of State, a

---

[5] The temporary abandonment of gold by the United States, though not the forced depreciation that followed, can be defended as a precondition of expansion. For efforts earlier in 1933 and in 1932 to expand the credit base had been accompanied by outward movements of gold.

bill to permit gradual tariff reduction was passed by Congress in 1934. Known as the Reciprocal Trade Agreements Act, it authorized the President to sign commercial agreements with other countries reducing existing U.S. duties by as much as 50 per cent, in exchange for parallel concessions. Since the study of proposed concessions and counter-concessions, as well as the actual negotiations in which they became realized, were to be carried out by committees made up of representatives of executive departments, this measure removed the making of tariffs from the political arena of Congress and made possible the beginning of a rational approach to this problem.

Especially in the depressed conditions of 1934, the bill could probably never have been sold to Congress had it not stressed the expansion of American exports by reduction of foreign duties. And since the Trade Agreements Act transferred from Congress to the executive responsibility for alterations in our tariff, there can be little doubt that this abdication of power was made attractive by the memories that many Congressmen had of their nightmarish experience in the year-long legislative tussle preceding the enactment of the Smoot-Hawley Tariff Act of 1930. For then they were subjected to the constant pressure of innumerable lobby groups and were "asked to pass judgment on the wisdom of thousands of different rates defined in the esoteric jargon of hundreds of different trades."[6]

In no sense did the Reciprocal Trade Agreements program contemplate the abandonment of protection, for a provision known as the "peril point clause" specified that duties were not to be cut if such action threatened serious injury to American industry. Moreover, an "escape clause" required an upward adjustment of a duty reduced as a result of negotiations if serious injury were shown to have resulted from that reduction. Yet in spite of these limitations, the Trade Agreements Act was a step toward the liberalization of trade—as Sumner Welles later characterized it, "one spot of sanity in a world outlook that seemed wholly and hopelessly dark."[7]

Originally enacted for a span of three years, the Trade Agreements Act was periodically reenacted (though modified somewhat after the war) until replaced by the more liberal Trade Expansion Act of 1962. Before war broke out, twenty-one agreements had been signed, under which average rates of duty on dutiable imports into the United States were substantially reduced, and corresponding reductions on our exports granted by other parties to these agreements.[8] By setting in motion a reversal of the trend toward ever-higher barriers, the program furnished the basis for a renewed and broader attack upon the problem in the years immediately after the war.

[6] Raymond Vernon, "America's Foreign Trade Policy and the GATT," *Essays in International Finance, No. 21* (October, 1954). Published by International Finance Section, Princeton University.

[7] Sumner Welles, "Postwar Trade Policies of the United States," *International Conciliation* (May, 1943), p. 394.

[8] For estimates of the extent to which the U.S. tariff has been reduced as a result of the Trade Agreements program, see page 538 in this book.

SELECTED REFERENCES

Ashworth, William, *A Short History of the International Economy, 1850-1950*. London: Longmans, Green & Co., 1952. Chapters VII and VIII provide, in brief compass, an excellent review of the major events between 1914 and 1950, together with an evaluation of their significance.

Bank for International Settlements, *Annual Reports* (Berne). For a review and evaluation of current developments, these reports are extremely useful.

Beyen, J. W., *Money in a Maelstrom*. New York: Macmillan, 1949. A lively account of monetary disturbances of the interwar period, by an insider.

Brown, William Adams, Jr., *The Gold Standard Reinterpreted, 1914-1934*. New York: National Bureau of Economic Research, 1940. A thorough study of the gold standard that focuses upon the changes it underwent after the first World War.

Harrod, R. F., *The Life of John Maynard Keynes*. London: Macmillan, 1952. The middle chapters of this book provide a vivid account of events of the interwar period from the point of view of one who was an active and influential participant.

Interim Report of the Committee on Currency and Foreign Exchanges after the War, reprinted in *British Banking Statutes and Reports, 1922-1928*, Vol. II, ed. T. E. Gregory. New York: Oxford University Press, 1928. The report of the Cunliffe Committee, which officially set the stage for Britain's return to the gold standard in 1925.

Kahn, Alfred E., *Great Britain in the World Economy*. New York: Columbia University Press, 1946. A well-documented and readable account of the post-1914 changes in the British economy and how they affected Britain's international position.

Keynes, J. M., "The End of Laissez Faire," in *Essays in Persuasion*. New York: Harcourt Brace, 1932. Reflections of a great economist on "possible improvements in modern Capitalism through the agency of collective action."

————, "The German Transfer Problem," *Economic Journal*, XXIX (1929); reprinted in *Readings in the Theory of International Trade*. One side of a famous debate on the operation of the adjustment mechanism with stable exchanges.

Lary, Hal B. and Associates, *The United States in the World Economy*, Economic Series No. 23. Washington, D. C.: U.S. Department of Commerce, 1943. A detailed analysis of the international transactions of the United States during the interwar period.

League of Nations, *International Currency Experience*. Geneva: The League, 1944. Especially good for its discussion of the changes in the operation of the gold standard, the history and effects of the devaluations of the 1930's, and the purposes and operation of exchange control.

————, *World Economic Survey*, annually. Geneva: The League, 1932-40. A current analysis of events during the years of the great depression.

Ohlin, Bertil, "The Reparation Problem: A Discussion," *Economic Journal*, XXXIX (1929); reprinted in *Readings in the Theory of International Trade*. The other side of the debate inaugurated by Keynes (see above).

Report of the Committee on Finance and Industry, Cmd. 3897. London: H.M.S.O., 1931. An analysis by Britain's leading experts of the monetary problems posed by the depression, and of alternative policies.

PART VI

Reconstruction, Change, and Reform

25

RECONSTRUCTION AND ITS
AFTERMATH

Our review of the interwar period has shown it to have been dominated by the legacy of war and by the impact of the depression. World War I brought in its train disruption and disequilibrium. Looking back nostalgically to the simplicity and certainty of a world firmly bound together by a gold standard centering in the London money market, the world's political and economic leaders struggled uncertainly to reconstruct the past. Their efforts, however, were overbalanced by structural and political changes as yet imperfectly understood. They restored the gold standard, but not London's position of pre-eminence, nor the close financial integration of prewar days. They sought to free trade from its increasing shackles, but were repeatedly balked by the irresistible forces of nationalism unleashed by the war.

Because its great economic strength was now apparent, the United States might have led in forging a world economy more suited to the changed circumstances. Yet its people, having just completed a long period of internal development, shrank from the responsibilities their new position thrust upon them. The automobile age had arrived, and they exploited to the limit the opportunities it afforded.

From the point of view of what forces were to be allowed to determine the course of trade, the decade of the 1920's was inconclusive and contradictory. Impulses and efforts toward establishing greater freedom for comparative costs competed with nationalistic policies with respect to money, trade, and immigration. Less free than in the Victorian Age, far more free than under Mercantilism, the world economy moved uncertainly toward reliance upon the impersonal price mechanism.

This phase ended suddenly with the outbreak of the Great Depression. One of its chief manifestations, the sharp decline in income, now seized the center of the stage. Imports followed the curve of production; the ranks of the unemployed swelled everywhere. To combat unemployment and to safeguard its currency, one nation after another adopted more and more stringent controls. With few exceptions, goods or capital could move only when governments gave

[427]

their permission. The forces of nationalism dominated almost all channels of international trade and payments.

Again during the second World War, the channels of trade and even its composition were shaped by the division of the world into warring blocs and by the insatiable needs of the armed forces. Because more nations and more people were drawn into this struggle, and because the complexity and costliness of armaments had greatly increased, the demand for goods to feed the war effort was far greater and more disruptive to the peacetime structure of production than in 1914-18. On the other hand, to obtain the needed supplies became more difficult, because the Axis powers dominated most of Europe, North Africa, and the East beyond India. The consequent search for substitutes for rubber, tin, quinine, hemp, and a long list of strategic materials furnishes a vivid illustration of the vital role played by international trade.

EFFECTS OF THE WAR

Despite the wholesale reorganization of production and severance of markets and suppliers occasioned by six years of global war, restoration of market connections and reconversion to peacetime production occurred with remarkable speed and without any general interruption of employment. It was the impact of war upon productive capacity, upon the conduct of national finances, and upon the pattern of international debt that had the most disruptive consequences for the functioning of an already badly weakened world economy. Some of these effects, and the degree of recovery as compared with the 1914 war, are shown in Table 25.1.

Table 25.1. RELATIVE RECOVERY IN THE SECOND FULL YEAR AFTER THE TERMINATION OF WORLD WARS I & II

	Industrial Production	Agricultural Production	Livestock Numbers	Population
1913	100	100	100	100
1920	76	63	90	99
1938	100	100	100	100
1946/7	80	75	81	97

SOURCE: United Nations, Department of Economic Affairs, *A Survey of the Economic Situation and Prospects of Europe*, Geneva, 1948. Tables 8, 11, and 16. The data refer to Europe, and cover the same countries for both periods. Population comparison from United Nations, Economic Commission for Europe, *Growth and Stagnation in the European Economy*, Geneva, 1954, Table A.4.

INTERNATIONAL PAYMENTS DIFFICULTIES

It is in western Europe's balance of payments that the international consequences of subnormal production and other war-induced changes are mirrored (see Table 25.2). With production low and income and employment high, goods that might have been exported were retained for domestic use, and imports were badly needed to supplement scanty domestic production. For the first three years after fighting stopped, Europe's trade deficit exceeded $5 billion; in the three years before the War, the trade deficit had been only $2 billion. Whereas the current account as a whole was in balance in 1938, for five years after the war it showed a large, though gradually diminishing, deficit.

Table 25.2. EUROPE'S BALANCE OF PAYMENTS ON
CURRENT ACCOUNT, 1938 AND 1946-50

(in billions of current dollars)

	1938	1946	1947	1948	1949	1950
Imports, f.o.b.	$ 5.8	$ 9.4	$ 13.7	$ 14.4	$ 13.5	$ 12.5
Exports, f.o.b.	3.7	4.3	6.4	8.8	9.4	9.6
Balance on trade account	$ −2.1	−5.1	−7.3	−5.6	−4.1	−2.9
Income from investments (net)	1.4	0.5	0.4	0.4	0.4	0.5
Other current invisibles (net)	0.7	−1.2	−0.5	0.3	−0.1	−0.1
Balance on services account	2.1	−0.7	−0.1	0.7	0.3	0.4
Balance on current account (goods and services)	0.0	−5.8	−7.4	−4.9	−3.8	−2.5

SOURCES: United Nations, *A Survey of the Economic Situation and Prospects of Europe*, p. 54; *Economic Survey of Europe in 1949*, p. 109; *Economic Survey of Europe in 1950*, p. 114.

Since almost three-fourths of Europe's cumulative deficit (1946-50) of $24.4 billion was with the United States alone, the deficit was often called simply "the dollar shortage." This phrase did not mean, of course, that Europe was spending more dollars than it had, for that would be impossible. What it did mean was that Europe was unable to earn enough dollars from normal sources to meet its expenditures, and so was forced to draw heavily on reserves, borrow what it could, and rely on large extraordinary grants to make up the balance.[1] Nor was this so-called dollar shortage a purely European phenomenon. Until 1950, Canada, Latin America, and all the major areas of the world had a dollar deficit on current account.

Causes of Europe's Deficit

Precisely what forces, unleashed by the war, brought Europe's current account from a condition of balance in 1938 to one of serious disequilibrium in 1947? Certainly a major share of the change must be attributed to *inflation*. But *structural changes* were also important.

[1] Neither should "dollar shortage," applied to this period, be taken to imply an insufficient supply of dollars made available by the United States through normal channels. Europe's payments difficulties arose from inadequate amounts of goods and services available for export, combined with an exceptional need for imports. Because its dependence upon the United States as a source of supplies was unusually great, its deficit was focused primarily upon this country.

Look first at the trade deficit, which rose by $5.2 billion in this interval. Had prices remained constant from 1938 on, the trade deficit would have been larger than the prewar one by $1.5 billion, for while the volume of imports increased, that of exports actually fell. This leaves $3.7 billion, or almost three-quarters of the deficit in trade, to be laid at the door of price changes. The prices of both exports and imports approximately doubled under the impact of worldwide inflation. Since imports exceeded exports in 1938 by over $2 billion, this force alone would nearly double the deficit.

Some part of the *real* rise in imports relative to exports is also attributable to inflation. Domestic pressure to restore standards of living after several years of austerity and hardship was heavy. Likewise, it was vital to replace and improve Europe's severely damaged capital equipment. These pressures led governments to finance excess demand instead of scaling it down to correspond to the resources available; the excess demand withdrew domestic production from export channels and also sucked in imports. Moreover, relative to the United States and Canada, where inflation was less severe, Europe's currencies became overvalued at existing exchange rates, making it difficult to export to the dollar area.

Also operating to stimulate imports and depress exports were various structural forces. The reduction of European productive capacity as a result of war damage and inadequate maintenance made imports more necessary and exports less available. Another factor affecting the physical volume of exports was the loss of overseas markets. Some of this loss disappeared with the restoration of trade connections, but some was more lasting, since it resulted from the expansion of production by former customers or from the replacement (as in Latin America) of European sellers by the United States and Canadian firms. On the side of imports, especially of timber and of wheat and other grains, western Europe had to rely more heavily on the Western Hemisphere, since the former suppliers, Soviet Russia and the countries of eastern Europe, could no longer be counted on.

The decline of $2.2 billion in receipts from shipping and other services had a very simple explanation. (1) Heavy wartime losses of tonnage left the European nations with far fewer ships to carry an increased volume of freight; they had to depend on the recently constructed (and heavily subsidized) American merchant fleet to bring their imports from overseas. Among "other" services, (2) credits earned from supplying tourists' wants were low just after the war, while Britain and the Netherlands, in particular, had to continue large military expenditures in the Middle East and in Southeast Asia.

EUROPEAN RECONSTRUCTION

A deficit must, of course, somehow be financed. During 1946 and 1947, the means of meeting Europe's huge excess payments came from an assortment of loans and grants and from further drafts on her badly depleted reserves. Some $4 billion was provided by the short-lived United Nations Relief and Recovery Administration (UNRRA), established during the war to prevent starvation, disease, and economic collapse in the immediate postwar period of maximum disruption. Under the Anglo-American Financial Agreement, the United States and Canada together advanced $5 billion to the United Kingdom. Additional stopgap aid came from various sources: $400 million to Greece and Turkey for military and economic assistance; Export-Import Bank loans of approximately $2 billion; and nearly another billion from the International Bank and the International Monetary Fund.

The European Recovery Program

By the summer of 1947, it had become clear that relief works and emergency loans were totally inadequate means for coping with Europe's difficulties. The mounting international deficit, inadequate supplies of fuel and raw materials, slackening industrial production, and a shortage of foodstuffs intensified by the worst harvest in years—all pointed to the need for a more drastic and far-reaching attack. This the European Recovery Program, or the Marshall Plan, aimed to provide.

In his commencement address at Harvard University on June 5, 1947, Secretary of State Marshall, after reviewing the breakdown of the European economy, stated the concern of the United States for this condition and its willingness to cooperate fully in a coordinated recovery effort. Insisting that "the initiative . . . must come from Europe," and that they should agree on requirements and on the action they would take, he pledged United States aid in drafting a program and in later financial support thereof.

The response was immediate. Out of a conference lasting all summer, there emerged a Committee, later crystallized as the Organization for European Economic Cooperation (OEEC), whose report analyzed Europe's problems and formulated a program of recovery to extend over the four years 1948-51. Financial aid needed was estimated at $22.4 billion, most of which would have to come from the United States. As their contribution, the participating countries[2] undertook to do everything in their power to make Europe productive, so that it could sell enough to pay its way in the world. This meant raising output and increasing efficiency of production, both of exports and of articles hitherto bought outside the European trading area. As means to this major goal, OEEC members were to cooperate in every way possible, in particular to eliminate restrictive trade barriers, and each was to check inflation as a precondition to the effective use of Europe's resources.

[2] The participating countries, all of which became members of the OEEC, were: Austria, Belgium, Denmark, France, Greece, Iceland, Ireland, Italy, Luxembourg, Netherlands, Norway, Portugal, Sweden, Switzerland, Turkey, and the United Kingdom. Western Germany was always included in the proposals made, and became a member upon achieving independence of Allied military control.

Parallel committees in the United States wrestled with cost estimates, the availability of American resources for aid, and the probable impact of a major aid program on the U.S. economy. From $12 billion to $17 billion was suggested as the necessary American contribution to a really effective undertaking. Congress passed legislation providing interim aid and $4 billion for the first year's operations of the Economic Cooperation Administration, the administrative counterpart of the OEEC in Europe.

The story of the ERP is a fascinating one. A flood of American administrators and experts, including businessmen, college professors, industrial and agricultural technicians, and publicity agents, crammed into offices in the European headquarters, Paris, and in the capital of every OEEC member country. Their job was to schedule Europe's needs in cooperation with the OEEC, to approve orders for goods ranging from wheat to tobacco, from tractors to locomotives and freight cars, and to see that these goods got to where they were needed.

By late 1951, although the recovery program was not yet completed, mutual defense against Communist aggression overshadowed economic aid and the ECA was merged in a new organization, the Mutual Security Administration, which administered both military and economic assistance. The cause of this change in direction and in organization was, of course, the outbreak of the Korean war in June, 1950, and the resultant emphasis on rearmament.

Up to mid-1951, the ECA had spent a total of $10.3 billion. Approximately 90 per cent of this was in outright grants, only $1.1 billion being advanced as loans.

Europe's Recovery

PRODUCTION   With the crucial aid supplied by the United States, Europe made rapid progress. Industrial production in the OEEC countries, some 17 per cent below prewar production in 1947, almost closed this gap in 1948. From then on it rose about 10 per cent each year until 1951, when it stood 35 per cent above the level in 1938. Agricultural production behaved similarly, though it moved at a slower rate.

CONTROL OF INFLATION   Inflation, which was open and unrestrained in some countries, notably France and Italy, and suppressed by price controls and rationing in England and the Netherlands, was brought rapidly under control. The increasing abundance of goods as production rose helped substantially to slow down the rise of prices, but deliberate use of monetary and fiscal policy was at least equally important. Drastic currency reforms in Germany and Austria, were inflation had progressed farthest, canceled the larger part of the old and excessive currency issues and replaced them with new ones. By early 1950, a decade of rapidly rising prices had given way to price stability.

With the outbreak of the Korean war in June of that year, a sharp spurt of buying generated inflation anew. Because of its threat to their balances of payments, most European countries applied credit restraints promptly and effectively. The renewed rise in prices slowed down and came to a halt within a year or two; thereafter, prices remained stable until 1956.

INTRA-EUROPEAN TRADE   Trade among western European nations stood in 1947 at about 60 per cent of its prewar volume. Reduced production, both in industry and agriculture, partly accounted for this sharp decline. More important was an imbalance in production and therefore in the ability to supply exports. Industrial output was especially low in Germany, whose large export surplus with other European countries formed the basis on which the prewar trade pattern rested. With this pattern disrupted, there developed a general tendency toward the close bilateral balancing of accounts between European trading partners. By 1948, some 200 bilateral agreements, backed up by rigorous quantitative restrictions, governed intra-European trade.

With the growth in production came the physical means to restore intra-European trade. But the bilateral arrangements and the trade restrictions remained stubborn obstacles. To combat the latter, the OEEC adopted a Code of Liberalization under which each member obligated itself progressively to eliminate restrictions on private trade. By 1955, the greater part (84 per cent) of quantitative restrictions on trade had disappeared. At least equally important was the establishment of the European Payments Union, which provided an effective means of clearing intra-European payments and thus of doing away with the bilateral channeling of trade. These collective measures, together with the steady increase in production, resulted in an increase in intra-European trade (by 1955) to almost 90 per cent above the prewar level.

DEVALUATION   A combination of eager buyers and handicapped suppliers created a typical sellers' market during the immediate years after the war. By 1949, with the increased availability of goods both in Europe and in North America, this suddenly became transformed into a buyers' market. Price considerations again came to the fore. Overvalued European currencies, not a serious hindrance to exports as long as supplies of all kinds were short, now became a primary obstacle. It became increasingly clear that currency values simply must be revised.

On September 18, 1949, Britain took the plunge, devaluing the pound by 30.5 per cent. Within a few days, some 27 nations followed her example, including all the sterling area (except Pakistan) and 11 western European nations. Most of the countries devalued by the same amount; a few—notably Belgium, France, Western Germany, and Italy—chose a substantially smaller figure.

THE BALANCE OF PAYMENTS   Each aspect of European recovery so far considered singly—the increase in production, the ending of inflation, the resurgence of intra-European trade, and the correction of currency overvaluation—worked jointly with the others to restore balance in Europe's international accounts. Steadily rising receipts from shipping and from tourism helped.

By 1950, the huge 1947 current account deficit had been cut by two-thirds, to $2.5 billion. Thereafter, progress was steady, with rising military expenditures in Europe by the United States contributing increasingly to Europe's dollar receipts. Including these expenditures, the OEEC countries from 1952 through 1955 had a surplus on current account. Since economic aid continued to be received, though in diminishing amounts, it was possible to add to reserves of gold and foreign exchange. These climbed steadily from $9.8 billion at the end of 1951 to $15.3 billion in 1955.

CHRONIC DOLLAR SHORTAGE?

Despite the steady improvement in production and in the competitive position of western Europe, and despite also the visible evidence of rising reserves of gold and foreign exchange, there were few who believed, in 1957, that western Europe's international payments problem had been solved. It was widely urged that the balance achieved was temporary and apparent rather than lasting and real, since it rested in considerable part on uncertain United States foreign expenditures and was supported by quantitative restrictions on dollar imports. With any significant decline in these expenditures, or with the removal of these restrictions, a persistent tendency toward dollar shortage would reassert itself.

This view undoubtedly underestimated the permanence of the forces underlying United States outlays on military establishments abroad and on foreign aid. More important, however, was an inability to appreciate the strength and vigor of Europe's recovery. Instead, many economists expressed a basic pessimism by contending that the problem of dollar shortage extended back at least to 1914, and that it rested upon the previous and continuing superiority in the competitive position of American industry, based on more rapid technological progress in the United States.

Today we know this view was exaggerated and unreal; but even as late as 1957, there was a good deal of evidence to support it. Certainly over the entire 37 years between 1914 and 1951, Europe's balance of payments with the United States had been adverse, except for a brief period in the 1920's. It was also true that technological progress in the United States had been rapid for a half century, during which it had increased its share of world trade in manufactures from approximately 11 per cent to 29 per cent.

But as was pointed out at the time, even four decades of recurring balance-of-payments troubles, when each recurrence can be explained by a distinct cause, no more establishes a state of chronic disequilibrium than a series of fortuitous illnesses constitutes chronic invalidism. As for the increase of productivity in the United States, a detailed statistical study failed to show that this was more rapid there than elsewhere except during both world wars.[3]

[3] G. D. A. MacDougall, "Does Productivity Rise Faster in the United States?" *Review of Economics and Statistics*, **XXXVIII** (May, 1956).

FROM DOLLAR SHORTAGE TO DOLLAR GLUT

Just as the debate over a presumed chronic dollar shortage began to die down, events were taking place that silenced it and that replaced a supposed European with a very real U.S. balance-of-payments problem.

Even during the years 1950-57, when serious concern over a presumed chronic dollar shortage continued to be expressed, the United States ran a series of deficits totaling $10 billion. Although exports of goods and services exceeded similar imports by a comfortable annual margin of more than $3 billion, U.S. military expenditures abroad, foreign aid, and net private capital exports topped this sum by approximately $1.2 billion. Other countries— mainly European—were thereby enabled to add to their reserves. But since the dollar remained the world's strongest currency, the greater part of excess dollar payments was taken in the form of deposits in United States banks or of short-term government securities. United States gold exports amounted to only $1.7 billion in this period.

Serious Disequilibrium Appears

Then, beginning in 1958, the situation changed suddenly. For four successive years, the U.S. deficit ranged from over $3 billion to over $4 billion. In place of a dollar shortage, there was now very clearly a dollar surplus. The earlier impregnable reserve position of the United States changed drastically. Whereas in 1949 United States gold reserves amounted to $24.6 billion and foreign short-term claims amounted to only $8.2 billion, by the end of 1960 reserves had been pulled down to $17.5 billion while foreign short-term claims, at $18.5 billion, now exceeded reserves. Two years later gold reserves had fallen to $16 billion, while short-term foreign liabilities stood at $22 billion.

What had happened to cause this striking change? Two factors appear to have been mainly responsible. Although overseas military expenditures and foreign aid rose but little, capital exports remained close to the high level attained in 1957, when abnormally large merchandise exports provided a sufficiently large current account surplus to finance them.[4] Meanwhile exports fell some $3 billion below the 1957 level in 1958 and 1959, while imports increased by more than $2 billion in 1959, reenforced by the steel strike of that year. The U.S. trade position, as reflected in the current account balance, was simply not strong enough to support a substantial increase in private investment abroad, in addition to continuing large foreign government outlays. The consequence was a deficit of $3.5 billion in 1958, and of $4.2 billion in 1959.

---

[4] Exports of $26.7 billion in 1957, nearly $7.5 billion greater than the 1951-56 average, were caused by exceptional demands in Europe during the Suez crisis, especially for petroleum products and the services of U.S. tankers. The large capital exports of 1957 and 1958 reflected growing interest of U.S. investors in the rapid expansion of European industry, reenforced in 1957 by the formation of the Common Market.

The slump in U.S. exports, together with the rise in its imports, suggests a possible worsening of the nation's competitive position in world trade. Changes in the distribution of trade among the leading industrial nations support this suggestion. Of the total exports of the nine leading industrial countries, the share of the United States declined from 36.3 per cent in 1952 to 29.4 per cent in 1959, or by 6.9 per cent.[5] With respect to the important category of manufactured exports, the decline in the U.S. share was even more marked— 8.8 per cent.[6] As Baldwin points out, little of this decline can be attributed to changes in the composition of trade due to changes in world demand; nearly all of it must be laid at the door of a weakened competitive position.

Why, then, did the ability of the United States to compete in world trade deteriorate? The answer provides an interesting commentary on the postwar European fears of a chronic dollar shortage due to more rapid technological progress in the United States. It is principally a lag in productivity in this country relative to its competitors that accounts for its reduced competitiveness. As Table 25.3 shows, productivity (output per man-hour) increased least in the United States of all the seven countries compared. Wages (hourly earnings), it is true, rose less in the United States than in any other country

Table 25.3. PRODUCTIVITY, EARNINGS, AND LABOR COSTS
IN MANUFACTURING, 1958 vs. 1953

(1953 = 100)

	U.S.	Belgium	France	Germany	Italy	Japan	U.K.
Output per man-hour	109	127	145	129	138	123	112
Hourly earnings	121	131	132	138	128	125	137
Labor costs	111	103	91	107	93	102	122

SOURCE: Bela Balassa, "Recent Developments in the Competitiveness of American Industry and the Prospects for the Future," Joint Economic Committee, op. cit., p. 36.

except France, but even so, they increased more rapidly than productivity, so that labor costs rose considerably relative to America's industrial competitors. The only exception is the United Kingdom, whose competitive position deteriorated even more than that of the United States, and for similar reasons.

If we pursue our enquiry into labor costs one step further, we see that the

[5] The countries included in the data are Belgium-Luxembourg, Canada, France, Germany, Italy, Japan, Sweden, the United Kingdom, and the United States. Together they accounted for approximately 52 per cent of world trade. See Robert E. Baldwin, "Implications of Structural Changes in Commodity Trade," Joint Economic Committee, Factors Affecting the United States Balance of Payments, 87th Congress, 2nd sess., Washington, D. C., 1962.

Also relevant to this discussion is the fact that since 1954, even the declining share of the U.S. in world exports had been supported by the sale (often at subsidized prices) of agricultural products for inconvertible currencies under Public Law 480. In the period under survey, these commodities accounted for about one-third of total U.S. exports.

[6] Ibid., Table 3.

trouble was concentrated in one important sector—in basic metals, and particularly in steel. Whereas the rise in productivity was identical for basic metals and for manufacturing as a whole (109 in 1958 vs. 1953), hourly earnings rose to 129 and labor costs rose to 118. This contrasts with an actual decline in labor costs in the basic metals industries in Belgium (94), France (92), and Italy (75), and a smaller rise in Germany (112) and in Japan (111).[7] Since steel is an important raw material for many industries, its price movements have special importance. Added to the general lag in productivity and the disproportionate increase in wages, it accounts for the fact that the decline in the U.S. competitive position was concentrated in metal manufactures, machinery, and vehicles.[8]

It is hardly necessary to look further for an explanation of the serious U.S. balance-of-payments disequilibrium of 1958 and 1959 and succeeding years. Subject to a heavy burden of payments for military and economic aid and with a large outflow of capital, the weakening of the nation's competitive trading position prevented it from generating a current account surplus adequate to offset these huge charges.

The problem could have been solved by a drastic cut in overseas military expenditures, in foreign aid, or both, or by measures to check the overflow of U.S. capital. Any such solution, however, was ruled out because of the paramount role of defense and foreign economic policy. Or the Government could have adopted the alternative of deflating costs and prices, thereby improving the nation's competitive status. Or it could have accomplished the same result by devaluing the dollar, which at current cost and price levels appears to have been appreciably overvalued.[9]

Reaction to the Deficits

At first, the Government took no action. Reserves were large, and even though the huge deficit might be due to a fundamental disequilibrium such as overvaluation of the dollar, the purpose of reserves is, among other things, to provide breathing space while underlying adjustments are set in motion. Indeed, official circles showed little concern until the summer of 1959; this concern did not become serious until the following year.

The deficit mounted in 1959 and remained high in 1960. Unwilling or unable to set in motion a true adjustment process, both the Eisenhower and the Kennedy administrations adopted a policy of "defending the dollar" through a series of measures that sought to reduce U.S. international payments

---

[7] *Ibid.*, Table 4.

[8] *Ibid.*, Appendix, Table A-3:

[9] Two responsible economists estimated that as of 1962, the dollar was overvalued by some 15 per cent. See Jaroslav Vanek, "Overvaluation of the dollar: Causes, Effects, and Remedies," p. 274; and H. S. Houthakker, "Exchange Rate Adjustment," p. 301, in *Factors Affecting the United States Balance of Payments*, 87th Congress, 2nd Session, Washington, D. C.: Government Printing Office, 1962.

and increase receipts. These measures took three principal forms: (1) mildly protectionist moves, such as tying foreign aid more closely to U.S. supplies, diverting military expenditures abroad to the United States, and reducing the duty-free imports allowed returning American tourists; (2) an appeal to European nations to carry more of the burden of mutual defence and of aid to underdeveloped countries; and (3) attempts to stimulate exports by improving government services to exporters, by an improved system of export credits and of credit guarantees, and by appealing to our trading partners to eliminate remaining discriminatory restrictions on imports from the United States.

While these measures were being discussed, prepared, and gradually put into effect, everyone hoped the competitive pressures, both domestic and foreign, and the progress of technology would effect a reduction of U.S. costs and prices. So far as concerns productivity and labor costs, these hopes achieved modest realization. A somewhat more rapid rise in U.S. productivity combined with a slower rate of increase in wages caused labor costs to fall moderately (see Table 25.4). In Europe, however, with full employment and labor shortages common, wages tended to rise faster than in the earlier period. Between 1958 and 1961, labor costs in the United States approximately held their own with similar costs in Belgium, France, and Italy, and actually fell appreciably relative to Germany and the United Kingdom. (A startling rise is productivity in Japan, even with a 30 per cent increase in hourly earnings, enabled her to improve her competitive position against all rivals.)

Table 25.4. PRODUCTIVITY, EARNINGS, AND LABOR COSTS
IN MANUFACTURING, 1961 vs. 1958
(1958 = 100)

	U.S.	Belgium	France	Germany	Italy	Japan	U.K.
Output per man-hour	114	112	114	117	121	160	109
Hourly earnings	110	109	105	133	116	130	120
Labor costs	96	97	92	113	95	80	109

SOURCE: Derived from Balassa, op. cit., Table 3.

This modest reduction in U.S. labor costs was certainly not sufficient to correct the payments imbalance, but at least it kept an underlying difficulty from getting worse. Elimination of the balance-of-payments disequilibrium by this route would require continuing prosperity with tight labor markets in Europe, persistence of the excessive unemployment (above 5.5 per cent from 1957 on) in the United States, and no offsetting changes in relative productivity. And above all, it would require time.

Partly in response to the steps taken to "defend the dollar," partly because of extraneous forces, the trade balance and therewith the basic deficit—that resulting from trade, government operations, and long-term investment—improved substantially. U.S. exports rose sharply in 1960, by $3.2 billion, while imports declined by a half billion, giving rise to a favorable trade balance of

$4.7 billion. The principal explanation of this improvement was a continuation of the rise in productivity and incomes in Europe, coupled with a mild recession in the United States.

Table 25.5. SELECTED U.S. BALANCE OF PAYMENTS ITEMS, 1958–1963

(in millions of dollars)

	Exports	Imports	Trade Balance	Basic Deficit*	Recorded Net Short-term Capital Outflow (—)	Unre- corded Transac- tions	Gross Deficit*
1958	16,202	12,867	3,335	−3,655	− 362	488	−3,529
1959	16,211	15,207	1,004	−4,667	77	412	−4,178
1960	19,401	14,654	4,747	−1,900	−1,433	− 592	−3,925
1961	19,819	14,449	5,370	−1,216	−1,332	− 602	−3,150
1962	20,566	16,193	4,373	−1,173	− 674	−1,000	−2,847
1963†	10,454	8,105	2,349	−1,540	− 519	− 54	−2,113

* After deducting unscheduled repayment of foreign obligations to the U.S. government of the following amounts: 1959, $435 million; 1961, $764 million; 1962, $666 million.

† First six months.

Sources: Data for 1958 through 1961 from Hal B. Lary, *Problems of the United States as World Trader and Banker*, Table 1. Published by National Bureau of Economic Research, New York, 1963. Data for 1962 and 1963 from *Survey of Current Business*, March 1963 and September 1963. Published by U.S. Department of Commerce, Washington, D. C.

The trade balance and the basic deficit improved still further in 1961, but with a sharp rise in imports in 1962, both receded again. The basic deficit, through much improved, held fast at a figure well over a billion dollars.

Meanwhile, recorded short-term capital movements of some $1.4 billion, together with $600 million of "unrecorded transactions" (probably in large part short-term capital), raised the total deficit to $3.9 billion in 1960. Although a considerable part of this large short-term capital outflow can be attributed to interest-rate differentials and to speculative transactions against the dollar, at least half and perhaps more consisted of short-term loans to foreigners that financed, directly or indirectly, an equivalent amount of U.S. exports.[10] Had it not been for this movement of short-term funds, U.S. exports would have been substantially less, and therefore the *basic* deficit would have been that much larger.

[10] This conclusion is the outcome of Philip W. Bell's painstaking study, "Private Capital Movements and the U. S. Balance of Payments Position," in *Factors Affecting the United States Balance of Payments*, op. cit., pp. 395-481. He suggests that perhaps $300-400 million of the net short-term capital exports of 1960, and a similar portion of the approximately equal short-term capital exports of the following year, may have been in response to interest differentials. This indicates far less sensitivity to international differences in interest rates than had been generally supposed, for in June 1960, the rate on 3-month Treasury bills stood at 2.7 per cent in New York, at 4.8 per cent in London, and at 5.5 per cent in Frankfurt.

Here we have an illustration of the interdependence of the various components of a country's balance of payments. It is also true of long-term capital movements, of military expenditures abroad, and of foreign aid that they cannot be counted at face value in assessing responsibility for a deficit. For some part of U.S. long-term investments come back immediately as expenditure for industrial equipment, a large part of foreign aid goes to finance U.S. exports, and the same is true of military expenditures.

Short-term capital movements continued in large volume in 1961 and 1962, putting the total deficit in the neighborhood of $3 billion. Preliminary figures for 1963 suggest a similar outcome for that year. Clearly, after six years of temporizing measures,[11] the United States balance of payments problem was still far from a solution. In the latter part of this period, it became increasingly intertwined with the even broader problem of international monetary reform (see Chapter 27).

SELECTED REFERENCES

Economic Commission for Europe, *Economic Survey of Europe in 1949*. New York: United Nations, annually since 1949. An analytical discussion of current developments in Europe.

————, *Economic Survey of Europe Since the War*. New York: United Nations, 1953. A thorough review of Europe's progress through 1952, and an analysis of its problems of trade and payments and of industrial development.

Harris, Seymour E., ed., *The Dollar in Crisis*. New York: Harcourt, Brace & World, Inc., 1961. The first several essays deal with various aspects of the dollar crisis in a lively fashion.

Lary, Hal B., *Problems of the United States as World Trader and Banker*. New York: National Bureau of Economic Research, 1963. The most thorough discussion of the U.S. balance of payments problem yet to appear.

MacDougall, Sir Donald, *The Dollar Problem: A Reappraisal*. Princeton, N. J.: International Finance Section, Princeton University, November, 1960. A brief pamphlet reviewing the position of the dollar as of 1960.

United States Congress, Joint Economic Committee, *Factors Affecting the United States Balance of Payments*, 87th Congress, 2nd sess. Washington, D. C.: Government Printing Office, 1962. An excellent collection of essays covering various aspects of the dollar problem.

[11] In July, 1963, President Kennedy advanced a proposal to Congress of a more drastic character than any yet tried. This was to introduce, as a means of checking the outflow of long-term capital from the United States, an "interest equalization" tax on the purchase of foreign securities by U.S. residents. The tax was to be 15 per cent on foreign equities (stocks); on foreign bonds of more than three years maturity the tax was to rise gradually from 2¾ per cent to 15 per cent on bonds of a maturity of 28½ years or more. Exempted were purchases of foreign securities by one U.S. resident from another, the securities of underdeveloped nations, and direct investments, defined as the purchase of 10 per cent or more of the shares of a foreign corporation. Since the bill contained retroactive provisions, it had an immediate depressing effect on the leading foreign stock markets. As of early 1964, the bill still remained in Committee in Congress.

26

POSTWAR MONETARY
PROBLEMS

The preceding chapter concentrated upon two major international problems of the postwar years and of the means devised for dealing with them. Now it is time to examine certain institutional changes that took place during the period and that led to a reshaping of the international monetary system.

When the war ended, and for many years thereafter, the world's currency system was in complete disarray. Two currencies—the United States dollar and the Swiss franc—stood out as the only stable and fully convertible monetary units. True, the sterling area—a group of countries consisting of the British Commonwealth (except Canada) plus a few other nations with close trading and banking connections with the United Kingdom—provided free transfer of payments throughout the area through changes in reserve deposits held in London. But payments to other countries, especially to the dollar area,[1] were subject to strict though varying exchange controls and import restrictions. As for the rest of the world, each country pursued its own goals independently. In western Europe, the general shortage of goods, inadequacy of export capacity, and excess of purchasing power forced the maintenance of fixed exchange rates at overvalued levels, backed up by extensive systems of controls and trade restrictions. Many other countries faced a comparable situation and adopted similar measures. Bilateral trading arrangements, adopted as a device to ensure minimum essential imports, were widespread.

THE INTERNATIONAL MONETARY FUND

Even while the war was still in progress, it was apparent that in view of the disruption and dislocation certain to exist upon its termination, deliberate and strenuous efforts would be necessary to bring some degree of order out of the threatened chaos of worldwide restrictionism. Sharing such convictions, experts in the United States and the United Kingdom during the war prepared compre-

[1] The United States, Canada, and countries (primarily in Latin America) that financed their trade through New York banks.

[441]

hensive plans for postwar international monetary cooperation. At first working independently, then together with representatives of other countries, they drafted the elements of a common plan for the establishment of a new and unique institution, the International Monetary Fund. At an international conference held at Bretton Woods, New Hampshire, in July, 1944, the delegates hammered out its Articles of Agreement, together with another Agreement establishing the International Bank for Reconstruction and Development.

The creation of the Fund represents a major effort at international cooperation. Though by no means the first in its field, it is the most detailed attempt deliberately to organize the conduct of international monetary affairs. Before World War I, there was international cooperation, but it relied upon impersonal market forces and not upon the establishment of specific institutions with directors, staff, and powers of action. The cooperation between central banks of the 1920's was informal and relatively loose. The IMF, however, strikingly embodies the trend that has become so prominent in recent years, of deliberate and conscious organization to achieve certain agreed international goals.

Purposes

The three main purposes of the Fund clearly reflect the lessons of the interwar period.

1. Perhaps most apparent was the need for worldwide convertibility of currencies, for this would recreate a multilateral system of payments and therewith a trading system which would permit the fullest advantage to be taken of the possibilities of international specialization. Therefore the Articles of Agreement made the *elimination of exchange controls* a major objective of the Fund.

2. To guard against the unsettling effects of unstable exchange rates and especially against competitive depreciation, another task assigned the Fund was to restore *reasonable stability of exchange rates*.

3. Most difficult of all, the Fund was to undertake to reconcile the apparently irreconcilable—*to combine exchange rate stability with national independence in monetary and fiscal policy*. The latter is essential if nations are to pursue the generally accepted goal of full employment. Yet such independence is inconsistent with any truly international currency system with stable exchange rates, which adjusts balance-of-payments disturbances by invoking deflation or inflation with accompanying variations in employment.

Powers

To realize these difficult objectives, the Agreement establishing the IMF replaced free-wheeling national exchange and payments policies with a code for international cooperation by which members agreed to abide.[2] This code

---

[2] In 1947, when the IMF began operations, it had 39 members; ten years later 68 nations had joined; by 1963 total membership was 82.

consisted of detailed provisions specifying the means available to the Fund to realize its assigned objectives.

ELIMINATION OF EXCHANGE RESTRICTIONS   To eliminate foreign exchange restrictions and thus eventually to restore convertibility, it was stipulated that no member was to impose *new* exchange restrictions on current international transactions without the approval of the Fund, and that after a period of readjustment and adaptation ending in 1952, members still retaining exchange restrictions were to consult with officers of the IMF with respect to their continuance.

An exception was made, however, for unwanted capital movements—that is, speculative or politically motivated flights of capital. Members could be requested to introduce controls to prevent such movements—a provision of dubious effectiveness unless exchange controls were extended into the prohibited area, over current transactions.

STABILITY OF EXCHANGE RATES   In approaching the twin problems of restoring stable exchange rates and providing an acceptable means of international adjustment, the Fund Agreement showed great ingenuity. It borrowed some elements from the gold standard, and some from the rival system of fluctuating exchange rates, combining them in a compromise solution—one achieving flexible stability of exchange rates.

Gold is retained as a base by the requirement that each member shall establish, in cooperation with the Fund, a par value for its currency expressed in terms of gold or the United States dollar. To ensure that these par values are maintained, members must not permit maximum and minimum spot rates of exchange to vary from them by more than 1 per cent.

ADJUSTMENT: A COMPROMISE SOLUTION   To deal with the less serious short-run disturbances or with the early stages of more deep-seated difficulties, the Fund acquired sizeable resources upon which members could draw. As a condition of membership, each country had to subscribe an individual quota, based on its relative size and economic strength, of which 25 per cent must be in gold, the remainder in its national currency. From these subscriptions, the IMF acquired (as of 1957) resources totaling $9 billion ($1.7 billion in gold). Any member could, in effect, borrow from these resources up to 25 per cent of its quota each year for a period of five years.[3] These "drawing rights" provided a form of reserve supplemental to members' own international reserves. Later on, the Fund furnished an additional means of supplementing reserves in the form of "standby agreements," whereby it undertook to make available sums in excess of the regular drawing rights.

For combating the more serious or "fundamental" types of disequilibrium, the IMF abandoned the objectionable deflation-inflation mechanism required

---

[3] Literally, a member does not borrow, but purchases with additional deposits of its own currency the currencies of other members with which it is running a deficit.

by rigid exchange rates and turned to supervised flexibility of exchange rates. When a member confronts a "fundamental disequilibrium" in its balance of payments, it must consult with the Fund. If the governing board of the IMF agrees that "fundamental disequilibrium"[4] exists, and that devaluation is necessary (likely to prove appropriate and effective), then it must concur with any proposed devaluation not in excess of 10 per cent. Greater degrees of devaluation are subject to negotiation.

Monetary and fiscal independence of members is guaranteed by a clause which provides that if the Fund is satisfied devaluation is necessary, it "shall not object to a proposed change because of the domestic social or political policies of the member." Can a member, then, follow an inflationary monetary policy, even though it may neutralize the corrective effect of a devaluation? Not necessarily, for members also undertake "to collaborate with the Fund to maintain exchange stability," with which internal inflation would clearly be inconsistent. In practice, the Fund has attempted with considerable success to persuade members to follow domestic policies consistent with external stability; it has also provided them with technical assistance in designing and applying appropriate policies.

TOWARD A MULTILATERAL PAYMENTS SYSTEM

Establishment of the International Monetary Fund gave the free world a respected international institution dedicated to the restoration of a fully multilateral payments system. During the early years of its operation, the IMF was able to achieve relatively little, but after the lapse of the five-year transition period in 1952, more and more countries abandoned rigid exchange controls and moved toward the operationally simpler and less restrictive system of multiple exchange rates. For this and for a general relaxation of restrictions, the Fund can certainly take part of the credit.

For almost a decade after the war, the sterling area, although it permitted free transfers among members, severely limited transfers to other areas, especially to the dollar area. In 1954 the system was greatly simplified and liberalized. Sterling acquired by any of 51 countries with "transferable" accounts in London could be transferred freely for current transactions, not only anywhere in the sterling area, but also to any other transferable account. Administrative regulations controlling capital transfers also became subject to frequent relaxation.

Certainly the most striking move toward convertibility and free international payments came in Europe with the inauguration, in 1950, of the European Payments Union. This short-lived institution did away, at one stroke, with the bilateral balancing of trade into which the nations of Europe had been

---

[4] This concept is not defined in the Articles of Agreement, but presumably means disequilibrium of a serious and enduring character.

forced by postwar shortages. Backed by a grant of $350 million in United States currency, the Union undertook to advance limited credits to members with deficits in their balances of payments, while members with surpluses agreed to extend credit to the Union. As the size of these credits increased, it was provided that a rising proportion were to be liquidated in gold or dollars. With this important supplement to their own inadequate reserves, members could and did gradually reduce the stringent restrictions on intra-European trade. Nations with considerable exporting capacity had hitherto limited their exports to avoid the accumulation of unusable currencies of countries with low export capacity. Now they could relax their restrictions, receiving a stipulated portion of increased exports in Union credits, the rest in gold or dollars.

Liberalization of exports had a sort of multiplied effect on intra-European trade. Those nations now enabled to buy essential goods more freely could recover their economic potential more rapidly, while the nations with larger exports could afford to spend an increasing part of their receipts even on luxuries. This furnished countries which produced such commodities (wines, perfumes, subtropical fruits) with the means of acquiring—perhaps in a third market—basic industrial supplies needed for their reconstruction.

Aided greatly by the European Payments Union, intra-European trade grew rapidly, while the economies of Europe increased in strength and competitive ability. By the end of 1958, some eleven of the OEEC group felt sufficiently sure of themselves to restore full currency convertibility for nonresidents, though residents remained subject to certain restrictions with respect to capital transfers and travel expenditures.

Among nonindustrial countries, from the mid-fifties on there took place a gradual shift away from the complexity of multiple exchange rates toward the simplicity of a single fluctuating rate. By 1962, out of 32 such countries, 16 still adhered to exchange controls in support of a single fixed rate; 4 had single stable rates but with nearly free payments; 8 had adopted freely fluctuating rates; 3 used a fixed official rate for prescribed transactions but with a free rate for all others, while only one continued with a multiple rate system.

THE DOLLAR BECOMES A RESERVE CURRENCY

Until 1958, when most European currencies became convertible, the dollar was the world's strongest and most wanted currency. Therefore during the years after 1949, when the heavy commitments of the United States for military support, foreign aid, and private investment abroad placed at the disposal of other countries more dollars than they needed for their purchases, they were glad to accumulate them. They could, of course, have converted the dollars acquired into gold to add to their own gold reserves. But they did so only to a minor degree. In the period 1950-57, United States deficits—which were surpluses to the rest of the world—totaled approximately $10 billion. Of this large sum, only $1.7 billion was converted into gold and withdrawn. The remaining $8.4 billion continued to be held by its recipients, either as dollar deposits or, more commonly, in the form of short-term government securities. These dollar holdings became part of their owners' international reserves, playing the same role for the nonsterling world as did sterling deposits and government securities for the sterling area.

The monetary system of the free world was now the gold-exchange standard, with gold still the main form of reserves, supplemented by foreign exchange holdings, principally in one of two reserve countries—the United States and the United Kingdom.

Indeed, had it not been for the substitution of foreign exchange for gold holdings, it is doubtful if world reserves would have increased sufficiently to avoid widespread deflationary pressure. As Table 26.1 shows, gold reserves rose only $4,925 million, or 14.8 per cent, during the nine years from 1949 to 1958, or by 1.6 per cent a year. In this interval the volume of world trade increased at a compound annual rate of 5.8 per cent. Foreign exchange reserves, however, came near to doubling: they grew by 84 per cent, or at an annual rate of 9.3 per cent. Thus aggregate reserves of gold and foreign exchange together rose by 31 per cent, or 3.4 per cent a year. Of the increase in the foreign exchange component of reserves ($8,810,000,000), over 60 per cent ($5,445,000,000) is attributable to the growth in dollar holdings. The remainder came mainly from increased holdings of other convertible currencies such as the Swiss franc and from rising credits with the European Payments Union.[5]

Table 26.1. RESERVES OF CENTRAL BANKS AND OTHER NATIONAL
MONETARY AUTHORITIES OF THE FREE WORLD

(millions of dollars, end of year)

		1949	1950	1951	1952	1953	1954	1955
1.	Gold reserves*	33,150	33,830	33,935	33,920	34,360	34,970	35,445
2.	Exchange reserves†							
	(a) U.S. Dollar	3,071	4,440	4,014	5,254	6,016	7,067	7,878
	(b) U.K. Pound Sterling	7,856	7,775	8,694	7,596	8,148	8,157	8,095
	(c) B.I.S. and E.P.U.	100	541	794	1,286	1,485	1,432	1,258
	(d) Others, minus adjustments	−527	1,939	1,583	1,474	1,491	1,589	1,529
	Together	10,500	14,695	15,085	15,610	17,140	18,245	18,760
	Gold and exchange	43,650	48,525	49,020	49,530	51,500	53,215	54,205
3.	Gross I.M.F. position‡	7,891	7,905	8,183	8,265	9,028	9,690	9,757
	Total	51,541	56,430	57,203	57,795	60,528	62,905	63,962

[5] With the liquidation of the EPU in 1959, these credits disappeared, remaining credit and debit balances being converted into long-term bilateral obligations.

Table 26.1. (continued)

	1956	1957	1958	1959	1960	Increase 1949-60
1. Gold reserves*	36,095	37,360	38,075	37,870	38,050	4,900
2. Exchange reserves†						
(a) U.S. Dollar	8,612	8,231	8,516	9,419	10,484	7,413
(b) U.K. Pound Sterling	7,807	7,222	6,955	7,448	7,563	−293
(c) B.I.S. and E.P.U.	1,352	1,541	1,877	378	477	377
(d) Others, minus adjustments	1,964	1,921	1,962	1,925	3,121	3,648
Together	19,735	18,915	19,310	19,170	21,645	11,145
Gold and exchange	55,830	56,275	57,385	57,040	59,695	16,045
3. Gross I.M.F. position‡	9,813	9,491	9,849	16,148	17,224	9,333
Total	65,643	65,766	67,234	73,188	76,919	25,378

* The *gold reserves* are only those of the national monetary authorities, and therefore exclusive of the gold stocks of the international monetary institutions.

† The *exchange reserves* are the foreign-exchange holdings of national monetary authorities—that is, their deposits in the U.S.A., U.K., and a few other countries, plus credit balances with the Bank for International Settlements (B.I.S.) and the European Payments Union (E.P.U.).

    (a) The holdings of U.S. dollars by the national monetary authorities equal the liabilities of the banks and the U.S. Government, to wit, (1) liabilities of the Federal Reserve Banks and other American banks to foreign monetary authorities, (2) official foreign holdings of short-term government securities and other short-term liabilities, (3) official holdings of U.S. securities with original maturities greater than one year; all these minus the U.S. liabilities to international organizations.

    (b) The holdings of pounds sterling by the national monetary authorities equal the liabilities of the U.K., to wit, (1) net holdings in sterling or Sterling Area currencies by foreign monetary authorities with banks in the U.K., (2) their holdings of British government securities, (3) funds held with the Crown Agents and Currency Boards, (4) certain intergovernment loans, (5) sterling securities issued by Commonwealth countries that are included in holders' Foreign Assets; all these minus U.K. liabilities to international organizations. (The net total includes some holdings by foreign individuals and corporations.)

    (c) Balances with the B.I.S. are the B.I.S. liabilities that are counted as monetary reserves by the creditor countries. The E.P.U. liabilities reflect accumulated balances of E.P.U.-members acquired in the course of financing trade surpluses with other members. When the E.P.U. was liquidated in 1958, remaining debtor and creditor positions were converted into bilateral claims and debts, which are not included among the monetary reserves.

    (d) Other foreign-exchange holdings are deposits in other countries with convertible currencies. Certain divergences between claims reported by creditors and liabilities reported by debtors were deducted from this item.

‡ The *"Gross I.M.F. Position"* of a national monetary authority is calculated by doubling that member's quota and subtracting the I.M.F.'s holding of its currency. The result is a measure of the member's drawing potential. The Fund began publishing this series in August, 1961, in *International Financial Statistics*.

SOURCE: Fritz Machlup, *Plans for Reform of the International Monetary System*, p. 3. Published 1962 by International Finance Section, Princeton University.

There was an actual decline of $900 million in the size of sterling exchange holdings.

NEW PROBLEMS

Until a substantial number of European currencies became convertible in 1958, the emerging gold-exchange system had no chance to operate freely, since the larger part of international payments were subject to restrictions of one kind or another. But when a number of major currencies were made convertible, these restrictions disappeared, payments could be freely made, and the state of each country's reserves became the principal criterion of its balance-of-payments policy. In particular, with convertibility, not only could goods and services be bought and paid for in any currency, but capital markets also became closely linked again, so that relatively small differences in interest rates could set in motion large international movements of short-term capital.

It took only a short time to demonstrate that the new gold-exchange standard fell far short of providing a smoothly operating international monetary framework. As we have seen, for five consecutive years the principal reserve-currency country ran large annual deficits.[6] While this could not be charged against the system itself, it presented a serious dilemma which pinpointed a major defect of the system.

If the free world were to rely solely on additions to the gold stock to provide for growth in international reserves, this would likely prove quite inadequate. The monetary gold stock had been increasing only at the rate of 1.6 per cent a year. Excluding that part of the increase due to sales of gold by Russia, upon which little reliance could be placed, the annual additions from production to the monetary gold stock amounted to only $440 million or 1.2 per cent per annum (1951-62). World trade, as we have seen, rose annually by 5.8 per cent. While it is probable that economies in the use of reserves may be expected to result from improvements in the international clearing mechanism, so that an exactly parallel movement in reserves and in the volume of trade is unlikely to be necessary, any disparity as large as that indicated would almost certainly result in a mounting shortage of reserves. Worldwide price deflation would eventually become necessary, for with stable prices and a steady increase in the value of world trade, reserves would decline in relative size. At some point, even moderate balance-of-payments deficits would become too large to be tolerated. The competition for reserves would lead to almost universal restriction of credit.

Under the gold-exchange standard, the alternative is for the reserve-currency countries to add to reserves by increasing their liabilities to the rest of the

[6] Deficits in 1961 and 1962, amounting to $2.5 billion and $2.1 billion respectively, reached totals of $3.2 and $2.8 billion when large advance debt repayments to the U.S. by European governments are deducted (Table 25.5).

world. This, however, requires complete confidence in the stability—ultimately, the convertibility into gold—of the reserve currency, combined with willingness to hold it in steadily increasing amounts. In the circumstances of the early 1960's, this essential combination became less and less possible of realization. Before 1958, the supply of dollars made available by U.S. deficits was welcomed as a means of building up shrunken reserves. But the return of so many countries in that year to convertibility was in itself a sign that reserves were now adequate. The much greater outflow of dollars from 1958 through 1962 was unneeded and unwanted by most recipients. They accepted additional dollar balances "with formal politeness . . . in accordance with the customary etiquette practiced by central banks."[7] And they converted a much larger proportion into gold.

Table 26.2. PERCENTAGE OF U.S. PAYMENTS DEFICIT TAKEN IN GOLD

1950-57	17	1960	43
1958	64	1961	35
1959	20	1962	(40)

SOURCE: S. E. Harris, "The U.S. Balance of Payments: The Problem and Its Solution," in *Factors Affecting the United States Balance of Payments,* Joint Economic Committee, 87th Congress, Second Session, Washington, D.C., 1962, p. 4.

Besides a declining willingness to hold the dollar, there were many signs of reduced confidence in its stability: a flurry of speculation in the London gold market in the autumn of 1960, the numerous and sometimes undignified attempts to reduce the U.S. deficit, and President Kennedy's assurance early in 1961 that convertibility of the dollar would be maintained.

Even though U.S. gold reserves remained large by any test,[8] the accumulation of foreign dollar holdings could not go on forever. At rates then current, it was unlikely to continue much longer.

Here, then, is the first major defect of the postwar gold-exchange standard. There must be provision for adequate growth of international reserves, but the means established by that system is unacceptable. To solve the problem, some new method of ensuring reserve growth must be found.

A second defect of the gold-exchange standard of the early 1960's is the *extreme instability engendered in individual countries' balances of payments by large speculative capital movements.* With the return to convertibility, the capital markets of the western world are once again linked with one another. Small differences in interest rates induce interest arbitrage—a flow of capital to take advantage of the opportunity for gain. Such flows alone could probably be tolerated; but when they are imposed on top of an already existing deficit,

---

[7] Fritz Machlup, *Plans for the Reform of the International Monetary System,* p. 10. Published 1962 by International Finance Section, Princeton University.

[8] At the end of 1962, U.S. gold reserves stood at $16 billion, while total foreign short-term claims against them amounted to approximately $22 billion.

and especially when such flows are aggravated by a low discount policy in the deficit country aimed at stimulating employment, they generate fears of devaluation. The basic conflict between external and internal equilibrium comes into the open. Speculative capital movements, which can be of massive proportions, then reenforce those of more normal character, causing what may be an intolerable loss of reserves.

Clearly, here is another problem calling for solution. It centers around the incompatibility of simultaneous external and internal equilibrium with stable exchange rates. To maintain such stable rates, a nation suffering a balance-of-payments deficit must take effective action to stem the deficit, which may include restriction of credit. If it does not, its devotion to the principle of exchange rate stability is put in doubt; if it does, its unemployment problem may be worsened.

Still a third defect of the existing international monetary system is what Machlup terms its *fragility*—its likelihood of collapsing under the pressures to which it is subject. This is really only another consequence of the forces we have already considered. The constant and, after 1957, rapid increase in foreign dollar holdings posed the problem of devising satisfactory means of ensuring adequate growth in international reserves. At the same time, the growing reluctance of foreign central banks and even of private banks and firms to increase their dollar holdings, together with their tendency to convert a larger proportion thereof into gold, bred and will continue to breed fears as to the long-run ability of the United States to maintain the gold parity of the dollar.

Likewise, when short-term capital movements add to the difficulties of a reserve currency country, as they did with the United States in 1960–61 and with Britain in 1961, that country's individual problem becomes a problem of the entire system. Fears as to the stability of the reserve currency arise from this source, too.

Given such fears as to the vulnerability of the monetary system caused by its very method of operation, intermittent—and, in such circumstances, inevitable—suggestions that the price of gold be raised or the dollar or the pound be devalued give still additional ground for doubt.

But any monetary system except a purely metallic one, since it contains an element of credit, rests on confidence. If that confidence is shaken, the system quakes; if it disappears, the system collapses. The doubts and fears engendered in the early 1960's weakened the base of confidence upon which the gold-exchange standard rested. This made it a fragile system, not a sturdy one.

REMEDIAL MEASURES

Enlargement of Fund Quotas

The readily apparent defects of the international monetary system stirred much discussion, but also some action. One of the first forward steps occurred in 1959, when the IMF enlarged the quotas of its members by approximately 50 per cent. This raised the resources of the Fund, consisting of gold and national currencies, from $9 billion in 1958 to over $14 billion the following year.

We should not conclude from this that the useful reserves of the free world were increased by some $5 billion, or that effective supplementary reserves supplied by the Fund amounted to $14 billion. For the majority of the currencies deposited with the Fund, which can be "borrowed" in case of need, would be of little interest to a country in need of additional international means of payment. Only the currencies of the leading industrial nations, generally accepted and widely used for international payments, could serve its purpose. Even so, the increase in the quotas of Fund members constituted an important contribution to international liquidity. Between 1958 and 1959, IMF holdings of gold and of the major national currencies increased from $6.2 billion to $10 billion. Or consider the change in the position of the United States. Its pre-1959 drawing rights (125 per cent of its quota of $2,750,000,000) were $3,437,000,000.[9] In 1959, its quota was raised to $4,125,000,000, with an accompanying increase in its borrowing power to $5,156,250,000.

Although members' drawing rights at the Fund constitute a form of reserve supplemental to their own holdings of gold and foreign exchange, for many years they were not actually counted as reserves. Beginning in 1962, however, the practice of so counting them began to spread. Conscious acknowledgement of this source of support should make some modest contribution to international confidence.

An International Standby Pool

During 1961 and 1962, there was wide-ranging discussion of the problems of international monetary reform. One aspect in particular—how to check or offset disturbing speculative capital movements—received a major share of attention.[10] Moreover, a critical situation that developed in 1961 forced action to deal with the problem.

Early in March, the German mark and the Dutch guilder were revalued upward 5 per cent. This step was taken to combat excessively large balance of payments surpluses, which were threatening to generate inflation in these coun-

---

[9] Normally, drawing rights can be exercised only at the rate of 25 per cent a year, so that a period of five years would elapse before a country could use these rights in full. The Fund may, however, waive this time limitation, especially for members that have not made large or continuous use of the Fund's resources.

[10] See, for example, Philip W. Bell, "Private Capital Movements and the U.S. Balance of Payments Position," in *Factors Affecting the United States Balance of Payments,* op. cit., p. 395; also Edward M. Bernstein, "Interest Rates and the U.S. Balance of Payments," in Carl J. Friedrich and Seymour E. Harris, *Public Policy, A Yearbook of the Graduate School of Public Administration.* Cambridge: Harvard University Press, 1961.

tries. Many felt, however, that the change in the value of the mark and the guilder would prove insufficient and would be followed by still more appreciation. To profit from this anticipated move, speculators shifted funds from other currency centers to Germany and the Netherlands. In particular, holders of sterling deposits, which had risen in previous months because of relatively high interest rates in London, now withdrew them in large amounts. The Bank of England defended the pound vigorously by making foreign exchange readily available. Meanwhile, European central bankers meeting at the Bank for International Settlements in Basle announced their conviction that no further currency adjustments were needed and stated that they were "cooperating closely in the exchange markets." Speculation against the pound continued, however, probably reflecting longer-run fears based on Britain's rising costs, sluggish exports, and declining competitiveness.

Despite this reassurance, the drain on sterling continued for the next four months, totaling (for the first half of 1961) approximately £600 million. Of this, some £265 million was in gold. Most of the remainder, from £250 to £300 million, the European central bankers provided under the Basle Agreement. Even with this help, the British government had to raise Bank rates from 5 to 7 per cent, supplementing this with other measures to restrain demand. Funds now began to return from abroad; the immediate crisis had been brought under control.

United Kingdom reserves, however, were low, and the central bank credits could not be renewed indefinitely. At this point, in early August, the IMF stepped into the breach. It authorized Britain to draw immediately up to $1.5 billion, and supplemented this with a one year's standby credit of $500 million.[11] To avoid simply transferring exchange pressures to the dollar, the Fund made available only $450 million of the drawing in this currency. By using $500 million of its own gold reserves to buy European currencies, the Fund managed to raise nearly a billion dollars in eight other currencies.

The British crisis made it clear that two tasks needed to be faced. To avoid reliance upon voluntary and perhaps unwilling cooperation in the future, it was essential that some regular means for meeting such a situation be established. And to prevent a mere shift of the problem to the dollar, it was imperative that whatever steps were taken should include arrangement for making available the currencies of several creditor nations.

At the annual meeting of the IMF in September, 1961, Per Jacobsson, the managing director of the Fund, introduced a proposal to set up a multicurrency standby pool to cope with similar future crises. Accepted in principle, his proposal continued to be discussed in succeeding months. In its final shape, the standby pool included ten industrial nations as members who undertook—

---

[11] By this emergency action, Britain was permitted to draw almost its entire quota immediately.

with important reservations—to contribute a *maximum* total of $6 billion to help any member to meet a crisis of liquidity.[12]

Administration of the pool was entrusted to the Fund, though not the decision as to what each member's contribution would be in any concrete instance. When in serious payments difficulties, a member is to request of the managing director of the Fund permission to draw on the pool. He in turn must consult with the other members of the pool, who are to "inform" him (if two-thirds of them agree to the drawing) of the amounts of their currencies they can make available. These amounts are to depend on their reserves and external payments positions at the time. The borrower is to pay a fixed charge of ½ per cent plus 1½ per cent interest a year, with repayment within a maximum of five years in convertible currencies.

This arrangement marks a modest step forward toward providing more adequate international credit to meet crises of liquidity such as Britain encountered in 1961. For all members other than the United States, the credits provided would probably be sufficient. Should that country experience a serious drain, however, it would need access primarily to additional Common Market currencies, and of these, the pool provides slightly less than $2.5 billion at a maximum. Thus the new arrangement moves only part way toward a system of international credit fully adequate to meet any emergency.

Further International Cooperation

Another move toward increased international cooperation also resulted from the anticipated further appreciation of the German mark in early 1961. There developed a large-scale flow of speculative capital from the United States into Germany, reenforced by the existence of a premium on forward marks that approached 4 per cent. A suggestion made by the German Federal Bank enabled the U.S. Treasury to provide ample supplies of forward marks and thereby to bring the premium down to less than 1 per cent within a matter of six months. This dampened the speculative outflow, supported confidence, and strengthened the dollar. The arrangement was simple: the German Federal Bank merely undertook to supply the U.S. Treasury with marks, when forward contracts matured, at the same rate at which the Treasury had sold them. In this same period, a somewhat similar arrangement with the Swiss National Bank enabled the Treasury to conduct parallel operations in Swiss francs.[13]

Mention should also be made of an international body that, although it has no powers of action, has proved and should continue to prove of great value

[12] The members, with their prospective contributions, were: the United States, $2 billion; the United Kingdom, $1 billion; Germany, $1 billion; France, $550 million; Italy, $550 million; Japan, $250 million; Netherlands, $200 million; Canada, $200 million; Belgium, $150 million; and Sweden, $100 million.

[13] For a fuller discussion of these operations, see Charles A. Coombs, "Treasury and Federal Reserve Foreign Exchange Operations," in *Factors Affecting the United States Balance of Payments*, Joint Economic Committee, 87th Congress, 2nd sess., 1962.

as a forum for consultation. This is the Organization for Economic Cooperation and Development. The successor to the Organization for European Economic Cooperation, it includes the 17 member nations of the latter plus the United States and Canada. Its task is to discuss economic problems confronting members and to formulate proposals for dealing with them. By providing for constant exchange of ideas among the leading industrial nations, it serves a useful purpose. Its recommendations—in the fields of financial and balance-of-payments problems, of its working party assigned thereto—can also be expected to carry considerable weight. This organization could become an effective, though informal, means of developing an increasing degree of coordination of national monetary and fiscal policies. At the very least, it should promote a better understanding of the particular problems of individual countries and of the policies they adopt, and perhaps serve to harmonize these policies in some degree.

A PECULIARITY OF THE POSITION OF THE UNITED STATES

Submission to balance of payments discipline is a condition of membership in any international monetary system that seeks to preserve stability of exchange rates. Yet under the system in force in the early 1960's, there existed a distinct difference in this respect between an "ordinary" or nonreserve member and the United States as the leading key-currency nation. The Agreement establishing the International Monetary Fund, which had not foreseen the emergence of the United States as the principal key-currency country, provided that any member when confronted by a "fundamental" disequilibrium could devalue. Restoration of international equilibrium was to be achieved through exchange rate adjustment rather than through the difficult path of enforced deflation (or, in the case of a persistent international payments surplus, through inflation). This solution, however, presents special problems for the United States.

A special responsibility to maintain the gold parity of the dollar because it is used as a reserve currency would not appear to be one of them. Choice of the dollar as a reserve currency was based on its strength when, after 1953, supplies of that currency became relatively abundant. The United States did not invite its use and gave no guarantees against changes in its par value. As a member of the IMF, the United States has the same right to devalue as any other member. Neither does the fact that foreign central banks continued to hold dollars when, after 1957, the dollar became weaker, give them any claim to special treatment. Aware of some risk of devaluation, they nonetheless chose—somewhat more reluctantly than before—to continue to maintain large dollar balances, on a major portion of which they were able to earn interest. If, however, because of the assurances given against devaluation by high American officials, including the President, one holds that it would be a breach of faith to devalue the dollar, a simple means of compensating foreign central banks would be available. The U.S. government could divert part of the gold profit resulting from devaluation to raising their dollar balances to a level equivalent to their previous value.

It is the practical difficulties of devaluing the dollar that would be serious. If such a step is not to induce heavy withdrawals of gold, it must be taken suddenly; there must be no intimation of its imminence. For the United States to change the price of gold, however, Congress must amend the 1946 Act ratifying the Bretton Woods Agreement. To prevent a run on the dollar that would dissipate gold reserves, the President would first have to declare an embargo on gold sales or purchases. He has the authority to do this under the Trading with the Enemy Act of 1917, but only under extraordinary conditions. For him to invoke this Act, there must be a "national emergency." Such a situation could doubtless be said to exist if U.S. gold reserves were threatened with exhaustion. But it is dubious if a gold embargo would be legal under circumstances less critical than this A cool and calculated devaluation, undertaken in accordance with the provisions of the IMF to correct a "fundamental" disequilibrium before it erupts into a crisis, does not seem to be a practicable alternative for the United States.

UNRESOLVED PROBLEMS

Reforms of the gold exchange standard already undertaken provide means for minimizing the impact on national reserves of large short-term capital movements. In countering one important source of instability, they should thereby reduce the danger of collapse and strengthen the international monetary system. Yet they fail to come to grips with its more basic defects.

First, though providing additional supplementary reserves to meet a crisis of liquidity, the new arrangements do nothing to ensure a steady growth of the world's primary reserves of gold and foreign exchange. These depend, as in the past, upon the normal but small additions to the monetary gold stock, and for any more substantial increase, upon further expansion of reserve currency holdings—that is, of dollars and sterling. The problem of finding a stronger backing for the world's monetary system has not been squarely faced.

Second, the conflict between internal and external equilibrium remains unresolved. So long as, under the present system of the adjustable peg, exchange rates are fixed, disequilibrium in a country's balance of payments must be eliminated by deflationary measures. Only after evidence of fundamental disequilibrium has accumulated can the peg be removed and the currency devalued. In the interval during which the exchange rate remains stable and deflationary policies are applied, considerable harm may befall the domestic economy from reduced output and increased unemployment. For the United States in particular, even the ultimate remedy of devaluation appears ruled out except under circumstances of severe crisis. We may add that even the remedies so far devised for countering short-term capital movements are of doubtful certainty and sufficiency.

SELECTED REFERENCES

Economic Cooperation Administration, *The Sterling Area, An American Analysis*. London and Washington, D. C.: The Administration, 1951. Contains much detailed information about the sterling area, its operation, its trade, and its resources. Exceptional diagrammatic illustrations.

Gardner, Richard N., *Sterling-Dollar Diplomacy*. New York: Oxford University Press, 1956. An illuminating study of Anglo-American collaboration in the attempt to reconstruct multilateral trade after the war.

Mikesell, Raymond F., *Foreign Exchange in the Postwar World*. New York: The Twentieth Century Fund, 1954. An excellent source on international currency problems until 1954.

Harris, Seymour E., ed., *The Dollar in Crisis*. New York: Harcourt, Brace & World, Inc., 1961. See especially the essay by Wallich on "Government Action."

Tew, Brian, *International Monetary Cooperation, 1945-1952*. London: Hutchinson's University Library, 1952. An excellent, brief discussion of the machinery and operation of the IMF, the sterling area, and the EPU.

United States Congress, Joint Economic Committee, *Factors Affecting the United States Balance of Payments*, 87th Congress, 2nd sess. Washington, D. C.: Government Printing Office, 1962. See especially Part 5.

27

INTERNATIONAL MONETARY
REFORM

Persistence of large United States payments deficits, relatively slow growth in the two key-currency countries, together with failure of the world's monetary authorities to adopt any but limited stopgap remedies, stirred mounting dissatisfaction and concern in economic circles. There has resulted an eruption of articles and books, both critical and constructive, exceeded in volume only by the literature directed toward that other major current problem, the economic development of the underdeveloped nations. The critical and the constructive suggestions have focused upon the main problems outlined in the preceding chapter: (1) how to devise an acceptable means of ensuring adequate growth in the world's monetary reserves; (2) how to reconcile substantial national monetary and fiscal independence with the requirements of balance-of-payments equilibrium; and (3) how to eliminate or reduce the instability engendered in the international monetary system by the impact on national reserves of sudden short-term capital movements.

Concrete proposals for reform of the international monetary framework cover a wide spectrum, ranging from financial unification of the western world to the adoption of a system of fully flexible exchange rates. Within the limits of a single chapter, it is impossible to present more than a sample of the widely divergent suggestions for reform. The sample chosen—five types of proposals—is, I believe, reasonably representative. Each type, however, permits many variations that are either conceivable or have actually been proposed. With these variations we cannot concern ourselves; the interested reader can consult the references at the end of the chapter.

Each of the proposals for reform has merit. Their authors differ, not so much in the economic principles on which their proposals rest, as in their evaluation of the causes at work, of the relative importance of the goals sought, or of the effectiveness of a specific mechanism or institutional change.

CLOSE FINANCIAL INTEGRATION

Of all the suggestions for the reform of the international monetary system, there is one that with its emphasis on fixed exchange rates furnishes a logical starting point for our discussion. Through a combination of unchanging exchange rates in a framework of complete financial integration of the Atlantic Community, this proposal seeks to establish a smoothly operating mechanism of international adjustment.[1]

Meaning of Financial Integration

What is meant by financial integration? Its essence is complete freedom of capital movements within the Community, to the end that there would exist a single great market for the securities of all members. In this market, all security issues would have to compete for funds, so that for each class of securities of given quality and maturity, a single rate of return would emerge. With the existing integration of commodity markets, which ensures that commodity prices differ within the Community only by the amount of transport costs and normal customs duties, together with some advance in monetary integration, balance-of-payments adjustment would be effected in the easy and inconspicuous manner now characteristic of adjustment between the different regions of a single country.

Consider, for example, the mechanism of regional adjustment in the United States, which depends in large part upon the close financial connections between all parts of the country. Variations in the receipts and payments of a region give rise, as with a nation, to deficits and surpluses in its balance of payments. But no intervention of central banks is required or occurs. Commercial banks in a region experiencing a deficit must obtain funds with which to meet the excess payments. Such funds can readily be acquired by selling some part of the portfolio of federal, state, or local securities that each bank holds. Because there exists a nationwide integrated capital market where securities sell at competitive prices and yields, buyers are always available to absorb securities offered at only a fractional price discount.

Banks in the deficit region experience an equal decline in assets (securities) and liabilities (demand deposits). But there is no loss of reserves (who even knows what a region's reserves are?) and no pressure to contract credit. The deficit is financed by a private inflow of capital that is equilibrating because it eases the balance of payments pressure. There is some contraction in the local money supply (through the cancelation of demand deposits); if the deficit-creating situation persists, this contraction will continue, with eventual pressure transmitted to local incomes and prices.

[1] For a fuller explanation of this proposal and the arguments supporting it, see James C. Ingram, "Proposal for Financial Integration in the Atlantic Community," in *Factors Affecting the United States Balance of Payments*, pp. 177-207.

Integration of the Atlantic Community

It is true that the various states of the American Union share not only well-integrated commodity and financial markets, but also a common currency. The Atlantic Community, although the liberalization of trade has proceeded to the point where an integrated market for traded goods exists, lacks a common currency, although the return to convertibility at fixed rates amounted to an approximation thereto. Financial markets, however, remain far from unified. Thus the capital markets of the European countries continue to be kept apart by both formal and informal exchange controls, while even in the United States there are many informal controls that inhibit the free international movement of capital.[2] These include the rules of federal and state regulatory bodies that prohibit or severely limit the investments of various classes of financial institutions,[3] as well as lack of knowledge, absence of adequate marketing facilities, business custom, and even "mercantilistic patriotism."

Professor Ingram, the author of the plan under discussion, believes that these shortcomings could be overcome. Besides abolishing all remaining restraints on international transactions, the nations of the Atlantic Community would have to alter inhibitory domestic legislation and take steps to reduce ignorance and to create a more effective international market in securities. A single currency in all but name could be achieved by fixing exchange rates *rigidly,* without any fluctuation permitted, not even the 1 per cent plus or minus variation now allowed.

Introduction of these reforms would create an international monetary system that would restore to operation, in a strengthened framework and in a more perfect form, the actual adjustment mechanism of the pre-1914 gold standard. Once financial integration and currency unification had been realized, the balances of payments of members would adjust to changing conditions as regional balances of payments do now. The system would have the great advantages that: (1) central bank intervention to support a currency's value would become unnecessary; (2) capital movements would be equilibrating, or helpful to the balance of payments. Disequilibrating movements could not occur so long as absolute rigidity of exchange rates could be relied on.

Adjustment with Integration

Imagine the proposed system in operation. Securities markets in every country would be closely linked with those in other countries, as the foreign

[2] The United States applies formal exchange controls only to capital transactions with the Communist bloc and to gold holdings abroad by U.S. residents.

[3] Thus Ingram notes that only $5 billion out of $120 billion of the assets of life insurance companies were invested in foreign securities (end of 1960); of $267 billion of commercial bank assets, virtually none was invested in foreign bonds and only $4.7 billion in short-term claims on foreigners, mostly in trade credits denominated in dollars (end of 1961). Ingram, *op. cit.*, pp. 188-89.

exchange markets are today, into one great financial market. To find buyers,
·a security of a specific quality and maturity would have to compete with all
other issues of comparable grade and duration. Therefore interest rates in
any country could depart from the common level only momentarily. A rise in
one nation would start an international flow of capital, large if necessary
but more likely marginal in magnitude, that would quickly bring interest rates
there into line. Banks in each country, guaranteed against the slightest fluctuation in exchange rates, would hold among their earning assets not only
the securities of their own national and local governments, but also those of
other governments in the Community.

Should any country, say the United States, develop a deficit in its balance of
payments, dollar checks drawn by Americans in favor of foreigners would
exceed the value (at the fixed exchange rates) of checks drawn in foreign
currencies in favor of Americans.[4] Foreign banks would acquire clearing
balances equal in amount to the U.S. deficit. They could liquidate these balances in various ways. If they wished to add to their holdings of U.S. securities, they could use the dollar balances acquired to buy them in the New
York market. European (or Canadian) banks would then have increased
their long-term assets and their liabilities to depositors (for example, exporters) equally. In U.S. banks, assets and liabilities would remain unaltered;
demand deposits would change hands, being transferred from the accounts of
U.S. importers, for example, to the accounts of New York security dealers.
Alternatively, foreign banks would notify U.S. banks of the claims held
against them. The latter could then authorize correspondent banks abroad to
sell foreign securities held by American banks, and to transfer the proceeds
to the creditor banks. Long-term assets of U.S. banks would fall, as would
demand deposits held by American firms making foreign payments. Foreign
banks would experience an increase in demand deposits held by exporters and
others with claims on the United States, a decrease in demand deposits held
by local security dealers.

To ensure such smooth functioning of the international payments mechanism, with little need for transfers of reserves, belief in the fixity of exchange
rates must be firmly established. If this were achieved, there could be no
speculative flights of capital; international payments would be limited to
merchandise transactions, equilibrating capital movements, and government
transfers. Not only is fixity of exchange rates with unlimited convertibility
essential to the system, but also equally essential are the integration of financial and of commodity markets.[5]

---

[4] With foreign exchange rigidly fixed, there would be no need for a foreign exchange
market. Instead of buying foreign bills of exchange to make payments, an importer would
simply mail his check, denominated in his own currency, to his foreign creditor. The latter
would deposit the check in his bank, which would credit his deposit account in local
currency, holding the foreign balance acquired for later disposal.

[5] As an exercise, assume that any one of the three forms of market integration is completely lacking; then work out the effects of a balance-of-payments disturbance.

Contrast with the Present System

Under the present international monetary system, which has evolved as a result of a series of compromises and unforeseen developments, there is relatively complete integration of commodity markets and partial integration of money markets. But exchange rates, though fixed within narrow limits, must be given official support when they reach the gold export point or its equivalent. Moreover, when a country's balance of payments is under heavy pressure, doubts as to the maintenance of the fixed rate arise. As for capital movements, although these are subject to both formal and informal restraints, both types can be evaded or overcome.

Like most compromises, our present system fails to give us the benefits that might be obtained from a more consistent model, combining either substantial integration with rigid exchange rates or monetary independence with fluctuating rates. In recent years, short-term capital movements, instead of helping to stabilize the U.S. balance of payments, have been a disequilibrating force. Capital moving outward in response to a deliberately established interest differential has aggravated the payments deficit. Fears as to the stability of the dollar have from time to time stimulated an additional export of speculative capital. Besides increasing the country's external deficit, they have hampered its attempts to cope with the problems of employment and growth.

Gains from Integration

Viewing the proposal for financial and monetary integration of the Atlantic Community in relation to the problems created by the existing monetary system, we can chalk up two tallies in its favor.

1. Large short-term capital movements, which have been such a disturbing influence in recent years, would be greatly reduced in size. With no possibility of the slightest variation in exchange rates, there would be no motive for speculative capital flows. On the other hand, interest arbitrage, or capital movements in response to interest differentials, would be sensitive to even small differences in interest rates. Prompt response should mean prompt correction; the flow of funds would therefore not need to be massive, but only marginal.

2. Such short-term capital movements as continued would provide a prompt and ready means of financing deficits or surpluses in the balance of payments, replacing the need for official compensatory financing, or use of a country's gold and foreign exchange reserves. Therefore nations would not need to keep large reserves, nor concern themselves overmuch with their variation.

Thus financial and monetary integration would be a most effective means of meeting two of the three principal problems that confront us: the inability of the existing system to provide for adequate growth of reserves, and its instability in the face of short-term capital movements.

It is important to note, however, that in a financially integrated community, short-term capital movements would be "equilibrating" only in the very limited sense that they provide a means of *financing* a balance of payments deficit and thereby reduce the need for a nation to draw upon its reserves. Although, by making unnecessary a multiple contraction of credit, this provides more time for any needed fundamental adjustments to work themselves out, it in no way contributes to those adjustments. In other words, short-term capital movements would not be equilibrating in the sense of contributing to the correction of a deficit.

Integration and National Autonomy

We have still to consider what contribution the proposed plan makes toward reconciling monetary and fiscal independence with the needs of balance-of-payments equilibrium. Clearly, national autonomy in monetary policy would be impossible. Since capital markets would be closely linked, a country that attempted to enforce a policy of low interest rates and easy credit would be faced, far sooner than at present, with an outflow of capital that would drain its reserves. Adherence to a rigid exchange rate would compel prompt alignment of monetary policies throughout the Community.

To deal with localized unemployment, much greater reliance would have to be placed on fiscal policy. Ingram contends that members of the Community would retain a limited degree of fiscal independence, perhaps as much as they enjoy at present. A nation undertaking to eradicate unemployment could engage in deficit financing, though only with a distinct difference from current procedures. It could not finance its increased expenditure out of newly created credit, but would have to raise the funds through the sale of its securities in the common capital market at a competitive rate of interest. The larger the sum the government wished to raise, the more attractive would it have to make the yield. Thus the cost of a program to counter unemployment would be increased, and would be more apparent than when based on an increase in the supply of money. Both the visibility of the cost and the need to maintain its credit rating would restrain governments pursuing such expansionary activities.

Such a limitation on fiscal autonomy may seem excessive. A government could spend in excess of revenues only as much as it could finance without injury to its credit status—that is, a sum on which it could pay interest and amortization charges. This could be substantial, however, given the taxing power of a strong government and the effect on tax yields of income raised through increasing employment.

It is important to remember that under the existing system of pegged exchange rates, governments by no means have complete fiscal autonomy. Attempts to maintain low interest rates to facilitate deficit financing are likely to cause an outflow of capital and a worsening of the balance of payments. Unless the drain on reserves is checked, fear of devaluation will intensify the capital flow and require either closer alignment of monetary and fiscal policies or the introduction of restrictions on trade and exchange transactions. Complete monetary and fiscal independence is compatible only with a regime of rigorous and effective exchange controls.

Practicability

Is the financial and monetary unification of the Atlantic Community politically feasible? This is, at the least, dubious. It may be that the logic of experience will convince central banks that their independence of action is largely illusory. But can national governments be persuaded to allow attainment of the goals of full employment and economic growth to be determined by impersonal market forces? This would require them to surrender sovereignty over vital economic policy. True, six nations of western Europe have agreed to merge their tariffs and gradually to intensify the extent of their integration. But there were strong and unique political and economic reasons for this decision. Conditions for the voluntary sacrifice of national autonomy, by a much larger group of nations and over more jealously guarded prerogatives, are far less favorable. Financial integration of the entire Atlantic Community is not a feasible proposal for the foreseeable future, though one day it may be. The plan has merit, however, as well as theoretical interest. Its serious discussion is warranted, and may win it support.

A MULTIPLE-CURRENCY STANDARD

Since governments surrender their sovereignty over important areas of decision only with great reluctance, proposals to patch or modify the present international monetary system are more likely candidates for acceptance than drastic reforms. Retention of the present system, though in modified form, ensures against the sacrifice of sovereignty. Among all the reforms suggested, the one that involves the least institutional or procedural change proposes the extension of the reserve-currency principle to a wider base.

At present, holdings of only two currencies, the dollar and the pound, serve in the place of gold as international reserves. If other currencies could also be used for this purpose, available reserves could be very substantially increased. Concern for international liquidity would tend to recede into the background.

Not just any currency would do. Potential reserve currencies would have to command confidence in their convertibility at existing exchange rates, and ultimately, in their redeemability in gold at par. This automatically limits their number to not more than a half dozen or so—those of France, West Germany, Italy, the Netherlands, Belgium, Switzerland, and in the Western Hemisphere, Canada.

Changes Required

Only minor change would be needed to introduce the proposed reform.[6] Countries that were willing to become key-currency centers would announce their readiness to sell gold to foreign central banks at a fixed price.[7] Thereafter, any country that developed a surplus in its balance of payments and that acquired holdings of one or more of the new key currencies could simply add these to its reserves. Owing to the declining acceptability of further dollar deposits as international reserves, this step should require little urging. The transition from a dual-currency to a multiple-currency standard should take place smoothly and inconspicuously, merely as a result of the desire to reduce the risk inherent in a continuing rise in foreign-owned dollar balances.

Spreading Reserve Risks

Thus suppose that a multiple-reserve currency system had been in operation in the years prior to 1962 and that the short-term foreign liabilities accumulated by the United States and the United Kingdom had been spread instead among nine countries—these two and the seven just mentioned. Table 27.1 shows how such a redistribution of short-term claims would have altered the ratio of reserve liabilities to gold reserves.

Table 27.1. EFFECT OF A REDISTRIBUTION OF SHORT-TERM
INTERNATIONAL LIABILITIES

(in billions of dollars, as of December, 1962)

	United States	United Kingdom	Nine Countries*
1. Gold holdings	16.0	2.9	34.1
2. Official short-term foreign liabilities	12.1	6.8	18.9
Ratio of 2 to 1	0.7	2.07	0.55
3. Total short-term foreign liabilities	20.1	9.8	29.9
Ratio of 3 to 1	1.26	3.37	0.88

* The nine countries are: United States, United Kingdom, Canada, Belgium, France, Western Germany, Italy, the Netherlands, and Switzerland.

SOURCE: *International Financial Statistics.*

[6] Among its supporters are Robert Roosa, Undersecretary of the U.S. Treasury, Dr. Posthuma, a director of the Netherlands Bank, and Friedrich A. Lutz, Professor of Economics at the University of Zurich. For a brief exposition of the merits of the proposal, see Professor Lutz's monograph, *The Problem of International Liquidity and the Multiple-Currency Standard*, Essays in International Finance No. 41. Published 1963 by International Finance Section, Princeton University.

[7] See Lutz, *op. cit.*, p. 13. Some supporters of the multiple-currency principle have recommended a gold guarantee. Professor Lutz rejects this suggestion as likely to make any needed devaluation so costly that it would freeze the existing pattern of exchange rates.

Official claims against U.S. gold reserves amounted to 70 per cent of the latter; for the United Kingdom, the corresponding figure is 207 per cent. Had these claims been spread among all nine countries, short-term official liabilities would have been only 55 per cent of aggregate gold reserves.[8] Since nonofficial liabilities can quite readily become official by their sale to the monetary authorities of a country, the ratio of total short-term foreign liabilities to gold reserves is perhaps more significant. For the U.S., this was 126 per cent; for the United Kingdom, 337 per cent. Spread over all nine countries, the figure is only 88 per cent. Insofar as a high ratio of liabilities to reserves weakens confidence in international monetary stability, multiplying the number of reserve currencies would have helped minimize this source of danger.

Introduction of such a system could not occur all at once. Balances in the United States or the United Kingdam could only be transferred by their holders withdrawing gold and depositing it in another country, a procedure that would merely weaken the reserve position of these nations. The system could be introduced gradually, however, and the further accumulation of dollar and sterling balances could thereby be retarded. This would require that countries with balance of payments surpluses vis-à-vis any of the new key-currency countries be willing to accept balances with them, instead of taking payment only in gold or in dollar or sterling deposits. In addition to spreading liabilities against world gold reserves, this would add to the total of international reserves rather than just reshuffle them.

Recent Developments

A number of steps toward the inauguration of a multiple-currency system were actually taken in the early 1960's. Thus in late 1961, when the German mark temporarily weakened, the U.S. Treasury acquired $55 million in marks, using these later to support the dollar when it came under pressure, then replenishing its mark holdings when the pressure eased. In January, 1962, the Bank of Italy extended a $150 million line of credit to the U.S. Treasury for use in support operations.

A more important move came during 1962, when the Federal Reserve authorities negotiated a series of reciprocal credit or "swap" facilities with seven foreign central banks and the Bank for International Settlements for a total of $700 million. The Federal Reserve and the Bank of England, for example, each agreed upon request to exchange its currency for the other's up to $50 million for a period of three months. If the dollar needed support, the Federal Reserve would credit the Bank of England with $50 million at a rate, say, of $2.80/£ while the Bank of England simultaneously credited

---

[8] Since none of the seven countries other than the U.S. and the U.K. had any appreciable short-term foreign liabilities of their own in 1962, the figures for these two countries can be taken to be total reserve liabilities for the entire group.

the Federal Reserve for about £18 million. With the demand for foreign currencies strong, due to an adverse temporary movement in U.S. payments abroad, the Federal Reserve could then sell the borrowed sterling, averting the need for an export of gold or an increase in foreign-held dollar balances. At the end of the three months, the transaction would be reversed, or repaid, and a new swap arranged if necessary.

Toward the end of May, 1963, the Federal Reserve and the Bank of England announced that they were increasing their reciprocal credit facilities from $50 million to $500 million, thus raising the total mutual credits available to the Federal Reserve or to its partners from $700 million to $1,150 million.

The first of the steps described, the acquisition by the United States of marks at a time when Germany's balance of payments was temporarily adverse, established the beginnings of a multiple reserve-currency system. The swap arrangements that followed, based on an exchange of credits, furthered the use of a number of currencies in international settlements. If the practice of accepting deposits in marks, lire, and other strong currencies in the settlement of balance-of-payments surpluses becomes general, we shall have moved from a dual-reserve to a multiple-reserve currency standard. This shift could probably be hastened were the strong currency countries to declare their willingness to sell gold at a fixed price, in lieu of their present undertaking to provide dollars at a maximum exchange rate.

Evaluation

Conversion of the present gold-exchange standard to a multiple-reserve currency form would contribute in two ways to easing international monetary problems. First, additional sources of foreign exchange reserves would be created, thus increasing the total of world reserves. The nation acquiring a new reserve currency adds to its reserves; the nation whose currency is acquired issues its promises to pay in lieu of exporting gold or drawing on its dollar holdings.[9] Therefore the reserves of both lender and borrower are increased. Contrast this with loan transactions that merely enable the borrower to exercise his borrowing power, but create no additional reserves for the lender.[10] This happens whenever the borrower's obligation to repay is not *itself* a reserve currency, as when a nation uses its drawing rights with the IMF or borrows dollar deposits from another nation.

A second gain would result from the increased confidence in the world's monetary system that would come from spreading the burden of reserve-currency liabilities over a larger base of gold reserves, as also from reduced

---

[9] Recall that foreign-owned deposits are a demand obligation of banks in the country in which they are held to residents (normally, banks) in the country that holds them. Thus the deposit-holding country is *lending* to the depository country; it holds the latter's obligations instead of requiring their payment in gold or in a reserve currency.

[10] See Lutz, *op. cit.*, pp. 6-9, where this distinction is worked out at some length.

anxiety about the adequacy of world reserves. Speculative capital movements would be reduced, and while interest arbitrage would continue, the larger world reserves would make such capital movements more manageable. The conflict between national monetary and fiscal autonomy and the need to submit to balance-of-payments restraints would remain unaffected except in the short run, when one reserve-currency country could use deposits in another to moderate a rise in the ratio of its foreign liabilities to gold.

RAISING THE PRICE OF GOLD

Of all the various means of increasing world liquidity, the simplest would be for the leading nations to raise the price of gold by concerted agreement. Were they to double the price from the present figure of $35 an ounce to $70 an ounce, the value of world gold reserves would automatically double. The effect on total reserves, though less, would still be striking. At the end of 1962, aggregate reserves—including gold, foreign exchange, and gross IMF positions—amounted to $78.7 billion, of which gold comprised $39.2 billion.[11] Doubling the price of gold would raise the total to $117.9, or by almost exactly 50 per cent. This could be achieved by a mere human decision, followed by simple numerical changes in the ledgers of central banks and treasuries. It makes the many devices to augment reserves by international lending seem painfully unnecessary. Why not, instead, adopt this simple and straightforward procedure?

Besides its important contribution to the problem of reserve adequacy, the proposal has much logic behind it. As Harrod argues, mankind has assigned to gold the role of acting as the ultimate medium for the settlement of international indebtedness. Having assigned gold this role, and having no complete substitute for it, it seems stupid not to give gold a sufficient value so that it can play its role effectively.[12] Moreover, gold is probably the only commodity whose price has not been substantially raised since 1934. The dollar has lost more than half its value in terms of commodities since before the war; other currencies have lost even more. Common sense would suggest that gold be brought into line with other commodities by raising its money price substantially.[13] (As noted, any such increase in the price of gold would have to be multinational. For the United States alone to raise this price would be to devalue the dollar.)

Doubling the price of gold, however, would do more than double the value of existing gold reserves. It would also double the money value of

[11] *International Financial Statistics*, June, 1963.

[12] Sir Roy Harrod, "The Role of Gold Today," *South African Journal of Economics* (March, 1958).

[13] See Sir Roy Harrod, "The Dollar Problem and the Gold Question," in *The Dollar in Crisis*, Seymour E. Harris, ed. Published 1961 by Harcourt, Brace, & World, Inc., New York.

current gold production and thus of the annual increments to gold reserves. Unless and until the cost of producing gold also doubled, it would afford a vigorous incentive to increase gold production. At a conservative estimate, this might rise by half, trebling the value of current gold output. Finally, all those individuals who have hoarded gold in anticipation of an increase in its price would be tempted to take their profit and place their hoards at the disposal of the monetary authorities.

Thus we can distinguish two direct effects of raising (say doubling) the price of gold. First, as an immediate, once-for-all effect, the value of the world's gold reserves would be doubled. Including the sizable but unknown disgorging of hoards that would occur, total world reserves would be raised by something more than 50 per cent. Second, as a continuing effect, persisting indefinitely, annual increments to the gold stock would be doubled and for some time perhaps trebled. The distinction between these two effects must be kept in mind, for monetary authorities can decide how the once-for-all effect shall be allowed to influence their reserve position, but they can only accept the continuing additions to gold reserves as they come.

Some Alternatives

If they wished, the monetary authorities of any country could prevent a doubling of the money value of gold reserves from having any effect whatsoever on their reserve position. They could do so by sterilizing, in one way or another, the profit from the revaluation of their gold stock. The simplest method would be to transfer half the gold in the vaults of the central bank to the Treasury, then require the latter not to part with the gold in its possession.[14] The monetary position of the central bank would be the same as before; the money value of its gold reserves would be unchanged, their weight cut in half.

This treatment of the initial impact of a doubled price of gold on reserves would appeal to monetary conservatives, who fear a resurgence of inflation whenever reserves expand. But it would be rejected by those who see an expansionary policy as the answer to stagnation and unemployment. Since conditions differ among countries, some might choose to sterilize the gold profit, some might not.

A more interesting alternative would be open to the present key-currency countries. They could use the gold profit to pay off the holders of official balances. This would reduce greatly the ratio of short-term foreign liabilities to gold, thus improving the liquidity of these countries. Thus if the U.S. gold reserve of $16 billion were increased to $32 billion, and $12 billion of this diverted to the repayment of official balances, the United States would be left with $20 billion of gold reserves unencumbered by any official claims.

---

[14] This sterilized gold could be used as a stabilization fund to support the currency's value when necessary, or to pay a subscription to a possible future world central bank, or held back for later transfer to the central bank when additional reserves might be needed.

The proportion of the remaining unofficial short-term foreign liabilities to reserves would be only 50 per cent. (These liabilities, amounting to $10 billion in 1962, would now constitute total liabilities.)

Such action would have a sharper purpose if considered together with one of the consequences of the up-valuation of current gold production. As we have noted, annual increments to gold reserves would be at least doubled. Since about half of recent additions to total reserves have come from gold production, half from the rise in dollar balances, the world could now dispense with the latter source of increased reserves. Should the key-currency countries liquidate existing official balances, then with future additions to world reserves supplied from gold production, the gold-exchange standard would give way to a reconstituted gold standard. In the eyes of some, this would be the principal gain from a revaluation of gold.

We should note that, although raising the price of gold would greatly improve the net reserve position of the United States, it would in no way contribute to the solution of the latter's balance-of-payments deficit. That problem and the problem of world liquidity, or the adequacy of world reserves, are distinct. Unless the forces giving rise to recurring U.S. deficits are counteracted, these will continue. Since, with the revaluation of gold, surplus countries would generally have more ample gold reserves, they would have less incentive than formerly to add to their dollar holdings. Continuing U.S. deficits would then intensify the drain on that country's revamped gold reserves.

A final point: the relative proportion of gold and of foreign exchange in national reserves varies widely from country to country.[15] Those fortunate enough to have a high ratio of gold would find their reserves approximately doubling if the price of gold were doubled. At the other extreme, countries such as Japan, with gold reserves only one-fifth of foreign exchange reserves, would improve their reserve status only fractionally. In the light of these facts, Machlup comments:

> If central banks had taken the repeated forecasts of an increase in the price of gold seriously, and were selfish enough to have their reserve position improved in the process, they would have tried to convert all their foreign-exchange holdings into gold and the present international monetary system would have long since collapsed.[16]

Evaluation

Raising the price of gold could contribute significantly to the solution of current international monetary problems. First and foremost, it would pro-

---

[15] At the end of 1962, the ratios of gold to foreign exchange reserves for a number of countries were, in round numbers: Switzerland, 14:1; the Netherlands, 8:1; South Africa, 5:1; Belgium, 4:1; France, 2.6:1; Germany, 1.3:1; Canada, 1:2.6; Sweden, 1:3; Japan, 1:5.

[16] Fritz Machlup, *Plans for Reform of the International Monetary System*, p. 46. Published 1962 by International Finance Section, Princeton University.

vide adequate reserves for most of the industrialized countries for some time to come. By improving the reserve position of the key-currency countries, it would lessen fears as to the stability of their currencies and thereby reduce the danger of speculative capital movements; and if desired, the gold-exchange standard could be transformed into a full gold standard.

Gold revaluation, however, would do nothing to resolve the conflict between national autonomy and restraints imposed by balance-of-payments discipline; for exchange rates would remain fixed, compelling nations sooner or later, depending upon the size of their reserves, to bring their domestic economic policies into line with their balances of international payments and receipts. Nor would a higher price for gold help to eliminate recurring deficits of the United States or the United Kingdom, though it would give them more room for maneuver. With ample reserves, these nations could adopt expansionary policies to stimulate employment and economic growth. Initially, higher incomes might intensify any balance of payments drain, but if rising profits and growing markets stirred investment in plant modernization, this could in the longer run improve their competitive position. A more profitable environment would also tend to check the outflow of long-term capital and even perhaps to attract foreign investment.

Such a happy outcome of enlarged reserves and greater short-run freedom would require moderation in monetary and fiscal policy, as well as restraint by labor and business alike with respect to wages and prices. Otherwise, either demand inflation or wage-cost inflation would neutralize the favorable effects of rising incomes and profits.

Some economists fear the general increase in reserves, particularly the steady increase in their size from enlarged current production, would be an invitation to inflation that would be welcomed everywhere. But this is to ignore the strong public support for stable monetary policies and to assume a governmental irresponsibility for which there is little evidence. Witness, for example, the alarm expressed by west European governments at the rising trend of wages and prices in late 1962 and early 1963. Moreover, unless inflationary policies were universal—a possibility made dubious by the uneven distribution of reserves—the retention of a fixed exchange rate system would soon bring the balance-of-payments check to bear upon the more feckless.

Closely related to the monetary behavior that followed the expansion of reserves is another danger—a renewal of speculation in gold, in anticipation of another increase in its price. If monetary authorities acted conservatively, preserving relative stability in the world price level, a long period could pass before further revaluation of gold would need to be considered, by which time more basic improvements in the international monetary system might make it unnecessary. Irresponsible action leading to a rapid rise of prices would, of course, be sure to stir renewed speculation.

A more immediate objection to raising the price of gold is that it would give an unmerited reward to gold speculators and to gold producers such as South Africa and the Soviet Union, while imposing an unjust penalty on countries that had supported the international monetary system by continuing to hold dollars and sterling. A bonus to gold speculators would be a cheap price to pay. So would any gain to the Soviet Union, since as Harrod has pointed out, the free world would be giving itself a far larger present. As for South Africa, that nation's government would profit only from the increased value of its gold reserve (some $500 to $600 million in 1962) and from higher tax yields from gold producers. It is the gold-mining companies and their Bantu workers who would chiefly benefit, and these companies "may be reckoned upon as a powerful force of enlightenment in the Union."[17] Perhaps there is no answer to the charge of unfairness to holders of the key currencies, except that they, like all nations, would have been worse off had a scramble for gold reserves brought about monetary collapse.

A practical difficulty is possibly the most serious obstacle to changing the price of gold. Before government officials can agree on such a step, they must discuss it at length. To prevent a rush to buy gold, with chaos in foreign exchange markets, any such discussion would have to be kept secret. But to maintain secrecy in such a wide-ranging discussion would be impossible. The proposal therefore cannot receive serious consideration where it counts.

TOWARD A WORLD CENTRAL BANKING SYSTEM

Many regard such devices as increasing the number of reserve currencies, raising the price of gold, and establishing a standby credit pool as essentially patchwork remedies designed merely to shore up an international monetary system that badly needs more fundamental reform. Recalling the great contribution to national monetary stability made by the establishment of national central banks, they have advanced a number of proposals for the creation of a world central bank, to perform functions for the world community similar to those performed on a smaller stage by a national central bank. Since space does not permit our undertaking a comparison of several alternative plans, let us consider the one that has received the widest attention, that advanced by Professor Robert Triffin of Yale University.[18]

Basis

Triffin's proposals for international monetary reform stem directly from his concern over the inadequacy of world monetary reserves and over the vulnerability of an international monetary system based in large part on official holdings of foreign exchange. As a closely related problem, he stresses the

[17] Cf. Harrod, in Harris, *op. cit.*, p. 60.
[18] For an excellent brief comparison of a number of proposals for the creation of a world central bank, see Fritz Machlup, *op. cit.*

need to protect the freedom of U.S. internal economic policies against the threat posed by large and growing dollar balances.

On the weakness of the gold-exchange standard, Professor Triffin is especially eloquent. Although he regards the monetary use of gold as an "absurd waste of human resources," nonetheless its replacement in international reserves by national currencies has been a haphazard development forced by circumstances. *Their* use in this role, Triffin contends, is totally irrational— they constitute a "built-in destabilizer" in the world monetary system.[19]

Content of the Triffin Plan

Accordingly, the keystone of Triffin's proposals is to transform balances of national currencies now held as international reserves into international balances. First, all nations would renounce the use of national currencies as international reserves, while the United States and the United Kingdom would prohibit such use of the dollar and the pound. Second, the International Monetary Fund would (after appropriate changes in its constitution) exchange its own deposits for official holdings of dollars or sterling. These international deposits "should be made equivalent in all respects to gold itself and as widely usable and acceptable in world payments."[20] To ensure this, deposits with the IMF would be given exchange rate and convertibility guarantees. Moreover, they would earn interest as determined by earnings of the Fund on its own loans and investments. The dollar and sterling assets acquired by the IMF it would liquidate at its discretion, at a rate not to exceed five per cent a year.[21]

To give the reconstituted Fund adequate initial resources, members would be required to deposit with it 20 per cent of their monetary reserves.[22] Any deposits in excess of this amount could be converted into gold, though this would be made unattractive by the interest earned on Fund deposits, which could be used, equally with gold, in all international settlements. A central bank holding them could exchange them for any currency needed or draw upon them to stabilize its currency in the exchange markets.

As members became accustomed to settling international balances by the transfer of Fund deposits, the simplicity and convenience of this procedure

[19] Robert Triffin, *Gold and the Dollar Crisis*, p. 87. Published 1960 by Yale University Press, New Haven, Conn.

[20] *Ibid.*, p. 102.

[21] This might create something of a problem, since to liquidate these dollar and sterling holdings, the United States and the United Kingdom would either have to pay them off out of their existing gold reserves, or develop a balance of payments surplus. This problem could be readily resolved if the price of gold were raised simultaneously with the introduction of the Triffin plan, for then the gold profit on reserves could be used to effect their liquidation painlessly.

[22] Existing net claims of members against the IMF would count as part of these initial deposits; to bring them up to 20 per cent of monetary reserves, additional deposits of gold and foreign exchange would be required.

might lead them to keep the major share or eventually all of their reserves in this form. In any event, a rising proportion of world reserves would take this form as a result of the IMF's contribution to their growth.[23]

The Triffin Plan provides for the secular expansion of reserves in a manner similar to that now employed by national central banks. The IMF could make loans to member nations, subject to agreement with respect to duration and interest charges, and, as in recent years, including provisions regarding economic and financial policies of the member designed to preserve long-run balance-of-payments equilibrium. Or the Fund could invest in various kinds of assets in the financial markets of member countries, including securities channeling funds into economic development, such as the bonds of the International Bank for Reconstruction and Development. Both loans and investments would create new IMF deposits, thus adding to the outstanding total of world reserves.

Since an incautious rate of lending and investing by the International Monetary Fund could generate a plethora of reserves, to guard against this inflationary danger Triffin suggests that the expansion of world reserves be limited to some arbitrary maximum figure of 3 to 5 per cent a year. This would restrict net Fund lending to the difference between the agreed rate of growth and the annual increment to gold reserves. What the actual rate of reserve increase might be would rest with the discretion of the Fund's management; it need not be the prescribed maximum should less appear adequate.

Evaluation

Triffin's plan for the centralization of world reserves would substitute a strong for a vulnerable international monetary system. Once the new system was established and in efficient operation, the dilution of its assets by the steady reduction in the proportion of gold and the attendant rise in the proportion of national currency holdings and long-term securities should be no cause for concern. What is needed for international settlements is some medium of exchange that is generally acceptable. If the IMF limited its investments to assets denominated in currencies that were in steady demand, its deposits would retain their value in international settlements. ("Distress" loans to countries in difficulties would, of course, have to be safeguarded, as we have noted, and limited in duration.)

Growth of world reserves is amply assured, with provisions to guarantee against overexpansion. Moreover, the flexibility to changing conditions now provided by the IMF would be retained and strengthened.

[23] Once confidence in IMF deposits as a means of international settlement were fully established, the need for gold in international reserves would no longer exist. In the meantime, however, gold could be retained in the system "as a harmless example of cultural lag and as an inexpensive subsidy for the production of something that the world wants but does not need." (Oscar Altman, "Professor Triffin, International Liquidity, and the International Monetary Fund," in Harris, *op. cit.*, p. 246.)

As with the proposal to raise the price of gold, the Triffin plan would relieve the United States from the immediate severe restraint imposed on its economic policies by the overhanging short-term foreign liabilities. But like all the proposals so far considered, it would leave the underlying trend of the U.S. balance of payments unaffected, for this is a problem of combating longer-run disequilibrating forces. This conflict between internal policies and external equilibrium, in general as well as in the particular case of the United States, would remain unresolved.

FLUCTUATING EXCHANGE RATES

At the end of the spectrum of alternatives for international monetary reform comes reliance upon fluctuating exchange rates. Not that this alternative is the worst because in this presentation it comes last; many economists think it is the best.[24]

Logically, the case for flexible exchange rates focuses upon the problem that other proposals, which embody fixed rates, pass over lightly or ignore: the conflict between freedom to determine national monetary and fiscal policies and the needs of balance-of-payments equilibrium. If exchange rates are allowed to vary, deficits will be eliminated by the consequent stimulus to exports and check to imports. Nations can then relegate balance-of-payments considerations to a position of secondary importance, and direct their major efforts to ensuring a state of full employment and to realizing their full potential of economic growth; to reducing the barriers to international trade; and to eliminating nationalistic restrictions on the use of loans and grants to underdeveloped countries.[25] It is far more important that these vital goals of policy be realized than that exchange rates remain fixed—not, be it noted, forever, but only for indeterminate periods. There has always been an element of the ridiculous in a state of affairs that requires the wealthiest nation in the world to suffer unemployment and heavy loss of production because of an imbalance in its international accounts of the order of one-half of one per cent of its gross national product. As one economist remarked in this connection, this is a case "not of the tail wagging the dog, but the tail of the flea on the dog wagging the dog."[26]

[24] Among economists who have sponsored some form of fluctuating exchange rates are: Milton Friedman, Frank D. Graham, Gottfried Haberler, George N. Halm, Erik Lundberg, Friedrich A. Lutz, Lloyd W. Mints, James E. Meade, Egon Sohmen, and Charles R. Whittlesey. For a list of their, and other, contributions to this topic, see Fritz Machlup, *Plans for the Reform of the International Monetary System*, pp. 57-58.

[25] For an especially vigorous presentation of this point of view, see James E. Meade, "The Future of International Payments," in *Factors Affecting the United States Balance of Payments*, Joint Economic Committee, 87th Congress, 2nd sess. (Government Printing Office, Washington, D. C., 1962).

[26] J. M. Culbertson, statement before the Joint Economic Committee, August 14, 1962.

To establish a case for fluctuating exchange rates, however, it is not enough to assert or even prove that under such a regime nations would be free to pursue national goals of paramount importance. For this freedom could be misused. Overzealous pursuit of full employment or economic growth could bring on serious inflation, speculation in the exchange markets, and wild fluctuations in exchange rates or constant and rapid depreciation of a country's currency. This would merely replace one kind of instability with another. It must be shown that the danger of such instability is nonexistent or grossly overrated, and that the danger of destabilizing speculation is either unreal, or if real, subject to effective control.

In considering this problem, it will be helpful if we first clear up some related issues. Therefore let us direct our attention once more toward the problem of international liquidity. Why is there such concern with liquidity, or the adequacy of international reserves? Wherein consists the the need for large international reserves, toward whose provision so much attention and effort has been devoted in recent years?

Liquidity Once Again

International reserves are, it is generally agreed, needed to tide a nation over temporary imbalances in its international accounts. They are a principal means of financing a short-run deficit in the balance of payments. These temporary deficits that are financed by reserve movements may result from any one of a number of causes: seasonal or cyclical fluctuations in the value of a country's exports or imports, the initial effects of a more basic source of disequilibrium, and especially in recent years, short-term capital movements caused by divergent national monetary policies or by the fear of currency devaluation. In discussions of liquidity, the emphasis is and must be on the *temporary nature* of the imbalance, for in the face of a persistent disequilibrium, no level of reserves would be large enough.

What amount of reserves is "adequate" for the financing of temporary deficits will, of course, vary from one nation to another, depending upon such factors as the stability or variability of its international payments or receipts, its holdings of financial assets that could be used to supplement reserves, and the responsibilities it has to bear. The reserve requirements of a reserve-currency country, for example, would be much greater than of a country that was not a recipient of the international reserves of other nations.

To an extraordinary degree, discussion of the major problem of international monetary reform has focussed upon one particular aspect of that problem: international liquidity. Practically none of the articles and books dealing with monetary reform fails to accord this topic sympathetic treatment; many give it top billing. But if liquidity, or adequacy of reserves, is related to the short-run or temporary aspects of balance of payments disequilibrium, why such great concern for what at bottom is ephemeral? Surely of far more lasting importance are deep-seated causes of disequilibrium and means of coping with them. It would seem that merely because of the frequency and size of recent short-term capital movements, economists, bankers, and government officials have permitted themselves to become hypnotized by this minor part of a much larger problem. If attention were focussed instead upon major causes of disequilibrium and means of effecting smooth adjustment to them, solution of this problem would in itself serve to diminish the frequency and size of short-term swings in capital movements.

Is it not possible that behind this preoccupation with the ephemeral there is a more fundamental but unexpressed concern—a concern for the maintenance of fixed exchange rates, which are coming increasingly to be regarded as something inviolable, almost sacred? This was certainly not the view of the economists and government officials who participated at Bretton Woods in framing the constitution of the International Monetary Fund. There concern was centered on finding a better means of dealing with fundamental balance of payments disequilibrium than the deflation called into play by the then emphatically rejected gold-standard mechanism. They thought they had found it in the procedures for controlled devaluation written into the Fund's charter.

Devaluation, however, has turned out to possess two basic defects. (1) It cannot be used, in practice, by a reserve-currency country because of the losses this would inflict on official holders of reserve deposits. (2) Any suspicion that devaluation is about to be invoked leads to immediate speculative capital movements. The threat of such capital movements, which have appeared from time to time in recent years, reenforces the search for means of raising the level of world liquidity, which have increasingly taken the direction of a move toward establishment of a multiple-reserve currency system. But establishment of such a system, by multiplying the number of nations that would be inhibited from resorting to devaluation, is the surest way of riveting fixed exchange rates onto the world's monetary arrangements. This may not be what some proponents of the multiple-reserve currency system want, but it is what they are likely to get. And it seems to be what many of its proponents *do* want. What a distance we have come from Bretton Woods! Must we learn its lessons all over again?

The Positive Case for Fluctuating Exchange Rates

In a market economy such as is predominant in the western world, it is anomalous to fix, officially and for long periods, such an important price as an exchange rate. Probably the reason for doing so is rooted in our attitude toward money. The *price* of any country's currency, say a dollar, is fixed by definition. When the domestic price level is stable, there is some justification for also regarding the *value* of a dollar as fixed. But in a world where economic policies differ, where the forces affecting the value of national currencies vary, there can be no justification for regarding the *relative value* of any two currencies as fixed.[27] This relative value in fact alters with every change in the forces of demand and supply in the foreign exchange market. A foreign currency is wanted, moreover, not just for its purchasing power or internal value; it is also demanded as a means of acquiring foreign assets, of remitting gifts, of paying debts, or remitting interest and profits. A free exchange rate responds to these forces and establishes equilibrium between them; it reflects the true relative value of a currency to buyers and sellers.

In a market that comes as close to perfect competition as any in the world, these responses to changing market conditions are prompt and continuous. It is probably this very fact that forms the basis for the major objection to a system of fluctuating exchange rates—that these rates *will* fluctuate, and that this means instability. But fluctuations are one thing; instability is, or can be, another. Businessmen are accustomed to price fluctuations. Besides, they have a ready means of hedging against exchange rate fluctuations in the forward markets, which would become highly developed were a free exchange rate system in force. A moderate degree of short-run instability, moreover— that is, of fluctuations above and below a currency's long-run equilibrium value—is desirable. With a fixed par value, even though in the long run it is the correct equilibrium value, a currency will always be somewhat overvalued or undervalued.[28]

As for instability over the longer run, if the leading countries pursue their avowed goals of full employment and optimum growth with price stability together, this would ensure reasonable stability of their exchange rates. Should one country expand too rapidly, its balance of payments would turn adverse and its currency would depreciate. Since this would stimulate exports and raise prices, it would signal the need for a policy of monetary restriction, which would induce a capital inflow that would stabilize exchange rates. Failure to take this action would be inconsistent with the accepted goals, which include price stability, and certainly do not sanction monetary and fiscal irresponsibility.

There is always present, of course, the special danger of a wage-cost-push type of inflation, due to the monopoly power of business or of strong trade unions. For dealing with this phenomenon, monetary policy is ineffective, being likely only to cause unemployment without checking the rise of prices. To obtain both full employment and stable prices, governments may be compelled to introduce direct controls over key wages and prices. But this problem is not unique to a system of fluctuating exchange rates; it is an equally intractable source of difficulties for a fixed exchange rate system.

If a country is irresponsible in its monetary and fiscal policies, or institu-

---

[27] For a more thorough development of this point, see George N. Halm, "Fixed or Flexible Exchange Rates?" in *Factors Affecting the United States Balance of Payments.*

[28] See Egon Sohmen, *International Monetary Problems and the Foreign Exchanges,* p. 71. Published 1963 by International Finance Section, Princeton University.

tionally incapable of combating inflation effectively, its currency will tend to depreciate continually under a regime of free rates.[29] But no other monetary system will work for such a country either. An attempt to maintain a fixed parity while inflation is rampant leads inevitably to repeated devaluations or to exchange controls. For *any* international monetary system to function effectively for a participating nation—that is, for it to effect adjustments in its balance of payments smoothly—that nation must behave responsibly, which means that it must not depart too far from current monetary and financial orthodoxy. If that orthodoxy is annually balanced governmental budgets, then an unbalanced budget will disrupt the international monetary mechanism for the nonconforming nation. If, as today, orthodoxy means full employment and optimum growth with price stability, serious departure from pursuit of these goals will likewise cause that mechanism to malfunction. In other words, whether the international monetary system is based on fixed exchange rates or on flexible rates, there must be reasonable harmony among domestic monetary and fiscal policies or there will be serious discord in the international sector.

Long-run forces causing disequilibrium in a country's balance of payments, such as technological change or shifts in world demand, are, however, an ever-present possibility in a changing world. Under a fixed exchange rate system, a country adversely affected by such a development finds its currency becoming overvalued; its exports shrink and its reserves decline. To maintain the external value of its currency, it must adopt a deflationary monetary policy. It is this enslavement of domestic policy to external forces that flexible exchange rates can prevent. Overvaluation of the currency is corrected unobtrusively by gradual depreciation, enabling the country to avoid enforced deflation and to follow instead the path of stable growth.

Speculation

So far we have made little mention of speculation. Yet opponents of flexible exchange rates contend that speculation would tend to be destabilizing: instead of helping to restore equilibrium, it would intensify an existing disequilibrium. In this prospect they see one of the most serious objections to a flexible rate system.

We can rule out at the start perverse speculation, or speculation based on overoptimistic or overpessimistic views—more simply, speculation based on bad judgment. Speculators who consistently exercise bad judgment will be driven out of business and replaced by others whose judgment is better.

If speculators must judge the facts correctly if they are to survive, their activity should stabilize exchange rates against temporary dislocations (sea-

---

[29] Such continual depreciation has characterized the currencies of Brazil and Chile for a good many years.

sonal influences, effects of strikes or natural disasters) or once-for-all changes (exhaustion of a natural resource, loss of markets due to technological change or increased tariffs). Foreseeing the reversal of a temporary cause of currency depreciation, they would support the forward exchange rate against heavy sales, which in turn would help maintain the spot rate. Similarly, with once-for-all adverse (or favorable) change, they would profit by recognizing ahead of others the limited impact of that change on the country's balance of payments and by foreseeing, as well, that the ultimate depreciation required will be less than the immediate. Any excessive depreciation of the currency affected would cause them to become buyers, thus helping to sustain the exchange rate.

There is one situation, however, in which speculation could be destabilizing. This situation occurs when a country has embarked upon the path of inflation. Prices and money incomes rise; its balance of payments becomes adverse; and its currency depreciates. Import and export prices rise, intensifying the inflation. If now speculators estimate (correctly) that inflation is going to continue, they will sell the currency, both spot and forward, thus increasing the degree of depreciation and adding fuel to an inflammatory situation. But this is our old friend, fiscal irresponsibility. This is the real culprit to be charged with disruptive depreciation. Speculation merely makes matters a little worse; it would make them a great deal worse in a similar situation with fixed exchange rates.

Even though fears of destabilizing speculation are grossly exaggerated, their very existence would prohibit most governments from permitting exchange rates to fluctuate freely. Moreover, they would regard recurring daily fluctuations as undesirable. Therefore they would probably engage in stabilization operations. Each government would establish a fund consisting partly of its own national currency, partly of gold and foreign currencies, selling its own currency on the foreign exchange market to prevent unwanted appreciation, buying its own currency with its other assets to offset depreciation.

An International Authority

Stabilization operations could be made international in character and therefore more potent, and international liquidity in addition to that furnished by private capital movements could be made available, by establishing an international monetary authority. An interesting proposal to this effect, which would soften many of the objections to a system of freely fluctuating exchange rates, has been advanced by Professor Meade.[30] According to his plan: (1) All monetary authorities of the participating countries would pay into a reformed IMF all their reserves of gold and foreign exchange, receiving in return gold certificates which would henceforth be their sole form of reserve. (2) All

[30] James E. Meade, "The Future of International Payments," in *Factors Affecting the United States Balance of Payments.*

national currencies would then be allowed to fluctuate in value in terms of gold certificates. Each national monetary authority could now use these certificates to support its currency, or it could buy certificates with national currency to depress its value. (3) Besides the gold and national currencies previously paid to the IMF as national contributions, it would add thereto huge further sums. It could use these resources as a giant international stabilization fund, supporting currencies it had reason to believe were undervalued, acting to depress those it believed were overvalued. By these actions, the IMF would supplement private capital movements that were stabilizing in nature, offset those that were destabilizing. (4) The IMF could control the total amount of funds available to national monetary authorities for stabilization operations (international liquidity) by purchasing national currencies with newly issued gold certificates or selling its holdings of national currencies against outstanding certificates.

Such an institutional arrangement would possess two important advantages: (1) It could counter any attempt at competitive currency depreciation (an unlikely development, but feared by some), and (2) if the IMF kept the value of its gold certificates constant in terms of national currencies in general, these certificates (which could be held by commercial banks and individuals) could become the measure of value of international contracts, which might facilitate the flow of international investment.

Conclusion

A system of fluctuating exchange rates, with or without a reformed IMF at the center, affords the only international monetary mechanism that will allow nations to pursue the vital national goals of full employment, price stability, and economic growth, unhampered by excessive concern for the status of their international accounts. Balances of payments, reflecting changes in relative international demands and supplies—in market relations—would be adjusted consistently with a market system by changes in the relative prices of currencies—that is, in exchange rates. Reduced concern for the balance of payments would also permit nations to consider the removal of restrictions on both aid and trade in a more liberal spirit, and to relate aid to underdeveloped countries to the supplier's wealth and not to the momentary overvaluation or undervaluation of its currency.

Given, however, the normal obstacle of inertia, together with the enormous difficulty of obtaining agreement among first the central bankers and Treasury officials and then the legislatures of, at the minimum, a dozen countries, realization of international monetary reform of this scope and character appears highly improbable in the foreseeable future. Yet opinions change, often as a result of continuing efforts to change them. Until they do, compromise is inevitable. As for the direction of compromise, it is already apparent: extension of the reserve-currency system, augmenting international liquidity in various ways, and, in general, adoption of devices that disturb the *status quo* as little as possible.

SELECTED REFERENCES

Friedman, Milton, "The Case for Flexible Exchange Rates," in *Essays in Positive Economics*. Chicago: University of Chicago Press, 1953. A brief and persuasive statement of the case for flexible exchanges rates.

Harris, Seymour E., ed., *The Dollar in Crisis*. New York: Harcourt, Brace & World, Inc., 1961. In addition to Harrod's discussion of an increase in the price of gold, contains a chapter by Triffin sketching his plan, another by Altman criticizing the proposal, and a reply by Triffin.

Joint Economic Committee, *Factors Affecting the United States Balance of Payments*, 87th Congress, 2nd sess. Washington, D. C.: Government Printing Office, 1962. Parts 3, 4, and 7 consist of articles expressing a wide range of views by monetary experts on the problem of international monetary reform.

Lutz, Friedrich A., *The Problem of International Liquidity and the Multiple-Currency Standard*, Essays in International Finance No. 41. Princeton, N. J.: International Finance Section, Princeton University, March, 1963. Advocates extension of the multiple-currency standard as a second-best solution of international monetary problems.

Machlup, Fritz, *Plans for Reform of the International Monetary System*, Special Papers in International Economics No. 3. Princeton, N. J.: International Finance Section, Princeton University, August, 1962. An excellent treatment of the subject, within the relatively brief compass of 60-odd pages. Footnotes contain an extensive bibliography.

Sohmen, Egon, *International Monetary Problems and the Foreign Exchanges*, Special Papers in International Economics No. 4. Princeton, N. J.: International Finance Section, Princeton University, April, 1963. An able analysis of the problem of international monetary reform from the point of view of a supporter of a system of free exchange rates.

———, *Flexible Exchange Rates: Theory and Controversy*. Chicago: University of Chicago Press, 1961. A theoretical analysis of the operation of systems of fixed and of flexible exchange rates.

Triffin, Robert, *Gold and the Dollar Crisis*. New Haven, Conn.: Yale University Press, 1960. In addition to a detailed statement of Triffin's proposal for reform, there is an enlightening discussion of the changed meaning of convertibility, and of reserve adequacy.

28

ECONOMIC DEVELOPMENT

Although the problem of international monetary reform is both persistent and pressing, and may well become critical, it is also highly technical in nature and limited in scope. Even the most drastic reform would entail comparatively little change in the habits or outlook of those it affected, in the institutions that influence their daily lives, or in the uses to which economic resources are put. By contrast, the problem of quickening the development of the economically retarded regions of the world is unsurpassed in its demands for the mobilization of resources, for the reconstruction of social and economic institutions, and for changes in people's habits and attitudes.

THE MEANING OF ECONOMIC DEVELOPMENT

Consider for a moment what economic development implies. By some it has been taken to mean closing the gap between per capita incomes in the advanced and the underdeveloped countries. That this gap is wide cannot be denied. Table 28.1 gives some idea of its size: in 1955, since when conditions have changed but little, average per capita income in the most developed countries (at $1,228) was over twelve times that in the poorest nations (at $97). Even after allowing for some exaggeration due to differences in climate, in consumption habits, and in the activities included as contributing to income, the disparity would still be striking.

The level of national per capita income, though it provides some measure of the stage of a country's economic advance, gives no clue as to why income is high or low, nor does a rise therein throw any light on the reasons for the change. To understand the process of economic development, we must go behind this simple index of progress or lack of progress to the conditions on which it rests. These conditions consist of all the elements that affect a nation's capacity to produce goods and services: its natural resource base; the quantity and quality of its labor force; the amount and kinds of capital available to its industry and agriculture; and the institutions, attitudes, and

[482]

Table 28.1. MEASURES OF MATERIAL WELFARE, 1955

	National Product Per Head (dollars)	Caloric Intake Per Person Per Day (numbers)	Protein Consumption Per Day (grams)	Infant Mortality (number of deaths per 1000 live births)	Literacy (per cent of population 10 years and over)	Inhabitants Per Physician (number)	Per Cent of Gross Investment of GNP (1954)
I. Countries with per capita incomes above $750	1,288	3,078	90	33	98	953	18.8
II. Countries with per capita incomes between $750 and $300	470	2,761	84	57	84	782	20.7
III. Countries with per capita incomes between $300 and $150	229	2,369	70	72	55	4,129	14.9
IV. Countries with per capita incomes below $150	97	2,048	55	114	38	14,388	9.8

Note: The countries included in the income groups are as follows: I. United States, Canada, France, United Kingdom, Denmark, Germany; II. Uruguay, Israel, Austria, Italy, Argentina, Cuba; III. Turkey, Brazil, Japan, Greece, Philippines, Iraq, Mexico; IV. Egypt, Indonesia, Ceylon, Syria, Thailand, India, Burma, Pakistan.

SOURCE: *The Role of Foreign Aid in the Development of Other Countries*, a study prepared at the request of the Special Committee To Study the Foreign Aid Program, United States Senate, by the Research Center in Economic Development and Cultural Change of the University of Chicago, 85th Congress, 1st Session (Government Printing Office, Washington, D. C., 1957).

[483]

habits that determine the effectiveness with which all these economic resources are used.

Compare, for example, the United States with a "typical" underdeveloped country. The United States is large in size and rich in natural resources. Capital accumulation over the past century or more has provided it in abundance with many forms of social overhead capital: an extensive network of railways, highways, and airlines; ample electric power facilities; schools and colleges adequate to provide a basic education to all and advanced training to many; hospitals and medical facilities sufficient to maintain high standards of health. Private investment has furnished the means for incorporating into its factories and farms the most advanced and productive technology. The nation's labor force is skilled, disciplined, and energetic. Its business leaders are numerous, enterprising, and highly respected. Its government is stable, efficient, and comparatively honest. Constant change, though resisted by certain vested interests, has become generally accepted as normal.

Most underdeveloped countries, in contrast, enjoy a relatively poor resource base, though there are exceptions. The rate of capital accumulation has been slow, the results apparent in a transportation network ranging from fairly good (India, Argentina) to miserable, in recurrent power shortages and interruptions in service, in such a scarcity of schools and teachers that illiteracy remains high, in few doctors and fewer hospitals. In many underdeveloped countries "industry" still means handicraft production, though in some, modern steel mills and cement plants stand alongside small workshops. Except on large plantations, agricultural methods are generally primitive. Labor is mostly unskilled and unproductive, unaccustomed to the demanding routine of modern industry, and often lacking in energy because of malnutrition or chronic illness. Tradition favors such occupations as estate management, the priesthood, the military, or government administration, but counts commerce and industry as unworthy or demeaning. Entrepreneurial talent is therefore notably lacking; often it is supplied by alien groups: the Chinese in Indonesia, Thailand, and Malaya; the Indian or Arab in Ceylon; the Levantine or newly-arrived European until recently in much of Latin America. Government is often unstable, or if stable, is authoritarian. Corruption is widespread, and efficiency is rare. The vested interests opposed to change are frequently very powerful: the landed aristocracy and the religious leaders in Iran, the rich landowners in many Latin American nations, the castes of India, the tribal leaders of west and central Africa.

This brief study in contrasts suggests rather clearly what is meant by economic development. It is simply the transformation of a backward, sometimes primitive, and always unproductive society into a modern and productive one. In the advanced countries, this transformation has been going on since the Middle Ages, though with greatest intensity during the past century-and-a-half. Today's underdeveloped countries are unwilling to wait that long; the arrival of the "revolution of rising expectations" has altered the timetable. Altering the timetable, however, does nothing to affect performance. Some trains are going to be missed; all of them are going to be late. Much can be done, however, to improve performance. Most of this improvement will have to be accomplished by the underdeveloped countries themselves. They have the advantage, however, of being able to draw upon the immense accumulation of technology and knowledge in the developed nations. They can also tap the savings of the richer countries to supplement their own meager supplies of capital. And they can utilize the channels of trade to obtain materials and equipment essential to their accelerated growth. It is to these international aspects of economic development that this chapter is devoted.

IMPROVING TECHNIQUES OF PRODUCTION

It is to be expected that the techniques of production employed in the underdeveloped countries would differ appreciably from those in use in advanced economies, if only because of the wide difference in factor proportions that exist. Most underdeveloped countries have an abundance of labor, whereas in most of the industrial countries capital is the abundant factor, labor relatively scarce in comparison. This fact alone would dictate economy in the use of capital and the substitution of labor-intensive for capital-intensive processes or techniques in the underdeveloped regions of the world.

But actual differences in techniques go far beyond what could be explained in these terms. Most underdeveloped countries use a technology, both in agriculture and in industry, that in general is out-of-date by any standards, and often primitive. Modernization of certain procedures, at little cost in terms of resources, often produces striking results. Thus in agriculture, adoption of improved seed, careful breeding of livestock, or proper rotation of crops have been known to raise yields markedly. In industry, simple changes such as better inventory control, improved accounting records, more careful inspection of output, and greater attention to the training of workers also can pay off handsomely. Technical assistance programs have for some years now been a major feature of United Nations efforts to aid the underdeveloped nations and of the Colombo Plan for the Southeast Asian countries of the British Commonwealth; they have also played an important role in the aid extended individually by the United States, the United Kingdom, France, and other countries. These programs have done much to raise productivity in the receiving countries at relatively low cost.

Although there is still plenty of scope for continued technical assistance, there is a distinct limit to what it can accomplish. Only a small part of the highly productive modern technology can be transmitted without substantial investment in capital equipment. Thus major irrigation works require costly dams, barrages, and canals. Introduction of tractors and other mechanized equipment, where suited to the terrain, the crops, and the landholding pattern, is also expensive. Blast furnaces and rolling mills, if they are to be efficient, must be relatively large; they require heavy capital investment, as do modern cement plants. And substitution of electricity for steam or animal power in industry calls for large sums for dams, generators, distribution networks, and relay stations.

INVESTMENT AND ECONOMIC DEVELOPMENT

If a poor nation is to raise the standards of living of its people, it must increase their productivity. To accomplish this, it must ensure the introduction of improved methods of production. Since the most efficient known techniques require substantial amounts of capital, it is not surprising that we should find developing countries incorporating expanded programs of investment into their plans. More often than not, such a program constitutes the very core of an economic development plan.

The Balance of Payments

A common feature of underdeveloped countries, however, is a relatively low level of current savings. Indeed, the sequence low saving, low investment, low productivity, low incomes, low saving is frequently mentioned as one of the "vicious circles" that handicap underdeveloped economies.

To overcome this shortage of voluntary saving, many countries have attempted to generate forced saving and a higher rate of investment through inflationary methods. The excess investment, financed by an expansion of credit, raises money incomes, of which some part spills over into increased imports. Total expenditure on domestic goods and services increases, diverts exportables into domestic consumption, and raises prices all round. Exports decline, and the country faces a balance-of-payments deficit. Even if the underdeveloped countries had ample reserves of gold or foreign exchange, which they do not, such a condition could not for long be tolerated. Something must give. Usually it is not the investment program that is sacrificed, but the freedom to trade. Imports of consumer goods tend to be limited to essentials, and capital-goods imports tend to be given a strong preference. The idea seems to be that indulging investors (public or private) while denying consumers will somehow augment the capital supply.

This idea is at best a quarter-truth. Import restrictions can suppress the deficit, but they can increase the supply of capital only if they cause savings to rise. Consumers who are denied their accustomed imports are likely to seek the best possible substitutes at home. If they can no longer obtain automobiles, nylons, canned goods, and Scotch whiskey from abroad, they are likely to turn to domestic products and to increase their outlays on such alternatives as better housing, entertainment, and sports. This shift of expenditure onto domestic goods will draw resources away from capital production within the country. All that will have been accomplished is a substitution of imported capital goods for locally created capital goods. Only if consumers cannot find a satisfactory set of alternatives for goods formerly imported will they appreciably increase their savings. Coupling import restrictions with a wide range of heavy consumption taxes might force a sizeable reduction of consumption, but import restrictions alone will not normally do it.[1]

An alternative means of speeding the process of capital formation is the expansion of exports, financed, say, by increased bank loans. By increasing its exports, a country acquires additional foreign exchange with which to purchase capital equipment. This, however, turns out to be no more satisfactory than restricting imports, which likewise permits the acquisition of foreign exchange. It fails to call into being an act of saving, which is essential if there is to be any *net* increase in capital formation.

Where are the resources to produce the increased exports to come from? We may assume the economy to be fully employed, since it is engaged in inflationary financing of a capital expansion program. With increased funds at their disposal, exporters could hire factors of production away from domestic producers of capital goods. Again, there is a mere substitution of foreign for domestic capital. Or exporters could try to bid factors away from the production of consumer goods. But since nothing has been done to reduce consumers' spending, the rise of prices will be aggravated. Few resources will be diverted from satisfying consumers' wants; more likely is a shift of the pressure onto the capital goods sector.

The Role of Foreign Capital

By now it should be apparent that the problem of capital formation in a poor country involves three basic types of shortage. (1) There is a shortage of savings in the financial sense: the average propensity to save is too low to provide sufficient funds to finance an investment program of the desired size. (2) There is a shortage of savings in the real sense: people are unwilling to release from the production of consumer goods enough resources to carry out the programmed investment. (3) Since domestic resources are inadequate to produce the capital goods desired, they must be obtained from abroad.[2] As-

[1] For a more extended discussion of import restrictions in relation to capital formation, see R. Nurkse, *Capital Formation in Underdeveloped Countries*, pp. 109-116. Published 1953 by Basil Blackwell, Oxford.

[2] Even if all investment projects were labor-intensive, with no imports of capital equipment required, the inadequate supply of domestic resources for investment would necessitate the importation of foodstuffs and other wage goods to support labor engaged in capital-goods production. If, as is usually the case, imported capital equipment is needed, this merely determines the character of the imports; it does not alter the basic nature of the problem.

suming there was no surplus in the balance of payments to begin with, the country encounters a shortage of foreign exchange.[3]

Since virtually no developing countries have more than minimal reserves of gold and foreign exchange to draw upon, there is only one practicable means of combating these crucial shortages. This is to attract an inflow of foreign capital. If foreigners can be induced to invest, lend, or extend financial aid to a developing country in sufficient amounts, all three shortages can be overcome. Foreign capital provides the foreign exchange needed to buy the necessary imports; the imports thus acquired constitute the supplementary resources that were lacking; and the funds made available from abroad take the place of the missing domestic savings.

In terms of the national income equation, the effort to execute an investment program in excess of a country's voluntary capacity to provide savings amounts to spending a total sum greater than the value of national output. Starting with the familiar equation

$$Y = C + I + G + (X - M),$$

we can isolate $(C + I + G)$ as total domestic expenditure or absorption (A).[4] In the absence of capital movements in either direction, $(X - M)$ is the balance of payments (B). Therefore

$$Y = A - B, \text{ or}$$
$$B = Y - A.$$

Starting with full employment and, for simplicity, with imports and exports equal, if one component of absorption, investment, is increased, total absorption (in real terms) of goods and services will exceed total output (Y). The shortage of domestic goods implies a real deficit in the balance of payments; B becomes negative. In money terms, if absorption rises, the money value of $C, I,$ and G is raised, but since the value of output (Y) cannot be increased, the excess purchasing power drains away abroad and pushes up imports. A deficit appears in the balance of payments.

All this can be prevented by an inflow of foreign capital. (Suppose it to consist of foreign aid in the form of grants and loans, D.) If absorption, because of an augmented investment program, rises by dA, but foreign aid (D) of an equivalent amount is forthcoming, our equation becomes

$$B + D = Y - (A + dA).$$

Interpreted broadly, this states that the inflow of foreign capital permits national absorption or expenditure to exceed national output without giving

[3] This formulation of the three shortages, or gaps, may be found in S. Kuznets, "International Differences in Capital Formation and Financing," National Bureau of Economic Research, *Capital Formation and Economic Growth*, pp. 34-35. Published 1955 by Princeton University Press. See also Gerald M. Meier, *International Trade and Development*, pp. 85-89. Published 1963 by Harper & Row, New York.

[4] This includes expenditure on imports by consumers, investors, and the government, which have to be deducted to obtain net national product or national income.

rise to a balance of payments deficit. More specifically, the foreign capital (D) finances an excess of imports. The current account of the balance of payments (B) becomes negative, but is offset in the total balance of payments ($B + D$) by positive foreign investment, which thus prevents a shortage of foreign exchange from arising. The additional imports made possible by foreign investment provide the wherewithal to offset the shortage of real resources apparent in the excess of absorption ($A + dA$) over output (Y). Finally, the foreign investment makes good the shortage of domestic savings. (In terms of the savings-investment equation, $S = I_d + I_f$, foreign investment, I_f, is identical with D. The country can undertake aggregate investment in excess of its savings by this amount.)

On our assumption of a fully employed economy, it is clear that any expansion of investment (represented by dA) can be no greater than the foreign financing made available. For since there are no free resources in the economy to produce output in response to increased expenditure, the marginal propensity to import is unity. Through the inflationary price mechanism, any additional expenditure will be diverted abroad.

A different outcome is possible if unemployed labor, capital, and natural resources exist, capable of augmenting output in response to increased demand. Then an increase in domestic investment can be some multiple of the foreign capital inflow. This expansion can go on until it is checked by the effect of rising income on imports. When these rise to equality with the capital inflow, any further expansion of investment will bring about a balance-of-payments deficit. This noninflationary limit to an investment program—the maximum expansion ratio, or the permissible ratio of investment to foreign lending, dI/dD—will be established by the equality: $dI/dD = dI/dM$. What this limit is, will depend on the values of the marginal propensity to save (s) and the marginal propensity to import (m).[5] We know that $dM = m \cdot dY$, and that $dY = k \cdot dI$. Therefore: $dM = m \cdot dY = m \cdot k \cdot dI = m \cdot dI/(s + m)$. It follows that

$$\frac{dI}{dD} = \frac{dI}{dM} = \frac{dI}{m\left(\dfrac{dI}{s + m}\right)}.$$

To illustrate, assume that $s = \frac{1}{4}$ and $m = \frac{1}{4}$. Then the multiplier, k ($=1/s + m$) has a value of 2. Substituting these values in the last equation

$$\frac{dI}{dD} = \frac{dI}{\frac{1}{4}\left(\dfrac{dI}{\frac{1}{4} + \frac{1}{4}}\right)} = \frac{dI}{\frac{1}{4}\,(2dI)} = \frac{dI}{dI/2} = 2.$$

With these values of s and m, any *increase* in investment (in addition to

[5] For a small country, we can safely ignore foreign repercussions and attend only to domestic propensities.

that already being undertaken) must be limited to twice the inflow of foreign capital if a balance-of-payments deficit is to be avoided.[6]

Net Investment

There is also a point that may seem obvious but that is often overlooked. An inflow of foreign capital contributes nothing *net* to a country's development if it merely displaces domestic investment. This is unlikely to occur if funds are borrowed abroad for investment in private enterprise, or if a foreign capitalist invests in an enterprise in a developing country. But it has frequently happened in connection with foreign aid. Thus U.S. aid administrators discovered that a project to construct a hospital in a Latin American country was to be followed by a transfer of local funds from the health budget to military expenditure. To ensure that the U.S. project made a net contribution to economic development, it was necessary to link its construction to maintenance of local capital outlays for health. This could not, of course, prevent the diversion of funds from some other type of development expenditure. To do that would require scheduling aid in accordance with a development plan agreed in advance, which is precisely the direction in which the programming of aid has been moving.

Capacity to Assimilate Investment

A noninflationary limit to investment in economic development such as we have just described is a maximum to be observed if a balance-of-payments deficit is to be avoided. Although observance of this limitation can prevent inflation, with its adverse effects on the balance of payments, as well as its tendency to divert investment into inventory accumulation, luxury building, speculation, and an outflow of capital into safer havens abroad, it will not insure against wasteful investment. If investment is to be economical,[7] there is another, less precisely definable, limit that must be observed that will vary from country to country. This limit is set by the capacity of an economy to assimilate investment—that is, its capacity to put capital to effective use. What this capacity is will depend upon a wide range of conditions. Some of the more imporant are: the stability and efficiency of government; the supply of enterprise and administrative ability, in or out of government, needed to plan, carry out, and operate investment projects efficiently; the supply of other complementary factors; the size of the market for specific goods and services; social overhead capital—such as railways, roads, harbor facilities,

[6] Capital imports are assumed to be zero at the outset. It should also be noted that the reasoning of this section applies only so long as there are free resources in the economy. Once they are fully employed, the marginal propensity to import becomes unity; domestic investment can then exceed domestic savings without adverse balance-of-payments effects only by the amount of foreign capital currently made available.

[7] For investment to be economical, it must pay its way; that is, it must contribute to the value of output enough to offset the marginal disutility of saving.

and communications—upon which depends the mobility of goods and people; and finally, such social factors as the attitude toward change and institutions and habits that influence productivity. In brief, a country's capacity to assimilate capital depends upon its stage of economic development.

Thus a primitive society like New Guinea can assimilate very little capital. Any attempt to invest large sums in modernizing agriculture, in establishing industries, or even in constructing railways and modern highways would be utterly wasteful. The population must first be made ready for these things—by education to implant literacy, dispel stone-age superstitions, and introduce a more modern outlook; by simple vocational training; by extension of orderly government from the coastal fringe into the interior; by the construction of simple roads geared to the character and volume of traffic; and so on.

New Guinea is, of course, an extreme illustration. But there are regions of other countries that are not greatly dissimilar. In any event, the point is clear. A nation cannot assimilate investment beyond its capacity; to undertake more, it must first be prepared.

Dependence on Foreign Investment

Fears have been expressed that underdeveloped countries will come to depend upon foreign capital assistance, and that this state of dependence will never end. This outcome need not be expected if the development plans of individual countries attain their goal of appreciably raising productivity and income. For this will create a source of potential saving that can at some point take over the burden of supplying the capital needed for continuing development. Prospects for this outcome will increase as the capitalist, in contrast to the subsistence, sector grows in size. In the capitalist sector, a larger share of income produced takes the form of profits, of which a greater proportion tends to be saved.[8] Moreover, should the desired rate of saving not be realized, the government can use its taxing power to increase public savings. As domestic savings grow, the country can gradually reduce its dependence on foreign aid and investment.

Failure to attain this happy result might occur from either one of two causes. Even if incomes rise appreciably, the potential savings may not become actual, though if rising profits provide attractive investment opportunities, this is unlikely. Or the government may respond to political pressures to expand welfare expenditures at the expense of capital formation. A second, more threatening possibility is that because of steadily increasing population pressure, per capita incomes may rise but little or not at all. Improvements

---

[8] See W. Arthur Lewis, "Economic Development with Unlimited Supplies of Labor," *Manchester School of Economics and Social Studies* (May, 1954). Reprinted in part in Okun & Richardson, *Studies in Economic Development*; published 1961 by Holt, Rinehart & Winston, Inc., New York.

in health and sanitation have greatly reduced the death rate in underdeveloped countries, with the result that annual rates of increase in population of 2.5 to 3 per cent are common. To achieve an increase in annual output in excess of such figures, even with substantial foreign aid, may be beyond the capacity of many developing societies.[9] If so, continuance of foreign aid would be nothing but a subsidy to overpopulate an already crowded planet. Surely this would guarantee its early cessation. We can only hope that current efforts to devise inexpensive, effective, and acceptable means of checking the population explosion will be successful.

Even though a developing country realizes a sufficient increase in productivity within the foreseeable future to finance by itself its continuing capital requirements, its need for imports of *capital goods* may actually rise, especially as it becomes more industrialized. Though investment fully backed by savings could not cause inflation, could there not arise a shortage of foreign exchange? This is possible, but it could be avoided by incorporating into the development plan provisions for the local production of the required capital goods, as India is doing under her series of Five-Year Plans. Or other types of imports could be reduced by the production of import subtsitutes, thus releasing foreign exchange for the purchase of capital goods imports. An increase of exports would serve the same purpose. Finally, as a last resort, restrictions could be placed on general imports for the period of especially heavy demand for capital goods imports.

Service Charges on Foreign Capital

The direct cost to a country of borrowed capital consists of the interest and dividends that have to be paid for its use. In addition, loans have to be amortized, although repayment of equity investments is necessary only in the event the foreign investors decide to withdraw their capital. Moreover, often a considerable part of interest and dividends earned will be reinvested by the lender or investor.[10] Despite these considerations, a country receiving foreign investment, as current loans and grants taper off, may one day expect to see

[9] If the annual rate of saving and investment is represented by s, the average social productivity of investment by e (the ratio of additional output accompanying current investment to that investment), and the rate of increase in population by r, the attainable growth of income (dY) is: $dY = s \cdot e - r$. A figure of $\frac{1}{3}$, or 33 per cent, is not untypical for the efficiency of investment. Thus if 10 per cent of income is saved, and the rate of population increase is 3 per cent: $dY = .10 \times .33 - .03 = .003$. The rate of increase in income exceeds the rate of population growth by only $\frac{3}{10}$ of 1 per cent; income per capita is virtually stationary. To achieve an annual rate of increase of only 2 per cent would require that savings (and investment) reach a level of 15 per cent per annum.

[10] In the period 1956-59, fourteen industrial OEEC countries and the U.S. and Canada together provided private investment in underdeveloped countries of $7,492,000,000. In the same interval, reinvested earnings amounted to $3,658 million, or almost half as much as current new investment. What proportion reinvested earnings bore to total earnings is not stated. OEEC, *The Flow of Financial Resources to Countries in Course of Economic Development* (Paris, April, 1961), Table 2.

itself obligated to make payments abroad for the service of previously invested capital in excess of any current capital inflow. (It is then said to have achieved the status of a "mature" debtor nation, as contrasted with its "immature" status when the current capital inflow exceeded service charges on previous investments.)

The question arises: is there any assurance that a debtor country will be able to service its foreign debt when this becomes necessary? Stated differently, what conditions must be met if it is to do so?

In its essentials, the situation that arises when a country must meet net service charges is the reverse of the one that existed when there was a net capital inflow. We showed earlier that an inflow of foreign capital provides the real resources, the finance, and the foreign exchange to counter a shortage of real savings, of money savings, and of foreign means of payment. By so doing, the foreign investment enables a country to undertake an investment program in excess of domestic saving, and thus to spend (absorb) more than it produces, without getting into balance-of-payments difficulties. By a contribution from abroad to its balance of payments, a developing country is enabled to overcome serious shortages and accelerate its growth.

In its later role as a debt-servicing nation, it confronts the opposite problem. It must somehow generate a surplus of foreign exchange receipts that exceeds imports of goods and services by the amount of service payments to be made.[11] This implies that it must expand exports or contract imports, or both. To make this excess of exports over imports possible, the country must produce more than it absorbs (that is, total production must exceed total consumption and investment by the required surplus of exports). Finally, to ensure that a sufficient part of current production is actually released for export, the community must raise its savings to the point where they are greater than domestic investment by the needed excess of exports.

In sum, whereas a foreign capital inflow *enables* a developing country to overcome shortages of resources, savings, and foreign exchange, the obligation to service accumulated debt *requires* that it create corresponding surpluses. Is there any reason to believe that it will do so? The answer depends upon whether the execution of its development plan satisfies the three conditions set out above.

Let us start with savings. The source of increased saving is to be found in rising per capita incomes. With higher individual incomes, the marginal rate of saving may be expected to increase; if not, the government can use its power of taxation to capture some part of the increase in incomes. The more successful the development program, the more rapidly will per capita incomes

---

[11] To reduce the problem to its essentials, I assume that net capital inflow has ceased, and that the country has no surplus foreign exchange or gold reserves upon which it can draw to pay service charges. Inclusion of these items would complicate the argument without altering it in any important way.

rise, and the greater will be the increase in marginal private or public savings. Provided the investment scheduled in the plan does not anticipate using the increased savings resulting from rising incomes, these new savings will constitute a net addition to the supply thereof.[12] Their existence ensures the release of a corresponding value of real resources, which can be exported or can substitute for imports. Therewith, there also appears a similar surplus of foreign exchange receipts over payments for imports, which can be used to cover debt service charges.

Although the attainment of some annual rate of increase of per capita incomes will provide some of the needed surpluses, will it provide enough to cover a prescribed amount of service charges? This depends on how speedy the rate of economic development is—that is, on the caliber of the development plan and its execution, and on the political, social, and economic conditions that influence its outcome. No general answer can be given. It would be necessary to evaluate all these determining elements for any individual country. Some of the more important are: the growth of the labor force, the abundance of natural resources, the rate of technological progress, and the availability of management and skilled labor—all of which serve to determine the output that will accompany an increment of investment.[13] Other important determining elements are the initial proportion of national income saved and the rate of population increase. If an evaluation of these factors suggested that per capita incomes could be expected to increase at a fairly high rate, there should be available each year a sufficient surplus of foreign exchange to cover an appreciable amount of service charges.[14]

If a country meets this very broad test of ability to service capital charges, it is unnecessary for it deliberately to direct foreign capital into the production of exports or of import substitutes. It will suffice if it is invested so as to yield the greatest possible increase in the social product. If, however, a country's

[12] Such anticipatory budgeting of savings would be hazardous, since the hoped-for rise in incomes is a target, not a datum.

[13] This increment of output, the marginal social productivity of investment, is the reciprocal of the "incremental capital output ratio," K/O, a concept extensively (and often carelessly) used in the literature of economic development.

[14] Thus Alter shows that, with population growth at 2¼ per cent a year, the initial average saving ratio 8½ per cent, the output-capital ratio 1:3.5, and the rate of growth of per capita income ½ per cent a year, it would require a per capita marginal saving ratio of only 0.23 to service a capital inflow extending over 25 years, comprising 7 per cent of aggregate net investment, and carrying an interest rate of 4½ per cent. If per capita incomes rise by 2 per cent a year, a capital inflow of similar duration and cost, but comprising 22 per cent of aggregate net investment, could be serviced if the per capita saving ratio were 0.31. (It is noteworthy that incomes grow faster and servicing the debt becomes relatively easier, the larger the preceding capital inflow.) Gerald M. Alter, "The Servicing of Foreign Capital Inflows by Under-Developed Countries," Chapter 6 in *Economic Development for Latin America*, Howard S. Ellis, ed., p. 151. Published 1961 by Macmillan & Co., Ltd., London. See this chapter for more extended discussion of this topic.

economic development lags, or if population grows too rapidly, it can only ensure that service charges will be covered by such directed investment, or by the imposition of restrictions upon both imports and consumption.

THE CONTRIBUTION OF FOREIGN CAPITAL TO ECONOMIC DEVELOPMENT

Since foreign capital entails a cost in the form of interest or dividends, a capital-importing country will receive no direct benefit unless the imported capital raises national product by more than enough to cover this cost. Normally, it will do so; for an increase in the supply of capital means that labor is more amply provided with tools, equipment, and other aids to production. The productivity of labor, and of the land or other resources with which it is combined, will be raised.

A Simple Model

Consider the simplest case, where a country's labor and capital are fully employed. In Figure 28.1, domestic capital in the amount *OD* is combined

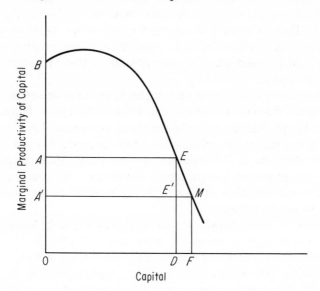

FIGURE 28.1 Foreign Investment with Labor and Natural Resources Fixed

with a given quantity of labor and natural resources to yield a total output represented by the area *OBED*. The marginal productivity of capital is *DE;* the total return to capital is *OAED*. The portion of national product *ABE* goes to labor as wages and to owners of natural resources as rent.

If foreign capital in the amount *DF* is now imported, and either combined

in existing enterprises with domestic capital or used to establish new enterprises employing similar techniques, the greater abundance of capital drives
down the marginal return on all capital, both domestic and foreign, to *FM*.
Total national product is increased to *OBMF,* or by *DEMF.* Of this, *DE'MF*
constitutes the cost of employing foreign capital, leaving a net increment of
product *EE'M* to be shared between labor and the owners of natural resources. This is the net benefit to the economy from the employment of foreign capital.

With the fall in the marginal productivity of capital, the total earnings of
domestic capitalists shrink, to *OA'E'D,* resulting in a transfer of income to
labor and owners of natural resources.

A More Realistic Model

Such a simple model is not very realistic, for investment is unlikely to be
attracted into an underdeveloped country if the principal effect to be anticipated is a decline in the return on capital. True, even this prospect might
still be attractive if the reduced yield, after allowing for risks, remained above
the return obtainable at home. But this implies that the return on capital in
the underdeveloped country, before any inflow of foreign funds, is exceptionally high. There is nothing to suggest that this is so. Although profits per
unit of goods sold tends to be high, because of a high markup over cost,
volume of production and sales are generally low, so that the return on investment is not excessive.

If, however, foreign capital can find employment at the going rate earned by
domestic capital, this may be sufficient to induce investment. Suppose that—
as in India, Egypt, and many Latin American countries—labor is not fully
employed, or is employed in occupations where its productivity is very low.[15]
If in addition there are available natural resources comparable in productivity
to those already employed, foreign capital can obtain a full complement of the
necessary factors. The inflow of such capital then results in increased employment of all the productive agents.

In diagrammatic terms, besides the production attributable to domestic capital combined with a given amount of labor and land (Figure 28.1), foreign
capital combined with formerly idle or unproductively employed labor and
natural resources now adds a new segment of production to the economy
(Figure 28.2). This foreign segment may consist partly of new firms in existing
industries or of indigenous firms expanded through foreign investment, partly

---

[15] Evidence of unproductive employment is to be found in the large numbers engaged
as messengers, car watchers, bearers, shopkeepers, and domestic servants whose time is
mostly occupied in waiting for something to do. Shining shoes, gathering and selling
bottles and petrol tins, and stealing for later sale such objects as garden tools and automobile accessories are other symptoms of poverty and low productivity. This phenomenon
of low productivity is often referred to as underemployment or disguised employment.

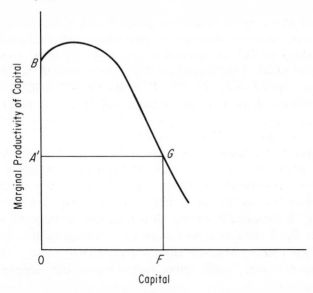

FIGURE 28.2   Foreign Capital Combined with Unemployed Labor and Natural
Resources

of new firms making new products, and partly of additional government
undertakings.

Adding this production attributable to this new foreign segment to the
previous domestic production, as in Figure 28.3, we obtain a new national

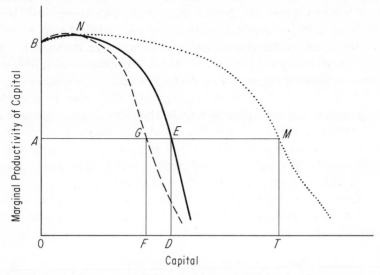

FIGURE 28.3   Productivity of Capital in the Foreign Sector, in the Domestic Sector,
and in the Entire Economy

product curve, shown by the dotted line *BNM*. Assuming that foreign investors are content with the return obtained by indigenous capital, they will carry investment to the point *OF*, where the marginal return *GF* is the same as in the domestic sector (*ED*). Total capital employed is *OT* (= *OF* + *OD*). Output in the foreign-financed segment is *OBGF*, in the domestic segment *OBED* (as before), while total national product is the sum of the two, or *OBMT*. Of this, the total amount going to domestic capital is the same as before, *OAED*, while foreign capital receives *DEMT* (= *OAGF*).

The net gain to the economy in terms of product consists in the enlarged earnings of labor and owners of natural resources, represented either by *ABNG*, or its (approximate) equivalent, *ENM*. Labor gains partly from increased employment, partly from its more productive employment.[16] If natural resources are all domestically owned, their increased earnings are part of the national gain. But if some have been acquired by foreigners, it is they and not nationals of the country who will enjoy the additional income. This can, of course, be taxed, as can—within rather narrow limits—the earnings of foreign capital.

The entire population of the country may also benefit as consumers, both from a wider range of choice as new commodities are produced and from an improvement in the quality of existing products. And since employment and incomes have been increased, the consequently enlarged market may permit the introduction of economies of scale, resulting in lower commodity prices.

Another important class of gains normally accompanies the import of foreign capital—a whole series of external economies. Thus foreign firms, with access to modern techniques, import them along with the capital, and frequently bring in highly qualified management and technical staff as well. As long as the improved techniques and management are confined to branch plants of foreign enterprises, the gain to the local economy consists only in lowered prices or improved quality of products. But local businessmen will tend to imitate the new methods; workers acquire skills, often through a deliberate training program, and carry them with them when they change employment.

Even without any improvement in methods, the supply of qualified labor is increased as a direct result of fuller and more productive employment. So too is the supply of experienced management, which may consist partly of foreigners, partly of local people who obtain managerial positions.

Introduction of new products may lower the costs of industries in higher stages, as when a cement plant enables the building industry to avoid payment of transport costs on imported supplies. Or producers of primary or intermedi-

---

[16] Clearly, some allowance must be made for the output, small as it may have been, that is lost when workers are transferred from unproductive to more productive occupations. To be accurate, therefore, we should have to lower slightly the productivity curve for domestic capital and consequently also the total product curve.

ate products who enjoy a larger market may be able to introduce economies of scale.

Finally, if foreign capital is invested, or releases domestic capital for investment, in roads, railways, power plants, and other forms of social overhead capital, the productivity of all industries served by them is increased.

A great deal of foreign investment fits this model. In Mexico, Brazil, Venezuela, India, and many other countries, domestic enterprises, foreign enterprises, and enterprises partly financed by foreign capital exist side by side, served by an infrastructure of public works that also embodies much foreign capital. All forms of enterprise compete with or supplement one another; they earn similar profits; and they are often indistinguishable except for the foreign names of some or the alien appearance of a few managerial employees.

The Dual Economy

Foreign capital may, however, be almost exclusively directed into a specific area of an underdeveloped country, one where rich natural resources promise a high return from their exploitation. Often this area is remote from the main centers of population, such as the copper mines of Chile, the oil deposits of Venezuela, the tea plantations of Ceylon and India. There develops an economy within an economy, one capital-intensive, modern, and highly profitable, the other labor-intensive, traditional, and yielding relatively low returns to each of the factors. Figure 28.2 could be used to represent this foreign sector of such a "dual economy," though the height of the curve should be raised to reflect the superior productivity of the natural resources. The marginal return on capital might be no higher than in the domestic sector, but either through ownership of the natural resource or through the acquisition of exploitation rights, the foreign investor would obtain all or part of the rent of the natural resource. (This consists of part, probably the major part, of the area $A'BG$.) Since this rent, together with the return on capital, would probably mostly be remitted overseas as a component of the total profits of the enterprise, the income accruing to the local economy from the operation itself would be limited to the wages of the labor employed. Often, especially if the project is very capital-intensive, relatively little labor is required. On the other hand, it is also often paid higher wages than it can obtain in alternative employment, and sometimes is better housed and cared for. Such practices are simply good business, a means of avoiding the high costs of a rapid labor turnover.

Benefits from the diffusion of technical training acquired by the labor are likely to be smaller than when the foreign sector is indistinguishable from the domestic, either because the skills may be highly specific or because the workers tend to stay put.[17] There may, however, be a gain from secondary

[17] On this and related points, see the interesting article by Robert E. Baldwin, "Export Technology and Development from a Subsistence Level," *Economic Journal,* **LXXIII** (March, 1963).

employment, as when local contractors are hired or farmers in the area discover a new market for their produce. Moreover, when the foreign enterprise
is engaged in exploiting an exhaustible natural resource, there is a strong case
for the taxation of its earnings. For many years, governments of the petroleum
producing countries have typically obtained, either from royalties or from
income taxes, 50 per cent of the earnings of the oil companies. As a result in
part of the recent establishment of the Organization of Petroleum Exporting
Countries (OPEC) to bargain with the producers, Middle Eastern governments now get approximately 55 per cent of realized profits, while in Venezuela
the government takes 67 per cent.[18] Inasmuch as practically all the oil produced
is sold abroad, these revenues are an important source of foreign exchange as
well as a major contribution to government budgets.

FOREIGN AID

What has been said in the preceding pages applies with equal force both to
foreign aid to developing countries in the form of public grants and loans and to
private investment. There is a difference, however, in that private capital
moves in response to the lure of profits, whereas foreign aid results from
policy decisions taken by governments. This raises the question of the purposes
to be served by foreign aid, and the criteria according to which it is to be
administered.

Purpose

Since 1950, when aid to underdeveloped countries first became an important
issue, it has been harnessed to various purposes: the support of allies in the
cold war, often, as in Korea and South Viet Nam, at the hot fringes; gaining
adherents to one side or the other in that struggle; obtaining strategic materials;
rescuing nations on the verge of economic collapse; as well as promoting a
nation's economic development. As it has become apparent that aid to the
developing countries is going to continue to be a major issue in the foreign
policies of the advanced nations, promotion of their more rapid development
has increasingly become the central objective. Emergencies will continue to
arise, however, that may require temporary departures from pursuit of this
goal.

Economic development, as we have seen, has many facets. These include
improved technology, greatly increased investment, the acquisition of many
kinds of skills, the conquest of illiteracy, the eradication of disease, and many
others. Developmental aid could be directed toward any one of them, and
frequently is. A program of aid as distinct from a particular project, however,
like the program of economic development it seeks to support, succeeds or

[18] *The Economist* (June 29, 1963), p. 1396.

fails according to the change in the developing country's total economic situation. Since the only reasonably satisfactory measure of such change we have is the change in per capita incomes, this is usually taken as the general criterion of the effectiveness of a development program and of the foreign aid that supports it.

Planning and Foreign Aid

A program of development and a program of aid—the two go together. Since economic development unavoidably extends over many years and encompasses many aspects, its realization implies a coordinated effort and the promise of continuing financial and human support. Development programming, or planning, is therefore essential. Without it, individual projects are haphazard and unrelated. With it, they become intelligible parts of a whole that has purpose and direction. But if development must be planned, foreign aid will only be fully effective insofar as it is geared into the scheduled program. If a development program calls at a particular time for a major power project upon whose output depends the expansion of the fertilizer industry and therewith of agricultural production, willingness of a grantor nation to supply only railway equipment or educational facilities is likely to appear headstrong and uncooperative.

The validity of these conclusions has been borne out by U.S. experience in rendering aid. The project-by-project approach, though it contributed many useful components of development in many countries, was seen to lack consistency and unity of purpose. Following a thorough reappraisal of foreign aid in the first year of President Kennedy's administration, it was decided in formulating the Alliance for Progress in Latin America to make U.S. aid conditional upon submission of a plan for development, to be approved by a committee of experts appointed by the Organization of American States. The experience of the World Bank led to similar conclusions. Its economic survey missions have uniformly recommended organized planning of development; its Economic Development Institute provides training for prospective planners in many nations.

Objections to the planning or programming approach have not been lacking. One of the most forceful regards it as certain to hamper and confine private enterprise while strengthening the autocratic powers of central government.[19] It has also been accused of committing grantors of aid to underwriting plans in whose formulation they participate. The first of these objections attacks a straw man. Development planning need not be central planning of the Communist variety. Usually it is far less comprehensive—"a framework within which the country can think in an orderly way about its economic future. . . . Program-

[19] See M. Friedman, "Foreign Economic Aid: Means and Objectives," *The Yale Review* (June, 1958). Reprinted in DeVere E. Pentony, ed., *United States Foreign Aid.* Published 1960 by Howard Chandler, San Francisco.

ming of this kind is compatible with wide latitude for private enterprise and is capable of revealing actions that should be taken to liberate and activate the private sector."[20] As for underwriting plans, aid-receiving nations know well that the legislatures of the grantors recognize no such commitment.

Besides such broad policy questions as the purpose of aid and its relation to development planning, there are many secondary policy issues of considerable interest. One of these is whether to emphasize grants or loans as the form in which aid is given. Under congressional pressure, the United States has moved increasingly from grants to loans at the same time that the International Bank, through its recently created affiliate the International Development Association, has gone in the opposite direction. Here the relevant issue, rarely considered in official discussions, would appear to be the need of the aid recipient for capital. If it must repay loans, it must divert to this purpose savings that could otherwise be devoted to its investment program. This could slow down appreciably its rate of future progress.

Many other questions—such as the relative merits and practicability of a multilateral, as contrasted with a bilateral, administration of aid; the economic significance of loans repayable in local currencies; and the criteria to be used in evaluating both programs and individual projects—would require consideration in a full discussion of foreign aid.[21] I feel obliged to conclude this section, however, with a brief glimpse at the estimated magnitude of the global need for foreign aid.

GLOBAL CAPITAL REQUIREMENTS FOR ECONOMIC DEVELOPMENT

A number of estimates have been made of the total amount of foreign capital likely to be required for their development by the underdeveloped countries of the world.[22] Although the bases used in computing these estimates differ, as well as the period from which reference data were derived, they show, when they are adjusted to make them comparable, a surprising unanimity in their conclusions.[23] To attain an annual increase of 2 per cent in the per capita

[20] Robert E. Asher, *Grants, Loans, and Foreign Currencies*, pp. 83-84. Published 1961 by The Brookings Institution, Washington, D. C.

[21] Excellent brief surveys of these and other related matters can be found in Robert E. Asher, *Grants, Loans, and Local Currencies*, in *Framing a Development Program*, Gustav F. Papanek, ed. (Carnegie Endowment for International Peace, International Conciliation Series No. 527, March, 1960); and in Andrew Schonfield, *The Attack on World Poverty* (Chatto & Windus, London, 1960).

[22] The four best known, by a committee of experts appointed by the United Nations, by Max F. Millikan and W. W. Rostow, by Paul G. Hoffman, and by P. N. Rosenstein-Rodan, have been summarized and compared in a United Nations pamphlet, *The Capital Development Needs of the Less Developed Countries* (Sales No.: 62.II.D.3).

[23] The U.N. committee of experts assumed a capital-output ratio of 6:1, two of the others a 3:1 ratio, and the last, that of Rosenstein-Rodan, one of 2.8:1. With regard to the last study, inclusion of certain expenditures listed separately raises the estimate of additional foreign capital required to approximate equality with the others. (*Ibid.*, p. 13n.)

incomes of the underdeveloped nations, the total foreign capital estimated to be needed each year for a ten-year period falls within a range of $5.7 to $7.0 billion. According to the three later studies (based on more recent data than the first), the current inflow of development capital was calculated to range from $3 to $4 billion. Additional capital required therefore came close to $3 billion on all four estimates. Since this is close to double the computed current inflow, these estimates suggest that a major effort needs to be made to raise the flow of foreign capital to an acceptable level.

Table 28.2. CAPITAL CONTRIBUTIONS TO UNDERDEVELOPED
COUNTRIES AND MULTILATERAL AGENCIES BY 14 INDUSTRIAL
OEEC COUNTRIES AND THE UNITED STATES AND CANADA

(in billions of U.S. dollars)

BILATERAL CONTRIBUTIONS

| | Official | | Private | | | | |
	Grants	Net Lending	Guaranteed Export Credits	Other New Lending and Investment	Reinvested Earnings	Contributions To Multilateral Agencies	Total
Average 1950-55	1.2	0.6	0.2	0.7	0.6	0.2	3.5
Average 1956-59	2.3	1.3	0.4	1.5	0.9	0.5	6.8
Total, 1956-59							
OEEC countries	3.6	1.7	1.4	2.6	2.2	1.6	12.8*
U.S. & Canada	5.4	3.4	——	3.4	1.4	0.8	14.4

* Sub-totals do not add to total, owing presumably to "adjustments" mentioned but not explained.
SOURCE: Organization for European Economic Co-operation, *The Flow of Financial Resources to Countries in Course of Economic Development, 1956-1959* (Paris, April, 1961), Tables 1, 2. Transactions with the IMF and lending of less than one year are excluded, as are all expenditures of a military character.

Additional reliable data on the movement of foreign capital into underdeveloped countries were published almost simultaneously with the latest of these studies.[24] They bring together all private and public grants, loans, and contributions made bilaterally to underdeveloped countries, together with those made through multilateral agencies such as the IBRD and the United Nations. It is noteworthy that total average annual contributions for the years 1950-55 tally closely, at $3.5 billion, with the inflow estimated by the earlier studies (see Table 28.2).

But see what happened in the next four years. Average annual contributions nearly doubled, to $6.8 billion. This increase cannot be explained by price

[24] OEEC, *The Flow of Financial Resources to Countries in Course of Development, 1956-1959* (Paris, April, 1961).

changes, for indexes of export and import prices for various parts of the world either remained relatively stable or declined moderately. There was localized inflation in some countries, but no worldwide inflation. What had taken place was a substantial rise in the flow of long-term capital.

For the United States, there is direct evidence. Nonmilitary assistance to countries in Asia, Africa, and Latin America rose from $4.5 billion in 1951-55 to $7.6 billion in 1956-59. Private direct investment to the same areas increased from $1.2 billion in the earlier period to $2.8 billion in the later.[25] The first half of the decade of the 1950's was a time when foreign aid programs were just getting under way. In the latter half, they became quantitatively and politically far more important. As for Europe, it was able only in the later period to lend or invest large sums abroad.

Certainly there was a strong response to the challenge of economic development. Was it fully met, as the figures just cited seem to indicate? Not if we judge by the fact that India is encountering great difficulty in financing her development effort, especially its foreign requirements; that the Alliance for Progress is only beginning to get under way in Latin America; and that the development efforts of many African countries have scarcely started. Perhaps the estimates of need, based in part on uncertain national income data and possibly overestimating rising marginal propensities to save, were too low. Moreover, the OEEC figures contain elements usually not counted in estimates of foreign capital assistance. They include purely commercial credits of relatively short (two to five years) duration, and reinvested earnings, which contribute to capital growth but not directly to the foreign exchange needs of the developing countries. If we make a rough deduction of $1.8 billion for these doubtful elements, the total annual capital contributions during the late 1950's still amount to $5 billion, considerably higher than the UN estimates.

Additional funds are undoubtedly needed; the exact amount is in question. More significant than the total is its distribution. Government aid in particular, to yield the maximum results, should be directed toward those nations that are promoting their own development most effectively. As development proceeds, selectivity becomes of increasing importance.

TRADE AND ECONOMIC DEVELOPMENT

From our study of the theory of international trade, we learned that nations can maximize their incomes by specializing in production and exchanging their specialized products with one another. Free trade, by promoting the most efficient worldwide allocation of resources, effects an upward shift in the world's production possibilities curve in which all nations share. Protection, which interferes with this efficient resource allocation, can be justified only under limited and highly restrictive circumstances.

[25] U.S. Department of Commerce, *Balance of Payments Statistical Supplement*, Tables 46 and 49.

This analysis, though valid, has its own limitations: it applies to a given moment or a short interval of time; it reflects a cross section, static point of view that makes no allowance for the passage of time and the changes that it brings. Economic development, however, is a process, a dynamic unfolding of interrelated events that contrasts sharply with the static character of the traditional doctrine of comparative cost.

There are, however, elements of a dynamic theory in some of the classical literature of international trade, elements that strongly suggest that trade exerts an important influence upon economic development. Thus it has been noted that trade opens up markets for a country's specialized production, increasing employment, raising profits, and providing the basis both for larger savings and their investment in expanded output. As production grows, economies of scale may be realized, innovations stimulated, and productive efficiency raised. Without trade, the importation of capital goods, so essential to a nation's growth, would be impossible. Trade also acquaints people with new and attractive goods that act as incentives to greater effort. According to a later but not inconsistent view, trade may even induce capital, enterprise, and labor to migrate to the site of natural resources, there to develop a thriving export industry. In all these ways, trade acts as an "engine of growth," in Sir Dennis Robertson's phrase, that powerfully stimulates a country's development.[26]

During the nineteenth and early twentieth century, this "engine" functioned efficiently. Large and growing markets in Britain and Europe led to rapid expansion of the exports of primary producing countries, principally the newer countries in the temperate zones: the United States, Canada, Australia, New Zealand, Argentina, Uruguay, and South Africa. Opportunities to improve their lot attracted a huge flow of immigrants, bringing with them skills, the culture of western Europe, and some capital. By 1870, a third of British capital exports went to these regions to build railways, sink mine shafts, and finance cattle and wheat ranches; by 1913 it amounted to two-thirds.[27] As the new nations grew in population and wealth, local markets became large enough to justify the rise of manufacturing industries.

Since World War I, international trade has been far less effective in transmitting growth from an expanding center to outlying areas. For one thing, the rate of growth of trade has slackened off. The focal center of world advance, though still progressing vigorously, has emitted a stimulus of diminishing intensity to the rest of the world. Whereas between 1850 and 1880, the volume of world trade rose by 270 per cent, and between 1880 and 1913 by 170 per

---

[26] D. H. Robertson, "The Future of International Trade," *Economic Journal* (March, 1938). Reprinted in American Economic Association, *Readings in the Theory of International Trade*. For a more extended discussion of the dynamic aspects of trade theory, including the contributions of earlier writers, see Gerald M. Meier, *International Trade and Development*, pp. 153-59. Published 1963 by Harper & Row, New York.

[27] R. Nurkse, *Patterns of Trade and Development*, p. 17. Published 1961 by Basil Blackwell, Oxford.

cent, from 1928 to 1958 it increased only 57 per cent.[28] Instead of expanding more rapidly than world output, it has grown more slowly.

The reasons for this development can be found in a combination of forces tending to depress the demand for primary products.[29] (1) Technical change has reduced the relative industrial use of raw materials: improved processes have achieved large economies in raw material consumption; synthetics have increasingly displaced natural raw materials (silk, wool, nitrates, rubber, hides and skins); heavy industries (engineering and chemicals), whose raw material consumption is relatively low, have grown faster in the industrial countries than light industries. (2) As incomes have risen in the industrial countries, an increased proportion has been spent on services. (3) The income elasticity of demand for many agricultural commodities is low. (4) High duties in western Europe, partly for revenue and partly for protection, have impeded the import of agricultural products.

If the stimulus to growth that operated so effectively in the nineteenth century has waned, it is also true that the character of the economies stimulated is different today. The newer nations that grew so rapidly before World War I were in the temperate zones; they inherited the culture, the skills, and the institutions of a dynamic civilization. The emerging nations of the mid-twentieth century are mainly in the tropics; they consist of traditional peasant societies, countries that inherited and still retain in large part a feudal system of great landed estates, and primitive tribal economies. Their nature is such that they respond with far less vigor to a stimulus that has weakened. It is therefore no mystery why international trade is a less effective "engine of growth" than in earlier decades, why the underdeveloped nations of today remain stagnant, while continued progress in the advanced countries still further widens the gap in standards of living.

Given these facts of life, what alternatives, in terms of their orientation with respect to international trade, are open to the underdeveloped nations?[30]

They could continue to specialize in the production for export of primary commodities. Even from the purely economic point of view, this appears most unattractive—a path likely to lead to declining prices, glutted markets, and continued stagnation. Though a general intensification of primary specialization may not be warranted, this is no reason for abandoning the specialized production that already exists. The need for imports of the developing countries is continually rising; they will require all the exports they can command; and making the most of comparative advantage still pays dividends. As new markets for primary products appear or are discovered, moreover, some further specialization may be worthwhile. It may be that the recent recovery of world trade will improve the position of raw material producers. Since 1953,

[28] *Ibid.*, p. 19n.
[29] *Ibid.*, p. 23.
[30] See Nurkse, *op. cit.*, second lecture, for a fuller discussion of these alternatives.

the volume of world exports has increased twice as fast as world output. Moreover, the growth of exports has not been confined to manufactures: total exports have expanded almost as fast, both in volume and in total value, so that primary exports have enjoyed a substantial rise (see Table 30.1).

A second alternative would be for the underdeveloped countries to move in the direction of industrialization for export. Potential markets exist in the developed countries, which exchange an immense volume of manufactures with one another. With their abundant labor, the underdeveloped countries are potential sources of supply of the lighter, less capital-intensive goods. Potential is one thing, however; its realization is another. It is precisely light manufactures that are suffering a relative, and in some instances an absolute, decline in the industrial countries. They are sure to offer strong resistance to any invasion of their markets. Moreover, though labor is abundant in the underdeveloped countries, it is not necessarily cheap. (India, for example, though able to sell textiles in international competition, has met little success with such articles as bicycles, electric fans, and sewing machines.) A further increase in the productivity of their labor will be needed before these countries can export a substantial range of manufactures at competitive prices.[31]

Finally, the underdeveloped countries could undertake industrialization for the home market. Here the principal difficulty is that two-thirds or more of the population of these countries is employed, at low levels of productivity, in agriculture. It is because they are so unproductive that so many must devote their labor to growing food. Until techniques in agriculture are improved, the local market for manufactures will support only the simplest varieties. To raise the level of agricultural practices is a formidable task, as may be seen, for example, in the snail's pace of rural change in India.[32]

Economic development by means of industrialization for the home market thus presupposes a prior, or at least simultaneous, development of agriculture. As progress goes on in this sector, more and more industries can be started with some hope of achieving reasonable levels of cost. The best prospects would be in commodities where imports have first shown that a market exists. Infant-industry protection will doubtless be necessary at the beginning; but

---

[31] Hope for a more liberal attitude of the industrial nations toward the exports, both primary and manufactured, of underdeveloped countries, received support in resolutions adopted at a meeting of Ministers in Geneva in May, 1963, under the auspices of GATT. The industrial nations agreed in principle, with reservations by the EEC group in Europe, to an Action Program to eliminate duties and restrictions on imports of primary products and to reduce by 50 per cent within three years duties on semiprocessed and processed products from underdeveloped countries. Negotiations on these and related matters were scheduled for May, 1964.

[32] Per capita income in the rural areas is only about one-sixth of per capita income in the urban areas of India. See Alvin H. Hansen, *Economic Issues of the 1960's*, Chapter 11 (McGraw-Hill Book Co., New York, 1960), for a vivid contrast of these two sectors of that country. An intensely interesting book on the subject is Kusum Nair, *Blossoms in the Dust*. Published 1961 by Gerald Duckworth & Co., Ltd., London.

as experience is accumulated and skills are acquired, it should be possible to dispense with this prop. Industrial growth in one field will justify the emergence of industries supplying raw materials or components, as also of industries carrying out more advanced finishing processes. (Growth of a beverage industry may warrant the manufacture of bottles; a textile or leather industry may be complemented by a clothing industry or the manufacture of shoes.) A linked expansion of agriculture, of industry, and also of social overhead facilities is indispensable if this choice of alternatives is made, as it is increasingly being made by many developing countries.

We should not forget, however, the great diversity of conditions in the countries we call underdeveloped. Some, such as Mexico, Brazil, and Argentina, are already well along the road of parallel industrial and agricultural development. Others, such as many of the new African nations, are only in the first stages of acquiring basic skills and of overcoming a glaring lack of social overhead capital. The abundance and richness of natural resources and the size of the economy also affect the direction its efforts must take and the likelihood of major advance. Some may find that exploitation of export markets for primary products, old or new, offers the greatest immediate promise. The smaller nations, such as the Central American Republics, may discover in economic union the means of creating markets large enough to support both expanding industry and a more diversified agriculture (on this point, see Chapters 29 and 30). Surely in view of the differences in their resources, in their stage of advancement, and in their social culture, there will be similar differences in the nature, the speed, and the extent of their economic growth.

SELECTED REFERENCES

Asher, Robert E., *Grants, Loans, and Local Currencies*. Washington, D. C.: The Brookings Institution, 1961. A lively and interesting little book on the economics of foreign aid.

Haberler, Gottfried, *International Trade and Economic Development*. Cairo: National Bank of Egypt, 1959. Defends the position that international trade has contributed greatly to economic development.

Meier, Gerald M., *International Trade and Development*. New York: Harper & Row, 1963. The most comprehensive treatment of the subject yet available.

Myrdal, Gunnar, *An International Economy*. New York: Harper & Bros., 1956. A wide-ranging study of the relations between trade and development that challenges the view that trade has helped, not hindered, economic growth.

Nurkse, Ragnar, *Patterns of Trade and Development*. Oxford: Basil Blackwell, 1961. Reprinted in *Equilibrium and Growth in the World Economy*. Cambridge: Harvard University Press, 1961. The Wicksell Lectures on changing trends in world trade and their relation to economic growth.

———, *Problems of Capital Formation in Underdeveloped Countries*. Oxford: Basil Blackwell, 1953. Chapters V and VI offer much of interest on the international aspects of capital formation.

Tinbergen, Jan, *Shaping the World Economy*. New York: The Twentieth Century Fund, Inc., 1962. Chapter 4 has a brief survey of commodity agreements as a means of stabilizing the export earnings of primary producers; Chapters 5, 6, and 7 deal imaginatively with the need for broader world goals and the policies to attain them. Appendixes I to IV provide regional surveys of the state of economic development.

29

REGIONAL INTEGRATION

Contrasting Trade Policies: 1500-1939

In the course of our historical survey, we have encountered three periods during which the attitude of governments toward international trade has differed widely. The first of these, the Mercantilist era, was a phase of close regulation and control, with the regulation undertaken in the interest of supporting the power of the state. In the course of the two-and-a-half centuries during which Mercantilism held sway, the middle class of merchants and manufacturers, hitherto small in numbers and of little importance, became increasingly numerous and prosperous. Yet because the restrictive features of Mercantilism hampered expansion and enterprise and held down their profits, the new middle class came more and more to oppose and evade its prohibitions and requirements. The merchant-capitalist class, steadily growing in economic and political influence, found its interest better served by economic freedom. Under its pressure, the internal restrictions of Mercantilism gradually broke down. Finding wider and wider acceptance, the new laissez-faire philosophy was given vigorous expression in the writings of Adam Smith. In Britain, it became the dominant point of view, and even on the continent it found increasing numbers of influential adherents.

After the Napoleonic wars, the steady shift in the political strength of conflicting economic interests led to the extension into foreign trade of the liberal ideas hitherto applied only to the internal economy. Trade was freed from its centuries-old bonds by one country after another. The nineteenth century saw trade freer than it had been since Roman times. Both the direction of trade and the character of national specialization became dominated almost exclusively by market forces. Under the new regime, the volume of international commerce expanded by leaps and bounds, making it possible for western Europe to become a highly specialized manufacturing center and thereby to support a huge increase in population.

This remarkable era was marred toward its close by a resurgence of nationalism, which brought with it the beginnings of a return to trade restriction. This movement became intensified with the outbreak of war in 1914 and the inflammation of nationalist sentiments that this entailed. The nostalgia of the 1920's for the comparative simplicity of the Victorian era met only disappointment in the mounting forces of nationalism, in growing economic rigidity, and in a widening range of sensitivity to disturbance. The shock of world depression speeded the disorganization of the world economy and ended in the dominance of nationally oriented policies. Although demand and supply still continued to function, they did so within narrowly constricted areas; the broad world market, which had served so well before 1914 to allocate production and to ensure steady supplies of every imaginable commodity, no longer existed.

Cooperation to Restore a World Economy

The difficulties encountered during the 1930's showed conclusively that the specialization of the nineteenth century and the growth of population it had engendered had gone too far to permit this disorganization to continue. The dependence of western Europe and Japan upon a wide-flung network of trade made efforts to repair that network imperative. Even while World War II was raging, extensive discussions were undertaken and plans laid to reconstruct a wider market area, and at the same time, to effect the minimum essential compromises between the requirements of a multilateral trading system and national demands for reasonable economic stability.

Some of these efforts were on a regional scale, some much broader. We have called attention to the sterling area, which provided a degree of financial unity, stability and convertibility of currencies, and comparative freedom of trade and payments over a large area. We are also acquainted with the efforts of the OEEC to liberalize the trade between European nations, and with the role played by the European Payments Union in easing their payments problems. And the European Recovery Program not only made the last two institutions possible by assisting European reconstruction, but also set the EPU in operation with a grant of funds. Moreover, in its administration, the European Recovery Program constantly stressed the need for the liberalization of trade and for a closer integration of the European nations.

As institutions serving to restore a more efficiently operating world economy, we have noted the contributions of the International Monetary Fund and the International Bank for Reconstruction and Development. The first of these aimed to replace chaotic currency conditions with some degree of stability, and by constant pressure on members to eliminate exchange controls and encourage a movement toward convertibility. The principal function of the International Bank is to foster the development of the less advanced nations: Indirectly, economic growth will enable them to lower their trade barriers and to move toward currency convertibility.

Proposal for an International Trade Organization

In view of the success that attended the discussions leading to the Bretton Woods Conference, the question naturally arose: if international cooperation can work in the monetary and financial area, why not in the field of international trade? Prolonged discussion of this question eventuated in the publication by the United States Department of State of a brochure entitled "Proposals for Expansion of World Trade and Employment." These proposals covered a wide range of topics in the realms of commercial policy: tariffs, preferences, quotas and licensing systems, restrictive business practices, the maintenance of full employment, and the establishment of an International Trade Organization to administer any agreements that might be reached.

After endorsement by the executive branch of the United States government and the government of the United Kingdom, the proposals underwent discussion at an international Conference on Trade and Employment that first met in London in the autumn of 1946, adjourned to Geneva the following year, and concluded in Havana in the winter of 1947-48. Some 53 nations there signed the resulting Charter for an International Trade Organization (ITO), which would go into effect upon its ratification by a prescribed number of nations.

But the ITO never became translated from provisions on paper into a functioning organization. Serious opposition to its wide-ranging provisions developed in the United States Congress. It failed of ratification and ceased therewith to be a live issue.

THE GENERAL AGREEMENT ON TARIFFS AND TRADE

Anxious to get about the business of reducing trade barriers regardless of what happened to the proposed International Trade Organization, some of the participants in the London Conference urged that extensive tariff negotiations be inaugurated simultaneously with the continuing discussion of the trade Charter at Geneva. These negotiations, participated in by some 23 nations, resulted in an extensive set of bilateral trade concessions which were then extended to all participants and incorporated in a General Agreement on Tariffs and Trade. Since the initial conference in Geneva in 1947, multilateral tariff negotiations have been successfully carried out in 1949, 1951, 1956, and 1961. A conference called for the spring of 1964 promised to be of outstanding importance.

To protect the rights and enforce the obligations of the nations signing the tariff agreement, the Contracting Parties of the original 1947 Geneva agreement also adopted a set of rules embodying the ITO provisions on commercial policy. To ensure the enforcement of these rules, they provided for annual (later, twice yearly) meetings of the Contracting Parties, for a modest secretariat, and (after 1954) for a permanent Council of Representatives. Thus, although GATT is essentially a contractual arrangement among a number of nations (increased since its inception to 44 as of early 1963), it is also a permanent international organization with continuing duties to safeguard the conduct of international trade. In its relatively brief life, it has emerged as the principal force in the world working for the multilateral expansion of trade.

Main Principles

In the rules adopted by GATT, three principles predominate: (1) trade is to be conducted in a nondiscriminatory manner; (2) the use of quantitative restrictions is condemned; and (3) disagreements are to be resolved through consultation.

To ensure against discrimination, the Contracting Parties agree to apply the most-favored-nation principle to all import and export duties: each nation shall be treated as well as the most favored nation. So far as quantitative restrictions are permitted, they, too, are to be administered without favor. To meet specific difficulties, however, carefully guarded exceptions to the rule of nondiscrimination are allowed. Thus dumping and export subsidies may be countered by measures limited to the offending country. And although the creation of new partial tariff preferences is prohibited, arrangements designed to establish systems of complete preference—that is, customs unions or free-trade areas—are permitted, provided their purpose is "to facilitate trade between the constituent territories and not to raise barriers to the trade of other . . . parties."

As a matter of principle, GATT rules prohibit the use of import quotas, seeking to limit restrictions on trade to the less rigid tariff. Though hedged with safeguards, three important exceptions to this prohibition are granted. (1) Countries confronted with balance-of-payments difficulties may use quantitative restrictions. They must, however, be limited to the extent necessary to stop a serious decline or forestall a threatened decline in reserves, or to achieve a reasonable increase in abnormally low reserves. Moreover, the International Monetary Fund is to be consulted as to whether quantitative restrictions are really necessary. (2) Underdeveloped countries may apply quantitative restrictions to further their economic development, but only under procedures approved by GATT. (3) Finally, import restrictions may be applied to agricultural or fishery products if domestic production of these articles is subject to equally restrictive production or marketing controls.

In practice, the exceptions allowed for balance-of-payments reasons and to further economic development have not been seriously abused. But many countries, notably the United States, have adopted agricultural price-support programs unaccompanied by production controls. To prevent a flooding of their markets, they have felt obliged to impose quantitative restrictions on imports. It is not too much to say that with respect to trade in agricultural products, GATT rules have been largely inoperative.

Besides arranging a series of multilateral tariff negotiations, whose comprehensive nature led to a lowering of duties on trade including more than two-thirds of the world total, GATT's principal accomplishment has been to establish a forum for continuing consultation. Disputes that might otherwise have caused continuing hard feeling, reprisals, and even diplomatic rupture, have been brought to the conference table and compromised.

In the early years of GATT, if one member felt that another had violated the rules, withdrawn a valuable concession, or otherwise acted in a manner conflicting with the agreement, it brought its complaint to the annual meeting. The disputants were urged to attempt to settle their differences bilaterally. If this failed, the contracting parties formed a working committee, which after studying the matter would make a recommendation or a ruling. If the offending member then refused to change its ways, the aggrieved party could retaliate by withdrawing some concession. More often than not, offending members could and did comply with a recommendation by some change in administrative procedure.

GATT proved so useful in bringing issues to a head and in settling a reasonable proportion of them that, in 1953, the contracting parties set up a panel to act as an informal court to handle disputes. This panel listens to the disputants, formulates and considers the issues, and drafts a report—all the while consulting with the disputing parties. With this change in procedure, the number of complaints brought before GATT and successfully resolved increased markedly.

TOWARD A COMMON MARKET IN EUROPE

Ten years after the establishment of GATT, six nations of western Europe decided, after long negotiations, that the continuation of national boundaries was no longer consistent with the economic and political needs of the area. In a treaty signed in Rome on March 24, 1957, they agreed to merge their separate economies into a single economic unit.[1] This decision promises to have effects of great importance on the economies of the participating countries, on their future political organization, on the trade and welfare of other free nations, and on the strategy of the free world in its rivalry with the Communist powers.

Although the Treaty of Rome comprised the major step in the creation of a European Economic Community, it was not the first one. This had been taken with the establishment in 1952 of the European Coal and Steel Community. A bold and imaginative scheme, the ECSC aimed, through the elimi-

[1] The Six include Belgium, Netherlands, and Luxembourg (the "Benelux" countries), and France, Germany, and Italy.

nation of trade restrictions and the encouragement of the free movement of resources, to stimulate the concentration of the coal and steel industries of the Six in the hands of the most efficient producers. With a common market kept competitive by the policing action of a central authority, it was hoped that members would be assured of abundant and cheap supplies of these essentials of modern industry. Instead of confining itself to the liberalization of trade, the ECSC set up an International Authority with substantial powers. It was to do away with all tariffs and other restrictions on trade, eliminate a maze of discriminatory transport rates and establish an equitable system, and allocate funds to alleviate the impact of the common market during a five-year transitional period. To police the common market once established, it was authorized to prohibit mergers and even to dissolve existing combinations and to set maximum prices. Finally, the Authority was given important powers over investment: it may require the submission of information about plans, forbid a firm to seek outside finances for any project it deems unwise, and make loans to firms for modernization or expansion.

A strong hint that the Coal and Steel Community was intended only as a first step in economic and political union, together with some indication of the powerful motivation underlying it, is contained in the Treaty establishing that Community. The six signatories:

> Resolved to substitute for historical rivalries a fusion of their essential interests; to establish, by creating an economic community, the foundation of a broad and independent community among peoples long divided by bloody conflicts; and to lay the bases of institutions capable of giving direction to their future common destiny; have decided to create a European coal and steel community.

Progress toward further economic integration began three years later with the Messina Conference, which set up a committee under the chairmanship of Henri Spaak, Foreign Minister of Belgium, to consider ways and means of establishing a common market and of pooling European resources for the development of atomic power. There followed the drafting of the Treaties of Rome, which set up two new agencies of integration: the European Economic Community and the European Atomic Community. Signed in 1957, these treaties were put into operation on January 1, 1958.

EUROPEAN ECONOMIC UNION

Purpose

The main economic purpose of establishing the European Common Market was to realize the advantages of increased specialization. It was hoped that a market embracing a population of over 160 million people would permit the more rapid development of the most economical sectors of each industry, as well as the use of the most modern production techniques. Its sponsors contended that existing national markets were too small for economical operation of certain industries except as monopolies. A large market would make possible mass production without this drawback. Attainment of these ends should, it was argued, make the unified area a more powerful unit, ensure continual expansion, increase economic stability, raise standards of living, and develop harmonious relations between its component states.[2]

Customs Union

The crucial provision of the Common Market is the one establishing a customs union of the six nations. This means that all tariffs between members are to be abolished, and a uniform tariff adopted vis-à-vis other nations. To allow time for adjustment, a transition period of twelve to fourteen years was agreed on. During this period, duties on the trade between members were to be eliminated in three stages of four years each, in installments of 30, 30, and 40 per cent in the successive stages.

Overseas territories (or former territories) of members may, if they wish, associate with the Common Market. Imports from these territories receive the same treatment as those from the metropolitan country, while territorial duties (with exceptions for local overseas industries) are to be gradually reduced to the level applying to imports from the parent country.

The uniform external tariff is to be no higher than the average of the previous tariffs of members. In practice, this means that it will be somewhat higher than the tariffs of Benelux and Germany, somewhat lower than those of France and Italy. As for quantitative restrictions, the Treaty specifies their gradual elimination. (All the foregoing provisions relate to industrial products only. Although agricultural products are not exempted from these provisions, they raise so many problems as to require special treatment. See below.)

Economic Integration

The Common Market is far more than a customs union. Both as a means of ensuring the smooth flow of intra-union trade and as a basis for a closer future political relationship, the Treaty of Rome contains provisions for making the Common Market area into a unified economy. Mere elimination of frontier barriers to trade, it was felt, would be appropriate only for laissez-faire economies. But in each of the six member nations, government intervention, varying in degree and kind, strongly affected the operation of the economic system. National tax systems, especially those aspects relating to the financing of social security programs, bore with different weight on different industries. Both taxes and subsidies were used to support certain industries in one country, but not in others. And national policies for dealing with

---

[2] Organization for European Economic Cooperation, *Report Prepared by the Heads of Delegations of the Intergovernmental Committee Set Up by the Messina Conference to the Ministers of Foreign Affairs* (Paris, 28th August, 1956).

inflationary and deflationary conditions could differ, especially with respect to their timing.

Unless these national policies were "harmonized," a labor-intensive industry subject to abnormally high social security charges would operate at a disadvantage; unsubsidized but efficient producers would be at the mercy of their subsidized rivals, while unsynchronized monetary and fiscal policies could provoke unwanted balance-of-payments disturbances. Moreover, monopolistic organizations in one country might, with the opening of the gates of trade, lead to the domination or possibly the extinction of competitive industry in another. Therefore, "to promote throughout the Community a harmonious development of economic activities," and "closer relations between its Member States," the Community undertook a "progressive approximation" of their economic policies.

To accomplish this, the Treaty of Rome (Article 3) provided for:

(1) the abolition, as between Member States, of the obstacles to the free movement of persons, services and capital;
(2) the inauguration of a common agricultural policy;
(3) the inauguration of a common transport policy;
(4) the establishment of a system ensuring that competition shall not be distorted in the Common Market;
(5) the application of procedures which shall make it possible to co-ordinate the economic policies of Member States and to remedy disequilibria in their balances of payments;
(6) the approximation of their respective legislations to the extent necessary for the functioning of the Common Market.

These provisions are very general. They were left to be worked out through hard bargaining around the conference table.

Special Aid Funds

As tariffs are gradually abolished, industries hitherto dependent on protection are likely to be injured, even though they may be able to adjust over time by intensifying their specialization, improving efficiency, or converting to other lines of production. To help workers in these industries over their difficulties, a European Social Fund was established which meets half the costs of retraining employees and, if necessary, of moving them to new locations.

Aid to industrial proprietors is part of a larger project. This is the European Investment Fund, which has one primary function and two secondary functions. Its most important task is to furnish aid to improve conditions—as by financing basic community facilities—in the underdeveloped regions of member states. In addition, it is to help finance projects of European importance that are too large to be handled alone by the individual states, and to advance funds to firms encountering difficulties in reconversion. The Fund has a capital of $1 billion, supplemented by loans raised in international capital markets.

Another fund with a special appeal to France, the European Development Fund, put up nearly $600 million for investment, through 1962, in the overseas territories. France contributed only $200 million, the same as Western Germany, but her territories got the lion's share of the expenditures—over $511 million.

Organization

With the entry into effect of the Treaty of Rome in 1958, the European Economic Community immediately confronted a great variety of tasks—establishing administrative agencies and their procedures, determining rules for the regulation of competition and of agriculture, and preparing for the first installment of duty reductions. Since the Community was to be a sort of super-government with respect to economic affairs, like any government it needed specific agencies to act, to legislate, and to settle disputes. The Treaty provides for a full complement of the necessary agencies.

The principal administrative body is the European Council, a sort of economic cabinet of the six states. It consists of one member from each state, and is the executive agent of the Community, making daily decisions, formulating rules of conduct, preparing new legislation, and prodding members to carry out the provisions of the treaty. Aiding the Council in its work is a nine-man European Commission, which oversees the application of the treaty, studies special problems, and makes recommendations to the Council. As advisory bodies, there is a Monetary Committee to watch over balances of payments, examine disturbing developments, and recommend remedies, and the European Economic and Social Committee. The latter consists of representatives of industry, workers, farmers, retail trade, and the liberal professions; its area of concern is virtually unlimited.

The legislative branch consists of an Assembly of 106 members, which takes final decision on recommendations of the Council, embodying these in new laws. The Assembly is also the legislative body for the European Coal and Steel Community and for Euratom, the organization created to plan and administer the development of atomic energy resources for the six states.

Finally, there is a Court of Justice to adjudicate disputes, also shared in common with the Coal and Steel Community and Euratom.

PROGRESS TOWARD UNION[3]

In 1962, the European Economic Community entered the second four-year stage of its transitional period. By the end of that year, it had many

[3] Any discussion in book form of a topic that changes as rapidly as the Common Market is bound to be out of date by the time it is published. For the student or instructor who wishes to familiarize himself with the latest developments, an excellent source is the *Bulletin from the European Community*, published by the Information Service, European Economic Community, 235 Southern Building, Washington 5, D. C.

achievements to its credit. Although difficult problems still confronted its leaders, it was in important respects ahead of schedule.

Elimination of internal duties

As of July, 1963, duties on internal trade in industrial products had been reduced by 60 per cent, well in advance of the time table. Moreover, the EEC Commission had earlier stated that it would propose complete abolition of these duties by the beginning of 1967 if the current economic progress of the Community continued. If this proposal is realized, customs union will be achieved three years ahead of time.

External Tariff and Trade Policy

During 1962, the first alignment of the common tariff was completed, with a second alignment planned for July, 1963, and the final one, establishing a full Community tariff, scheduled to be completed simultaneously with the elimination of internal duties by the beginning of 1967.

An offer by the Community to cut a wide range of Common Market duties up to 20 per cent on a reciprocal basis had been negotiated at a GATT conference in mid-1962. This resulted in tariff reduction on trade worth approximately $5 billion a year with the United States and the United Kingdom.

The European Council also laid down a program for the gradual adoption of a common policy for Community exports and imports. This would mean a single system of export aids and promotional devices, the elimination of bilateral trading arrangements between member countries and third countries, and the termination of quotas on trade with GATT members.

Agriculture

A combination of severe postwar shortages of foodstuffs, lack of foreign exchange to pay for imports, and political demands of farmers for increased incomes had caused the individual members of the EEC to impose a wide variety of complex import restrictions and to adopt differing kinds and degrees of price supports. There resulted in each nation a pattern of agricultural production unsuited to its resources, an increase in output to satisfy domestic needs in many products, and much uneconomic production.

Harmonization of the widely divergent policies, essential if trade in agricultural products was to be freed, presented the most difficult obstacle for the Community to overcome. Prolonged negotiations finally in January, 1962, led to agreement on the procedures to be followed in attaining the goals laid down in the Rome Treaty. These were (1) to increase productivity by means of technical progress and the optimum use of resources; (2) to realize a fair standard of living for the agricultural population; (3) to stabilize markets; (4) to guarantee regular supplies; and (5) to ensure reasonable prices to consumers.

Commodities were divided into two main groups for procedural handling. The first, consisting of cereals, pork, poultry, eggs, fruits and vegetables, were to come under a scheme to take effect at the end of July, 1962. The second group—rice, beef, dairy products, and sugar—were postponed for detailed consideration until the following year.

For the first group of commodities, the agreed program contained the following essentials: (1) the establishment of a single target price for each commodity for the entire Community; (2) maintenance of this price by a system of variable import levies equal to the difference between the world market price and the target price, and, where necessary, by purchase of price-depressing Community surpluses.

Target prices were not to be set immediately; they were to be negotiated, presumably some time in the following year. In the interim, each nation was to determine its own level of support prices. Also during that period, variable import levies (administered by the Community) were to apply not only to external trade but also to internal trade, though with somewhat lower rates on the latter.

To provide the financial resources for administering the program, a European Guidance and Guarantee Fund was established. It is to receive a portion of the proceeds of the variable import levies and possibly also direct contributions from governments. The Fund may also play a role in providing training to agricultural workers, in furnishing advisory services, in establishing improved credit facilities, and other matters with respect to which the EEC Commission was preparing proposals.

How restrictive the Community's agricultural policy is to be depends upon one crucial consideration: the height of the target prices adopted, and therewith of the import levies that are to equalize import and domestic prices. Low target prices could leave room for substantial imports, but high prices would tend to eliminate imports and might even lead to such an increase in European production as to generate surpluses that could be disposed of only by means of export subsidies.

Other Aspects of Integration

As of the spring of 1963, most other common policies of the EEC were in the stage of partial implementation, with proposals for further progress coming forward at a rapid rate.

Substantial movements of labor, especially from Italy northward, had already occurred. Domestic workers still received some preference at local labor exchanges, but for most practical purposes free mobility of labor had been attained.

Improvements in the transport system had already been made through investments by the European Investment Bank, while the European Commission had made concrete proposals for harmonizing all technical, fiscal, and social regulations affecting transport operations.

Provisions with respect to monopolistic practices are stated in the Rome Treaty in very general terms. Certain practices likely to interfere with competition are prohibited, but with exceptions where they contribute to technical progress or improved production or distribution of goods. Taking "unfair" advantage of a "dominant" position by one or more firms is also prohibited, but the crucial terms are not defined. The character of the Community's antimonopoly policy remains to be determined in the settlement of concrete cases that will reflect whether a tough or a soft policy is to be followed.

In a Memorandum of October 24, 1962, the European Commission forecast its intention to make proposals for economic programming for the Community as a whole—that is, to establish the course economic activity should follow, in terms of projected GNP, investment both public and private, consumption, and the policies needed to reach the stated objectives. This would mean applying to the Community as a whole the sort of mild economic planning used successfully in France in recent years.

Another striking proposal of this Memorandum projects the establishment of a Council of central bank governors to review monetary problems, meet with the ministers of finance of the Community countries, and work out a coordinated monetary and fiscal policy, with monetary union to be considered for the third stage of the transition period.

Finally, a proposed agreement with the 18 Associated African countries provided for abolition of all duties on imports from these countries of coffee, tea, cocoa, bananas, pineapples, spices, and tropical woods. Duties in the common external tariff would be reduced 40 per cent on the first three commodities. Aid to the African countries for the five-year period 1963-67 was set at approximately $800 million. The EEC nations also gave to the African countries of the British Commonwealth an option to associate with the Common Market on the same terms as the 18 already so associated, to do so on somewhat looser terms, or to conclude trade agreements with the Six.

Summary

In the central area of customs union, the Six had reached the halfway mark by the fifth year of the proposed twelve-year transition period. Agreement had also been reached on the basic principles and procedures for dealing with the problem of agricultural policy. Steady progress had also been recorded with respect to most other matters of concern.

Most important, perhaps, a prediction made in 1958 by an American economist[4] has come true: that the increase, in a broad sense, of competition, would bring closer economic, social, and intellectual contacts and thereby change policies, institutions, and attitudes toward production.

[4] Tibor Scitovsky, *Economic Theory and Western European Integration.* Published 1958 by Stanford University Press, Stanford, Calif.

The Common Market has triggered off all kinds of Community meetings between young people and University teachers, lawyers and designers, civil servants and trade unionists. From the new meetings new ideas are sprouting up at every turn. There is a general will to reform outdated organizational structures. The establishment of the Community is forcing every Member to compare its institutions and development with every other: it is calling old-established habits into question and opening up channels for new, often young men to take charge of new and formidable tasks. At times it may assume the form of a mystique: but this liberating experience is one that must have been lived through on the spot, shared with continental friends and colleagues, for its significance to be fully grasped. The spirit of awareness of their great work-shop in which new shapes are being forged, a sense of achievement, a sense of their mastery over their destiny, a sense even of world mission has come over the new generation of Frenchmen and Germans, Dutchmen and Italians, who operate the system and who are converting old national institutions and found-ing new industrial enterprises to meet the new challenge.[5]

THE PROBLEM OF BRITISH ENTRY

During the years preceding the signing of the Treaty of Rome, when the European Coal and Steel Community was launched and discussion of a Com-mon Market was under way, Britain showed little interest in joining the endeavors of the Six. Indeed, unwillingness even to consider supranational regulation of coal and steel production caused the Government to refuse an invitation to join in the negotiations on the ECSC. It likewise declined to join in preparing the Treaty of Rome, but proposed a counter-plan for a larger Free Trade Association. This provided for elimination of custom duties between members on industrial products, but there was to be no com-mon tariff or any of the measures looking toward harmonization of national policies. Britain was unwilling to include agricultural products because its own agricultural policy gave consumers the benefit of prices kept low by duty-free imports from the Commonwealth, whose advantage would have been seriously diminished by similar treatment of European producers. Do-mestic agriculture in Britain was supported by direct payments from the Treasury.

In 1959, faced with the Common Market as an established fact, unwilling to join, and fearful of its effect on her trade, the British Government, with six other nations, formed the rival European Free Trade Association.[6] Start-ing with a 20 per cent cut in duties on intra-area trade in industrial products, the reductions were thereafter to keep pace roughly with those made by the EEC. Each nation retained its own external tariff. As of 1963, EFTA had

---

[5] U. W. Kitzinger, *The Challenge of the Common Market*, p. 47. Published 1961 by Basil Blackwell, Oxford.

[6] The members are: the three Scandinavian countries—Denmark, Norway, and Sweden —and Austria, Switzerland, Portugal, and the United Kingdom.

proceeded with its tariff cuts as rapidly as had the Six, with complete free trade among members scheduled for the end of 1966.

Only two years after inaugurating the EFTA, joining the Common Market acquired an overpowering appeal to Britain. In July, 1961, Prime Minister MacMillan announced that his Government had officially applied for membership. What caused this change in attitude? In large part, fear of exclusion from a large and expanding Common Market was responsible. In particular, many proponents of British membership stressed the importance, especially to the newer industries employing the most advanced technology, of access to the Community market in order to realize economies of large-scale production. There was also a recognition that the British economy, many sectors of whose industry remained unenterprising and stagnant, needed a dose of the chill but energizing wind of competition. French industry, with even more conspicuous areas of inefficiency, had feared the competition of its more progressive neighbors, but had been rejuvenated by it.

In the negotiations between British officials and representatives of the Common Market that continued over the next year-and-a-half, three main problems had somehow to be solved. One was how to align, by a programmed adjustment of some sort, Britain's agricultural policy with that of the Six. In the United Kingdom, the consumer of farm products enjoyed the benefits of low, relatively free market prices, while the farmer was compensated by deficiency payments equal to the difference between the market price and a calculated support price. As we have seen, the Common Market countries intend to maintain prices above the world level by a combination of government price support backed by import duties.

A second difficulty was how to minimize the impact of Britain's entry upon members of the Commonwealth, especially upon the Australian and Canadian producers of wheat and the New Zealand producers of dairy products, who enjoyed Imperial Preference in the British market.

Finally, the United Kingdom had an obligation to its partners in the European Free Trade Association. Two of them, Denmark and Norway, had also applied for membership in the EEC. Not to make every possible effort to safeguard the interest of these and other EFTA members would have been highly irresponsible.

After months of tough bargaining in Brussels, by the end of 1962 many complexities had been resolved. The outlook for British entry appeared moderately optimistic. Then, in a press conference in mid-January, President de Gaulle challenged Britain's readiness to become a member of the Community on terms acceptable to France and rejected the concept of an economic community more diverse and less cohesive than the existing one. While stating that "it is possible that Britain would one day come round to transforming itself enough to belong to the European Community without restriction and without reservation," when "France would place no obstacle in its path," he nonetheless slammed the door on further current negotiations.

ECONOMIC UNION IN LATIN AMERICA

The Latin American Free Trade Area

With their wide differences in governmental structure and in political temper, the nations of Latin America have not had a comparable political basis for forming an economic union. They share, however, a common interest in protecting and expanding their trade and in promoting their economic development. Although their trade has been growing, its rate of expansion has been slow. During the 1950's, Latin America's share of free world exports actually fell from 11 to 8 per cent. Moreover, a quarter of Latin American exports goes to the European Common Market, and of this, half consists of commodities likely to be displaced because of European preference for the products of associated African nations.[7] The low level of intra-Latin American trade, too—only about 10 per cent of total trade—has been a cause for concern.

Discussion of the possibility of establishing arrangements that would strengthen the Latin American trade position—in particular, any that would stimulate increased intra-area trade and contribute to regional economic development—began in 1954. For several years, ideas on this topic were exchanged, with the Economic Commission for Latin America playing a leading role. Finally, seven countries—Argentina, Brazil, Chile, Paraguay, Peru, and Uruguay in South America, and Mexico—reached sufficient agreement to formalize their views in the Treaty of Montevideo, which was signed on February 18, 1960, and entered into force on July 1, 1961. Two additional countries, Colombia and Ecuador, later joined the original seven. Open to further adherents, it is hoped many more countries will sign the Treaty in the future.

Declared purposes are the liberalization of intra-Latin American trade, the promotion of complementarity of industrial production, and the coordination of agricultural development and trade. Trade liberalization is to be achieved through the gradual elimination, over a period of twelve years, of all duties and restrictions on mutual trade. Although there is no provision for a common external tariff, the Treaty urges members to work toward uniform treatment of imports of capital, goods, and services from third countries, with the prospect at some later date of establishing a Common Market of all twenty Latin American countries.

[7] The principal commodities in this group are coffee, cocoa, bananas, hides and skins, vegetable oils, sugar, wheat, meat, hardwoods, lead, and zinc. Data from Walter J. Sedwitz, "A Common Market for Latin America?", *Current History* (July, 1962).

It is hoped that a more economic allocation of manufacturing industries may be realized, with accompanying internal and external economies, through national specialization. To this end, the Treaty authorizes "complementarity agreements," which would presumably reserve certain industries to some countries, others to different countries.

The goal of coordinating agricultural development and trade policies is expressed in very general terms. Much more specifically, the opposite goal of national insulation is then supported by a provision that enables a member to limit agricultural imports to the amount by which customary consumption exceeds home production.

The Treaty of Montevideo provides a framework which could eventually lead to the formation of a true common market for all Latin America. There are, however, many obstacles to be overcome: the vested interests of national producers, both industrial and agricultural; the continuance of bilateral trading and payments arrangements by many countries; and a vague feeling of distrust and uncertainty among the members of negotiating bodies. It is still too early to judge clearly as to the prospects of this nascent free-trade area.

Central American Economic Integration

Integration has moved much faster in Central America. Three separate agreements were signed by five countries (Costa Rica, El Salvador, Guatemala, Honduras, Nicaragua) in 1958 and 1959, but in the following year these were incorporated in a more comprehensive document, the General Treaty of Central American Economic Integration.[8] Aiming at the creation within five years of a customs union with a common external tariff, it established free trade immediately in all products originating in the five member countries, barring a rather large number of exceptions to be liberalized gradually.

There is also provision for economic integration through the agreed assignment of certain industries to specific countries. A Central American Economic Integration Bank, established in May, 1961, with a capital of $16 million, stands ready to support closer economic union by helping to finance agricultural, industrial, or social overhead projects of interest to the entire community.

Considering the relatively low stage of development of the Central American republics, even their union into a group with a population of 10 million will not guarantee a prosperous market for industrial production. Current exports consist, to the extent of approximately 80 per cent, of coffee and bananas; there is little industry in the area and that small in scale; and economic growth is inhibited by illiteracy, primitive agricultural methods, a small and comparatively unenterprising middle class, poor communications, and a general power shortage. Yet there are a few efficient light industries; greater competition

[8] All had ratified by the summer of 1962.

could stimulate others to improve, and with financial help still others may emerge. The least one can say is that the union of the five small countries into a single market should afford some additional stimulus to growth, a stimulus that should increase as basic economic development proceeds.

SELECTED REFERENCES

Benoit, Emile, *Europe at Sixes and Sevens.* New York: Columbia University Press, 1961. An excellent, wide-ranging discussion of the problems arising out of the division of western Europe into rival trade areas.

Kitzinger, U. W., *The Challenge of the Common Market.* Oxford: Basil Blackwell, 1961. Chapters I-IV provide an excellent statement of the economic and political significance of European Union; the last four chapters deal with the problems of British entry.

Lamfalussy, A., *The United Kingdom and the Six.* Homewood, Ill.: Richard D. Irwin, Inc., 1963. A penetrating discussion of the reasons for the contrast in the rate of growth in the United Kingdom and the Common Market countries.

Mikesell, Raymond F., "The Movement Toward Regional Trading Groups in Latin America," in *Latin American Issues,* Albert O. Hirschman, ed. New York: The Twentieth Century Fund, 1961. A critical evaluation of the Montevideo Treaty and the prospects of Latin American economic union.

Sannwald, Rolf F. and Jacques Stohler, *Economic Integration.* Princeton, N. J.: Princeton University Press, 1959. Mainly a theoretical discussion of the problems of economic integration, with special reference to western Europe.

Scitovsky, Tibor, *Economic Theory and Western European Integration.* Stanford, Calif.: Stanford University Press, 1958. A thorough analysis of the probable effects of economic integration in Europe.

Urquidi, Victor L., *Free Trade and Economic Integration in Latin America.* Berkeley, Calif.: University of California Press, 1962. A relatively optimistic statement of the case for economic integration in Latin America.

Vernon, Raymond, *American Foreign Trade Policy and the GATT.* Princeton, N. J.: Princeton University Press, 1954. Analyzes U.S. participation in GATT.

United States Tariff Commission, *Operation of the Trade Agreements Program.* Washington, D. C.: Government Printing Office, issued periodically. Report on the operation and effects of the Trade Agreement programs and description of the work of GATT.

30

REGIONAL INTEGRATION AND TRADE EXPANSION

EFFECTS OF A CUSTOMS UNION

Economic integration, already well advanced in western Europe and under way in Latin America, is a new and striking development. Hitherto independent economies, often bitter rivals in the past, are merging their differences and either forming an economic union or tearing down the tariff walls that have separated them. Surely such actions are bound to have significant effects, both upon the participants and upon outsiders. Can we say what these effects are likely to be?

Formation of a customs union or of a free-trade area entails the elimination of all artificial barriers to trade within the region.[1] This is bound to affect prices, the volume and composition of trade, the allocation of resources, and with these changes, the efficiency of production and the welfare of consumers. Over the longer run, the creation of a large regional market may permit the extension of large-scale methods of production and the realization of external economies. It is clearly impossible to predict with accuracy the effects of such widespread changes. Much will depend upon the specific circumstances under which they occur.

Intensive study of this complex subject has indicated, however, the most likely consequences of the formation of a customs union, and the conditions that will determine how strong their effects will be.[2] Here we shall attempt only to summarize the main guidelines established by recent analysis.

[1] As in EFTA, some commodities may be excluded from the agreement, but on those included, all barriers must be removed. Otherwise the agreement conflicts with the provisions of the General Agreement on Tariffs and Trade, which regard a partial reduction of duties as establishing preferential treatment, which is prohibited.

[2] Among the more important contributions to this study are the following: Bela Balassa, *The Theory of Economic Integration* (Richard D. Irwin, Inc., Homewood, Ill., 1961); James E. Meade, *Problems of Economic Union* (University of Chicago Press, 1953): James E. Meade, *The Theory of Customs Unions* (The North Holland Publishing Co., Amsterdam, 1955); Rolf Sannwald and Jacques Stohler, *Economic Integration* (Princeton University Press, 1959); Tibor Scitovsky, *Economic Theory and Western European*

Consider first the static effects of establishing a customs union—those that take place before one allows for the changes induced by a reallocation of resources and alterations in the structure of production. We can distinguish two sets of static effects: those on production and those on consumption.

Production Effects

When members of a customs union dissolve their tariffs on intra-union trade, new sources of supply of many commodities are opened up within the union. Substitution of the new sources of supply for the old occurs. Two types of substitution may be distinguished.

1. The new supply from within the union may displace high-cost domestic production, hitherto supported by a member's tariff. Thus, if before union French producers of plate glass had been supplying their domestic market at relatively high cost, after union they would be displaced by the low-cost Belgian producers. Where international trade did not exist before, it has now been created. This *trade creation* results in an increase in the efficiency of world production; total world output is greater, since output within the customs union has increased, with no offsetting diminution elsewhere.

2. The new intra-union supply may, however, displace a member's imports from a lower-cost foreign source. If France, for example, had been importing aluminum from Canada and the United States at a price of $100 a ton plus a 30 per cent duty, with the elimination of this duty on intra-union trade, Italian producers with a cost of $120 a ton could now displace the previous imports into France. The actual cost to France of her aluminum is now $20 a ton higher than before. Trade has been diverted from a low-cost to a high-cost source. This trade diversion reduces the efficiency of world production, since to produce the same output as before, a larger quantity of resources has to be used. (Alternatively, one could say that to acquire the same quantity of imports as before, France must now use a larger amount of resources in producing the exports to exchange for the imports.)

Whether the favorable effects of trade creation are greater or less than the adverse effects of trade diversion will depend not only on the change in the volume of trade, but also on the differences in unit costs. Even a large volume of trade created, if the cost saving were relatively small, could be offset by a comparatively small volume of trade diverted, if the difference in unit costs were relatively large. The relevance of both these elements to the question of net gain or loss in world efficiency suggests the sort of considerations that need to be taken into account in judging the impact of a customs union on this score.

Integration (Stanford University Press, 1958); Jan Tinbergen, *International Economic Integration* (Elsevier, Amsterdam, 1954); Jacob Viner, *The Customs Union Issue* (Carnegie Endowment for International Peace, New York, 1950). The discussion that follows owes much to several of these sources, particularly to the works of Meade and Balassa.

(a) If the economies merged in a customs union are *competitive* in the sense that they produce a wide range of similar goods, there will be many opportunities for the substitution of the products of one union member for those of another, and thus for trade creation rather than trade diversion. Where the lowest-cost producer is outside the union, this will, of course, constitute an exception causing trade diversion.

The union of complementary economies, producing very dissimilar goods, would, on the other hand, provide few opportunities for intra-union substitution. There would be little reallocation of production between high-cost and low-cost sources of supply, such as would tend to occur with a union of competitive economies. Though elimination of tariffs would increase the trade of existing low-cost suppliers, it would do little to *create* trade by causing the substitution of a low-cost for a high-cost source. A considerable amount of trade might, however, be *diverted* through the substitution of high-cost internal for low-cost external suppliers.

(b) Any gain from the union of competitive economies would be augmented by the existence of large differences in unit costs. Not only would there be a large gain for each unit of goods traded, but there would also be a substantial reallocation of resources.

(c) Tariff levels are another important determinant of the effect of customs unions on world efficiency of production. (1) If pre-union tariffs of members were high, thus restricting imports in general, their removal would permit the substitution of many lower-cost sources of supply within the union for high-cost domestic supplies. This would favor trade creation. (2) After the union is established, a low tariff against the outside world will be favorable to efficiency, for this will minimize trade diversion. There will be less likelihood that low-cost outside producers will be excluded from the union market, whereas with a high tariff wall around the union, its market will tend to be reserved for relatively high-cost suppliers inside the union.

(d) Other things equal, the larger the market formed by a customs union, the more numerous will be the opportunities for a more productive reallocation of resources. Whereas the unification of Belgium and Luxembourg resulted in inappreciable change of this kind, formation of the Common Market is leading to the elimination of many inefficient producers and the concentration of production in the more efficient units.

Relative transport costs have a distinct bearing on the size of the market resulting from a customs union. Since high transport costs act as a barrier to trade, the unification of economies separated by high costs of this kind will be less effective in creating a large market than the unification of economies between which transport costs are low.

SUMMARY   We may summarize the effect on production of the formation of a customs union by saying that an expansion of trade from this cause may, by permitting a reallocation of resources into a more efficient pattern of spe-

cialization, effect an increase in the efficiency of world production. If it does
so, welfare is increased because of the larger volume of goods available for
consumption. Total output, the efficiency of production, and welfare may,
however, be diminished if instead of a net increase in trade there is a mere
diversion, causing a reallocation of resources into a less efficient pattern of
specialization.

Consumption Effects

Alongside its effects on production, the expansion of trade has equally
important effects on consumption. In essence, trade consists in buying commodities where they are cheap and selling them where they are dear: in other
words, transferring goods from where a relatively low value is put upon them
to where their value is relatively high. The consumer, whose enjoyment is the
ultimate concern of both production and trade, is enabled by trade to increase
his satisfaction, for he can thereby raise his consumption of articles upon
which he places a relatively high value.

It stands to reason that trade will be optimized, or carried to the point
where it cannot increase the welfare of consumers any more, only when it has
equalized the relative marginal value of all commodities to all buyers. So long
as any consumer places a relatively higher value on additional purchases of a
given commodity than do other consumers, exchange will be beneficial. Thus
suppose the marginal value to A of phonograph records is $10, of a pound of
smoking tobacco, $5; while to B the marginal value of each is $5. If A exchanges with B a pound of tobacco for a record, A obtains $10 worth of
satisfaction while giving up only $5 worth, for a net gain of $5, while B
neither gains nor loses.

Now just this essential equalization of relative marginal values is brought
about in a freely competitive market. Any given consumer will continue buying each commodity until its marginal value to him is equal to its price. Then
the marginal satisfaction he derives from each dollar spent will be the same,
and his satisfaction will be maximized. But since, in a competitive market, all
buyers confront the same prices, what is true for any single buyer is true of
all. Marginal value is equal to price for all buyers. Moreover, under conditions
of perfect competition, price is equal to marginal cost. Buyers are therefore
enabled to extend their purchases to the point where the marginal value of
each commodity corresponds to the cost of producing it.

The introduction of monopoly, of an excise tax, or—on an imported article
—of a customs duty, will raise the price and marginal value of that article
above its marginal cost. If, at the new higher price, the consumer still buys
the *same quantity* as before, the marginal satisfaction derived from a dollar
spent on this commodity will be less than for his other purchases. To ensure
that each dollar spent yields the same satisfaction, he must reallocate his
expenditure, reducing his purchases of the now more costly product and in-

creasing his purchases of those that are cheaper. But this lowers the marginal satisfaction on each purchase. The imposition of a customs duty, by introducing a divergence between marginal value and marginal cost, thus prevents the realization of maximum satisfaction in consumption. Conversely, the removal of such a duty will permit consumers' satisfaction to be increased.

Stated more broadly, the point just made is simply an illustration of the reduction in consumers' satisfaction that comes from narrowing the range of consumers' choice. To take an extreme case, suppose a large proportion of articles currently consumed were taxed so heavily as to make them prohibitively costly. Consumers would then have to spend their incomes on larger amounts of a limited range of commodities. The principle of diminishing marginal satisfaction would operate, and total satisfaction would decline sharply.

Now let us relate these concepts to the formation of a customs union. When the tariff on intraunion trade is abolished, a low-cost source within the union may displace a domestic high-cost source of supply (trade creation), or a second-best source within the union may displace imports from a lower-cost source outside the union (trade diversion). Under either circumstance, however, the price in the consuming country of the commodity now available duty-free within the union will fall. Consumers "get a break." The divergence between marginal value and marginal cost will be eliminated if the lowest-cost producer is inside the union. If the union supplier is only second-best, the divergence between marginal value (the former price) and the lowest attainable marginal cost will be reduced. So far as concerns the commodity directly affected, consumers' satisfaction will tend to increase, since expenditure on this relatively highly valued commodity will rise. How large a *net* increase in consumers' welfare occurs, however, will depend upon the kind of goods whose consumption is *displaced* by the increased consumption of the commodity in question. For what kinds of goods is the new imported product a substitute?

It may be a good substitute for goods already available in the importing country from domestic suppliers. If so, buyers will reduce their consumption of commodities on which they had brought marginal value, price, and marginal cost into equality, in favor of the commodity for which marginal value has been held artificially high because of the tariff. By increasing their consumption of a good upon which they place a relatively high value, at the expense of others for which their valuation is relatively lower, they can enjoy a net increase in satisfaction.

The newly imported product may, however, be a good substitute instead for some commodity that is imported from outside the union and which is subject to a restrictive duty. If so, then although consumers will enjoy additional (though diminishing) satisfaction from increased consumption of the new duty-free import, up to the point where marginal value is equated to the new lower marginal cost, they will suffer an offsetting loss from reduced consumption of the dutiable and still highly valued article. The duty on this article maintains a divergence between marginal value and marginal cost; the size of this divergence is a measure of the loss in consumers' satisfaction on each unit by which its consumption is diminished.[3]

To illustrate, suppose before the formation of the Common Market, France was importing cameras costing 200 francs from Germany and watches (with the same unit cost) from Switzerland, each commodity being subject to a 50 per cent duty. After the removal of the duty on union products, cameras sell for 200 francs, while the price of watches remains unchanged at 300 francs. Let us assume, as in Figure 30.1, that before the Common Market was formed,

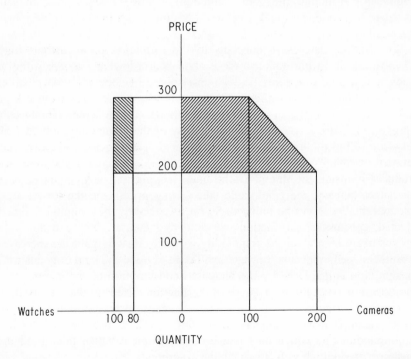

FIGURE 30.1   Consumption Effect of Elimination of a Duty on One of Two Substitutable Imports

100 units each of cameras and watches were sold in France, but that afterward, at the new low price, sales of cameras doubled, to 200, while sales of watches (for which cameras are highly substitutable) fell to 80. The elimination of the divergence between the marginal value and marginal cost of cameras yields

[3] The loss from reduced consumption of the still dutiable article, however, can never exceed the gain from increased consumption of the now duty-free commodity. Such an outcome would reflect irrational consumer, behavior—a failure to allocate expenditure so as to equalize the *value* of each dollar spent.

consumers an increase in welfare represented by the irregular area in the diagram. But there is an offsetting loss of welfare from the reduced consumption of watches, represented by the rectangular area on the watches side of the diagram. Since the divergence between marginal value and marginal cost for watches remains at the original level, there is a loss of welfare corresponding to this divergence on each unit by which the consumption of watches is reduced. As for cameras, consumers' satisfaction is increased on all units purchased—both those bought at the old price and (at a diminishing rate) on the additional consumption at the new, lower price.

In estimating, for any customs union, its probable impact on consumers' welfare, it is clear that tariff levels would be of primary importance. If before the union high duties prevailed on trade between members, the likelihood of gain would be increased, since this would ensure a large displacement of high-priced domestic or imported supplies by lower-priced supplies from within the union. Low tariffs against outside countries *after* the formation of the union, however, would favor a gain in welfare, since then the divergence between marginal value and marginal cost on imports would be relatively small. Any reduction in imports caused by expanded intra-union trade in substitutes would now entail less offsetting loss.

As with production effects, the competitiveness of the economies of union members is highly relevant. The greater the similarity in the range of commodities produced, the greater would be the possibility that high-cost domestic suppliers would be displaced by lower-cost sources within the union.

DYNAMIC ASPECTS OF UNION

We have seen that when a customs union replaces several small national markets by a single large one, production tends to become more specialized, while consumers enjoy an increase in satisfaction. These effects are static, in the sense that they involve no changes in the structure of industry, in its technology, or in patterns of behavior. Everything goes on as before, except for a reallocation of productive resources into more efficient combinations and of consumer expenditure into a more satisfying pattern.

But the dynamic effects of a large expansion of the market area can be far more important than the static effects. The basis for dynamic effects is to be found in the increased competition generated by the opening up of new market opportunities. Firms hitherto excluded from protected national markets now have the chance to offer a comparison, on even terms, of their prices, the quality of their products, servicing facilities, terms of credit, speed of delivery, and advertising and marketing assistance.

1. *Competition and emulation.* When their customers are given a choice of new and superior alternatives, hitherto protected producers, if they are to survive, must either imitate or innovate. Emulation of their competitors leads

to the spread of the best practices. There occurs not just a mechanical re-shuffling of resources from inefficient firms and industries into those more efficient and capable of meeting or of extending the new competition, but a change in attitudes, habits, and organization. Conservative and traditional in-dustries are forced to become progressive, active rather than passive, and to adopt improved methods if they are to stay in business. Older men tend to be replaced by younger men, willing and able to change, who with the stimulus of rivalry, improve upon the new practices they are forced to meet.

When a customs union is reenforced by economic integration, with the free movement of capital, labor, and enterprise, and with cooperation in shaping government policies and in establishing common institutions, the competition of ideas generated by product competition is extended over a far wider range. Capital that is free to move shuns repressive or discriminatory tax laws, while labor seeks not only higher money wages but also better working conditions and the most attractive fringe benefits. Enterprise goes where, given equal prospects of profits, freedom to operate is greatest. Governments therefore are pressed to reform tax laws, social security provisions, and legislation affect-ing enterprise—that is, to copy or improve upon the best existing practices. International conventions replace national conventions of engineers, salesmen, executives, and accountants, affording a wider forum for the exchange of ideas. Although its effects are difficult to measure, surely the inauguration of a spirit of emulation is one of the most beneficial effects of economic union.

Emulation may, of course, extend to bad as well as to good practices. If before union national markets were dominated by cartels, these may merely be replaced by larger international organizations, perhaps restricting output and maintaining prices even more effectively. This suggests that in this area, whether only a customs union or full economic integration is being attempted, a common policy is needed if the welfare of the community is to be served.

2. *Economies of scale.* A number of recent studies[4] show a high correlation between market size and productivity. A basis for a causal relationship is to be found in a number of different directions: in the economies permitted by large-scale operations, in external economies, in the stimulus to technological change, and in an increased rate of investment. With respect to economies of scale, the risks of establishing even a single large-scale industry are less in a large than in a small market, while the range of industries that can schedule a large output is much greater.

We have seen that economies derived from large-scale operations, or econ-omies of scale, are associated with the use of expensive, specialized equipment, the specialization of labor, savings on inventories and from bulk handling, and from relatively smaller outlays for nonoperational activities such as research, planning, and the like (Chapter 8). The possibility of realizing these economies is by no means universal. Recent studies of German, American, and New

---

[4] Cited in Balassa, *op. cit.,* pp. 109-112.

Zealand industries, however, indicate that productivity increases with the size of the plant in a substantial proportion of the industries surveyed.[5] In the United States, for example, the production of pig iron, crude petroleum, sugar, paper, electricity, and creameries shows increasing returns to scale, but there is little or no evidence of such economies for fertilizers, bakery products, or tires.[6]

3. *External economies.* As market size increases, economies external to the plant may also arise. Industrial growth creates a pool of skilled labor and of managerial talent, and causes technological knowledge to spread and to develop. Expansion of one industry may permit its supplier to introduce more economical large-scale methods, or it may be able to increase its own specialization and to subcontract for specialized parts and components with other specialized firms.

4. *More rapid technological advance.* We have seen that, as a market grows, some industries at least are likely to realize economies of scale. In these industries, large firms will increase their share of the market. Given the combination of economies of scale in research, the larger financial resources and better access to the capital market of the large firm, and its "longer time horizon," then, as Balassa contends, it is probable that the larger firm will spend more freely on research activities.[7] This will tend to promote more rapid technological progress. Moreover, if large producers are relatively more numerous in a large economy, and if they spend more freely on research, the large economy will have the advantage of discoveries over a wider field, for whose application its very size affords more opportunities.

5. *Investment.* If economic union produces the favorable effects on productive efficiency suggested in the forgoing pages, aggregate income will rise, savings will increase, and the aggregate volume of investment will be larger. A rise in the *proportion* of income saved and invested may be encouraged by a number of forces: by the increased confidence generated by the expansion of and stability in intra-union trade, by the average increase in the productivity of investment that comes from the elimination or the upgrading of inefficient firms, and by the larger proportion of investment that goes into large-scale, more productive equipment.

To higher savings and investment in the unified community may be added an inflow of foreign funds, attracted by the prospects of producing and selling in the enlarged market and by a rising rate of economic growth. Witness, for example, the rise in U.S. direct investment in the six nations of the EEC from $637 million in 1950 to $2,194,000,000 in 1959.[8]

[5] *Ibid.*, p. 126.
[6] *Ibid.*, p. 128.
[7] *Ibid.*, pp. 174-5.
[8] *U.S. Business Investments in Foreign Countries*, Office of Business Economics, Department of Commerce (U.S. Government Printing Office, Washington, D. C., 1960), Tables 1, 3.

MULTILATERALISM VERSUS REGIONALISM

We have noted at many points in earlier chapters the progress made in restoring a worldwide multilateral trading system. Especially noteworthy has been the great reduction in the use of quantitative restrictions by the main trading nations, the restoration of convertibility to their currencies, and the persistent and successful efforts of GATT to reduce tariff barriers and to settle disputes through conciliation and compromise. The increasing liberalization of trade, together with recovery and expansion of production in Europe and Japan, was accompanied by remarkable growth in the volume and value of world trade. Table 30.1 shows this vividly.

Between 1953 and 1961, while world commodity output rose 35 per cent, the volume of world exports increased by 73 per cent, or more than twice as fast. Thus the proportion of world output entering international trade climbed steadily during this nine-year period. Liberalization of trade has in fact led to a great expansion of trade.

Equally noteworthy is the even greater increase of the trade between the six members of the European Economic Community. The value of the exports of these countries to one another nearly trebled between 1953 and 1961.[9] Partly, of course, this was due to the rapid recovery of European economic activity. But in the later years, the anticipated and actual effects of the formation of the Common Market undoubtedly provided an added stimulus.

Does this development foreshadow a trend toward increasing self-sufficiency and isolation of the new regional groupings—the EEC, the EFTA, LAFTA, and the Central American common market? The answer depends mainly on the height of the external tariffs established by the regional groups and upon their willingness to participate in multilateral negotiations.

Thus the EEC tariff on industrial products promises to be moderately protective. But if high target prices are set for agricultural products, the variable import levies will be correspondingly high and restrictive. This could cause a substantial degree of trade diversion in temperate agricultural products, or even such an increase in European output of some products as to aggravate the world surplus problem.

A first test of future prospects will be provided by the GATT negotiations scheduled for 1964. Here representatives of the Common Market will for the first time confront, in the person of the U.S. negotiators, a revised American trade policy.

Before considering the "new look" in U.S. trade policy, let us review the development of this policy from where we left it in Chapter 24.

[9] The increase was 197 per cent. Since prices were relatively stable during this period, this corresponds fairly closely to the change in volume. (Even manufactured exports rose in price only 9 per cent.)

Table 30.1. VALUE, PRICE (UNIT-VALUE) AND VOLUME OF INTERNATIONAL TRADE, AND VOLUME OF WORLD PRODUCTION

(1953-1961)

	1953	1954	1955	1956	1957	1958	1959	1960	1961
Value of world exports[a] (thousand million dollars f.o.b.)									
Total	77.6	82.3	90.8	100.5	108.8	104.8	113.1	125.9	131.3
Manufactured goods[b]	35.0	38.0	44.0	49.8	54.5	54.1	59.6	67.8	(70.8)
Unit value of world exports[c] (1953 = 100)									
Total	100	99	99	101	103	100	98	99	98
Manufactured goods[b]	100	98	99	103	106	106	105	107	109
Volume of world exports (1953 = 100)									
Total	100	107	118	128	136	135	149	164	173
Manufactured goods[b]	100	111	127	138	147	146	162	181	(186)
Volume of world commodity output[c] (1953 = 100)									
All commodities	100	101	110	114	116	116	125	132	135
Mining and manufacturing[d]	100	101	112	117	121	118	130	139	144

[a] Excluding United States special category exports.
[b] Including base metals.
[c] Excluding Eastern trading area.
[d] Value added.
SOURCE: *International Trade 1961* (The Contracting Parties to the General Agreement on Tariffs and Trade, Geneva, September, 1962).

U.S. TARIFF POLICY, 1934-1962

United States tariff policy from 1934 onward can be briefly summarized as paring off the protective fat by negotiation. The Trade Agreements Act of that year, renewed periodically thereafter, authorized the President to reduce existing duties by as much as 50 per cent, in exchange for similar concessions by other countries. In a series of bilateral negotiations with a number of countries, a considerable number of such concessions were exchanged, then extended to other countries by means of the most-favored-nation principle. In 1947, authority to cut duties by 50 per cent from the new, lower level was granted; in 1956 further duty reductions were limited to 20 per cent.

In the 28 years during which the Trade Agreements Acts shaped U.S. tariff policy, there occurred a very substantial lowering of the average level of U.S. import duties. Responsibility for this reduction was divided about equally between price increases, which lowered the *percentage* rate of the predominantly specific duties in the U.S. tariff, and negotiated duty cuts.[10] Thus in 1934, the average duty on dutiable imports was 46.7 per cent. At the end of 1952, the duties in effect in 1934 would have amounted to only 24.4 per cent at the higher level of prices then ruling. The actual average rate of duties, however, was only 12.2 per cent. Trade agreements had therefore brought about a 50 per cent reduction of the U.S. tariff level. Between 1952 and 1962, the average duty on dutiable imports was further reduced to approximately 12 per cent.

Although this appears to be quite low, and by comparison with the tariff level in the early 1930's *is* low, an average of a wide range of duties is deceptive.[11] It conceals *all* duties that are prohibitive, since only duties actually levied on imports are counted. Some duties included in the average are high though not prohibitive. And many low duties afford substantial protection when international cost differences are slight. It is the consensus of experts that as of 1962, the U.S. tariff was moderately protective.

Moreover, the Trade Agreements Acts in force from 1947 on contained an "escape clause" which practically guaranteed domestic producers against injurious foreign competition. Upon a finding by the Tariff Commission that a product on which a concession had been granted was, due *even in part* to the concession, being imported in such increased quantities, either actual or *relative*, as to cause or threaten serious injury to the competing domestic industry, the President was authorized to withdraw or modify the concession. With increased imports defined in relative terms, this meant that protection could be restored even though output of the American industry was growing, provided only that imports were growing faster.

---

[10] Thus in the 1930 tariff, the specific duty on garlic was 1.5 cents a pound. Converted into an *ad valorem* figure, it amounted to 40 per cent. By 1950, the price of garlic had risen to the point where the 1.5 cent duty amounted to only 22 per cent *ad valorem*.

[11] In 1962, U.S. duties ranged from 1 per cent to nearly 100 per cent.

Later extensions of the Trade Agreements Act went further by defining an industry as the producers of a single product. This led to the absurdity that an industry producing multiple products could apply for tariff relief even though a *relative* increase in foreign competition was limited to only one of its several products.[12]

Reenforcing the protectionist policy embodied in the escape clause were two other legislative provisions. One authorized the withdrawal of a concession or the restriction of imports by quotas if imports increased in such quantities as to threaten the national security. Watches, which obtained relief under this provision, are undoubtedly important to national defense, though the need for maintaining a protected industry as a source of supply is certainly dubious. But the connection between clothespins (which qualifies under the national defense provision) and national security would seem to be somewhat indirect. The law (National Defense Amendment of 1955), however, defines almost any adverse effect on economic welfare, such as increased unemployment, loss of government revenues, or loss of skills or investment, as constituting impairment of national security. A coat of national security paint is a feeble camouflage for the underlying protectionism.

Finally, the "Buy American" Act, passed by Congress during the depression to give preference to American producers, requires Federal agencies to award government contracts to American firms unless foreign bids are 6 per cent lower (in some cases, 12 per cent).

In sum, the Trade Agreements Acts and related legislation sought to expand American exports by an exchange of concessions. In the progress of negotiating them, the U.S. tariff was reduced very substantially from its inordinate height of the early 1930's; but it continued to afford effective protection for most domestic industries encountering foreign competition. Most importantly, U.S. legislation refused to tolerate injury to domestic producers from such competition. Any such injury, real or threatened, was to be—not compensated —but prevented.

THE TRADE EXPANSION ACT OF 1962

In 1962, President Kennedy advanced to Congress proposals for legislation to replace the expiring Trade Agreements Act that represented, if not a revolution, at least an important shift in American tariff policy. After extensive hearings and debate, Congress passed the Trade Expansion Act of 1962 embodying most of these proposals.

The new law differs from its immediate predecessors in two principal ways: it grants the President much greater authority to lower or even eliminate U.S.

---

[12] A finding of injury, coupled with relief, occurred in such individual items of multiple product lines as watches with seven but not more than seventeen jewels, flax toweling, safety pins, clinical thermometers, and garlic.

import duties, and it substitutes for the negative policy of *preventing* dislocation the positive one of *promoting and facilitating* adjustment to dislocation
caused by foreign competition.

Tariff Reduction

Tariff reduction by negotiation is retained as the basic goal. A more vigorous pursuit of that goal is made possible, however, by more generous provisions for cutting duties. Four specific provisions express this feature of the
Act.

1. The President may, through trade agreements with foreign countries, reduce any duty by 50 per cent of the rate in effect on July 1, 1962. Thus duties
lowered through trade agreements before that date may be cut in half again,
or duties hitherto untouched may be similarly reduced.

2. The President may, in a trade agreement with the European Economic
Community, reduce or eliminate the duties on any category of commodities
in which the EEC and the United States together account for 80 per cent of
the value of world trade. This important section would make it possible, if
Britain became a member of the Common Market, to establish free trade
in some 30 categories of goods, including such important commodities as
agricultural machinery, aircraft, passenger automobiles and buses, metalwork-
ing machinery, rubber products, and many chemicals. These are goods in
which the United States or the European nations, or both, are efficient producers. Successful negotiations on these categories would serve the interest of
each party by guaranteeing access to the market of the other.

Without British membership, however, the list of commodities subject to
such liberal treatment is severely restricted, being limited principally to aircraft, vegetable oils, and perfumes.

3. Duties on tropical agricultural or forestry products may be reduced or
eliminated if the EEC accords them comparable treatment. The purpose of
this section is to keep open the Common Market to the products of underdeveloped countries other than the favored associated African nations.

4. Finally, any duties amounting to 5 per cent or less may be eliminated
through the trade agreement procedure.

Before undertaking negotiations looking toward an exchange of concessions
in a trade agreement, the Tariff Commission must investigate and advise the
President as to the probable economic effect of prospective concessions on
the competing domestic industry. Hearings must then be held before an inter-
agency committee, after which negotiations are conducted by a Committee
consisting of two members of the House Committee on Ways and Means, two
members of the Senate Committee on Finance, and a Special Representative
for Trade Negotiations appointed by the President. Changes in the tariff made
in a trade agreement must be spread over five years, to minimize any dislocation.

Provisions relating to injury resulting from a tariff concession still contain elements akin to the old escape clause, though much restricted in scope. An injured party may petition for tariff adjustment, thereby setting in motion a Tariff Commission investigation. This body is to judge whether, "as a result in *major* part of concessions granted under trade agreements," increased imports are "the *major* factor" causing (or threatening to cause) serious injury to the domestic industry. In other words, injury must be serious; it must in major part be traceable to increased imports; and the increased imports must be due to the concession. This is a far more tightly drawn escape clause than the old one.

Even if the Tariff Commission report recommends tariff adjustment, the President need not follow its advice, but he must explain to Congress why he has not done so. Congress may then override his decision by majority vote of both houses. But if tariff relief is given, it is limited to four years, unless extended by the President, and may be ended before then if he determines this to be in the national interest.

Owing to the stiffened requirements for tariff adjustment, recourse to this alternative would appear likely to be much less frequent than in the past. Even under the earlier and far looser provision, adjustment was granted rather sparingly under both Democratic and Republican administrations. There appears to be a good prospect that more frequent resort will be had to a second alternative, adjustment assistance.

Adjustment assistance reflects a refreshingly new attitude toward the dislocation caused by foreign competition. It regards that competition as essentially no different from domestic competition—a consequence of change and a spur to increased efficiency. Dislocation, or injury to the sluggish competitor, is its unavoidable companion and therefore not to be avoided but welcomed. President Kennedy expressed this viewpoint well in a broader context in his message to Congress accompanying his tariff proposals:

> The discipline of the world market is an excellent measure of efficiency and a force to stability. To try to shield American industry from the discipline of foreign competition would isolate our domestic price level from world prices, encourage domestic inflation, reduce our exports still further, and invite less desirable governmental solutions.

There is, however, one major difference between foreign competition promoted by tariff reduction and the familiar domestic competition. The latter is a normal feature of everyday business life; it must always be taken into account by existing firms or by new entrants. But when an industry has for long been sheltered by protection, businessmen will have been led in good faith to invest large sums in fixed equipment, while employees will have acquired skills that may be of little use in other occupations. Therefore when the government, in the national interest, alters its established policy of protection, it incurs a responsibility toward those injured by its action. This principle of responsibility underlies the provisions in the Trade Expansion Act of 1962 for adjustment assistance. Instead of maintaining the status quo, these seek to promote adaptation to the increased competition by stimulating the mobility of resources and their prompt reallocation to more efficient uses.

Adjustment assistance under the new tariff law may be provided to both firms and their employees in several forms. Firms may obtain technical assistance—in management, marketing, organization, or research and development —either from existing government agencies or from private consultants. The government may render financial aid by making or guaranteeing loans up to 25 years in duration to purchase land, plant, or equipment or to acquire working capital. Finally, tax assistance may be provided in the special form of carrybacks and carryovers of losses. Losses incurred in any year as a result of tariff concessions may be carried back over the preceding five years, thus resulting in tax rebates if the preceding years had been profitable. Or such losses may be carried forward over the ensuing five years.

Workers who lose their jobs as a result of tariff concessions may obtain three kinds of help. They may obtain "trade readjustment allowances" for a period of 52 weeks, of an amount equal to 65 per cent of the average weekly manufacturing wage. They will be retrained for another occupation at government expense. The government will also pay the costs of relocating workers if suitable jobs are not available where they live.

In emergency situations, when the President judges adjustment assistance would be inappropriate, he may negotiate international agreements with foreign countries limiting the export of any article whose increased importation would cause (or threaten) serious injury to the industry affected.

The act also contains provisions relating to national security (section 232) that could, in the hands of a protectionist-minded administration, be used to obstruct the basically liberal intent of the law. National security is defined just as broadly as before, to include "economic welfare." But the President is not required to withdraw concessions granted; if he determines that the national security is being impaired, he may "take such action, and for such time, as he deems necessary to adjust the imports of such article and its derivatives so that such imports will not threaten to impair the national security." Whether this clause is used to negate the clear intent of the law, or as a necessary means of safeguarding the national security, will depend upon circumstances. We can only wait and see.

CONCLUSION

There can be no doubt that the Trade Expansion Act has equipped the U.S. government with the means for effecting a negotiated liberalization of world trade of large proportions. Whether it is able to do so depends, first, upon its own willingness to put its avowed principles into practice, and second, upon the attitude of the European Economic Community and of other countries of the free world. That Community is itself divided. Some of its leaders are outward-looking; while dedicated to ultimate political union of the Six, they have no desire to isolate the Community economically behind a high tariff wall. Others tend to regard economic union as the primary objective, with the fruits thereof to be enjoyed by the participants. Fear of American dominance, national self-assertiveness, a desire to create a "third force" influencing the balance of world power—all play a part in determining the attitude of the EEC toward the United States, toward the United Kingdom and other western European nations, and toward the free world as a whole. A similar divergence of attitudes and interests exists in other regions, notably Latin America, which will be strongly influenced by developments in Europe. It is only as these conflicting views are resolved that we shall know whether the trend is to be toward free multilateral trade, with equal access to markets for all, or toward a system of relatively self-contained regional blocs.

SELECTED REFERENCES

Balassa, Bela, *The Theory of Economic Integration.* Homewood, Ill.: Richard D. Irwin, Inc., 1961. A most useful survey of the static and dynamic effects of economic integration and of the policy problems raised by integration.

Humphrey, Don D., *American Imports.* New York: The Twentieth Century Fund, 1955. A thorough study of the U.S. Trade Agreements program in relation to American imports.

————, *The United States and the Common Market.* New York: Frederick A. Praeger, 1962 (paperback). A more recent study covering some of the same ground as the preceding book, but including also an examination of trade relations between the United States and the Common Market.

Meade, J. E., *Problems of Economic Union.* London: George Allen & Unwin, Ltd., 1953. A brief, nontechnical study.

————, *The Theory of Customs Unions.* Amsterdam: North Holland Publishing Co., 1955. A classic work dealing with the static effects of customs union.

Commission on Foreign Economic Policy, *Staff Papers.* Washington, D. C.: Government Printing Office, 1954. Chapters IV to IX contain a useful discussion of various special aspects of U.S. trade policy.

Sannwald, Rolf E. and Jacques Stohler, *Economic Integration.* Princeton, N. J.: Princeton University Press, 1959. Compares the theory of free trade with the theory of regional trade; discusses methods of integration and monetary and fiscal policies of economic union.

Scitovsky, Tibor, *Economic Theory and Western European Integration.* Stanford, Calif.: Stanford University Press, 1958. Is especially good on the dynamic aspects of integration.

United States Congress, Senate Committee on Commerce, *The United States and World Trade*, 87th Congress, 1st sess. Washington, D. C.: Government Printing Office, 1961. Analyzes the challenges to U.S. trade policy and the need for change therein.

United States Congress, Joint Economic Committee, *Factors Affecting the United States Balance of Payments*, 87th Congress, 2nd sess. Washington, D. C.: Government Printing Office, 1962. See Part II for chapters by Kravis, Krause, Markham, and Kindleberger dealing with the challenge of the Common Market to U.S. exports.

INDEX